Warners Wiseguys

Warners Wiseguys

All 112 Films That Robinson, Cagney and Bogart Made for the Studio

Scott Allen Nollen

McFarland & Company, Inc., Publishers
Jefferson, North Carolina

Selected Other Works by Scott Allen Nollen
and from McFarland

Chester Morris: His Life and Career (2020)
Karloff and the East: Asian, Indian, Middle Eastern and Oceanian Characters and Subjects in His Screen Career (2020)
Takashi Shimura: Chameleon of Japanese Cinema (2019)
The Making and Influence of I Am a Fugitive from a Chain Gang (2016)
Three Bad Men: John Ford, John Wayne, Ward Bond (2013)
Abbott and Costello on the Home Front: A Critical Study of the Wartime Films (2009; paperback 2019)

Frontispiece, top: Edward G. Robinson and James Cagney in their only film together, *Smart Money* (1931). Bottom: Robinson and Humphrey Bogart in their second cinematic collaboration, *Kid Galahad* (1937).

The present work is a reprint of the illustrated case bound edition of Warners Wiseguys: All 112 Films that Robinson, Cagney and Bogart Made for the Studio, *first published in 2008 by McFarland.*

Library of Congress Cataloguing-in-Publication Data

Nollen, Scott Allen.
Warners wiseguys : all 112 films that Robinson, Cagney and
Bogart made for the studio / Scott Allen Nollen.
p. cm.
Includes bibliographical references and index.

ISBN 978-1-4766-8516-8
softcover : acid free paper ∞

1. Warner Bros. 2. Motion pictures—United States—Plots, themes, etc.
3. Robinson, Edward G., 1893–1973. 4. Cagney, James, 1899–1986.
5. Bogart, Humphrey, 1899–1957. I. Title.
PN1999.W3N65 2020 791.43'75—dc22 2007033257

British Library cataloguing data are available

© 2008 Scott Allen Nollen. All rights reserved

No part of this book may be reproduced or transmitted in any form or by any means, electronic or mechanical, including photocopying or recording, or by any information storage and retrieval system, without permission in writing from the publisher.

On the cover: Edward G. Robinson, Alice White and Neil Hamilton on a lobby card for the 1930 fiilm *The Widow from Chicago* (Front cover design by Trudi Gershenov)

Printed in the United States of America

*McFarland & Company, Inc., Publishers
Box 611, Jefferson, North Carolina 28640
www.mcfarlandpub.com*

For "those who dared to whack HUAC,"
the 140 courageous members of
the Committee for the First Amendment,

especially
Lauren Bacall
Humphrey Bogart
Philip Dunne
Henry Fonda
Ira Gershwin
Benny Goodman
Paul Henreid
John Huston
Danny Kaye
Gene Kelly
Myrna Loy
Fredric March
Gregory Peck
Edward G. Robinson
Gladys Lloyd Robinson
Frank Sinatra
Billy Wilder
William Wyler

plus
James Cagney
Glenda Farrell
and
Mae Clarke
(I would have served a nicer breakfast, Violet)

Contents

Preface	1
Introduction: Like a Wiseguy	5
1. Little Tough Guys	9
2. Taking Over the "Talkie" Racket	15
3. Mugs' Gallery	34
4. Playing All the Angles	57
5. Crime *Must* Not Pay	83
6. Real American Killer	99
7. Whaddaya Hear? Whaddaya Say?	137
8. Bogie in Purgatory	145
9. Eddie G., Boss of the Biopic	171
10. Perilous Pard and That Bastard Bogart	193
11. The Black Bird	214
12. Whacking the Axis	222
13. Bogie and Baby	255
14. Protecting the Goods	283
15. Cagney Apocalypse	303
16. Three Wiseguys *Who Knew Jack*	312
Appendix: The Warners Bros. Wiseguys Films	345
Chapter Notes	348
Bibliography	351
Index	353

Preface

Warner Bros. Wiseguys has been in the planning stages for more than two decades. Though there have been previously published volumes on James Cagney, Edward G. Robinson, Humphrey Bogart, the gangster genre, and Warner Bros., no single volume has focused on the *entire output* of these three top stars who are synonymous with the studio. This book covers, in depth, all 112 motion pictures featuring the "Wiseguys" and their various travails with the powerful Jack L. Warner.

Thanks to modern video standards, I was able to obtain the finest quality prints of 101 of them (90 is an extraordinary percentage, when titles beginning in 1930 are the subject). The majority of the book focuses on the era of the studio system from 1930 to 1949, with all the films released by Warners from 1950 to 1964 featuring the Wiseguys also included. Films with relatively simple plots include a basic synopsis, while complicated narratives (the most incomprehensible being *The Big Sleep* [1946]) receive a detailed treatment. Full biographies of all three actors, as well as mentions of their work for other studios, are intertwined through the entire Warners experience.

When I began collecting and writing about films in 1979, a few of the classic Warner Bros. greats were still on the planet. The first Warners-connected filmmaker who wrote to me wasn't an actor, but *the* director, John Huston, who sent a signed photo from his personal collection on February 15, 1982. At that point, I didn't think directors even answered "fan" mail, so hearing from the man responsible for *The Maltese Falcon, Across the Pacific, The Treasure of the Sierra Madre* and *Key Largo*, not to mention the screenplays for *The Amazing Dr. Clitterhouse, Dr. Ehrlich's Magic Bullet* and *High Sierra*—and these are just his "Warner Bros. Wiseguys" credits—blew my 18-year-old mind.

John Huston's personal publicity photograph, signed in February 1982 (courtesy of John Huston).

Then living in Puerto Vallarta, Mexico, Huston wrote, "Receiving letters such as yours is one of life's true pleasures.... It was generous and gracious of you to write me and I thank you very much. Much success to you in your future endeavors."[1] Later on, Huston offered to sign a *Key Largo* lobby card for me, but he passed away before I could send it to him.

The formidable Bette Davis wrote that same year, as did Ralph Bellamy, who appears with Cagney in *Picture Snatcher* and *Boy Meets Girl*, and with Robinson in *Brother Orchid*. The year 1983 brought letters and signed photos from the unforgettable Mae Clarke, receiver of the grapefruit from Cagney in *The Public Enemy* and the by-the-hair dragging in *Lady Killer*, plus supporting Robinson in *The Man with Two Faces*; Lew Ayres, the unlikely Mob boss in *Doorway to Hell*; David Manners, who has a much larger role than does Cagney in *The Millionaire*; and Martin Kosleck, as the iniquitous Dr. Joseph Goebbels in *Confessions of a Nazi Spy* and a Third Reich fifth columnist battling Bogie in *All Through the Night*.

Bette Davis' personal publicity photograph, signed in 1982 (courtesy of Bette Davis).

That same year also inaugurated a decade-long, warm friendship with ubiquitous character actor Ian Wolfe, who continued to write to me until he gave up the ghost at the age of 96. His entire "Wiseguys" contribution amounts to a single line in the outlandish *The Return of Doctor X*, when Dennis Morgan and Wayne Morris do a little "graverobbing" at the bogus burial place of Bogie!

In 1985, I received a wonderful letter and signed photo from the exotic Zita Johann, who memorably played Quita, the conflicted wife of Robinson, in *Tiger Shark*. For three days during the summer of 1988, I enjoyed several memorable conversations with menacing, Berlin-born character actor Henry Brandon, discussing his work with Laurel and Hardy (*Babes in Toyland*, 1934) and John Ford (*The Searchers*, 1956), among so many others. Though he has a sole Wiseguys credit — *The Black Legion*, in which he plays Joe Dombrowski, the unfortunate immigrant terrorized by Bogart — Henry, a brilliant, outspoken liberal, recalled his experiences with some of the Warners actors he knew. His comment that Ward Bond (the reactionary nemesis of so many Hollywood actors) was "the most loathsome human being I've ever known"[2] is unforgettable! Until his death at age 77 in February 1990, Henry and I remained close friends, maintaining our cinematic discussions by phone and mail.

In 1992, I met Ronald Reagan for the second time. With his presidency behind him, he enjoyed recalling his early days at Warner Bros., which included contributions to four "Wiseguys" films. Another first-rate Red baiter during his post-Warners days, he became rather infamous to Robinson, Cagney and Bogart.

In 1995, I corresponded with the soft-spoken, underrated Eddie Albert, Robinson's lazy assistant in *A Dispatch from Reuters* and the lion tamer nearly mauled to death by Bogie's big cats in *The Wagons Roll at Night*. And, in 1999, I was honored to meet the ever-lovely Anne Francis, who, very early in her career, played Cagney's *young* girlfriend on the side in *A Lion is in the Streets*.

Sadly, aside from Miss Francis, these irreplaceable performers all have left us. They were all very nice people as well as wonderful artists, and I wish they'd been here when I finally decided to write this book. The biggest thrill of all was receiving a package from James Cagney himself, mailed from his beloved Verney Farm in New York in August 1983.

Rather than gathering a group of film "experts" to aid this project, I wanted to reflect the populist nature of the original Warner Bros. studio, and organize a union of "everyday" folks from various backgrounds to comment on specific films. These wonderful Warners films were not meant solely for stuffy ivory-tower scholars trying to wring every last frame of significance from them. They *were* meant for anyone who loves a great story told cinematically by the best actors, technicians, writers and directors.

Among the comments that follow my own on particular Robinson, Cagney and Bogart classics are those from a Catholic priest; a National Archives customer service program analyst; an African American history professor; the proposal manager at a major Los Angeles law firm; a film buff who maintains county roads; a movie memorabilia collector; and a movie star's daughter, each bringing a unique perspective to the book.

Henry Brandon and the author, St. Paul, Minnesota, July 1988.

There are some corrections of myths and inaccuracies found in earlier published sources (most notably a clearing up of the truth behind Cagney's famous phrase, "You dirty rat!" which the actor claimed he *never* used). While a previous Cagney scholar pinpoints the film *Taxi!* (1932) as originating the phrase, the actor already had used a version of the expression in an *earlier* Warners film. Yes, that's right, you guys—Cagney said it, not once, but *twice*. Three more Cagney films feature characters referring to *him* or others with a variation of the phrase. That makes a total of *five* Cagney films incorporating a version of "you dirty rat." You get the true dope here, for the first time. Sorry, Jim…

I'd like to extend my heartfelt thanks to the following friends, colleagues, correspondents and institutions, who in some way contributed to this book over the past quarter century: Barton H. Aikens, the late Henry Brandon, the late James Cagney, the late Mae Clarke, David Craft, the late Bette Davis, the late Midge Farrell, Thomas Fortunato, the late John Huston, Todd ("Dane") Jacobsen, Harriet Jenkins, John ("The Slack") Jensen, Sara Jane Karloff, Harold N. Nollen, Shirley A. Nollen, Rudy Pearson, Tom A. Pennock, Reverend David J. Polich, the late Ronald Reagan, David Ressler, the University

James Cagney's personal publicity photograph, signed in August 1983 (courtesy of James Cagney).

of Southern California, the University of Wisconsin Center for Film and Theatre Research, and Valerie Yaros, archivist at the Screen Actors Guild. No dirty rats here!

What a subject for a book. These three actors who became the most famous of all cinematic wiseguys were, not only great actors, but — more importantly — wonderful human beings who really gave a damn.

I hope all you *mugs* and *molls* enjoy it.

Scott Allen Nollen
September 2007

Introduction: Like a Wiseguy

Warner Bros. has always been my favorite studio. Together with their certifiable masterpieces, many titles made by contract "hacks" at this unique film factory are often as captivating as the works of great directors who worked elsewhere. While certain genres developed and championed by other studios—MGM's Technicolor musicals and Universal's horror films, for example—are fascinating, scores of films made by Warner Bros. from 1930 to 1949 warrant attention: particularly the early, gritty, streetwise productions released during the Great Depression and before the Red Scare that followed World War II.

Though glitzy escapist fare made at MGM and Paramount is enjoyable, it's the Warners world, with its thrills and sins, joys and problems, flighty loves and violent hates, that caught my attention as a youngster and still does today. Even when the Warners films contain cliches and unconvincing plots, there is enough of that Darryl Zanuck-inspired "realism" to keep them grounded. As soon as sound arrived, the studio began releasing uncompromising, hard-hitting fare with such titles as *Doorway to Hell* (1930), James Cagney's second film.

From 1930 until Cold War hysteria led to blacklisting—the shameful *un*-American crackdown on any Hollywood artist who drew even a hair's breadth left of right—Warner Bros. was *the* anti-establishment studio, even after the ultracensorial Production Code finally kicked in on July 15, 1934. A former socialist who became more conservative over the years, James Cagney escaped most of the witch-hunting fervor, while Edward G. Robinson was "graylisted" and Humphrey Bogart, who attended the 1947 HUAC hearings as a member of the Committee for the First Amendment (CFA), was painted as the poster boy for those Hollywood types who, according to some fanatical Red-baiters, were trying to "bring down the United States government!" By that time, liberal Jack Warner had joined the other studio moguls—all of them staunch conservatives—in bowing to the blacklist.

In their seminal study *Radical Hollywood*, Paul Buhle and Dave Wagner note:

> [W]ithin the limits of the commercial enterprise, Warners management cared for something rather beyond the bottom line, or more properly committed themselves to a certain kind of quasi-politics, which, even in its turn to anti-Communist films, expressed a commitment generally lacking at other studios.[1]

In the tradition of Robinson, Cagney and Bogart—and that early Warners studio led by Zanuck—I'm beginning this book *like a wiseguy*, being so bold as to challenge a cinematic sacred cow with my choice for the "best" American film of all time. Like the film-connected people who compiled the "100 Best" lists for the American Film Institute, I have my own favorites. Not necessarily "the best," but my *favorites*, for a myriad of reasons.

If I were to compile a list of "100 Best Films," it would not be the same as my "100 Favorite Films" list. For example, *Citizen Kane* (1941) wouldn't be among my favorites, but it *might* be one of the best.

Do I agree with the AFI that it's the greatest American film?

No.

I think *Citizen Kane* is an extremely well-made, brilliant motion picture, but also a self-indulgent monument to the ego of its rebellious, youthful maker, Orson Welles, who, I believe, made films as good as or better than his maiden effort. Film historians like to hail it as the ultimate *auteurist* work, simply because *it is*, made under the 25-year-old Welles' near-Machiavellian control during the heyday of the Draconian studio system.

To me, *Citizen Kane* isn't very entertaining. If the viewer is so busy admiring all the cinematic tricks of the *Wunderkind*—impressive though they are—does he or she notice that Welles' demonization of William Randolph Hearst, though psychologically complex for 1941, goes on for an awfully long time?

But I'm not writing here to criticize Welles, an artist I admire. Check out *Lady from Shanghai* and *Touch of Evil*—and even *The Stranger*, starring Edward G. Robinson.

Now, *Casablanca* ranked number two on the "Best" list? Perhaps, but I'll save *all* my praise for this magnificent film for its proper sequence in this book. *No other director* made more great films in more Hollywood genres than Michael Curtiz. He was the Studio System *Man*, if ever there was one.

Other filmmakers I'd put in that same class are Raoul Walsh and (*nearly* beside John Ford) John Huston, director of my choice for the best American film, *The Maltese Falcon*, released the same year as *Citizen Kane*, but the absolute polar opposite in terms of style and storytelling. (The AFI ranks *Falcon* number 23.)

Falcon is unadorned, intense and hard-boiled, while Kane is ponderous, sprawling and made to show the egg on a powerful man's face. As influential as any motion picture, *Falcon* looked ahead to the forthright filmmaking of Don Siegel, John Cassavetes, Francis Ford Coppola and Martin Scorsese, while *Kane* foreran the often over-the-top, sometimes sleep-inducing, indulgence of Stanley Kubrick—and many major post-1970 directors (especially number-one ranked AFI darling Steven Spielberg).

Falcon is still in the rarity of *untouchable cool*. Arguably, no film will ever catch up to it. *Forget about it.*

John Huston's straightforward storytelling in *Falcon* only enhances Dashiell Hammett's thick-as-pea-soup mystery novel, far more fascinating than a child's wooden sled on fire. The viewer can't help but feel for tough yet vulnerable dame Brigid O'Shaughnessy (Mary Astor) at the end of *Falcon*, but what would it take for anyone to empathize with Charles Foster Kane, or that dizzy broad who marries him? In the first place, *Kane*—no matter how wonderful was Orson Welles—doesn't have an incendiary Bogart to set the final scene truly ablaze.

Though John McCabe and I had a little tussle over the significance of Laurel and Hardy decades ago, I agree with him that Cagney is probably the greatest screen actor of all time. And Bogart consistently has been named the greatest of all movie stars.

Edward G. Robinson? He may be the best damn actor of his time—period. Like Cagney and Bogart, he was 100 percent unique and far more versatile than anyone could have imagined. He could be just as tough, intense, and electric as the other two, but he regularly delivered a quality that Jim and Bogie didn't often depict on the screen. Eddie G.—"Little Caesar" himself—could be *lovable*. Glimpses of this quality distinguish many of his Warners performances, but he really let it shine—in a perfectly nuanced and naturally controlled manner—in MGM's *Our Vines Have Tender Grapes* (1945).

To Midge Farrell, the original secretary of the Screen Actors Guild in 1933, Cagney was "Lightning in a Bottle." To the often disagreeable Jack Warner, he was "The Professional

Againster." I feel *electricity* when I watch Cagney. In 1996, while I ate lunch with a SAG contingent in Hollywood, Ms. Farrell told me:

> Jim was the same way in life as he was on the screen. Even if my back was turned away from the door, I always knew when he came into the room. Just by looking at other people's reactions. They all could feel his presence, and you could hear a pin drop. He *was* lightning in a bottle.[2]

On Easter Sunday 1986, when I saw the news of Cagney's death, I felt as if I'd lost a close friend. I never actually met him, but I'd lived with endless images of the persona, as well as a good knowledge of the "real" man, for a long time. When the report flashed on television, I was sitting in my living room, playing a mandolin. (Cagney was an aspiring guitarist.) As if I was channeling a riff from some Cagney karma, I instantly improvised an Irish-style tune later recorded as "James Cagney."

The Warner Bros. Wiseguys' effect on popular culture — and life itself — is impossible to chronicle completely. Traces of Robinson and Cagney can be seen dramatically during the first season of the acclaimed TV show *NYPD Blue* (1993), with Dennis Franz and David Caruso (a Cagney disciple), who are occasionally reminiscent of Eddie and Jim, respectively — and Bogart's influence has been all-pervasive. Not surprisingly, the Wiseguys' photos briefly appear during a scene in the premiere episode of the television Mob phenomenon *The Sopranos* (1999). Life imitates art, and it's no secret that real-life gangsters have patterned their own behavior after characters in *Little Caesar*, *The Public Enemy*, *The Petrified Forest* and — later — the *Godfather* films.

1

Little Tough Guys

Edward G. Robinson

Edward G. Robinson was born Emmanuel Goldenberg in the Jewish section of Bucharest, Rumania, on December 12, 1893. The Goldenberg family endured virulent anti-Semitism in Rumania, including a total ban on educational opportunities for Jewish children, a reality denying any opportunities for bright young "Manny."

From 1900 to 1906, 35 percent of Rumanian Jewry emigrated to the United States. After three of Manny's uncles sailed for New York, his father, Morris, joined them, leaving the boy, his mother, two brothers and maternal grandmother behind. Two years passed before Morris sent for the family, who made their way to Vienna and then to LaHavre, France, where they settled into a crowded steerage area during the long sea voyage to the Big Apple, arriving in February 1903. On the Lower East Side, they set up house in a slum tenement.

While his father worked various jobs, including running a candy store, Manny, who spoke no English but was fluent in Yiddish, Rumanian and German, enrolled at P.S. 137. He learned the language very quickly and began to read voraciously, including the *New York Evening Journal*, a paper published by the Hearst empire. In 1909, at age 15 — while attending Townsend Harris high school — he became a soapbox campaigner for William Randolph Hearst, who ran (and lost) a second time as an independent mayoral candidate. He also devoured *The Saturday Evening Post* and Jack London's *The Sea Wolf* (a novel that later would provide one of his greatest film roles).

In 1910, after considering a career as a rabbi, then a lawyer, Manny entered the City College of New York, where he auditioned for the Elizabethan Society by reciting Antony's soliloquy from Shakespeare's *Julius Caesar*. Intrigued by the stage, he read whatever plays and books on actors he could find in the college library, then began attending productions on Broadway and in the Bronx.

Prior to his junior year, he auditioned at the Sargent School, later known as the Academy of Dramatic Arts, where he began studying during the autumn of 1912. After a few weeks' work, at the suggestion of Franklin Sargent, he decided to Anglicize his name, choosing "Edward G. Robinson": "Robinson" from a character in *The Passerby*, a comedy he had seen at the Criterion Theater; "Edward" after King Edward of England; and "G" after Goldenberg.

After "Eddie" played a conspicuous role in an Academy production of Henrik Ibsen's *The Pillars of Society*, he impressed casting men at the Loew's Theater chain, who gave him a chance to perform his one-man play, *The Bells of Conscience*, based on Henry James' *The Bells*, at the Plaza Theater on Lexington Avenue. Though he now considered himself a professional actor, he continued to attend classes at the Academy.

Following a one-off Yiddish part (using the name "Edward Golden") in *Number 37* for

Rudolph Schildkraut at the West End Theater, Robinson accepted other acting jobs in New York and with road companies, establishing himself as a versatile performer who could play several roles in the same play. In 1918, he enlisted in the U.S. Navy, but did not ship out to fight in World War I. Seeking a position with the Intelligence Bureau Service — for which he was recommended by none other than George M. Cohan — he instead was assigned to clerical duties at Pelham Bay in the Bronx, where he saw enough disfigured soldiers to make him a lifelong pacifist. To escape these "miserable days," he often went to the movies: "I disliked them, and except for an occasional Chaplin or Keaton or Fatty Arbuckle film, I thought them badly acted, insipid, and scarcely an art form."[1]

Edward G. Robinson, USN, 1918.

In 1920 he accepted a small part in a film, *Fields of Glory*, starring Dorothy Gish and produced by Sam Goldfish (a.k.a. Samuel Goldwyn), who asked him to drop out of the production, which was being shot in Fort Lee, New Jersey. Ironically, Eddie, who was uncomfortable with performing his scenes out of continuity, had just walked into Goldfish's office to quit.

He soon was back treading the boards, but again was unemployed by late 1922, when he was persuaded by director John Robertson to try another film, *The Bright Shawl*, to be shot in Havana, Cuba, where he was pleased to acquire some choice cigars (other than collecting art, his favorite weakness). For the next four years, he played a variety of roles in more New York stage productions, including a major part as General Porfirio Diaz in *Juarez and Maximilian* for the Theater Guild.

Having some free time before *Juarez* opened, he accepted a choice role in *We Americans* during its trial run in Atlantic City. He enjoyed playing Morris Levine, the head of a Jewish clan, so much that he tried to get out of the *Juarez* production, to no avail. Interestingly, the Levine part was given to Yiddish Theater star Muni Wiesenfreund (his future Warner Bros. rival, Paul Muni) for the New York run.

James Cagney

James Francis Cagney, Jr., was born July 17, 1899, at 391 East Eighth Street on the Lower East Side of New York City. His mother, Carolyn Nelson Cagney, was a loving and hard-working woman, who valiantly supported the struggling efforts of her husband, James, Sr., a bartender who suffered alcoholic fits yet maintained a kind demeanor, and cared for Jim and his three brothers, Harry, Edward and William. Jim, with characteristic offhanded wit, later claimed, "My childhood was surrounded by trouble, illness, and my dad's alcoholism, but ... we just didn't have time to be impressed by all these misfortunes."[2]

Young Jim Cagney was shaped profoundly by his environment, both from the singing and storytelling of his father at home and the tough-guy characters populating the mean streets outside. One rough character, "Moishe," taught the seven-year-old to fight, emphasizing effective footwork and strategic punches. The boy developed his first dance steps while learning to street fight. Soon, "Carrie" Cagney took up the mantle of boxing teacher, instructing the diminutive Jim and his brothers in proper technique while refereeing bouts in the living room.

Eventually Jim became one of the toughest scrappers in the neighborhood, standing up to larger bullies and braving a local saloon to purchase "hair of the dog" for his father on particularly painful mornings. During the spring of 1907, Jim, acclimated to this raucous urban lifestyle, visited Carrie's aunt and uncle, Jane and Nick Nicholson, in Flatbush — then a rural area of Brooklyn — where he received a welcome dose of pastoral splendor that instilled a lifelong love of the countryside and agriculture.

Though he didn't like attending P.S. 158, he enjoyed studying languages, having grown up hearing so many on the neighborhood streets. He later said, "I was twenty-two before I ever met an elderly man who spoke without an accent."[3] He developed a fascination with Yiddish, and was growing fluent when he entered Stuyvesant High School in 1913. He also landed a part-time copy-boy job at the *New York Sun*, joining his brothers in contributing much-needed cash to the Cagney "kitty."

In 1916 Jim applied to the Farmington School of Agriculture on Long Island, but was rejected after an admissions counselor visited the Cagney home. Early the next year he took a job as a doorman at The Friars actors' club, making his first contact with theatrical people. Soon he was grabbing free passes to Broadway shows and reading plays at the local settlement houses. At Lenox Hill, he began designing and painting scenery for plays staged by Florence and Burton James, future founders of the Seattle Community Theatre.

Following the sudden death of James, Sr., during the influenza epidemic of 1918, Carrie gave birth to a girl, Jeanne Carolyn Cagney, on March 25, 1919. (Two other children, Gracie and Robert, had died in infancy.) Jim had been recruited by the Student Army Training Corps (SATC, a forerunner of ROTC), which offered him a scholarship at Columbia University, where he studied German with Professor Franz Mankiewicz (father of future film notables Joseph L. and Herman J. Mankiewicz), but he left after his father died.

Working to beef up the kitty, Jim snagged a small singing-and-dancing part in *Every Sailor* at B. F. Keith's 86th Street Theatre, for eight weeks (at $35 per). Appearing *in drag* in his first stage jaunt, he developed his trademark "quick, jerky" walk while mastering the wearing of high heels. He turned down a spot in the vaudeville tour version, then auditioned at the Longacre Theatre for a chorus boy part in *Pitter Patter*, first observing the other tryouts before landing the gig with his own variation on the Peabody dance step.

While appearing in *Pitter Patter*, he met Frances Willard ("Willie") Vernon, an Iowa farm girl born in Des Moines on June 19, 1899 (less than a month before his own nativity), and now beginning to make it as a Broadway chorus girl. He also became friends with fellow chorus boy Allen Jenkins (born Alfred McGonegal on Staten Island), who would be a lifelong friend and colleague (particularly at Warner Bros.). Following a tour of *Pitter Patter*, Jim and Willie decided to create their own vaudeville duo, a truly threadbare prospect.

In September 1922 they both won parts in *Ritz Girls of 19 and 22*, a touring show produced by the popular Lew Fields, who also was re-teaming with former partner Joe Weber for *Reunited* on Broadway. During the run, Jim and Willie got married at New York City Hall on September 28. When the tour ended, they moved into the family apartment on East 78th, an arrangement that was awkward at best.

The couple toured vaudeville venues with Wynne Gibson, landing parts in *Snapshots of 1923*, another Lew Fields show (in which Jim played *eight* different parts, as well as dancing), before seeking Los Angeles film work in 1924. Bunking in Hawthorne, California, with Willie's mother, who recently had relocated from the Midwest, they found it impossible to gain unagented access to the studios. Following a disastrous one-off gig with vaudeville pal Harry Gribbon, Cagney wired Jim Fair, a New York buddy, for enough dough to return home; and, in Chicago, Willie watched as he briefly teamed with Victor Kilian for yet another vaudeville attempt.

The young James Cagney, dressed to the nines (courtesy of James Cagney).

With Kilian's help, Jim won his first legitimate acting part after returning to New York. Director Kenneth MacGowan, casting redheaded actors in his production of Maxwell Anderson's *Outside Looking In*, paired him with the formidable Charles Bickford. Both actors received rave reviews, but publicity about the show's uncensored content and dialogue limited the run to 113 performances. During the engagement, Cagney learned an acting lesson that became an integral part of his own performance style —*listening*— by watching Irish actor Barry McCollum, who always looked as if he was hearing the other actors for the first time. When the show closed in January 1926, Jim was offered a contract by the Theatre Guild, but turned it down in the hope of continuing as a song-and-dance man.

Rejected by George M. Cohan himself, Jim teamed with Willie to create a vaudeville routine for *Lonesome Manor*, which they performed on several occasions with Bill ("Bojangles") Robinson. Jim then landed the lead role of Roy Lane (based on song-and-dance man Roy Lloyd) in the London-bound version of the hit show *Broadway*, though eventually lost it to the actual Lloyd through the machinations of shifty producer Jed Harris. Frustrated by this ridiculous Broadway snub, he and Willie opened the "Cagne School of the Theatre" (using the Gaelic spelling of the family name) in Elizabeth, New Jersey. They also bought a house at Free Acres, a socialist "single tax colony" in nearby Scotch Plains.

Humphrey Bogart

Humphrey DeForest Bogart was born at Sloan's Maternity Hospital in midtown Manhattan on Christmas Day 1899. In a West 103rd Street townhouse on the Upper West Side, he lay in his crib as his prominent parents—Dr. Belmont Bogart and the popular artist Maude Humphrey—celebrated the turning of the new century. Educated at the prep schools of Delancy and Trinity, "Hump" was a quiet, orderly, somewhat withdrawn child who cared little for academics but enjoyed staging his own dramatic "productions" on the beach during holidays at Seneca Point.

Hump and his friends improvised their dialogue but wore actual Broadway costumes supplied by William A. Brady, a producer who was a patient and friend of his father's, and lived just a block away on Riverside Drive. Other than acting and directing, Hump's favorite pastime was sailing aboard the *Comrade*, the champion-class yacht owned and operated by his father. The sea would provide Humphrey with a relaxing escape for the rest of his life.

Hump spent as much free time as possible at the Brady household, indulging his love for the stage and developing the liberal, anti-establishment attitude for which he would become famous (and, in some quarters, infamous). He attended Broadway shows with Bill Brady, Jr., and dropped nickels to watch "flickers," as well as hitting the newfangled movie theaters, including the Hippodrome on Sixth Avenue.

Though Humphrey's grades were sub-par, Belmont's influence resulted in his acceptance at the old alma mater, Phillips Academy, in Andover, Massachusetts, in 1917. Hump hated the Puritanical environment, but mainly was bored out of his skull by the antiquated academic program. Placed on probation, he was dismissed from the school, which he characteristically called "this fucking place."[4] After spending four unpleasant days with his parents, Humphrey "redeemed himself" by signing on for a four-year hitch in the U.S. Naval Reserve, rated Seaman 2nd class, on May 28, 1917.

He reported for training at Pelham Park on July 2; and, on November 9, received his orders to ship out on the troop carrier U.S.S. *Leviathan*. Two days later, World War I ended, and Hump was assigned to help transport the troops home, steaming between New York and Europe for the next six months. Like his future Warners costar Edward G. Robinson, he was greatly affected by the constant sight of maimed and psychologically disturbed veterans, which he witnessed during shore leave in Paris. Back in the States, on February 15, 1919, he was declared a deserter after the U.S.S. *Santa Olivia* sailed from Hoboken without him.

Bogart spent the next six weeks explaining that he'd merely been late, so the charge was downgraded to AWOL, and he was sentenced to three days solitary confinement. Ten days later, he was honorably discharged and sent home to Belmont and Maude, though he again spent as much time at the theater as possible, usually with his buddy, Bill Brady.

To dissuade him from partying all night in speakeasies, Brady's sister, Alice, a successful actress, suggested that he tread the professional stage. When William Brady, Sr., who owned the new company World Films, offered him a job as an office boy, he accepted, then became a filmmaker over night when the director of *Life* was fired suddenly. Brady moved Bogie into the director's chair, but — not surprisingly — the cinematic neophyte quickly had the entire cast chewing the scenery, and the boss had to take over.

Following an attempted screenplay — which ended up in the hands of producers Jesse Lasky and Walter Wanger, who dumped it — he then was re-hired by Brady, this time as stage manager for *The Ruined Lady*, starring Grace George, at $50 per week. Bogart also understudied all the male parts and, when star Neil Hamilton became ill, was forced to perform in front of an audience for the first time. Much to his relief, George also got sick, closing the production.

In May 1921 Bogart made his official stage debut — as a *Japanese* butler — in an Alice Brady play, then moved on to *Drifting*, *Up the Ladder* and *Swifty* during the next 18 months. By November 1923, he was able to leave behind his stage manager status for a role in *Meet the Wife*, a comedy starring Clifton Webb and Mary Boland, who flew into a rage when he forgot his lines.

Bogart now was making enough money to drown such sorrows at Manhattan's more "elegant" speakeasies, and at Connie's Inn and the Cotton Club in Harlem, where he reveled into the wee hours. His drinking soon would begin to cause problems, including numerous fights, one of which apparently led to the famous scar on his upper lip. (Bogart may have been genetically predisposed to alcoholism. Both parents indulged serious drug addictions; and his sister was clinically bipolar, a malady that received major financial attention from Bogie over the years.)

While appearing in *Meet the Wife*, Bogart met actress Mary Phillips, who was cast in *Nerves*, produced by Bill Brady, Jr. Bogie and his friend Kenneth MacKenna both landed roles in this World War I drama that unfortunately was killed off by the overwhelming success of the blockbuster *What Price Glory?* After receiving positive reviews for his performance, Bogie managed a road production of *Drifting* for the elder Brady. When scenery fell on the play's star, Helen Mencken, she got into a fight with Bogart, who eventually made the logical decision to marry her!

In January 1925 he costarred with Shirley Booth in *Hell's Bells*, then was back with Mary Boland (who had vowed never to work with him again) in *Cradle Snatchers*, also featuring Edna May Oliver and Gene Raymond. Following her Broadway triumph in *Seventh Heaven*, Helen Mencken married Bogie on May 20, 1926, but the relationship quickly became rocky, resulting in numerous conflicts and brawls (a trait that characterized all of his marriages).

Bogart kept busy on the stage, in Maxwell's Anderson's *Saturday's Children* (later filmed by Warner Bros. with John Garfield), and costarring with Roscoe "Fatty" Arbuckle (whose Hollywood film career had ended when the 320-pound actor allegedly raped and killed actress Virginia Rappe six years earlier) in *Baby Mine*. During the summer of 1927, he separated from Helen, traveling to Chicago for another production of *Saturday's Children*, while she went abroad for a London production of *Seventh Heaven*. Later that year, he made his film debut in Paramount's two-reel *The Dancing Town* (now a "lost" film) with Helen Hayes.

2

Taking Over the "Talkie" Racket

If the family from Poland had retained its ancestral name, the studio would have been called "*Eichelbaum* Bros. Pictures." Three of the Eichelbaum siblings, Hirsch, Albert and Samuel, were born in Krasnosiek between 1881 and 1887. By the time Jacob was born on August 2, 1892, the family had migrated to London, Ontario, Canada, where the patriarch favored the surname "Warner." Little Jacob was still an Eichelbaum, but would be known as "Jack L. Warner," while Hirsch became "Harry," Albert became "Abe," and Samuel remained "Sam."

In 1903 Harry and Sam entered the nickelodeon business, traveling through Ohio and Pennsylvania exhibiting short films, including Edwin S. Porter's seminal *The Great Train Robbery*. Four years later, they had saved enough profits to open the Cascade Theater in New Castle, Pennsylvania, where Harry and Abe sold tickets, Sam cranked the projector, and Jack sang to the accompaniment of sister Rose's piano during intermissions. In 1908 they established the Duquesne Film Exchange, distributing a catalog of 200 titles throughout western Pennsylvania, then opening branch offices in Norfolk, Virginia, and Atlanta, Georgia.

In 1912, with Abe serving as treasurer in New York, Harry, Sam and Jack began producing their own motion pictures in Culver City, California. By 1918 they were able to invest $25,000 in property at 5482 Sunset Boulevard, where "Warner Bros. Pictures" was born. In New York, Harry ruled as President, while Abe, with his financial prowess, served as Treasurer. In Hollywood, Jack and Sam focused on production, officially opening the studio on April 4, 1923. Their early films ranged from *The Beautiful and the Damned*, adapted by F. Scott Fitzgerald from his own novel, to a series of "Rin Tin Tin" box-office favorites, starring the cinema's first "four-legged star"—a German Shepherd—beginning in 1924.

In April 1925 Warner Bros. publicity chief Hal B. Wallis announced that the studio would adopt a policy of producing "talking pictures." Harry Warner intended to compete with the other majors by bringing the greatest musical and stage stars to the public. At the Warner Theatre in New York, the studio publicly demonstrated "the second turning point in the story of film entertainment," the Vitaphone sound system, in August 1926.

Vitaphone, a division of the Western Electric Company, had approached several producers, but Sam Warner was the only mogul gutsy enough to buy a license for the invention, which played back a film's soundtrack on phonograph records. After his three brothers accepted this "sound idea," Warners produced the epic *Don Juan* (1926), starring John Barrymore, featuring a complete synchronized score recorded for Vitaphone by the Philharmonic Symphony Orchestra.

Following similar efforts for other feature films, Warners adapted the system for important prestige productions. Though *The Jazz Singer* (1927) features only a few musical numbers and dialogue scenes with Al Jolson, this groundbreaking film was a smash hit, placing the studio at the forefront of the sound revolution. At the time, Jolson was known as "the foremost personality in the entertainment world," and audiences who had no chance to see him perform live could now see *and hear* him sing his hit songs on the silver screen. Produced for $500,000 (a large portion of which went to Jolson), the film was the studio's most expensive to date, but a profit of $250,000 made it possible for the brothers to expand production and convert their soundstages and theaters for sound.

Sam Warner didn't live to see the success of their new venture, tragically dying of a cerebral hemorrhage the day before *The Jazz Singer* premiered. The following summer, the remaining brothers unleashed the first "all-talking" feature film, *The Lights of New York* (1928), which grossed $1 million on a $75,000 budget. Jolson's second film, *The Singing Fool*, also was released, trumpeting him as a "truly great artist" and Vitaphone as inaugurating "The New Era in Motion Pictures." The souvenir program for *The Singing Fool* includes the dedication,

To S. L. Warner:—
   Whose faith and foresight made Vitaphone possible. He died before his dreams came true. But the marvel of science which gives immortality to the voice is an everlasting memorial to him.[1]

In fact, by the time *The Singing Fool*— billed as "a greater motion picture than ... *The Jazz Singer*"—was released, every production made by Warners was a "Vitaphone Picture."

Aside from dealing with company executives in New York, Jack Warner managed the Sunset Boulevard studio, handled contract negotiations and made casting decisions. The youngest but dominant brother, he oversaw the most important productions, often claimed others' ideas and innovations as his own, and put on a heavy Yiddish accent for visitors. Lesser projects—the bread-and-butter melodramas and action pictures—were entrusted to Darryl F. Zanuck (then billed as "Darryl Francis Zanuck"), a wily Nebraskan who also was responsible for the majority of day-to-day studio operations, including screenplay development.

While the suits were experimenting with Jolson and sound, Edward G. Robinson was back in Atlantic City, starring in *The Kibitzer* by Jo Swerling, and in New York, playing Nick Scarsi, a Capone-like gangster, in Bart Cormack's *The Racket*, the play that made him a big star on Broadway. Portraying a Mob boss finally got him there, so he took the show on the road to Philadelphia, Chicago and, fatefully, to Los Angeles, where both Mervyn LeRoy and Irving Thalberg saw his performance. Soon, offers of film contracts came his way, but he turned them down, moved on to San Francisco and then back to the Big Apple.

By autumn 1928 Warners was fully equipped for sound production, and far ahead of the competition in releasing talkies to its theaters. The brothers had bought a controlling interest in First National, a Burbank studio with large, newer production facilities and an extensive distribution system. During the day, the Sunset studio was hooked to the Burbank audio equipment via telephone wire. In the evening, the First National crews would take over and shoot through the night. By the year's end, Harry Warner had paid all the debts and still enjoyed a $2-million profit. Following the stock market crash in October 1929, he increased Warners power even further by buying the remaining First National stock from the financially strapped William Fox.

In late 1928 Robinson had appeared in a Walter Wanger film, *The Hole in the Wall*, shot in Astoria, Queens, playing a gangster named "The Fox" opposite Claudette Colbert. The Depression hit Broadway hard, too, and Eddie finally was persuaded to try his luck in Hollywood, where *Bright Shawl* director John Robertson welcomed him to Universal for the role of a gangster in *The Night Ride* (1930). Following a trying experience filming *Sunkissed* [a.k.a. *A Lady to Love*] (1930) for Irving Thalberg and MGM, he was ready to bolt from Tinsel Town, but stayed to star in Tod Browning's *Outside the Law* (1930), a sound remake of the Lon Chaney silent thriller. Eddie's role? Cobra Collins, a hood. So far, cinematically, he had remained 100-percent gangster, so he bought a train ticket and headed for New York.

En route, he was barraged by telegrams from Universal's Carl Laemmle, who eventually offered him $100,000 to replace Jean Hersholt as a "Chinese chop suey king" in *East Is West* (1930), costarring the amorous Lupe Velez as his slave. After *A Lady to Love* proved a box-office hit, Thalberg offered him $1 million to sign a three-year contract with MGM. Wanting more time to appear on the stage, Eddie turned it down.

Back in New York, Robinson starred in the play *Mr. Samuel*, which flopped almost immediately. Instead of basking in the glow of a $1-million contract in sunny Tinsel Town, he was busted in the Big Apple. Fortunately, Hal Wallis, in the audience for the fifth performance, went backstage to offer him a Warners contract. The deal was for less money than Thalberg had offered, but Wallis agreed to let him have ample time off for stage productions. Eddie signed and returned to Hollywood, this time to meet the brothers Warner.

Though James Cagney enjoyed teaching dance at his socialist school, he necessarily moved back into active stage performance, including roles in *Women Go On Forever* (during which he met lifelong friend Pat O'Brien, who visited backstage), *The Grand Street Follies of 1928* and *Maggie the Magnificent*, which paired him with the "perfectly beautiful" Joan Blondell for the first time.[2] In March 1930, he (playing a murderous bootlegger) and Blondell moved on to *Penny Arcade* under the direction of William Keighley at the Fulton Theatre, where Al Jolson attended on opening night. Impressed by the production, Jolson bought the film rights, then sold them to Warners, asking Jack to attend the play, particularly to check out Jim and Joan. After signing both to short-term Warners contracts, the mogul then repeated the act for Pat O'Brien, who was appearing in *This Man's Town* at the Ritz Theatre.

In April 1928 Humphrey Bogart had married Mary Phillips. The following January, he costarred with her in the mediocre play *The Skyrocket*— for which they both received good reviews— then appeared in *A Most Immoral Lady*, with Alice Brady, and *It's a Wise Child*, produced by David Belasco. In 1930 he again tried his hand at film acting, appearing with Joan Blondell in the Vitaphone one-reeler *Broadway's Like That*.

Bogie's brother-in-law, Stuart Rose, who then was the Eastern story editor for Fox, recommended him for the lead in the sound remake of *The Man Who Came Back*. Desperate to find a capable *talking* actor, the studio was impressed with his screen test and signed him at $750 per week. His move to Los Angeles created the expected marital problems when Mary Boland refused to abandon her New York stage career. Then, after making the journey, he lost the promised part to silent star Charles Farrell, whom he actually had to coach before production began.

Bogie did appear in two 1930 Fox films, *The Devil with Women*, starring Victor McLaglen, and *Up the River*, in which he was cast as a rich kid turned convict. The latter film was an incredible experience for a fledgling film actor. He began a lifelong friendship with Spencer Tracy, who starred as hardened criminal "St. Louis," *and* a study of the craft of filmmaking from director John Ford.

The Depression had forced Harry Warner to curtail his former heavy investment in sound production, abandoning plans for elaborate, expensive musicals for more economical contemporary, realistic film plots. In November 1930 Darryl Zanuck was promoted to head of production at the studio, reigning over all operations, now housed at the First National facility.

Zanuck became responsible for the "Warner Bros. style," a genre-based approach to filmmaking emphasizing current social issues, gritty streetwise characters, hardboiled dialogue and fast-moving plots—the antithesis of the positive, glitzy, naïve screenplays filmed by MGM and Paramount. While the other studios primarily promoted escapism as an "antidote" to the Depression, Warners showed the underbelly of American society, its hard-working everyday folk, its socioeconomic outcasts and losers.

Jack L. Warner, the youngest and most powerful of the four brothers, ruled the studio for a half century.

Though actors were kept on a tight rein, writers and directors often enjoyed the Zanuck approach, which allowed them to demonstrate range and versatility while working within a variety of genres. Though directors didn't usually participate in the pre-production writing process, they were left alone to shoot as efficiently as possible. Warners was a picture *factory*, with top staff directors like Michael Curtiz and Archie Mayo being assigned to four or five films per year, moving from one shooting schedule to the next, and not having time to sit in on post-production editing sessions. One notable exception was Mervyn LeRoy, the studio's most powerful director, who specialized in hard-hitting, realistic "social problem" films right up Zanuck's alley.

Cagney's short-term Warner Bros. contract paid his transportation to Los Angeles, plus a guarantee of three weeks' work (at $500 per). Joan Blondell received less, and had to find her way to Tinsel Town separately from Jim, who left Willie behind while he made his silver-screen debut. Zanuck adapted *Penny Arcade* into a screenplay titled *Sinners' Holiday*, depicting Ma Delano (Lucille Laverne), a tough old broad who runs a carnival attraction while attempting to protect her son, Harry, from a bootlegger.

In their first on-screen teaming, Cagney and Blondell demonstrate the chemistry they would carry over into six more films. Joan not only became Jim's most frequent female costar, but also the "toughest dame" he ever would work with, and she was one of the few actresses who effectively played characters who could successfully stand up to his wiseguys and roughnecks.

Ironically, the future "broad basher" of 1930s cinema took a shot *from* a woman (the first of several significant on-screen mothers) in his film debut. Cagney remembered Lucille Laverne as a robust "farm woman type" with large forearms that reminded him of Jim Jeffries, a boxer he knew in his youth. Before shooting a scene in which Ma hits Harry, Jim told her to use only her fingers, while leaving the thumb extended. "She agreed, but didn't control it," he explained, "and the heel of her hand hit me on the jaw, belting me to a fare-thee-well."[3] In the finished film, Ma slaps her son, who breaks down sobbing.

Sinners' Holiday, set on Coney Island, where Ma Delano runs a penny arcade, features no above-the-title stars. Cagney is billed fourth in the credits (featuring amusement-park sounds rather than music), with Blondell below him, though she appears on screen first. Jim's introduction to the cinema is an effective one, with director John G. Adolfi first showing the back of Harry Delano's head as he plays poker at the Palace of Joy, the park's speakeasy, run by bootlegger Mitch McKane (Warren Hymer). After Harry turns around to reveal his face (a forerunner to James Whale's introduction of Boris Karloff's monster in *Frankenstein*, filmed the following year at Universal), Harry puts on his hat and coat, then quits the game he had joined the previous afternoon. As he leaves, he confers with McKane, then runs into Ma at the penny arcade. In his first few moments on screen, in a scene accomplished with impressive narrative economy, Cagney's cinematic persona and his career motif of "the Mother" are established instantly.

Ma, fearing that he is involved in the "booze racket," also is concerned about his association with Myrtle (Blondell), the carnival's "Little Happiness Girl," who provides brief companionship for male patrons. Referring to her as the "Tenth Avenue Cruiser," Ma doesn't believe a word Harry tells her. "You're getting to be as big a liar as your old man was," she accuses. Walking toward the stairway leading to the family apartment above the arcade, Harry motions to Myrtle, who is standing at an adjacent attraction. This first scene pairing Cagney with Blondell is done, sans dialogue, as Harry and Myrtle communicate with pantomime to set up a late-night date.

The resilient Ma tells her employee, Buck Rogers (Noel Madison), that booze ruined her husband and set Harry on the wrong path before he was born. Later, discovering Rogers' connection to McKane, she fires him. Ironically, another McKane underling, Angel Harrigan (Grant Withers), an ex-con fired from his job at the Palace, is hired by Ma, who is unaware of his strong attraction to her daughter, Jenny (Evalyn Knapp).

Following a scene in which hooch is hoisted through a trap door at the Palace, McKane is pinched by Detective Sikes (Purnell Pratt), but released after a "sap jury" finds him "not guilty." When the cop tells Ma to keep her son away from the bootlegger, she replies, "Harry's all right. He's a good *boy*."

But Harry hasn't been a good boy, and McKane discovers that the upstart mug skimmed from the racket during his absence. Approaching Harry, Rogers asks the reluctant would-be bootlegger to convince Ma to rehire him.

In Ma's room, Harry sits on her lap as she questions him about booze. "If you're in a jam," she tells him, "let me help you. Ain't I always been your pal? Ain't I deserted everybody else for you?" (In retrospect, this image of Cagney and his cinematic Ma, filmed nearly two decades before *White Heat*, appears prophetic.) Treating him like a child, she orders him to bed, but he pretends to go to his room. Carrying a rod that his brother, Joe (Ray Gallagher), had loaned to Harrigan to protect the arcade during his absence, he sneaks into the street, where McKane is waiting.

As Jennie watches from her bedroom window, McKane emerges from a panel in Buck Rogers' joint. "You dirty, double-crossing little rat," he growls at Harry while pulling a gun. (In Cagney's first film, *he* is on the receiving end of a version of "you dirty rat." Though he later claimed he never spoke these words on-screen, he would use variations on the line in two subsequent Warners films.)

John J. Adolphi—here working during the first full year of "talkie" production—directorially demonstrates an adept use of sound. As the scene cuts to a reaction close-up of Jennie, a shot is heard on the soundtrack; then another rings out as the killing is shown from her point of view. A second reaction shot then cuts to a medium shot of Harry leaning over the body, frantically crying out, "Mitch! Mitch!" Finally, Harry drags the body out of the road and through the panel on Buck's joint.

Harry hides the rod under his mattress, planning to feign illness the next morning. Myrtle, stood up while awaiting their 12:30 a.m. rendezvous, accuses him of being out with "another dame." Handing her some dough, Harry asks her to provide him with the alibi that they were "together on the beach until 3 a.m."

Angel attempts to open the lock on Buck's joint, but Jennie stops him. Buck then breaks it off with a hammer, just in time for the arrival of Sikes, who discovers McKane's body, "stiff as a board." As a small crowd gathers, Ma comments, "That mug in there had it comin' to him."

The police close down the amusement park to conduct a thorough investigation, while the Delano family remains in the apartment, playing cards. Intent on "frisking" every joint, Sikes arrives to question them.

Noticing Harry's nervousness, Ma nags, "You oughtn't to smoke so many of those cigarettes." (The script obviously required Cagney to smoke. He hated smoking all his life, and went to great lengths to tolerate his wife, Willie's, tobacco habit. Occasionally, begrudgingly, he would light up on screen.)

When they are alone, Ma tells Harry, "I don't want you running around with that gutter floozy," just as Myrtle walks in. Referring to Ma as "an old bat," she then calls Harry "Baby."

"Don't you call him 'Baby,'" Ma orders her. "I'm the only one who can call him that."

Myrtle leaves, and Ma, realizing that her efforts to save her son from the wages of sin have failed, asks, "Did you do it?" then slaps him hard. He breaks down, crying, then confesses. Hugging her around the waist, he hysterically pleads, "Help me, Ma. Help me. I'm scared, Ma."

"All right," she finally capitulates. "I'll help ya."

As if the criminal ruination of her beloved son isn't enough, Ma receives another familial blow when Jennie tells her that she is going to marry Harrigan. When Harry gives Ma the rod, she — knowing that it came from Angel — plants it in the prospective bridegroom's suitcase. Sikes, who has reappeared to question Myrtle a second time about Harry's alibi, discovers the rod, and Joe admits that he had given it to Angel.

Sikes begins to take Angel away, but Jennie, swearing that he is innocent, is forced to tell the truth about her brother. "Forget about it, old sweetheart," Harry consoles Ma. "You aren't gonna quit me now, are ya? You know I love you."

"My boy. My boy," Ma laments as Sikes takes him away. Then, as a huge crowd pours into the reopened park, she returns to business as usual.

In his very first role, Cagney — playing a punk scarred by experiences with an alcoholic, now dead, father — delivers the kind of brilliantly shaded intensity for which he became famous. And right there, from the very moment he hit celluloid, as a misguided young man forced to kill, he grabbed the sympathy of the audience. In an era still affected by the histrionic overacting styles of the silent period, his performance, even in the heartrending confession scene, is believable and natural — an archetype for the talkies.

Cagney's "dese, dem and dose" East Side pronunciations would influence countless actors, especially the gang who became the future "Dead End" Kids. Most importantly, for the moment, Darryl Zanuck and Jack Warner were impressed enough to extend his contract another three weeks while mulling over a long-term deal.

The Doorway to Hell (1930), starring the boyishly handsome Lew Ayres as Mob boss Louis Ricarno, was already in production, so Zanuck cast Cagney as Steve Mileaway, the gangster's right-hand man. Concerned about his kid brother, Jackie (Leon Janney), and new bride, Doris (Dorothy Mathews), Ricarno decides to go straight, but matters are complicated by his wife's love for Mileaway, who has taken over the gang. When Mileaway loses control and confesses his way into the slammer, Ricarno returns, only to be whacked by his foes.

The Doorway to Hell (1930): Lew Ayres as Mob boss Louis Ricarno, and James Cagney as his lieutenant, Steve Mileaway, in Warners' first sound gangster drama (original lobby card).

Referring to the irrevocable one-way step taken by those who join the Mob, *Doorway*, Warners' first major gangster film, opens with Zanuck's "ripped from the headlines" style, showing the titles printed in a newspaper hot off the press. In fact, much of the plot is presented through headlines and bylines, a technique that adds to the terminal staginess of the film. While there is one brief depiction of "gang war," the remainder of the action is described in newspaper articles and photographs. Glimpses of the Cagney to come lend Mileaway charisma, and the actor gives the film its only energy. Whenever he disappears, *Doorway*, confined to interior sets, is utterly typical of most "talkies" released in 1930.

The opening sequence is the most exhilarating. Fading in on a close-up of a billiard shot, the scene cuts to Mileaway, whispering into the ear of Monk (Dwight Frye, months away from eternal horror-film typecasting in Universal's *Dracula* and *Frankenstein*), a little weasel-like wiseguy. Collecting his violin case, Monk, vowing "to teach a guy a lesson," leaves for the apartment of Whitey Eckhart (John Kelly), whom he guns down with a Thompson.

Though this scene suggests further gangland potential, the move through *Doorway* quickly goes downhill after Lew Ayres appears. Though he gives an effective performance as the naïve German soldier in Universal's *All Quiet on the Western Front* (1930), here he is irritatingly miscast as the feared gangster, a character who would have been ideal for Cagney had the production not been set in stone by the time *Sinners Holiday* was in the can. When Captain Pat O'Grady (Robert Elliott) tells Ricarno, "It's too bad to see a swell kid like you in this racket," he could be speaking for every film viewer. Cagney called Ayres "one of the pretti-

The Widow from Chicago (1930): Edward G. Robinson in his first Warners appearance, as a Mob boss, with Alice White and Neil Hamilton (original title lobby card).

est guys in all Hollywood," noting, "That will indicate how they did things at the studio then. Lew was hot at the box office."[4]

Briefly, Cagney develops some of his magnetic hand gestures and movements, including tapping one character on the shoulder with his fist, and pulling down the suspenders of another. But this edgy attitude quickly gives way to a lackluster gathering of the Mob bosses, where Ricarno supposedly brings them under his protective wing. Dialogue that could have been fun in Cagney's mouth — "Any mug that don't think so will be subjected to the swellest mob that ever stopped traffic" — is completely ludicrous when delivered in Ayres' wimpy monotone.

Cagney takes part in the film's most blatant pre-Production Code scene. Riding in a car's back seat with Doris Ricarno, Mileaway is tempted by forbidden fruit. When asked where he wants to hang out, he replies, "I could think of a thousand places if you weren't married to Louis." Doris then *licks* her wedding ring before handing it to him. Their adulterous affair eventually forces him to confess to the murder of "The Midget" (Edwin Argus), an overweight goon who had intended to double-cross Ricarno, rather than allow the Mob boss to learn the truth. Later, Mileaway discovers that the coppers have framed him. The jailed Ricarno had been arrested, not for whacking The Midget, but for killing "Gimpy."

A dull film, *Doorway*, opening with such promise, closes with Ricarno walking from an apartment to his (off-camera) death, as the sound of machine-gun fire accompanies a moralistic subtitle directed toward equally lifeless viewers, driving home the significance of the "one-way door." The tedium of this conclusion gives no indication that Warner Bros. was soon to unleash revolutionary gangster epics with unforgettable, uncompromising endings.

Robinson's first Warner Bros. contract was a major deal from the outset: one-year, for four pictures at $35,000 each. His inaugural film, *The Widow from Chicago*, released in December 1930, gave him second billing and predictably required him to play a Mob boss, a slight variation on his character in *The Racket*. He didn't relish the role; and, to make matters worse, his gangster is foiled by a typically bloodless "romantic" couple.

The film opens on May 3, 1930, with James "Jimmy" Henderson (Harold Goodwin), "the newest and best detective on the New York City police force," telling his sister, Polly (Alice White), about the nefarious activities of "Swifty" Dorgan (Neil Hamilton) and the gang of Dominic (Robinson). Following a flashback, she watches from the apartment window as Jimmy is whacked on the front steps. The actor is so bad that the hit seems like a mercy killing.

At the Crystal Dance Palace, "Get Happy" plays in the background as Slug O'Donnell (Frank McHugh), "the Eastside Whirlwind," is dressed down by Dominic, whose plans have been fouled by the apparent demise of Dorgan. On a mission to snare her brother's killers, Polly, posing as Dorgan's widow, arrives at the speakeasy. Sarcastically insulting the Mob boss, she observes, "He looks like the heavy in *Way Down East*." Dominic ultimately responds by hiring her to perform as "Palpitating Polly Dorgan."

Dominic pretends to fire Polly so she can infiltrate the rival gang of Chris Johnson (Lee Shumway), but changes his mind after Swifty shows up at the speakeasy. Though it depends on a back-screen projection process, the following scene, set atop a two-tier bus, lends *Widow* a spaciousness totally lacking in *Doorway to Hell*. Swifty (actually a cop posing as the dead thug) eventually falls for "his widow," then phones to inform Dominic that she will no longer report to work. However, when Swifty is cornered by a cop, she shoots the flatfoot in the back. Having witnessed the whole affair, Dominic assumes he is dealing with an ignorant female, but she soon turns the tables on him by planting a bug on his phone, tricking him into confessing to every crime he's committed.

Except for Robinson, who is electric as Dominic (a far more substantial character than Cagney's in *Doorway*), the acting in *Widow* is uniformly wooden; but the plot of a major mobster brought down by the ploy of a woman was an unexpected development this early in the history of the gangster genre. The film mercifully runs a mere 62 minutes, and is made tolerable by the razor-sharp delivery of Eddie, whose characterization provides a glimpse of things soon to come.

Robinson, who worked hard to improve the scripted dialogue, referred to *Widow* as a "hokey-pokey" affair, Alice White as "almost entirely without any acting ability," and, as for the director: "Nice man, Cline, but I liked my mother better, and I wouldn't let *her* direct a picture."[5]

Eddie looked forward to taking time off for stage work, but was side-tracked by a meeting with Hal Wallis. The new script Wallis handed over was an adaptation of W. R. Burnett's *Little Caesar*, a crime novel sent to Robinson a few months earlier by his friend Leah Salisbury, whom he had met in Canada during his early days on the road.

Wallis initially told Robinson that he was being considered for the role of Otero, the loyal henchman of Cesare Enrico Bandello, or "Little Caesar," based on Al Capone. But director Mervyn LeRoy, remembering Robinson in *The Racket*, had been discussing the casting of "Rico" with Jack Warner, who lobbied for a newcomer named Clark Gable (until he saw the actor's enormous ears sticking out during his screen test). Though Warner claimed it was his idea to cast Robinson as Rico, the decision was made after Eddie stormed into Wallis' office, cigar in hand, demanding the part. Robinson recalled:

Little Caesar (1931): Robinson, as Cesare Enrico Bandello, survives an attempted hit by a rival gang (original lobby card from the 1954 re-release).

> Hal listened carefully to my ravings, made a few notes, then reminded me that my contract gave me no approval of roles. Were I to refuse Otero, I could be put on suspension and no other studio would be able to use me — and no theatrical producer either.... Hal then said he would take the matter up with Mr. Warner, and within a matter of hours I was cast as Little Caesar.[6]

Following a screen test, both Warner and Wallis had no doubt that Robinson *was* Rico.

LeRoy shot *Little Caesar* over 31 days in July and August 1930, during which a "spy" planted by Al Capone observed the production. This fact made Robinson a bit nervous, as did the scenes in which he had to fire a gun. During the scene in which Rico murders Crime Commissioner Alvin McClure (Landers Stevens), his eyelids had to be taped open so he wouldn't blink when he blasted away with his rod. "Special effects," involving the use of blank cartridges, were primitive at best in 1930, and Eddie had to be fitted with steel plates for the scene in which Rico meets his end from a hail of machine-gun bullets. His nervousness caused him to move off his mark, but technician George Daly compensated, thus preventing the death of the actor himself!

In the original script, Rico's final line was "Mother of God, is this the end of Rico?" but a censor's objection reduced it to "Mother of *Mercy*, is this the end of Rico?" for the retake tacked onto the ending. The film opens with a far more pious Christian reference, the quote from Matthew: 26.52 referring to "all who take the sword shall perish by the sword." This blatant foreshadowing of Rico's destiny is depicted more subtly in the narrative. Later, a cathedral provides further spiritual symbolism as Rico guns down Tony (William Collier, Jr.) on the steps leading to the entrance — a scene recalled by Francis Ford Coppola more than 40 years later in *The Godfather* [1972]).

The film opens with a gas station robbery; then Rico and Joe Massara (Douglas Fairbanks, Jr.) are seen in a roadside diner, discussing their future as criminals. When Joe speaks of his love for dancing and dames, Rico replies that his pal is "soft." *Little Caesar*'s oft-repeated mantra, "You can dish it out, but you're getting so you can't take it no more," ultimately becomes his own epitaph after Joe, egged on by his doll, Olga Stassof (Glenda Farrell), survives, while Rico — having selfishly shunned romantic attachments — lies dead in the gutter behind a billboard promoting the loving couple.

Unlike many subsequent gangster films, *Little Caesar* avoids any mention of Prohibition, an association that may have created viewer sympathy with the ruthless Rico, who, at one point, warns his underlings about booze: "That's the way a lot of guys get bumped off." The only criminal activity depicted in the film is the gang's heist of the gambling joint of Little Arnie Lorch (Maurice Black) — including the Crime Commissioner whack — depicted by LeRoy in a brief montage.

Little Caesar romanticizes the criminal antihero, but its conclusion supports law and order brought about by a former gangster and his assertive girl, who turns stoolie to save her man. At one point, Rico confronts Joe, accusing Olga of turning him into a "sissy" and threatening, "It's suicide for both of you." Later, when he arrives at the couple's apartment to kill them, he is unable to pull the trigger. Here, Robinson's ability to infuse a character type with a genuine, subtle and effective range of emotion is brilliant. LeRoy uses a tight close-up to accentuate the actor's nonverbal use of his watery eyes and slightly trembling mouth — the perfect complement to the dynamic, fast-talking, take-charge gang leader of the earlier scenes. In an archetypal role, Robinson creates a depth rarely seen on the screen up to that time, alternating his confident animalism with an equally effectual boyish innocence.

Rico's avoidance of women, and his close relationships with Joe and Otero (George E. Stone), have led some film historians to brand the mobster a closet homosexual, an element actually mentioned by W. R. Burnett after he saw the finished film. This overtone is certainly present (Otero crawls onto Rico's bed while hanging out at his apartment), but any further comment remains pure speculation. Rico and Joe genuinely care for each other; and when the mobster is unable to whack his pal, Otero tries to shoot him, claiming that his boss has "gone soft." Rico's inability to be completely ruthless is his tragic flaw, a sentimental action leading directly to his downfall.

Rico quickly scales the gangland ladder through sheer fortitude, intimidation and murder, but slides into the gutter even faster. The scene depicting verbal abuse from haggy old Ma Magdalena (Lucille Laverne, fresh from playing Cagney's Ma), who allows him only $150 of the 10 Grand he's stashed at her greasy crib, is surpassed in inevitable tragedy by a sequence in a filthy flop house, where he overhears a bum shakily reading an unflattering newspaper article about him just as he pounds down a few last drops of bootleg hooch. Finally, enraged by the police-planted press coverage, he phones Sgt. Flaherty (Thomas E. Jackson), who quickly takes to the streets with a Tommy gun to mow down the former Mob boss.

The overall tone of the film is hard-edged, dark and violent, but a few moments of humor provide occasional respite. The fact that the Chicago Mob is overseen by a boss called "The Big Boy" (Sidney Blackmer) is indicative of the absurdity of Mafia monikers; and it comes as no surprise that Little Caesar quickly takes over a gang including such members as "Killer Peppi" (Noel Madison) and "Scabby" ("What a smart guy he is!" mocks

Little Caesar (1931): Rico cannot force himself to whack his pal, Joe Massara (Douglas Fairbanks, Jr.), who is comforted by stand-up dame Olga Stassof (Glenda Farrell) (original lobby card from the 1954 re-release).

Sam Vettori [Stanley Fields]). Flaherty's seemingly ambiguous sexual orientation is also a curiosity.

While Robinson's innate magnetism dominates the film, the supporting performances of George E. Stone and Glenda Farrell also stand out in a somewhat stage-bound production. In her first major screen role, Farrell plays a sympathetic stand-up dame, a contrast to the tough as nails, fast-talking gold diggers she often played in subsequent pictures at Warners (being particularly memorable as Paul Muni's nemesis in *I Am a Fugitive from a Chain Gang* [1932]).

At the Los Angeles premiere of *Little Caesar*, W. R. Burnett made a Rico-like move, exclaiming, "Screw you!" after the emcee, following the studio suits' introduction of the actors, director and cinematographer, finally acknowledged the writer's existence . When the film was released in January 1931, audiences beaten down by the Great Depression immediately identified with the iniquitous gangster, who was seen as the underdog, a rugged individualist who, for a time, successfully deals with the establishment. Though *Little Caesar* and the Warners crime epics that followed offered little hope for a better society, they gave filmgoers an outlet for their dissatisfaction with the current economic disaster. As a result, Robinson, a diminutive dynamo, quickly shot to the zenith of the Warners galaxy of stars. The following month, he negotiated a two-year contract, signing for six films at $40,000 each.

In public, Eddie caused small children to scamper away at the sight of him. Store clerks

Other Men's Women (1931): Cagney (far right) in the small supporting role of railroad worker Ed Bailey, with Grant Withers (center) as his down-and-out pal (original lobby card).

waited on him first, nervously trying to get the words out. The Warners publicity machine saw that no merchandising opportunity was missed; and, in interviews, Robinson was cautioned to claim he had considered becoming, not a rabbi, but a "minister," a denial of his Jewish background that he tolerated for about a year. Gladys, his wife of four years, added to his mystique by writing a fan-magazine article called "Confessions of a Gangster's Moll" (though Rico has no moll in the film).

On June 23, 1930, Cagney signed his first year-long Warner Bros. contract at $400 per week, with options for yearly renewal over the next six years. *Other Men's Women* (1931), a strange mess of a film shot as "The Steel Highway," happily features his friend Joan Blondell, but offered him only a small supporting role as a railroad foreman.

Grant Withers, the star of *Sinners' Holiday*, again receives top billing while Cagney is listed fourth, though he has little screen time until the final reel. Blondell is billed seventh, yet appears throughout the 70-minute running time. The "plot"— two railroad men love the same broad — makes little sense until mid-point, and the direction of William A. Wellman, who had been working in Hollywood for a decade, is surprisingly amateurish, until the bizarre, frightening climactic scene involving the wreck of a train during a torrential flood.

The film opens with Bill White (Withers) running along the top of a moving train. Cinematographer Barney McGill executed some good location shots, with his fluid camera mounted to a train car, then moving along the tracks and station platforms — a strategy that provides a stark stylistic contrast to the many stagey interior scenes typical of a 1930 production. Cagney first appears, as Ed Bailey, six minutes in, also running along the tops of the cars, describing a recent boxing bout to White. During their playful discussion, both actors pull off a dangerous stunt, ducking just in time to miss being decapitated by a bridge (a foreshadowing of the tragedy that occurs in the climactic action scene). Following this brief sequence, Cagney disappears for the next 35 minutes.

At a station lunch counter, White hits on Marie (Blondell), the waitress, but she says she's "A.P.O.—Ain't Puttin' Out." He responds by buying a bottle of bootleg hooch, getting plastered and summarily thrown out of his lodgings. Taken in by Jack Kulper (Regis Toomey), his coworker and pal of 20 years, White falls in love with Kulper's wife, Lily (Mary Astor), who returns his affections. After a kiss, White, unwilling to ruin his buddy's marriage, bolts from the house.

During a late-night railroad run, White tries to ignore Kulper's probing questions. A fight breaks out, Kulper goes down, and they collide with another train. White takes the rap, and faces losing his job. Again hitting the bottle, he accompanies Marie to a dance, drunkenly mentions marriage, then quarrels with her. Here, Bailey makes his second appearance (as Cagney does some fancy steps onto the dance floor). Noticing his friend's inebriated condition, he mentions that Kulper is in the hospital and offers an escort to the Y.M.C.A.

White pays a visit to Lily, who is now tending to her convalescent husband. She informs him that his old pal doesn't want to "see" him; but, in reality, Jack has been blinded by the accident. (Toomey's portrayal of blindness merely consists of trying to keep his eyes closed.) Jack, unable to tolerate any more of Lily's constant attention, sends her to stay with her family.

Bailey takes over for Kulper, joining White, who volunteers for the dangerous task of driving a train across a bridge while the massive flooding continues. Overhearing this plan, Kulper stumbles out into the pouring rain, falling down several times as he feels his way along the tracks and trains. This harrowing scene features him staggering directly in front of an oncoming locomotive at one point. When White tries to stop him from taking the train across, Kulper tosses him beside the tracks. As the rest of the railroad men rush to the scene, he nearly makes it across before the entire bridge collapses in the torrent. At the station lunch counter, Lily returns to find White, whom she invites back to the house. The films ends as it begins, with a happy-go-lucky White running along the top of a moving train.

Consigned to play himself in a few insignificant scenes, Cagney does very little, while Withers dominates with an often irritating performance filled with odd effeminate gestures in the scenes featuring White's wooing of women. Like much of the narrative, this element makes no sense. (A hard-drinking "man's man," Withers, whose best buddy was John Wayne, was married and divorced five times, including a 1931 annulment from Loretta Young, who had just turned 18. At age 55, he committed suicide with an overdose of barbiturates.)

"The Steel Highway" would have been a far better release title, since *Other Men's Women* implies a plural amount of affairs, when only a singular situation occurs. But perhaps the element that makes the least sense was Warners casting of Cagney and Blondell in the same film, then preventing them from sharing a single word.

Jim began to wonder why the studio was barely using him under the new contract, but was pleased to be interviewed by George Arliss, Warners' top star, who was planning his fourth sound film, *The Millionaire* (1931), adapted from the story "Idle Hands" by Charlie Chan-creator Earl Derr Biggers. The 62-year-old Arliss—whom Cagney called "a most pleasant, very dignified man"[7]—was casting the small but important role of Schofield, an insurance agent, who is integral to his own character's motivation, and was instantly impressed by Cagney's naturalistic acting style.

Arliss plays James Alden, a nationally known auto engine manufacturer, ordered to retire

The Millionaire (1931): Cagney memorably appears in one scene of this George Arliss starring vehicle (original herald).

by his doctors. Turning the reins over to his assistants, he "goes West," spending six months doing nothing but taking pills and tonic while being waited on hand and foot. Ordered not to smoke, he announces to his wife, Laura (his real-life spouse, Florence Arliss), "I feel like Hell!"

Alden's attitude changes after a surprise visit from Schofield, who, realizing that a life insurance policy can't be sold to a retired man, persuades him to look for a "new job." "I wouldn't sit around and wait for the undertaker," the fast-talking salesman advises. The scene lasts only three minutes, but Cagney's effortless performance rubs off on the usually mannered Arliss, whose portrayal becomes more relaxed during the remainder of the film. Not only does the briefly seen Schofield drive Alden's subsequent behavior, but the supporting actor's style influenced that of the star. This single, short sequence provides an on-screen glimpse at the far-reaching, magnetic influence Cagney would exert on the future of cinematic acting.

Alden stops at a small service station, which he discovers is for sale by the owner, L. Peterson (Noah Beery, Sr.). Using the name "Charles Miller," he pays $2,500 for a half-interest in the business. The other half was just bought by young Bill Merrick (David Manners, fresh from playing Jonathan Harker in Universal's *Dracula*), who needs to raise $12,000 to put his architecture degree into practice.

Keeping his new "position" a secret from his family, Alden-as-Miller — discovering that Peterson, having just built Palm Service, a large station on the new highway, pulled a fast one — asks Merrick to borrow $1,000 from his aunt to help buy the property across the road. "Miller" tells his partner that he mortgaged the balance, then opens Mission Service, using the competitive publicity, "Don't buy cheap fuel." Moreover, he proceeds to work the gas pumps like the rest of the staff.

The Public Enemy (1931): Tom Powers (Cagney) sweet-talks blonde bombshell Gwen Allen (Jean Harlow) as fellow wiseguy Matt Doyle (Edward Woods) pines away.

Eventually, his daughter, Barbara (Evalyn Knapp), in love with Merrick, discovers "Dad" working at the station. Later, after pulling a similar surprise on his unamused wife, he enjoys inflicting the biggest shock on his partner, who has been convinced (by "Miller" himself) to ask "Babs'" father for her hand. Having sold the business to Peterson for $13,000, which is turned over to Merrick to start his architecture firm, the Millionaire — now the very picture of health — accepts an offer to return to the Alden Motor Company.

Cagney made a 180-degree turn from this brief comic role when he was cast by William Wellman as gangster Tom Powers in *The Public Enemy* (1931), Warners' follow-up to *Little Caesar*, scripted by two Chicago writers, John Bright and Kubec Glasmon. Though Zanuck originally had cast Edward Woods as Powers, Bright, Glasmon and Wellman (who had seen *Doorway to Hell*) preferred Cagney, who had the essential street-bred wiseguy qualities that Woods lacked. The two actors switched parts, with Woods moving into the supporting role of Powers' pal, Matt Doyle.

Cagney based Powers on Jack "Dirty Neck" Lafferty, a friend of his father's, who wound up in Sing Sing after murdering a man during a car theft. Though Lafferty had positive qualities, Cagney considered him a "damned soul." From the outset of his film career, Cagney had the ability to portray iniquitous characters with an underlying depth, including sympathetic and likeable qualities, arising naturally from his personality. These qualities created, in this film, a new screen archetype that would influence the American cinema more than any other.

Like *Little Caesar*, *The Public Enemy* opens with a disclaimer, but differs in its build-up to the gangster's life of crime. While the previous film, devoid of a sociological premise, opens with Enrico Bandello as an adult, quickly rising to power by murder and usurpation, this "follow-up" film explains Tom Powers' experiences as a child, growing up in a slum environment, beginning a criminal lifestyle long before he joins the Mob. The influences a young person might have on the mean streets is obvious in the scene, set in 1909, in which the adolescent Tom hangs out in a saloon with a "family entrance." A later sequence actually includes a joint called the "Family Liquor Store."

As soon as Cagney appears as the adult Tom, his expressive hand gestures are in full force. In a particularly unusual moment, as he and Matt talk to local mobster "Putty Nose" (Murray Kinnell), Cagney is shown in close-up as the pool-shooting wiseguy sticks his bum right in Tom's face (one of many pre–Production Code "treats" offered by the film).

But the "subversive" content of *Public Enemy* is not always so blatant, as Glasmon and Bright occasionally managed to work in some subtle socialist material. When Tom and Matt first accept the support of Paddy Ryan (Robert Emmett O'Connor), who later becomes their boss, the saloon owner tells them, "Nobody can do much without somebody else," a comment that, on the surface, refers to the Mob chain of command, but also is an underlying jab at the myth of American individualism.

The Public Enemy takes a direct shot at the 18th Amendment—then still the law of the land—which had led directly to bootlegging and the creation of the modern Mafia. When the film was made, Prohibition still had two years to run its course before the progressive FDR supplanted the conservative Herbert Hoover. And the film makes no bones about the fact that just about *everyone* was breaking the law. Even Tom's Ma (Beryl Mercer) accepts a glass of bootleg brew when he brings home a keg to celebrate his brother's return from the Great War. The straight-laced, shell-shocked Mike (Donald Cook), however, vehemently refuses to drink, shouting that the barrel is filled with "beer and blood—blood of men!"

Disgusted by his brother's moral outrage, Tom counters, "Your hands aren't clean. You killed and liked it."

In a blatant, pre–Production Code scene, Tom is being fitted for some new, expensive clothes by a tailor who is a flaming Queen. After Tom states that he needs plenty of room "in here" (his pants), the tailor feels his biceps, remarking that this bulge necessitates such spaciousness. Before the sequence ends, Cagney again gleefully reprises the room-in-the-pants request. (This scene was heavily edited before the film was reissued, first in the late 1930s, then in 1954.)

Though Cagney imbues Tom with "positive" qualities—decisiveness, independence, charisma, and concern for his Ma ("He was a no-good bastard but he loved his mother," said Darryl Zanuck[8])—his ability to inject sudden, startling acts of viciousness set his gangster apart from Robinson's and, simultaneously, established the screen persona that would dominate his entire career. After discovering that a speakeasy owner has bought kegs from a rival gang, Tom spits an entire mouthful of beer in the terrified man's face—the first of several instances of his attacking someone else's pan. When Mike objects to the dirty money he has given to his Ma, Tom tears the wad of bills in half, tossing them into his brother's mug. And then there is the infamous action with the *citrus*.

The grapefruit scene is a fictionalized version of an actual incident in which Chicago gangster Hymie Weiss (who was machine-gunned by the Capone gang in 1926) rubbed an omelet in his moll's face. Bright and Glasmon changed the omelet to a half grapefruit; and, according to Mae Clarke, Cagney tossed it at her face on the first take. After conferring with Wellman about a second take, Cagney, with Clarke's permission, rubbed it in her face. Bright claimed that Clarke, who had a cold, asked Cagney to "fake" the action with the help of cin-

The Public Enemy (1931): The legendary grapefruit scene depicting Tom Powers' callous mistreatment of whining strumpet Kitty (Mae Clarke) was based on an actual incident in which Chicago Mob boss Hymie Weiss rubbed an omelet in his moll's face.

ematographer Dev Jennings; but when Wellman would have none of it, Cagney ground it in and infuriated Clarke.

Tom's absolutely stone-cold approach to murder is depicted stunningly when he whacks Putty Nose, who had abandoned him and Matt during a heist-gone-wrong. Suspecting that the end is near, Putty, having entered his apartment with his two former underlings, sits down at the piano to play a song he had sung to them during their youth. After the camera pans away from him, Tom, with Matt beside him, quickly drills him dead, then nonchalantly speaks of phoning his latest flame (Jean Harlow): "I guess I'll call Gwen. She ought to be home by now."

Just prior to this scene, he commits what may be an even more heinous act. After Mob captain "Nails" Nathan (Leslie Fenton) — based on Chicago Mob boss Samuel "Nails" Morton — dies after being kicked in the head by a horse, Tom arrives at the stables, pays the attendant $1,000, then guns down the helpless equine. In 1923 Morton's minions, including "Bugs" Moran and Hymie Weiss, emptied four slugs into the head of their dead boss' horse after he had been thrown while riding in Lincoln Park. (Later, *The Godfather* would depict an even worse gangland abuse of a horse.)

Though Harlow became Hollywood's best-loved blonde bombshell, she shares Jim with two other light-locked loose broads in this sexed-up Mob opus. While Mae Clarke portrays Kitty, the first cast-off strumpet — playing one scene with her back to the camera, giving the viewer an extended gaze at her spectacular derriere — Rita Flynn plays Molly Doyle, the more overtly amorous whore hired by Paddy Ryan to occupy Tom while he goes out to calm his men, who have scattered in the wake of a hit by the Burns mob. After getting Tom sloppy drunk, she follows him into the bedroom, kisses him on the bed, then turns off the light. The next morning, after she refers to their session, he slaps her in the face — the fourth such action in the film. At other times, Cagney uses his trademark knuckles-to-the-chin gesture, Tom's streetwise version of a handshake.

But Harlow grabs the prize as the most overt "bad girl" of the bunch. In one scene, after pushing Tom's face into her breasts, Gwen admits to having been with "dozens" of men. (Barefaced dialogue such as this certainly supplied plenty of ammunition to those calling for enforcement of the Production Code.) Cagney called Harlow "a very, very distinct type of gal. Brand new in the business, she didn't much know the acting end, but she certainly was a personality *and* very pleasant to work with."[9]

Tom escapes from Ryan's den of hooch and hookers, then enters a pawn shop, where he pulls a fast one on the clerk. Inquiring how to load a pistol, he orders, "Stick 'em up." As a heavy rain falls, he (shown in a menacing advance toward the camera, during which Cagney's face is the very acme of evil) struts into the joint patronized by the Burns mob. Again, the gun play, accompanied by painful wails, is heard off screen; then Tom staggers out, bleeding, onto the sidewalk, where he falls. "I ain't so tough," he admits. (Like the horse scene, this sequence, set in a restaurant, was an obvious influence on *The Godfather*.)

Heavily bandaged in the hospital, Tom apologizes to his brother, while Beryl Mercer is absolutely pitiable as Ma, admitting, "I'm almost glad this happened" and wanting "Tommy" to come home "to stay." Cagney completes the scene with a gentle rap on her chin. Earlier, Tom actually had shoved her after tossing the torn bills into Mike's face.

The remainder of the film contains some of the most memorable and powerful drama in all American cinema, set up by a visit to the Powers home by Paddy Ryan, who, claiming that the Burns mob has kidnapped Tom, has agreed to quit the racket if they'll "bring him home." The truth of who actually pinched him, however, remains ambiguous.

The closing scene is utterly spine chilling, as riveting today as it was in 1931. As the tune of "I'm Forever Blowing Bubbles" and the sight of Ma readying "Tommy's" room provide stark counterpoint, Mike answers a knock at the door to discover the bloody corpse of his brother, trussed up like a hideous mummy — only his staring face being visible. As Mike steps back to reveal this moribund spectacle, the body falls forward, landing flat on its mug (an ironic end for the repeat facial offender).

The final shot shows the "Bubbles" record silently spinning as the needle grinds away. The sequence, relying very little on acting or editing, is cinema in its purest form. It is a combination of grace and horror, like etching poetry with a sledgehammer. This single image of Cagney, which *must* be emblazoned on the memory of every viewer, is perhaps rivaled in his career only by the final apocalyptic closing image of *White Heat*, the postwar film noir version of *The Public Enemy*.

3

Mugs' Gallery

Robinson, having called upon the Mother of Mercy, remained idle for the next five months, reading his voluminous fan mail, but was called back with a script tailored to unite both of the studio's inaugural Wiseguys. In *Smart Money* (1931), he would star as gambler Nick "The Barber" Venizelos, with Cagney cast as "Jack," his right-hand man. *Public Enemy* partners Kubec Glasmon and John Bright also returned to hammer out the screenplay. Before shooting began, Robinson persuaded Hal Wallis to cast his wife (as Gladys Lloyd) in a small part as a cigar-stand clerk — a move allowing them to smooth out lingering marital problems while driving to the studio together.

Although Cagney watched few of his films, he enjoyed *Smart Money*, later claiming it "gave (him) the pleasure of seeing Robinson as his usual sharp self, that always solidly reliable self." Recalling their only on-screen pairing, he referred to Eddie as a "fine gentleman and splendid actor."[1]

Cagney appears in only a few scenes at the beginning and end of *Smart Money*, but Robinson's engaging performance and the tight direction of Alfred E. Green combine to make Venizelos' plunge into the world of illegal gambling consistently entertaining. Though Robinson enjoys far more screen time, the inclusion of Cagney makes the film important as a document of the star system during the heyday of the Hollywood studios. At this stage, with the success of *Little Caesar* a sure thing, and *Public Enemy* beginning to percolate in theaters, Warners placed its payoff on Eddie, while adding some protection with Jim.

Boris Karloff has a tiny part in *Smart Money* as "Sport" Williams, who incurs the wrath of Venizelos during a crap game. The sequence lasts one minute, but the tell-tale, bowlegged gait of the actor who soon would rise to stardom in *Frankenstein* makes it look as if the Monster is already on the screen, shooting dice. Nick, who had just given a streetwalker a mended $100 bill, is angered when Williams shuffles to the table, holding the same, taped-together c-note. After winning back the dough and ordering the two-bit crapshooter to blow the joint, he claims, "I don't like the way he parts his hair."

Encouraged by his Irontown barber-shop pals, Nick, posing as a big-time poker player, travels to "The City" to seek out the permanently floating game of Hickory Short. At the hotel, he charms the necessary information from Marie (Noel Francis), the cigar-counter girl, during two scenes including some entertaining improvisation. While Mrs. Robinson briefly appears as an assistant, Francis is quite effective in the meatier role, with Eddie referring to her as "a cute little package" and "a cute little trick," and buying her a $6.00 box of candy, which Nick rejects because it "gets stuck in [his] teeth."

Cleaned out during the poker game, Nick discovers that the real Hickory Short was just released from a 30-day stint in a Florida slammer, and that Marie had acted as the "shill for the burglars," including the ringleader, Sleepy Sam (Ralf Harolde). Back in Irontown, he meets up with Jack, who, tired of the small burg, is no longer working as a barber at the shop.

Smart Money (1931): "Sport" Williams (Boris Karloff) crashes the crap game of Nick "The Barber" Venizelos (Robinson) and his right-hand man, Jack (Cagney).

Persuading two Greek businessmen to supply him with a large wad of dough, Nick moves on to "Another City," this time with Jack and another rod-packing associate in tow. Following a thorough cleaning out of Sam and the boys, he admits to having shaved the cards, then opens the door to reveal his bodyguards, brandishing their cannons.

In an effort to add Marie to his winnings, he buys a diamond bracelet, then hits the road with her and Jack, quickly becoming the top professional gambler. According to a newspaper headline, he is "running wide open [with] police unable to cope with his activities." Now the proprietor of several major joints, he hands out cigars to everyone, repeatedly claiming, "A fellow in Havana makes them up for me."

Burned by one too many broads, Nick plays his romantic cards close to the vest. When District Attorney Black (Morgan Wallace) sends a sequin-dripping blonde (Margaret Livingston) to ask for a handout, he plays her, then administers a swift kick out the door. Prior to her entrance, Jack cleverly mimes the news: Cagney enacts some hilarious effeminate gestures and dancing (unique moves he had honed on the stage), answered by Robinson's own distinctive non-verbal shtick.

Many of Robinson and Cagney's best moments together occur after Venizelos aids Irene Graham (Evalyn Knapp), a young woman dragged from the river following an apparent suicide attempt. The actors' respective distinctive personalities are further developed here, pitting the sucker-for-dames Eddie against the cynical, cocky Jim. At one point, after Nick orders Jack to leave the room while he speaks with Irene, Cagney rubs Robinson's head and, with that classic smirk, sarcastically says, "Mother knows best." In their only teaming, Eddie winds up playing Jim's figurative Ma!

A later exchange, also referring to Irene, is another treat: "Where is she, then?" asks Jack.

"In the bedroom, Wiseguy," Nick replies. "She'll be gone in a couple days, and you can be my sweetheart again, Dearie."

First, Eddie is Jim's mother; but now, his dame! This is pre-Production Code dialogue at its apex, delivered by two masters early in their screen careers.

The D.A., after admitting to Nick that Irene is wanted for extortion, compounds a felony by blackmailing her into planting a racing form in his suit jacket while the cops raid his main joint. Irene, the one woman who ever truly cared for him, refuses, saying, "He's the only person who's ever been kind to me." Of course, she can't escape the long arm of John Law, and feels even worse when Nick proposes to her, calling her the "sweetest" girl he's ever known. "I used to be a sugar taster," he adds.

In contrast to the cold-blooded killers of *Little Caesar* and *The Public Enemy*, Nick and Jack are likeable law-breakers in *Smart Money*, never resorting to outright intimidation or murder. When the cops harass Irene and break up the joint with axes, viewer identification is solidly with the Wiseguys this time around. Unfortunately, after Jack confronts Irene about the racing form, he is punched by Nick, who sends him crashing to the floor. The cops enter to arrest Nick on an "old blue law" regarding gambling, then discover that Jack was killed when his head struck a door stop. Robinson's watery-eyed, non-verbal emotion as Nick looks down at his dead friend (a variation on his memorable moment with Douglas Fairbanks, Jr., in *Little Caesar*) is touching, providing a poignant end to Eddie and Jim's sole cinematic collaboration. They are so good that Warners' (presumably economic) decision not to team them again seems a pity.

Nick's combination of affection and disdain for the African American characters in the film is a curious, uneasy element of the film, and somewhat atypical of Warners' screenplays of the period. There is some racial "humor" common to 1930s films (Warners' admirable *Wild Boys of the Road* [1933] does include a "*wauda*melon-eatin'" scene), but Nick inspires genuine affection from "Snake Eyes" (John Larkin), the one Black member of his entourage. After offering his boss a rabbit's foot (a repeat of an incident early in the film) and being turned down, Snake Eyes sincerely adds, "I didn't mean no harm. I loves you, Mr. Nick." Robinson could not have been too comfortable participating in some of these scenes.

This ethnic insensitivity, however, is unexpectedly combined with a maturity in Venizelos' attitude toward women. After displaying all the chauvinistic mannerisms expected of a wiseguy, he ultimately forgives Irene for her actions, and enjoys a sincere farewell from the rejected Marie at the train station, just before he heads up the river to serve his sentence for manslaughter.

Warners sent Eddie and Gladys to New York to attend the June 18, 1931, premiere of *Smart Money*, an event that assured Robinson of his status as, not just an A-list actor, but a major Hollywood star. Thousands of fans had gathered to see Eddie when he stepped from his limousine onto the red carpet outside the Winter Garden Theater. When they turned into a screaming mob, mounted police intervened.

Robinson recalled, "I was surrounded by autograph hunters, redcaps, crowds, people shoving me, pushing me, stealing my handkerchief, and tearing off my shirt buttons. I'd never known anything like it; I was frightened, and, deep inside, a little excited."[2] Taking advantage of his popularity, he accepted an offer from the RKO Theaters to make a personal appearance tour through Brooklyn, Boston, Newark and other cities, paid $5,000 a shot to dress as Rico Bandello and refer to audience members as mugs!

Smart Money bit player Boris Karloff sparred much more substantially with Robinson

Five Star Final (1931): *New York Gazette* editor Joseph Randall (Robinson) issues an order to bogus preacher T. Vernon Isopod (Boris Karloff) in Warners' groundbreaking exposé on tabloid journalism.

while shooting *Five Star Final*, which re-teamed Eddie with Mervyn LeRoy. Darryl Zanuck had convinced Jack Warner to pay $50,000 for the screen rights to *Late Night Final*, a London-based play by Louis Weitzenkorn, who had served as managing editor for the *New York Evening Graphic*, a tabloid specializing in scandal and sensationalism. He then instructed screenwriters Byron Morgan and Robert Lord to re-tailor the lead role to suit Robinson's streetwise talents.

Eddie, who relished being in a project "about something," noted, "Weitzenkorn posed a dilemma that has to be considered along with the First Amendment. Does freedom of the press not carry with it some freedom of compassion, some freedom concerning the rights of the innocently involved?"[3] Excited about reuniting with LeRoy, whom he considered "special"—"He is morally indignant about injustice ... he feels deeply that in the end justice must be triumphant"[4]—he also convinced the director to cast Gladys in a small role.

LeRoy took only one day to rehearse, beginning the shoot on April 14, 1931, with a four-week schedule and a $290,000 budget. The entire production was atypically filmed in continuity, and the director was so efficient that its release had to be delayed for two months to honor the studio's agreement with Weitzenkorn that it not compete with a stage run in any major U.S. city. The New York premiere was held September 10, 1931, at the Winter Garden. Critics loved the film, which became Warners' longest-running picture of the year.

Robinson portrays *New York Gazette* editor Joseph Randall, ordered by his publisher to increase citywide circulation by serializing the story of Nancy Voorhees Townsend (Frances Starr), a woman who murdered a man 20 years earlier. With the aid of expelled divinity student T. Vernon Isopod (Karloff), who masquerades as a preacher, Randall sets off a chain reaction culminating with the double suicide of Nancy and her husband (H. B. Warner). After being confronted by Townsend's hysterical daughter (Marian Marsh), Randall resigns.

Isopod's repellent personality, magnified by Karloff's overacting, provides perfect counterpoint to Robinson's balanced blend of nonverbal intensity, rapid-fire delivery and moral shading. While Isopod enjoys the sensationalism he creates, Randall is often shown washing his hands, a symbolic attempt to purge himself of guilt. Robinson consistently gives a double-layered performance. While his more overt remarks represent Randall's "loyalty" to his employer, Bernard Hinchecliffe (Oscar Apfel), whom he refers to as "The Sultan of Slop," his subtle nonverbal expressions reveal the character's pangs of conscience — a quality also reflected in the behavior of his secretary, Miss Taylor (Aline McMahon), the only truly decent character in the newspaper office.

Robinson's complex performance is a specific representation of the film's general conflict. As the story begins, Hinchecliffe, frantic to jack-up circulation, cannot find Randall, whose absence suggests that he doesn't belong in the same league as the suits at the paper. The others are simply concerned with numbers and revenue, but the editor has a code of ethics, albeit one compromised by his work for the *Gazette*. While Hinchecliffe, Brannegan (Robert Elliott) and French (Purnell Pratt) discuss reviving the Nancy Vorhees story, they agree that the paper represents, not "sensationalism," but "human interest."

Although much of *Five Star Final* resembles a filmed stage production, it is a powerful and engrossing film, featuring a host of pre–Production Code references and double entendres. Early in the film, when Kitty Carmody (Ona Munson) applies for a job, Miss Taylor, staring at her breasts, tells her she'll get the job, and mentions that the last young woman was "fired ... because she was flat-chested."

Throughout the film, Randall makes sarcastic remarks about Isopod. After telling his employers of the bogus preacher's indiscretions, he adds, "He didn't get shot, so he became a newspaper man." Later, he tells Isopod, "You're the most blasphemous thing I've ever seen. It's a wonder you're not struck dead." When Randall is told that Isopod will have to conduct an investigation with little preparation, he replies, "Well, he'll have to *feel* his way. He's good at that."

Karloff's exaggerated characterization is both repulsive and humorous. In one scene, after the drunken Isopod stumbles into Randall's office, he is reprimanded for his inebriated behavior, especially his need for "stimulation."

"Very well," Randall says. "Stimulate *me*."

There are plenty of sexual references — many involving Carmody and the lecherous Isopod — but Taylor delivers a real peach to Randall: "A secretary only *secs* for pay." Though these comments reflect the "gutter" audience to which the newspaper panders, the script also takes some shots at religion. When Arthur Goldberg (Harold Waldridge) wants to "change [his] religion," Miss Taylor advises, "New York's too full of Christians as it is."

The acting in *Five Star Final* ranges from the realistic (the perennially understated Aline McMahon) to the stylized (Frances Starr as Nancy Voorhees is histrionic yet sympathetic), but Robinson carries the entire film with one of his finest performances. Nearly eight decades later, his powerful summation in the closing scene is as riveting as ever.

Sara Jane Karloff
daughter of Boris Karloff
on
Five Star Final

A wonderful film. My father's character is one of those you love to loathe. What a slimy fellow he is.

3—Mugs' Gallery

Blonde Crazy (1931): Cagney shows off those expressive hands while sandwiched between two knockout blondes, Joan Blondell and Noel Francis (original lobby card).

> Daughter or not, I wouldn't have wanted to ride in a taxi with him either! What a wonderful, lecherous, unscrupulous performance he delivered! You just knew he'd do anything for a buck! I loved it.
> Part of the magic of the scenes with Robinson and my father is that my father's sleazy character mirrors what Robinson fears he is becoming himself, and both men play off that chemistry beautifully. The script is written and crafted so that these two actors could draw out the worst in each character and the best in each other's talent.

After shooting his brief role in *Smart Money*, Cagney re-teamed with Joan Blondell for the aptly titled *Blonde Crazy* (1931), playing a breezy comic role that is the antithesis of his *Public Enemy* pug. Again, the script was written by Kubec Glasmon and John Bright (who, this time, crafted the material specifically for Jim and Joan), with director Roy Del Ruth maintaining a brisk pace.

The film is primarily lighthearted, but the writers still worked in plenty of "commentary," depicting Ann Roberts (Blondell) seeking to escape the grifter's life of Bert Harris (Cagney), only to become disillusioned with the dull, bourgeois existence offered by her stockbroker husband. She attempts to get Bert to go straight, but he can't bear to become a wage slave, preferring instead his Robin Hood-like life of robbing from the rich (those who steal from everyone else). In fact, at one point, Bert informs Ann that he is "Santa Claus, Robin Hood and the Goose That Laid the Golden Egg all put together."

"When Your Lover Has Gone" accompanies the titles, foreshadowing the final scene of the film. Opening in "The Leading Hotel of a Small Mid-Western City," the narrative focuses on working stiffs who aspire to beat the Depression by becoming con men and women. Bert is posing as a bellhop when Ann arrives at the hotel, seeking the "linen job" under the supervision of "Old Lady Snyder" (Maude Eburne), who is snow-balled by Harris' story about the blonde bombshell's "extensive experience." Informed about Bert's "crooked dice" and "booze peddling" by Peggy (the incomparably dumb Polly Walters), Ann, lured up to the sixth floor with "fresh towels," hauls off and slaps the womanizing scoundrel.

Ann is propositioned by jewelry entrepreneur A. Rupert Johnson, Jr. (Guy Kibbee), whom she spanks after stuffing pearls down his pants. Bert convinces her to become his "partner," and their first con is a simple one. While she "parks" with Johnson, a bogus cop (Nat Pendleton) arrives to arrest them, then is "persuaded" by Bert to accept a bribe of five grand to forget the whole thing. Now the couple of cons have enough bread to become Chicago-bound.

At "The Leading Hotel of a Big City," referred to as "Larceny Lane" (the film's working title) by the house dicks, the clientele are "worse than all the gangsters and hoodlums put together." Soon, Bert and Ann ingratiate themselves with racketeer "Dapper" Dan Barker (Louis Calhern) and Helen Wilson (Noel Francis), who eventually clip them for the entire five G's after pulling a counterfeiting scam. To restore their lost fortune, Bert engineers an equally bold theft by masquerading as the "personal secretary" of a jewelry store owner. Managing to lay his mitts on a $15,000 bracelet, he (in fine Cagney style) slaps a pawnbroker into handing him another five G's. Called a "tough guy," Bert counters, "Not tough, just mercenary," before smacking the coerced clerk across the kisser with the dough.

During a train trip, Ann "accidentally" sits on the lap of Joe Reynolds (Ray Milland), claiming she has "something in her eye." After being introduced to Reynolds, Bert shakes hands, then (in another of Cagney's trademark gestures) "shakes off" his own mitt. This train sequence features several such Cagney movements, including Bert smashing his hand down onto Ann's head and slapping a deck of cards out of her hands. Later, in a hotel room, Cagney performs an eccentric recitation as Bert attempts to read from a book of Robert Browning poems that Ann received from Joe, who "gives [him] the cramps."

Bert admits stealing the necklace, and Ann vows to pull a fast one on Dan, who forced him into "common thievery." They hire a counterfeit "colonel" and chauffeur, then soak the racketeer for several grand with a horseracing swindle; but, when Bert asks Ann to marry him, she reveals her love for Joe. During their ceremony, Bert sits in a taxi outside the church; and, when the cabbie (Richard Cramer) asks, "What is it, a wedding or a funeral?" he replies, "Both."

One year later, Bert returns from a trip to Europe, declaring that the continent "stinks." Equally stinky was a scene requiring Cagney to light up a cigarette. The health-conscious, athletic actor was basically a non-drinker, enjoying only an occasional glass of wine, and he absolutely detested smoking.

Ann arrives at Bert's flat, begging him to help her husband, who embezzled 30 G's and then lost it in a bad investment. Bert admits that he hasn't pulled a job since she left him, but agrees to help by staging a cover-up with a robbery of the stock company's safe. True to his word, he is set up by the shiftless Joe, who hides out around the corner with a pair of policemen. After a high-speed chase, Bert, shot with a Tommy gun, crashes his car into a store front.

Though Cagney insisted he never said, "You dirty rat!" he does use a version of the phrase in the closing slammer scene. When Ann visits the recuperating Bert to tell him the truth about Joe's sell-out, he responds with "That dirty, double-crossing rat!" This phrase is the first of two such "rat" references the actor would make during his early Warner Bros. career.

Ann vows to tell the truth about the set-up, but Bert refuses to allow her to reveal their criminal past. She has always loved him, and will wait for him, she admits, before Bert sends her on her way. Glancing up at the nurse-jailer, he smiles into the final fade-out, inexplicably waxing a paraphrase of incarcerated 17th-century English Royalist versifier Richard Lovelace's 1642 poem "To Althea from Prison": "If I had the wings of an angel, Honey, over these prison walls I would fly!" (What? Warner Bros. had some erudite chaps on the payroll in those days.)

While Robinson and Cagney were ascending the stardom stratosphere, Bogart was costarring with Charles Farrell and Myrna Loy in Fox's *Body and Soul* (1931) and with Bette Davis on a loan-out in Universal's *Bad Sister* (1931). He then continued his Fox contract with *Women of All Nations* (1931), another Victor McLaglen vehicle that placed him under the direction of Raoul Walsh for the first time. He even attempted to play a *cowboy* in the George O'Brien Western *Holy Terror* (1931), then abandoned Tinsel Town for New York. But after one play, the mediocre *After All*, and being subjected to more marital woes, he returned to Hollywood, where Columbia had signed him to appear in *Love Affair*. Like Fox, Columbia decided that Bogie was difficult to cast and loaned him to Warner Bros., where he signed for small parts in the upcoming Joan Blondell vehicles *Big City Blues* and *Three on a Match*.

Robinson's next film, shot in the autumn of 1931, required him to play an "ethnic" role, a Chinese gang lord in *The Hatchet Man*, directed by William Wellman and costarring Loretta Young as his wife! He didn't think much of the project when it wrapped, and he and Gladys left for Europe in November. In London, he was heralded as "The Al Capone of the Screen"; in Paris, he enjoyed purchasing a choice Renoir for his growing art collection; and, in Rome, the Jewish boy from Bucharest had an audience with the Pope. Back in Hollywood in January 1932, he was declared one of the top six box-office draws of the previous year, and Warners promoted *The Hatchet Man* as "the greatest picture of his career."

A Tong was a protection racket organized by residents of a U.S. Chinatown that collected fees from immigrants in exchange for "security." Leaders of the Tong were called *Boo How Doy* or, in English, "Hatchet Men." During the 1870s and 1880s, organized gangs waged "Tong Wars," during which hatchets would be left in the skulls of murdered victims who had opposed the rackets.

During a Tong War in San Francisco's Chinatown, number-one *Lem Sing Tong* hatchet man Wong Low Get (Robinson) is ordered to kill his best friend, Sun Yat Ming (J. Carroll Naish). Before the execution can be carried out, Sun offers to bequeath Wong all his property if he will agree to raise Sun's six-year-old daughter, Sun Toya San, as his own, then marry her when she comes of age.

Many years later, Wong, now a prominent man in the community, is in love with his foster daughter (Loretta Young). She marries him out of obligation, but has secretly fallen for Harry En Hai (Leslie Fenton), a handsome, young Chinese gangster from New York, hired as one of Wong's bodyguards during a recent Tong War. When Wong travels to Sacramento to eliminate "Big Jim" Malone (Ralph Ince), the mobster who started the war, Toya San and Harry go dancing at a local club, then are discovered upon his return. Wong plans to kill Harry, but recalls his promise to Sun Yat Ming to always keep Toya San happy. After Harry makes the same pledge to Buddha, Wong releases them, a decision decried by his fellow Chinese. Soon, his business fails, and he is reduced to working as a field hand.

Harry is deported to China, taking Toya San with him. Years later, Wong is given a letter sent by Toya, whom Harry has sold to Madame Si-Si (Blanche Friderici), the owner of an opium den. Working his way to China by shoveling coal on a steamship, Wong finds Toya and demands that Si-Si honor his rightful claim as her husband. The old woman doesn't recognize his status as a hatchet man, so he flings his weapon at the painting of a dragon on the wall. After Wong and Toya leave, Si-Si enters the adjoining room to rebuke Harry for losing the girl. Staring blankly, he nods slightly, then falls forward, the hatchet having cleaved the wall and (coincidentally) his skull!

The Hatchet Man (1932). Robinson as Wong Low Get, the only "Asian" character of his Warners career.

The Hatchet Man marked the only time Robinson played an "Eastern" character during his Warners career. A common practice at the time, the casting of actors of European origin and heritage in Asian roles was part and parcel of the pre-"politically correct" studio contract system.

The most glaring problem with *The Hatchet Man* is Robinson's reckless miscasting (a problem that later would befall Bogart, cast as a Mexican bandit, in *Virginia City* [1940]), along with Loretta Young and the other major supporting actors. Robinson's wife, again working as Gladys Lloyd, appears as a Chinese, Fan Yi. The only performers of Asian origin (Anna Chang, Willie Fung, James B. Leong, Miki Morita, Toshia Mori and Otto Yamaoka) are kept in the background in uncredited bit parts—a practice that prevented their authentic features from standing out against those created for white actors by the makeup artists.

In April 1931, when *The Public Enemy* had become a smash hit (raking in more than $1 million on a $151,000 investment), Cagney realized that his $400-per-week contract was in sore need of renegotiation. *Blonde Crazy* also made a tidy profit, providing further evidence that he was a major moneymaker for the studio.

While Willie Cagney went house hunting in Beverly Hills, Jim began shooting *Taxi!* (1932), with Roy Del Ruth directing a Glasmon and Bright script inspired by current labor conflicts in the transportation industry. Aware of Cagney's fluency in Yiddish, Bright wrote a humorous opening scene in which cabbie Matt Nolan aids an Ellis Island-bound visitor who speaks the language to a confused Irish cop (Robert Emmett O'Connor). Cagney liked the idea so much that he expanded the Yiddish dialogue, ending the scene with the Russian man inquiring if he's Jewish, and the cop asking him what part of Ireland his folks came from. "Delancey Street, denk you!" he replies.

Taxi is another of the few films that required Jim to smoke. A second worry was the dance contest involving the Peabody step, one of his specialties. He was stepping out on screen for the first time; and, though Loretta Young was a whiz at the maneuver, he needed a worthy male dancer for the competition. Knowing that George Raft was in Hollywood to costar in Howard Hawks' *Scarface* (1932), Cagney suggested that Warners hire him for the scene, resulting in a truly realistic dancing duel between two New York tough guys.

The two couples maneuver the floor to "Darktown Strutter's Ball," and the winner is chosen by the spectators' applause. The Raft character wins, and Cagney's Matt punches him

Taxi! (1932): Matt Nolan (Cagney, with right fist at the ready) ignores the pleas of his level-headed wife, Sue (Loretta Young), as his pal "Skeets" (George E. Stone, right) intercedes.

out, incurring the wrath of Sue Reilly (Young), who refers to "that insane temper of yours," a character defect that repeatedly plagues the hot-headed cabbie. Cagney later called Raft "one of my nicest working companions ... the only other one in California who knew the Peabody well."[5]

In classic Warners style, the story begins with a newspaper headline announcing, "War Declared! Rival Taxicab Companies Contest Bitterly for City's Business." The conflict soon results in street violence. Matt brawls with agitators from the Consolidated Cab Company (one of whom is played by Frank McHugh); and Sue's father, Michael (Guy Kibbee), has his taxi wrecked by another goon (Nat Pendleton), whom he guns down, receiving 10 years in the slammer in return.

At a labor meeting, Matt speaks out against Consolidated, claiming, "We live in the United States. We're free and equal, or so they tell us."

Sue then joins in, saying, "If my father hadn't shot that man, I might have shot him myself"; but when she speaks out against further violence, Matt is outraged, especially since her father has died in the Big House. Arbitration brings a truce, but Matt is even angrier, threatening to "run Consolidated cabs into the East River."

During a date at the movies (Warners plugs its own *The Mad Genius* with John Barrymore), Matt's temper aggravates Sue, who slaps him. Later, she gives him "one more chance" if he'll curb his violence, and he responds by placing a ring on her finger as they dance to music on the apartment radio.

While celebrating their wedding at the Cotton Picker's Club (a true sign of the times), scantily clad dancing girls perform to a rousing pre-Production Code version of Hoagy Carmichael's "Georgia on My Mind." As the band tears through a hot "Dinah," Matt is angered by the obnoxious Buck Gerard (David Landau), the thug who was responsible for "sending" Sue's old man up the river.

Gerard insults Sue, snarling, "I bet you had to marry the bim," and Matt delivers that ferocious Cagney right to his chin, knocking him to the floor. Unfortunately, Matt's kid brother, Danny (Ray Cooke), steps in and is knifed in the back for his trouble. The poor lad dies at the hospital, and Matt refuses to identify the killer to the cops; but Slats, a fellow cabbie, names Gerard.

Sue, tired of Matt's all-consuming vendetta against Gerard, gives the $100 he was saving for Danny's headstone to "Buck's girl," Marie Costa (Dorothy Burgess), who wants to get the killer out of New York. With Sue and her friend Skeets (George E. Stone) in pursuit, Matt drives to Gerard's hideout, where the cops soon arrive. Sue reveals the truth, but Matt shoots through a closet door, causing Buck to fall through a window to his death on the sidewalk below.

Here, Cagney makes his second "dirty rat" reference. Before Matt blasts away, he fumes, "Come out and take it, you dirty, yellow-bellied rat, or I'll give it to you through the door!" Cagney's characters shoot through doors in several of his films, but here he actually does no killing, and the "dirty rat" falls from a window to his death.

Sue plans to leave Matt, but changes her mind after he returns to their flat. Movers have loaded nearly all their possessions into a truck, and Matt (using another classic Cagney gesture, the playfully raised fist) threatens, "If I thought you meant that ..." (the third and final time he says it in the film). Cagney later revealed:

> [I] used one of my pop's favorite gestures ... Pop had an affectionate thing he did with his four sons; he'd put one hand behind the back of our necks, ball his other fist as if he were about to clout us, then say, "If I thought you meant it —" It was always good for a laugh, for afterward he'd put his arm around us.[6]

Matt Nolan, responsible for starting the fracas that leads to his brother's death, is another complex Cagney character, possessing both likeable and distasteful (yet strangely appealing) tough-guy qualities. Containing some of the strongest left-wing sentiments in all the Warners Depression-era classics, *Taxi!* was praised in *The Nation*, to which Darryl Zanuck reportedly responded, "I'll be a son of a bitch. I thought it was all cops and robbers."[7]

Working for Warner Bros. on a freelance basis, Howard Hawks also enjoyed the rare artistic freedom lavished on Mervyn LeRoy. In 1932 Hawks was paid $50,000 per picture to direct *The Crowd Roars* with Cagney and *Tiger Shark* with Robinson. He also was allowed to participate in scripting and editing, though Jack Warner had approval of the shooting script and final cut.

"The moment I saw Cagney, I wanted him for a picture," Hawks recalled, "because he did things completely differently from anybody else."[8] While shooting *The Crowd Roars*, Joan Blondell again added some enjoyment to Cagney's work, and he was pleased to share scenes with Frank McHugh, who would support him in many future Warners films.

After the first day on location, Jim and Frank bunked together at the Santa Barbara Hotel, where they became fast friends as they lay awake talking until it was time to report back to the set the following morning. "We worked the next day through without sleep," recalled Cagney, "but we were young and thought little of it."[9]

Hawks and Seton I. Miller wrote the original story, but the screenplay by Kubec Glasmon, John Bright and Niven Busch presents few surprises. Besides the dynamism of Cagney as racer Joe Greer (a true dramatic stretch, since the actor was a self-confessed terror behind the wheel), some interest is generated by a dozen professional drivers who come and go, awk-

The Crowd Roars (1932): Lee Merrick (the incomparable Ann Dvorak) provides redemption for has-been dirt-track driver Joe Greer (Cagney) in Howard Hawks' first Warners Wiseguy film.

wardly delivering a line or two. A true highlight are the racing scenes shot on location in Indianapolis and at the Ventura and Ascot tracks in California. Hawks said:

> Cagney was so much fun to work with because you never knew what Cagney was gonna do.... Cagney had these funny little attitudes, you know, the way he held his hands and things like that. I tried to make the most of them, and I think we did pretty well even though I didn't know how he worked.
>
> Jim Cagney worked with movement. He didn't work with lines. I don't ever remember him suggesting a line — it's the way he *does* the line, the stuff you feed him, that makes him so good. Whenever I work with a fellow who was as good as Cagney — let's include Bogart there — I make sure that they feel free to try anything.[10]

The Crowd Roars opens with *roaring* engine sounds, a violent car crash and a shot of a *roaring crowd* in the stands before music and the title credits fade in. The first scene is characteristically set up by a newspaper headline trumpeting, "Indy champ to return to home town" as Joe and his pal, racer and mechanic "Spud" Connors (Frank McHugh) travel by train to visit Pop Greer (Guy Kibbee) and Joe's kid brother, Eddie (Eric Linden), whom he hasn't seen in four years.

Playing Joe's girlfriend, Lee Merrick, Ann Dvorak makes her second appearance in a 1932 Hawks film, the first having been the groundbreaking gangster masterpiece *Scarface*, shot the previous year. The conflict between the couple is immediately established when Lee attempts to convince Joe to stop racing *and* drinking. Soon, the discord is amplified when Pop and Eddie unveil the race car they have built from an old wreck owned by Joe, who tells his brother not to get involved in the sport. "You're a hero today and a bum tomorrow," he explains.

The initial racing scene illustrates the terrible conditions endured by the dirt-track drivers. Joe and Spud, engulfed in an enormous dust cloud, both crash out of the first heat, and Eddie takes first place. The combination of the constant maelstrom of dirt and the driver's only protection — a small pair of goggles — suggests that participating in the sport may be the result of either courage or insanity. During the second heat, after Ed cracks up his car, Joe places him under contract, promising his own racer to his brother.

While Lee is partying with her pal Ann (Blondell), Joe, out of respect for young Eddie, arrives to tell his girl to "cool down" on their romance. In another classic Cagney "broad bashing" sequence, Joe first checks out Ann's gams (featured prominently in the shot), then drags her across the room and out the door. Angry about Eddie's boozing with the women (which amounted to *one* drink), he breaks up with Lee, who slaps him, then becomes hysterical when he leaves.

As in *Scarface*, Hawks was able to direct Dvorak into hysterics. Interestingly, in a reversal of the earlier film's sibling subplot — in which Tony Camonte (Paul Muni) is incestuously overprotective of his sister, Cesca — Joe threatens to destroy relationships with everyone around him by obsessively sheltering his brother.

Ann nonetheless works her wiles on Eddie, who quickly falls for her. Spud warns Lee that "Joe's on the warpath," and the drunken driver arrives at the apartment to order Ann to leave his brother. Admitting that she had intended to use Eddie to prove a point, she now confesses her love for him. Following Eddie's pathetic attempt to start a fist fight, Joe walks out.

During the Ascot 100, the inebriated Joe tries to terrorize his brother, but Spud drives his car between them. Joe will have none of it, however, and pulls a "Ben-Hur" by grinding his front right wheel into Spud's left rear axle. The sparks ignite the gas tank, and Spud's car explodes into flames, roasting him alive (McHugh screams hideously in a graphic tight closeup). Shattered, Joe quits, allowing Eddie to win the race. This scene is quite shocking, particularly since McHugh and Cagney were now bosom buddies. Joe Greer is another of Jim's characters, an essentially decent person flawed by selfish and violent behavior, whom the viewer struggles to like.

Several months pass, and Eddie, now the racing champion, is hired by Fred Duesenberg to drive a hot new car at the Indianapolis 200. Joe has been missing for months, and Lee borrows money from Ann to pay for transportation to the race track, where he — fresh from riding the rails in a filthy suit — futilely attempts to find a car to enter in the race. In one of those moments only possible in a Hollywood script, Joe is spotted by the owner of a lunch counter, who insists that he enjoy a free meal, served by none other than — Lee!

Joe tells Lee that he hasn't had a drink since the Ascot tragedy (and gains a sympathy point from the viewer). During the Indy race, Eddie's tire tread splits off, seriously whipping his arm bloody. Joe comes to the rescue, taking over for his brother, then winning in a photo finish just before the right front tire blows out. Following yet another crash, the two brothers reconcile on the way to the hospital as Joe encourages a final race, this time between their *ambulance* and another carrying the injured mechanics. Though the script includes improbable elements and a plot that already had become a Cagney standard, *The Crowd Roars* features one of the actor's finest early performances.

Robinson's effective performances as a gangster, a gambler and a muckraker led to a real cinematic sentence in his next Warners film. In the opening scene of *Two Seconds* (1932),

Winner Take All (1932): Bruised and battered Jimmy Kane (Cagney) and his trainer, "Rosebud" (legendary actor and songwriter Clarence Muse), in Roy Del Ruth's often risqué pre-Production Code boxing drama.

directed by Mervyn LeRoy, Eddie's character, John Allen, goes straight to the electric chair! As a university student (William Janney) joins a group of journalists in the death chamber, one of the reporters explains that the condemned convict's brain functions for "two seconds" after the executioner throws the switch, "long enough to relive his entire life."

In a lengthy flashback, John Allen is depicted as a bashful, thoughtful construction worker with aspirations for an education and a better lot in life. However, his pathetic marriage to Vivienne Osborne (Shirley Day), a gold-digging dance-joint dame, leads to the accidental workplace death of his best pal, Bud (Preston Foster), and his eventual mental breakdown. After he murders his wife for her immoral activities (adultery, prostitution), he frantically informs the judge that he is being killed "at the wrong time," claiming that his elimination of a woman who was a corruptive influence on other girls was justified.

Two Seconds, an unconvincing and outlandish melodrama, is one of LeRoy's lesser works, featuring over-the-top performances (even Robinson, who is excellent in a change-of-pace role, chews the scenery during the surreal courtroom scene) and a disjointed script. Preston Foster's character actually becomes so obnoxious, constantly complaining about Allen's wife, that it seems a blessing when he plunges to his death (via a laughable process shot) from a skyscraper beam. The film's best moments are contributed by Robinson during the early scenes, demonstrating his ability to convey a natural, warm innocence while Allen waxes philosophical to Bud and politely courts Vivienne. He also plays one of his first excellent drunk scenes, after Allen, having unknowingly married her while in an alcoholic blackout, returns to the apartment he shares with Bud.

Cagney was able to rely on past urban experience while portraying a boxer in *Winner*

Take All (1932), though he thought little of the hoary plot about Jimmy Kane, an honest Joe corrupted by a pompous society woman. The script features some choice dialogue by Wilson Mizner, a writer (and former con man) whom Cagney remembered as "fabulous ... the great raconteur and adventurer in living ... fascinating to hear, fascinating to see."[11]

During the shooting of *Winner Take All*, Cagney was visited by a professional pugilist who, after observing his footwork, assumed he'd been in the ring as a pro himself. "Only a street fighter," Jim told him. "I'm a *dancer*. Moving around is no problem."

"Oh, I get it," the boxer replied. "When I first saw you doing your stuff, I said this son of a bitch has been at it. Now I get it."[12]

Directed by Roy Del Ruth, the film opens with Kane, *way* down on his luck, put on display in the boxing ring as the announcer (Selmer Jackson) begs the spectators to donate dough to help the completely exhausted athlete regain his once-awesome strength at the Rosario Ranch and Hot Springs in Arizona: "He gave you all he had, in a dozen tough fights, right here in this arena. But he fought too often."

Compared to Cagney's previous rapid-fire tough guys, Jimmy Kane is another character altogether. Sporting a smashed nose and cauliflower ear, he is a man of few words with a limited vocabulary, speaking as if his sinus cavities have been radically rearranged by *a lot* of punches to the head.

Kane is seen off at the train station by his manager, "Pop" Slavin (Guy Kibbee), and trainer, "Rosebud" (Clarence Muse), who, knowing his destination, gives him some advice: "Don't mess around with those Indian squaws. You might get tomahawked." (One of Golden Age Hollywood's most respected African American actors—as well as an accomplished songwriter—Muse rarely played down to stereotypes.)

During his first evening at Rosario, Kane hears strange sounds emanating from the desert. Investigating, he meets another lodger, Peggy Harmon (Marian Nixon), who explains that the howls are made by coyotes. "I thought the joint was haunted," admits Jimmy.

The pleasant young woman seems very familiar; and, indeed, the two had met in New York, when Peggy was working as a singer at Texas Guinan's nightclub. She also had seen him box at Madison Square Garden. Now, she is seeking a cure for her ailing little boy, Dickie (Dickie Moore).

Jimmy becomes attached to the mother and child, and she reluctantly admits that her insurance has run out, leaving her unable to pay for the remaining three months of Dickie's "cure." To raise the necessary $600, Jimmy secretly signs on for a "winner take all" fight at the Tia Juana Sports Club, where his nose is broken and ear disfigured further before he finally manages to win the bout. Packed and ready to leave, Peggy is surprised by a "paid in full" receipt, then realizes that the injured Jimmy was responsible.

"Oh, come on, Kid," he implores. "Don't get sloppy. I cry easy."

When Pop Slavin reads about Kane's bout in the papers, he initially sends a telegram ordering him to get back on his rest program, then sends another, this time telling him to take a train to Chicago, where his first new official fight has been booked. Peggy and Dickie are paid up, so he decides to go, but plans to marry her after the three months of treatment are completed. At this point, Cagney seems to be playing the first truly "positive" leading role of his career; but, beware, there's a bad broad just waiting around the next corner to trip him up. And what viewer would want him to be so two-dimensional, anyway?

Back on top in New York, Kane attends a party at the Stork Club, where he meets young and beautiful society dame Joan Gibson (Virginia Bruce). At a subsequent uppity soiree, a pompous Soviet pianist informs him that "Russia today is the laboratory for the world's greatest economic experiment" (a typically direct leftist reference written by Mizner and allowed by Warners in the year that elected FDR, still two years prior to the Production Code). Asked what he thinks of the "Five Year Plan," Jimmy replies that people who buy on such a drawn-out "installment plan" get robbed of their money. A tuxedo-clad guest who laughs at him *laughs last*, after taking a quick smack to the head.

Given a shot at the championship, Kane turns it down, claiming that he'll be going out of town for at least a month. "You ain't gonna be two-timing me while I'm gone," he tells Joan on the telephone. Pop and Rosebud try to talk some sense into him, but his mind is set, and he secretly pays Dr. Wilson Kendall, a plastic surgeon (who is mentioned but never shown), to fix his nose and ear. While his new features are still bandaged, he attempts to take lessons from an etiquette teacher (Alan Mowbray), who asks if he wants to read some Shakespeare.

"I don't want any part of that Shakespeare guy," Kane replies. "He's the one who ruined Gene Tunney."

Jimmy (now sporting the actual Cagney face but the same altered voice) returns to the city and drops in on Joan, who not only teases him half to death but invites an older friend to stay the night, leaving her bedroom door open. Fed up, Kane storms out, prompting Joan to tell her intrusive pal that, without his beaten-up nose and ear, Jimmy's no longer of any interest to her. This scene is a pre-Production Code *killer*. Backlit while wearing a sheer nightgown, the stunning, 21-year-old Bruce can be viewed nearly *au naturel*; then, during a close two-shot with Cagney, she shows more cleavage than would be seen in the mainstream Hollywood cinema for another 35 years. Kane's frustrated reaction and departure is understandable following a close-up in which Joan, while reclining on a divan, steams up the camera with an expression hot enough to melt the boxer's new plastic "shnozzle."

Kane's aggravation is now doubled by Pop, who objects to his association with a "no good" broad and his new status as a "dancing master" afraid to let an opponent near his new facial features. Making matters worse, the old man sends for Peggy, whom Jimmy first gives the bum's rush; then, the following morning, attempts to pay off with a fistful of dough. His intention to marry a "swell society dame" provides the final straw, and she throws him out. Kane's transformation from sensitive, potential "family man" to womanizing cad is now complete.

Joan doesn't arrive at the championship fight, but instead telegrams that she must rush to help her sister in Havana! Jimmy knocks out his opponent in short order, takes a taxi to the pier, brawls his way onto the ship and into her cabin, punches out her male companion, and kicks her in the bum. The final scene shows him in Peggy's apartment, dressed to the nines, his nose bandaged, handing her a hot ring he had bought from "Legs" Davis (Ralf Harolde) while having his tuxedo made. As she kisses him, he (repeating an earlier remark) warns, "Watch the shnozzle. It's full of firecrackers."

There are obvious, large gaps in the narrative (a complete neglect of Peggy and Dickie, only to have her shoehorned back in at the last moment to set up the hasty, unconvincing conclusion), but *Winner Take All* features an excellent Cagney performance, well-paced direction by Roy Del Ruth and believable boxing scenes in which Jim's electricity is crackling: dancing and bouncing around the ring, he lands some believably real punches on his opponents.

With *Winner* in the can, William Cagney tried to wangle his brother another raise, pointing out that singer-actor Dick Powell was raking in $4,000 per week while Jim, a box-office powerhouse, was pulling in a paltry $1,250. Jack Warner refused, placing Cagney on suspension.

Tiger Shark (1932): Mike Mascarenhas (Robinson), "the best fisherman in the Pacific," protects Quita Silva (Zita Johann) from the lecherous Tony (J. Carroll Naish) in Howard Hawks' exciting maritime melodrama.

In a subsequent press release, Cagney explained that he deserved to be paid what he was worth, and offered to act for free in three Warners films (including *Blessed Event* and *20,000 Years in Sing Sing*) in exchange for a new, adequate contract at the year's end. Warner responded by threatening a law suit (and casting Lee Tracy in *Blessed* and Spencer Tracy in *20,000*), so Cagney headed back to New York, where he considered enrolling in Columbia's medical school. Following intervention by Frank Capra, representing the Academy of Motion Picture Arts and Sciences, a new contract was hammered out (with Bill Cagney now acting as Jim's manager) in September 1932, raising Cagney's salary to $3,000 per week, with incremental options to reach $4,500 by 1935.

After production began on *Tiger Shark* (1932), Howard Hawks realized he disliked how Robinson's Portuguese character had been written by Wells Root and John Lee Mahin. Mike Mascarenhas was depicted as a pessimistic, bitter man, and the director wanted to rewrite him as "happy-go-lucky" and "talkative."[13] When Robinson agreed, Hawks wrote new dialogue on a daily basis, handing it to his star on yellow sheets, encouraging him to create a believable character through improvisation.

Unlike Steven Spielberg's *Jaws*, released 43 years later, *Tiger Shark* uses, not a huge rubber—often unconvincing—shark, but real 18-footers captured in the Pacific. (In 1932 filmmakers didn't worry about the "rights" of fish. The modern animal-rights movement was developed during the 1970s, hence Spielberg's really bad shark.) Though Robinson later claimed that Hawks let him chew more scenery than the fearsome fish, the director's suggestion that he improvise added the naturalism they were seeking.

"He's a fine actor, and I thought he did a great job," Hawks said. "But I hate to think of what the picture would have been if we'd done the dour, sour man instead of this rather gay, futile man, because the whole tenor of the picture changed."[14]

Hawks had Robinson outfitted with a hook to replace the hand that Mascarenhas loses during a vicious shark attack. This necessitated close collaboration with cinematographer Tony Gaudio to mask the extension added to his full-length arm. The prosthesis didn't bother Eddie as much as the *water*, which reminded him of a near-drowning swimming pool accident during his youth. Hal Wallis assured him that the dangerous work would be done by a stunt man; but, while filming on location off Catalina, he had to perform Mascarenhas' death scene during a four-hour session in shark-infested water.

The film opens on the San Diego waterfront — home port of the tuna fishing fleet — then superimposes a newspaper report about the wreck of the *Santa Maria* in Mexican waters, where Mascarenhas, Pipes Boley (Richard Arlen) and a third sailor lie unconscious in a small fishing boat. When the parched sailor attempts to brain Mascarenhas with a club, the captain kicks him overboard, where he instantly is devoured by a school of sharks. The exhausted Mike then collapses with his left arm over the side. Pipes tries to rouse him, but a shark quickly bites off his appendage at mid-forearm. The next scene shows Mike using his hook to scratch Pipes' back.

Mascarenhas first meets Quita Silva (the exotic Zita Johann, who also costarred with Boris Karloff in *The Mummy* that year) after her father, Manuel (William Ricciardi), is bitten in two by a shark. Calling himself "the best fisherman in the Pacific" with "the biggest boat on the California coast," he nurses the ailing lass back to health with fresh food and "insurance money," then asks her to marry him. Prior to the wedding, a humorous sequence shows a manicurist polishing his detached hook.

After his first fishing voyage away from Quita, Mike returns a very happy man, waving to a mother carrying a child, announcing, "There's going to be some more." Though she has been enduring the marriage, Quita, utterly miserable, confesses her love for Pipes, who then tells Mike that he will remain in Mazatlan after their next trip. His plans change, however, when, impaled in the neck by a fishing hook, he is forced to return to San Diego for treatment.

Following his recuperation in the Mascarenhas household, Pipes is joined by Mike *and* Quita on the next voyage. While Mike stands on the bridge, shooting at tiger sharks with a rifle, Quita kisses Pipes. Here, Hawks expertly uses sound — or, rather, the absence of sound — to suggest, off camera, that Mike has discovered the embracing couple. The shooting stops, but the kissing continues; then the scene cuts to an enraged Mascarenhas, who pummels Pipes and drags him out on deck, where he tosses him into a rowboat and harpoons the wooden hull.

The sharks "settle everything," he rants, describing that the fish first took his hand, leaving him a hook — then Manuel, giving him Quita. Thinking the sharks now can settle his marriage dilemma, he instead is dragged overboard by the harpoon rope. Pipes attempts to haul him back in, but he — like Manuel — is bitten in two, ultimately becoming "the best bait in the Pacific Ocean." Claiming that the definitive fisherman, St. Peter, will rescue him from the pits of Hell, Mascarenhas puts his arm around, not Quita, but Pipes before he dies.

The romantic triangle depicted in the film was resurrected three times by Warner Bros. in the ensuing decade, for Pat O'Brien and Henry Fonda in *Slim* (1937), Bogart and Eddie

Big City Blues (1932): Humphrey Bogart (left) made his Warner Bros. debut alongside (standing) Joan Blondell, Eric Linden, and (seated) Ned Sparks.

Albert in *The Wagons Roll at Night* (1941), and Robinson and George Raft in *Manpower* (1941). In *Tiger Shark*, it is done in classic Howard Hawks style, with the male bonding in full force.

As in nearly all of Hawks' films, *Tiger Shark* depicts a group of men working closely together to get a job done. Aboard the boat, they are seen joining in a sing-along with Pipes, who strums a guitar. (Hawks would effectively reprise this scene 27 years later in Warners' *Rio Bravo*.) Later, they are seen fishing, then as they toil to remove scores of tuna from the icy hold. Hawks brilliantly captured realistic scenes at sea, lending the film an authentic documentary quality.

Mascarenhas' married mate doesn't love him, but his first mate truly does; and, while the jealousy-crazed Mike nearly succeeds in getting Pipes killed by sharks, the conclusion shows Boley pulling his lifelong friend out of the water and holding him as he dies on the deck. His wife merely looks on as Pipes puts his arm around Mike, who—as he does twice earlier in the film (including during his wedding)—scratches his friend's back. It's the final thing Mike does. This is vintage Hawks, who captured fine performances by Robinson and Arlen.

Directed by Mervyn LeRoy, *Big City Blues* (1932) covers 72 hours in the life of Bud Reeves (Eric Linden), a naïve lad from Indiana who experiences the urban dangers of New York. Led astray by his cousin, "Gibby" Gibboney (Walter Catlett), he loses all his dough and falls for Vida Fleet (Joan Blondell), an attractive chorus girl. During a wild hotel-room party financed with his inheritance, Shep Adkins (Bogart) and Len Sully (Lyle Talbot) initiate a drunken brawl ending with the accidental death of a hot young dish. Hummell (Guy Kibbee), the house detective, sees Vida leaving the scene, then describes her and Bud to the police, who find them at a local gambling joint.

The cops suspect Bud, but he is cleared after Hummell pins the crime on Sully, who is found hanging in the hotel broom closet. Bud returns to Indiana, but plans to raise more bread to return to Vida in the Big Apple. Making his Warners debut as Adkins, Bogart briefly demonstrates the volatile temper that would empower his later gangster characters.

Three on a Match (1932)—from a story by Kubec Glasmon and John Bright, who also wrote the dialogue—is one of the most bleak Warners social melodramas, featuring Joan Blondell, Bette Davis and Ann Dvorak as three former school mates who meet a decade later to recount their respective triumphs and troubles. Dvorak is excellent as Vivian Revere, a socialite who parties her way into adultery, association with criminals, the loss of her young son and, ultimately, suicide.

Like the studio's *Wild Boys of the Road*, *Three on a Match* is an uncompromising depiction of Great Depression tragedy with documentary-like sequences. By the time Mervyn LeRoy directed this exciting trio of women, the Warners talkie technique had become more refined, and the slow pacing of *Little Caesar* and *Public Enemy* had given way to a fast-moving, economical style. *Three on a Match* runs only 63 minutes, but covers an impressive span of material.

The film opens in 1919, with images of Prohibition and women's suffrage prefacing scenes depicting the trio as children. Young Vivian (Anne Shirley—then known as Dawn O'Day) is voted the most popular girl in school, and Ruth Wescott (Betty Carse) is valedictorian, having scored the "highest marks ever," while Mary Keaton (Virginia Davis), though "not a bad girl," is "not serious enough—too full of fun." After graduation, Vivian (now played by Dvorak) attends Miss Jason's School for Young Ladies, Ruth (Bette Davis) studies at Metropolitan Business College, and Mary (Blondell)—as predicted by the other two—winds up in reform school, where Glenda Farrell has a small part as a wisecracking inmate who warns her not to get "mixed up with a man—any *man*."

At this point—1930—an editorial newspaper cartoon depicting World War I soldiers is shown, accompanied by the following caption:

> The saying "Three on a Match means one will die soon" did not originate in the war, where it was said that to hold a match burning long enough for three lights would attract enemy gun fire.
> It did originate with Ivan Kreuger, the Swedish Match King, who wanted the world to use more matches. It is reported that the saying brings his companies $5,000,000 more revenue annually.

Three on a Match (1932): Mervyn LeRoy's hard-hitting Depression opus features (left to right) Lyle Talbot, Bogart, Allen Jenkins, Buster Phelps, Ann Dvorak and Jack LaRue.

Not surprisingly, Glasmon and Bright couldn't resist taking a shot at capitalism with this little interlude. In fact, *Three on a Match* may be Warners *most* politically pessimistic Depression opus.

The three now meet again, sharing the same match as they demonstrate their status as "modern" liberated women who smoke cigarettes. Mary is now a performer, Ruth a stenographer, and Vivian the wife of Robert Kirkwood (Warren William), a prominent lawyer, and mother of a 5-year-old boy called Junior (Buster Phelps). Mary and Ruth are content, but Vivian — whose life has been "too easy for her" — is very unhappy in her beautiful home.

With her husband's permission, she and the boy leave on a cruise to last "a few weeks." After only one day, she disappears with Michael Loftus (Lyle Talbot), a con man introduced to her by Mary just before the ship sailed. Now living together, Mary and Ruth discover Vivian's profligate partying and inform Kirkwood, who retrieves the neglected Junior while the adulterous alcoholic is passed out in bed. As soon as Robert is awarded a divorce, he weds Mary and hires Ruth as the boy's governess.

In 1932 Vivian — at the urging of Loftus, who owes two grand to mobsters — hits up Mary for some dough. Forty-six minutes into the film, Bogart finally appears as Harve, right-hand man to Ace (Edward Arnold), who is *not* pleased with the rubber check he received from Loftus. The $80 now offered by the pathetic hell-raiser amuses the Mob boss even less. After trying to blackmail Kirkwood into giving him two grand — and getting the bum's rush — Loftus kidnaps Junior. In a dingy apartment, he is strong-armed by Harve and three other goons, including Dick (Allen Jenkins in his first of many appearances with the

Wiseguys), who, wanting to grab a piece of the action for Ace, demand a ransom of 25 G's from Kirkwood.

These gangsters mean business, and the humor that soon would begin to creep into Warners' Mob depictions is nowhere to be seen in this unrelenting film. When Vivian pathetically cries out for booze during a bout with the DTs, she is beaten (off camera) by Dick, who receives his orders from Harve. In this brief role, Bogart already displays the rock-solid screen persona that would lead to his typecasting a few years later.

After 10 days in the filthy sty, the goons

Silver Dollar (1932): Yates Martin (Robinson) strikes it rich, then abandons his practical wife, Sarah (Aline MacMahon), in Warners' fact-based reproof of good old capitalist values (original lobby card).

assign the job of whacking the kid to Loftus, who refuses. In a scene that rivals the ending of *Public Enemy* as the most spine-chilling in the entire Warner Bros. classic catalog, Vivian writes a note on her nightgown in lipstick; then, as the goons enter the room, she crashes through the window, falling several stories to her death on the sidewalk below. (Though an obvious dummy is used, the entire action is shown.) Vivian pays tragically for her innumerable sins, but Mary and Ruth are shown in the final sequence, enjoying cigarettes as their match burns out on Kirkwood's fireplace hearth.

Again unimpressed with the work he had received in Hollywood, Bogart made another trip back to the Big Apple, where the Depression had devastated the theater business. Scraping through with a few roles and those landed by his wife, he eventually would turn back to the cinema to make a living.

Robinson was reunited with *Smart Money* director Alfred E. Green for his next project, *Silver Dollar* (1932). Before shooting began, he threw himself into the campaign to elect Franklin D. Roosevelt. Warners was the only non-Republican studio in Hollywood, and Eddie's political activities would have incited turmoil at a right-wing haven like MGM. Simultaneously, he studied diligently for the role of Yates Martin, reading everything he could find on real-life Colorado silver baron H.A.W. Tabor, whose empire crumbled when the United States adopted the gold standard. Tabor's second wife, known as "Baby Doe," retained control of the Matchless Mine in Leadville, where she became the town's most famous eccentric (until she froze to death in her cabin in 1935). The screenplay by Carl Erickson and Harvey Thew was adapted from the novel by David Karsner, a fictionalization of Tabor's adventures, which was "absorbed cover to cover" by Robinson.[15]

Eddie — by avoiding "mug" roles whenever possible — proved he was less easily typecast than Cagney and, later, Bogart. Continuing his series of versatile star characterizations in *Sil-*

ver Dollar, he portrays Yates Martin as a Colorado boom-town grocer, Denver millionaire, United States Senator and, finally, ruined capitalist.

The film opens in 1876, following the discovery of silver, when Martin is persuaded to open a store by his practical wife, Sarah (Aline MacMahon), who becomes concerned over his acceptance of shares in miners' stakes rather than cash. When some of them hit silver, however, Martin becomes a partner in a major mine, attains public office, and builds an opera house for the people of Denver.

Sarah is faithful but uncomfortable with her husband's newfound wealth. Turning to the glamorous Lily Owens (Bebe Daniels), Martin travels to Washington, D.C., where he marries her and buys a temporary seat in the Senate. He loses his fortune when President Grover Cleveland accepts the gold standard, then accepts an appointment as Denver Postmaster. Before he can take office, he dies and, as he had requested, is buried in a silver casket, mourned by both Lily and Sarah. (Lily was based on Baby Doe, but all names and many details were changed to avoid possible legal ramifications.)

Produced during the last months of the Herbert Hoover administration, *Silver Dollar* premiered in Denver on December 1, 1932, less than a month after Franklin D. Roosevelt was elected in a landslide victory over the embattled President whose former popularity was undone by his conservative attempts to stem the monumental economic disaster. Depicting an earlier fiscal disaster prefaced by self-interest, ostentation and greed (good old capitalist values), Warners took another entertaining shot at the prevailing climate in contemporary Depression America. (President Chester A. Arthur [Emmett Corrigan], General Ulysses S. Grant [Walter Rodgers] and Congressman William Jennings Bryan [Niles Welch] are all depicted in the film.)

Eddie and Gladys went to Denver for the premiere. Robinson liked the film, and thereafter carried a silver dollar in his pocket, to remind him of the project *and* the fact that Gladys was pregnant. FDR was elected, but economic times were tough, and Eddie had to accept a 15-percent salary cut at the end of the year.

4

Playing All the Angles

By early 1933, Jack Warner had dubbed Cagney "The Professional Against-er," who in turn called his boss "The Shvontz" (Yiddish for "prick"). Back at the studio, Jim again went to work for Mervyn LeRoy, whom the actor disliked, mainly for marrying Harry Warner's daughter, as well as his penchant for strolling into camera range at the end of takes prior to yelling, "Cut!" In fact, Cagney had little appreciation for many directors, whom he thought "phony," of little help to talented actors, and rather superfluous when blessed with a good script.

The title of the new LeRoy project, *Hard to Handle* (originally titled "Bad Boy"), perfectly pertained to the management's opinion of Cagney, here playing Myron C. "Lefty" Merrill, a workaholic, fad-promoting publicist specifically written for him by his friend Wilson Mizner and Robert Lord. Mary Brian costars as Jim's love interest, Ruth Waters, whose mother, Lil, is played brilliantly by Ruth Donnelly, a stage veteran (only three years older than Cagney) who was cast in several Warners films as the witty, ascerbic sidekick of the female lead.

Making his first appearance in a Cagney film, Allen Jenkins plays the radio announcer at "Lefty Merrill's Dance Marathon" in Los Angeles, where couples, hoping to win a $1,000 prize, have been dancing for days. Unknown to them, Lefty has rigged the contest in favor of his girlfriend and a hired hoofer.

Lefty's partner, Ed "Mac" McGrath (John Sheehan), splits with all the bread, so the shifty sweettalker attempts to put off payment until the following day. "Do I look like a thief?" he asks Lil Waters, who responds, "You look like you'd steal two left shoes." Delivering dialogue at a staggering clip, Cagney races through asinine lines like "The public is like a cow, bellowing to be milked."

The crowd will have none of his nonsense, however, and chases him out of the dance hall to a train, which he repeatedly rides to the end of the line. Later, he appears at the window of the Waters apartment, climbs in, carries Ruth over to the bed and (in a bold pre–Production Code move) kisses one of her sore feet! Since Cagney disliked kissing scenes, this incident is all the more striking. However, one may assume that he was very fond of Mary Brian, whom he kisses more than any other actress in his films.

Lil walks in on them, declaring that she wants to leave town, but Lefty claims that he needs only 12 hours to raise the $500 he owes them. At the Sea Breeze Park Pier, he and a loan shark stage a "Treasure Hunt" with a promised payoff of five grand, though they have planted only two $5 bills on the grounds—with the other $490 going to pay off the Waters women. The crowd, again discovering one of Lefty's rip-offs, riots, destroying everything in sight.

Subsequently, Lefty learns that the broads are even better at the confidence game. While he was away, they sold all the furniture from the apartment, which actually belongs to someone else, then left for New York. His bad luck continues when the other dance marathon winner arrives, demanding his dough. Delivering a quick punch, Lefty takes it on the lam.

Hard to Handle (1933): Lil Waters (Ruth Donnelly) and her bombshell daughter, Ruth (Mary Brian), beat Myron C. "Lefty" Merrill (Cagney) at his own con game.

While sitting in his underwear at a Manhattan tailor's shop, Lefty sees a photograph of Ruth in the newspaper, then tracks her to the office of the photographer, John Hayden (Gavin Gordon), her latest flame. Later, he drops in at the Waterses' new digs, asking for a place to stay for a few days, but receiving $20 in return. When Ruth complains that her cold cream "won't rub in," he grabs the jar and undergoes a hyperactive fit while throwing Lil to the floor in an attempt to smear the worthless ointment into her skin. He then meets with suits at the cold cream company, pitching the goop as "reducing cream" that will cause users to burn off fat as they attempt to rub it in! Clearing $3,500, he hires the prominent socialite Mrs. O. H. P. Weston-Parks (Louise Mackintosh) to endorse the product.

Ready to move on to another, even more profitable, fad, Lefty joins Charles G. Reeves (Robert McWade) in promoting Grapefruit Acres, distributing brochures that guarantee a full repayment to investors after only one harvest. He then promises Ruth that they will be married following his return from Florida.

In his hotel room, Lefty is surprised by Reeves' daughter, Marlene (Claire Dodd), who easily persuades him to stay until breakfast, when he receives an even bigger bolt from the blue—the arrival of the Waters women, who run out, screaming. Back in New York, they discover him, having flown back ahead of them, sleeping on their bed.

Things really go to hell in a fruit basket when he is busted by the D.A. (Douglas Dumbrille) for using the United States Mail to commit fraud "from coast to coast." The citrus is worthless—"a drug on the market"—and Reeves has taken a powder for Rio de Janiero, leaving Lefty holding the bag. Claiming that he really had nothing to do with the scheme, he says, "I never even saw a grapefruit."

"Lock him up," the D.A. replies, "and *show* him a grapefruit."

Escorted to his new room at the cross-bar hotel, Lefty mumbles, "Show him a grapefruit" (a hilarious in-joke recalling the *Public Enemy* breakfast with Mae Clarke) before recognizing his cell mate: none other than "Mac" McGrath, the bum who had absconded with the marathon moola. Now suffering from a terrible toothache, Mac is "cured" by a punch to the jaw from Lefty, who then asks his "friend" how he managed to lose so much weight.

"By eating grapefruit," he admits. "It'll take off three or four pounds a day."

Lefty's bail is posted, so he kisses Mac on the head and runs out, giggling like a madman. Meeting with a room full of fellow con men, he claims, "It took fifty pounds off the crookedest guy I ever knew. What will it do for honest people?" As an alternative to serving five years in the Big House, he decides to "make grapefruit as expensive as orchids" by developing the "Eighteen Day Diet," which, according to a newspaper headline, soon "sweeps the country."

The D.A. drops the charges, and Lil attempts to stop the marriage she set up between Ruth and John Hayden. Accompanied by two "cops," Lefty arrives in handcuffs, claiming he'll be spending "ten years in Atlanta," but first wanted to see her before the wedding.

"I'll never marry anybody but you," she admits. "I'll wait ten years, twenty, forever. I love you. I always have."

"That's all I wanted to know," Lefty replies, glancing at his companions. "You guys are fired!"

Hayden, holding an enormous bouquet, knocks on the door, only to be met by a vicious shove to the floor by Lil. Lefty works in his final major kiss on Ruth, who complains, "Oh, you *hurt* me!"

"That's love," he explains, gesturing to Lil (with the Cagney hand movements in full bloom) to leave the room.

Mary Brian and Ruth Donnelly are a powerhouse dual version of the wisecracking, resilient Joan Blondell archetype. Then 27, Brian, a knockout from Corsica, Texas, shared a tangible chemistry with Cagney; and his obvious comfort in an effortless performance created one of the more convincing romantic relationships in his Warner Bros. films.

Disgusted with the Warners salary cut, Robinson accompanied his wife to New York, where she rested at Essex House, pending the birth of their child. Eddie asked Darryl Zanuck if he could remain there until the event, but Jack Warner insisted that he return to film *The Little Giant* (1933) with Roy Del Ruth. At first he refused but, threatened with suspension, reluctantly returned, realizing that—box-office king or not—he still was a servant to the Brothers.

Eddie's stardom also spawned unwanted attention back in the Big Apple. While strolling along Broadway, between 38th and 48th Streets, he was accosted by autograph hunters, some of them drunk, who stammered, "Tough guy, huh? Little Caesar, huh? Well, let's see how tough you are. I can knock you into Tuesday."[1]

FDR's promise to end Prohibition and the censorial powers of the time had affected Jack Warner's attitude toward the gangster genre he helped to create, and *The Little Giant* was the first film to reflect that reality. Robert Lord and Wilson Mizner's screenplay features Joseph "Bugs" Ahearn, a Chicago bootlegger forced to turn "legitimate," a new variation on Eddie's infamous screen persona. The majority of the film depicts Ahearn's attempts to fit into California high society, chasing Polly Cass (Helen Vinson) but ultimately winning the hand of Ruth Wayburn (Mary Astor).

Robinson appreciated *not* dying this time *and* ending up with the girl; but, again, he had been terrified by a dangerous filming situation. While shooting a polo sequence with Vinson, he had to rescue her when she was thrown from her horse. Rehearsals with mechanical horses and a moving backdrop had gone well; but, during the actual take, Vinson grabbed him hard, causing them to slip down toward the steel platform below. Robinson yelled for Del Ruth to cut, but the noise of the machines drowned him out. Both of them fell hard on the steel plates: Robinson was badly bruised, and Vinson suffered hairline fractures that sent her to the hospital for a week, causing time and budget over-runs. Eddie, however, was compensated an additional $3,000 before returning to Gladys in New York.

Fred Fisher's famous song "Chicago" appropriately accompanies *Little Giant*'s opening credits. A montage (obviously dear to Jack Warner) then swiftly recounts Franklin Roosevelt's landslide victory over Herbert Hoover, even mentioning the former president's home state of Iowa, which FDR captured in the November 8, 1932, election. Immediately after hearing of Roosevelt's triumph in a radio report, Ahearn dismisses his mob, announcing, "I came from the gutter, but I'm steppin' right out of it."

Pre-Production Code references saturate Lord and Mizner's script. While telling his right-hand man, Albert J. Daniels (Russell Hopton), about his aspirations toward high culture, Ahearn points out a cubist painting hanging on the wall. "Have you ever seen anything like it?" he asks.

"Not since I've been off cocaine," Daniels replies.

The film is a parody of the gangster genre, but also takes plenty of shots at the establishment. The plot amply demonstrates that "polite society" is just as corrupt and criminal as the mob life that Ahearn attempts to leave behind. Specific comic incidents depict the U.S. government buying left-over ammunition from the gangsters, who have peddled their "choppers" to Mexican rebels, and Ahearn realizing that he can't get a passport because he has evaded paying his income tax. Some gay overtones also spice up the mix: Daniels calls himself "Papa" and Ahearn "Mama," then is presented with a bouquet of flowers at the train station.

In a hilarious scene, Ahearn, incensed at being charged $45 per day for his room at the Santa Barbara Biltmore Hotel, turns on all the faucets and tosses the towels and rug into the bathtub as it fills up. Obviously enjoying her role as Polly, ringleader of the Cass family of gold-diggers who squeeze every possible cent from Ahearn, Helen Vinson appears semi-nude in several scenes, wearing a sexy backless dress at one point, and going braless throughout the film. Lying on her back in a sleeveless dress, with her arms raised behind her head, Polly quickly seduces Bugs in one sequence (with Eddie laying on a truly furious kiss). Later, when Ruth, posing as a real estate agent (the house, facing foreclosure because of back taxes, is actually her own), gives Ahearn a tour, the "art-loving" ex-mobster pats a nude statue on the bum, then tells her, "I'll get my money's worth out of you."

Checking out the master bedroom, Daniels remarks, "Boy, what a crib."

"Kind of gives you ideas," Bugs replies.

While Ruth develops true feelings for Bugs, Polly and the Cass clan, led by Donald Hadley Cass (Berton Churchill), continue to sell him frivolous and worthless items, including a 110-foot yacht and the entire Cass, Winter and Company for 600 grand. But when the District Attorney charges Ahearn with being responsible for the sale of bogus South American bonds, he remarks, "The toughest mug in Chicago comes out here and gets trimmed by a bunch of fags with handkerchiefs up their sleeves," then phones his former mob from the D.A.'s office.

After the goons punch out the Cass butler, they coerce Donald Hadley, his Vice President and Board of Directors (one of them while nude in his bathtub) into buying back 600

The Little Giant (1933): Helen Vinson heats up "gone-legit" bootlegger Eddie G. in this sexy pre-Production Code scene.

G's worth of bonds! Grabbing back the seven-grand engagement ring he'd given to Polly, Bugs then tosses it into the tin cup of a blind beggar on the street. As he and Ruth declare their love for each other, the mobsters all attempt to "play" polo, shooting at a ball on the field and nearly annihilating everything in sight.

The entire cast of *The Little Giant* is excellent, and Roy Del Ruth (a director admired by both Robinson and Cagney) moves the action at a brisk pace. Robinson is simply superb in his first comic role, delivering lines such as "The only school I went to is reform school" with a keen sense of timing. He loved working with Mary Astor, whom he considered a "vastly underrated actress": "She had then all the attributes that make for greatness ... beauty, poise, experience, talent, and, above all, she did her homework."[2]

On March 19, 1933, Gladys Robinson gave birth to a healthy son, naming him Edward G. Robinson, Jr., but agreeing to raise him as a Jew called "Manny." Eddie returned to Hollywood, shopping for a permanent family residence while beginning a new Warners project.

On April 15, Darryl Zanuck left Warners to form the independent Twentieth Century Pictures with former United Artists executive Joseph Schenck, who was threatened with a lawsuit by the Brothers. Harry Warner thought he'd been robbed of his production chief, but the system Zanuck left behind remained a solid, smooth-running operation.

Cagney's first assignment of the post-Zanuck era was *Picture Snatcher* (1933), directed by Lloyd Bacon (one of his favorite filmmakers) and costarring his pal Ralph Bellamy. As shooting began, Jim was pleased to hear news from several Tinsel Town colleagues about the possibility of forming a new actors' union. Inspired to aid the Warners players, he sometimes feigned illness in the late afternoon, requiring the shooting to be carried over to the next morning, ensuring another day's pay for the cast.

Allen Rivkin and P. J. Wolfson adapted their screenplay from a story by Danny Ahern, who based his material on the real-life experiences of Ben Hecht, who had begun his Chicago newspaper career as an intrepid photographer. Cagney plays Danny Kean, an ex-con who will do anything to make it as a newspaper man. Fresh out of Sing Sing, he ditches his old gang after being picked up by "Jerry the Mug" (Ralf Harolde), who ran out on him two years earlier, leaving him to take six slugs fired by Lieutenant Casey Nolan (Robert Emmett O'Connor).

Having received a tip in the Big House, Danny asks J. R. McLean (Bellamy), Managing Editor for the tabloid *Evening Graphic*, for a job. He soon impresses Grover (Robert Barrat), the owner, with his ability to talk his way into difficult and dangerous situations to "snatch" photographs that prove sensational in the paper. Danny's attitudes begin to change a bit after he meets Patricia Nolan (Patricia Ellis), a young college student, who just happens to be the daughter of the policeman who sent him up the river.

Initially rebuffed by Lt. Nolan, Danny is accepted after McLean convinces the cop that his captain's promotion resulted from the aspiring reporter's idea to have a "legitimate" paper publish a story on his career. Danny enjoys a homey atmosphere with the Nolans, but throws it all away when he lies his way back into Sing Sing to sneak a photo at a female murderer's execution. In charge of the electric-chair event, Nolan is demoted after the Kean catastrophe becomes public knowledge and the lurid photo hits the front page of the *Graphic*. Danny had told Pat, "It was a great feeling doing something that was never done before," and now becomes a drunken bum after she learns the truth about his unethical effort.

The scandal snaps McLean out of a long alcoholic binge, and he eventually finds Danny in a sleazy dive, where the inebriated picture snatcher (in an amazing pre-Production Code moment) pours a glass of brandy between the breasts of an on-the-prowl loose broad. Learning that Jerry the Mug has killed two cops, they plan to locate Danny's former associate and grab a major scoop and some photos. Danny finds the Mug, snaps a picture, and tries to leave; but when the police surround the hideout, Jerry insists that he help "shoot it out." Danny hesitates, then discovers Jerry's wife and two kids dodging bullets in an adjacent room. An extremely violent, brutal battle erupts, the Mug is hit, and Danny snaps a photo of him before he drops.

Thinking fast, Danny tells the cops that he was working with Nolan to find the killer. After he and McLean are hired by the *Daily Record*, the paper publishes the exclusive story and the shocking photo. Nolan is promoted back to Captain, and Danny and Pat are reunited, but only after McLean's amorous girl, Allison (Alice White), tries to make out with him (for the third time) while waiting in a car.

While shooting the car scene, during which Danny rebuffs Allison and is slapped in return, Cagney instructed White to sit still while he threw one of his fake punches. Bacon had set up a shot to make it look real, he assured her; but, rather than leave it up to Jim, she mistakenly stuck out her chin. "I really goaled her," recalled Cagney, "And there was poor little Alice down on the floor of the car, crying her heart out."[3]

Cagney received his own shot to the head while filming yet another sock scene, this time with Bellamy, who'd never acted in an on-screen fight. Bellamy was worried that he'd hurt his costar, but was assured that Cagney and Bacon's combined expertise would create a convincing shot even though the punch would miss by a mile. Misjudging the length of Bellamy's reach, Jim took it solidly on the chin, crashed into a chair, and chipped a tooth.

Picture Snatcher (1933): Allison (Alice White) repeatedly puts the make on Danny Kean (Cagney) in Lloyd Bacon's exposé based on the early news photo career of Ben Hecht.

Picture Snatcher features some of most risqué of all pre-Production Code incidents and one-liners. "Keep in step, bedroom eyes," Danny says to Allison at one point; and, when she tries to seduce him later, he snaps a photo of her wearing nothing but a slip. The sexual references also include the aforementioned brandy down the dress event, and a comment by Jerry the Mug that he, his wife and his lover had all been staying in "the same joint." The script bears similarities to *Five Star Final* and earlier Cagney efforts, including *The Public Enemy* ("I'm Forever Blowing Bubbles" is playing in a speakeasy) and his work in general (while alone in Allison's apartment, Danny does a few dance steps and boxes with himself in a mirror).

Danny Kean possesses a great deal of his wiseguy persona (a criminal past, current associations with gangsters, using unethical behavior and dishonesty as tools for success, slugging men *and* women) but allowed Cagney to play a character who essentially wants to "go straight" in a legitimate profession. His enjoyment during the production is obvious, and he bounces through the film in classic, electric Cagney form.

Cagney begins as a racketeer in *The Mayor of Hell* (1933), but goes on to become a deputy commissioner of state penal institutions who cleans up a corrupt boys' reformatory, winning Dorothy Griffith (Madge Evans), the school nurse, in the process. As Richard "Patsy" Gargan, he gives his usual polished performance, but top acting honors are shared by young Frankie Darro, who previously had given powerful performances in Warners' *The Mad Genius* (1931), with John Barrymore, *The Public Enemy* (as the young Tom Powers), and the unforgettable *Wild Boys of the Road*, directed by William Wellman. Cagney was pleased to share the screen with his pal Allen Jenkins, who plays "Uncle" Mike and subsequently would be

The Mayor of Hell (1933): Archie Mayo directed Cagney, young Frankie Darro and Madge Evans in this reformist "social problem" classic.

cast as his faithful sarcastic sidekick, as well as further support to Robinson, Bogart and other leading men, in a raft of Warners films.

Anxious to bring the production in under budget, Archie Mayo worked his cast and crew 18 hours each day, often wrapping in the wee hours of the following morning. Cagney and his cohorts occasionally would finish a scene, only to discover Mayo, sitting behind the camera, sleeping soundly.

Mayor of Hell is one of Warner Bros.' most powerful, unrelenting social problem films, thanks in large part to Edward Chodorov's screenplay, which created a precursor to the later "Dead End" Kids. The group of boys who are threatened with "reform school"—actually an abusive prison for minors until Gargan cleans up the joint—are a truly integrated bunch, including an African American, Joliet "Smoke" Hemingway (Allen "Farina" Hoskins); a Jew, Isadore "Izzy" Horowitz (Sidney Miller); an Irish-American, Tommy Gorman (Charles Cane); and an Italian-American, Tony Carmonotti (who is tried but not sent to the slammer).

In many ways, the film is *decades* ahead of its time. Not only does the Black kid (who is never depicted differently than the others) feature heavily in the narrative—including touching scenes in which he holds the hand of the frightened Johnny "Skinny" Stone (Raymond Borzage) and becomes the *defense attorney* at the school's court after Gargan institutes a self-governed system—but Miss Griffith is an amazingly strong female character. At Gargan's behest, *she* devises the new, reformed system for the school, then feeds him portions of his improvised speech to the boys when he first takes command from the corrupt Mr. Thompson (Dudley Digges). When Gargan is forced to stay away from the school to beat a bum rap—

the accidental shooting of Joe (Harold Huber)—she stands up to Thompson and is fired. Ultimately, she returns with Gargan to quell a riot sparked by Thompson's role in the death of the ailing Skinny.

In classic Warners style, *Mayor of Hell* depicts an array of corrupt and conservative authority figures, including Thompson and Judge Gilbert (Arthur Byron), who refuses to support Gargan's reform efforts (then apologizes to him at the film's end). Chodorov's screenplay also takes a shot at attorneys, when Mr. Hemingway (Fred "Snowflake" Toones, in the film's only overtly stereotypical characterization) is warned by the judge, "Tell me what you know, not what you *think*." His reply: "Excuse me, boss. I ain't no lawyer. I can't talk without thinkin'."

There are a number of memorable lines. At one point, Mike's girl (Sheila Terry) calls him a "dirty rat" (perhaps another reason this phrase became attached to Cagney). And in a hilarious pre–Production Code moment—when Mike is complaining about having to hang out in the hospital with the wounded Joe—Gargan orders his sidekick to "get in bed with him" (eliciting the kind of double take only Allen Jenkins could deliver).

The Cagney attitude is in top form. While Gargan is making demands to his gang, one of them attempts to cut in. "Now listen, Patsy ..." is met with a lightning-fast "push in the face" by Gargan's gloved right hand. Cagney again uses his hands throughout a performance, and his "face push" here is as impressive as the rapid-fire punches he threw.

On June 30, 1933, the courageous founders of the Screen Actors Guild, including Warners veterans Boris Karloff and Noel Madison, filed their articles of incorporation. As part of its by-laws, the Guild created a contract, specifying the rules and a fee of $25 for "Class A" membership, on July 8. Cagney joined at a special meeting on October 3, and posed for a publicity photo with Karloff, who became a good friend. Jim later wrote:

> The need for the Guild was dramatized for me by that very gentle gentleman, Boris Karloff ... [who] came to me one day saying, "Jim, I'm having a terrible time. Every morning I have to report three and a half hours before work commences in order to put on these fanciful makeups. By day's end, I'm thoroughly exhausted, and then it's another hour getting the damned stuff off. Sometimes they keep me working through to eleven or twelve o'clock at night. It's terribly, terribly trying." I said, "Boris, this is exactly what they're doing at Warner Bros., too.[4]

Midge Farrell, the original secretary of the Guild, recalled that Jim was a "very active and charismatic" member during the early days.[5]

In *I Loved a Woman* (1933), directed by Alfred E. Green from a script by Charles Kenyon and Sidney Sutherland, Robinson plays John Hayden, an aspiring art student in 1892 Athens who is forced to take over his deceased father's Chicago meat-packing empire. During preproduction, he did extensive research on 1890s Chicago, specifically studying the packers' struggle with the federal government and President Theodore Roosevelt's efforts to break the meat monopoly.

Eddie disliked the melodramatic screenplay, and worked to improve his dialogue before setting foot on the soundstage, but Green repeatedly ignored his "suggestions." Finally, he approached Hal Wallis, who ordered Kenyon and Sutherland to retool portions of the script. Robinson was pleased, but his artistic satisfaction was dimmed by a knee injury that became another bone of contention with the studio. Eventually Warners agreed to pay a $30 medical bill in return for his approval of a four-week contract extension.

"Did you ever in your life see such squalor?" Hayden asks his coach driver as they attempt to move through the muddy Chicago streets. Rather than attend a meeting with Hayden and Company's board of directors, he stops to aid Martha Lane (Genevieve Tobin), daughter of his meat-packing rival (Robert Barrat). When Hayden finally reaches the office, revealing his plan, not to create the monopoly envisioned by his father, but to blow the company's dough rebuilding the slums to improve conditions for the workers, he receives a 100-percent walkout.

Smitten with Miss McDonald (Kay Francis), an ambitious, gold-digging opera singer, Hayden winds up a war-mongering capitalist, killing Spanish-American War soldiers with "embalmed" meat and threatening to sell the same to both sides during the Great War. Indicted for a major book-cooking effort to cover his myriad of sins, he returns to Athens, where, unable to recognize the visiting Miss McDonald, he dies.

One of golden-age Hollywood's star curiosities, Kay Francis was Warner Bros.' top actress at the time. Later, Robinson remembered, "Despite her lisp, despite her background as a model, despite her inexperience in the theater, she had that indefinable presence that somehow enabled her to be convincing as well as beautiful."[6]

Forty years after the fact, Eddie may have been overly generous with his praise. Francis' speech problem was a enduring impediment that defies explanation in classic Hollywood terms. (If she — like the ill-fated John Gilbert — had begun her career during the silent period, justification for stardom in the early 1930s might make some sense; but she appeared only in sound films, beginning with the Marx Bros.' *The Cocoanuts* in 1929.) She literally could not pronounce the letter R; and, in intimate scenes with Robinson, what should be taken seriously is instead totally ludicrous. After all, this character is supposed to be a professionally trained *vocalist*. Hearing Europe pronounced as "Uwope" and other such words as "gwate," "vewy" and "pwobly" spoken in short order, combined with a bombastic, pseudo-operatic performance of the cowboy classic "Home on the Range" (dubbed by an uncredited vocalist), makes the film a trying viewing experience.

An over-long soap opera, *I Loved a Woman* is interesting as a forerunner to the biopics that would star Robinson a few years later; and Hayden's problematic relationship with his wife is another role that cast Eddie as a pleading, scraping shmuck in a loveless marriage (a character he often would play in the future).

After demanding more artistic freedom, Robinson signed a new Warners contract on July 11, 1933, requiring him to appear in three films each year, but now granting him story approval. He enjoyed rejecting most of the treatments and scripts sent to him, nearly all of them dealing with crime, corruption and gambling. He did approve a dream project — the life of Napoleon — but this expensive idea would continually be pushed back by Jack Warner.

Fresh from his successes with *42nd Street* (1932) and *Gold Diggers of 1933*, choreographer Busby Berkeley was planning his next lavish Warner Bros. musical, *Footlight Parade* (1933), which finally gave Cagney what he wanted: the lead role as a song and dance man. As stage musical maven Chester Kent, he would be supported by his pal Joan Blondell, Ruby Keeler and Dick Powell, under the direction of reliable Lloyd Bacon during the dialogue scenes, which screenwriters Manuel Seff and James Seymour based on Fanchon and Marco, a vaudeville enterprise located near Warners on Sunset Boulevard.

The long working hours continued, but Cagney didn't care. He was dancing; and audiences, for the first time, would literally be shocked into realizing that he was much more than a "gangster actor." Curiously, he was never formally introduced to Ruby Keeler (then married to Al Jolson), who spent some time rehearsing the "Shanghai Lil" number with him, but only nodded and moved on. Even while shooting their dialogue scenes, they had no time to speak off camera, hard evidence of the hurried, factory filmmaking approach at Warner Bros.

Jim also recalled that working with the svelte Claire Dodd (as Vivian Rich, his gold-dig-

I Loved a Woman (1933): Robinson and Kay Francis in Warners' "soap opera meets greedy capitalist war profiteers" opus (original lobby card).

ging would-be fiancée) posed a problem unique in his career. She was too tall for him; so, in the close-ups, he stood on a two-inch apple box. Working with the cast was a pleasant experience, and he was particularly impressed with the underrated Dick Powell, whom he remembered as "a nice, nice guy ... one of the remarkable people, and Warners was full of them."[7]

Footlight Parade opens with the announcement that talking pictures are now the vogue. Chester Kent dismisses the innovation as "a fad," but soon realizes he'd better adjust to the times to put groceries on the table. "Bread line, I hear you calling me," he announces.

Kent creates a new company to produce stage prologues for talking pictures on a "chain store" basis, sending his various units out on tour. Such unlikely units as "The Russian Revolution" (undoubtedly a Manuel Seff leftist inclusion) are followed up by (proposed but unrealized) units like "Frankenstein" and "Slaves of Old Africa," in which a line of chorus girls would have appeared in blackface. Here, Seff may have taken an underhanded shot at the studio, which recently was still making films with a blacked-up Jolson.

The entire film focuses on Kent's efforts to create successful, sensational prologues. Eventually he puts an entire army of Depression outcasts to work, drilled by the neurotic, stressed-out, whiny hypochondriac-choreographer Francis (Frank McHugh), who threatens to quit. When Kent accepts his resignation, Francis (in classic McHugh comic style) nearly has a heart attack.

Kent's secretary, Nan Prescott (Joan Blondell)—in love with her boss—has her hands full trying to sabotage the gold digging of Vivian Rich while running the day-to-day operations of the busy studio. In 1933 Blondell was one of the few actresses who could pull off such a "tough" role; and this film is further proof that she was Cagney's finest on-screen partner, and perhaps his female equivalent. "That looks vaguely familiar," Nan says while gazing at Vivian's bum; then, later, after threatening to "wrap a chair around [her] neck," tells her, "As long as there are sidewalks, you've got a job." But all Blondell's pre–Production Code magnificence reaches its apex when Nan, introduced to Vivian by Kent, responds, "I know Miss B—*rich*."

Kent realizes that a "spy" has been leaking his concepts to a major rival, so he restricts the entire cast and crew to the studio for three days, to hammer out three astounding new prologues featuring his young leads, Bea Thorn (Ruby Keeler) and Scotty Blair (Dick Powell). Here, Busby Berkeley's booze-fueled surrealism really shines, as the company takes off by bus for three major Broadway theaters to present the production numbers. "Honeymoon Hotel" ends with Keeler and Powell in bed as the camera moves to a magazine featuring the picture of a baby; and "By a Waterfall" is an excuse for Berkeley to show off his amazing synchronized-swimming cinema.

"Shanghai Lil" offers song-and-dance man Cagney, warbling and hoofing for the *first* time on the silver screen. The scene opens with Kent finding the leading man loaded, then trying to force him down a ladder. After *someone* falls down to the stage, the camera remains at waist level on the tux-clad actor until, at the bar, it tilts up to reveal Chester himself. Finishing the scene in a sailor suit, Cagney dances across the bar top and a table with Keeler (in "Chinese" makeup); then they finish the film in a Navy parade featuring huge images of the American flag, Franklin D. Roosevelt, and the National Recovery Act (NRA) eagle. No other mainstream Hollywood feature film of the period features more blatant political grandstanding, and the effect of these images on Depression down-and-outers may have been immeasurable.

Many critics over the years have noted that Cagney's Kent is actually Warners' cinematic version of FDR, the strong leader with new ideas who attempts to stand up to whatever fearsome depressive forces come his way. Prior to the institution of the Production Code, World War II, and the blight of HUAC and McCarthyism — before Jack Warner defected to the right wing — the critics were right. Regardless of its content, *Footlight Parade* is a visual and verbal delight, one of the best examples of James Cagney unbound, and a must-see product of early 1930s Warner Bros.

Cagney was re-teamed in powerhouse fashion with Mae Clarke for the seriocomic *Lady Killer* (1933), in which he plays Dan Quigley, a New York criminal who becomes a Hollywood movie star. Originally, Warners had planned to make a film called "Fingerman," based on an idea by writer Rosalind Keating Schaefer, about an aspiring dancer who becomes a hood after unwittingly falling in with criminals in his New York neighborhood. By the time Roy Del Ruth called, "Action!" the entire enterprise had been transformed, and Jim was cast, not as a dancer, but as an *usher* in a movie theater!

A fast-paced, fun satire of Hollywood filmmaking, ripe with choice pre–Production Code dialogue, *Lady Killer* is also one of the more implausible early Cagney pictures, featuring plot contrivances galore. Though the opening scene showing the Bijou ushers lining up in military fashion is set in New York, the rooftop on which they are standing is so *obviously* in Los Angeles. Warners couldn't resist plugging another picture, and the "coming" placard outside the theater shows a gun-wielding Eddie G. in *Dark Hazard* (though no such action appears in that film). A moviegoer, while walking toward the entrance where Cagney is standing, mentions "Edward G. Robinson" to his companion.

Following theater policy, Quigley refuses to admit an elderly woman (Grace Hayle) car-

Footlight Parade (1933): Cagney proved he really was a song and dance man, in the ultimate Warners Busby Berkeley musical, supported by Joan Blondell and Claire Dodd (original lobby card).

rying a little dog, and is fired by the manager (Edwin Maxwell), who agrees to keep "Fido" until the film is over. Now unemployed, Quigley loiters in a hotel lobby until he sees Myra Gale (Mae Clarke) drop her purse as she is leaving. In her apartment, while returning the purse, he accepts a drink. "Chaser?" she asks.

"Always have been," he replies, with the charming Cagney smirk.

In the next room, a "five-cent ante" poker game is being waged by Spade (Douglas Dumbrille), Duke (Leslie Fenton), Smiley (Russell Hopton) and Pete (Raymond Hatton), who quickly fleece Quigley of $50. On the way out, he notices an old geezer (Harry C. Bradley) returning a purse to Myra. Hip to their two-bit racket, he returns, demanding his dough and a 10-percent piece of the action, then poses as Myra's brother-in-law to draw in the new sucker.

In no time, Quigley juices up enough action to open a large gambling joint, but the gang becomes too greedy for its own good. After devising a car-accident racket to gain entry into the home of a wealthy socialite (Marjorie Gateson), they commit a burglary during which one of them brutally beats a maid. Then, during the "Crosby job," a butler is whacked. (Both incidents are mentioned but not shown.) The cops raid the joint, Duke guns down an underling who squealed to the D.A., and the gang takes it on the lam.

In Chicago, Quigley and Myra decide to move on to Los Angeles, where the "bulls" are waiting for him at the train station. Myra eludes them and — in the script's worst contrivance — immediately runs into Spade, who convinces her to flee to Mexico with him, rather than stay behind and spend five grand to bail Dan out of the slammer. When the New York police can't "quite get the goods" to extradite him, he is given 48 hours either to find a job or get out of town. Reduced to pounding down bad hooch at a pool hall, he is spotted by a producer from National Studios who is casting "tough guys for a gangster picture."

Cagney's favorite scene in the film features Quigley in costume as a Native American chief. After riding a mechanical horse in a shot using a back-projection screen, he staggers into a dressing room to eat his box lunch. A costumed woman (Margaret Lindsay) he assumes is an extra reveals herself as Lois Underwood, the studio's top actress. Asked about his attire and condition, he replies that his name is "Big Chief Es-Tut-Mir-Vay-in-Tuchas" ("Big Chief Pain in the Ass"), then adds, "It's *Sioux*— Sioux you for anything." (This Yiddish in-joke added by Cagney incited roars of laughter from Jewish filmgoers.)

Lady Killer was the first of four films that cast Margaret Lindsay as Jim's romantic interest. He was not fond of the actress, who often was a cold fish on screen. Born Margaret Kies in Dubuque, Iowa, she affected pompous diction learned while studying in England, though her performance appropriately fits the role in this film.

Quigley continues to play bits and small parts, while receiving "hundreds" of fan letters (actually created by himself and a letter handler [Harold Waldridge]). A quick montage of magazine articles culminates with his stardom, proved by the fact that he now wears a pencil-thin mustache (the first of Cagney's career). Now Lois' official squeeze, he organizes her birthday party; and, when she tells him she wants Tyrolean yodelers, a dozen monkeys and an elephant, he — replying that "this is Hollywood" — gets her just that, adding another dozen wild simians for good measure. An unqualified success (or disaster, depending on one's viewpoint), the soiree is reduced to total bedlam as the monkeys trash everything in sight, including the birthday cake.

Taking another shot at Hollywood behavior, the narrative shifts to the famous Cocoanut Grove, where Quigley complains to Lois about a bad review that attacks her on a personal level. Seated just a few tables away (smack dab in the middle of another contrivance) is the critic, who is escorted to the men's room by Dan. Forced to eat the newspaper clipping, the wide-eyed journalist then receives a push in the face, sending him crashing into a toilet stall. A flushing sound fills the soundtrack as Quigley exits.

While showing Lois through his new, posh apartment, Dan discovers none other than Myra lounging on his bed. Understandably offended, Lois leaves, prompting him to pack Myra's clothes (which she arrogantly had already hung in the closet). Angered by her bold attempt at blackmail, he then (in Cagney's second career act of Mae Clarke abuse) drags her across the apartment floor by her hair, gives her a swift kick out the door, and tosses her suitcase into the hall. (A later comment by Clarke, claiming that she actually was dragged by her arms, is borne out by a close viewing.) Just before the scene fades out, Myra shouts, "You son ..." Perhaps the most famous of the pre-Production Code "immoral acts" filmed at Warners, it certainly is the most drawn-out and vicious of all the Cagney "broad bashing" scenes (which the actor quickly grew tired of performing). It is also one of those rare sequences that simultaneously evoke shock *and* laughter.

The following day, Myra, backed up by the entire gang, returns to hatch another blackmail attempt. In a reprise of the *Public Enemy* grapefruit incident, Dan initially responds by dropping a pineapple onto her lap. (One wonders if this was a Cagney improvisation; but his naturalistic performance, as usual, makes everything seem ad libbed.) In exchange for their silence regarding his connection to the New York burglaries and murder, Spade demands that Quigley provide them with access to movie stars' homes. His counter-offer is a check for 10 grand, if they'll blow town. Spade accepts, asking, "Where would you like us to go from here?"

"Need I say?" Dan replies.

The next Underwood-Quigley epic, an "Italian" costume drama, allows the estranged couple to take respective shots at each other. Required to eat cloves of garlic before shooting an intimate scene, Dan, dressed like a fop and wearing an awful wig, wrenches tears from Lois, who retaliates by shoving him into a fountain.

Meanwhile, the gang, still very much in Tinsel Town, begins hitting the stars' homes. When Lois' jewels are stolen, Dan tracks them down, but is pinched by the cops on his way out with the retrieved rocks. The gang escapes, bumping off one of the officers in the process. With Quigley in the can, Spade, fearing that he will squeal, has Myra bail him out so they can take him for a ride.

But Quigley is too clever for them, and tips off the cops before he exits the slammer. During the ensuing high-speed chase, Spade and the boys blast away at Myra's car, now driven by Dan. Immediately behind the gang are the bulls, who force them off the road and into a tree.

"Quigley Hero of Gun Fight; Cleared of All Charges," trumpets the next day's headline. Accounting for her help during the attempted hit (and perhaps making up for his previous Neanderthal behavior), he asks for leniency in Myra's case. In another of those hastily tacked-on "Hollywood embrace" endings, Dan, unwilling to wait the three days required by California law, and Lois are flying to Nevada to tie the knot.

Despite its flaws, *Lady Killer* is an unfailingly entertaining satire of an industry in which its star had been involved for only three years. Though most of the violence is suggested, the gangster elements are played straight by the somewhat inept, small-time mob, the most impressive aspect of which is Mae Clarke's superb performance as Myra. An underappreciated actress with great beauty and skill, she was allowed to develop a real character in this Warners film (and was only marginally utilized at Universal, in the controversial, long-suppressed *Waterloo Bridge*, *Frankenstein* and *Impatient Maiden*, all directed by James Whale during 1931–32).

Fifty years after *Lady Killer*, Clarke, with characteristic eloquence and graciousness, wrote, "It is nice to be remembered. Thank you. My working days, years, were fun, and my retirement years just begun, will be Paradise; a time for me to remember, too—oh so *many*, and all *wonderful* people."[8]

Having lived in a socialist community, Cagney considered himself a liberal, but was not usually active in political causes. He had become friendly with John Bright and another screenwriter, Samuel Ornitz, both of whom were "card-carrying" Communists, and joined them at a few meetings of the Film and Photo League, a leftist filmmakers' group. The two men also enlisted Jim to help aid the Scottsboro Boys, nine young African Americans in Alabama, eight of whom had been sentenced to death for supposedly raping two white girls (actually prostitutes) on a freight train in 1931. Their convictions by all-white juries eventually were overturned by the U.S. Supreme Court, who ordered new trials.

Cagney wasn't alone in his support for the railroaded Black youths. By the mid-1930s, the Hollywood film community had established a committee that included a struggling Warners actor named Humphrey Bogart. Eventually, one of the "rape victims" recanted her testimony, but the jurors, assuming that she had been bribed by the Communist International Labor Defense (ILD), again voted for capital convictions. The "Boys" spent many years in prison before being pardoned, released or paroled. One of them, Haywood Patterson, who had been sentenced to death *four* times, escaped to Detroit, where, 20 years later, he was arrested by the FBI. Michigan Governor G. Mennen Williams, however, refused to allow Patterson to be extradited to Alabama.

Lady Killer (1933): Myra Gale (Mae Clarke) and Dan Quigley (Cagney), covered with dough in the sack, featured on one of the hottest pre-Production Code Warners posters (original lobby card).

Cagney also sent a check to striking Mexican cotton workers in the San Joaquin Valley in October 1933. This largest agricultural strike in U.S. history involved 18,000 members of the Cannery and Agricultural Workers Industrial Union (CAWIU). Hundreds of migrants were injured and three died before the growers agreed to a raise. The workers had asked for $1.00 per 100 pounds of picked cotton. They were assured of 75 cents.

Jim's name eventually reached the hands of Sacramento D.A. Neil McAllister, who was organizing an effort against "Communist sympathizers" in Hollywood. However, after the names of all those who supported the San Joaquin strikers were published — and Cagney personally charged McAllister with attempting to generate publicity for himself — the case was abandoned.

During 1934, Cagney (and his *Public Enemy* costar, Jean Harlow) became publicly involved in protesting the "Merriam Tax," a skimming of one day's salary from the highest paid actors then under contract to the major studios, to be donated to the campaign fund of California Republican gubernatorial candidate Frank E. Merriam. This unconstitutional proposal, cooked up by two of Hollywood's premier conservatives, Louis B. Mayer and William Randolph Hearst, angered Jim, who preferred the radical candidate, Upton Sinclair, whose proposed End of Poverty in California (EPIC) program struck terror into the hearts of the studio bosses. Mayer and Hearst not only raised $500,000 for Merriam, but they also produced their own right-wing propaganda films: bogus newsreels depicting armies of homeless and unemployed Depression victims poised to flood into California if Sinclair won the election.

A Warner Bros. project that initially appealed to Robinson was *Dark Hazard* (1934), a touching dog-racing odyssey adapted from W. R. (*Little Caesar*) Burnett's novel by Ralph Block and Brown Holmes. Though Eddie's performance is subtle and likeable, the film did not fare well with audiences. Remarkably, decades after the film bombed, Robinson claimed he "loathed it."[9]

Dark Hazard chronicles the exploits of Jim "Buck" Turner, a compulsive gambler, who, in the opening scene, accompanied by Valerie Wilson (Glenda Farrell), a gambling groupie, wins 20 grand at a horse race, then blows the entire roll at an after hours casino. At a local boarding house, he rents a room-with-breakfast for $9.00 weekly, then lands a job as cashier at the Bel Port race track.

Seeking "respectability," Turner marries Marge Mayhew (Genevieve Tobin), the "proper" daughter of the old boarding-house broad (Emma Dunn), then attempts to go straight by working as a hotel clerk. His job ends quickly, however, when he tosses a key at John Bright (Sidney Toler), a boarder who has continually taunted him. Later, Bright, admitting, "I've been riding you for weeks, just for a gag, see?" hires Turner to inspect—of all things—a dog racing track in California.

The stilted nature of the Turner marriage is depicted in a scene set in the front yard of their new Los Angeles home. When Buck tries to make out with Marge, she refuses, advising, "Jim, don't do that. The neighbors will think we aren't married." Even when successful, Turner remains a rather pathetic character (the dialogue of Block and Holmes simultaneously creates pathos and pre-Production Code innuendo).

Now Turner has no way to break his addiction, particularly after he falls in love with a black greyhound named Dark Hazard! To make matters worse, Valerie (who continually shows up from coast to coast), makes casino sobriety impossible. "Don't tell me you turned decent on me?" she tells him.

Suffering through her marriage, Marge tells Buck that she is "going to have a baby"; then, upset by his continued wagering, orders, "Go away! I never want to see you again." Out on the town with Val, he gambles until 6 a.m., winning another 20 G's before he goes home with her. Back at his own digs, while in a deep sleep, he finally loses Marge when she runs off with his dough, leaving only $500 behind.

For the next two years, Buck rides the rails, trying to raise enough lettuce to get back to his wife and the tiny son he has never seen. In his scene with the little boy, Robinson is brilliant, and his emotions are identical to those he demonstrates when acting with the dog. (This performance offers a glimpse at the innate goodness of the "real" Edward G. Robinson.) Marge claims she will avoid a divorce if Buck reforms, and he accepts a cashier job from Pres Barrow (George Meeker), his wife's "friend."

At the Bel Port track, Buck runs into Tex Willis (Robert Barrat), the owner of Dark Hazard, now "practically a three-legged dog." When the leg bone snaps during a race, Buck saves his beloved pooch from the gas chamber for $25. Back at home, he complains about the family while getting loaded with Marge's brother, George (Hobart Cavanaugh), then punches out Barrow and leaves with Dark Hazard. Bumming rides, he eventually gets the dog back in racing trim; then, after winning a fistful of dough, he happily walks into the final fadeout with Val on his arm!

Dark Hazard casts Robinson as yet another character who, due to his seemingly irredeemable behavior, suffers through a doomed marriage with a woman who seeks, not love, but respectability. Unable to experience true affection from his wife, Turner receives his only real moments of pleasure from either Valerie or the dog (both of them cast-off characters). In

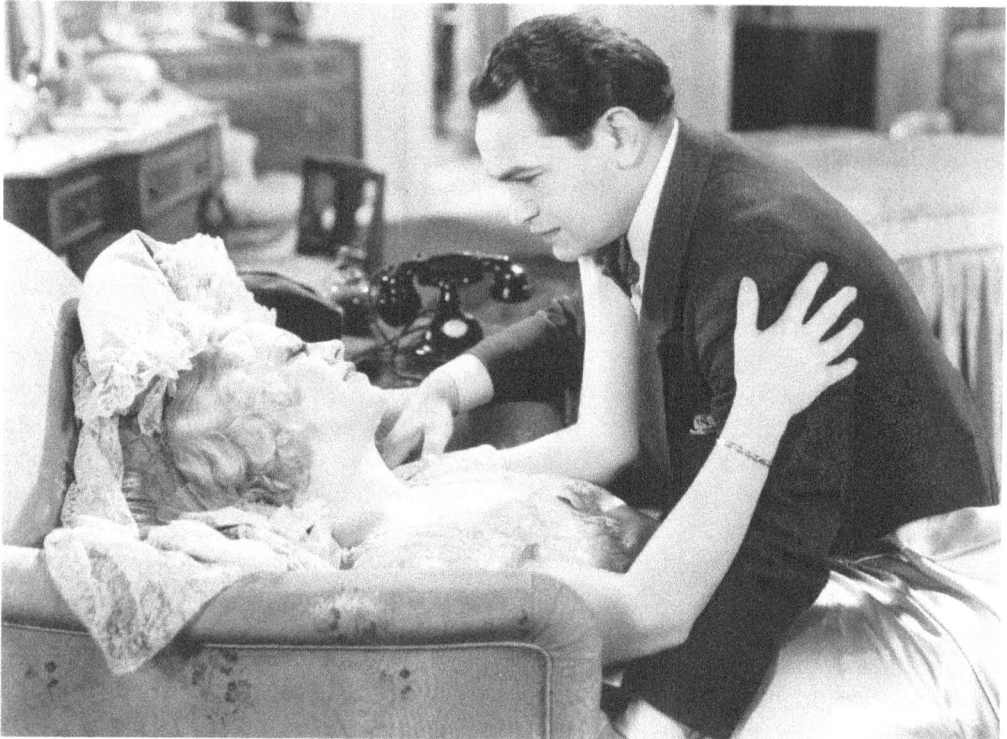

Dark Hazard (1934): Unforgettable Warners dame Glenda Farrell, in a typically snappy performance, works her wiles on Eddie G.

spite of an outlandish story, the film benefits from the effective, subtle work by Eddie (who is genuinely in love with the dog) and Farrell (in one of her best performances), whose Val, according to Marge, is a "frowsy, over-painted creature." No other actress of the period could better deliver lines like, "Heads up, you dimwits. A lady's comin' in"; "I didn't do anything to him (or vice versa)"; and (as Val and Buck stroll into the fade) "C'mon, let's go home. I have an idea." Farrell was inspired to become even more creative after the Production Code took effect on July 15, 1934.

Cagney's next film, *Jimmy the Gent* (1934), paired him for the first time with Bette Davis and director Michael Curtiz, whom Jim praised for his cinematic prowess but disdained for his cavalier treatment of actors. Expected to reprise his hoodlum routine, he played a powerful joke by reporting to Perc Westmore's makeup chair ahead of time to have his head shaved on the sides, Prussian style, and some scars added to the back. Curtiz was flabbergasted, but it was Jack Warner whom Cagney set out to irritate. Hal Wallis simply responded, "What is that son of a bitch trying to do to me now?"[10] Davis also disliked the assignment, but enjoyed working with Cagney, who, as James Corrigan, operates an agency that locates heirs for people who die in testate, then collects a hefty commission.

In classic Warners montage style, the film opens with several fatal accidents, including a boating disaster, a plane crash, a horse racing death and a plane collision, all juxtaposed with newspaper articles referring to the victims' lack of obvious heirs. Ira Morgan's camera tracks into a window advertising "James Corrigan — Personal Contacts," and "Jimmy" (who is not yet "the Gent"), sitting at his desk, is introduced from *behind* (proving that Curtiz couldn't have been too upset by Cagney's haircut stunt), revealing his numerous head scars.

Soon, the acquisition of these healed wounds becomes apparent when his boisterous and violent nature is revealed. This is one of Cagney's most brash and loud "dese, dem and dose" Warners performances.

After a secretary announces, "*It's* here," in strolls the very late Lou (Allen Jenkins), Jimmy's sidekick, who proudly announces, "I've been looking up an heiress." Slapping him into next week, Jimmy severely chastises him for fooling around with a dame named Mabel (Alice White); after all, he'd been sent to locate "a guy."

Meanwhile, at the office of the gentlemanly Charles Wallingham (Alan Dinehart), a rival ambulance chaser, Joan Martin (Bette Davis), Jimmy's former secretary, has discovered an informer, Ronny Gatson (Philip Reed), who has been phoning Corrigan on a regular basis. Having spent 10 months with Jimmy, Joan knows that "he'd bribe a corpse to sit up and telephone."

Based on Laird Doyle and Ray Nazarro's story "The Heir Chaser," Bertram Millhauser's screenplay is peppered with memorable dialogue. After Jimmy tells Lou that he is upholding "the NRA, liberty and democracy" (an obvious Warners reference to FDR), Joan arrives to deflate his mock delusions of grandeur. When she accuses, "Your business is crooked," he counters (in another choice Depression reference), "*All* business is crooked." He explains further that "There's only two kinds of guys in business. Those who get caught and those who don't."

One of Warners' more colorful depictions of unethical business practices, *Jimmy the Gent* consistently benefits from Millhauser's sarcastic one-liners that provide humor *and* character complexity. The extent of Jimmy's sleazy side is vividly suggested after Joan realizes *how* he thinks about her. "I'm liable to catch something, hanging out in your mind," she tells him. After she hits him with her purse and leaves, Jimmy takes it out on poor Lou, giving him another sound thrashing (with those Cagney hands).

Trying to locate the true heir to the Barton estate (the matriarch died from a cyanide-tainted cheese sandwich!), Jimmy offers to exchange what he knows for Wallingham's tips on how to inject class (like the constant serving of jasmine tea) into "his joint." He finds Monty Barton (Arthur Hohl), a.k.a. Joe Rector, who is wanted for "moider," then devises a plan to grab half of the 200-grand inheritance. He pays the ditzy Mabel $500 to marry Barton/Rector, then convinces Gladys Farrell (Mayo Methot), the only witness to the (self-defense) killing, to do the same — but for the promise of half the loot: 100 G's. When the murder case is dismissed, Gladys, exposed as a bigamist, is left high and dry.

In a splendid pre-Production Code moment, when Jimmy asks Mabel, "Listen, Baby. What would you do for 500 bucks?" she replies, "Well, I'd do my best."

Jimmy finally becomes the Gent after he and Joan expose Wallingham as the true crook: a racketeer who used his overstaffed "tea room" as a front. Joan then convinces Jimmy to turn over his 100 G's to Monty's sister, Sarah Posy Barton (Nora Lane), who first appeared as the potential heir. In golden-age Hollywood style, Jimmy and Joan plan to marry, kissing into the fadeout as she, no doubt, is ready to hang out in places other than his mind.

Slight hints of the Bette Davis to come can be seen early in the film, when she (in Joan Blondell fashion) stands up to Cagney; but, like Loretta Young and his other female costars, she ultimately becomes the romantic object. Davis, as in all her early Warners films in which she plays a "type," gives a thoroughly likeable performance. Perhaps the most distinguishing aspect of her character is the fact that she goes upside Cagney's head, while he (much to his satisfaction during production) breezes through an entire film without striking a woman. (After all, he was able to work out all his tension on good old Allen Jenkins!)

Jimmy the Gent (1934): As ambulance chaser James Corrigan, Cagney displays the Prussian-style haircut that so exasperated Michael Curtiz, Hal Wallis and Jack Warner (original lobby card).

On May 15, 1934, the official publication of SAG, *The Screen Player,* reported on "The Film Stars Frolic," an elaborate show intended to raise money for the union. Working closely with his pal Boris Karloff, Cagney was in charge of all "arena activities," including circus and rodeo performers, for whom he worked out some of his trademark choreography.

After working for the dictatorial Michael Curtiz, Jim enjoyed reteaming with Lloyd Bacon — and Joan Blondell — for *He Was Her Man* (1934), though he again was cast as an ex-con, "Flicker" Hayes, a former safecracker who sacrifices himself to save Rose Lawrence, a reformed streetwalker, from his murderous former "colleagues." After making himself fairly hideous in his last film, he now adopted a suave look, including another pencil-thin mustache. He also wisely created a character who is the behavioral opposite of Jimmy the Gent, a testament to his versatility. Corrigan is a hyperactive, fast-talking bully who slaps what he wants out of others, but Hayes is a calm, deliberately considerate gent (in the true sense of the word) who has abandoned his wiseguy ways.

The first image of Cagney in *He Was Her Man* is that of the semi-nude Hayes lounging in the Manhattan Turkish Bath with mobsters led by Dan Curly (Bradley Page). Initially Hayes, fresh from the Big House, appears to be joining them on another heist, demanding "15 grand in advance" for his help in knocking over a warehouse. After Hayes takes a shower (Cagney seems to enjoy the continued "nudity" as he unleashes his trademark, high-pitched laugh), he turns stool pigeon by phoning the coppers.

Hayes joins the mob at the warehouse, but quickly blows the joint, climbing out a skylight, laughing as the police arrive. One of the officers gets whacked during the bust, and the killer is quickly convicted and sentenced to burn in the chair. When the gang orders a hit on Hayes, he lams it to San Francisco, where, using the moniker of "Jerry Allen," he hides out in a hotel.

Rose Lawrence unexpectedly sneaks into Hayes' room to retrieve her wedding dress, which she had hidden in the bed. She plans to hitchhike 100 miles south to Santa Avila, where her fiancé, Nick Gardella (Victor Jory), awaits. Hayes calls for room service, then later plants a kiss (very passionate for Cagney, but this *is* Joan Blondell) on the grateful dame. When two locals recognize Hayes, one of them, Pop Sims (Frank Craven), phones the Mob back in the Big Apple.

After "Jerry" and Rose take a bus to a diner 12 miles north of Santa Avila, they catch a ride with a buck-toothed cabbie called Dutch (John Qualen, in a surreal performance). At the Gardella home, they meet the kindly Nick, a Portuguese fisherman, and his equally benevolent mother (Sarah Padden), who invite Hayes to stay for fishing and the forthcoming wedding. Rose appears to disapprove of his hanging on, then discusses her "past" with Nick, who insists that their marriage will give her a "new start." Here, the screenplay, involving a Portuguese fisherman and a developing love triangle, sails very close to *Tiger Shark* territory.

Soon, Pop Sims, calling himself "Jim Parker," arrives, feigning an interest in fishing. While staying in the bunkhouse, he steals the .45 hidden in Hayes' suitcase. After Nick and the crew sail out on a night trip, Rose confesses her love for "Jerry," and they plan to leave together the next morning, just before the wedding is to take place.

Sims sneaks out and heads to the diner, where he meets up with J. C. Ward (Harold Huber) and Monk (Russell Hopton), two hitmen sent by the Mob, then quickly boards a northbound bus. Meanwhile, Hayes grabs a ride with Dutch to the diner. When Rose is ready to leave, the two thugs arrive, and she stalls by claiming Jerry will "be back any time." Realizing that they plan to whack the dame, their driver returns to the diner, where he warns Hayes.

"She doesn't know a thing about me," Hayes tells the hitmen, then pretends that he is no longer interested in taking Rose with him. After "getting the girl" in numerous Warners films, here Cagney gives his own life to save the woman he loves, allowing her to build a life with a truly decent man who has been working extra hard to "provide for her." Nick is so understanding that he doesn't care if his wife-to-be planned to run away with someone else.

Lloyd Bacon's direction and George Amy's editing in the final scene is a superb combination of visual economy and narrative restraint, as Hayes, walking toward a roadside cliff, says, "I'm going *that* way" as he points toward the ocean. After the goons follow him with their rods drawn, the scene cuts to the tower of the church where the wedding is now under way.

This film was the first to bump off Jim since *The Public Enemy*, and the characters and the endings could not be more dissimilar. Flicker Hayes was Cagney's first ex-criminal to reform *completely*. After doing his time, he returns to society to put the finger on mobsters, aid a young woman in distress, act with consideration toward others and—ultimately—sacrifice his love and life. Perhaps Cagney's constant complaining finally resulted in this script; and, though he again plays a "wiseguy," he achieves true redemption by the film's end. Hayes actually commits no real criminal acts in *He Was Her Man*, the final film Cagney and Blondell would make together. It is their most moving team effort, and they both give superb performances. (Ironically, the film has rarely been shown since its initial release.)

Cagney and Bacon immediately moved on to *Here Comes the Navy* (1934), a service picture offering some real treats for the actor—a teaming with buddies Pat O'Brien and Frank McHugh, and a chance to work on the ocean, including scenes shot on the U.S.S. *Arizona*, then docked in San Diego (and more than seven years before she was sunk at Pearl Harbor, killing some of the men included in these sequences). In their first screen teaming, Cagney

He Was Her Man (1934): In the final James Cagney–Joan Blondell film, Jim's reformed wiseguy, "Flicker" Hayes, sacrifices his life to save Joanie's reformed streetwalker, Rose Lawrence (original lobby card).

plays smart aleck Chester "Chesty" J. O'Connor, while O'Brien is stern military man Biff Martin, with McHugh expert comic relief as Wilbur "Droopy" Mullins.

On location during a rare day off, Cagney and O'Brien decided to visit Bing Crosby at his estate near Rancho Santa Fe. Though the crooner wasn't home, they convinced the servants to let them explore the house and grounds. Less pleasant was an incident that occurred after their return to work. While filming a low-angle shot of O'Brien being hauled off the ground by a rope dangling from the dirigible *Macon*, Cagney was to climb down and tie another rope around his pal's waist. Jim clamped his legs around Pat, but they both plummeted, burning their hands on the rope as they went. After being treated, Cagney noticed that his famous mitts looked "like hamburger."[11] However, accidents such as this did not dissuade him from performing his own stunts, something the fitness-minded actor continued to do throughout his career.

The film opens in Seattle, where Martin is stationed aboard the *Arizona*. While strolling along the waterfront, he notices some civilian workers, whom he calls "scaffold monkeys," earning the instant enmity of O'Connor, who returns the sarcasm.

At the Iron Workers' Frolic, where O'Connor is sponsoring a waltz contest (giving Cagney an excuse to dance), Martin cuts in on him and his girl, Gladys (Dorothy Tree), provoking a fight, which they take outside. During the brawl, Gladys yells to Chesty that the contest is starting. Hesitating, he is punched out by Biff, who joins Gladys to win the competition. Insult is quickly added to Chesty's injury: He had personally purchased the trophy cup with his hard-earned pay. Even worse, his girl leaves him for Martin, just after he is fired from his job!

Here Comes the Navy (1934): In their first on-screen teaming, Cagney and Pat O'Brien, at odds aboard the U.S.S. *Arizona*, are joined by Gloria (*Titanic*) Stuart.

Intending to "get back" at Martin, Chesty enlists in the Navy, hoping to be assigned to the *Arizona*. Outraged that he must spend 90 days at the Naval Training Station in San Diego, he gets his wish upon graduation. Aboard the *Arizona*, he learns that Martin is his senior officer. During their tense encounters, some humor is provided by McHugh's "Droopy," who is saving his pay to buy a set of "choppers" for his "Old Lady."

Granted his first liberty, Chesty walks home with Dorothy Martin (Gloria Stuart), not realizing she is Biff's sister. During his next night ashore, he is invited to her apartment for dinner, but is asked to leave when he gets too fresh. He manages an apology, is allowed to stay, then gets into another fight when Biff arrives to throw him out and order his sister never to see him again. Soon after, she sends Chesty a telegram with an urgent request to meet, but Biff won't approve special liberty.

Determined to go ashore regardless, Chesty pays Cookie, an African American sailor (Fred "Snowflake" Toones, in a typical Stepin Fetchit-like performance), $10 for his pass, then dons blackface before lining up for the liberty boat. Incredibly, Biff, even while straightening his tie, doesn't recognize him. Even more incredible is the fact that Cagney agreed to do this scene (but then, seven years later, Bing Crosby, who was directly responsible for helping to erode the "color line" in Hollywood, did a far worse blacking-up for a minstrel scene in Paramount's *Holiday Inn* [1941]). Cagney plays the scene in a straightforward manner, and Chesty is not condescending to the Black sailors.

For all his trouble, Chesty receives the "important news" that Dorothy wants him to bury the hatchet with Biff, who, back on the *Arizona*, discovers that Droopy has been stand-

But it's all in the movie "The Man With Two Faces," First National drama now at the Strand. Looking them over, starting at the left, we find Ricardo Cortez, Arthur Byron, Mae Clarke, Edward G. Robinson, John Eldredge, Mary Astor and Emily Fitzroy. And did you know that the film was adapted from the Broadway stage success by Alexander Woollcott and George S. Kaufman?

The Man with Two Faces (1934): Ricardo Cortez, Arthur Byron, Mae Clarke, Robinson, John Eldredge, Mary Astor and Emily Fitzroy, in Archie Mayo's screen version of the George S. Kaufman–Alexander Woollcott play (original press book publicity).

ing watch in his stead. Chesty pays a speedboat pilot to approach the ship with the lights off, then jumps into the water, yelling, "Man overboard!" Court-martialed for being AWOL, he is confined to the ship for two months and fined $72.

Chesty takes out his frustration on his shipmates, telling them that he hates the Navy. With the exception of the faithful Droopy, they all avoid him. When Dorothy comes aboard, she defends her brother's actions as "just doing his duty," and Chesty breaks up with her.

A fire erupts in the gun room during battle maneuvers, and Chesty puts it out by rolling on top of the burning gunpowder. Seriously injured, he earns the admiration of his fellow sailors and is decorated by the brass. As defiant as ever, he tells Droopy that he did it only to save himself. Reassigned to the U.S.S. *Mekong* in Los Angeles, he performs a second heroic act when Martin hangs dangerously from the *Macon*. They are both injured after parachuting down, and Chesty is promoted to boatswain.

Referring to Dorothy, Biff orders, "You'll marry her, or I'll slug you with a crutch!" Unable to walk, Chesty is wed in a wheelchair, as Droopy's "Old Lady" (Maude Eburne), now fitted with her new choppers, horribly warbles a song, the lyrics of which are tattooed on her son's belly and back!

Here Comes the Navy, the first and best of the Cagney-O'Brien service pictures, moves at a brisk Lloyd Bacon clip, and features excellent performances by the entire cast. Cagney is in top form as Chesty, playing the character with just the right blend of intensity and devilish, sarcastic charm (and never resorting to the over-the-top shenanigans that mar his similar characterization in the next military opus with O'Brien, *Devil Dogs of the Air*). The film is also significant as an historical document, providing a visual record of the *Arizona* before she was permanently sent to Davy Jones' Locker by Japanese Zeroes.

Cagney's old "opponent," Mae Clarke, was cast as stage actress Daphne Flowers in Robinson's next Warners film, *The Man with Two Faces*, a Tommy Reed–Niven Busch adaptation of the popular George S. Kaufman and Alexander Woollcott play, directed by Archie Mayo, who began shooting on March 5, 1934. Warners' extensive promotion of the film suggested:

> If genius may still be correctly defined as "an infinite capacity for taking pains," Edward G. Robinson qualifies as one of the modern geniuses in the art of characterization.
> The modern portrayal of a character may take the First National star fifteen to twenty days of actual performance in front of the camera.
> His preparations for that portrayal require weeks of preliminary work and study.
> There is no more painstaking or thoroughgoing artist in Hollywood. Once he knows the character he is going to play next, Robinson becomes as insatiably curious about every detail of that character's life, every point of view and attitude he may conceivably have, every trait and peculiarity of his nature, as a detective on the trail of an elusive criminal ...
> There is nothing accidental about Robinson's attitude toward his art. He is thorough and methodical by nature. But his inborn attitude toward whatever he does is re-enforced and intensified by years of schooling in the most exacting fields of drama.[12]

Damon Wells (Robinson) is the most brilliant actor and director on Broadway, but his theatrical world is shattered when his sister, Jessica (Mary Astor), the top actress on the stage, experiences a complete mental and physical breakdown. Soon after, her Svengali-like husband, Stanley Vance (Louis Calhern), disappears, and she eventually recovers, again becoming the toast of New York. But when Vance reappears, admitting that he's been in the Big House, Jessica relapses.

In the suite of a fashionable hotel, Vance attempts to sell the rights to his wife's current hit show to a Mr. Jules Chautard. Later, an incoherent Jessica returns home in a daze, while Vance's body is found stashed in the closet of the suite. Chautard cannot be located, nor can any information on his identity be discovered by the police. One officer, Curtis (David Landau), remains on the case, learning that Vance had committed several crimes, including the murder of a former wife. While searching the hotel room, Curtis finds a false mustache in a Gideon Bible, leading him to surmise that the killer is an actor.

Recalling a stage character who matches the description of Chautard, Curtis haunts the theater scene, eventually reaching the dressing room of Damon Wells. One night, Curtis hands Wells the mustache, advising more caution in the future. Sweating profusely, the actor breathes easier when he is assured that the world is better off without Vance and that the case has been closed. (Had the film gone into production three months later, the Production Code would have required that Wells burn for his crime.) The only other person privy to the killer's true identity is Ben Weston (Ricardo Cortez), theatrical producer and Jessica's lover, who had provided his office to Wells when he made himself up as Chautard. (The photographs hanging on the walls of Weston's office include two stills of Robinson in *The Hatchet Man*.)

Eddie, publicized as "undoubtedly one of the most finished and talented actors on stage or screen," enjoyed playing a powerful thespian who literally gets away with murder while leading a double life.[13] The supporting players also appreciated being cast in good roles, particularly Ricardo Cortez, who was able briefly to escape being typecast as a villain, and Mae Clarke, who, as Jessica's humorous friend, escaped the abuse she had received in previous Warners Wiseguy efforts (fortunately for her, Cagney didn't play Damon Wells). Despite Warners' ambitious multimedia campaign, including an Eddie G. "disguise contest," radio spots, large "animated" street displays, newspaper contests, and the marketing of an official Superior "Ricardo Cortez shirt" ("It won't shrink!"), *The Man with Two Faces* fared poorly at the box office.[14]

Pleased with his characterization, Robinson rejected several scripts from Jack Warner, and was suspended on April 28, 1934. Having moved into spacious new digs at 910 Rexford Drive in Beverly Hills (described by Warners publicity as "resembl[ing] a beautiful but impenetrable jail, with double locks on the doors, steel bars outside all the windows, and the sleeping porch screens backed by formidable steel grills") he looked forward to spending a little time with Gladys, Manny and his growing art collection.[15]

5

Crime Must *Not Pay*

On July 15, 1934, Joseph Breen's official enforcement of the Production Code literally wiped out the antisocial tough guys pioneered by Robinson and Cagney. An improving economic situation at Warner Bros. also affected the narrative content of the studio's screenplays, and Harry Warner was anxious to switch from gritty, urban "social problem" films to prestige productions on par with those at the other Hollywood majors. With Robinson on suspension, Cagney appeared in even more films, becoming one of the top 10 box-office draws during the coming year.

Cagney's first "Code film" was *The St. Louis Kid*, released in November 1934, a project apropos of his recent election to Vice President of the Screen Actors Guild. Under the direction of Ray Enright, Jim and Allen Jenkins portray truckers straddling the line between bosses and labor — scabs — a reality that later troubled him, after he learned that the script had been drawn from current problems in the dairy industry.

The content and tone of *The St. Louis Kid* are established in the opening scene, in which Buck Willetts (Jenkins) bails Eddie Kennedy (Cagney) out of jail for "wrecking a dance hall." Soon, Kennedy reveals that his actions were necessary to get his friend "out of a tight spot."

Like the real Cagney, Eddie Kennedy professes a love of the country, as the two truckers haul a load of machinery from St. Louis to Chicago. Following an accident on the road, Eddie meets Ann Reid (Patricia Ellis), who has slammed her car into the back of their truck. Soon, Brown (Addison Richards), arrives, and is head-butted by Eddie (another of Cagney's rapid-fire fighting moves).

Eddie and Buck are arrested and thrown into the Ostopolis slammer. Learning that Brown is "the tool" of a powerful corporate milk company "squeezing the local farmers," Eddie uses the issue to persuade Judge Jeremiah Jones (Arthur Aylesworth) to set them free. After the magistrate initiates a "milk war" between the corporation and the farmers, the trucking company orders Eddie and Buck to drive out-of-state milk through the "war zone" to Chicago. They are soon stopped at a road block by irate farmers who dump the milk and start a brawl that lands all of them in Jones' court.

While in the crossbar hotel, Eddie sneaks out at night to soften up Ann, whose iciness is eventually melted by his incendiary charm while hoofing at a local dance. Farmer John Benson (Robert Barrat) is gunned down by Louie Munn (Harry Woods), an armed scab hired to drive the contraband milk to the Windy City, and Eddie is accused, but he escapes at a gas station. Cagney again does the personally unspeakable by smoking a cigarette in the scene.

When the dust settles, Eddie rescues Ann from Munn, who had kidnapped her after killing Benson, and he and Buck are cleared of all charges. But the trouble continues even after Eddie and Ann are married. In their hotel room during the honeymoon, they are waylaid by the suspicious innkeeper, who has them busted and tossed into jail! This ending is an obvious example of the type of film Warners began producing after the Production Code was

The St. Louis Kid (1934): Eddie Kennedy (Cagney) and Ann Reid (Patricia Ellis), busted on their honeymoon (original lobby card).

enforced. *St. Louis Kid* is a prime example of the studio's blend of compromised liberalism, cocky tough-guy action and situation comedy that emerged after mid-1934.

A truly tough guy, Robert Barrat, who had developed enormous forearms from frequent work-outs, presented Cagney with yet another unexpected punch. Perhaps Jim should have learned better by this point in his career, but he again calmly assured his fellow actor that he'd take care of any blow aimed at him. "I reckoned without that big forearm," he remembered, "which hit me on the side of my head, damn near taking it off."[1]

In New York, Bogart landed a major part in the All Star film *Midnight* (1934), starring O. P. Heggie and released by Universal, then was back on Broadway in *Invitation to Murder*. Following the play's brief run, he was devastated by the death of his father, who left behind a substantial debt that the actor vowed to pay. Now the depression really set in, and he spent much of his time self-medicating with booze, until his friend, playwright Robert Sherwood, suggested that he play ex-football star Boze Hertlinger in the forthcoming *The Petrified Forest*. But after seeing Bogart, Arthur Hopkins, the show's producer, was convinced that he'd be much better in the colorful role of vicious gangster Duke Mantee, patterned after John Dillinger. Instead of wearing makeup, Bogie took the realistic approach of playing the part with stubble, and his powerful performance received rave reviews.

But not even *The Petrified Forest* could pull Bogie out of his mental quagmire. After the play opened, his best buddy, Bill Brady, Jr., burned to death in a New Jersey cabin, an event that made his already substantial personal and financial problems too difficult to bear without the application of liberal amounts of alcohol.

When no suitable projects could be found at Warner Bros., Robinson was loaned out to

Harry Cohn at Columbia, where he starred as two characters—vicious gangster "Killer" Mannion and his milquetoast look-alike, Arthur Ferdinand Jones—in the hilarious screwball comedy *The Whole Town's Talking* (1935), directed by John Ford and costarring the irresistible Jean Arthur. Robinson personally chose Ford for the project, a move that helped create an unforgettable screen performance, including one of the most convincing, subtly comic drunk scenes ever filmed.

Back at Warners, he was offered a script called "Stiletto," about a Sicilian marked by the Mafia who moves to the States and fights gangsters. He liked the idea of playing the hero for a change, but after he referred to the role in an interview, the project was put on hold by Jack Warner, who then offered him *Dr. Socrates*, a script planned for Paul Muni, who was proving at least as difficult as Robinson. Muni demanded the title role—a doctor who experiments among the underworld—so Eddie was offered the supporting role of a mobster. Outraged at the prospect of playing second fiddle to his "rival," he turned it down.

More disagreements led to another loan-out, this time to the man who had let him go 15 years earlier, Samuel Goldwyn, for *Barbary Coast* (1935). Jack Warner didn't care if the big star was working at his studio or not; while Eddie received $80,000 from Goldwyn, the mogul landed a cool $160,000. Robinson appreciated a reunion with Howard Hawks, but hated the experience of playing opposite the insufferably self-absorbed Miriam Hopkins, whom he considered "a horror."[2]

The success of *Here Comes the Navy* led to the inevitable: Lloyd Bacon's direction of Cagney, Pat O'Brien and Frank McHugh in another service picture, *Devil Dogs of the Air* (1935). One of Jim's weakest 1930s Warners efforts, the film suffers from a nearly plotless Malcolm Stuart Boylan and Earl Baldwin screenplay offering poorly developed, two-dimensional characters and tedious incidents involving the training of Marine Corps flyers.

Lieutenant William R. Brannigan (O'Brien), a 16-year veteran, is excited about the impending arrival of his boyhood neighbor, Thomas Jefferson ("Tommy") O'Toole (Cagney), but his expectations prove unwarranted when "The World's Greatest Aviator," flying like a "swell-headed trick circus performer," arrogantly buzzes the base during a formal presentation ceremony. The film alternates O'Toole's egotistical efforts to fly "his own way" while constantly hitting on Brannigan's girl, Betty Roberts (Margaret Lindsay), with training exercises and maneuvers. Including no actual combat scenes, the narrative never takes off; and O'Toole, who ultimately kisses his way into the final fadeout with Betty, may be the most obnoxious and unlikable non-wiseguy character in Cagney's career at Warners. He is little more than an annoying attitude in a uniform.

Devil Dogs is neither preparedness nor propaganda film, having no actual point to make. Some of the well-staged aerial scenes provide momentary excitement, but none of the character relationships convince. When O'Toole first arrives at the base, literally jumping into the arms of Brannigan (who cradles him like a baby!), the Cagney-O'Brien chemistry briefly burns (like their plane later on), but is quickly extinguished by the inadequate script. The dialogue is often ludicrous. Near the film's end, when Brannigan finally pops the question to Betty, he sappily says, "I'm *daffy* about you. Will you marry me?" Would any intelligent woman reply affirmatively to such a proposal? Betty then replies that she loves Bill "like a brother" but really has fallen for O'Toole.

Again working with Margaret Lindsay, his least favorite actress, perhaps Cagney consciously chose to overemphasize Tommy's harassment of Betty, who calls his behavior "contemptible, swell-headed, fresh and conceited." (Lindsay, however, doesn't use her "British" pronunciations in this film.) Cagney did enjoy working with his two best pals, particularly

McHugh, who pioneered his trademark "one-two-three" laugh for his character of "Crash," a frustrated ambulance driver. Unfortunately, his incessant singing of "Merrily We Roll Along" is exasperating. Equally annoying is Cagney's high-pitched laugh, on which he relies far too often. The quality of the film is illustrated by one of the more convincing performers: Ward Bond, in the small supporting role of Jimmy, the senior flight instructor. (Bond, who would become a true reactionary nemesis of Cagney, Robinson and Bogart during the HUAC period, appeared in seven films with the Wiseguys, as well as many other Warners productions, beginning with *Doorway to Hell* in 1930.)

For the prestige project *G-Men* (1935), Hal Wallis ordered director William Keighley to make certain that Cagney, although cast as a federal agent (based on Chicago FBI agent Melvin Purvis, who pursued and "eliminated" John Dillinger in July 1934), emphasize his East Side wiseguy persona. After all, his character, James "Brick" Davis, is a Mob-sponsored attorney who turns G-Man. Cagney (who considered the project "a step up the ladder artistically"[3]) took none of Keighley's suggestions, and — as usual — played the role his own way.

On March 28, 1935 — the final scheduled day of shooting — assistant director Chuck Hansen, on orders from Wallis, told the cast and crew to break at 5:40 p.m. and to return an hour later to complete the last scene. SAG Vice President Cagney refused, forcing the angry Wallis to pay for another day's work, including more cash for Jim, Keighley, Ann Dvorak, and eight extras and crew members.

The U.S. Department of Justice had established the Bureau of Investigation (BOI) in 1908. J. Edgar Hoover served as Director from 1923, constantly agitating to create an actual national police force, rather than hiring attorneys and accountants to assist law enforcement at the local level. Though the American public originally viewed rural, bank-robbing gangsters such as Dillinger, Ma Barker, Bonnie Parker and Clyde Barrow as modern folk heroes, events of the mid-1930s began to disgust people throughout the nation.

On June 17, 1933, BOI agents were ambushed while attempting to return escaped mobster Frank Nash back to the U.S. Penitentiary at Leavenworth, Kansas. Prior to being sentenced to 25 years for assaulting a mail custodian, Nash already had been pardoned twice, for murder and burglary, respectively. Dubbed the Kansas City Massacre, the hit, organized by Charles "Pretty Boy" Floyd, left two agents, two local police officers, and Nash dead. Floyd and his two goons, Vernon C. Miller and Adam C. Richetti, took

Top: Warner Bros. publicity portrait of Cagney, 1934. *Bottom:* Warner Bros. publicity portrait of Robinson, 1934.

Devil Dogs of the Air (1935): Cagney and Pat O'Brien truly go *over the top* in this tedious and often annoying service picture (original lobby card).

it on the lam but soon came to violent ends. Miller made it to Detroit, but was whacked by a rival gang from New Jersey five months later. Richetti was captured in October 1934, after he and Floyd crashed their car, then shot it out with Ohio cops. Though his boss escaped, Richetti was returned to Kansas City, convicted of the killings, and later executed in 1938. Floyd escaped once again, but was apprehended just two days after the Ohio shootout. This time, during another battle, his luck ran out when he was fatally gunned down.

Popular myth credits the coining of "G-Man" to George "Machine Gun" Kelly, who, unarmed when apprehended by BOI agents for kidnapping on September 26, 1933, reportedly shouted, "G-Men! Don't shoot, G-Men!" Truth to tell, it was J. Edgar Hoover himself who invented the term, as part of an ongoing publicity campaign to draw attention to the Bureau.

Public outcry, in part, led to the Congressional passage of the Omnibus Crime Bill, which finally created the type of agency favored by Hoover. From then on, agents were allowed to carry guns and pursue criminals across state lines. Concerned about the types of crime films traditionally produced in Hollywood, Hoover didn't offer BOI cooperation to Warners during the making of *G-Men*; but after the completed film proved an enormous box-office success, he endorsed it as a positive depiction of the Bureau and a valuable publicity tool. By the end of 1935, the agency was known as the Federal Bureau of Investigation (FBI).

G-Men opens in the New York office of "Mr. James Davis, Attorney at Law," where "Brick," bored from a year's lack of cases, attempts to kill a fly by hurling a letter opener into the wall. After punching out a politician who offered favors in return for the defense of a drunken man who pistol-whipped his own mother, who lies critical in the hospital (an incident personally added to the film by Hal Wallis), Brick is visited by his old college roommate, Eddie Buchanan (Regis Toomey), who is in the Big Apple to arrest Durfee (Noel Madison), a notorious bank robber. Buchanan tries to recruit him for the Department of Justice's Bureau of Investigation, but he declines. Brick quickly changes his mind, however, after Eddie is gunned down by mobster Brad Collins (Barton MacLane).

These early scenes provide an indication of the high level of violence that permeates this film. More brutal than any gangster picture made up to that time, *G-Men* was passed by the Production Code Administration for glorifying the "good guys," law enforcement officers, rather than romanticizing criminals. The murder of Buchanan, however, is depicted with shadows only—a visual element demanded by Joseph Breen, who reminded Warners that the murder of a cop by a criminal could not actually be shown.

At the nightclub of "Mac" McKay (William Harrigan), Brick pays his respects to singer-dancer Jean Morgan (Ann Dvorak) before meeting with the boss, who was responsible for paying for his extensive education, which earned him Phi Beta Kappa honors, a law degree and a PhD. Having refused to be "a shyster or an ambulance chaser" ("I grew up in too many dirty back alleys to go back to them," he explains), Brick tells McKay that he was accepted by the Justice Department.

"I've been in rackets all my life. They don't pay off, except in dough," says McKay, claiming that he didn't spend 20 grand on a capable young man, expecting him to be dishonest. Collins threatens Brick as he leaves, then is informed that McKay is "selling out," making the joint and command of the mob available. "Mac," a "traditional," bootlegger-type gangster, is the only sympathetic criminal in the film. The new breed, represented by Collins and his mugs, is a more vicious type involved in less savory activities.

In Washington, Brick meets Jeff McCord (Robert Armstrong), the agent responsible for his training. During a boxing "lesson," Brick first feigns inexperience, then quickly punches McCord to the mat. Moments later, during a jujitsu demonstration by Hugh Farrell (Lloyd Nolan), he receives payback by being thrown to the floor three times and hitting his head on a fixture. His final test is pistol target practice, "in case they change the law" and allow federal agents to carry firearms. Expected to be unfamiliar with a rod, Brick fires all six bullets into the heart of the dummy. "I used to be marble champion of the Bronx," he claims.

A carry-over from the service pictures, Cagney's familiar attitude toward authority graces these training scenes (which were groundbreaking in 1935), with Armstrong taking over for Pat O'Brien. Though a supporting character, Hugh Farrell provided the film's working title, "Mister Farrell," a tactic used by Jack Warner to hide the actual content of the script from rival studios who might have jumped on the G-Men bandwagon.

Again paired with the dreaded Margaret Lindsay (who slips in some pompous pronunciations this time), Cagney must have enjoyed the next scene, during which Brick shoves open a door, slamming it into the bum of Kay McCord, Jeff's sister, knocking her to the floor. Pretending to read a text book on character types, he then "analyzes" her face, making several facetious remarks.

An armored car is fatally hit, and Brick, hearing about a discarded gardenia, recognizes the trademark of New York wiseguy Danny Legget (Edward Pawley). Unable to follow up, due to his in-training status, he is disappointed when the Bureau sends Farrell to apprehend the gang. Following a surprise visit from McKay at the train station, Brick is accused by

G-Men (1935): James "Brick" Davis (Cagney) is pushed in the face by Danny Leggett (Edward Pawley), manhandled by Gerard (Russell Hopton), and threatened by the heater of wannabe Mob boss Brad Collins (Barton MacLane) in Warners' anti-gangster opus praised by none other than J. Edgar Hoover *after* it created positive publicity for the FBI (original lobby card).

McCord of being a Mob stool pigeon, but explains his connection to the former boss, who has retired to run a vacation lodge at Pine Crest, Wisconsin.

A newspaper headline reads, "Crime Wave Sweeps Midwest" as Legget and his crew continue to knock over banks. Farrell and several agents apprehend him, but, during the transport process, are viciously hit by a car load of gangsters with Tommy guns (Ward Bond can briefly be spotted among the killers). The headline "Machine Gunners Butcher Officers" prefaces a Congressional meeting, during which the Director of the Bureau argues for the passing of new federal criminal laws, including the arming of all agents. "This is war!" he declares, and Legget is now branded "Public Enemy Number One."

McCord and Brick are assigned to head the division in Chicago, where (on a tip from a florist) they break into Legget's apartment. While McCord blasts away, Brick climbs in the window and beats the mobster senseless. Collins' wife is detained, and Brick recognizes his old flame, Jean Morgan, whom he questions alone, discovering that Collins and crew are hiding out at McKay's lodge in Wisconsin. During a ferocious battle, McKay is killed when the gang uses him as a human shield, and all but one of the gang (Collins, of course) is wiped out. Brick, shaken by the senseless death of his benefactor, turns in his gun and shield, but McCord won't accept his resignation.

The shootout was based on the April 1934 "Raid on the Little Bohemia Lodge" at Manitowish Waters, Wisconsin, a BOI debacle during which agents gunned down three innocent

Civilian Conservation Corps workers (one fatally), while Dillinger and his gang, including Lester J. Gillis, a.k.a. George "Baby Face" Nelson, escaped. During the brief battle, "Baby Face" killed agent W. Carter Baum. The event was a public relations nightmare for J. Edgar Hoover, who, after nearly being fired by the Department of Justice, understandably preferred the cinematic version.

During a visit to Jean's apartment, Brick, after knocking McCord down to save his life, is shot twice by Collins: once in the upper chest, with a second bullet "creasing his skull." At the hospital, Jean reveals the hideout location used by her criminal husband, whom she plans to desert. Kay McCord, working as a nurse, leaves the building, and is kidnapped by Collins, who imprisons her in an auto garage.

While Collins is away from the hideout, Jean arrives, sees Kay, and quickly leaves to phone Brick at the hospital. Collins discovers her in a phone booth and shoots her twice at close range. The film's most shocking moment, it is followed by a tender scene of Brick gently kissing her as she dies. Again, a Warners film (as in *Three on a Match*) sends the magnificent Ann Dvorak to a tragic, violent end; and she (as always) plays it perfectly. One of the finest actresses of the 1930s, she spoke every line with documentary realism and, more than 70 years later, can still break a viewer's heart with those huge, doe-like eyes. The *anti*-Margaret Lindsay, she was a true Warner Bros. treasure, and Cagney is always at his apex in his scenes with her.

Brick leaves the hospital, bandaged after surgery, to shoot it out with Collins, who, while trying to escape in a sedan, is machine gunned, meeting his end as he crashes into a light pole and building. Though the film ends with Brick and Kay discussing the obligatory climactic marriage, the scene fades out, not on them, but on Jeff McCord, who is pleased with the performance of his new star agent.

With *G-Men*, Cagney had made the complete transition from vicious Public Enemy to the eliminator of this "scourge of society." In four years (thanks in part to religious groups and the PCA), he had moved from gangster, to reformed gangster, to military officer, to federal agent. Inspired by the fine script of Seton I. Miller (who co-wrote *Scarface*, as well as working on seven Warners Wiseguy efforts) and the hard-hitting direction of William Keighley, he created a fully realized character, light years ahead of the cardboard smart ass he'd played in his previous Warners vehicle.

Cagney became a member of the Motion Picture Hall of Fame in July 1935, appearing with a host of other actors, including Warners vets Bette Davis, Joe E. Brown and Boris Karloff, at the California Pacific International Exposition in San Diego, where they happily spoke with fans and signed autographs. Cagney and Karloff also were elected officers of SAG — Treasurer and First Vice President, respectively — joining Warners players Warren William and Noel Madison.

Though saddled with stereotypical situations and dialogue, Cagney loved making *The Irish in Us* (1935), in which he, Pat O'Brien and Frank McHugh are the East Side Irish O'Hara brothers. He again appreciated Lloyd Bacon as director, who shot quickly but didn't object to Jim and his pals improvising dialogue. Cagney and O'Brien both were aghast at the casting of Scottish actress Mary Gordon as their mother, Ma O'Hara. Gordon, who had a thick Caledonian accent that obscured some of her dialogue, was consistently cast as Irish women, a fact that angered Irish actresses who were under contract. Cagney complained, and achieved some satisfaction when Earl Baldwin worked a reference to her "Scotch" ancestry into the script.

Cagney didn't object one bit to Danny O'Hara winning the hand of Lucille Jackson (Olivia de Havilland), finding the actress a delightful improvement on his previous teamings with Margaret Lindsay. (The English de Havilland had a lovely natural accent that Lindsay apparently tried to emulate.) A second treat was another chance to box on screen, during a scene in which Danny replaces fighter Car-Barn Hammerschlog (Allen Jenkins), who has pounded down a half bottle of gin to kill toothache pain.

Not surprisingly, the Irish-American standard "When Irish Eyes are Smiling" accompanies the opening credits, which feature a few shamrocks. This tune is followed by "Too Ra Loo Ra Loo Ral" as Ma is shown in the kitchen, and "The Minstrel Boy," which Pat O'Hara (O'Brien) whistles as he readies himself for his job as (what else?) a cop. While Mike O'Hara (McHugh), who would rather remain in bed, is a firefighter, Danny (Cagney) has a "career" attempting to manage prize fighters. At breakfast, Pat audibly complains about his youngest brother's refusal to get a real job, staying out all night and sleeping late.

Danny tells Ma that he finally has discovered a "champ," Hammerschlog, who is crashed in his room. Incorporating an element worthy of the Three Stooges, Danny explains, "Every time he hears a bell ring, he starts sluggin'." Offering her a 10-percent interest in the fighter for a $15 investment, Danny gets a counter offer of $14. "There's that wee bit o' Scotch comin' out again," he observes. The best reference Earl Baldwin could devise plays on the old stereotype of the Scots being cheapskates.

Pat believes that Lucille, daughter of the police commissioner, Captain Jackson (J. Farrell McDonald), is "his girl," and has mentioned marriage to his family, but the fetching young lass becomes instantly smitten with Danny after he and the "in-training" Hammerschlog fix a flat tire for her while they are out running. Pat invites Lucille to the O'Hara apartment for dinner, during which the fighter hears a bell and goes berserk, clocking both Mike and Pat, who is bedridden for the rest of the night. Danny happily offers to drive Lucille home and, on the way, buys her dinner at Joe's Steak House. At the Fireman's Ball, he and Lucille step outside, proclaim that they're "falling" for each other, and kiss passionately. Of course, Pat steps out just in time to witness the torrid scene.

Danny moves out of the apartment, nearly breaking Ma's heart. Before he leaves, they have a tender parting (allowing Cagney ably to demonstrate his subtle side). Jim may have disapproved of the casting of Mary Gordon, but none of this attitude seeped into his characterization, another testament to his professionalism. In fact, he kisses her several times. (After all, it was smooching in *romantic* situations that made him uncomfortable.) Gordon's Scots burr is ever-present, but she occasionally attempts to mask it with an "Irish" accent on certain words. This affinity between Danny and Ma is another in Cagney's catalogue of mother relationships. Later, when Ma questions him about Lucille, he hugs her and replies, "What do I want with a wife? I've got you, haven't I? You're my sweetheart."

Still angry, Pat recommends Hammerschlog as the contender for the Middle-weight World Championship against the defender, Joe Delancy (Harvey Parry), sponsored by Captain Jackson. Of course, Delancy's mobster promoter requests a push-over, and Pat reveals that Hammerschlog is "just some slug my brother picked up — punches guys around car barns." In fact, Hammerschlog hates to train, and is fond of eating, smoking and chasing broads. While waiting for the fight to begin, he writhes in pain, having sent Mike out to get some medicine for his tooth. Unable to find it, Mike returns with gin, telling him to wash the booze over the tooth and then spit it into a bucket. In no time, they have drained the entire bottle; and, when Hammerschlog hears the phone ring, he attempts to sock Delancy, who has arrived to check the challenger's taped hands. Defending himself, Delancy knocks him cold with a single punch.

The Irish in Us (1935): Danny O'Hara (Cagney) demonstrates the boxing moves of his "champ," Car-Barn Hammerschlog, to his Ma (Mary Gordon), who offers to invest $14 in the sporting enterprise.

Unable to rouse Hammerschlog with smelling salts, Danny smashes the bottle against the telephone, which he tears off the wall. Then, at the approval of Jackson, he enters the ring as Car-Barn's substitute. During the bout (in which former middle-welterweight champion Mushy Callahan appears as the referee), Danny has a rough time, until (at the behest of Ma) Pat rushes to tell his brother about Lucille's true feelings and that he'll "step down." Managing a knock-out, Danny, the new world's middle-weight champion, also has a new fiancée.

Before entering the ring, Ma happily punches out an inebriated spectator. When a microphone is shoved in his face, Danny sums up the victory by announcing, "Folks, I want you to meet the champion of the world — my mother!"

Regardless of the clichés permeating the screenplay, *The Irish in Us* is an immensely entertaining, fast-paced comedy with serious overtones. Lloyd Bacon (the same director who oversaw the poor character development and overacting in *Devil Dogs of the Air*) helped to create a fine blend of naturalistic performances and believable action scenes in this film. Frank McHugh is insufferable in the earlier Bacon effort, but he is at his best here (unleashing his famous laugh only once), especially when trying to learn table manners from Ma and during the drunk scene at the boxing match. Many actors overplay inebriation, but McHugh — continually attempting to enter the arena, Mike runs afoul of cops— primarily relies on a nonverbal, physical performance worthy of Stan Laurel or Charles Chaplin.

Incorporating familiar "Irish" melodies and contemporary tunes like Ray Noble's "The

Very Thought of You" and Harry Warren's "Lullaby of Broadway," the musical score blends well with the action (when it would have been easy to over-emphasize the more sentimental material during the family scenes).

During the autumn of 1934, Harry Warner had signed legendary German expressionist stage director Max Reinhardt to helm a lavish $1 million adaptation of William Shakespeare's *A Midsummer Night's Dream*, to feature Cagney as Bottom, "the Weaver," Dick Powell as Lysander, Joe E. Brown as Flute, Olivia de Havilland as Hermia, 14-year-old Mickey Rooney as Puck, and Frank McHugh as Quince. Reinhardt had produced the play in Austria, England, and at the Hollywood Bowl, staging spectacular scenes to the classical score by Felix Mendelssohn.

Cagney hadn't read the play, having no real desire to interpret Shakespeare, but was intrigued by a comic character possessed of infinite ego. Hal Wallis wanted Guy Kibbee, whose fuzzy-headed style would have been painfully out of place, but Reinhardt lobbied for Jim, whom he considered the best actor in Hollywood. In a February 12, 1935, studio memo to Henry Blanke, Wallis complained that Cagney was chewing the scenery (something Reinhardt wanted *all* the actors to do), but it was too late for co-director William Dieterle to do anything about it. Uncomfortable in the role, Cagney claimed he was never directed by Dieterle, and by Reinhardt only once, when Bottom reaches up to see if the ass's ears are still on his head.

The most pleasant aspect of the production for Jim was an opportunity to spend time with the "tremendous" Austrian composer Erich Wolfgang Korngold, whose scoring of Mendelssohn's music became his Hollywood debut. Cagney noted, "[F]ortunately for Warner Bros., he was to remain and write scores for some of their best pictures."[4]

Shakespearean scholars may forever debate the actual publication date of *A Midsummer Night's Dream*, but the play was first performed around 1600, to celebrate "a wedding somewhere."[5] It includes three separate plots: (1) the main, sentimental plot of the court of Theseus, Duke of Athens, and the four lovers; (2) the comic plot of Bottom and his fellows; and (3) the fairy plot. The film opens with:

> WARNER BROTHERS
> HAVE THE HONOR TO PRESENT
> A
> MAX REINHARDT
> PRODUCTION

No one else's name arrives before the title, and Shakespeare — rightfully — prefaces Cagney, who gets the top "with" spot, just above Joe E. Brown, Dick Powell and Mickey Rooney. The other performers' names appear in their proper places in the official "cast of characters" just before the action begins. Cagney first appears as Bottom, flanking Joe E. Brown's Flute, during the opening tribute to Theseus (Ian Hunter).

The contrast between a legitimate Shakespearean actor (Hunter) and the Warner Bros. players is painfully apparent from the outset, and it's no surprise that the studio avoided the Bard for the rest of its days. Cagney's pseudo-psychotic overacting is nearly unbearable, challenged only by Hugh Herbert's eternally intolerable laugh and Mickey Rooney's sheer, spurious snickering as Puck, who justly casts the fairy dust that transforms Bottom into an ass. With the donkey's head covering his face, Cagney makes the most of his expressive hands and familiar gait (including a few dance steps), and he actually achieves moments of thespian subtlety when reacting to the rampant overacting of his colleagues.

Bottom weds the stunning Titania, Queen of the Fairies (Anita Louise), a luminous, opaquely draped creature stunningly rendered by Reinhardt and cinematographer Hal Mohr. While embracing in the verdant green, Titania asks Bottom, "Whilt thou hear some music, my sweet love?"

"I have a reasonable, good ear for music," replies the ass-headed Bottom, who then attempts to sing, his headache triggering a surrounding gnome chorus and orchestra. Celebrated dwarf actor Billy Barty (1924–2000), then 10 years old, plays "Mustard Seed."

Ultimately, Titania flies away with Oberon (Victor Jory), King of the Fairies, and Puck restores Bottom to his mortal form. "Man is but an ass," he says, while trying to find his furry ears. He chews away just a bit longer, as he mingles human laughter and donkey braying.

The end to the phony laughing of "Bottom's Dream" is a blessing. Bottom and Flute engage in a bit of semi-homosexual playfulness, followed by a soliloquy, during which Cagney literally hams it to the hilt of his sword. "Now, am I dead?" asks Bottom. Perhaps, but the audience still must experience Joe E. Brown — in *drag*.

In the final scene, Theseus proclaims some pompous drivel, Puck giggles like a moron, and "all is mended" before Mendelssohn's "Wedding March" plays for a few minutes. A noble but nonsensical cinematic experiment, *A Midsummer Night's Dream* is a bungled blend of Shakespeare and the star system, and 1935 filmgoers may have struggled to grasp the pretentious display they had just seen.

On July 19, 1935, Warners' period costume consultant Dwight Franklin, then working on the Michael Curtiz-Errol Flynn swashbuckler *Captain Blood*, wrote a memo to Jack Warner, suggesting that the studio produce a follow-up film about Robin Hood, starring none other than James Cagney! Since Jim had tackled Shakespeare, it seemed natural to cast him in another English extravaganza. And to support him, Franklin thought it best to feature his fellow cronies Frank McHugh, Allen Jenkins, Ross Alexander and Hugh Herbert. Jack Warner bought the proposal for two reasons: romantic adventure epics were again in vogue, and Cagney consistently had been agitating for non-criminal roles. In August, Hal Wallis assigned primary research to Herman Lissauer while hiring English screenwriter Rowland Leigh to prepare a script for Cagney as Robin and Guy Kibbee as Friar Tuck. However, when Jim threatened Warners with another walkout, the casting took a completely different, and more reasonable, turn. (The film, eventually released as *The Adventures of Robin Hood* in 1938, directed by Michael Curtiz and William Keighley, with Errol Flynn in the title role, became one of Warner Bros.' greatest masterpieces.)

Robinson's appearance in Goldwyn's successful *Barbary Coast* induced Jack Warner to release his own San Franciscan opus set in 1854, *The Frisco Kid* (1935), directed by Lloyd Bacon and starring Cagney (making his second actual appearance in a period picture). Though he considered the script banal, and again was saddled with Margaret Lindsay as his romantic interest, he agreed to do the film, one of the most consistently violent released by Warners during the Golden Age.

As Barbary Coast sailor Bat Morgan, Jim, bound for the California gold fields, is nearly pressed into service by Slugs Crippen (Joseph Sawyer), an underling of the Shanghai Duck (Fred Kohler), a notorious scoundrel with a prosthetic hook, whom he later kills in a furious bar fight. Aided by Solomon "Solly" Green (George E. Stone), a kind Jewish tailor (perhaps the only truly decent character in the film), and offered help by Charles Ford (Donald Woods), editor of the *Tribune*, who wants to clean up the Coast, Bat accepts a bouncer job from Paul Morra (Ricardo Cortez), owner of Morra's Palace.

Ford, who works for Jean Barrat (Margaret Lindsay), "the first managing editor that wore skirts," writes an editorial asking Big Jim Daley (Joseph King) and the Board of Supervisors to take action, so Bat approaches the crooked politician. He asks Daley to put him "in charge of the Coast" and pitches his plan for a protection racket to provide a bulwark against the newspaper and the police. He also *tells* Big Jim to build him a brand-new joint, the Bella Pacific, which will be more lavish than the finest establishment in the "respectable" part of town.

All the proprietors on the Coast, except one, Spider Burke (Barton MacLane), agree with the plan; but after his joint is raided twice, he, too, pays off Morgan. Tired of interference from the newspaper, Daley orders Bat to kill Ford in a duel, but he refuses. Daley hires Burke for the dirty deed, and Bat, as a favor to Jean, confronts the would-be assassin in his dingy flop, knocking him cold with one overhand punch. Later, Solly, who reports that Burke "is on the warpath," threatening to kill Morgan "on sight," takes a bullet meant for Bat, who hugs him as he dies. This effective, touching scene culminates with a powerful close-up in which Cagney brilliantly registers a subtle expression of sorrow as he places his cheek against Stone's.

"You were very fond of him," observes Jean as Bat stands beside the majestic headstone, engraved with a Star of David, marking Solly's grave.

"He was my friend," Bat replies. Later, as they look out at the horizon together, he opines, "The only thing you get for helping others is a kick in the face." When Jean tries to temper his statement, he adds, "He'd be alive today, if he hadn't met me."

Appointed to look after Jean by her late father, Judge Stephen Crawford (Robert McWade) violently disapproves of her association with Morgan, whom he considers beneath her station. When Bat pays her a call, Crawford refuses to shake hands (giving Cagney an opportunity for some subtle hand ballet), then threatens to "shoot [him] down like a dog, if he tries to see Jean again." A thorough hypocrite, the Judge occupies the bench while perpetrating a pathological prejudice against the working-class "low-lifes" who populate the Coast.

In an effort to draw the "young blades" of San Francisco society away from the dens of iniquity, Crawford sponsors the high-brow McGuire's Opera House, and is appalled when Morgan attends, followed by Paul Morra and his wife, Bella (Lili Damita, who recently had married Errol Flynn). Further outraged by the Morras' audacious entry into his private box, the Judge attempts to throw them out, but is shot down by Paul.

"This finishes the Coast," Ford tells Morgan. "You and your *tribe* are through." Initially appearing as a level-headed journalist, Ford becomes less appealing in every scene, here revealing his veiled racism, indirectly equating the Coasters with Native Americans. Truth to tell, as depicted in the film, most of the "low-lifes" are pretty heinous. When a mob gathers to lynch Morra, the newspaper man reasons with them to "uphold the law."

Morgan and Daley try to free Morra from the slammer, but Ford intervenes, punching the politician, who shoots him in the back. As the "martyred" editor dies, he implores Jean to "keep the paper going." Jean blames Bat, claims she was wrong to have loved him, and insists she *never* wants to see him again. Lindsay's histrionics and pompous diction rise to the fore during this tirade.

As an alternative to "the mob, with anarchy," the denizens of society create "vigilance, with law," actually a vigilante mob using a kangaroo court to pass sentences of "hanged by the neck until dead." Joined by the police, they "try" Morra and Daley, then hang them from windows on the top floor of the "judicial" building. Bacon suggests the lynchings by cutting from the noose-bedecked men to overhead reaction shots of the huge crowd gathered below.

Now, the Barbary "mob, with anarchy," with torches ablaze, storms into town, ready to burn it to the ground, starting with the newspaper building. Morgan intervenes, telling them to return to the Coast to stop the vigilantes; then, after pleading with them not to use violence, is shot in the back for his trouble. He survives and, also "tried" by the kangaroo court, is sentenced to swing, while the rest of the Coasters are ordered to leave the city.

"The only thing I'm guilty of is trying to make good," Bat says, as Jean informs them of his intervention that saved the town from being torched. Insisting that he has "no connections," they want to exile him from San Francisco.

"He has *me*," says Jean, convincing them to parole Bat "in her care." In fact, Jim had Margaret Lindsay for the fourth and (perhaps to his eventual relief) final time in *Frisco Kid*. First appearing as a weary sailor, dressed in pea coat and stocking cap, then gradually gaining more "class" in his attire throughout the film, he ultimately is dressed like a dandy, complete with wavy, foppish hairdo. Bat Morgan, a characterization unique in his career, is completely believable, and a far cry from his over-the-top turn in *A Midsummer Night's Dream*.

In November 1935 Harry Warner made an agreement with William Randolph Hearst, whose Cosmopolitan Productions previously had been in league with MGM. Retaining total production control, Warner Bros. would finance, produce and distribute 12 Cosmopolitan films, four to star Hearst's beloved Marian Davies, and evenly divide the net profits, in exchange for the vast publicity and story material afforded by the Hearst publishing empire. This merger resulted in Warners' impressive series of historical epics and biopics starring Errol Flynn, Paul Muni and — Edward G. Robinson.

Naval aviator Frank "Spig" Wead, who had broken his back in a freak fall down a staircase, turned to writing after being confined to a wheelchair. Howard Hawks, who saw action as a World War I pilot, had seen Wead's 1935 Broadway play *Ceiling Zero*, starring John Litel and Osgood Perkins, and thought it would make a good film. Hawks thought Wead's writing was "damn good," but disliked the womanizers that populated the airman's work, an aspect he believed resulted from the disability.

Ceiling Zero (1936) features Cagney as "Dizzy" Davis, another smart ass who eventually becomes heroic with the aid of Pat O'Brien (as his supervisor, Jake L. Lee). Davis constantly makes passes at women, a trait that Hawks thought ludicrous in the hands of Cagney.

"Jim, we're in trouble," he told the actor. "You're too smart to make a second pass. There's about three of them written in the script, and it's getting ridiculous. You make your first pass so good, what are you gonna do?"

Cagney replied, "I guess I didn't read it carefully," then joined Hawks in a brainstorming session.

Finally, a property man approached them, offering, "If I miss out on my first pass, I say to the girl, 'Look, I was wrong,' I apologize, and then I blame everything on her. I say, 'I promise to behave myself, you oughta behave yourself too.' It always works."

In the original script, Davis was to give the young woman his room key. By the time Hawks and Cagney had shot the scene, she had given *her* key to Davis.

"It was all switched around," remembered Hawks. "We had fun doing it."[6]

Davis and Lee were fellow hot-shot World War I pilots, but now the hell-raising "Dizzy" delivers airmail for his old pal, who manages Federal Airlines in Newark, New Jersey. In the opening scene, hampered by poor visibility, Davis chooses to save his own skin by bailing out of his plane, which then crashes, destroying the company's valuable cargo. Without Lee to cover for him, his career would meet the same fate at the hands of company president Al Stone (Barton MacLane).

Due to his supercilious squiring of aviatrix "Tommy" Thomas (June Travis), Davis fakes a heart condition to convince "Texas" Clarke (Stuart Erwin), another war veteran, to fill in

The Frisco Kid (1935): Cagney, dandily dressed as Bat Morgan, with his least favorite actress, Margaret Lindsay, in Warners' answer to Samuel Goldwyn's *Barbary Coast* (which stars Robinson).

for him. Clarke successfully completes the flight, but is critically injured while trying to land in impenetrable fog. Commerce Department Inspector Joe Allen (Craig Reynolds) revokes Davis' license, then asks Lee to buy a fleet of second-rate aircraft from Fred Adams (Addison Richards), who could use his influence in Washington, D.C., to reinstate Dizzy. Davis refuses to accept this corrupt plan, then is put in charge of operations after Tex dies and Lee leaves to console Lou (Isabell Jewell), the grieving widow.

Davis disregards Lee's orders to cancel a night flight scheduled for Tay Lawson (Henry Wadsworth). Racked with guilt over Tex's demise, he (in typical Cagney fashion) knocks Lawson unconscious, then impulsively takes off in freezing rain to test a de-icing device. During the hazardous trip, he demonstrates his own design modification, but sacrifices his life in the process. Free from Davis' dizzy antics, Tommy marries Lawson, while Lee returns to his managerial position.

A forerunner to Hawks' *Only Angels Have Wings* (Columbia, 1939), *Ceiling Zero*, though dealing with aviation, is a very stage-bound exercise primarily confined to an unconvincing airport control room. Frantically parrying loads of Wead's dialogue at each other, Cagney and (especially) O'Brien nearly chew art director John Hughes' bad set to its very foundations.

Ceiling Zero was a commercial and critical success, but Cagney was still dissatisfied with the types of roles the studio was offering. After driving to New York with Willie, he bought a 100-acre farm near the sea on Martha's Vineyard, including a run-down house built in 1728. Meanwhile, backed by his brother Bill, he successfully sued Warner Bros. to be released from his $4,500-per-week contract.

On January 28, 1936, he and Willie attended a Beverly Hills cocktail party thrown by SAG colleagues Jimmy and Lucile Gleason. Joining Mr. and Mrs. Frank McHugh, Mr. and Mrs. Pat O'Brien, Mr. and Mrs. Basil Rathbone, and many other Tinsel Town heavyweights, they participated in an elaborate send-off for Boris Karloff and his wife, Dorothy, who were catching a train to New York, where they would sail to England for the "horror star's" upcoming role in the thriller *The Man Who Changed His Mind* (1936).

As a free agent, Cagney signed with Grand National Pictures, an independent outfit owned by former Warners sales executive Edward L. Alperson. Over the next two years, he would star in *Great Guy* (1936), with old "pal" Mae Clarke, and the musical *Something to Sing About* (1937), on which he collaborated with his favorite dance instructor, Johnny Boyle. Jim personally helped develop the scripts for both films, which feature content deliberately "non-Warners" in nature. *Something to Sing About* also allowed him to take an indirect shot at Jack Warner, in its depiction of arrogant studio mogul "B. O. Regan" (Gene Lockhart).

6

Real American Killer

Robinson had enjoyed his loan-out to Columbia, but was pleased to accept Warners' offer of the Duke Mantee role in *The Petrified Forest*. If the material was superior, he didn't mind playing an evil bastard. The cast was to include Bette Davis and Leslie Howard, who had starred in the hit Broadway version and controlled the movie rights, as well as choice of screenwriter, producer and director.

But there was a serious problem. The role of Mantee already had been promised to Bogart. In September 1935, Bogie, excited about his impending return to Tinsel Town, opened an issue of *Variety*, only to see that Warners had cast Eddie G! Furious, then depressed, he went out and got drunk, certain that Robinson — after all, a huge star — would play the part *he* had created so powerfully on the stage. But he didn't just get soused; he made sure to cable Howard, who was on holiday in Scotland.

This request prompted a stern telegram from Howard, who stood up to Jack Warner, telling him that, without Bogart, there would be *no film*. Making certain that studio publicity claimed that Robinson, refusing to play another gangster, had backed out, Warner tried to save face, but Eddie accepted the decision diplomatically. Robinson's association with "Little Caesar," a character who *wants* to be a gangster, made him utterly wrong for Mantee, whose criminal ways are the result of a bad upbringing in a mean old world. If Eddie G. had played the part, Warner, who was selling the production as a Leslie Howard-Bette Davis film, would have been faced with a billing dilemma.

Bogie signed a one-picture deal with Warners, guaranteed $750 per week (the exact sum he'd been paid for *Three on a Match* three years earlier) for three weeks' work. Following another career-oriented argument with his wife, he left for Hollywood. On Saturday, October 26, 1935, he reported for work on Stage 8 at the Burbank studio, and his lifelong conflicts with Jack Warner began when the mogul asked him to change his name. Fortunately, Bogie had his substantial Broadway career to back up his absolute refusal. With this move, Bogart joined fellow Wiseguys Cagney and Robinson in standing up to the "boss."

Archie Mayo wanted to shoot the film on location, but budget constraints relegated nearly all the shooting to the soundstage, where the production was plagued with problems. Since he had the real power, Howard took his sweet time arriving on the set each morning, prompting futile memos to Mayo from Hal Wallis, who also was concerned when the actors became ill from inhaling the trucked-in desert sand made airborne by the studio air conditioners. Ignoring his temperamental costars, Bogie simply soldiered on.

During the shoot, Jack Warner welcomed a visit from H. G. Wells, who observed work on *The Petrified Forest* and *The Walking Dead*, starring Boris Karloff and directed by Michael Curtiz. (At that time, Wells was embarking on a screenwriting career, for London Films' adaptations of his novels [*The Shape of*] *Things to Come* [1936] and *The Man Who Could Work Miracles* [1937].) At one point, Karloff (in full zombie makeup) and fellow cast members Ricardo Cortez, Marguerite Churchill, Henry O'Neill, Barton MacLane and Warren Hull visited Mayo's desert set. For a few moments, Warner Bros. was both *Dead* and *Petrified*.

Only Howard and Davis are billed above the title in the credits of *The Petrified Forest*, and Bogart is fifth in the cast listing. A long shot of the bleak Arizona desert opens the film, as disillusioned and depressed author Alan Squire (Howard) walks along a hot, dusty, windswept road. Though a car eventually appears, its driver does not stop to pick up the hitchhiking "gypsy," as he later calls himself. Mayo, using Howard's double, filmed the long shots on location at Red Rock Canyon State Park in Mohave, California.

At the "Last Chance" Bar-B-Q in Black Mesa, has-been football player ("almost" an All–American) Boze Hertlinger (Dick Foran) tries to relive past glories while running among the cacti before approaching young Gabrielle "Gabby" Maple (Davis), daughter of the owner and his employer, Jason Maple (Porter Hall), who objects to a local lineman's opinion that "our government's nothing but a gangster's joke."

Nick, the lineman (Eddie Acuff, who replaced Ward Bond), reveals that the first message sent over the wire was "God save the Republic!" and comments that it's in dire need of saving again. Maple is glad to see him go, then informs Gabby that he will be putting on his uniform to attend the Black Horse Vigilante meeting. Unimpressed with such reactionary shenanigans, family patriarch Gramp Maple (Charley Grapewin) is thrilled by the headline in the Denver Post—"Oklahoma City Massacre: Six Killed, Two Wounded"— and the accompanying photograph of Duke Mantee. Later, Gramp, praising the dying breed of the rugged individualist, refers to Mantee as an "old-time desperado": "Gangsters is foreigners, and he's an American." Claiming to have been shot at by Billy the Kid, he adds, "Sure does feel good to have a real killer around here again."

While serving Squire the first food he's eaten in days, Gabby reveals her romantic dream of studying in France, where she was born. Her World War veteran father returned to the States after her birth, but her mother remained in Bourges, where she hopes to visit—to escape "the sun-baked, ignorant desert rats" surrounding her. Picking up the volume of Francois Villon poetry she is reading, Squire learns that it was sent by her mother.

Squire, dumped by his weathy wife, has wandered across the United States, trying to discover "something worth living for ... or dying for." He has a desire to see the Pacific Ocean, "or perhaps drown in it." A failed intellectual, he doesn't "know anything," but tempers his incessant fatalism by mentioning his one achievement: "I once actually did write a book," which sold a whopping 600 copies.

Gabby accounts for a great deal of human behavior when she observes, "You talk like a darn fool. It's no wonder your wife kicked you out. It's no wonder she fell for you in the first place." She asks him to stay with her at Black Mesa, but he declines, instead kissing her goodbye (much to the dismay of Bose) before he leaves. When the Chisholms (Paul Harvey and Genevieve Tobin), a tourist couple, and Joseph (John Alexander), their African American driver, arrive, Gabby asks them to give Squire a lift. "He hasn't got a car right now," she says. "He's an author." (Her statement is a perceptive commentary on the status of those who attempt to live by the pen.)

On the road, the Chisholm car is waylaid by Mantee and his crew, who were stranded when their own ride broke down. Leaving the four travelers in the desert, the gang drives back toward the Bar-B-Q. "This is Duke Mantee, the world famous killer," announces Jackie Cooper (Joseph Sawyer) as the thugs enter the diner, "and he's hungry."

As Mantee, Bogart is instantly magnetic; like Howard, having had the advantage of honing the part during 197 Broadway performances. Though he doesn't appear until 30 minutes

The Petrified Forest (1936): Notorious gangster Duke Mantee (Bogart) pulls his rod while depressed author Alan Squire (Leslie Howard), idealistic diner waitress Gabby Maple (Bette Davis), and has-been football player Boze Hertlinger (Dick Foran) fear the coming explosion of violence.

have passed, the other characters provide a dramatic build-up for his entrance. Before Mayo actually shows him, he is introduced by a report on the car's radio. Holding his arms in an ape-like posture, he speaks slowly and deliberately, using only enough words necessary to convey the career criminal's intentions. At one point, he explains, "I spent most of my time since I grew up in *jail*. I guess I'll spend the rest of my life *dead*." There are several shots in which Bogart is positioned in front of a large moose head hanging on the wall behind him. Hal Wallis objected to these bizarre images, but Mayo ignored his complaints.

Aware of Gramp's possession of a stash of Liberty Bonds buried in the desert, Squire believes that the money should be given to Gabby, so she may pursue her artistic education in France. "Why in Heaven's name don't you die and do the world some good?" he tells the old geezer.

In a gesture proving he is not inherently evil, the outraged Mantee springs up from his perch above the others to question just "what kind of human being" is making such an insensitive statement. Waiting for his girl, Doris, and three others to arrive in another car, he has remained seated, while Jackie, Ruby (Adrian Morris) and Slim (Slim Thompson. who played the role on Broadway) have guarded the joint.

While Gabby is in another room, Squire endorses his $5,000 life insurance policy over to her, then asks Mantee to kill him. "I will be mourned by no one," he says. "There was an artist who died before his time." Gramp thinks he's drunk, and the Chisholms, who have arrived back at the diner, proclaim him "insane."

"Will you do it, Duke?" he asks.

"*Sure*, I'd be glad to," drawls Duke. Moments later, the "cold-blooded killer" adds, "You're all right, Pal. You got good ideas. I'll try to fix it so it don't hurt."

Meanwhile, Jason Maple and two of his lynch-mob confederates deliver news that the other carload of crooks has been apprehended. Mantee's girl "snitched" on him, they claim. A full-scale battle ensues after the law arrives, and Mantee orders the "civilians" to lie down in the middle of the floor, where Gabby and Alan kiss under a table. Jackie turns off the lights, and the scene is illuminated only by the flashing Bar-B-Q sign outside. Characteristically unconcerned with his guests' safety, Maple observes, "If they're not careful, they're going to wreck that neon sign." Perhaps justifiably, the gangsters decide to use the vigilantes as human shields during their escape.

Squire, realizing that Mantee has abandoned their pact, jumps up, refusing to let him harm the three men. Duke tells him to "get down," then is impelled to gut shoot him before fleeing the diner. Gabby cradles Alan as he dies, then vows to bury him in the Petrified Forest, the symbol of the inflexible society responsible for his—and the others'—frustrated lives.

Bette Davis (still a few years prior to her ascension to the throne of "Hollywood Bitch Number One") is superb as the pure and innocently naive Gabby, while Bogie is simply stunning as the simian Duke. Having carefully crafted the character on Broadway (and basing his look on Dillinger, a real member of the gangster "nobility"), he was able to leave an indelible, unique impression in his first portrayal of a cinematic gangster. Few of his future gangsters, particularly his simpering wiseguys whacked by Robinson and Cagney, share Mantee's traits.

Following Robinson and Cagney as a Warner Bros. Wiseguy was a tall order, but Bogie did so brilliantly, in a style avoiding any of the elements of the other actors' interpretations. Eddie's mobsters cannot avoid being likable, and Jim's are usually cracking wise and crackling with electricity, but Bogie's killer is a dark, obviously troubled creature who prefigures the anti-heroes of film noir. As good as Robinson is in his wiseguy roles, his casting as Mantee may have been disastrous; and, of course, Cagney was never considered. Risking the wrath of Cagney's ghost by bringing up The Method, it can be argued that only Bogart—having suffered a problematic past involving drug-addicted parents and child abuse—carried the proper psychological baggage to play the part.

Reflective of Robert Sherwood's authorship of the original source material, the film's inclusion of two African American actors in fairly non-stereotypical roles is a trail-blazing element of *The Petrified Forest* (made at the same time that Paul Robeson traveled overseas to seek dignified Black roles in the British cinema; he would, however, return to the States—to collect a large paycheck—for James Whale's *Show Boat* in 1936). Though John Alexander's Joseph is a chauffeur, he is a far cry from the usual "Black servant" characters prevalent in films released during the 1930s. Joseph is an intelligent, articulate man, though he *acts* like he "knows his place." When Slim tells him, "Have a drink, colored brother," Joseph automatically defers to Mr. Chisholm for permission.

"Haven't you heard about the big liberation?" asks Slim sarcastically. Arguably, this dialogue would not have made it into the final cut of a film produced at any of the other major Hollywood studios, and *The Petrified Forest* was perhaps the first mainstream Hollywood release to depict a Black character as being the equal of his white counterparts. Warner and Wallis could have cast a African American actor familiar to filmgoers, yet they made the admirable choice of bringing Slim Thompson from New York, along with Bogart and Howard. Though Slim calls Mantee "boss," all three members of the crew work for "the Duke," and it is the Black man who attempts to counsel him throughout their ordeal at the diner. It is Jackie, not Slim, who is gunned down during the shoot-out. Interestingly, Mantee, who never alters his attitude, makes no distinctions of any kind and treats everyone alike.

Due to its stage origins, most of the narrative is confined to the single diner set, but Mayo's direction (particularly his use of tight close-ups), the chiaroscuro lighting of Sol Polito (insisted upon by Hal Wallis), and the fine performances of, not only Bogart, Davis and Howard, but the excellent supporting cast — all of them handling a lot of dialogue — makes it a satisfying cinematic experience. Mayo and musical director Leo F. Forbstein's clever choice of using only music and news reports from the radio, as well as the incessant sounds of the sand storm outside, as the film's soundtrack (rather than a musical score) lends realism to what could have become a very stage-bound exercise.

When the film was released in February 1936, Warners was praised for its ability to transform stage plays into effective films, and the cast, including Bogie, was heralded far and wide. But it didn't take critical raves to persuade Jack Warner to offer the new "gangster sensation" a six-month contract. Two months before *The Petrified Forest* hit theaters, Bogie had signed a 20-page agreement guaranteeing him $550 per week ($200 less than he'd been paid while freelancing on the film) for the first 26 weeks, plus eight options for further 26-week periods (then 52-week periods), with a raise of $50 each time. The contract wasn't lavish — a sign that Warner intended to see what the new boy could do — but not bad for an actor who'd fallen on hard times in New York before being billed fifth in his first major effort for a Hollywood studio. (Joined by Tyrone Power and Joan Bennett, Bogie later reprised his Mantee role during a January 1, 1940, *Lux Radio Theater* broadcast of *The Petrified Forest*.)

Robinson returned to work on March 16, 1936, playing Johnny Blake, a cop (inspired by New York detective Johnny Broderick) who apparently loses his badge, but stays on the heels of numbers racketeers, in *Bullets or Ballots*, meeting his end from a bullet fired by Bogart's Nick "Bugs" Fenner. He hated the script (based on the experiences of journalist Martin Mooney, who had infiltrated the New York rackets), and refused to begin the project until several changes were made. Several bad working titles, including "All the Evidence," "The Showdown," "The Pigeon" and "In the Home of the Rackets," eventually gave way to *Bullets or Ballots*, which provides two opposing ways of dealing with gangsterism: violent action or established legal means. As the film demonstrates, it is the first, more sensational, choice, that necessarily wins out.

During production, the constant complaints of Joan Blondell, who was dissatisfied with the subordinate nature of her role as a small-time numbers runner, caused director William Keighley to run a week over his 27-day shooting schedule. To make matters worse, the Warners publicity department asked Eddie to meet with the personal ambassador of the King and Queen of Rumania. Learning that the royal representative wanted to be publicly photographed with "Little Caesar," he declined, then was forced to capitulate when the ambassador and his entourage appeared on the set. As the paparazzi flashed away, he reluctantly shook hands with the ambassador, who gave him inscribed photographs of "Their Majesties," then insisted that he receive an autographed image in return. Much to Eddie's chagrin, a publicity man handed him a *Little Caesar* still, which he signed, "Very truly yours, Emmanuel Goldenberg" before "stomp[ing] off the set."[1]

The opening credits read, "Edward G. Robinson in *Bullets or Ballots* with Joan Blondell," while Bogart arrives fourth (behind Barton MacLane) in the familiar Warners "parade of players" that includes an image of each featured actor. The cover of the official studio pressbook features the same billing, although it's "Edward G. ('Little Caesar') Robinson," just in case. And the first interior page of this elaborate, 32-page publicity release plays up "the greatest cast of strong arm 'killers' ever assembled in a single production":

EDWARD G. ROBINSON (Little Caesar)
BARTON MacLANE (He was Red Sebastian,
the killer, in "Dr. Socrates")
HUMPHREY BOGART (Who played Duke
Mantee in "The Petrified Forest")
GEORGE E. STONE (Famous for his many
gangster characterizations)
… And for romance you have JOAN BLONDELL
… And for comedy, FRANK MCHUGH[2]

The first scene shows Fenner and his boss, Al Kruger (MacLane), in a movie theater, watching a propaganda picture in which the Mob captain's recent trial is dramatized. (Kruger was based on real-life psycho-mobster Dutch Schultz.) Angered by this fabrication, Fenner (against Kruger's wishes) whacks the film's producer, publisher and "vice crusader" Ward Bryant (Henry O'Neill), who has been attempting to use legal means to end racketeering.

Detective Johnny Blake drops in at the Metropolitan Business Improvement Association, the front for Kruger's rackets, secretly supported by the board of directors of the Oceanic Bank and Trust Company. A follow-up to *G-Men*, *Bullets or Ballots* covers the same basic territory at the local level, with Robinson clandestinely working with Police Commissioner Dan McLaren (Joseph King) to bust the rackets and bring down the mob backing them. Though the film is another anti-gangster exposé, Seton I. Miller's screenplay depicts greedy capitalists as the real criminals who use mobsters to fill their coffers.

In their first scene together on film, Robinson and Bogart experience a tense confrontation. Though he is more clean-cut and varies his speech patterns, Fenner occasionally speaks in the deliberate Mantee manner; after all, this was Bogie's first post-*Petrified* performance. Reflecting the shift in Warners' depiction of organized crime since 1933, Kruger tells him, "That strong-arm gangster stuff went out with Prohibition."

A Grand Jury is established to investigate racketeering, and the police department undergoes a major clean-up, including the "firing" of Blake, who drops in on his friend Lee Morgan (Blondell), who runs the Bronx numbers game, and her partner, Nellie LaFleur (Louise Beavers), who manages the Harlem end. In the audience at a boxing match, Blake punches out McLaren in front of Kruger, who then hires him to "look over the whole set-up." While Blake surveils Fenner and the gang, Bugs in turn orders a stooge, Wires Kagel (George E. Stone), to check on his activities. During his investigations, Blake observes counterfeiting, loan sharking, the fleecing of minors with five-cent pinball machines, and Fenner's personal rackets involving milk and produce.

After Kruger is persuaded to infiltrate the numbers racket, Blake intends to run it, but Fenner tries to muscle in on the action. In a humorous scene, Nellie (another Warners depiction of a capable African American character) orders an enormous Black associate to manhandle the mobsters from the premises. After Fenner's milk racket is raided, he whacks Kruger, then takes over the numbers, claiming to return the Bronx and Harlem districts to Lee and Nellie.

Ordered to report to the Oceanic Trust, Blake is named the new boss by the bankers, who tell him, "You are the only one who will know who we are." At Mob headquarters, he signals the cops to begin their raid, and Fenner again has Kagel tail him. Thinking he is safe in his secret hideout, Blake leaves, only to be shot twice by Fenner, whom he manages to gun down before Lee, who has learned the truth, drives by to pick him up. In the car, Blake masks

Bullets or Ballots (1936): The first screen teaming of Robinson and Bogart, this follow-up to *G-Men* pits them against each other as "disgraced" cop Johnny Blake and Mob lieutenant "Bugs" Fenner, respectively. Barton MacLane plays racketeer Al Kruger, who is fronted by the board of a major bank, greedy capitalists who are this Depression film's real criminals.

his agony, then lives just long enough to expose the bankers. Crawling outside the Oceanic building, he again hails his fellow officers, giving his life to bust the rackets.

William Keighley maintains a brisk pace throughout *Bullets or Ballots*, providing a satisfying "first entry" in the eight films in which Bogart would appear with either Robinson or Cagney. Fresh from 198 performances as Duke Mantee, Bogie retained a minimal amount of his landmark characterization for his new gangster, who is a bit tougher than his subsequent wiseguys who die at Eddie and Jim's hands. In *Bullets*, Fenner does not cower before being killed; instead, he blazes away before falling dead at the foot of the stairs down which Eddie's Blake staggers. Like Cagney, Robinson had gone from Public Enemy to the ultimate authority figure, a law enforcement officer who annihilates the Big Boss.

However, official studio publicity advised theater owners to display a 40-by-60-inch "teaser" poster, plugging *Eddie* as "Public Enemy No. 1," plus a 24-sheet featuring "real smoke coming from the star's cigar." "*Bullets or Ballots*," the ballyhoo continued, "is said to be the most exciting and dramatic of all detective films, exceeding in thrills even the famous Robinson film, *Little Caesar*."[3] But, in its special "Hollywood After Hours" section, the pressbook presented the real "dope" on Eddie G.:

> You can't judge an actor by the character he portrays. Many motion picture stars have been embittered because the public insisted upon confusing their own personalities with those of the roles in which they have made conspicuous successes. But no actor, in pictures or on the stage, is so entirely different AFTER HOURS from his own characterizations as is Edward G. Robinson ... one of the

most cultured and scholarly gentlemen in the country ... books share with music and art the chief outside interest of E.G.R.[4]

The publicity concerning Bogart was confined to petty issues such as what his wife thought of journalists' comments about his screen roles—"Critics prais[ing] his work in *The Petrified Forest* ... have taken him to task for his work on other occasions"—and the ludicrous claim that "the only thing Humphrey Bogart ... doesn't like about Southern California is the sunshine. He complains about it, saying that he has lived in New York's shadows so long he finds he can't see very well in the sun. But he does say he likes his role of a double crossing gangster in the First National Picture."[5]

The same pressbook includes a major article, "Humphrey Bogart Rises to Top After Film Failure," listing the number-one appeal of Hollywood as "the weather—that is, the *good* weather."[6] One feature refers to his considerable prowess as a sailor, while another, titled, "Humphrey Bogart Prefers Surgery to the Theatre," quotes him as saying, "Acting essentially is a romantic profession ... and as such it leaves something to be desired—as a vocation. My father was a physician and a surgeon, and I would have followed him in his profession had it not been for the war."[7] Though including a kernel of truth, this sort of studio propaganda, cut into pre-packaged columns for newspapers, was always 90-percent nonsense (Bogie would have used a much stronger word).

Prior to the May premiere of *Bullets or Ballots*, which proved a huge box-office hit, Eddie, Bogie and Blondell performed a radio version on the *Hollywood Hotel* program that boosted its commercial potential, including a record-setting opening weekend in New York. (Later, on April 16, 1939, the two Wiseguys were joined by Mary Astor for another audio version on the *Lux Radio Theater*.)

Back at the studio, Robinson—whose participation in the Anti-Nazi League, which had been attracting other film-industry liberals wanting to persuade FDR to oppose the Third Reich and aid refugees now in the U.S., was gaining attention—met with Jack Warner, who told him he was supporting the Republican candidate, Alf Landon, in the 1936 election. (Some Democrats, impatiently disgusted with FDR, made pro–Landon statements during that campaign, but Robinson took Warner seriously.) When the German-American Bund held a convention in 1937, Eddie and other League supporters were joined in picketing by members of the American League for Peace and Democracy, the American Legion, the California Christian Church Council, and the VFW. Eddie recalled:

> [Warner] was advising me that he, personally, cared nothing about my political activities, but did I have to champion Roosevelt so visibly? After all, he and Louis B. Mayer were for Landon, and L. B. was the California man on the Republican National Committee and a great friend of Herbert Hoover's. While J. L. *hated* Hitler, wasn't it true that the Anti-Nazi League was full of Bolsheviks?[8]

"J. L." had put a scare into Robinson, but this political perplexity was matched by the mogul's *actual* indecisiveness on what to do with Bogart following his teaming with Eddie G. Much to Bogie's dismay, he was "exiled" to Bryan Foy's B unit, where he was assigned inferior scripts and roles. Worse yet, his first vehicle, *Two Against the World*, was a slapdash remake of *Five Star Final*, requiring him to play an updated, radio version of Robinson's original tabloid newspaper editor. Perhaps Warner and Hal Wallis believed that, if switching from playing a dynamic gangster to interpreting Louis Weitzenkorn's Joseph Randall had worked for Eddie, it might also work for Bogie, albeit as Sherry Scott, producer of radio programs at New York's United Broadcasting Company (WUBC), "The Voice of the People." After unleashing incredible animal magnetism on the screen in *The Petrified Forest*, here he was saddled with a totally thankless role.

Director William McGann, cinematographer Sid Hickox, editor Frank Magee and most of the principal actors studied *Five Star Final* before shooting began. Although producing such a remake aping the compositions, staging, art direction and performances of the original may have seemed expedient to Warners in 1936, the material already had to seem antiquated to filmgoers. The play transferred to the screen powerfully in 1931; but, five years later, it was dead in the water. For instance, the atmospheric illegal speakeasy of the original is now a nondescript cocktail lounge where the drunken employees are no longer breaking the law (but perhaps only slightly aggravating the PCA.)

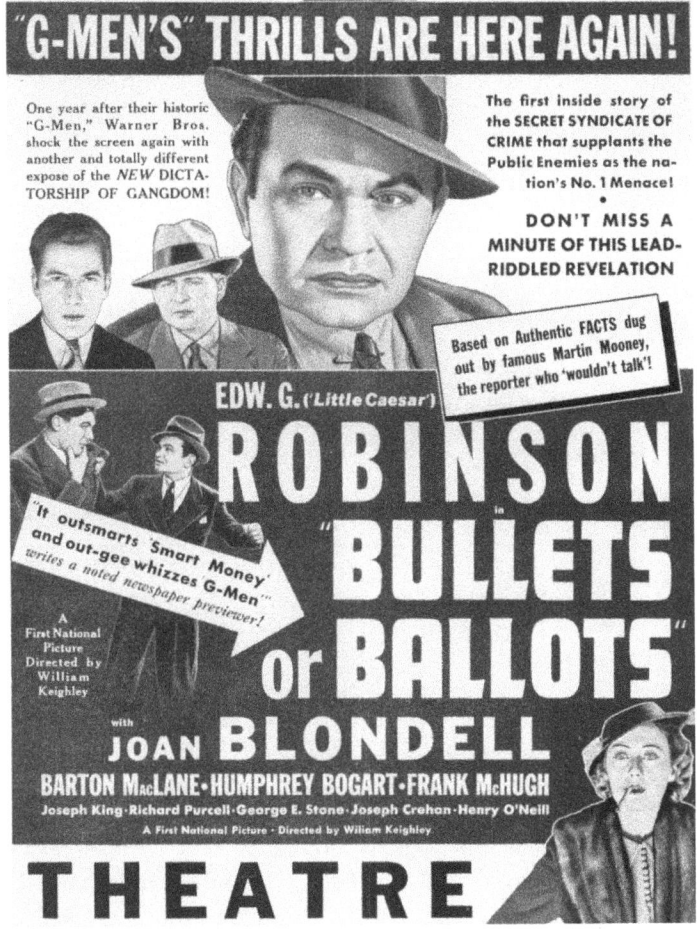

Bullets or Ballots (1936): Bogart is billed fourth, his name dwarfed by those of Robinson and Joan Blondell [original press book publicity].

Jack Warner could have cared very little about the Foy unit, other than hoping his B product would turn a profit. More than seven decades later, with the superior *Five Star Final* available for viewing, there is no reason to watch *Two Against the World*, other than to see what Bogart was able to do in such a situation. He is very good in every scene, but with no creative opportunities, he offers a performance that is only a flicker of that created by the electric Eddie.

The scenes involving the Carstairs family (Townsend in the original) could almost have been lifted directly from *Five Star Final*. Aside from different actors giving slightly less melodramatic performances, the scenes are nearly identical to Mervyn LeRoy's originals. As young Edith Carstairs, Linda Perry, though different in physical appearance, directly reproduces Marian Marsh's Jenny Townsend performance, especially in the scene where she confronts the muckrakers at their office building, accusing them of murdering her parents (Henry O'Neill and Helen MacKellar).

The acting is uniformly excellent; and, though Harry Hayden is good as Dr. Martin Leavenworth, the writer of the 15-chapter radio serial recreating "The Notorious Gloria Pembroke

Two Against the World (1936): In this "radio remake" of *Five Star Final*, Bogie was put in the improbable position of reinterpreting the character originally played by Eddie G. (original lobby card).

Murder Case," he is not nearly as colorful as Boris Karloff's deliberately overplayed, sleazy T. Vernon Isopod in *Five Star Final*. The only real variations on the original are the more modernized radio setting — bringing into play the FCC (established by the Communications Act of 1934), which, at the behest of the Carstairses' clergyman, Dr. Maguire (Howard C. Hickman), launches an investigation — and the running time. While *Five Star Final* clocks in at 90 minutes, *Two Against the World* is crammed into a mere 56 (and it still seems overlong!).

The studio was unsure of Bogart's appeal, but the Foy unit kept him working constantly, cranking out a programmer every six weeks. Released in July 1936, *Two Against the World* was followed by *China Clipper* in August and *Isle of Fury* in October. Bogie is billed fourth in *China Clipper* as Hap Stuart, an intrepid pilot who flew alongside Dave Logan (top-billed Pat O'Brien) in the Great War. The film opens with a disclaimer, "This photoplay is not historical in any sense," but the screenplay, written by Frank Wead, presents a fictionalized version of early aviation developments, specifically the first Transpacific air route from California to China via the South Pacific islands.

In 1927 aspiring businessman Logan, inspired by the Transatlantic flight of Charles Lindbergh, tries his hand at commercial aviation, but his Philadelphia to Washington, D.C., route proves a financial disaster, much to the dismay of his backer, B. C. Hill (Addison Richards). Encouraged by "Dad" Brunn (Henry B. Walthall), a visionary aircraft designer, to build a "flying boat," Logan opens Trans-Ocean, an airmail service between Key West and Havana, to establish a "Caribbean loop." Thanks to the tireless efforts of his top pilots, Hap Stuart and Tom Collins (Ross Alexander), Logan becomes a hero after devoting his service to hurricane relief work; but he also becomes a slave-driving workaholic intent on further success, regardless of the cost in lives.

Logan opens a school for pilots, riding them relentlessly. Pushed to the limit, Stuart alleges that he's been transformed from a "regular guy" into something "not even human." When Stuart is fired for his remarks, he punches out Logan, who decides to offer a career track and insurance benefits to his pilots, only two of whom remain at the school. Logan refuses to ease up on his demands for results, and insists that Dad complete his work on a large sea plane capable of flying across the Pacific. Even after his doctor diagnoses a serious cardiac condition, Dad continues his long work hours and ultimately gives his life for the cause. Hap returns and, against all odds, successfully flies the "China Clipper" from Alameda to Macao via Honolulu, Midway, Wake Island, Guam and the Philippines, just beating a November 30 deadline by a few minutes after miraculously surviving a major typhoon.

A well-made but formulaic aviation film directed by Ray Enright, *China Clipper* was an improvement on the pointless *Two Against the World*, offering a heroic Bogart whose determination in the face of an abusive taskmaster makes the airline a success. He appears in only half of the film's 85 minutes, but his role is memorable and a far cry from his iniquitous gangsters and the Robinson-redux role of the previous film. In an example of Frank Wead's clichéd dialogue, Stuart, after completing the flight to Macao, radios Logan to ask, "How do you say 'Toots' in Chinese, you mug?"

After playing his sidekick, Bogart took over a leading role originally intended for Pat O'Brien in *Isle of Fury*, another remake, this time of *The Narrow Corner*, a 1933 Douglas Fairbanks vehicle based on the novel by Somerset Maugham. First, Bogie complained about the terrible script, then followed this exercise in futility by protesting the grueling shooting schedule, which ran from 9 a.m. to 7 p.m. for 16 days. July 3 promised to be the worst of all, with director Frank McDonald pushing the cast and crew for 15 hours to make up for their time off for the Independence Day holiday. But July 5 was even worse, clocking in at 17 hours, with McDonald finally shutting down at 2 a.m. Having informed the assistant director that he would be leaving after supper, Bogie relented when he realized his militancy would make his colleagues' jobs even tougher.

The *Isle of Fury* shoot had one bright spot for Bogie, however. Five of the 16 days were spent on Catalina, where he could indulge his lifelong obsession with the sea. He also was pleased when his first Warners contract option was exercised, giving him an additional $50 per week.

The South Seas "unmarked island" created by screenwriters Robert Hardy Andrews and William Jacobs is an outlandish B-film setting. Aside from sporting one of the worst pencil-thin mustaches in history (not just in the cinema, but in *all* of history), Bogart gives a fine performance as Valentine Stevens (perhaps the worst character name in his career), an amiable pearl harvester who uses native divers to provide capital for his attempt to buy the island!

During Val's wedding to Lucille Gordon (Margaret Lindsay), a ship wrecks off shore. Moments after the ceremony, he rescues Captain Deever (Paul Graetz) and Eric Blake (Donald Woods), who instantly is attracted to Lucille. Concerned about making his next payment, Val asks Blake to accompany him on a visit to the natives, who, because of "something under the water," are refusing to dive. Forced to go underwater himself, Val is attacked by a savage octopus (actually a fairly lethargic one), but is saved by Blake, who is now "even" in the lifesaving department.

Blake saves Val a second time (from two native servants who attempt to steal the pearls) but turns down the offer of a "50–50 partnership." "Doc" Hardy (E. E. Clive), the island's resident philosopher, tells him, "Ask for nothing you know you can't have," so he plans to leave rather than risk a relationship with Lucille. Back on the island, Captain Deever tells Val that Blake is wanted for murder, then adds, "He's at your house right now, making love to your wife!"

A genuinely decent, though naïve, guy who trusts everyone at face value, Val is pushed to the breaking point. Forced to end the showdown, Blake reveals his true identity as an officer sent to the island to arrest Val for murder. Now believing him to be innocent, Blake plans to leave without him. Captain Deever bursts in waving a rod, but is gunned down by Antvar Anderson (Gordon Hart), an old buzzard who occasionally rears his head. When he returns to civilization, Blake's report will read, "The man I was after is dead."

Isle of Fury features a comic-book B plot, but it is a well-acted, fast-moving (60-minute) programmer. Even Margaret Lindsay, avoiding any pretensions in her speech, is convincing. She may have been more comfortable with Bogart than she was with the more intense Cagney.

With the exceptions of the lackluster octopus scene and some footage shot on location at Catalina unconvincingly intercut with a "native village" filmed in the studio, Frank McDonald's direction is a vast improvement over William McGann's "one-shot" approach in *Two Against the World*. Though another B film gave Bogie a non-wiseguy role, Val Stevens is an alleged murderer; and one scene, set on the boat as he and the crew are ready to sail to the diving spot, features Lucille inquiring about his gun. In a response that could have been improvised by Bogie, Val says, "I'm so used to wearing one of these things, I feel undressed without it."

Bogart couldn't help feeling frustrated, but Robinson—a major star—may have been just as aggravated as his B-film colleague. Eddie had wanted the title role in *The Story of Louis Pasteur* (1936), but this became another prize grabbed by Paul Muni, who edged him out as Warner Bros.' "prestige star." The Napoleon biopic was never taken seriously, nor was a similar project about Ludwig van Beethoven, though, during an interview, Jack Warner had mentioned Robinson's "involvement." With more free time on his hands, Eddie joined Gladys in London, where he starred in *Thunder in the City* (1937) for producer Alexander Esway, another unsatisfying filmmaking experience.

Since the spring of 1936, Bogart had been living at the Garden of Allah, where he began an affair with actress Mayo Methot, prompting the arrival of Mary, whose relationship with him had remained problematic. He spent the remainder of the year acting in *Black Legion*, another B film but one of a powerful, "social problem" nature; *The Great O'Malley*, another Pat O'Brien vehicle; and *Marked Woman*, an A production starring Bette Davis which also provided Mayo with a supporting role.

Black Legion was completely topical, presenting a hard-hitting, straightforward look at American fascism, in the form of Detroit-based "night riders" modeled on the Ku Klux Klan who had been terrorizing immigrants in the Midwest. Particularly, the script by Abem Finkel and William Wister Haines, based on a story by Robert Lord, dramatizes an actual kidnapping and murder case that had landed the Black Legion in the headlines and the slammer.

Reunited with *Petrified Forest* director Archie Mayo, Bogart received top billing as Frank Taylor, a thoroughly decent working man who turns to a "100-percent American" organization after losing a promotion to Joe Dombrowski (Henry Brandon), an immigrant with far less time at the factory. Friendly and playfully sarcastic in the opening scenes, Taylor, called a "wiseguy" by his pal and next-door neighbor Ed Jackson (Dick Foran), joins the Black Legion after hearing anti-immigrant propaganda on the radio and a pitch from Cliff (Joseph Sawyer), a member who takes him to a meeting in the back room of a local pharmacy. "How's

Black Legion (1937): Bogart stars in one of Warners' most courageous "social problem" films, a denunciation of a Ku Klux Klan–like organization that briefly terrorized immigrants in the Midwest. As the Legion-poisoned Frank Taylor, he menaces Erin O'Brien-Moore as his wife, Ruth.

it feel being pushed around by a Honyock?" asks Moore. (Though the Sawyer character is listed as "Cliff Moore" in the end credits, he is called "Cliff Summers" by Jackson in the actual film.)

Taylor is told that foreigners are "openly plotting to overthrow our government," and that the Legion is dedicated to keeping the country "free, white, 100-percent American!" In a secret, nighttime ceremony, surrounded by Klan-like hooded figures, he is held at gunpoint as he swears, on pain of death, an oath never to betray the trust of his fellows. He tells his wife, Ruth (Erin O'Brien-Moore), that he is attending "lodge meetings," then exacts terror by night with the Legion, first running Dombrowski and his father (Egon Brecher) out of town after burning their farm to the ground, then vandalizing and torching immigrant businesses in the area.

After a radio announcer mentions the existence of a "new Ku Klux Klan," three "prominent" businessmen led by Mr. Brown (Robert Barrat) are shown discussing how to raise even more revenue through their organization of the Legion. Following their order to "recruit two new members in the next ten days," Taylor, now foreman at the factory, is demoted after causing an equipment breakdown while attempting to enlist Ted Metcalf (Eddie Acuff), a recent hire. Old Michael Grogan (Clifford Soubier), father of Ed Jackson's girl, Betty Grogan (Ann Sheridan), accepts the foreman position, and is severely flogged by the Legion in return. "That ought to give the Irish something to remember us by," shouts Cliff.

Ruth — having witnessed Frank's quick descent into anger, drunkenness and violent behavior — confronts him, receiving a slap in the face for her trouble. That night, she and their young son, Buddy (Dickie Jones), leave for her parents' home. Fired from his job, Taylor goes on a bender with Pearl Davis (Helen Flint), a local floozy who had been pursuing Jackson. Tired of all the bad singing coming from next door, Jackson tosses Pearl into Taylor's yard before attempting to sober him up. Bogart (having plenty of real-life experience) plays an expert drunk scene as Taylor babbles on about the Black Legion to his pal, who vows to inform the police. "I tried to get out. They wouldn't let me out," he struggles to explain.

Events bring tragedy after Jackson is kidnapped by the Legion, who intend to flog him. He tries to escape, and is gunned down by Taylor, who then runs off into the woods. After he is apprehended at a roadside diner, he is visited in the slammer by Brown, who, posing as his attorney, threatens to kill Ruth and Buddy if he doesn't plead self-defense. For good measure, Brown also enlists Pearl Davis to tell the same bogus story of how Taylor and Jackson had been fighting over her. At the conclusion of the trial, when Taylor finally reaches the stand, he confesses, identifying every Black Legion member in the courtroom. All are convicted of Jackson's murder and sentenced to life in the Big House.

Addressing the lineup of killers, the judge (Samuel S. Hinds, who was born for the cinematic judicial bench) tells them, "Your idea of patriotism and Americanism is hideous to all decent citizens. It violates every protection guaranteed them by the Bill of Rights contained in our Constitution." Mentioning unacceptable "racial and religious hatreds" propagated by "hooded terrorists," he completes his sermon by quoting Abraham Lincoln. A wordless sequence ends the film, as Ruth watches Taylor (subtly played by Bogart at his nonverbal best) being led out of the courtroom. This conclusion is one of many powerful scenes expertly framed and lit by Mayo and cinematographer George Barnes, using dramatic shadows in the Michael Curtiz tradition.

Black Legion gave Bogart his best acting opportunity since *The Petrified Forest*, and he was unanimously praised by critics. The film didn't rocket Bogie to stardom, nor rival the films of Cagney and Robinson at the box office, but did respectable business and stirred things up a bit. Having used the actual insignia of the KKK — a red circle decorated with a white cross and a black triangle in the center — Warners was sued by the "Knights of the Ku Klux Klan, a corporation chartered under the laws of the State of Georgia" (the modern KKK had been founded on Stone Mountain). This ridiculous suit was dismissed in 1938, with all legal costs to be footed by the Klan.

Interestingly, Warners included the usual disclaimer at the beginning of the film, stating that none of the characters or events had been based on reality. Regardless of this claim that *The Black Legion* is purely fiction, it was the studio's most compelling depiction of a serious social problem since *I Am a Fugitive from a Chain Gang* and *Wild Boys of the Road*. Even without Darryl Zanuck on board, Warner Bros. proved that it was still the only Hollywood studio bold enough to expose such unsavory goings-on existing under the "respectable" surface of American WASP culture.

A half century after he played Joe Dombrowski in *Black Legion*, the erudite Henry Brandon (born Henry Kleinbach in Berlin) — a naturalized citizen who emigrated to the United States in the wake of the Nazi terror — revealed:

> My agent in the Thirties, Abe Sugarman, suggested a name change quite casually one day. I asked him why. With only the slightest hint of a twinkle in his eye, he answered, "Let's say it's too long for a marquee."
>
> I had very little objection to changing my name. Ever since I can remember, it was mispro-

nounced—"Kleenback," "Klineback," "Klinebok," even "Kleenbitch." Brandon is a corruption of my mother's even more Teutonic maiden name, Brandenburg.

The "dirty" words—"too German"—were never mentioned. I have never been ashamed of being German—only ashamed of a very corrupt and evil German government. [During World War II] I even got the guys in my barracks in the Signal Corps at Fort Monmouth, New Jersey, to say, "dirty Nazis" instead of "dirty Germans."[9]

A versatile character actor, Brandon, during the days of the studio system, made his living by portraying characters of every ethnic group imaginable. He explained, "There are good and bad people of all races. I have played countless heavies of various nationalities, and never felt that I was maligning any race by doing so. This includes Germans, and my adopted nationality—Americans."[10]

In *The Great O'Malley* (1937), Pat O'Brien plays the classic Hollywood Irish cop to perfection. As James Aloysius O'Malley, a rookie patrolman in New York's 7th Precinct, he stops John Phillips (Bogart) for driving with a loud muffler. Phillips agrees to fix the problem, but O'Malley insists on writing a ticket, causing him to be late for a new job at a factory where the gate has been locked. To provide for his wife (Frieda Inescourt) and disabled daughter, Babs (Sybil Jason), Phillips hocks his Army pistol and World War I medals, then resorts to a pawnshop robbery, during which he injures the owner. Again he is busted by O'Malley, this time receiving a two-year stretch in the Big House.

O'Malley is so obsessed with the letter of the law that he continually refers to the police manual, accusing his mother (Mary Gordon, of course) of littering when she tosses bread crumbs to some birds, and earning the published jibes of reporter Pinky Holden (Hobart Cavanaugh). O'Malley is despised in his own neighborhood, but his rigid attitude begins to soften after he is demoted to crossing guard duty at a school where he meets young Babs. Eventually he discovers that she is Phillips' child, secretly arranges treatment for her injured knee, and requests an early parole for her father. Unaware of O'Malley's efforts, Phillips panics when he appears on the doorstep, shoots him, then saves his life with a blood transfusion. Back on his beat with a new attitude, O'Malley becomes a role model for his fellow officers.

The Great O'Malley is a somewhat atypical "feel good" variation on the Warners prison vehicle. O'Brien again plays an inflexible authority figure who attempts to force a "wiseguy" onto the straight and narrow path, but here is shown the moral error of his ways by an innocent child (another classic Hollywood element). Following this film, O'Brien was able to temper his strict, military-based character (established in *Here Comes the Navy* and *Devil Dogs of the Air*) with compassion (transforming him into the tough but tolerant warden in *San Quentin* and priest in *Angels with Dirty Faces* and *The Fighting 69th*).

Following *Black Legion*, in which Bogart played a decent family man corrupted by a heinous influence, *The Great O'Malley* (billing him below O'Brien and Ann Sheridan) allowed him to create a more sympathetic version of the average Joe struggling to provide for his wife and child during the Depression. Phillips is not the innocent Warners character railroaded to the slammer on a bum rap (like Karloff in *The Walking Dead* and Cagney in *Each Dawn I Die*), but the desperation that drives him to commit a crime is clearly depicted; and, unlike Karloff's John Elman and Bogie's Frank Taylor (in *Black Legion*), he is ultimately set free, rather than being sentenced to Life or, worse, Death.

More predictable and sentimental than William Dieterle's "prestige" projects at Warners (*The Story of Louis Pasteur*, *Dr. Ehrlich's Magic Bullet*), *The Great O'Malley*, enhanced by the moody style of cinematographer Ernest Haller, nonetheless features some of the German director's "clinical" touches in the blood transfusion scene involving O'Brien and Bogart.

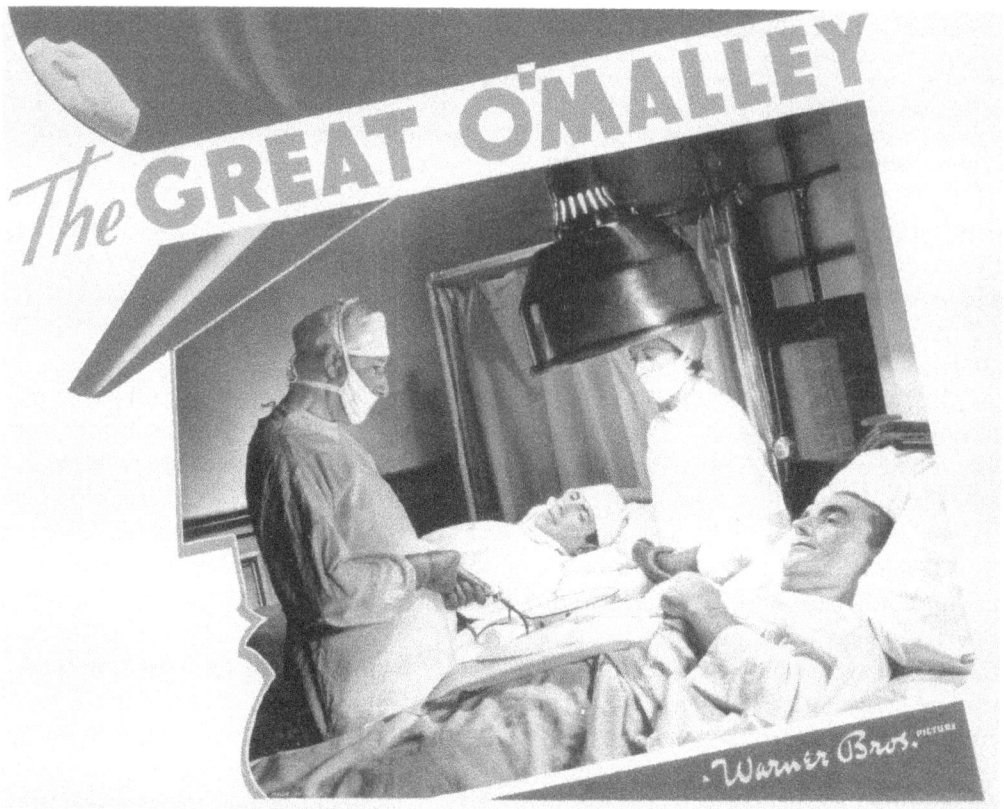

The Great O'Malley (1937): John Phillips (Bogart) gives blood to save the life of James Aloysius O'Malley (Pat O'Brien), the overzealous cop who sent him to the slammer (original lobby card).

For *Marked Woman*, Bette Davis was cast as nightclub "hostess" Mary Dwight Strauber, while Bogart enjoyed another good part: crusading assistant D.A. David Graham, a character based on Thomas E. Dewey, then District Attorney of New York County. Robert Rossen and Abem Finkel used the saga of Charles "Lucky" Luciano as resource material for their screenplay depicting five barroom hostesses who attempt to survive a Mob takeover of their club. After viewing some of the dailies, Hal Wallis advised Lloyd Bacon to spiff Bogie up a bit, complaining about his unkempt clothes and perpetual five o'clock shadow.

Marked Woman is Bacon's hardest-hitting film, and one of Warners' most straightforward post-1933 gangland depictions, nearly devoid of humor. Except for a brief scene in which the ubiquitous Allen Jenkins appears as Louie, a clothing "designer" who brings the girls some stolen garb, the portrayal of the five women — Mary, Gabby Marvin (Lola Lane), Emmy Lou (Isabel Jewell), Florrie Liggett (Rosalind Marquis) and Estelle Porter (Mayo Methot) — is consistently serious, punctuated with moments of tension and brutality.

The Mob boss, Johnny Vanning, has none of the curious charm of Rico Bandello and Tom Powers, nor any of the animal magnetism of Duke Mantee. As played by Eduardo Cianelli, he is nothing but a sadistic racketeer who orders his hoods, particularly Charlie Delaney (Ben Welden), to dish out the violence and murder necessary to protect his interests. He merely announces that he is taking over the Club Intime, one of the joints he is organizing for gambling purposes, then informs the hostesses that they are now working for him. "Anybody that sticks with me gets taken care of," he tells them. Taking a gander at Estelle,

Marked Woman (1937): As Betty Strauber, Bette Davis chews the scenery while Bogart, as Assistant District Attorney David Graham (based on Thomas E. Dewey), plays it cool in Lloyd Bacon's hard-hitting Mob film.

he adds, "Hey, you. Yeah, you. You're kind of old, aren't you? I need young dames here, the kind men go for in a hurry."

Later, Estelle asks the other women, "I don't really look old, do I?" Even before meeting Bogart, Mayo Methot's career had begun to falter, due to her constant abuse of alcohol and frequently violent temper tantrums, and the effects are apparent in her puffy, sad face, which was quite unattractive at this point. In every scene, she appears to wear a perpetual scowl, and she actually drinks a beer in an early morning scene.

A customer, Ralph Krawford (Damian O'Flynn), is whacked by Vanning's goons after a night of gambling with Mary, who is arrested for the crime. Making his first appearance 30 minutes into the film, Bogart's Dave Graham vows to go after Vanning, who sends a mouthpiece to visit Mary in the slammer. She stages a hysterical show for Graham (Davis continually shouts at Bogie, who provides quite a controlled contrast to her deliberate histrionics), then agrees to testify against Vanning, who is acquitted by the jury. "My mistake," Graham tells her. "Thanks for the ride."

Mary's naïve sister, Betty Strauber (Jane Bryan), who had arrived on the day of her arrest, is too ashamed to return to college. Soon, she is caught up in the Vanning web, is attacked by the lecherous Gordon (John Litel), and receives a tumble down the stairs from the Mob boss. Graham sees the coroner's report and tells Mary about Betty being found "in the river, dead." Again, Bogie provides subtle, nonverbal counterpoint to Bette's scenery-chewing response.

Graham tries to enlist the hostesses' help in nailing Vanning, but they refuse. In a shocking scene (the actual violence is off-screen, with Davis' wails providing the necessary effect), Mary is nearly beaten to death by Charlie. A subsequent scene in the hospital, showing her swollen and bandaged, provides the female equivalent of Tom Powers' post-beating "mummy" image in *The Public Enemy*. Eventually, the women agree to testify, and are placed in protective custody.

Dave Graham, a two-dimensional "good guy," was Bogart's first "cop" role, allowing him (just one year after *The Petrified Forest*) to join Robinson and Cagney in moving 180 degrees away from the gangster archetype. Graham's questioning of Estelle during the trial allows a glimpse of the future "Battling Bogarts" on screen together, and his summation to the jury demonstrates Bogie's subtle but powerful ability to build a dynamic intensity throughout a lengthy speech. After all the gangsters receive 30 to 50 years in the Big House, Graham offers to help Mary. "No matter what you do, or where you go, we'll meet again," he says, just before the press surrounds him on the courthouse steps. The final image shows the five women, still together, disappearing into the fog.

An interesting 1937 release, *Marked Woman* pulls no punches in its portrayal of the Mob's harassment and terrorism of the female gender. While Cagney's wiseguys had committed some unsavory moves against his molls and companions in several films, these events are tempered by his characters' slightly "redeeming" qualities. In *Marked Woman*, the violence against dames is pure torture and murder, committed, not by the star, but by a supporting actor in a totally unsympathetic thug role. And who sends that vicious bastard up the river? Bogie and a bunch of broads.

In April 1937, while Cagney was working at Grand National, threats of mass support for a film industry strike were voiced. On May 1, 3,000 technicians and workers picketed the major studios, inducing the Screen Actors Guild to throw its weight behind the effort. Ninety-six percent of the major stars and players were ready to strike. Proposing a contract for actors working in feature films (including a closed shop, minimum wage rates, a 10-percent pay increase for extras, and a 12-hour rest period between calls), the Guild completed successful negotiations without resorting to an actual strike. On May 15, the new agreement, signed by 13 producers, went into effect. Two weeks later, when SAG held its annual elections, those who retained their offices were Boris Karloff and Cagney, whom the *New York Times* described as "the most ardent proponent of unionism among the stars."[11]

"I guess I would be drawn and quartered if I passed *Kid Galahad* without telling you that its leading lady was Bette Davis,"[12] writes Robinson in his autobiography. In January 1937 Eddie finally went back to work at Warner Bros., again supported by Bogart, in *Kid Galahad*, the story of shifty boxing manager Nick Donati and his moll, Louise "Fluff" Phillips (Davis). At that time, Robinson considered Davis "hard as steel," and had asked Warners to test Jane Wyman for the part. Nonetheless, Davis was cast, and complained that she was being paid only $18,500 while Eddie was landing $50,000. Perhaps she shouldn't have grumbled quite so much: Bogie only grabbed a paltry $3,185!

Kid Galahad marked the first time Robinson and Bogart acted for Michael Curtiz. Limited by Seton I. Miller's formulaic script, the director's work falls somewhat short of his usual standard; but, collaborating with cinematographer Tony Gaudio, he created one of the first memorable boxing films.

After serving the law in *Marked Woman*, Bogie is solidly back in stone-cold killer mode as "Turkey" Morgan (a contender for his most ridiculous character name). Though Robinson's "Nicky" Donati is far more developed than Turkey, both fight promoter-gangsters use naïve bellboy-cum-boxer Ward Guisenberry (Wayne Morris) for their own selfish ends. Donati

Kid Galahad (1937): Robinson, Bette Davis, stiff-as-a-board Wayne Morris, and Bogart pose for a Warners publicity photograph.

occasionally shows a humorous side ("Did you ever see a bellhop who didn't want to be a fighter?"), but he is dead serious about his opposition to Guisenberry's romantic interest in his young sister, Marie (Jane Bryan, in another innocent sibling role). Fluff (who is also in love with the lad) mentions the King Arthur legend, so Donati dubs the boxer "Kid Galahad."

In 1937 realistic fight sequences had yet to be developed for boxing films. Guisenberry becomes a fighter after punching out the current heavyweight champion, Chuck McGraw (William Haade), at a Donati party crashed by Morgan and his mugs. No training is ever shown, and most of the bouts are covered in montages featuring the classic Warners newspaper headline technique. Morgan acts like a tough guy, but is knocked cold while attempting to put the squeeze on Guisenberry in New York; and it's Nicky who proves truly tough, by taking no guff from Turkey and roughing up Buzz Stevens (Ben Welden, billed as Buzz Barett in the credits). Bogart is confined to a one-note performance, but Robinson demonstrates a wide range of emotion in a familiar role.

Of course, Morgan expects "the Kid" to throw the championship fight against McGraw (who is more concerned with booze and broads), especially after Donati decides to teach "Gooseberry" a lesson for messing with his sister. When the Kid takes a beating during the bout, Nicky begins to show remorse; and, after Fluff pleads with him at ringside, he coaches the grateful aspiring farmer to a K.O. right cross. As in *Bullets or Ballots*, Eddie and Bogie shoot each other dead in the end, with the former dying in the arms of "his" woman after his nemesis bites the dust. Nicky gives his blessing to Marie and the Kid, then tells Fluff, "We did what we set out to do. We got a champ." As for Morgan, he truly dies like a turkey, grimacing in pain as he falls dead under the dressing-room sink. Robinson revealed:

Bogie had a manner, a personality — yes, an immense talent — that has made him almost immortal. Working with him, I understood it better than his fans. For all his outward toughness, insolence, braggadocio, and contempt (and those were within Bogie), there came through a kind of sadness, loneliness, and heartbreak (all of which *were* very much part of Bogie the man). I always felt sorry for him — sorry that he imposed upon himself the façade of the character with which he had become identified.[13]

Two of Robinson's most appealing scenes depict Nick speaking Italian, including a pleasant meeting with his immigrant mother (Soledad Jimenez) at the family farm. Having objected to the casting of Davis, Robinson demonstrates the same relaxed rapport he shares with his leading ladies in earlier films, and Bette delivers a likeable, warm performance including none of the scenery chewing that occasionally mars *Marked Woman*. One of her finest moments in *Kid Galahad* is a brief scene with the dependable Harry Carey (as boxing trainer Silver Jackson). After she tells Jackson that Guisenberry "would never be in love with me," he thoughtfully replies, "Don't kid yourself. They don't come any better than you.... I've known you a long time. They can't beat aces."

With *Kid* in the can, roles at the studio again dried up for Robinson, but the Napoleon idea was batted around for another spell after Jack Warner saw Eddie dressed as the Emperor at a costume party at Basil Rathbone's house! Following another trip to New York, he was loaned out to MGM for *The Last Gangster* (1937), an uneven revenge tale costarring James Stewart. Robinson hated the right-wing atmosphere around the fiefdom of Louis B. Mayer, who had told fellow conservatives Stewart and director William Wellman to avoid any discussions of a political nature.

Bogart again played second fiddle to Pat O'Brien, in *San Quentin* (1937), another tough, fast-paced Lloyd Bacon production. Inspired by recent reform efforts aimed at the corruption and brutality of California's prison system, John Bright was back, this time cowriting the script with fellow leftist and former San Quentin inmate Robert Tasker (who would die mysteriously in Mexico City a few years later). The warden of San Quentin allowed some location shooting on the prison grounds, including exteriors and long shots of the yard and cell blocks, under a provision that the faces of actual inmates would not be visible. Bacon, art director Esdras Hartley and cinematographer Sid Hickox did a remarkable job of integrating these shots with their backlot and studio recreations of the Big House.

The film opens at San Quentin, where sadistic Acting Captain of the Yard Druggin (Barton MacLane) is informed of the impending arrival of his replacement, Army Captain Stephen Jameson (O'Brien), a training officer intent on bringing humane rehabilitation to the Joint. Jameson is discussing his new job with fellow officers at a nightclub, where sexy May Kennedy (Ann Sheridan) is singing "How Could You?" Responding to Jameson's obvious interest, one of the soldiers warns, "Training one woman is worse than a whole company of citizen recruits."

May sings directly to Jameson, then refers to him as a sergeant.

"Do you know what two bars means?" he asks.

"Sure," she responds cockily. "Twice as many drunks as one bar."

Enter May's brother, Joe "Red" Kennedy (Bogart), telling her he needs some dough to get to a "job in Seattle." Moments later, he is pinched by the cops for "trying to stick up a restaurant." Having spent five years at reform school and one in the county jail, he now receives a 10-year stretch at San Quentin, where he and repeat offender Carl "Sailor Boy" Hansen (Joseph Sawyer, again playing a troublemaker who leads Bogie astray) arrive to serve their sentences. In the prison yard, after Red boasts, "I got pals on the outside that can pull wires," he takes the bait that he's been pardoned. When all the inmates laugh, he

San Quentin (1937): Captain of the Yard Stephen Jameson (Pat O'Brien) does his best to reform repeat offender Joe "Red" Kennedy (Bogart) during his 10-year stretch in the Big House.

punches out Hansen, losing his privileges for one month and receiving a four-day trip to solitary.

May, dining with Jameson at her apartment, is surprised to discover his status as a prison officer, a type for whom she has no respect. She then visits Red and slips him some money, resulting in another month-long revocation. Assigned to a job in the jute mill, he is advised by Hansen to work for a transfer to the road gang, which offers escape opportunities. But, after Red witnesses Jameson standing up to a fanatical inmate who shoots a guard, he decides to do his time, hoping that good behavior will reduce the length of his sentence.

May eventually apologizes to Jameson, who gives Red a spot on the road gang. (Bacon shot the scene at Bronson Canyon in Los Angeles.) Seeking revenge, Druggin secretly adds Hansen's name to the list and spreads a rumor that Red is receiving special treatment because of May's involvement with the Captain. When Hansen's girl, Helen (Veda Ann Borg), stops by the work site with a flat tire, he and Red grab two rods from the car, take Druggin prisoner, and cruise down the road. During the high speed chase, Hansen shoves the shiftless screw down an incline to his death. Due to an objection from the Breen Office, the shot of Druggin was edited to show only his ejection from the car.

The pursuing guards shoot their gas tank, so they switch to another car while Helen drives off into the woods. They barely slip past an oncoming train, then plummet down a hill and crash. Hansen is killed, but Red escapes, bent on whacking Jameson, whom he confronts at May's apartment. Learning the truth, he climbs out a window, but is shot by a cop. He painfully makes his way out of town and hitches a ride back to San Quentin, where he falls at the prison gate, muttering, "Tell Jameson I come back. Tell the cons to play ball with him. He's a swell …" before cashing in his chips.

A fast-moving, 70-minute vehicle, *San Quentin* provided Bogart with his first actual prison role, blending elements of his previous gangster parts with some of the more positive aspects of the characters he'd played over the past year at Warners. Here, he isn't a criminal because of the environment in which he was raised or because he believes it's his lot in life. Red Kennedy is a character with a bit more depth who aspires to go straight but is foiled by current circumstances, namely the conniving of a truly self-interested offender. While undoubtedly dissatisfied with the role in another B film, Bogie nonetheless delivered the goods.

Warners, avoiding any offense to the actual San Quentin, was careful to depict the abuse at the prison, not as the result of the system, but as the work of one unethical individual, and only a lieutenant to boot! Solitary confinement is never shown, nor is any actual punishment. This choice may also have been budgetary, since costs were held down by using only a few primary sets.

The studio wouldn't be quite so cautious a year later, when the Bryan Foy-produced *Devil's Island* went into production. Starring Boris Karloff as a doctor who is imprisoned and eventually sentenced to the guillotine after treating a notorious revolutionary, the film was intended to criticize the horrendous conditions at the French penal colony. But by the time *Devil's Island* finally was released in 1940, the abuse and torture was attributed solely to the actions of a sadistic commandant (who cuts his cigars with a miniature guillotine!) and his lackeys. Had *Devil's Island* been an A film, Robinson may have been a top choice to play Dr. Charles Gaudet, though he is portrayed very strikingly and quietly by Karloff (sporting a near-afro), who had been signed to a B contract.

Warners played it relatively safe with *San Quentin*, but the film was banned in several European countries, including Sweden and Finland. Several Canadian provinces, objecting to the very notion of films depicting prison life, also condemned it.

On September 27, 1937, Robinson began playing Steve Wilson, editor of the *Illustrated Press*, on the radio show *Big Town*, sponsored by Lever Brothers. As he had done in *Bullets or Ballots*, here he was able to fight evil forces—crime, gambling, corruption—but on a weekly basis. Eddie loved the content of the program, the money ($4,000 per show for the first year, to increase to $6,000 the second and $7,000 the third), and his status as executive producer. Warner Bros. balked at letting him devote time to the show, but he made a deal allowing him to leave at noon on Tuesdays in exchange for working on Saturday mornings. Lever Brothers also agreed to promote his current Warners film at the end of each show.

Bogart was pleased to be loaned to Samuel Goldwyn for the colorful part of "Baby Face" Martin in *Dead End* (1937), William Wyler's film version of Sidney Kingsley's Broadway smash. Though he again played a gangster, this proved a gritty, extremely well-written one, sharing tough scenes with Claire Trevor, as a former girlfriend reduced to prostitution, and the "Dead End" Kids in their first screen appearance.

Back at Warners, Bogart unsuccessfully attempted to wangle a raise from J. L., who again loaned him out, this time to producer Walter Wanger for *Stand In* (1937), as a booze-swilling, movie producer opposite his pal Leslie Howard and Joan Blondell. The sting of Warner's refusal to give him a salary increase was still fresh when he returned to the lot in January 1938 to star in the ridiculous *Swing Your Lady*, perhaps the only "hillbilly musical wrestling film" ever made. At first, he had refused to appear in the picture, prompting an order from J. L.'s executive assistant, Max Arnow, that he report to the studio at exactly 9:45

the next morning. Bogie showed up, still adamant about turning down such an inane project.

Contract players often rejected roles, but usually received a suspension without pay in return. Warner and Hal Wallis both were surprised by Bogart's repudiation, the first time he had acted in such a stubborn manner. The truth was that Bogie needed the dough, finally prompting Wallis to increase his salary to $1,000 per week *if* he'd star in *Swing Your Lady*. His new contract guaranteed 40 weeks, with an option to follow for another two years at $2,000 per week.

As Ed Hatch, a small-time promoter, Bogie "tours the Ozarks" with two-bit imbecile wrestler Joe Skopapoulos (1920 Olympic silver medalist Nat Pendleton) and endures the atrocious musical numbers of the Weaver Brothers and Elviry. Also on hand are Warners' perennial sidekicks Frank McHugh (in his first film with Bogart) and Allen Jenkins, and a 27-year-old actor making his A-film debut: Ronald Reagan, who had signed with the studio three months earlier.

Why Warner and Wallis, the creators of so many gritty, streetwise productions, wanted to make this film boggles the mind. This cinematic misadventure cleared only $24,000 over its costs, and Bogart thereafter referred to it as the worst film of his entire career (and there were still a couple of Warners miscasting excursions to come).

The film opens with Spike Jones-like "hick" music by Adolph Deutsch featuring ludicrous sound effects, followed by equally preposterous dialogue rattled off by Bogie: "Joe Skopapoulos himself ... the ponderous pachyderm of grunt and groan, the wrestling Hercules, is the next heavyweight champion of the world." Stopping off in Plunkett City, Missouri, to search for a challenger, Hatch vows to promote a bout for Skopapolous, "even if he has to wrestle an overgrown rooster." No male prospects can be found, but they offer $100 to Sadie Horn (Louise Fazenda), a rather masculine "lady blacksmith," who sings "Dig Me a Grave in Missouri" and single-handedly lifts Hatch's car out of the mud on a dirt road. She then pins Hatch to the ground, forcing him to capitulate by saying, "Hootie Owl." Dusting himself off, he offers her a c-note if she can stay in the ring with Skopapoulous for 30 minutes.

This plotless mess is padded with the worst caricatures of country music, including a production number during which hillbillies play saws. After observing a parade of stereotypes, Hatch enters the scene, praising, "That's mighty fine music, folks! Very entertaining." One of the most obvious abominations produced by the studio system (especially for a major like Warners, when this material would have made a *little* more sense at a Poverty Row outfit like Monogram), this effort must have necessitated gallons of whiskey being consumed by Bogie during the evenings at the Garden of Allah! *Swing Your Lady* is not only arguably the worst film starring Bogart, but also the most appalling product in the entire Warner Bros. Wiseguys catalog.

In another musical sequence, Cookie Shannon (Penny Singleton), Hatch's matrimony-minded girlfriend, sings "Hillbilly from 10th Avenue," claiming to have been born "in the hills of Manhattan" and admitting, "I guess I'm just a hillbilly at heart." In the tradition of Warner Bros. boxing films, Skopapoulous goes for a run with "Popeye" Bronson (McHugh) and "Shiner" Ward (Jenkins) in the countryside, where they meet up with Sadie. Unable to pronounce his own name, the mentally challenged wrestler asks her, "How much do you weigh?" then declares, "I like big girls." After they feel each other's biceps, he adds, "You're a pretty one, all right."

Sadie reveals that her Old Man "went possum huntin' ... eleven years ago," and hasn't returned. Responding to Hatch and the boys, she uses colorful hick sayings like "Well, shuck my corn!" and "Chisel my tombstone!" While rehearsing for the big bout, Skopapoulous, after practicing on poor Popeye, says he can't wrestle her. During a later negotiation, the Old Man returns after his 11-year hunt, to take several shots at Hatch from a nearby bush. Skopapoulous, reassigned to wrestle Noah Wulliver (Daniel Boone Savage; called Noah Webster in cast listings), receives the honor of having the contest announced by Jack Miller (Ronald Reagan).

Swing Your Lady becomes even more notorious when the imminent world's greatest movie star is joined on screen by the future President of the United States. Perhaps the strangest commingling of cultures and styles accomplished in Golden Age Hollywood, the film is worth viewing solely for the scene in which Bogie gives press advice to Ronnie!

Finally, Hatch gets Sadie all jacked up by telling her that Skopapoulous is married. Then, when Joe pops the question to her, she flips him. "She's just giving you the Ozark raspberry," Hatch inanely explains. This series of events is capped off by yet another hideous musical number, "Swing Your Lady," including an absurd square-dancing sequence.

In classic "pro wrestling" style, the entire bout is choreographed, including a dive to be taken by Skopapoulous. Shiner Ward provides protection from the excitable Noah by wielding the rough-hewn Ozark equivalent of a baseball bat. During the actual "Battle to the Death" (in which no "gouging, kicking or biting" is allowed), the plot apes *Kid Galahad*. At the last minute, Hatch, receiving an offer from Madison Square Garden, shifts the strategy so Skopapoulous can win, but then makes the mistake of telling Sadie he isn't married. Joe ends up as an Ozark blacksmith with a passel of kids, while Noah joins the mugs on the road as the new wrestling sensation.

Just who comprised the studio's target audience for this picture? Were Warner and Wallis trying to appeal to rednecks who didn't go to see their urban films? What appeal was generated by blending country music with their Big Band song-and-dance formula and transplanting it to the Ozarks? Truth to tell, the anomaly that is *Swing Your Lady* only raises more questions than it answers. Hopefully Bogart didn't spend too much time sobering up to think about any of it.

In early 1938 Robinson was back at Warners, starring in *A Slight Case of Murder*, based on the successful play by Damon Runyon and Howard Lindsay. Eddie's comic timing was exquisite, and it's demonstrated brilliantly throughout this consistently hilarious film, the best of all the satirical gangster films he starred in at the studio.

Cagney possessed great versatility, and Bogart created powerful, interesting variations on his indelible persona, but Robinson could be absolutely chameleonic when tackling a role. Just as Rico Bandello in *Little Caesar* is the archetype for the cinematic gangster in a serious context, Remy Marco is the ultimate "Mob boss gone legit" in a humorous vein. Jim and Bogie share the pantheon with him, but Eddie is the preeminent Wiseguy. One of the traits that makes him so special is that, while holding this distinction (and playing off it throughout his career), he also portrayed so many other types of characters, often of a benevolent disposition, in a variety of genres.

Damon Runyon began his career as a journalist, then wrote fascinating short stories based on actual people he had known and observed on the streets of New York. In 1935 he devised the story for *A Slight Case of Murder*, which he then entrusted to Howard Lindsay, a master of comic and satirical playwriting, who was particularly adept at crafting witty dialogue. The play premiered on Broadway at the 48th Street Theatre on September 11, 1935, and ran for 69 performances. Warners purchased the film rights for $50,000, then assigned the

Swing Your Lady (1938): This "hillbilly musical wrestling" film — singled out by Bogart as the worst project of his entire career — features bout promoter Ed Hatch (Bogie), his sidekick, "Shiner" Ward (Allen Jenkins, brandishing the Ozark equivalent of a baseball bat), and Neanderthal grappler Noah Wulliver (Daniel Boone Savage) (original lobby card).

adaptation to Earl Baldwin and Joseph Schenck, who were ordered to juice up the action, most of which had only been suggested in the stage version.

A Slight Case of Murder is a pleasure to watch, and audiences can't help but love Remy Marco, a humorous cinematic representation of the Prohibition bootlegger whom working-class Americans viewed as an industrious individual providing a valuable service during tough times. "It's the end of Prohibition!" announces a bartender as the film opens in a crowded speakeasy. After the final keg of Marco's beer is *given* away, a true brew connoisseur exclaims, "Thank Heaven we don't have to drink his beer anymore!"

At Marco's headquarters, Remy, informing his mob that they are "going legitimate," orders them to hand over their "artillery," which, much to their chagrin, will be "dumped in the river." Possessing the foresight to prepare for such a situation, he unveils his new, sure-fire campaign for the "Gold Velvet Brewery," which will peddle the same brew, only now it will be "legitimate."

"It's a good thing the boss never drinks beer," muses "Lefty" (Edward Brophy).

Remy's wife, Nora Marco (Ruth Donnelly), when hearing the news of "legitimacy," replies, "I don't know hardly how to act." As usual, Donnelly is a superb female comic complement to the male lead. Perfectly teamed with Robinson at the top of his game, she effortlessly alternates between her "natural" gangster's wife lingo and affected "society" diction, often during the same sentence, throughout the film.

Four years after going legit, Remy, "worse off than when [he] started," is threatened with foreclosure by his bankers, Mr. Post (John Litel) and Mr. Ritter (Eric Stanley). But his daughter, Mary (Jane Bryan), having returned from school in Paris, thinks all is well as they plan a wing ding at their (rented) summer home in Saratoga.

Before leaving the city, Remy revisits his "alma mater," the Star of Good Hope Orphanage, where he plans to select a needy boy who will spend the next month with them. "Let me have a look at the little mob," he tells Mrs. Cagie (Margaret Hamilton).

With all young eyes trained on him (in typical 1930s Warner Bros. style, Lloyd Bacon focuses on the lone African American boy in the bunch), Remy orders, "Now, look here, you mugs—I mean, you *guys*!"

Mrs. Cagie has picked four candidates, "all perfect little gentlemen," but Remy admits, "That's what I was afraid of.... I want the *worst*. You know, some little mug that nobody else wants.... Now, give me the ugliest and toughest little *gazaebo* you got. I want to mold him, see?"

"Go down to the cellar and unlock Douglas," Mrs. Cagie tells some of the boys.

Enter Douglas Fairbanks Rosenbloom ("Dead End" Kid Bobby Jordan), who tells Remy, "I'll go up and give your joint the once over."

In the car on the way to Saratoga, Douglas sits in front with Mike (Allen Jenkins), who puts him to sleep with a Mob-vernacular version of "Little Red Riding Hood." As usual, Jenkins' faithful sidekick is a supporting-cast highlight.

Unknown to them all, a gang of armored-car robbers led by "Little Dutch" (George Lloyd) is waiting to get even with Remy for some past outrage. Toting a satchel loaded with 500 $1,000 bills, "Innocence" (Joe Downing) overhears the four goons saying they "don't like him no more" and whacks the lot of them! Intent on adding Marco to his collection of stiffs, he stashes the dough (which belonged to a group of bookies) under the bed in another room.

Upon arrival, Mike is put in charge of Douglas, whom he plies with beer. After checking upstairs, he comes down to tell Remy that the kid's room is occupied, by "four guys ... they don't seem to be alive." Recognizing the mob, he identifies the mugs as Little Dutch, "No-Nose" Cohen (Joe Caites), "Black Hat" Gallagher (John Harmon) and a "stranger" (Harry Tenbrook).

"Let's take these fellas and throw them away somewhere," says Marco, who decides to plant each one in the domain of some *deserving* individual. "You know, we don't want to waste these fellas."

Considering their current predicament, "Gip" (Harold Huber) laments, "It's the life I'm leadin.' I was much better when I was *illegitimate*." When they return, everyone is is good spirits. "We ain't had so much fun since we shot up Little Dutch's headquarters!" exclaims Remy, revealing the reason the gang had wanted to whack him.

A state trooper, Dick Whitewood (Willard Parker, who beat out Ronald Reagan for the role), has followed them to Saratoga and continually shows up at the door. The revelation that he is Mary's fiancé enrages Remy, who can't stand coppers. "It's your father," Nora tells her. "He doesn't like uniforms. He's a pacifist."

Innocence, still prowling around upstairs, sticks his head through the door of the room where he stashed the cash, and receives a pelting from Douglas' slingshot. Meanwhile, Remy's boys, having seen a newspaper article about a 10-grand reward for *each* of the armored-car robbers, are out retrieving the four corpses, which they subsequently stash in an upstairs closet.

At the party, while Remy vocalizes "It Had to Be You" with "The Singer" (Harry Seymour), Dick drags his father, Mr. Whitewood (Paul Harvey), a man who "can't take excite-

A Slight Case of Murder (1938) Gone-"legitimate" bootlegger Remy Marco (Robinson) creates endless hysterical problems for his wife, Nora (Ruth Donnelly), and daughter, Mary (Jane Bryan), in this brilliant post-Prohibition comedy, based on the play by Damon Runyon and Howard Lindsay (original lobby card).

ment," into the fray. A stuff-shirted sissy who keeps announcing that he's "going to faint," he tells Lefty, "This house seems to be full of idiots and lunatics."

Nora, simultaneously trying to maintain her "society" veneer while easing her husband's mounting stress, mixes her metaphors as she observes, "Why, Remy. You're sweatin' worse than a stuck hog!"

Remy realizes that going legit is equal to going broke, and yearns for his bootlegging days. "Starting right this minute, I'm going to be *illegitimate!*" he announces. In the library, he offers to make Whitewood a partner in his brewery business for "a half million," just what he needs to pay off his creditors.

One taste of Gold Velvet is all Whitewood needs to refuse absolutely. "It's absolutely rotten!" he shouts before Nora escorts him to the bedroom where the bodies are hidden. After taking one sip of the horrendous brew, Remy forces a bottle each on Lefty, Gip and Mike, who reluctantly admits he feels "cauterized."

Discovering Douglas carrying wads of $1,000 bills, Remy collects the satchel of dough. "Marco's gonna put over the sweetest little job you've ever seen," he announces, knowing the bankers will arrive at any time. But when the head bookie, Sad Sam (Bert Hanlon), examines a money band found on the kitchen floor, he asks Dick to arrest his genial host.

Post and Ritter, realizing that Remy's payoff of 500 G's will end their interest profits, offer him another year-long note. With the "sweetest little job" put over, he hands over the satchel

Crime School (1938): As social worker Mark Braden, Bogart is supported by the "Dead End" Kids in their Warner Bros. debut (original window card).

to Dick, whose father goes berserk after opening the closet to find the four mugs, who appear to be alive. "Go up to that room and start blazin' away!" Remy tells the copper, then helps him shoot all six slugs, the last one of which whizzes through the window and into the shoulder of Innocence, who has been creeping around on the roof!

Robinson counted *A Slight Case of Murder* among his favorite films: "I had absolutely no fault to find with the script because it was beautifully constructed and written and it was very funny."[14] The quality of Baldwin and Schenck's script benefited from the work of Howard Lindsay, who subsequently collaborated (with Russel Crouse) on the uproarious Broadway masterpiece *Arsenic and Old Lace* (1941), starring Boris Karloff, which features similar elements of dark humor, including the stashing of numerous bodies within a private home. The film received tremendous reviews when it was released in February 1938, getting Eddie's New Year off to a prosperous beginning.

After *Swing Your Lady*, Bogart was rushed into three more films, all of them better than his previous vehicle. He was reunited with the "Dead End" Kids (in their Warner Bros. debut) for *Crime School* (1938), a Production Code-friendly remake of *Mayor of Hell* directed by Lewis Seiler. The opening credits bill "The 'Dead End' Kids" above Bogart; but, in the classic Warners pictorial cast parade (framing each actor within a window of the reform school), Bogie appears first, followed by Gale Pale, then Billy Halop (as Frankie Warren), Bobby Jordan (as "Squirt"), Huntz Hall (as "Goofy"), Leo Gorcey (as "Spike" Hawkins), Bernard Punsley (as "Fats" Papadopolous) and Gabriel Dell (as "Bugs" Burke).

The boys are first seen on the streets of the East Side, trying to work some less than honest angles as they are harassed by Mrs. Hawkins (Sibyl Harris) and Officer Hogan (Ed Gargan). Indicative of an earlier, less politically correct era, Squirt threatens to "smack" his drunken Ma "in the kisser" and Goofy explains that his mother is doing 30 days in the county jail. "It's Pop's turn next," he adds, "'cause he's gonna beat up Mom when she gets out."

At Junkie's Pawn Shop, the gang tries to unload some hot rubbish. Offered only $5 for "the *woiks*," they protest until Spike hits the proprietor upside the head with a candle stick. When he doesn't move, they all take it on the lam, but Spike is immediately pinched by the cops.

"If you want to do something for them," Frankie's sister, Sue (Gail Page), asks Judge Clinton (Charles Trowbridge), "why don't you clean up the slums?" Replying that many upstanding individuals have emerged from the East Side, Clinton (who cannot get the guilty boy to confess) sentences them all to two years in reform school. Making his first appearance during the hearing, Bogart's Mark Braden is revealed as the director of a local settlement house.

Late that evening, the boys reach the "school," where they are refused their request for supper. Frankie is provoked into brawling with another inmate, then chased by guards and, after being caught on a barbed-wire fence, whipped with a cat o' nine tails by the sadistic Superintendent Morgan (Cy Kendall, who was particularly adept at playing brutal, fascistic authority figures). The next day, Braden — now the new Deputy Commissioner — hired to investigate rumors of terrible conditions at the school — is met by Morgan, who defends his beliefs in "law and order" and "patriotism."

In the film's first use of tension-relieving humor, Squirt — whose request for a belt to hold up his oversized trousers is ignored — appears in formation with the offending article down around his ankles. "We make the punishment fit the crime," Morgan explains.

"Why not make the pants fit the boy?" Braden replies.

In the infirmary, Braden discovers that Frankie's whip cuts have not been treated by the inebriated doctor (Spencer Charters). After firing the guards — ex-cons, disgraced cops and army deserters — he also dismisses the doc, whose license had been revoked six years earlier. "This is a school, not a prison," Braden says, citing a statistic that 60 percent of those incarcerated emerge as hardened criminals. Making a "clean sweep," he also gives Morgan the boot. Though Cooper (Weldon Heyburn), the head guard, tells Braden, "I'm with you right from the start," he makes a secret pact with Morgan to bring down the new deputy.

The boys initially resist Braden's more benevolent policies, even after he tells them he's from the same neighborhood. "I got to thinkin' that tough guys were fall guys," he says. Their icy resolve begins to melt into further "Dead End" Kid humor when he orders them to paint their own dormitory. Following an escapade of painting *each other* as well as creating a roomful of graffiti — culminating with a soaked brush in Cooper's face and a full bucket dumped into his pants — (they are exiled to the boiler room, which they blow up by laying on too much coal. After Braden rescues Squirt from certain death, Frankie shoulders the blame, then makes a deal to help turn the joint into a real school.

Cooper finally makes his move, blackmailing Spike into telling Frankie that Braden is making time with his sister in exchange for their decent treatment. Forcing the gang to accompany him, Frankie, armed by Spike, drives into the city to shoot Braden at Sue's apartment. (This sequence is a near-exact rehash of the climactic scene in *San Quentin*, with Bogart on the other end of the rod this time.) Discovering the set-up, Frankie tries to strangle Spike, who then tells Braden about Cooper's plot to bring the vicious Morgan back to power.

The boys quietly sneak back into the school and climb into their beds as Braden, accompanied by two cops, confronts Cooper, Morgan and the Commissioner (Frank Jacquet) with

Men Are Such Fools (1938): Advertising "idea girl" Linda Lawrence (Priscilla Lane) finds it difficult to resist the advances of office lothario Harry Galleon (Bogie) in Busby Berkeley's disappointing soap opera, a major contender for the worst "Bogart film" (original lobby card).

news of the embezzlement carried out prior to his arrival. Cooper tries to grab the cooked books from the desk, and Braden beats him to a pulp. (As Bogie assumes his tough-guy persona, the violence is relegated solely to off-camera sound effects.) "That's just Mr. Braden going over the books with Mr. Cooper," one of the cops explains.

In 1936 Bogart had played a role originally created by Robinson in a Warners classic made five years earlier; here, in 1938, he did the same with a Cagney role from 1933. He gives an excellent performance in his second "cop" role, a character far more warm and enthusiastic than his D.A. in *Marked Woman*. Unlike Cagney's earlier interpretation, Bogie's version is not a former criminal, but a social worker with a sense of humor. Unlike *Mayor of Hell*, *Crime School* is leavened by a lighter tone, and the ending requires a less violent resolution. Back in Judge Clinton's chambers, all the boys—now dressed in nice suits—are paroled, and Braden (in typical Hollywood fashion) ducks out with Sue, his future wife.

Though Busby Berkeley directed *Men Are Such Fools* (1938), it proved a far cry from his masterful musicals of a few years earlier. Billed below the ever-wooden Wayne Morris and perky Priscilla Lane, Bogart plays womanizing ad executive Harry Galleon, a slight improvement on his *Swing Your Lady* character, but the film was a major disappointment, making even less than the earlier production (only $10,000). Released on the heels of *Crime School*, the product was another embarrassment for Bogie, who, for the second time, was billed below Morris in what amounts to a small supporting role. He doesn't appear until 27 minutes have passed, and his four brief scenes merely require him to make unwanted passes at Lane.

Even in a thankless role, Bogart is the best thing about *Men Are Such Fools*. Morris is as stiff as mahogany in *Kid Galahad*, but he's a much lighter wood here. (Morris reportedly studied acting at Los Angeles Junior College and the Pasadena Playhouse, though his early performances suggest that he developed his style during his brief tenure as a forest ranger.) Lane, however, compensates for Morris' slight improvement with her annoying "playing hard to get" shtick, as 21-year-old advertising "idea girl" Linda Lawrence rebuffs the continual "romantic" overtures of his even more exasperating Jimmy Hall.

Based on the novel by Faith Baldwin, Norman Reilly Raine and Horace Jackson's screenplay hands the two lovebirds equally obnoxious dialogue. While maniacally driving to a pool party, Jimmy informs Linda that "weekends were invented to get drunk, to have fights and make love to your girl." But these inane words are followed by even more obtuse action. Stopping on train tracks, he coerces her into accepting his marriage proposal before he narrowly escapes an oncoming locomotive.

In the swimming pool, Harry Galleon (Bogie, in a pseudo-beefcake scene!) and Linda (indulging Busby Berkeley's obsession with cinematic swimming) play with a beach ball, an activity sufficient to elicit a real proposal from Jimmy. Now a wed woman working late hours in Galleon's office, Linda endures such enlightened remarks as "I'm definitely not an angel … I'm probably a cad."

Jimmy and his former fraternity buddies attend the annual Princeton-Navy football game, but Linda remains in New York, developing an ad campaign with Galleon, who impetuously kisses her, then offers to drive her to the Sea Horse Club, where she was supposed to meet her now-hammered husband. Missing her by seconds as they use different elevators, the couple converges at the club, where Jimmy punches out Galleon, then orders Linda to quit her job.

Relegated to a bourgeois existence outside the city, Linda attempts to land a new job for Jimmy, but he refuses the offer of a partnership with Mr. Nelson (Eric Stanley), owner of a major advertising firm. Mad as a hornet, she leaves him — immediately! (Rarely has there been so little motivation for a cinematic split.)

Whom does Linda choose for her new beau? "I want to be with you constantly," Galleon tells her over an expensive dinner. "It even interferes with my drinking." Did Bogie perhaps improvise this line? Or did Berkeley, a world class tippler, toss it in?

After running into Jimmy — who is squiring none other than Galleon's former fiancée, Wanda Townsend (Marcia Ralston) — Linda stages a bogus broadcast, during which she describes an upcoming "personal matter" to take place in Paris. In one final childish romantic pursuit, Jimmy follows Linda — who convinces some cops to transport her — to the docks, where a ship will sail within moments. When the dust settles, Galleon arrives to find Wanda in his cabin, while Linda sits on the dock, enjoying more starry-eyed shenanigans from her moronic hubby.

Far less entertaining than *Swing Your Lady*, *Men Are Such Fools* (an equally awful title) arguably is a contender for the worst Bogart film; but, then, it really isn't a "Bogart film" at all. The fact that Jack Warner even cast Bogie in *Men Are Such Fools* is another inexplicable move on part of the mogul. The actor's frequent threats to take a suspension rather than honor his Warners contract make perfect sense in light of this bad B film.

Perhaps the worst element of *Men Are Such Fools*— possibly inferior, even, to all the horrors of *Swing Your Lady*— is the supremely maddening "comic" character actor Hugh Herbert (as Harvey C. Bates), whose stylized laugh and shtick soliloquies permeate the film. At one point, Bates (who has taken Linda out to dinner) actually *writes* his hooting laugh on an index card before capitulating his "date" to Jimmy.

Released on the same day as *Men Are Such Fools*—July 16, 1938—*Racket Busters* put Bogart back in the hands of Lloyd Bacon, who ably directed (in less than four weeks) this tale of a D.A. who attempts to crack down on racketeering in the New York trucking industry. As gangster Pete Martin, Bogie received top billing, over George Brent, who plays his nemesis, Denny Jordan, a truck driver who develops the courage to stand up to the racketeers. Also on hand are the reliable Allen Jenkins (as Jordan's sidekick, "Skeets"), Walter Abel (as Special Prosecutor Thomas Allison) and Henry O'Neill (as the Governor). Robert Rossen again scripted (with Leonardo Bercovicci), working in enough facts to receive an endorsement from the Commercial Crime Commission and plenty of pro-labor material to earn the praise of *The Daily Worker*.

Unlike his previous film, which introduces him at the 27-minute mark, *Racket Busters* hits the viewer with Bogart in the very first shot. "Nothing's going to stop me," vows Pete Martin. "I'm going to make this whole town pay off to me, from boot blacks to bankers." The opening scene proves that, at this point in his career, Bogart was considered an urban bad boy. In a B potboiler, he might not appear in the first half of the film; but, in a crime melodrama, he now provided the main interest. Rossen's script and Bacon's direction add up to a brisk narrative that bogs down only when the focus shifts to the Special Prosecutor's Office.

When Thomas Allison accepts the prosecutor position, he refers to the racketeers as a disease. Indeed, Martin is a supremely confident and ruthless version of the Bogart Mob boss whose "takeover" of the fruit and produce market requires a 24–7 commitment to the "Manhattan Trucking Association." "Seven million people depending on us," he tells his minions, "paying off." Equally dedicated, Allison directly subpoenas the owners of companies doing business with the gangsters. "This time we're after the leaders," he announces, "the system of racketeering."

Martin launches a "recruitment campaign" for the M.T.A., utilizing announcers in radio trucks and hawkers passing out printed flyers. To counter this effort, Allison calls in truckers, who, fearing for their lives, refuse to act as "stool pigeons." Following a series of beatings and vehicle tamperings, the main drivers ally with Allison. A particularly effective, brutal scene involves Charlie Smith (Elliott Sullivan) being beaten into a brain-damaged state as his wife watches. At this point, *Racket Busters* becomes a remake of *Taxi!*, with Brent in a variation of Cagney's original character.

As the violence and intimidation continue, Jordan's truck is blown up outside his apartment, Skeets and Pop Wilson (Oscar O'Shea) cannot find work, and Jordan's pregnant wife, Nora (the gorgeous Gloria Dickson), is hospitalized after goons terrorize her at home. Completely broke, Jordan punches out an M.T.A. stooge and steals a satchel of cash to pay her medical bills. Soon he is visited by Martin, who "asks" him to keep the dough in exchange for displaying an M.T.A. sticker on the windshield of his new truck. Dumbfounded, his colleagues call him "yellow," while Allison questions him about his new allegiance. "If you think Martin gave me that money, prove it!" he dares the prosecutor, who then passes a law allowing indictments of witnesses who hold back information and refuse to testify. Martin responds by having businessmen beaten and their goods torched. In an expanded version of a scene from *Taxi!*, goons push Pop to his death on subway tracks.

Jordan is arrested, and Skeets (one of Allen Jenkins' best characterizations) rallies the truckers with a rousing speech delivered from the hood of a truck. As the drivers run to their rigs, Skeets is gunned down by Martin's trigger man. To cap off Bacon and Rossen's narrative expediency, the film concludes with a fierce fight convincingly carried out by Bogart and

Racket Busters (1938): Tough trucker Denny Jordan (George Brent) fights to the bitter end with New York racketeer Pete Martin (Bogart) in this *Taxi!*-inspired pro-labor film praised by both the Commercial Crime Commission and *The Daily Worker*.

Brent. "Nice job you did on Martin," Allison tells Jordan, who, now agreeing to testify, inspires the full support of his fellow truckers.

The casting of Bogart and Brent in the two lead roles was an interesting move by Warners. Both actors have the same tonal range, as well as a raspy vocal timbre, qualities that make them appear as opposing sides of one larger being, a sort of dual-personality Jekyll-and-Hyde entity embodied in two separate characters. *Racket Busters*, though an obvious remake of *Taxi!*, is an even more "proletarian" version of the earlier film, stretching the original citywide cab shutdown into a scandal that leaves people starving in a large geographical area.

From late February through early April 1938, both Robinson and Bogart reported to Warners for *The Amazing Dr. Clitterhouse*, released on July 20, just four days after *Men Are Such Fools* and *Racket Busters* hit theaters. Now one of Hollywood's busiest contract players, Bogie was one active criminal-cad, here playing career jewel thief "Rocks" Valentine, while Robinson has the title role as a physician-psychiatrist who joins the underworld to study the physiological basis of criminality. Some suits at Warners, believing that audiences would think Eddie was one of the gangsters, recommended Sir Cedric Hardwicke, who had played the role in the stage version by Barre Lyndon. Jack Warner, however, realized that Robinson smarted from Paul Muni's domination of the prestige pictures, and cast him as Clitterhouse, the first of Eddie's "man of science" roles.

The screenplay was cowritten by John Wexley and John Huston, the first time both actors worked with the latter, who began his longtime friendship with Bogart during the making of this film. Like Bogart and Robinson, Huston was assigned to the project by Henry Blanke; but, even in a genre film with specific conventions, he was able to create a major character who became one of his trademarks: a successful professional man who is defeated by his own ambition.

Robinson's name appears above the title, while Bogart is billed third, beneath Claire Trevor. The film opens during a vocal recital at the posh home of Mrs. Frederick B. Updyke (Georgia Caine), where a white-gloved figure wielding a flashlight is robbing the upstairs jewel safe. A burglar enters through the window, and the man with the gloves tells him to remain where he stands. A second thief, "Rocks" Valentine, looks in the window, then bolts. Soon after, the doctor's friend, Inspector Lane (Donald Crisp, sans toupee), assigned to solve a series of similar burglaries, arrives. Before leaving, Clitterhouse asks the cop to call him as soon as a suspect is identified.

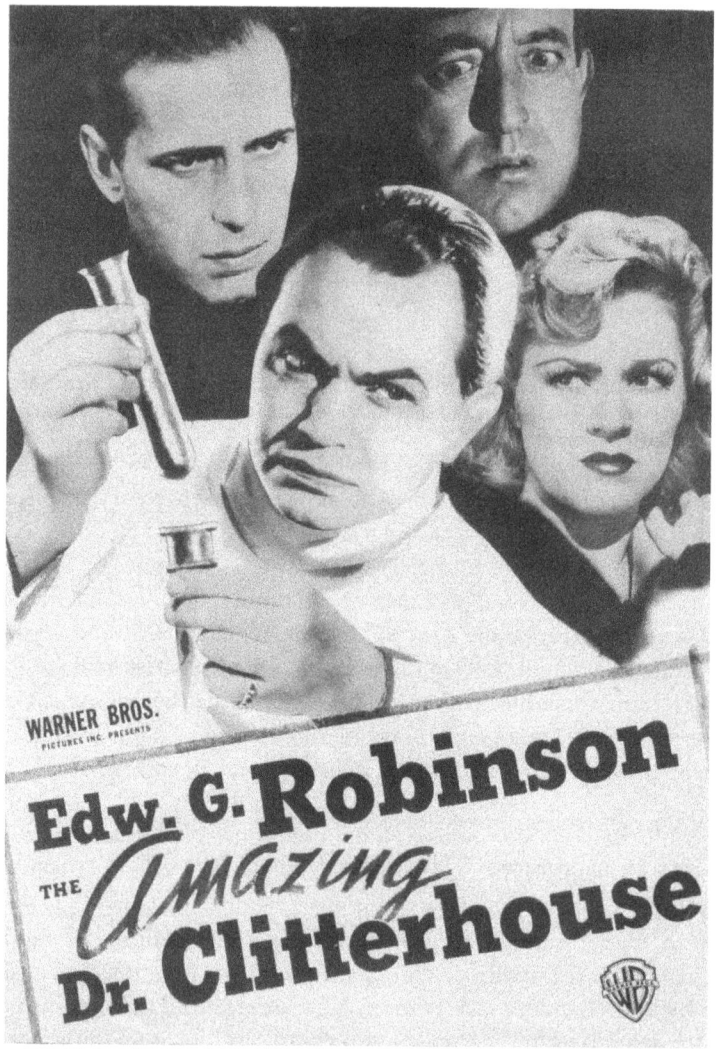

The Amazing Dr. Clitterhouse (1938): Robinson, playing a physician-psychiatrist who studies the physiological basis of criminality, is ably supported by Bogart, Allen Jenkins and Claire Trevor (original herald).

Later that night, on the way home in a taxi, the doctor confesses to his trusted nurse (Gail Page) that he is responsible for all four burglaries. Interested in preventing crime, he has been studying the "medical aspects" of criminal behavior, concluding that such activity actually changes the physical makeup of a person. Criminality, according to the erudite doc, is not a sociological problem, but a physiological one.

Tipped off by Lane, Clitterhouse visits "Jo" Keller (Claire Trevor), who runs a gambling operation at the Hotel Sequin. After leaving her apartment, he drops in on the gamblers to reveal his stash: all the jewelry from the four unsolved burglaries. Demonstrating his impressive intelligence and wit, he wins the admiration of Valentine's mob, including Okay (Allen Jenkins),

Butch (Maxie Rosenbloom) and Tug (Ward Bond), who refer to him as "The Professor." He joins forces with them, then follows up each "job" by performing a blood test on each of the goons in their secret apartment hideout, using "The Hudson River String Quartet" as a front. "Every time I see that needle, I get woozy," announces Tug before grabbing his violin. The image of Ward Bond masquerading as a chamber musician is one of the film's more amusing moments.

Rocks refuses to be a guinea pig, and Clitterhouse informs Jo that the gangster's "entire personality is distorted."

"I ain't no guy you can push around like these other dopes," Rocks tells the doc. During a heist of minks at the United Fur Building, he traps Clitterhouse in a refrigerated safe, but Butch, accidentally left behind, cuts through the door with a torch. Back at the apartment, Clitterhouse tells them he's quitting the mob, who are ordered to "blow town." The doc describes how Rocks' murder attempt "lacked ingenuity," then explains to Jo that he must leave due to a loss of objectivity. Experiencing true enjoyment while pulling the jobs, he is noticing a physical change in his own behavior.

Rocks, not nearly as ignorant as his underlings, manages to trace the phone number Clitterhouse called before blowing the flop. At the doc's Park Avenue office, he discovers the notebook containing the results of the tests on his boys, all of whom are listed by name. Hatching an elaborate blackmail scheme, he plans to make the joint his "headquarters," where the doc will work for him for 10 percent of the take. Clitterhouse calls the offer "very generous," and Rocks (unleashing one of Bogart's most famous lines) replies, "You'll take it and like it."

The doc, unwilling to do any such thing, slips the Mob boss a major mickey (a fatal overdose of paradol chloride), telling him that he now will research "the greatest crime of all ... homicide." Interestingly, Rocks, wanting to stick to burglary and blackmail, replies, "We don't have to give nobody the works," before lapsing into a coma.

The next morning, the police find Valentine's body floating in the river. Jo arrives at the police station to confess to the crime, but Lane, listening through a hidden microphone, overhears her subsequent conversation with Butch about Clitterhouse. Even confronted with possible conviction and imprisonment, the doc retains his calm demeanor, being so utterly convinced of the importance of the work that made him a criminal. His attorney, Grant (Thurston Hall), convinced that a man with such beliefs is "mad as a hatter ... a monomaniac," crafts a powerful insanity defense; but, when the doc testifies on his own behalf, he refers to his research, claiming, "It is impossible for an insane man to write a sane book."

The jury delivers a "not guilty" verdict, "on grounds of insanity." The foreman, explaining that the doc's defense depended on "proving himself insane," concludes that "only an insane man" would go to such lengths to prove he is actually *sane*! Rising from the witness box, Clitterhouse mutters, "Amazing, clearly amazing."

The Amazing Dr. Clitterhouse has the distinction of being the only Warners film in which Robinson deliberately murders Bogart to save his own skin, a cold-blooded act that is all the more shocking in light of the doc's initial benevolent reasons for studying crime and joining the Mob. In their earlier teamings, they wind up whacking *each other*. After appearing with Bogie in Goldwyn's *Dead End*, Claire Trevor, in one of her utterly convincing, cool "tough girl" characterizations, adds another level to the gangland plot, that of a female who is not merely a moll, but a smart *operator* who sees the merit in Clitterhouse's obsessive attempts to isolate the causes of criminality.

Having played Porfirio Diaz in *Juarez and Maximilian* on the stage, Robinson had been promised an appearance as the Mexican general in a Warner Bros. film; but he was frustrated again when John Garfield landed the role opposite Paul Muni in *Juarez* (1939). Robinson had written a letter to Jack Warner, claiming he could just as easily play Benito Juarez, but the mogul's reply consisted of loaning him to MGM for *I Am the Law* (1938). John Huston, who researched and cowrote the screenplay, also was frustrated when Muni, his colossal ego unchecked, insisted that it be rewritten to suit his persona.

Muni had a policy of never playing a Jewish character on screen. Robinson, however, looked forward to the prospect of representing his heritage, and was pleased to hear that writer Norman Burnstine (who used the Anglicized name "Burnside") had proposed to Jack Warner a biopic on Dr. Paul Ehrlich, a German Jew who had developed several revolutionary serums, including one that provided a cure for syphilis, and won the Nobel Prize. Burnstine believed that *Dr. Ehrlich's Magic Bullet* could help combat the rising anti-Semitism that was being affected by Hitler's Germany.

Muni turned down the role, so Robinson lobbied while Jack Warner ordered extensive research for the project. Years later, Robinson called Muni "my most potent competition": "He played *Pasteur* and *Zola*; I could have. I played *Ehrlich* and *Reuter*; he could have. The Brothers Warner regarded us as two sides of a coin and did not hesitate to exploit the situation. I disliked Muni and Muni detested me."[15] During pre-production on *Ehrlich*, Eddie and Gladys took a vacation to Mexico, where they enjoyed spending time with artist Diego Rivera and exiled Soviet revolutionary Leon Trotsky.

On August 20, 1938—one month after the release of *The Amazing Dr. Clitterhouse*—Bogart married Mayo Methot, capping off the day with a drunken fight at the reception. Happy in his own domestic situation, Cagney, after making two films for Grand National, realized that his new work wasn't receiving sufficient distribution. (A third film, "Dynamite," dealing with black-market oil dealings in Texas, was proposed but never made.) Following extensive negotiations by William Cagney, Jim returned to Warner Bros., armed with an excellent new contract guaranteeing $150,000 per picture (two or three per year, for five years), 10 percent of the grosses over $1.5 million, and script approval.

Cagney enjoyed the contractual terms, but Hal Wallis, intending to work him as much as possible, turned up the production pace, ordering Lloyd Bacon to shoot many retakes during the making of the screwball comedy *Boy Meets Girl* (1938), costarring Pat O'Brien, Ralph Bellamy and "dumb blonde" specialist Marie Wilson. (Marion Davies, who complained about the script, had been dropped from the project.) Wallis watched all the rushes, making notes on scenes in which the action "dragged," then expected Bacon to punch it up.

The occasionally clever script, by Bella and Sam Spewack, features Cagney and O'Brien as two screenwriters (based loosely on Charles MacArthur and Ben Hecht) who attempt to create a new major star with the forthcoming baby of studio waitress Susie (Wilson), whose husband, a bigamist, had returned to his first wife, only to be murdered! In the end, after she marries an English Lord (Bruce Lester) and leaves the studio, the baby of studio production chief C. Elliott Friday (Bellamy) achieves stardom instead! The zany plot and breakneck tempo worried both Cagney and O'Brien, who delivered dialogue with equally alarming velocity and were amazed at the way they sounded in the dailies. Regardless of Wallis' views on comic farce, the actors were right, and critics agreed that the pacing, which allowed no time for audience laughs, utterly doomed the film.

The first scene opens with an aerial shot of the Warner Bros. soundstages; although, when the sequence cuts to ground level, the gate is dressed as "Royal Studios," where Rosetti (Frank McHugh), an agent, arrives with cowboy star Larry Toms (Dick Foran), expecting to confer with the writing team of Robert Law (Cagney) and J. C. Benson (O'Brien), who are first seen hiding out as dancers in a musical currently in production.

"We're not writers! We're hacks!" shouts Law, as Cagney begins what is arguably his most shamelessly over-the-top Warner Bros. performance; at least, with *A Midsummer Night's Dream*, he had a legitimate excuse for such scenery chewing. "If we weren't," he asks Toms, "would I be standing here, listening to your inarticulate grunts?"

Indeed, "grunting" is not the problem with *Boy Meets Girl*. It's the out-of-control, rapid-fire dialogue, much of which is unintelligible. And some of the lines that are discernible are delivered in such an obnoxious manner (by both Cagney and O'Brien) that they are painful to the ear. It was one thing for Bogart and other Warners players to take part in a parody of Tinsel Town shenanigans in an independent film like

Boy Meets Girl (1938): Cagney and Pat O'Brien overact outrageously in this breakneck-paced screwball comedy also featuring dumb-blonde specialist Marie Wilson (original one-sheet poster).

Stand In; but, here, two stars are headlining a similar film actually produced at the studio. After failing to float his own independent enterprise, Cagney—who had taken his shots at Warners in the poorly distributed *Something to Sing About*—was making his studio comeback in an even more obvious satire. Perhaps Jack Warner, realizing that his own players were taking outside shots, decided to show his sense of humor by slamming his own house cinematically. Whatever the reason, *Boy Meets Girl* is approximately one-quarter charm and three-quarters torture. Most of it resembles a Poverty Row production, rather than an A film released by a major studio.

Marie Wilson's dumb blonde-ness is like a calming breeze wafting between the twin storms offered by the squalling Cagney and O'Brien. Susie's son, "Happy," appearing opposite Toms in "The Cowboy and the Baby," becomes an instant star, and the two writers are given power of attorney for the child. Unknown to them, when their provision expires, Rosetti negotiates a new contract for the kid at $300 per week. Outraged, Law reveals, "Why, *we* turned down $1,500 from Warners!"

Law tries to regain the upper hand by "casting" Rodney Bevan, an aspiring English actor, as Susie's long-lost husband, ordering him to crash the party at an upcoming lavish film premiere, where he will spill the beans that he didn't actually drown in a disaster at sea! As a huge crowd gathers outside the Carthay Circle Theatre, an announcer (Ronald Reagan) continuously plugs the new Warners epic "'The White Rajah,' starring Errol Flynn." (No such film was ever made.) Believing that they are shooting an upcoming attractions trailer, Bevan rushes up to the microphone, shoves the announcer away, and delivers the lines written by Law.

At the 50-minute point, the film finally becomes interesting, and the continuous bombast is leveled out a bit by the believable performance of Ralph Bellamy, who provides a stabilizing force among the frantic frolics. "Sometimes I wonder if this industry is worth the sacrifice," he says after speaking over the intercom with studio mogul B. K. (Pierre Watkin). Apparently, it isn't worth the effort, as the thoroughly insufferable antics soon return, thanks to — Cagney.

Friday, discovering the truth about the set-up at the premiere, fires Law and Benson. Toms is out with measles contracted from the kid, so Friday also sacks Happy, who, at eight months, is already washed up. In love with Susie, Bevan, revealing himself as an English Lord, asks her to marry him, and she agrees to give up the picture business for a life in London — proving Benson's belief that there is only one true scenario: "Boy meets girl; boy loses girl; boy gets girl." Quickly refocusing their innate bombast, Law and Benson hatch a new "baby star-making" scheme after Friday receives a phone call from his wife, who shares the news of her pregnancy.

Following this embarrassing effort, Cagney and O'Brien would collaborate on their greatest Warner Bros. film as a team. Aside from Marie Wilson, the acting highlight of *Boy Meets Girl* is provided by the 27-year-old Ronald Reagan, who is refreshingly naturalistic as the radio announcer (an early indication of just how effective he was with a microphone and an audience). Reagan, for the most part, enjoyed his years at Warner Bros. In 1992, with his presidency behind him, he recalled, "Well, you know, I was the only actor at the studio who was forced to use his *real* name. I wanted to be called 'Dutch,' and they insisted that I be billed as Ronald Reagan."[16]

7

Whaddaya Hear? Whaddaya Say?

Cagney's disastrous defection to Grand National Pictures—a premature attempt to go independent with his own crew—yielded unexpected fruit. At Jim's behest, Edward Alperson had purchased the original story "Angels with Dirty Faces" by Rowland Brown, but the fledgling studio didn't have enough dough to produce such an ambitious project.

J. L. welcomed Cagney back to Warner Bros.—and when he arrived, "Angels" came with him. Assigned to "script doctor" John Huston, the property was turned over to John Wexley, a founder of the Hollywood Communist Party, who teamed with Warren Duff to create an innovative and exciting screenplay. Wexley had written the anti-capital punishment play *The Last Mile*, which had been adapted for the screen in 1932. Unsatisfied with this watered-down film, he now set out to create a powerful setting for Cagney as a gangster destined to fry in the electric chair.

Warners spared no expense to create urban realism for *Angels*, building a tenement neighborhood covering four city blocks. To dress the set, they brought in four hurdy-gurdies and 56 push carts loaded with vegetables that were distributed to the needy after each day's shoot, a gesture that impressed Cagney, who created one of his most inspired, powerful and carefully crafted performances.

The spark for William "Rocky" Sullivan's physical hitching of his shoulders came from Cagney's memories of a pimp he had seen in Yorkville, a flamboyant hustler called "Smoke" who hung out on the corner of 1st Avenue and 78th Street, rolling his shoulders and addressing his pals with "Whaddaya hear? Whaddaya say?" At one point, Hal Wallis sent a memo to Michael Curtiz, complaining that Jim was doing the shoulder shrug too often.

Cagney and Pat O'Brien, both raised as Catholics, found several major problems with the script, particularly the confessional scene between Rocky and Father Jerry Connelly (O'Brien), which Jim considered "ludicrous." After discussing the unsatisfactory dialogue with Curtiz, the two actors were allowed to improvise their own material that recognized the proper ceremonial forms. Cagney explained, "[T]he director, the producer, and the writer were all Jewish, so how could they be expected to know?"[1]

The climactic scene, in which Rocky walks the last mile to the chair, was a major challenge, with Curtiz spending three days of shooting, during which Cagney dropped four pounds. Rocky's cell and the corridor down which he walks were exact replicas of those at Sing Sing, and though the electric chair was recreated, Curtiz chose not to show it on-screen. The sequence in which Father Jerry counsels Rocky in the cell was filmed in one 12-minute stretch, nailed by O'Brien and Cagney in a single take. Asked by the priest to end the boys' hero worship by dying a coward's death, Rocky goes to the chair pathetically pleading and wailing. Is he just putting on an act for the sake of the kids, or does he really "turn yellow"? Cagney explained:

Angels with Dirty Faces (1938): This publicity pose of Ann Sheridan, Cagney and Pat O'Brien gives no hint of the tragedy faced by their characters in Michael Curtiz's urban crime, capital punishment masterpiece (original lobby card).

> I think in looking at the film it is virtually impossible to say which course Rocky took — which is just the way I wanted it. I played it with deliberate ambiguity so that the spectator can take his choice. It seems to me it works out fine in either case. You have to decide.[2]

Cagney was intense on the set. When "Dead End" Kid Leo Gorcey copped an attitude like that of his character, improvising and trying to upstage the star, Jim rapped him in the face, telling him to knock it off. Bogie enjoyed hanging out with the boys, even joining in their stickball games between takes.

The important prologue, set in 1920, nearly was cut from the script following a lengthy, unsuccessful search for actors to play young Rocky and Jerry. Even after 23-year-old Cagney impersonator Frankie Burke (who had never appeared in a film) was cast, Curtiz still was unable to find someone who sufficiently resembled Pat O'Brien. Following William Tracy's successful audition, the footage finally was shot near the end of production.

Cagney and O'Brien are billed above the title, with ANGELS WITH DIRTY FACES followed by Bogart, Ann Sheridan, George Bancroft and the "Dead End" Kids. A medium close-up of a newspaper with the headline, "Harding Nominated for President" (indicating that the year is 1920) begins an impressive crane shot (lasting 29 seconds) spanning the tenement before it reaches street level, cutting to a closer shot of an organ grinder cranking out the tune "East Side, West Side." Young Rocky Sullivan appears, aggravating Laury Ferguson (Marilyn Knowlden) before heading off to burglarize a train car with his pal Jerry Connelly.

Because Jerry is able to "run faster," he makes it over the fence into their secret hideout in Hell's Kitchen, but Rocky is nabbed by a pursuing policeman. Later, at the Society for Juvenile Delinquents, Rocky greets his pal with "Whaddaya hear? Whaddaya say?" (the first time it is spoken in the film), then advises him to stay out of trouble: "Always remember — don't be a sucker."

As a result of his incarceration, Rocky sinks into an endless life of crime. During a classic, fast-moving Curtiz montage, he does several stints in the Big House for various felonies. Following shots of nightclubbing and street bombings, Rocky meets with his mouthpiece, James Frazier (Bogart), with whom he had pulled a heist for which he expects to be paid $100,000 upon his release.

At this point, the film shifts closer to the present day, back to the slum, where another 29-second crane shot begins with a newspaper headline and ends at street level, where it cuts in closer to a radio truck. This masterful shot is nearly a duplicate of the earlier one, paced identically and cutting when reaching the then-current technology for reproducing music.

At the Catholic Church, the newly sprung Rocky enters to listen to an angelic boys' choir, led by Father Jerry. Having escaped from the police, Connelly took his friend's advice, stayed out of the slammer and entered the priesthood. (Made the same year as *The Amazing Dr. Clitterhouse*, *Angels*, with its convincing emphasis on the environmental causes of criminality, is a serious, polar political opposite of its forerunner.)

Rocky is delighted when he sees two choir boys fighting on the way out of the church. Father Jerry, equally thrilled to be visited by his boyhood pal, suggests that he find a room in the parish. Taking his advice, Rocky meets up with Laury (Ann Sheridan), now Martin, having married a young man who was killed while mixed up in the rackets. After showing him a room at Mrs. Mangione's Boarding House for $5 per week, she slaps him and pulls his hat down over her eyes. "I've waited fifteen years to do that!" she shouts triumphantly before leaving the room. Sheridan truly earned her nickname as the "Oomph Girl" in this scene, both for her performance and for her going conspicuously bra-less, as she usually did on screen.

Three years following their Big House meeting, Rocky visits Frazier at his office behind the El Toro nightclub. "Where's that dough?" he asks, demanding to know his territory and his cut. Frazier responds by introducing him to Mac Keefer (George Bancroft), then orders a hit on his old "partner" as soon as he leaves the room.

All of the above action remarkably occurs in the first 21 minutes of the film. Having saved the dynamic *The Adventures of Robin Hood* for Warners from the schedule overruns of William Keighley earlier in the year, Curtiz now lent a similar extraordinary pace to *Angels*, using Sol Polito's camera, dramatically combining fluid movement with perfectly placed close-ups, to tell the tale.

The "Dead End" Kids make their entrance at this point, running into Rocky and picking his pocket before high-tailing it to their secret hideout, climbing the same fence over which Father Jerry had made his successful escape 15 years earlier. As the kids count the money in the wallet, Rocky walks down the stairs. "Stick 'em up!" he orders. "Say your prayers, you mugs!" Introduced to the gang — Swing (Bobby Jordan), Bim (Leo Gorcey), Patsy (Gabriel Dell), Crab (Huntz Hall) and Hunky (Bernard Punsly) — by Soapy (Billy Halop), he repays the leader with a swift kick in the ass. "Never bother anybody in your own neighborhood," he informs them, offering an essential piece of street advice before giving them a fin to buy some food.

At the boarding house, when Father Jerry crashes their party, Rocky talks the gang into participating in the church basketball game. Chaos ensues on the floor until Rocky steps in, slapping them around (in characteristic Cagney style) just enough to take the contest seriously. As Laury watches the game, Father Jerry observes, "Somehow, I feel that Rocky could be straightened out."

Following the game, as Rocky and Laury stroll down the sidewalk, Frazier's mob shadows him. Stepping into a drug store, Rocky shoves a goon into a phone booth, where he is shot down by his fellow wiseguys. Assuming that Rocky has been whacked, Frazier is surprised when he turns up at the office, demanding money from the safe. Frazier gives him two grand, with which Rocky (in another Cagney trademark) slaps him in the face. On the phone, Frazier orders Mac Keefer to withdraw 100 G's from the bank in the morning, then is taken hostage by Rocky.

The next day, Frazier returns, all stubble and dirt, to the office, while Rocky, about to be pinched by the cops, entrusts the envelope of dough to Soapy, who takes it to the hideout. Following the gangster's release, Patsy remarks (in a legendary line), "First you're in, then you're out. Boy, they can't hold you, Rocky." To repay the kids, he gives them all the cash in his wallet, then returns to his room, where he hides the 100 G's in the hollow metal posts of the bed.

Predictably, the bread burns holes in the boys' pockets. Trying to resemble real wiseguys, they buy fancy new clothes before hitting the local pool room, where they pass beer out to everyone. Father Jerry, asking Rocky to stop giving them money, tells him, "With them, it's kind of a hero worship."

"Well, you can't blame 'em for that, can you?" Rocky replies.

At the pool hall, Jerry's offer of another basketball game is turned down flat. On his way out, some of his old ways return when he punches an ill-mannered patron who insults him.

Rocky, demanding a piece of the action from Frazier and Keefer, sends 10 grand to Father Jerry to help build a new recreation center for the boys. The priest turns down the 10 G's, then informs Rocky he has decided to wage an all-out campaign to bust the rackets.

"Go ahead, Kid," Rocky approves, "and if I'm in your way, keep on stepping just as hard." Another fast-paced montage follows, juxtaposing headlines and Father Jerry's meetings with local newspaper publishers. Though Laury (reflecting the "good" part of Rocky's soul) pleads with the priest to ease up, he explains that he counts all of the lives of the current generation above Rocky's, then broadcasts his views about the Sullivan mob over the radio.

Keefer tells Frazier he wants to whack the priest. Rocky orders them to "lay off the rough stuff," then pretends to leave the office, but listens outside the door. When he bursts back in, Keefer pulls a rod, but is gunned down in return. Frazier kicks over a floor lamp and tries to run, but Rocky drills him.

During his escape from the El Toro, Rocky climbs through a skylight into another building, which is quickly surrounded by an army of policemen. A ferocious battle ensues, during which Rocky shoots two cops (a startling inclusion, since the Production Code forbade any such conduct by cinematic criminals). Placing their trust in the priest, they allow Father Jerry to go into the building, but Rocky chooses to use his friend as a human shield on his way out. Trying to run, in one last gasp of defiance, he throws his empty rod at the coppers as they apprehend him.

In yet another variation on the Warners headline style, the boys read a series of newspaper stories about the trial and fate of Rocky. At Sing Sing, 10 minutes before the execution, a "screw" informs him, "I'm going to tell the electrician to give it to you slow and easy, Wiseguy."

During their final conversation, Rocky tells Father Jerry, "I think, in order to be afraid, you've got to have a heart, and I don't think I've got one. I had that cut out of me a long time ago."

"I *want* you to let them down," Jerry says. "You see, you've been a hero to these kids, and hundreds of others, all through your life. And, now, you're going to be a glorified hero in death, and I want to prevent that, Rocky. They've got to despise your memory. They've got to be ashamed of you."

Rocky refuses, claiming that their admiration is the only thing he has left.

"Straighten yourself out with God," Jerry requests. "Outside of that, I can't ask for anything else."

"Well, *don't*!" Rocky replies angrily. While walking the last mile, he tells Jerry, "Promise me you won't let me hear you pray." Going out with yet another final act of defiance, he punches out a screw, adding, "I don't need anybody. Come on." The final image of Rocky is a tight, chiaroscuro close-up on Cagney's face, as resolute as ever.

A medium close-up of Father Jerry reading from the Bible cuts to a shadow (a Curtiz trademark) of Rocky, beginning to plead with the guards. A close-up of Jerry, beginning to tear up, is then followed by a close-up of Rocky's hands grabbing a wall radiator before the switch is thrown.

As depicted here, the electrocution lasts only a split second, while an actual electric-chair execution is a much more torturous affair, especially if not done properly. While Rocky's head is not shaved, which is always done for the application of an electrode, his pants leg is split, indicating where the other electrode would be placed.

The Production Code included prohibitions against depicting this sort of detail, but several compromises were made during production. Specifically, Rocky's shooting of the two policeman was probably allowed to provide sufficient reason for his execution. After all, audiences—like the "Dead End" Kids onscreen—viewed Rocky as a hero, particularly in the scene in which he gives Frazier and Keefer their just deserts.

Meeting with the gang at the hideout, Father Jerry tells them that the newspaper reports about their hero's cowardly, "yellow" departure are accurate, adding, "Let's go say a prayer for a boy who couldn't run as fast as I could."

Cagney and O'Brien give knockout performances that are the absolute antitheses of their rampant overacting in *Boy Meets Girl*. In his first appearance with Cagney, Bogart again does his best as a heartless mobster, meeting a cringing end similar to those at the hands of Robinson. Following their Warners "warm-up" in *Crime School*, the "Dead End" Kids give the film just the right touch of East Side atmosphere, and Ann Sheridan rounds out the main cast in fine fettle.

Cagney won the New York Film Critics Best Actor award, and was nominated for an Oscar, but lost to another Catholic priest characterization, that of Spencer Tracy as Father Flanagan, in MGM's sentimental favorite, *Boys Town* (1938). Lights years ahead of every other 1938 Warners release, *Angels* is arguably the best film the studio had released since the inception of the Production Code four years earlier.

Michael Curtiz sometimes gets his due as a Hollywood studio system director who was amazingly adept in all genres, yet rarely is he thought of as a film artist of *substance*, *Casablanca* notwithstanding. To the contrary, *Angels* and his other films dealing with capital punishment fly in the face of such a hasty evaluation. Prior to Cagney's tour de force, Spencer Tracy walked the last mile in *20,000 Years in Sing Sing* (1933), and Boris Karloff was railroaded to the chair in *The Walking Dead* (1936), then returned from the dead to wage God's own wrath on the gangsters who sent him up.

Angels with Dirty Faces (1938): At Sing Sing, Father Jerry Connelly (Pat O'Brien) prays as Rocky Sullivan (Cagney) stoically walks the last mile to the electric chair.

Curtiz's outstanding Warners film *Young Man with a Horn* (1949) is one of the best Hollywood depictions of a jazz musician ("Rick Martin," based loosely on Bix Beiderbecke and played superbly by Kirk Douglas) remarkably presenting a sensitive portrait of an African American character (Martin's mentor, Art Hazzard [Juano Hernandez, a master of quiet underplaying]) totally free of the racist stereotypes that lingered on for decades. This swingin' classic also features equally fine performances by Doris Day and Hoagy Carmichael.

On May 22, 1939, the *Lux Radio Theater* broadcast an audio adaptation of *Angels with Dirty Faces*, starring Cagney, O'Brien and Gloria Dickson as Laury. In his introduction, Cecil B. DeMille played up the Irish heritage and versatile talents of the two stars, noting that "both can sing and play the piano."

Father David J. Polich
Diocese of Des Moines, Iowa
on
Angels with Dirty Faces

The Cagney-O'Brien relationship really works. It is a believable friendship based on their growing up together and Cagney keeping O'Brien from going to jail. There is a strong loyalty but it does not stop the priest from fighting Cagney for the souls of the kids in the old neighborhood.

O'Brien's depiction of a priest rings true. His is a strong character, neither pious nor naïve. Given that the 1920s saw the defeat of Catholic Al Smith and the resurgence of the Klan throughout the South and Midwest, this very favorable and sympathetic characterization in a film is quite interesting. Continuing on with Bing Crosby, the Roman Catholic clergy did pretty well for a couple of decades. Pat O'Brien is compassionate but tough. He is principled and streetwise. He would have made a great pope!

Thomas M. Fortunato
National Archives, Washington, DC
on
Angels with Dirty Faces

I was raised a Roman Catholic in Brooklyn, and spent half the time wanting to grow up to be Father Jerry Connelly, and the other half wanting to be Rocky Sullivan.

Angels with Dirty Faces (1938): Warners' potent poster art depicts Rocky Sullivan (Cagney) between representatives of heaven (Pat O'Brien's Father Connelly) and hell (Bogart's James Frazier) as the "Dead End" Kids await their hero's fateful decision (original jumbo window card).

Whenever we played "cops and robbers," which, believe it or not, we New York kids actually used to play, everybody always wanted to be "the bad guy." Nobody ever wanted to be the cops!

If you were the bad guy, you were almost always Rocky Sullivan. That way, you could call the *coppers* "dirty screws" and tell them you were going to "spit in their eye." We used to say, "Whaddaya hear? Whaddaya say?" all the time, not just when we were playing.

I have to say that *Angels* was my favorite movie, not just my favorite Cagney movie, for most of my childhood. I remember, in my sixth grade autograph book, they had a cover page where you could list your favorite movie, your "hero," and your favorite saying.

My favorite movie was *Angels with Dirty Faces*. My hero was Rocky Sullivan.

Unfortunately, I didn't want the teachers to think I was a complete low-life juvenile delinquent, so, instead of my favorite saying being "You dirty screw, get your hands off me before I spit in your eye," I wimped out and wrote, "Keep your face to the sun, and the shadows will fall behind," a totally stupid piece of pap I got off a Tetley Tea bag tag!

I always wanted to cross it out and change it to the real one, but never did, and then lost the stupid autograph book before I even got to high school! So it goes ...

Michael Curtiz, at the height of his directorial powers.

8

Bogie in Purgatory

Angels with Dirty Faces was a hit, and Bogart worked steadily, appearing in supporting roles in three vastly different films released back to back. The first, *King of the Underworld* (1939), a remake of the 1935 Paul Muni film *Dr. Socrates*, gave him top billing as a Mob boss, costarring with Kay Francis. By the time the actress, who formerly had been one of the studio's biggest stars, saw the opening credits, which bill Bogie above the title, but list her underneath — "with Kay Francis"— she already had left Warner Bros., her contract expired.

An inappropriate title that suggests a major gangland epic, *King of the Underworld* is the cheapest, most poorly written, totally *unnecessary* Warners Mob film of the 1930s. After major supporting roles in several superb studio offerings, Bogart still was given "star" billing only when playing the lead in shoddy B films; and, with *King*, he again was saddled with a quickie remake of a Warners A film released just a few years earlier. Aside from Bogie (as gang leader Joe Gurney), the cast consists of a has-been actress and lukewarm players drafted from the second string.

The script by George Bricker and Vincent Sherman, with its emphasis on Gurney's simplistic obsession with Napoleon, is so bad that 65 minutes seems like an excessive running time (an element made even worse by huge gaps in the narrative occurring at regular intervals, as if only half the screenplay was shot or half the footage ended up on the cutting-room floor).

The opening scene set at "General Hospital" introduces the husband-and-wife, not-for-profit physician team of Niles and Carole Nelson (John Eldredge and Kay Francis), who are preparing to operate on a man with a bullet pressing his heart. During the surgery, one of Gurney's goons reports back to "da boss" on the patient's condition. Gurney is holding the gunman, who will be released "if Butch pulls through." When Butch survives, Gurney tells the goon, "Get that doc's name and address, and come on up here," then gives the shooter his "release": a bullet in the back. It's what Napoleon would have done, he idiotically tells his gang.

Gurney delivers $500 to Niles, suggesting, "There's plenty more where that came from." Carole assumes he won the windfall on a horse race, and instantly they are living in a ritzy apartment. She asks him to stop gambling and focus on his practice, but Gurney calls about another "problem" with "one of his boys." Niles initially refuses but, having no choice, goes out, with Carole close on his heels.

While he cares for the "patient," cops raid the joint and gun him down. Assuming Carole was privy to her late husband's gangland activities, they give her the third degree; and the D.A., having no evidence, puts her on trial, at which she is acquitted by a jury. However, the hospital, considering her "guilty until proven innocent," gives her three months to provide the proof to retain her medical license.

Carole reads a newspaper story about two members of the Gurney gang locked up in the small town of Wayne Center, where she, intent on retribution, immediately sets up a practice. On his way to the burg, Gurney is stalled by a flat tire he assumes was caused by a shot fired by a roadside bum — actually Bill Stevens (James Stephenson), an unemployed writer with an English accent (a ludicrous rip-off of *The Petrified Forest*). "He's one of them geniuses," proclaims Gurney, who takes him along. During the drive, while discussing Napoleon, they mention Waterloo.

"That's in Iowa, isn't it?" one of the mugs asks.

"It's in Europe," counters Gurney.

A shootout erupts at the Wayne Center slammer. Stevens is shot trying to run away, and Gurney is clipped in the arm while driving the getaway car. Carole treats Bill in his jail cell, then accepts a c-note from Gurney after patching him up. Responding to one of her facetious comments, he proudly informs his stooge, "Wait until I tell the boys. I'm a *moronic* type."

Released from jail, Stevens works as Carole's handyman, but is kidnapped by two goons ordered by Gurney to "grab the genius." Gurney wants Stevens to pen his autobiography, but when he is told that such a work is actually written by the subject, he insists that the scribe "front" for him.

"What you want is a ghostwriter," says Stevens.

"No, none of that mystery stuff," Gurney replies.

One of the script's few clever moments occurs when further discussion results in the proposed book title, "Joe Gurney: Napoleon of Crime." (Sir Arthur Conan Doyle's Professor Moriarty, in the 1893 short story "The Final Problem," is referred to as "The Napoleon of Crime" by Sherlock Holmes.) With Stevens serving as his amanuensis (a term utterly unfathomable to him), Gurney dictates his life story, mentioning that he went to reform school, where he "got a lot of angles." This comment, referring to the criminal-making nature of the penal system, and the earlier scene depicting a travesty of the due process component of American justice, are the film's only attempts at "social commentary."

A ridiculous incident involving Gurney giving a sleeping underling a "hot foot" is followed by the boss' admission that Stevens will be whacked after his work is done. Planning to have his memoirs published posthumously, he can't take the risk of the writer turning stool pigeon.

Another conversation about Napoleon results in Gurney placing his hand inside his coat and asking, "Why was he always standin' like this?"

"He was reachin' for a gat," replies one of his fellow morons.

When Carole arrives to change the dressing on Gurney's wound, he makes his most moronic comment of all: "Dolls is nice to have around the house, like pets, and dogs and cats and things."

Responding to his complaint of having an eye problem, Carole, claiming that he has caused his "highly contagious" infection to spread, suggests that she treat them all with "beledrine sulfate" (actually a chemical that will cause temporary blindness). Using Stevens as a guinea pig, she hits them all with eye drops, just in time for the coppers to surround the joint and start blasting away. Unable to see, the goons begin to bite the dust, but several manage to stumble their way to a surrender. As Gurney wanders around with his rod, he is shot, causing him to tumble down a flight of stairs.

"Hey, pal, do me a favor, will ya?" he asks Stevens. "Don't tell 'em that a dame tripped me up." This last gasp of bad dialogue from Gurney is immediately followed by perhaps the worst tacked-on ending in Warner Bros. history: Carole and Bill are not only (apparently) married, but also have a son who appears to be about six years old!

King of the Underworld (1939): As moronic Mob boss Joe Gurney, Bogart received top billing above the has-been Kay Francis, but still had to suffer through a shoddy B remake of an earlier Warners success, *Dr. Socrates* (original lobby card).

Robinson and Cagney, whose Warners stardom began immediately after their first big gangster hits, never had to suffer through anything a fraction as humiliating as *King of the Underworld*. Jack Warner's conflicts with Bogart are legendary, but the fact that the mogul approved him as the "star" of a straight gangster film that belongs at the bottom of the barrel with *Swing Your Lady* boggles the mind. Joe Gurney is simply the most *ignorant* character Bogie ever played in a Warners film, and he didn't even have the luxury of being miscast this time around (something that would be rectified in his very next film).

Critics noted that Cagney quickly slid from the sublime (*Angels with Dirty Faces*) to the ridiculous in *The Oklahoma Kid* (1939). While few could accept the Eastside kid as cowboy Jim Kincaid, the actor was upset that no one noticed what an accomplished horseman he'd become. (He handles his steed flawlessly throughout the film.) Interestingly, both audiences and reviewers considered Bogart, who plays Kincaid's rival-in-black, "Whip" McCord, the more convincing Westerner. Viewed today, there is little in the film to support this conclusion, as Cagney is very comfortable in his role, and Bogart is merely playing a Mob boss in a cowboy hat — a racketeer on the range.

Originally, Edward Paramore, Jr., had planned to write a film about legendary frontier scout Kit Carson, an idea that inspired Cagney to research the character, including his choice of an historically accurate costume. But by the time Lloyd Bacon began shooting *The Oklahoma Kid*, Jim was duded up in the most ridiculous B-Western outfit imaginable. Taking a look at his costar's huge 10-gallon hat, Bogart remarked that he looked like a mushroom.

The Oklahoma Kid (1939): Racketeers on the range: Jim Kincaid (Cagney) blasts the pistol from the hand of "Whip" McCord (Bogart) after tossing beer into the face of gang member Wes Handley (Ward Bond).

At one point during production, Hal Wallis ordered Lloyd Bacon to reshoot scenes in which Cagney was smirking during serious moments. Always ignoring the "advice" of executives who knew little or nothing about acting, Jim instead maintained his lighthearted approach, knowing that no one could possibly take the film seriously. He also added his own touch to the film's music, suggesting that the saloon pianist pound out "I Don't Want to Play in Your Yard," a song his father used to sing. In the scene, when the pianist refuses, Kincaid orders, "Play It!" then begins to sing. Though Wes Handley (Ward Bond), a member of McCord's gang, attempts to shut him down, Kincaid knocks the much larger man to the barroom floor with a right to the jaw, then resumes the song. Harassed further, he temporarily blinds the outlaws with beer and runs out of the barroom.

While shooting a scene in which McCord and Handley thunder by as Kincaid stands on a rock above, Cagney, who had never used a lariat, asked the wrangler if he could perform the lassoing of Ward Bond's horse himself. Getting a handle on the rope, he wanted to add some realism to the sequence; and indeed he did, tossing the loop directly over the horse's head and stopping Bond cold. After holding on for a second, he let go, prompting Bacon to yell, "Cut! Why didn't you hang on?"

"What did you want me to do?" asked Jim. "Kill Ward?"

"Why not?" replied Bacon.[1]

The film opens with President Grover Cleveland (Stuart Holmes) signing the bill opening the Oklahoma Territory for settlement. (Cleveland's successor, Benjamin Harrison, was

President when the "Land Run" began on April 22, 1889.) After reaching Cherokee City, where would-be "Sooners" are waiting for the gunshot beginning the rush, Kincaid tangles with McCord and his gang in the saloon, then explains his views on White settlement to Judge Hardwick (Donald Crisp). Interestingly, the conversation could just as easily have been improvised by Cagney and Crisp, a conservative who later joined the ranks of the witch-hunters.

HARDWICK: How come a strong, healthy young fellow like you isn't out there, up to his neck in this land rush?

KINCAID: Why? I'm doing all right.

HARDWICK: Those people are going out there to build a new empire.

KINCAID: Fine. Let them have it.

HARDWICK: You mean to say you've got no feeling for the country? No pride in seeing a civilization carved out of a wilderness? What sort of an American are you?

KINCAID: I like the country fine. As for civilization, I've got nothing particular against it. I can take it or leave it alone.

HARDWICK: What sort of folks did you come from?

KINCAID: (laughs) The most God-fearing, law-adibing, land-grabbing, empire-building fellows you ever saw. Suckers for this land rush stuff, too; but not for me. I crave a nice, easy-going existence, and I've got it.

HARDWICK: I see. No responsibility. No ambition. None of this get up and get it stuff that regular folks have.

KINCAID: Exactly, and that's why my folks and I have been on the outs for years.

HARDWICK: You seem like a very antisocial young man.

KINCAID: But I'm *not*. I'm as social as a set-up pup. I like all kinds of people. But I don't take to this itch of plowing up new empires, that's all.

HARDWICK: But why not?

KINCAID: I'll tell you why not. Now look — in the first place, the White people steal the land from the Indians, right?

HARDWICK: They get paid for it, don't they?

KINCAID: Paid for it? Yeah, a measly dollar and forty cents an acre, price agreed to at the point of a gun. Then the immigrants sweat and strain and break their hearts carving out a civilization. Fine, great. Then, when they get all pretty and prosperous, along come the grafters, and land grabbers and politicians — and, with one hand, skim off the cream, and with the other, scoop up the gravy. Not for me.

Listen, I learned this about human nature when I was about *so high*— and that is, that the strong take away from the weak, and the smart take away from the strong.

HARDWICK: I suppose you've never heard of the law that protects people's rights and property.

KINCAID: Yeah, I've heard of it. I've seen it work, too. Sometimes it's all right. In the cities, it may be fine — but here, you can't trust it. (pats holster) This is the only law I know that's worth a hoot in this part of the country. The *only law*.

After the Kid is arrested for having wagered newly minted "Indian money" in a poker game, he escapes, rides out of town, and holes up with a Mexican couple. In a charming scene, he plays the guitar and sings "Rock-a-bye, Baby" in Spanish to an infant. Meanwhile, McCord opens the Territory Saloon in Tulsa, where he becomes responsible for "an orgy ... of vice, crime, gambling and murder." When John Kincaid (Hugh Southern) and his son, Ned (Harvey Stevens), run for mayor and sheriff, respectively, McCord hatches a frame up to jail the old man for murder. While the gang railroads him to a first-degree murder sentence, the Kid waylays a stagecoach carrying Judge Hardwick and returns to Tulsa. Now revealing that the old man is his *Old Man*, the Kid tries to break him out of jail, but he refuses and is subsequently lynched by the four members of McCord's mob.

The Kid tracks down Indian Joe (Trevor Bardette; called "Indian Jack Pascoe" in the credits) and Ed Curley (Lew Harvey), whom he kills in duels, and Handley, whom he shoots from a train car, from which he falls to a grisly death (off camera). He then captures the exhausted and dehydrated Doolin (Edward Pawley), who admits the truth about McCord ordering the lynching. Following an extended barroom brawl with McCord, Kincaid is saved by his brother, who, mortally wounded, guns down the gang leader. The Kid tries to light out for Arizona, but is stopped by Jane Hardwick (Rosemary Lane)

The Oklahoma Kid (1939): A lifelong student of the guitar, Cagney strums a few chords as Jim Kincaid serenades a *niño* with a Spanish version of "Rock-a-bye, Baby."

and her father, who, as Judge, marries them where they stand.

Well-paced by Lloyd Bacon and atmospherically photographed by James Wong Howe, *The Oklahoma Kid* is a very entertaining oater. Cagney's performance and horsemanship are more than adequate; and, although Bogart is difficult to accept in his role, this bizarre casting (along with the occasionally thoughtful and witty screenplay by Paramore, Warren Duff and Robert Buckner) occasionally lifts the film above the level of "just another Western."

While appearing in *The Oklahoma Kid*, Bogart also shot his scenes as Michael O'Leary—this time awkwardly attempting to use an "ethnic" accent—for *Dark Victory* (1939). When originally presented with the property, Jack Warner wondered aloud just who would pay to see a depressing film about a selfish, 23-year-old socialite who goes blind and dies from a brain tumor. Seven decades later, the premise seems even more dubious for a feature film; but, at the time, *Dark Victory* proved an enormous box-office smash. With any other actress in the lead role, the film could have been a soap-operatic disaster, but Bette Davis' multi-layered performance is one of her finest, and still one of the best ever given by a Hollywood actress.

Bogart struggled with two difficult parts simultaneously. After playing scenes as a cowboy, he then had to attempt an Irish brogue (which constantly comes and goes) as O'Leary, the horse trainer unsuccessful in his attempts to woo Davis' Judith Traherne. At one point, Davis' tragic, emotional characterization led her into hysterics, and director Edmund Goulding fell two weeks behind schedule when she had to take time off for illness.

Billed third (below Davis and George Brent), Bogart appears in the very first shot of the film, calling Judith early in the morning after a wild night of partying. "I'd like to slap that man's face," Judith tells her best friend, Ann King (Geraldine Fitzgerald). Later, when he comes on to her in the horse stable, rather than slapping him, she tells him she's dying.

Judith's terminal illness is discovered after months of unreported headaches, double vision and, finally, an equestrian accident. Dr. Frederick Steele (George Brent) operates, consults a dozen other leading specialists to corroborate his negative prognosis; then, with the support of Ann King, decides not to tell Judith, who falls in love with him. Steele proposes, but she discovers the deceit; and, after a prolonged binge of drinking and alienating nearly everyone around her, she apologizes and lives out the rest of her days at the doc's home in Vermont, where he is conducting "cell research."

The final 20 minutes are the most powerful and enjoyable to watch, thanks to Davis and Brent, a fine leading man (whose quiet performance is occasionally reminiscent of fellow Warners star Errol Flynn). Judith, believing that a storm is brewing, actually begins to lose her eyesight while outdoors, planting hyacinths with Ann, who has paid a visit. Declining to accompany Fred to a conference in New York, she hides her condition from him (a highly implausible element, though a dramatic parallel to his earlier behavior), bids farewell to Ann, then climbs into bed, where she dies alone.

The film's ending originally included an additional scene intended to provide an upbeat antidote to the sequence showing Judith's death in isolation. After her prized Thoroughbred won a major race, O'Leary, tending to the animal, closed out the picture with a tearful tribute. The scene may have been great for Bogie; but, after the preview audience left unimpressed, the studio left it on the cutting room floor.

The supporting cast is excellent, including Geraldine Fitzgerald (in her American film debut) and Henry Travers (as Judith's family doctor). Ronald Reagan plays Alec Hamm, a terminally inebriated playboy, who gladly keeps Judith company during her drunken spree. (Though he's called "Hamm," Reagan gives his usual reliable, understated performance.) Bogart, sporting a wispy hairdo (rather than his usual slicked-back look) and riding breeches, appears in four scenes, doing his best with another dose of Warners miscasting.

Davis makes up for whatever shortfalls the film may have. She conveys a staggering array of moods and emotions, brilliantly using those famous eyes to communicate Judith's failing sight. Even before she begins to fade, when describing the inevitable process of "dimming vision, then blindness" to Ann, Davis' eyes visually match every word of dialogue. The final close-up, showing her face as she dies in bed, is chill-inducing. Having won her second Best Actress Academy Award for Warners' *Jezebel* (1938) the previous year, she was nominated again for *Dark Victory*, but no other actress stood a chance against Vivien Leigh in 1939, with MGM's technically stunning though overrated pro-Confederate soap opera *Gone with the Wind* cleaning up at the Oscars.

While MGM was producing a nostalgic whitewash of a former society founded on racism, Warners was ready to drop the hammer on a current one. When Robinson returned to Hollywood, Jack Warner awarded him the *Dr. Ehrlich* part, and went one better by asking him to star in "Storm Over America," an adaptation of Leon Turrou's book *The Nazi Spy Conspiracy in America*. Warner had been lukewarm about confronting the Third Reich directly, but the recent murder of a Jewish studio representative in Germany spurred him to produce a film exposing the German-American Bund.

There were extensive legal problems to work out on the Nazi project (including a $500,000 lawsuit by the Bund) and *Dr. Ehrlich*, which also had been planned by another studio. While waiting to begin, Robinson signed a new three-year contract, for two films per year at $85,000 each. The agreement, which would take effect on January 19, 1939, assured him of no more loan-outs and granted him the ability to approve of two films per year outside Warner Bros. For his Warners projects, he was to consider three scripts each May and September, giving him the power to select the "principal male role" in each — a clause assuring his stardom, rather than reducing him to the rank of character actor.

With his role in *Dr. Ehrlich* confirmed, Robinson agreed to star in *Brother Orchid*, a seriocomic gangster picture, at a later date. For the time being, he again focused on "Storm Over America," now re-titled less subtly as *Confessions of a Nazi Spy*, and became even more involved with the Anti-Nazi League, an organization intending to wage a personal appearance and radio campaign to persuade FDR to get tough with Hitler.

On the evening of December 9, 1938, Cagney dropped in at Robinson's residence, not to discuss Warner Bros. contract negotiations, but to support the League, which now had 4,000 members. Also among the convened "Committee of 56," named after the number of signers of the Declaration of Independence, were Joan Crawford, Melvyn Douglas, Henry Fonda, John Ford, Myrna Loy, Groucho Marx, Paul Muni, Claude Rains, Spencer Tracy, and even Jack Warner. Five days later, Robinson was directed by Frank Capra in a short dramatization celebrating Rededication Day, the anniversary of the signing of the Bill of Rights, on NBC Radio. On December 21, the Committee announced plans to produce film clips depicting Nazi activities. Soon, the FBI began a file documenting all of Robinson's activities, although he had been friendly with J. Edgar Hoover in the past.

Robinson began *playing* an FBI man on the *Confessions of a Nazi Spy* set on February 13, 1939, and immediately received threatening phone calls at home. Jack Warner and his wife, Ann, also received death threats, so the mogul quickly hired bodyguards to accompany him to and from the studio. German officials made protests to the U. S. State Department, but Warner stood his ground, refusing to be intimidated by the Third Reich's promises to make its own film exposing "American corruption."

Hal Wallis and director Anatole Litvak were dedicated to making *Confessions* a powerful work, and allowed Robinson to make dialogue revisions to Milton Krims and John Wexley's screenplay, which brings him into the action at mid-point. He had completed his scenes by March, when Wallis asked if he would approve a plan to pitch the film as a pseudo-documentary, featuring no "star billing" in the film's credits nor advertising campaign. Though his contract insured the billing, Robinson told him to forgo such ego-massaging. He did receive top billing, below the title, while no one's name was included on most of the posters and trade ads.

The plot was based on an actual case involving the German-American Bund, a fascist organization popular in Wisconsin and on Long Island (but no competition for that native group, the KKK, which had a general hold on hate). At one point, Wexley saw Martin Dies leaving Jack Warner's office, having just warned the mogul not to malign a "friendly country" like Germany. Apparently, the notorious witch-hunter also had requested that the script place some dreaded Commies alongside the Nazis, but Wexley characteristically refused.

The film's opening title leads directly to a "news reporter" (John Deering) in silhouette, recounting the past two years of Nazi espionage activity in Britain and the United States. Located in Argyll, Scotland, Mrs. Mary McLaughlin (Eily Malyon) serves as the official international mail liaison for the Third Reich, forwarding important information between Germany and the U. S.

In New York, Dr. Karl F. Kassel (Paul Lukas) speaks to a gathering of the Bund, insist-

Confessions of a Nazi Spy (1939): Most of Warner Bros.' advertising for this unapologetic anti-Nazi epic didn't focus on the actors, but one lobby card set included this title card featuring Robinson's name. In response, representatives of the Third Reich threatened to eliminate Eddie G., Jack Warner, and others involved in the production (original lobby card).

ing that "America's deepest roots are essentially German." Preaching against "democracy and racial equality," Kassel insists upon the need to "unite all those of German blood for the German future of America." His impassioned speech is met with "Sieg Heil!" and Adolf Hitler's favorite tune, "Deutschland Uber Alles."

In Berlin, Gestapo officers, stating that "the Americans are a very simple-minded people," discuss the Stateside activities of their number-one operative, Kurt Schneider (Francis Lederer). The ultimate worldwide goal is for all Germans *not* to assimilate with other cultures, no matter where they are living.

During another speech to German-Americans in New York, Dr. Kassel insists on the total destruction of "democracy … a fanatical faith," as represented by the Constitution and the Bill of Rights. Interrupting him, an American Legionnaire (Ward Bond) says that he will fight for these sacred American foundations. "We don't want any isms in this country except Americanism!" he shouts. As a fight breaks out, he adds, "I have a right to speak in an open meeting! This is a free country!"

Gestapo officer Franz Schlager (George Sanders) arrives on the *Bismarck* to meet with Kurt Schneider, a.k.a. "Sword," who has been receiving military information from his friend, Werner Renz (Joseph Sawyer). Kassel is called back to Germany, a "different Fatherland" from the one he'd left a decade earlier. "Inspiring. Positively inspiring," he tells Dr. Joseph Goebbels (Martin Kosleck), who puts him in charge of all National Socialist activity in the U. S., where "racial and religious hatreds must be fostered" upon his return. In the "ensuing chaos," the Nazis will "take control."

The Nazis' international scheme is already beginning to unravel, however, as British Military Intelligence arrests Mary McLaughlin in Scotland. Meanwhile, in Washington, G-Man Edward Renard (Robinson, making his first appearance at the 43-minute mark), "one of the oldest operators with the FBI," targets the "half-witted, hysterical crackpots" who are waging "war" on the United States. The first "crackpot" brought in is Schneider, whom Renard informs, "Don't worry. There's no Third Degree with the Federal Bureau of Investigation." Playing to the fact that the Nazi agent is an egomaniac, Renard uses a complimentary approach to obtain hours of secret information, including a full confession.

Schneider identifies his cohort, Hilda Kleinhauer (Dorothy Tree), who, in turn, helps nab Kassel. Using the same methods, Renard convinces the doctor to reveal the entire Nazi spy organization. As the operatives are rounded up, Hitler annexes Austria and invades Czechoslovakia; meanwhile, Stateside, Dr. Julius Gustav Krogmann (Sig Ruman) advises Hilda to say she was tortured by the FBI into signing a false confession.

During the subsequent trial of Schneider, Kleinhauer, Kassel and Renz, U.S. Attorney Kellogg (Henry O'Neill) describes the "ruthless march of the Nazi iron boot ... God alone knows what peace-loving nation will be next." Concluding his summation, he states, "America is not simply one of the remaining democracies. America *is* democracy." In the classic Warners headline style, the next day's newspaper declares, "Spies Convicted."

Meeting at a diner, the G-Man and the lawyer discuss the ideology of the Third Reich, which Renard describes as "absolutely insane." As patrons at the lunch counter discussing the trial's outcome agree that the U. S. "ain't Europe," Kellogg praises "the voice of the people."

"Thank God for such people," says Renard.

"Yes, thank God," replies Kellogg as the film fades to black.

One of the first feature films to save its credits for the end, *Confessions* awards Robinson the sole "starring" billing, then gives the rest of the cast a "with" designation. A 180-degree turn from his previous Warners character (Remy Marco), Edward Renard provided Eddie with an equally rewarding experience, this time on a much different level. An archetype for future figures of authority played by Robinson (the Nazi-war-criminal hunter "Mr. Wilson" in Orson Welles' *The Stranger* [1946], for example), Renard is thoroughly believable: cool, calm, intelligent and persuasive in his efforts to stem the tide of Nazi menace.

The first anti-Nazi propaganda feature produced in the United States, *Confessions* premiered on April 21, 1939, when policemen and plainclothes detectives were stationed throughout the theater. Jack Warner and Hal Wallis demonstrated sheer guts in giving the green light to the project, directly intended to alert the American public to the evils of fascism on a worldwide level. The power of the film was proved when the Third Reich banned it, followed by a denunciation from the German ambassador in Washington. Despite Hitler's own threat to "execute" the cast and crew, the film did very well at the box office and with critics, who praised its frank, hard-hitting approach. Not even the ridiculous Bund lawsuit could stop the film, especially after its leader, Fritz Kuhn, was arrested for embezzling the organization's funds.

Having impressed Hal Wallis in his *Dark Victory* scenes with Bette Davis, Bogart was cast as her tragic beau in *The Old Maid*, another Edmund Goulding effort. He began working on the film on March 15, 1939; but, by the end of the day, he'd been replaced by George Brent, whom Jack Warner originally had considered. Bogie, realizing that he'd been miscast as a romantic lead, apparently left the set, angry and thinking he'd be nothing but a character actor for the rest of his career.

Following a trip to Kansas to help publicize the latest Michael Curtiz-Errol Flynn spectacular, *Dodge City* (1939), during which Mayo tried to stab Bogie with a broken Coke bottle during a drunken brawl aboard the train, he was back at Warner Bros. for another B crime drama, *You Can't Get Away with Murder* (1939). Thoroughly sick of these cookie-cutter projects, Bogart (receiving top billing in another programmer) simply walked through it, and his disinterest was noted by more than one critic.

Robert Buckner's screenplay, based on the 1937 play *Chalked Out* by Jonathan Finn and Warden Lewis E. Lawes, recycles other Warners material, including the borrowed-gun device from Cagney's debut, *Sinner's Holiday*, and the reliable pawnshop-robbery-gone-bad angle (again involving a "Dead End" Kid). Billy Halop

You Can't Get Away with Murder (1939): Bogart walks through yet another programmer giving him top billing as a low-rent wiseguy (original window card).

plays Johnny Stone, a teenager who emulates Frank Wilson (Bogie), a local wiseguy who whacks the proprietor of the Chapin Loan Company (Robert Strange), then plants Johnny's rod, which the kid had scrounged from Officer Fred Burke (Harvey Stephens), the fiancé of his sister Madge (Gale Page, who also plays Halop's sister in *Crime School*).

Burke is convicted and sentenced to fry in the Sing Sing chair. However, when Wilson and Stone also end up in the Joint (for a gas station robbery), the kid, encouraged to go straight by "Pops" (Henry Travers), the prison librarian, struggles with his conscience. During an attempted jailbreak, Wilson shoots Johnny, who, as he dies, confesses the whole truth. Burke is sprung, while the wiseguy satisfies the Production Code by taking the cop's place in the electric chair.

After playing the reformer who aids Halop's character in *Crime School* and the cringing weasel who gets bumped off by the kid's hero, Rocky Sullivan, in *Angels with Dirty Faces*, Bogie returned to his evil thug persona to truly place Halop in harm's way in *You Can't Get Away with Murder*. The title says it all. Supporting Bogart and Halop (in roles they could have played in their sleep) is an impressive parade of Warners mugs, including Harold Huber, Joe Sawyer, Joe Downing and George E. Stone. On the "right" side of the law are several familiar faces of authority, including John Litel, Joseph Crehan and Herbert Rawlinson. Appearing in a small, unbilled role as "Sam"—what else?—Eddie "Rochester" Anderson provides some welcome comic relief each time he strolls into the library to hit up Pops for a new recipe.

Warner Bros.' "lesser" wiseguy, George Raft, was the studio's only major actor who had hobnobbed with real gangsters, including Al Capone, though he hadn't actually engaged in illegal activities. As a dancer, he had performed in mob-owned nightclubs before hitting the silver screen, most powerfully in Howard Hawks' *Scarface*.

Cagney admired Raft for his acting and terpsichorean skills, and was pleased to be teamed with him in *Each Dawn I Die* (1939), the story of Frank Ross, an investigative, public-minded reporter who gets railroaded to the Big House by gangsters and a D.A. on the take. In depicting an innocent man hardened by a brutal penal system, Cagney gives an understated but powerful performance, and Raft is strong and equally subtle (often needing no dialogue, but using only his eyes and slight facial expressions) as Stacey, a legendary criminal whose life is saved by Ross. In turn, Ross is freed by Stacey's later fatal sacrifice during a prison break. "George was a real pro," recalled Cagney, "letter-perfect in his lines every day, every word. I must say I can't say the same for myself."[2] Interestingly, Bogart had been Warners' first choice to play Stacey, while John Garfield had been considered for the Ross role.

A fascinating component of shooting *Each Dawn I Die* was the presence on the set of labor racketeer Willie Bioff, the head of the International Alliance of Theatrical Stage Employees (IATSE), who threatened studio moguls with shutdowns if they didn't grease his palm. Raft spotted Bioff, and later was told that Cagney's reputation for snubbing labor tough guys nearly had gotten him killed. Bioff admitted that a hit on Jim had been ordered when Jack Warner refused to pay, but Raft's participation in the picture kept the goons at bay. Cagney saves Raft cinematically; but, apparently, the latter saved the former for real. (In 1955 Bioff was whacked in classic Mafia style—blown up in his car—after hiding out in Arizona, posing as a grocer.)

Cagney and Raft are both billed above the title on the opening credits panel. William Keighley establishes solid narrative economy from the opening shot, which fades in on a campaign billboard for Jesse Hanley (Thurston Hall), an assistant district attorney running for the D.A. office. The shadowy lighting, combined with the juxtaposition of this image with the subsequent shot of Frank Ross slouched in his car, peering out the window at the headquarters of the Banton Construction Company, suggests that Hanley is a politician up to no good.

Keighley and cinematographer Arthur Edeson establish their effective moving camera style immediately, enhancing Ross' surveillance of Hanley and his "associates" burning the Banton books, the publication of the headline story, and the abduction of the reporter, who is knocked cold, doused with booze, and sent careening down the street in his car. Witnessed by a crowd of bystanders, the runaway vehicle crashes into another car, instantly killing three innocent passengers.

Ross desperately declares his innocence; but, framed by Hanley and W. J. Grayce (Victor Jory), he is convicted of manslaughter and sentenced to one-to-20 years at hard labor. On the train to prison, he is handcuffed to career criminal "Hood" Stacey, who has just been handed a 199-year sentence. At the Big House, they are immediately menaced by Pete Kassock (John Wray, who replaced Barton MacLane), the "toughest screw in the state," who delights in his sadistic treatment of the inmates.

In the twine mill, "Limpy" Julien (Joe Downing), Pete's pet snitch, lunges at Stacey with a shiv, but is tripped by Ross. After the fight is broken up by Pete, Limpy whips the shiv at Stacey, but hits a bail of twine fiber behind him.

Each Dawn I Die (1939): In the Big House twine mill, framed journalist Frank Ross (Cagney) throws in with "Hood" Stacey (George Raft) in the hope of being released from stir.

The effects of prolonged incarceration are demonstrated by Mueller (Stanley Ridges), who tells Ross and Stacey that he's going to attack Pete with "a steam hose … a blow torch … a hammer." Joined by his scar-faced pal, "Polecat" Carlisle (Alan Baxter), one of the goons who helped Hanley frame Ross, Limpy squeals on an inmate carrying contraband, but Stacey, knowing that the con is soon to be paroled, takes the rap. After serving time in the "Hole," where the prisoner is handcuffed to the bars for eight hours each day, he emerges, staring and ashen-faced, to retrieve the shiv from Fargo Red ("Slapsie" Maxie Rosenbloom), who had held it for him.

During an evening showing of Warners' *Wings of the Navy* (another of the studio's own "product placements"), Limpy is stabbed to death. No one is accused, and Stacey tells Ross that he had given the shiv to another inmate. "Someone else beat me to it," he claims, but nonetheless asks Ross to tell Warden Armstrong (George Bancroft) that he committed the crime, so he can escape during the trial and work "on the outside" to free his innocent partner. Ross refuses, but following a tearful visit from his mother (Emma Dunn, a docile, loving Cagney "Ma" in the *Public Enemy* vein) and girlfriend, Joyce Conover (Jane Bryan), he accepts Stacey's deal.

Stacey tells him, "No matter how tough, or how long it takes, I'll get you out." In the Warden's office, Stacey throws a punch at Ross, and they stage a convincing brawl. At the trial, the "Hood" jumps out a window into the box of a truck, then ducks into a getaway car. Back at the Big House, conditions worsen for Ross, whose participation in the escape is suspected by Lang, the Head Guard (Willard Robertson), who tells him, "We won't lose you, you dirty little rat." (*Each Dawn I Die* is the second Warners film in which Cagney is referred to with a variation on the phrase "you dirty rat.") Moments later, Lang, slapping him around, follows up with, "Don't lie to me, you little rat."

Polecat, who snitched about Stacey's plan, has again made Ross' life miserable, and the guards beat him until the Warden ends their abuse. Handcuffed in the Hole, he vows to ignore all the rules and do whatever he wants in the future. Five months after the escape, Joyce visits Lockhart (Clay Clement), Stacey's mouthpiece, to arrange a meeting with the "Hood." At the gang's hideout, Stacey vents his anger about Ross' decision to inform the newspaper about their plan. Many photographs taken at the trial are now in the possession of the Warden.

Joyce points out to Stacey that, although he and Ross both grew up as "slum kids," he chose a life of crime, while Frank opted to fight it as an investigative reporter. (This scene recalls the Rocky Sullivan-Jerry Connelly dichotomy in *Angels with Dirty Faces*.) During a meeting with the Warden, Joyce is told that Ross "is the most troublesome prisoner I've had in 35 years of penal work."

"I'll get out if I have to kill every screw in the Joint," Ross threatens after he is brought into Armstrong's office. Aware of the truth about the escape, the Warden offers to recommend parole in two months if Ross will willingly return to the Hole. In the twine mill, Pete beats ailing prisoner Joe Lassiter (Louis Jean Heydt), who falls and hits his head.

At the Parole Board hearing chaired by Grayce, Ross is shown no mercy. Denied another application for five more years, he breaks down. Cagney is heartbreaking in this scene, a milder, sympathetic forerunner to his later psychotic meltdown as Cody Jarrett in *White Heat*.

Stacey tracks down "Shake" Edwards (Abner Biberman), a member of the gang who framed Ross, and he spills the beans about Hanley and Polecat. In a remarkably selfless gesture, Stacey, claiming that he'll break out again, turns himself in at the prison.

Mueller, now totally insane, kills Pete with a tong, sparking a riot. Ross tries to intervene, but Stacey takes control of the mob. When an inmate mutters, "I don't want to get killed, Hood replies, "What do you want to do? Live forever?" At this point, Stacey obviously envisions a different way of "breaking out."

Under heavy fire from the guards, Stacey is shot but squeezes a confession out of Polecat that is overheard by the Warden. Tear gas is lobbed in; and, after Ross and Stacey say, "So long," Hood and Polecat are killed. Upon his release, Ross is presented with an inscribed photo of Stacey, who, the Warden says, wants him to live the kind of life the less fortunate guy would have, had there been "better breaks." Hanley and Grayce are charged with murder, and Frank, arm and arm with his sweetheart, gets a "fresh start."

Like *Angels with Dirty Faces*, *Each Dawn I Die* explores the environmental "causes" of criminal behavior, depicting two strong characters on opposite sides of the law who ultimately care for and help each other. *Each Dawn* offered Cagney an opportunity to play the character on the "right" side; and, though Ross is nearly "made" a criminal by a bad penal experience, the negative aspects of the system (as in *San Quentin*) are shown to be corrupt politicians, attorneys and law enforcement officers. Like Rocky Sullivan, Hood Stacey, a killer (who must die, according to the Production Code), ultimately sacrifices himself to help others. This time, Cagney, rather than frying in the chair, walks off with his girl.

Warren Duff and Norman Reilly Raine's screenplay offers few surprises, but Keighley's solid pace and fluid visual style, realistic sound effects that enhance a sparse musical score, and the performances of an outstanding cast (including the superb character actor Stanley Ridges) still make *Each Dawn I Die* a thoroughly satisfying 92 minutes in the Big House. (On March 22, 1943, the *Lux Radio Theater* resurrected the story for a broadcast version starring Raft and Franchot Tone.)

Mark Hellinger wrote the original story "The World Moves On" for the gangster epic *The Roaring Twenties* (1939), which combines newsreel-type montages recapping historical events with an opening World War I scene involving Cagney and Bogart, and a primary Prohibition plot about the rise and fall of Jim's character, Eddie Bartlett, King of the Bootleggers. Bogart essentially repeats his characterization from *Angels with Dirty Faces*, Cagney's insidious rival who gets gunned down just before Jim's mobster also takes a fatal hit. Impressively, *The Roaring Twenties* marked the Warner Bros. debut of powerhouse director Raoul Walsh, who had begun his Hollywood career acting for D. W. Griffith.

In 1914 the intrepid Walsh rode with Mexican bandit leader Pancho Villa during the Mexican Revolution, shooting footage for his directorial debut, *The Life of General Villa*, released by Griffith. The following year, he played the notorious John Wilkes Booth in Griffith's *Birth of a Nation* (1915). In 1924 he directed the epic Douglas Fairbanks fantasy *The Thief of Baghdad*. The eyepatch that became his trademark was a necessity, the result of losing his right peeper to a jackrabbit that crashed through his car windshield as he drove through the desert while directing *In Old Arizona* (1929). Walsh not only gave an obscure, Iowa-born actor named Marion Morrison his first big break, in the epic Western *The Big Trail* (Fox, 1930); he also invented a new name for his star: John Wayne.

Cagney and Priscilla Lane are billed on the opening credits panel of *The Roaring Twenties*, with Bogart receiving the top "with" spot after the title. The opening montage, moving backward in time from 1939, features images of Adolf Hitler, Benito Mussolini, Herbert Hoover and Calvin Coolidge (an interesting visual association of individuals, considering that Jack Warner was Hollywood's only "FDR mogul"; Roosevelt is saved for a subsequent, more

The Roaring Twenties (1939): As World War I veteran turned Mob boss Eddie Bartlett, Cagney electrifies Raoul Walsh's gangland epic. Though Bogart is billed (in much smaller type), he doesn't appear in the poster art (original jumbo window card).

positive sequence). Narrator John Deering's familiar voice accompanies similar historical transitions throughout the narrative.

The action begins in a 1918 World War I rat hole, where George Halley (Bogart) complains each time another doughboy dives in for cover. Bumming a smoke from Eddie Bartlett, he picks a "cootie" from the tobacco just as Lloyd Hart (Jeffrey Lynn), a terrified law-school graduate, comes crashing in.

Later, during a mail call, Halley receives a handful of letters, one of which includes a photo of an ugly dame that he quickly tosses to the floor. Eddie also gets a photo, but from a glamorous girl, Jean Sherman (Priscilla Lane), whom they refer to as "Mineola," from her address in New York. Bullied back into the trenches by Sergeant Pete Jones (Joseph Sawyer), whom Halley threatens to bump off some day, the three comrades fire at the enemy.

Bartlett follows orders, but Halley sadistically revels in the carnage. After gleefully dispatching a "Heinie," he announces, "That sucker jumped three feet in the air and come down as stiff as a board." Hart is sickened by the prospect of shooting at a German "who looks about fifteen," so Halley guns down the teenager. "He'll never see sixteen," he says, just as the armistice is declared.

A Prohibition montage segues to a New York street scene of Bartlett walking down the sidewalk as an organ grinder plays "I'm Forever Blowing Bubbles" (a tune often associated with Cagney's wiseguys). "I thought you were dead," says Mrs. Gray (Vera Lewis), his landlady.

"If I am, they forgot to bury me," he replies, then walks upstairs to find his best buddy, Danny Green (Frank McHugh), sitting at the table, exhausted from driving a hack. At this point, Jerry Wald, Richard Macaulay and Robert Rossen's final draft of the script originally included a different scene that failed to impress Cagney and McHugh. At their request, Walsh allowed them to concoct a replacement of their own. Filled with the unique humor for which McHugh was famous, the sequence is a beautifully timed repartee between the two real-life friends. After Eddie quietly enters the room, he lifts the coffee pot from the stove and pours his pal a cup. Danny accepts it as if Eddie had never left, then does his trademark double take, as believable as the joy he has for seeing his friend again.

Recalling several Warners classics from 1931–32 (especially *I am a Fugitive from a Chain Gang*), the film depicts the harsh reality faced by many returning World War I veterans. Bartlett is refused his old job, and the current workers whisper about the soldiers who sponged off Uncle Sam while they "stayed home and worked." In trademark Cagney style, Eddie punches one mug who, causing a "domino effect," takes another down with him.

Following a second Prohibition montage, Danny drives Eddie out to Mineola to meet Jean Sherman, whose mother (Elizabeth Risdon) practically drowns them with lemonade while they wait for her to return from "school." Eddie, surprised that the fresh-faced girl is a *high* school student, says he'll call her in "two or three years." In a well-timed close-up, Frank McHugh does a muted version of his famous "one-two-three" laugh when Danny observes his friend's predicament. As directed by Walsh, McHugh, much more subtle than in many of his other Warners films, gives one of the best performances of his long career.

Danny offers to split his taxi business with Eddie, who is asked by a passenger to deliver a brown paper bag to Panama Smith (Gladys George). In a speakeasy, he is pinched by two cops not at all interested in his status as a babe in the woods. Panama is found not guilty, but Eddie, defended by Lloyd Hart, receives a sentence of 60 days and a $100 fine for violating the Volstead Act. "Next time you get a client," he tells Lloyd, "make sure he's committed a crime. It's a whole lot easier to get him off."

The Roaring Twenties (1939): Eddie Bartlett (Cagney) and his pal Danny Green (Frank McHugh) are introduced to the bootlegging racket by speakeasy hostess and off-key canary Panama Smith (the inimitable Gladys George).

After a three-night stay in the slammer (during which he tries to talk sense to his suicidal cell mate [Elliott Sullivan]), Eddie is bailed out by Panama, who buys him a drink (a glass of milk) at the speakeasy. In no time, he becomes an ace bootlegger (described during another Deering voiceover as an "adventuresome hero" of the American people), first working out of an undertaking parlor, then making his own bathtub hooch.

Using the cab service as a front, Bartlett employs only honest criminals, and turns away an ex-con who claims he "was framed." Hiring Hart as his official mouthpiece, he hands him a wad of dough, insisting, "You hang onto my shirttails and you'll be using that as wallpaper."

While collecting money at a local theater, Eddie spots Jean Sherman in the chorus line. Unwilling to take "no" for an answer, he accompanies her home to Mineola on the train, but declines to go inside after she reveals that her mother has died. Eddie Bartlett, though possessing Cagney's ready-to-punch prowess, is a complete gentleman toward the ladies. At this point in his career, Jim was fed up with his "broad-bashing" persona, and he made Bartlett his most likeable gangster.

Eddie lands Jean an audition with Pete Henderson (Edward Keane), Panama's boss, *telling* him she's hired and how much to pay her. Having heard only one run through of "Melancholy Baby," he is reluctant to shell out $100 per week. "I don't even pay myself a hundred," he admits.

"You can't sing," replies Eddie, who, afterward, proudly shows Jean his bootlegging operation, which transforms "diluted New Jersey applejack" into "champagne." Deeply infatuated, he buys an engagement ring, a hasty move that worries Panama. Anxious to scale the bootlegging ladder, he drops in on top dog Nick Brown (Paul Kelly), who refuses to do business with him. In retaliation, he and his boys, posing as Coast Guard men, hijack a Brown shipment steaming down from Canada.

Discovering that the skipper on Brown's boat is his old "war buddy," George Halley, Bartlett forms a partnership to double-cross the arrogant bootlegger. Utilizing George's connections to procure the hooch, Eddie will use his extensive network to distribute it.

A montage recalling the 1924 arrival of the Tommy gun prefaces their heisting of a government warehouse containing 4,000 cases of whiskey confiscated from Brown. During the burglary, Halley meets up with "his old sergeant," Pete Jones, and executes him in cold blood.

The furious Brown arrives at the speakeasy to initiate a brawl, which concludes with Bartlett buying the joint. To avoid further violence, Eddie organizes all the bootleggers, but Halley is envious of his partner's newly won power. Tired of being "ignored" and treated like "a stooge," he tells Eddie, "My feelings is gettin' hurt."

Brown makes a bold move by whacking Danny and dumping his body in front of the speakeasy. The close-up of the dead Frank McHugh is one of the film's most unexpected, jarring images. Danny's demise marked the second time McHugh died a horrible death in a Cagney film, the first occurring in *The Crowd Roars* seven years earlier. "Well, Danny, I told you this wasn't your racket," Eddie says quietly before leaving to confront Brown. Halley, the "office boy," then phones the Mob boss to tip him off.

A full-scale battle erupts at Luigi's spaghetti restaurant, where Bartlett shoots Brown through a swinging kitchen door (one of several such "door shootings" in Cagney's films). Back at the speakeasy, he surprises Halley and the goons who have thrown in with him. "Take your hand off that heater, Lefty," he orders Halley's top stooge (Abner Biberman).

Panama informs Eddie that Jean is "in love," not with him, but with Lloyd Hart. "Shud up!" he replies violently (in the film's only moment of Cagney being verbally abusive to a female). Outside, he punches Lloyd, then apologizes. Here, Walsh includes a lingering close-up of Cagney, who registers a subtle array of expressions as he makes amends.

Taking up the bottle, Bartlett ushers in a montage of the October 29, 1929, stock market crash, followed by Halley's buyout of the cab company for 250 grand. Having turned down a $2-million offer from a Chicago firm, Eddie reluctantly accepts. Left a single taxi to drive, he lands in jail, but Panama is waiting when he is sprung.

A montage spotlighting FDR trumpets the repeal of Prohibition, leaving Bartlett with only the prospects offered while driving his cab. During the Christmas season, he picks up Jean, who lives in the suburbs with Lloyd, now an honest member of the D.A.'s office, and four-year-old son, Bobby (Don Thaddeus Kerr). Before leaving their home, Eddie warns Lloyd about building a case against Halley. On New Year's Eve morning, two of George's goons arrive to tell Jean of an impending hit on her husband.

Jean desperately searches for Eddie, who is stewed to the gills at "Flanagan's joint on Third Street," where Panama is attempting to sing. "Same old story," he laments. "Any time she wants anything, she comes to me."

Panama, advising him to stop drowning his torch for Jean with "a lot of cheap hooch," asks him to talk to George. "I'll be up there again," he dazedly tells himself before heading for the mob's headquarters, where Rocko orders, "Sure, take him up. Give the boss a laugh." George tells his former partner that he knows too much to live. "Goodbye, Eddie, and Happy New Year."

Snapping out of his stupor, Eddie punches out Lefty and — in a replay of the office shootout scene in *Angels with Dirty Face* — George tries to throw a wall sconce just as his executioner blasts away. "Eddie! You're crazy!" he groans just before he dies.

Eddie runs out, shoves one henchman over the balcony railing, then shoots another on the staircase as he makes his way down to the first floor. Heading out to the street, he is capped by the last remaining goon as the police drive up. Painfully scampering up the stairs of the "Community Church," he then stutter steps his way across toward the entrance, but falls, rolling over to die sprawled out on his back. Cagney's physical movements, though choreographed and perfectly executed for Ernest Haller's moving camera, look completely natural and unrehearsed. Another triumph for the "song and dance man," it is one of the most memorable, powerful closing scenes in cinema history.

Working closely with Raoul Walsh, Cagney's contribution to the outstanding quality of *The Roaring Twenties* went beyond his performance. He and Frank McHugh met with the script girl each evening, to improvise on the scenes and craft new dialogue for the next day (contributions that made Danny's violent death at the hands of Halley's mob even more poignant). Their dedication, combined with the usual kinetic excitement created by Walsh, transformed a mediocre screenplay into one of the great gangland epics and Cagney's most thorough depiction of a Mob *boss*. His gunning down of Bogie and then being killed on the church steps made the film a fitting epitaph for the 1930s Warner Bros. gangster genre and the transition for a new production unit at the studio, one that included Hellinger, Walsh, Wald, Macauley and — Bogart.

Capped by Cagney again, Bogie at least had been involved in a class production. His next assignment, *The Return of Doctor X* (1939), a *horror* film (unconnected to Michael Curtiz's original *Doctor X* [1932]), provided an even more hideous miscasting than *The Oklahoma Kid*! Originally offered to Boris Karloff (who had given a stunningly underplayed performance in Warners' *The Walking Dead*, directed by Curtiz three years earlier), the role of Marshall Quesne (pronounced "Cane"), a.k.a. Dr. Maurice Xavier — a vampiric zombie — is one of the most unbelievable examples of *insane* casting in Hollywood history.

Lee Katz's screenplay, one of the worst filmed by Warners during the 1930s, merges some back-from-the-grave elements from the superior *Walking Dead* with outlandish pseudoscience about "synthetic blood" and perfectly atrocious dialogue. Wooden Wayne Morris inexplicably receives top billing once again (above Rosemary Lane and Bogart), this time as *Morning Dispatch* reporter Walter "Wichita" Garrett (listed as Walter Barnet in the credits), who is repeatedly insulted by his "Chief" (Joseph Crehan), who never lets him forget he hails from a "hick" state. Referring to him as the "Kansas Sherlock" and the "Wichita Frankenstein," the editor fires him, threatening, "I want this Wichita brainchild *exterminated*."

What required extermination was this entire project. As if audiences would think that a man (Dr. Xavier) who had gone to the electric chair for starving a baby to death could actually be brought back from the dead after "six hours of the most intense work" by Dr. Francis Flegg (John Litel), the studio decided to include a disclaimer before the famous Warner Bros. opening logo: "The characters, names and events of this photoplay are entirely fictitious ..."

Intending to interview the "prominent actress" Angela Merrova (Lya Lys), Wichita discovers her stabbed to death in her hotel room; but when the police arrive, the body has disappeared. Soon after, when Merrova appears at the newspaper office to announce a lawsuit, Wichita loses his job. Remaining "on the case," he and his friend Dr. Mike Rhodes (Dennis Morgan) find "professional blood donor" Stanley Rogers (John Ridgely) murdered by the same method he had observed on the body of Merrova: a deep, surgically precise wound directly under the heart. Moreover, every drop of blood — "type one" — has been drained from Rogers' corpse.

The Return of Dr. X (1939): In an example of truly *insane* Hollywood casting, Bogart plays Marshall Quesne (pronounced "Cane"), a.k.a. Dr. Maurice Xavier, a vampiric zombie brought back to life after being fried in the electric chair — a role originally intended for Boris Karloff! Worse than the absurd pseudoscience about "synthetic blood" and the atrocious dialogue is Bogie's billing, beneath Rosemary Lane and — in the top spot — wooden Wayne Morris (original one-sheet poster).

Rhodes, seeking expert assistance at the laboratory of Dr. Flegg, meets his pallid assistant, Mr. Quesne. Making his first appearance 23 minutes into the film (which runs a mere 62), Bogie is quite a sight sporting deathly white facial makeup, a Bride of Frankenstein-like hair streak and wire-rimmed glasses with round lenses.

"His interest in blood almost equals my own," admits Flegg, who deliberately gives Rhodes erroneous information about the sample taken from the crime scene. In a lame narrative device (often used in Warners B films), Wichita, who has trailed Rhodes, observes the entire incident through a window, then makes the profound deduction, "You know, Mike, there's something awful funny going on in that joint."

Merrova arrives at Flegg's for a blood transfusion, so Wichita and Rhodes set up an interview with the zombie-like woman, who agrees to tell "all she knows" during a subsequent meeting at the newspaper office. Quesne pays her a visit before she can spill the beans, however, and the unfortunate actress is found dead. Aided by Pinky ("Dead End" Kid Huntz Hall), a young former colleague, Wichita discovers archival clippings about the Dr. Xavier child-murder case. That night, at Greenlawn Cemetery, he and Rhodes exhume the executed doc's empty coffin, prompting the caretaker (Ian Wolfe) to exclaim, "I've been robbed!"

Confronted with the evidence, Flegg admits resurrecting Xavier, whom he considers "a medical genius ... a martyr to science." The reason for reviving a convicted killer is Flegg's further research in the development of synthetic blood, which could save "thousands of lives." Unfortunately, Quesne needs to commit murder to provide the type-one blood necessary for his survival. Delivering dialogue worthy of Bela Lugosi in a Monogram Z-film, Flegg laments, "My experiments have turned into madness. I've created a monster."

In a conclusion combining horror and gangster elements, Quesne pulls a rod on Flegg, demands the list of blood donors, then guns him down. Kidnapping Joan Vance (Rosemary Lane), a nurse who gave type-one blood at the hospital, the crazed zombie heads for his New Jersey hideout where the baby was starved to death. Pursued by the police, he is shot off the roof while trying to escape. In the streetwise world of Warner Bros., a zombie can be eliminated with a regular old bullet.

"Tell Dr. Rhodes we'll have to postpone our talk on blood composition," Quesne says as he dies. Was the studio planning a sequel? Not if Bogie could help it.

Again, the blatant miscasting of Bogart gave a film a level of appeal that would otherwise not exist. If master "terror" interpreter Boris Karloff had played the part, it would have amounted to a colossol waste of his talent (as was often the case), a pathetic imitation of John Elman in *The Walking Dead*. Although the Xavier/Quesne character is far more ludicrous than Ed Hatch in *Swing Your Lady*, *The Return of Doctor X*— the only Warners horror film featuring one of the Wiseguys— is infinitely more watchable *because* Bogie is a reanimated corpse. Luckily, for the long-suffering actor (who was thrown a bone by receiving top billing in the end credits), he would never again have to appear in a film this awful.

After his sanguinary experience, Bogart was back in gangster form in *Invisible Stripes* (1939), directed by Lloyd Bacon. Warners continued its George Raft in the Big House campaign, this time — without Cagney — giving him top billing on the opening credits panel, above Jane Bryan and William Holden. After the title, Bogart again tops the "with" category, a slap in the kisser that irked him to no end. Handed the fourth spot after toiling for three years at the Warners factory was bad enough, but being billed below a 21-year-old, silver-spoon actor playing his second major film role was outrageous. Nonetheless, Bogie's character, Chuck Martin, a slightly more ambiguous mug than his other "supporting wiseguys," inspired one of his best performances since *The Petrified Forest*.

The film opens at Sing Sing with a Bogart and Raft "nude scene." As Martin and Cliff Taylor shower, they discuss their impending releases: the former having served his full five-year sentence; and the latter, after serving one year on a burglary conviction, awarded parole. When Alec (G. Pat Collins), one of the "new fish," recognizes Taylor, he claims, "I'll still be here when you come back."

In the office of the Warden (Moroni Olson), the grateful Taylor is congratulated on his successful rehabilitation. "I learned my lesson a long time ago," he admits, "I won't be back," while the spiteful Martin merely announces, "Me and the State is quits."

Unable to wish Martin luck, the Warden says, "I wouldn't relish the thought one day of escorting you to the electric chair, Chuck."

"If that's in the cards," he replies, "there ain't nothin' that you and I can do about it."

As the two ex-cons leave the Big House, Old Peter (Tully Marshall), the trusty at the gate, advises, "Have a good time, boys. Don't stay away too long. You'll be back."

Depicting the penal system as a "revolving door," *Invisible Stripes* presents an interesting variation on the "good" and "bad" criminal types consistently portrayed in the Warners gangster and prison films of the later 1930s. Taylor, a decent, poor person, believing that rehabilitation is possible, wants to go straight; while Martin, entrenched in behavioral determinism, thinks that any attempts at an honest life are futile.

During their train ride to Brooklyn, Martin explains, "You think changing your uniform means anything? You'll still be wearing stripes. You might not be able to see them, but they'll be there, all right."

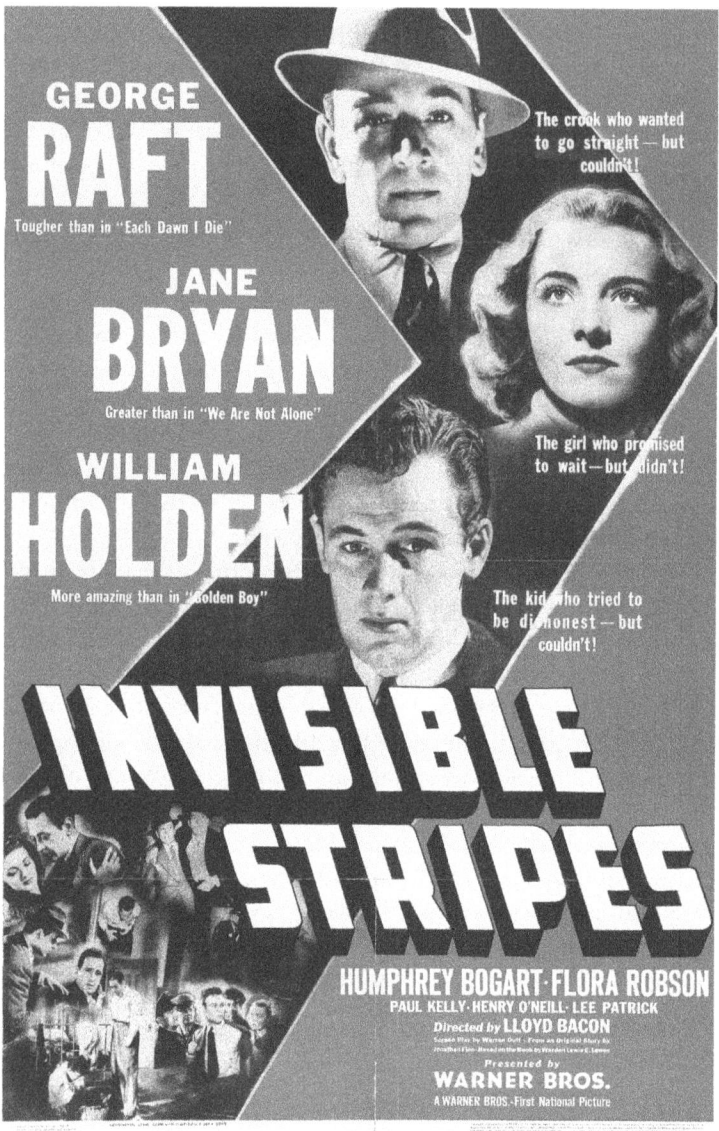

Invisible Stripes (1939): Bogart is *buried* beneath George Raft, Jane Bryan and punk pretty boy William Holden (in the second role of his film career) on Warners advertising for this crime melodrama (original one-sheet poster).

Martin's assessment seems like sheer pessimism when pitted against Taylor's naïve optimism; but when the career criminal calls himself a "realist," he sets the stage for the rest of the narrative, which makes a strong case that the only vocation open to an ex-con is further criminality. "I'm going to make them pay for every day I spent in that crummy stir," he swears.

Invisible Stripes inverts the casting of *Each Dawn I Die*, giving Raft the Cagney role, while Bogie plays a variation on Raft's Stacey, a hardened criminal who ultimately shows some heart just before he dies at the film's end.

Raft created a much more nuanced character for this film, and he demonstrates his talent for understatement during the quiet scene in which Taylor is reunited with his mother (Flora Robson), another element associated with Cagney. Joined by his brother, Tim (William Holden), and Tim's sweetheart, Peggy (Jane Bryan), he enjoys his first dinner back in the family home, but is disappointed by the cold shoulder he receives from Sue (Margot Stevenson), his own girlfriend, who admits, "I can't marry an ex-convict." He also is troubled by the hot-headed behavior of his brother, who has been hanging out in a pool hall and playing the numbers racket.

Martin also has reclaimed his old haunts, lazing around with Molly Daniels (Lee Patrick), a "natural blonde," and forming a "partnership" with Ed Kruger (Paul Kelly) and "Lefty" Sloan (Marc Lawrence). Cliff returns to his old job as an auto mechanic; but, unable to drive and unwanted behind the sales counter, he is fired after only four days' work. Other frustrated attempts at employment include a warehouse job, at which he is assaulted by his coworkers, and a factory position that amounts to playing stool pigeon for the unscrupulous boss, whom he punches out. A visit with Masters (Henry O'Neill), his parole officer, keeps him pounding the pavement.

At the local movie theater, which is showing *You Can't Get Away with Murder* (another of Warners' ubiquitous "product placements"), Taylor runs into Martin, whose offer of "a drink" he declines. (After Bogart walks off, the camera pans over to photos of him on the theater placard!) Desperate for any kind of honest work, Cliff accepts a stock boy position at a department store, where his young colleagues (one of whom is "Dead End" Kid Leo Gorcey), realizing his situation, offer their support. At a company dance, he happily jitterbugs with Ma (allowing Raft to display his terpsichorean talent), then returns home before his 9:30 p.m. curfew, just in time for the cops to bust him for masterminding a fur heist at the store.

Tim tries to raise the $100 bail; but, after being turned down by his boss, punches him out and is fired. Following a two-night stay in the slammer, Cliff is cleared by Masters. Released from parole, he throws in with Martin and "the boys," intending to grab enough dough to set Tim up in his own auto garage. "The Kid thinks I'm selling tractors," he tells Martin as they pull a series of bank jobs. At this point, Martin's "Invisible Stripes" theory has been proved, at least in Cliff's case.

Tim and Peggy are married, and Ma asks Cliff why he doesn't follow suit. Echoing Cagney's Danny O'Hara in *The Irish in Us* (also directed by Lloyd Bacon), he replies, "What do I want another girl for? I've got you, haven't I?" Having raised enough dough to open his brother's business, he quits the gang. Lefty tries to get tough, but Martin lets him go before they pull the heist of an armored car. The robbery is interrupted by the cops, who shoot Martin, then chase the gang through the city. Pulling into the Taylor garage, Martin tells Tim that his brother was involved in the holdup, then hitches a ride home in the sidecar of his motorcycle. (During the shoot, Bogie's enmity toward Holden was worsened when the young actor slammed the motorcycle into a wall.) When Tim returns to the garage, he is pinched by the police.

Cliff visits Chuck, who, according to his blonde moll, is "hurt bad." Always trying to save his own hide, Martin insists that "the Kid" lie to keep him and his mob from "going to the chair."

"He's gonna talk," replies Taylor, who makes a deal with the cops for Tim to testify in exchange for a dismissal of the charges. The Kid identifies the whole mob, and Cliff returns to Martin's apartment to help him escape, but the remainder of the gang arrives and starts blasting. Hit with two more bullets, the resilient Martin slithers along the floor. "The Kid deserved a break," he tells Taylor in a last-minute display of humanity. "What do I care? You can't live forever." Cliff tries to shoot the two remaining goons through the door, then defiantly throws the rod at them before he is gunned down. The cops then arrive to finish off the mob. A brief closing scene shows Tim unveiling a new neon "Taylor Bros. Garage" sign to Peggy, claiming to a bystander that his sibling is his "silent partner."

Due to Bacon's focus on Warren Duff's well-written characters, *Invisible Stripes* provided

George Raft with one of his best roles and Bogart with a wiseguy possessing a hint of the depth that would distinguish his masterful Roy "Mad Dog" Earle in *High Sierra* less than two years later. And Bogie was correct to complain about being billed beneath William Holden, who gives the film's one disappointing performance, his inexperience showing during extended dialogue exchanges when he annoyingly makes the same gestures over and over again.

In late 1939 William Cagney sent a memo to Hal Wallis, reminding him that Jack Warner had mentioned the role of American Naval hero John Paul Jones to Jim, who was eager to play such a drastic change from the succession of hoods and jailbirds he'd been portraying so powerfully for the past two years. Warner, however, characteristically changed his mind, no doubt fearing the huge expense of such a Technicolor epic, not to mention that filmgoers might not accept Cagney in the part.

Instead, Warner considered Cagney for the role of Notre Dame's most legendary football coach in the studio's upcoming action-filled biopic, *Knute Rockne, All American* (1940). Not surprisingly, Jim was rejected by both the widow of "The Rock" and university president Father Hugh O'Donnell. Their choice: Cagney's bosom buddy Pat O'Brien, who went on to "win one for the Gipper" (Ronald Reagan, in his most memorable role—other than that of President, of course).

This time Jim didn't care about losing such a notable part, and immediately sent a telegram to Pat, who also was cast as Father Francis Duffy, yet another priest who tries to "straighten him out," in the next Cagney opus, *The Fighting 69th* (1940), which chronicles the World War I service of the famous "Irish" Sixty-Ninth Infantry Regiment of the New York National Guard. As Jerry Plunkett, Cagney is *really* a rebel without a cause, appearing to care nothing about anyone or anything, and in turn despised by his comrades in arms.

Also in the cast are Jim's pals Frank McHugh, who again contributed to a screenplay, this time adding some needed humor to the downbeat ending, and George Brent, as well as Warners stalwarts Alan Hale, Jeffrey Lynn and Dennis Morgan. Cagney observed, "What with all the Micks in the stock company, it did seem a natural."[3]

Cagney, O'Brien and Brent are all billed above the title, and the impressive group of actors is featured in one of Warners' most stunning visual "cast parades" before the action begins. William Keighley's depiction of the "Rainbow Division" opens at Camp Mills, New York, in 1917, featuring Norman Reilly Raine, Fred Niblo, Jr., and Dean Franklin's fictionalized versions of real-life soldiers Father Duffy, "Wild Bill" Donovan (Brent) and Joyce Kilmer (Lynn), the poet best known for "Trees." Donovan, commander of the First Battalion of the 69th, was the most decorated American officer of World War I.

From the moment he arrives in camp, Plunkett is a cocky, boastful menace. Proclaiming his toughness in the immunization line, he then faints after receiving a shot. At morning reveille, he refuses to get off his cot, but is dragged out on his back by Sergeant "Big Mike" Wynn (Hale). During roll call, he speaks Yiddish to "Mike Murphy" (Sammy Cohen), a young Jewish man (actually named Moskowitz) who masqueraded as an Irishman to enlist in the 69th. Later, "Murphy" demonstrates the interdenominational nature of the regiment by acting as Father Duffy's aide.

While Big Mike and his brothers, "Long John" (Dick Foran) and Timmy (William Lundigan), joined to bring honor to the 69th, Plunkett, calling himself "Smilin' Jerry," signed up "to come back drippin' medals." After trying to get Duffy to go AWOL to help him score a date, he becomes involved in a brawl with an Alabama regiment. "Don't mind him, Sarge," says "Crepe Hanger" Burke (McHugh). "He's his own worst enemy."

"Not while I'm alive, he ain't," Big Mike replies.

The Fighting 69th (1940): Cagney signed this publicity still depicting the dejected Jerry Plunkett during the battlefield memorial attended by Major "Wild Bill" Donovan (George Brent), Paddy Dolan (Guinn "Big Boy" Williams), Father Francis Duffy (Pat O'Brien), Sergeant Joyce Kilmer (Jeffrey Lynn), Sergeant "Big Mike" Wynn (Alan Hale) and Lieutenant Oliver Ames (Dennis Morgan).

Later, Burke tells Plunkett, "You've got the loudest mouth in the Allied Army." Usually cast as Cagney's bosom buddy, Frank McHugh here had a rare opportunity to play a more disapproving character.

During his first day in combat, with the regiment pinned down, Plunkett recklessly shoots off a flare, then tosses a grenade at the enemy. Keighley's prowess as an action director shines in this scene, as the Germans (realistically speaking their native language) blaze away, collapsing the 69th's trench, burying several of the soldiers, including Timmy Wynn, alive. Duffy attempts to crawl into the rubble, but realizes that the men are dead.

In an equally effective scene, Duffy holds a memorial for the fallen soldiers. Kilmer recites one of his poems, while Plunkett sits off to the side, away from his comrades. Cagney subtly conveys remorse without using dialogue, relying mainly on his eyes.

Following a fist fight with Big Mike (which Plunkett insists was an "exhibition" for the men), Donovan decides to transfer him out of the 69th, but Father Duffy, believing "there's good in him" (a reprise of Father Jerry and Rocky in *Angels with Dirty Faces*), disagrees. Plunkett admits to Duffy that he is "yellow," but the priest counters that it was fear of an unknown situation that guided his actions. During another engagement with the Germans, Jerry shouts loudly, an irresponsible action that results in the death of Kilmer. Big Mike punches him out, he is arrested, court-martialed and sentenced to death. For the first time in his career, Cagney plays a true coward. As in *Angels*, Pat O'Brien again provides his "redemption" before he meets his maker.

While in the brig, Plunkett overhears just enough of Duffy's prayers to send him into action after he is freed by a German bomb blast. He saves Big Mike by frantically waging a mortar attack on the enemy, but is fatally wounded. "Father, I've just been talking to your boss," he tells Duffy, then adds, "Mike … I'm awful sorry about Tim," just before he expires. The film ends with a montage of the dead soldiers marching and the priest delivering a brief sermon superimposed over the statue of the real Father Duffy in New York's Times Square.

Warners waged a major publicity campaign for *The Fighting 69th*, including sending Cagney and O'Brien to New York, where they met with Father Duffy and surviving members of the actual regiment. When the two actors arrived at Grand Central Station, 5,000 enthusiastic fans were waiting to greet them. Subsequently, the film was a huge hit at the box office.

9

Eddie G., Boss of the Biopic

Robinson enthusiastically welcomed Paul Muni's recent arrogant departure from Warner Bros. *Confessions of a Nazi Spy* began his ascent as resident king of the Warners biopic, leading to *Dr. Ehrlich's Magic Bullet* and *A Dispatch from Reuters*. Perhaps the brothers Warner should have heeded his demands sooner, for all these films helped put the studio on a more equal footing with MGM and Paramount. With Robinson and Cagney enjoying new territory, George Raft and new Warners bad boy John Garfield filled the tough-guy void.

"A scientific discovery by a Jew is worthless," declared Adolf Hitler, referring to Dr. Paul Ehrlich's syphilis serum, and ordering all records of the scientist's work destroyed. After scoring a direct hit on Der Fuhrer in *Confessions of a Nazi Spy*, Hal Wallis moved ahead with *Dr. Ehrlich's Magic Bullet*. Having cleared up the legal mess, the producer oversaw several script rewrites: Norman Burnstine's original screenplay had been revised by Heinz Herald, whose clinical details would have incited PCA censors (and sailed over the heads of viewers), so the reliable John Huston, who had a knowledge of bacteriology, was brought in to work his dramatic magic. Still maintaining a scientific approach, Huston wanted to avoid the typical Hollywood love story for a focus on Ehrlich's actual experiments. Besides, Heinz Herald "couldn't write," he said.[1]

While Huston rewrote, Robinson accepted an offer from MGM to star in *Blackmail* (1939), an uneven but entertaining and well-acted semi-remake of Warners' *I Am a Fugitive from a Chain Gang*. He then took Gladys and Manny to Europe, where, due to recent events and the release of *Confessions of a Nazi Spy*, he often had to use police protection.

Excited about his first true biopic, Robinson returned to Warners in October 1939 to craft an uncanny performance as Ehrlich, aided in no small measure by makeup wizard Perc Westmore, who carefully worked from the doctor's photographs. Eddie also had spent time researching the role from material acquired from Ehrlich's daughter. The $765,000 budget also grabbed a top director, German refugee William Dieterle, and cinematographer, James Wong Howe. Dieterle wrapped *Dr. Ehrlich* on December 8, and Robinson joined his cohorts for a cast party.

The film opens with Ehrlich's examination of a patient whose illness is not disclosed, but the dialogue suggests that syphilis has been diagnosed. "I'm afraid marriage is out of the question," the doctor informs him.

"Does anybody ever get cured?" the young man asks. As Ehrlich confers with a colleague, the despondent man kills himself behind a dressing screen. Maintaining a strictly clinical attitude, Ehrlich comments that "now, there is no chance of his infecting someone else."

At home with his wife, Hedwig (Ruth Gordon), the doctor shows his emotional side as he runs around the dining table, giving one of his two little daughters a piggy-back ride. This, a rare domestic scene in Robinson's career at Warners, was a revelation to moviegoers in 1940.

Back at the hospital, Ehrlich spends his off-duty hours in the laboratory of Herr Sensen-

Dr. Ehrlich's Magic Bullet (1940): Dr. Paul Ehrlich (Robinson) shares a tender moment with his devoted wife, Hedwig (Ruth Gordon). For the rest of his life, Eddie referred to the role as his "proudest" moment on the screen (original lobby card).

brenner (Charles Halton), experimenting with dyes in an attempt to stain specific matter in slide samples. Unexpectedly visited by Dr. Emil Von Behring (Otto Kruger), who inquires if a particular microbe can be stained, Ehrlich is further inspired to continue his independent research on "the phenomenon of chemical attraction," or "affinity."

The scourge of disease is not the only enemy Ehrlich is up against. The hospital administration, interested only in the doctor knowing his proper place in the established order, disapproves of his renegade activities. The fascistic Dr. Hans Wolfert (Sig Ruman) complains about Ehrlich to Professor Hartman (Montagu Love), admitting to "a certain feeling against people of his faith in our profession."

This anti-Semitic remark is followed by Hartman's chastisement of Ehrlich. "I am not interested in your ideas and experiments," he tells his underling, "only in your conduct as a member of the staff of this hospital ... It's *conform* or suffer."

Ehrlich receives an invitation from Von Behring to attend a lecture at the prestigious Koch Institute. He goes AWOL from the hospital, then sits in the back of the hall to avoid Hartman. During his lecture on tuberculosis, Dr. Robert Koch (Albert Basserman) describes the bacillus he has isolated, then admits that most doctors, using a microscope, will be unable to see it on the slide. Ehrlich rises to reveal his staining theory; and Koch, realizing the usefulness of such a procedure, claims, "Your fame in science will be secured." Not so safe, however, is his position at the hospital, from which he is immediately sacked by the outraged Hartman.

Driving himself to the point of illness, Ehrlich relentlessly toils in his home laboratory, attempting to stain the tuberculosis bacillus. Visited by Von Behring, he places the slide on a stove before going to the kitchen to have coffee with his friend. Angered by his wife's lighting of the stove, he assumes the slide is ruined, then is delighted that the heat has affixed the dye to the microbe. Von Behring insists that Ehrlich take a culture from his own throat, and the doctor's contraction of tuberculosis is confirmed.

Koch examines the stained slide and immediately asks Ehrlich to join his staff. But first the infected doctor must take a rest cure in Egypt, where he makes an important discovery during his convalescence. After a father (Frank Lackteen) and son are bitten by an adder, the young boy suffers horribly and dies, while the man, having been bitten three times previously, shows no sign of sickness. Realizing that the man had developed an immunity to snake venom, Ehrlich returns to Germany, intent on experimenting with poison.

A raging diphtheria epidemic claims the lives of thousands while Von Behring labors to build up a serum in an animal to then inject into a human. Preoccupied with his snakes, Ehrlich first ignores his friend's plea, then agrees to apply his theory of gradually developing antibodies to creating a diphtheria serum in a horse's blood.

Hartman insists on a controlled experiment — injecting 20 children, while leaving another 20 to suffer — but Ehrlich, ignoring the cold-hearted rules, treats all 40. Every child, including the grandson of Minister Althoff (Donald Crisp), recovers, and Ehrlich is rewarded with his own laboratory, to experiment with "whatever he wants." A title card then announces that, over the next 15 years, the doctor's "Side Chain Theory" earns him the Nobel Prize and his own institute in Frankfurt, where he is "molding magic bullets," the inauguration of chemotherapy.

During an inspection headed by the ever-reactionary Dr. Wolfert, Ehrlich is criticized for hiring an "Oriental" researcher, Dr. Hata (Wilfred Hari). "You're not German, are you?" the arrogant administrator idiotically asks, then tells Ehrlich he should have filled the post with someone "of pure German blood."

"What has race to do with science?" Ehrlich asks. When Wolfert and his cohorts leave, he protests, "The nitwits! The *State*! *Un-German*!" Here, John Huston takes his second indirect shot at the Nazis, who were beginning to murder their "racially pure" path across Europe.

Using arsenic to develop a "magic bullet," Ehrlich has experimented on diseased mice to attack the microbe. Unfortunately, as a side effect, the poison also has driven the rodents "crazy." While reading an article about the cause of syphilis ("man's most vicious disease") and examining an image of the microbe, he realizes that it resembles the spirochete found in the mice. Devoted to finding a cure for syphilis, he advises his staff to develop a drug "one-hundred percent effective against the microbe" and "zero-percent harmful to the human cells." While experimenting, Ehrlich resembles Robinson himself: "I can't think without a cigar in my mouth. Tobacco stimulates me."

Asked to provide the budgetary committee with an opinion on the value of Ehrlich's work, Von Behring tells his friend that the "idea of injecting chemicals into humans" is horrific. Rejected by his closest colleague, Ehrlich undauntedly carries on. "He isn't the old Emil anymore," he tells his wife. "No use mourning the loss."

Hedwig offsets the 50-percent budget cut by approaching Frau Franziska Speyer (Maria Ouspenskaya), a widow with a sizeable fortune to invest in a worthy cause. At a dinner party, Ehrlich shocks all the guests with his mere mention of syphilis (Dieterle incorporates a rapidly cut montage of close-ups), but the Frau remains unfazed. Gaining her rapt attention, he then spends the rest of the evening sketching out his findings on the expensive tablecloth.

Dieterle concludes the scene with an effective reverse tracking shot, slowly pulling back to reveal the two of them, alone at the deserted table.

Following 605 failures, the new syphilis drug finally is administered successfully to a chimpanzee. Fearing that Ehrlich will become the human subject, one of his assistants, risking an injection on himself, survives. The winning mixture, "606," then is given to a volunteer who is going blind from the disease. Gradually the man's sight is restored, prompting him to offer all his worldly goods to Ehrlich in return. "Your complete recovery is all that I want," the doctor responds.

Reluctant to release "606" for public use until further tests have been conducted to account for patients with complications, Ehrlich is approached by two physicians (Louis Calhern, Frank Reicher), who, citing his diphtheria experiment of 17 years earlier, implore him to focus on "humanity" rather than science. As orders for the medicine flood in, Ehrlich collapses in the lab; then a scheduled rest trip to Egypt is cancelled after a patient dies while being treated with "606."

The dedicated fascist, Dr. Wolfert, is at it again, now bringing a list of 38 deceased victims of the drug to a local publisher. Ehrlich sues for libel; and, during the controversial trial, Von Behring arrives to testify that he is "convinced that '606' … a complete success … stops infectiousness." His remark that the 38 dead are "martyrs to the public good" is followed by a warm reconciliation with his friend. The trial concludes with Wolfert sentenced to one year in prison for criminal libel.

Dr. Paul Ehrlich is a role for which Robinson deserved a Best Actor Academy Award. In the film's final scene, he caps his magnificent, understated performance (Ehrlich looks a bit like Santa Claus after his hair and beard turn white) with a deathbed speech delivered to the institute's staff in a single take, a medium close-up beautifully composed and lit in the classic James Wong Howe style. Combining Ehrlich's historic quest with contemporary commentary on the Third Reich, he says,

> There can be no final victory over the diseases of the body unless the diseases of the soul are also overcome. They feed upon each other. Diseases of the body. Diseases of the soul. In the days to come, there will be epidemics of greed, hate, ignorance. We must fight them in life, as we fought syphilis in the laboratory. We must fight. Fight. We must never stop fighting.

After headlining a blatant propaganda film like *Confessions of a Nazi Spy*, Robinson was given a rare opportunity to convey a similar message, but in a far more indirect, subtle manner. Released in late February 1940, the film was a huge hit, with critics inevitably comparing him to Paul Muni; but no Oscar nomination for Eddie was in the offing, the short-sighted Academy having lost interest in prestige biopics. Robinson later said, "Among all the plays and films in which I've appeared, I'm proudest of my role in *Dr. Ehrlich's Magic Bullet*." Regardless of Eddie's opinion, John Huston, who did receive an Oscar nomination for Best Screenplay, believed that Dieterle had directed in a much too heavy-handed fashion. "It was a bit fucked up," he bluntly said.[3]

At least Eddie was on the prestige circuit. Poor Bogie couldn't get off the miscasting treadmill, now shooting scenes as a *Mexican bandit* in *Virginia City* (1940), Michael Curtiz's follow-up to *Dodge City*, a far superior Errol Flynn Western released the previous year. Robert Buckner based his screenplay on an incident that occurred in Virginia City in 1864, the year Nevada became a state in the Union. Southern sympathizers living in the area, seeking to provide the Confederacy with much-needed weapons and supplies, conspired to transport a stolen cache of gold to Mexico, where it would then be sent to Europe. Discovered by a spy, the plot was foiled by a Union agent stationed in Virginia City.

Flynn and Miriam Hopkins are billed above the title, with Bogart listed fourth, below Western star Randolph Scott, on the "with" panel. Following a Civil War battle at Morgantown, Kentucky, the film's opening line is spoken by Ward Bond, making a brief appearance as a Confederate sergeant checking the passes of travelers. Visiting "The Devil's Warehouse," Libby Prison in Richmond, Virginia, Julia Hayne (Hopkins) speaks with Captain Vance Irby (Scott) about stealing $5 million in gold at Virginia City to save the Confederacy. Meanwhile, Union prisoners Kerry Bradford (Flynn), Olaf "Moose" Swenson (Alan Hale) and "Marblehead" (Guinn "Big Boy" Williams) are attempting to tunnel their way out of the prison.

Locating the entrance to the tunnel under a stove, Irby tells the would-be escapees that he had discovered their plan three days after it began, thinking it appropriate that "their own punishment" would be three months of hard digging before he captured them. After Irby discusses the Virginia City plot with Jefferson Davis (Charles Middleton), Bradford and his two pals blow up the powder magazine above the tunnel and escape through a swamp.

Before he was taken prisoner, Captain Bradford had been assigned to track gold shipments to Richmond. Accompanied by Moose and Marblehead, he heads to Nevada, where he meets John Murrell (Bogart), the leader of a guerrilla band, on the stage to Virginia City. "What is your *bees*-ness, *Meester*?" the bandit asks Bradford before pulling his Derringer on them. The Captain catches him off guard, however, and Murrell orders his banditos to beat it, then starts a (very unconvincing) shootout aboard the stagecoach before jumping into a river. Bradford hops onto the galloping horses to stop the runaway coach (a very popular stunt following the release of John Ford's *Stagecoach* the previous year); then, before continuing on to "the richest, roughest town on the face of the Earth," he woos Julia Hayne, who happens to be traveling with them.

By the time they reach Virginia City, Vicksburg has fallen, Sherman has destroyed Atlanta, and some Yankees are hanging an effigy of good old Jeff Davis in the street. At the local blacksmith shop, Irby and his co-conspirators are loading wagon beds with gold bars, intent on claiming they are driving an "immigrant train" to California. Following Julia's performance of "The Battle Cry of Freedom" (an atrocious, off-key attempt by Hopkins, who is nearly as miscast as Bogie), Irby informs her that Bradford is a "Union spy," then attempts to head out with the wagons, but the town is soon surrounded by Union troops.

The wounded Murrell is patched up by Dr. Cameron (Moroni Olsen), the local sawbones, and Irby offers him $10,000 to attack the Union garrison. With Julia's help, Irby then captures Bradford, who escapes after Murrell arrives with his gang. Tumbling down a cliff on his horse, Captain Kerry plays dead while Irby continues on with the wagon train. At a telegraph station, Bradford, rejoined by Moose and Marblehead, contacts Major Drewery (Douglas Dumbrille), who sends troops to intercept the gold. When the mercenary Murrell attacks the wagons, Bradford and Irby join forces against the marauders. "Too bad you and I had to be on opposite sides of the fence in this," the Yankee tells the Rebel.

"I'd rather Murrell got it than the North," Julia tells Bradford, who, intent on providing the gold for Southern Reconstruction, buries it under a rockslide. The cavalry arrives in the nick of time, Murrell is gunned down, and Bradford announces, "There isn't any gold." Convicted of high treason, Bradford argues that his orders were to "keep the gold from prolonging the war," but is sentenced to be executed on April 9, 1865.

Insisting on a pardon, Julia meets with none other than President Abraham Lincoln (Victor Kilian) on April 8, who informs her that the surrender of the Confederacy will occur the next day. Claiming that she and Bradford are symbols of what is possible in reforming the Union, the President stops the execution. Shown only in shadow on a doc-

Virginia City (1940): Bogart's infamous turn as *Mexican* bandit John Murrell, surrounded by "Marblehead" (Guinn "Big Boy" Williams), Olaf "Moose" Swenson (Alan Hale) and Captain Kerry Bradford (Errol Flynn), in Michael Curtiz's ponderous follow-up to his superior *Dodge City*.

ument, and from behind as he speaks to Julia, Lincoln recites a few phrases from the Gettysburg Address.

A disappointing "successor" to *Dodge City*, *Virginia City* is a poorly written big-budget Western with insufficiently developed characters, gaping plot contrivances, and an overused, bombastic Max Steiner musical score that often overpowers the images and performances. Errol Flynn is given very little to do, and never really seems to be in much danger, particularly at the hands of Bogie's Murrell, a career embarrassment and arguably the worst performance he ever gave. Then 38 years old, Miriam Hopkins is the most unconvincing (and least attractive) of all of Flynn's Warners leading ladies, and the "relationship" between Bradford and Julia never stirs up a single iota of screen chemistry. Obviously rushed into theaters to capitalize on the success of the previous Flynn epic (shot in Technicolor), this murky black-and-white effort is one of Michael Curtiz's lesser Warners films.

Todd M. Jacobsen
Classic Film Buff, Harlan, Iowa
on
Virginia City

In *Virginia City*, the name "Errol Flynn" arrives on screen before those of Miriam Hopkins and Randolph Scott; then comes The Bronx Bandido. I know that Humphrey Bogart was under contract, but Warners should not have cast him as a Mexican bandit named Murrell.

It's a fun movie, and one would think Flynn would have been looking forward to working with Bogart; but when he appeared on the set as a bandit, Errol probably thought, "What in the hell is *this*?"

During the scene where Bogart is showing his gun to Flynn on the stagecoach, Bogie opens his mouth, and it is *ridiculous*. I think Michael Curtiz should have slowly panned the camera to the other side of the coach, where James Cagney could have been sitting with a Tommy gun. That would have made as much sense.

Bogie probably thought the whole thing was insane, but he needed the cash. I can imagine that he and Flynn had a really good time *off* the set.

Simultaneously, Bogart was appearing as yet another gangster, this time hiding out in a theatrical boarding house, in *It All Came True* (1940), directed by Lewis Seiler. Based on a story by Louis Bromfield, the script by Michael Fessier and Lawrence Kimble gave him an opportunity to create a comic variation on his familiar criminal character. "Chips" Maguire, a.k.a. "Mr. Griselli," is also notable for being the first of several Bogart roles originally turned down by George Raft.

Aspiring singer Sarah Jane Ryan (Ann Sheridan) arrives at the boarding house run by her mother, Maggie (Una O'Connor), and Norah Taylor (Jessie Busley), showing her grit by kicking a masher down the stairs to the street. "As if I didn't know how to handle a monkey with a gat," she informs Ma, then assures her, "Technically, I'm still a *good* girl."

Meanwhile, at the Cairo Club, Norah's son, pianist Tommy Taylor (Jeffrey Lynn), is playing "Danny Boy" as Chips Maguire enters to request that he play some original material. Tommy tries to tell Maguire that he is tired of holding a gun for him, but the police arrive. After setting the club's books ablaze, the "gambling czar" ducks into an alley, grabs the gun from Tommy, and whacks Monks (Herbert Vigran), the "squealer" who gave him up.

Returning to the boarding house for the first time in five years, Tommy reluctantly provides a hideout for Maguire, now using the Griselli identity, claiming he is recovering from a nervous breakdown. Suspecting foul play, Sarah Jane spies on the new boarder from the bathroom linen closet, then confronts him when she realizes that Griselli is actually her old employer, Chips Maguire. Eventually, the gangster, realizing that the house is full of old vaudevillians, proposes opening a "Roaring 90s" nightclub to pay off back taxes and avoid foreclosure by the bank.

All goes smoothly until Miss Flint (Zasu Pitts) sees Maguire's photo in *Perfect Detective* magazine. Though Sarah Jane frightens her with a tale about the "torture" and "garroting" of a stool pigeon by gangsters, she runs to the local police precinct after downing two bottles of champagne during the club's opening night. Originally planning to stay in his room during the show, Griselli can't resist going downstairs, where he is busted by two detectives. At first, he intends to tell them Tommy killed Monks with the gun, but then—softened up by the heartfelt thanks of Mrs. Taylor—he gives Tommy and Sarah Jane a break, planning to do about "125 years" in the Big House.

It All Came True, a somewhat uneasy blend of the gangster, musical and drawing-room comedy genres, borders on fantasy, and the theatrical sequences go on far too long, but the performances are consistently entertaining. Bogart benefits from a fair amount of screen time allowing him to build a characterization superior to his usual one-dimensional thug (as in *King of the Underworld*); and, in several scenes, he demonstrates flashes of the trademark timing (verbal and visual) he soon would demonstrate flawlessly in *The Maltese Falcon* and *Casablanca*.

While Robinson was being thrilled by his latest role, and Bogart was pulling another double duty, Cagney was suffering through the Richard Macauley and Jerry Wald potboiler, *Torrid Zone* (1940), directed by William Keighley. Jim hated the project from the moment he received the script, initially refused to do it, then capitulated when the studio had nothing else for him to do. To play Nick Butler, overseer of a Latin American banana plantation, he decided not to shave a pencil-thin mustache, just to aggravate Jack Warner and Hal Wallis, who thought the facial hair lessened his tough-guy appeal.

Cagney had to act in the film with a left-hand injury, the result of a shooting accident that occurred when he tried to drive coyotes away from the henhouse he kept on his Coldwater Canyon estate. Though he promoted the picture as "Horrid Zone" on *The Edgar Bergen and Charlie McCarthy Show*, he did appreciate spending more time with Pat O'Brien and Ann Sheridan.

The stunning cinematography of James Wong Howe is wasted on Macauley and Wald's atrocious script, an endless parade of ethnic stereotypes, unfunny attempts at humor, and dreadful dialogue adding up to one of the most embarrassing projects released by Warners during the Golden Age. Steve Case (O'Brien), manager of the Baldwin Fruit Company, tries to re-hire his top associate, Nick Butler (Cagney), after a blow-up involving the ex-Mrs. Case sends the cocky banana man packing for a job with the Coast to Coast food company in Chicago. Case, wanting to avoid trouble with the locals, is also intent on sending sultry singer Lee Donley (Sheridan), who has just arrived, back to the States.

The two travelers meet on the boat, but neither stays aboard. Butler accepts $1,000 from Case for just "two weeks" of work bringing in the banana crop at Plantation No. 7, while Lee secretly sneaks off to meet him for a date. Halfway through the 88-minute film, *nothing* has actually happened, except for Nick's realization that Lee is a "card cheat." The second half concerns the fruit company and local law enforcement's efforts to capture Rosario La Mata (George Tobias), a revolutionary who twice escapes by using a cigarette trick that wouldn't fool a child. In the closing scene, the banana man and bandito aid each other, and Nick embraces Lee in the final fade-out.

The nearly nonexistent plot of *Torrid Zone* isn't the film's biggest defect. The milieu involving white overseers and "native" laborers in a plantation system smacks of slavery, and the fact that Caucasian actors play all the Latino speaking parts makes this element even more obnoxious. Warners stalwart George Tobias portrays the rebel stereotype to the hilt, and Italian-American character actor Frank Puglia is all dim-witted ineptitude as Police Chief Juan Rodriguez. Worse yet are Rosario's two imbecilic henchmen, who seem to have stepped right out of a Warners "Merrie Melodies" cartoon: Sancho (future "Superman" George Reeves) and Carlos (Victor Kilian). White actors in brownface speaking pidgin English provide an ironic contrast to the actual Latino actors relegated to non-speaking extra parts. *Torrid Zone*'s facetious depiction of the ethnic characters differs from the serious portrayals in *The Hatchet Man* and *Virginia City*.

When Case is asked about his decision to "deport" Lee, he explains, "I just figured that redheads were more of a novelty down this way." Pat O'Brien's entire performance is consistently annoying, as he (obviously believing the material beneath him) practically yells his way through the entire film.

Cagney and Sheridan, on the other hand, appear to ignore the inferior script by giving their usual polished portrayals. In his trademark role of the rotund, whining sidekick, Andy Devine plays "I'm Forever Blowing Bubbles" (Cagney's unofficial Warners theme) on his harmonica, and Helen Vinson is predictably catty as the wife of Bob Anderson (Jerome Cowan), the employee Case wants Butler to replace at Plantation No. 7. Nick's romantic interest in Mrs. Anderson is superceded by the attractions of the unattached Lee.

Cagney works in his usual quota of physical action: kicking the boat's skipper overboard (twice); engaging in some "broad bashing" by holding Lee upside down to shake loose the

Torrid Zone (1940): Cagney, whose pencil-thin mustache indicates his disdain for the material, suffers through this plotless, ethnocentric mess with Ann Sheridan, Andy Devine and Helen Vinson (original lobby card).

$300 she won in her crooked card game; and punching out Sancho and Carlos, *two* men larger than himself. The white hat Jim wears throughout the film, rivaling his *Oklahoma Kid* 10-gallon in absurdity, adds some camp to his generally straightforward performance. The film's closing line also offers an in-joke, referring to Sheridan. Holding Lee in his arms, Nick admits he's staying for "you and your 14-carat oomph."

The ethnocentric dialogue (at one point, Devine's Wally Davis announces that "the natives are all lined up" for the overseers) contradicts Warners' traditionally progressive values. After the studio produced serious films exploring incarceration, institutional abuses and capital punishment, *Torrid Zone* (supposedly a comedy) arrived in theaters replete with *jokes* about execution: Case, too impatient to wait for the date specified by the sentence, demands that Rosario be shot immediately. After all, he's only a "native."

The revolutionary's response? "Sooner or later, everybody dies. Too bad I'm sooner." Case wants Rosario eliminated, but Butler ultimately helps him escape. During the Warners tenure of Darryl Zanuck, *Torrid Zone* would have proved an unlikely prospect. Hal Wallis, always concerned with the bottom line, was a far less sophisticated animal. At least Cagney wasn't required to become "ethnic," like Robinson and Bogart before him. Perhaps everyone connected with the film Jim called "Horrid Zone" would have benefited had the idea never been *executed* by Macauley, Wald and Keighley.

Torrid Zone proved to be the last of the Cagney-O'Brien films, a rare Hollywood series that, for the most part, honestly depicts true affection and loyalty between two men. Perhaps O'Brien's hammy performance in their swansong was a deliberate acting-out of a blunt comment he recently had told a reporter:

> I think one picture a year with Cagney would be fine. But, as it is, I've been with him in every uniform — the Army, the Navy, the police, the Marines, the Air Corps — and it's always a case of me falling in love with his girl, or him falling in love with mine. It gets tiresome.[4]

In March 1940 Robinson began playing, of all things, "Little Johnny" Sarto, a gangster-cum-*monk* in *Brother Orchid*, again falling afoul of Bogart, who, as Jack Buck, his former right-hand man, takes him for a ride, dumping him in the country, where he crawls and stumbles into a monastery. Lloyd Bacon planned to finish the shoot in a month, to allow Robinson to move on to his next biopic, *A Dispatch from Reuters*, an homage to the journalist who used carrier pigeons to create the famous news agency.

Of his contact with Bogart on the *Orchid* set, Robinson recalled, "He was a pro in the best meaning of the word and put the play above himself. We got along splendidly.... We were never close friends, but we respected each other."[5] Three decades after making the film, Robinson watched it on television: "I thought both Bogart and Robinson overacted, shouted a little too much, and occasionally were very good indeed. Robinson would have played the character quite differently today; I suspect Bogie would have too."[6]

Robinson and Cagney continued in their top-billed starring roles, but Bogart still was trying to avoid suspension by grabbing any bone tossed by Jack Warner, accepting another third position, below the title and under leading lady Ann Sothern. Lloyd Bacon again proved why he was one of Warners' top house directors by creating a fast-moving, entertaining 88-minute example of sheer narrative economy, combining a gangster story with serious overtones and straightforward performances, witty comic situations and dialogue, and a Good Samaritan subplot involving a monastery where the monks raise money for the poor by growing and selling flowers! More substantial action occurs in the first 10 minutes of *Brother Orchid* than in all 88 of *Torrid Zone*. The fact that the same studio simultaneously produced both films stretches the imagination.

Providing an interesting twist on the "going straight" premises of *The Little Giant* and *A Slight Case of Murder*, *Brother Orchid* begins at the John Sarto Protective Organization, where "Da Boss" has decided to quit the rackets because one of his mugs has, "for the first time in the history of this organization," used a rod. Like Eddie's "Bugs" Ahearn in *The Little Giant*, Johnny Sarto wants to seek "good taste and refinement." "Don't worry, pal," Jack Buck assures an associate as the boss departs. Foreshadowing things to come, he adds, "He'll never come back."

At his comfortable apartment, Sarto informs his fiancée, Florence "Flo" Addams (Ann Sothern), that he will be pursuing "class" in the capitals of Europe. Sothern brilliantly, subtly plays the beautiful "dumb blonde" to perfection, prompting Johnny to comment, "Sometimes you've got me guessin' if you're even a nitwit." She, too, gets to deliver some choice gangland levity when Flo, contemplating their future marriage, recalls, "Gee, I ain't been in a church since the night your brother was bumped off." Before he sails, Johnny magnanimously arranges a hat-check job for her at the Crescent Club.

For the next five years, Sarto meanders through London, Paris, Monte Carlo and Rome, attempting to buy "class" in the form of a huge diamond (actually a doorknob), antiques (the "Bed of the Borgias," made in Grand Rapids, Michigan), a prize race horse (a broken-down nag), and disastrous trips to gambling casinos. When all his dough has been fleeced, he returns home, planning to slip back into running the protection racket he had impulsively handed over to Buck. But "going back to be boss again" (the first time this move was depicted in a Robinson gangster spoof) isn't so easy. Some of "the boys" stage a big welcome, but Buck quickly gives him the business, inaugurated by a whoopee cushion attached to his old chair. Having changed the name of the joint to the Monarch Protection Association, Buck will never relinquish control.

"All right, Wiseguy," Sarto threatens, just before he is thrown out into the corridor. Learning that Flo has moved out of the apartment, he finds her living at the Parkway Biltmore, luxury digs made possible by Clarence P. Fletcher (Ralph Bellamy), a wealthy rancher from the Midwest who put up 10 grand for her to buy the Crescent Club. "He's interested in cows," she explains.

Brother Orchid (1940): In Lloyd Bacon's charming, seriocomic take on the gangster genre, Bogart takes Robinson for a ride; but, after Eddie becomes a *monk*, Bogie is hauled off to the hoosegow!

"Especially ones that wear petticoats." Johnny fires back.

Sarto's pal, Willie "The Knife" Corson (Allen Jenkins), trying to avoid Buck and stay loyal to his old boss, has committed himself to the Pattonsville Private Sanitarium, where he is "having a swell time with his mental disorder." Buck's mugs follow Johnny and Flo as they are driven to the hospital by the bird-calling Clarence, who is reassured by Sarto that he'll "meet the right girl. You just have to feel your way."

Reunited with his faithful sidekick, Sarto describes the new mob they will organize to remove Buck from power. Allen Jenkins effortlessly indulges his penchant for delightfully mangling the English language, while Robinson brilliantly demonstrates his talent for Buster Keaton-like physical comedy as Willie offers Johnny a chair with an overly springy seat cushion. Eddie all too rarely had an opportunity to display the physical aspects of his comic abilities at Warners, although his rapid-fire verbal wit required a formidable physicality of the face and vocal cords. (His finest physical comedy performance may be as his *two* characters in John Ford's *The Whole Town's Talking*; but, then, Ford usually *cajoled* the best performances from his actors.)

Setting up his new mob at the Crest Hotel, Sarto briefly gets tough as he slaps information out of former associate Mugsy O'Day (Richard Lane). At the Acme Paving Company, he and the gang throw out Buck's boys and peddle their own brand of protection.

Rehashing a scene from *The Amazing Dr. Clitterhouse*, Flo visits Buck, declaring that the racketeer rivalry is "all a lot of hooey."

"It ain't nice, is it?" Buck replies. "But Johnny don't like me no more. Makes me feel bad, too."

She reminds Buck about an unsolved hit the cops are still investigating, and he agrees to a "sit down" at Fat Dutchy's Tavern, 30 miles away. "I'll be the first guy to stick out my hand," he promises. "Don't let him know I'm gonna be there."

That night, Flo phones Johnny, pretending she's drunk and being pawed by some amorous mugs. At first he is reluctant to go, but her claim of having some dope on Buck is too much to resist. At the tavern, as the band plays a laid-back swing number, Buck tells him, "That music upsets me. It makes me nervous. My hands are shakin.'" Outside, Buck and one of his goons literally take Johnny for a ride, then stop in some woods to carry out the whack. Sarto runs away, but is shot in the back before he rolls down a hill into a creek.

Lloyd Bacon's pacing is so precise that the film shifts from the gangster plot to the monastery material *exactly* at mid-point. Discovered and brought to the Brother Superior (Donald Crisp, in one of his masterfully gentle performances), Sarto is near death. Nursed back to health, he awakens, sees two monks standing over him, and assumes he's in Heaven. Not quite, they tell him, but actually among the "Little Brothers of the Flowers" at the Floracian Monastery. Trying to understand their "racket," he recognizes Brother Wren (Charles D. Brown) as a former fighter, but the monk explains that he has chosen a new, charitable path in life. In a letter to Willie, whom he has "planted" in Kansas City, Sarto explains, "I'm in a swell hideout run by the biggest chumps in the world."

Brother Superior, having sold a truckload of flowers, announces that an extra $2 will be used to purchase watermelons, a beneficence they haven't enjoyed for the past two years. However, when young Joseph (Tommy Baker) arrives to reveal that his father has been laid off, the windfall is given to the child to buy a pair of shoes.

Now known as "Brother Orchid," Johnny goes to work, milking a cow (obtaining a record quantity by secretly watering it down) and planting a beautiful zinnia bed (promising Joseph 50 cents to tend it for him). Brother Superior is disappointed with his behavior; but, after reading a newspaper announcing Flo's marriage to Clarence, Brother Orchid is allowed to observe the selling of flowers in the city.

Johnny apologizes to his fellow monk, then enters Flo's apartment. Believing he is dead, she faints, then agrees to marry him in Kansas City, where Willie is still "planted." Back at the truck, he notices that the flowers haven't been sold. Brother Superior explains that the order must now join the "protective association"; and Johnny, knowing that Buck is wanted by the police, enlists Clarence and his fellow cowpokes—"in town to see [his] weddin'"—according to Curley Matthews (Tom Tyler), to "run these tough boys outta town." Flo reveals her true feelings, and is rewarded with the response, "Baby, when you speak like that, you're knocking at Johnny Sarto's heart with a sledgehammer."

Sarto and his new hayseed mob drop in at the Monarch Protective Association. A brawl erupts, and Johnny confronts Buck in his private office. Following an extended fist fight (the first ever between Bogart and one of the other Wiseguys), the cops arrive to arrest Buck and his boys. Pretending that he doesn't really love Flo, Johnny gives Clarence his blessing for their marriage, accepts $300, then gives it to a poor cleaning woman on his way out of the building.

Back at the monastery, Brother Superior is explaining the absence of Brother Orchid, who quietly enters the dining hall. Hat in hand, he humbly admits:

> Brother Superior, I'm such a guy that was looking for class. I once went halfway around the world trying to find it, because I thought that class came in dough and nice clothes and society. Well, I was wrong. I sure traveled a long way to find out one thing. This—this is the *real* class.

A film with a fantastical premise, *Brother Orchid* is made believable by superb acting, sharp writing, and sure direction. In its closing scene, when a former wiseguy voluntarily becomes a member of a commune of selfless men, the Warners cycle of 1930s gangster films has come to a fully "moral" conclusion. *No one* is killed in the film, and the only fighting is done by some innocent good ol' boys just having some fun while doing the right thing. Finally, Warners produced a Production Code-friendly Mob-oriented film. After all, Little Johnny Sarto refuses to use a rod!

Surrounded by an exemplary supporting cast, Robinson delivers a charming performance flawlessly blending mobster moxie, witty humor and subtle pathos in a unique film providing a satisfying climax to a long series teaming Bogie with Eddie G. and Jim, the two "original gangsters." Following this film, Bogart, aided by Raoul Walsh, finally began to climb toward the stardom he so richly deserved, while Robinson and Cagney, nearing the end of their respective Warners contracts, went on to two of their greatest performances and subsequent cinematic free agency.

While working on *Orchid*, Robinson visited with the daughter of Paul Ehrlich and her husband. After inviting them to the set, he arranged a special screening of *Magic Bullet*, which they enjoyed, then asked about Mrs. Ehrlich, who had left Berlin and was living in Geneva on very limited means. After refusing his offer of financial assistance, they asked Eddie if he could send her a letter and some stills from the film. He did just that, in return asking for a personal memento of Dr. Ehrlich.

On June 15, 1940, Frau Hedwig Ehrlich wrote to him from Switzerland, praising not only his resemblance to her late husband, but also mentioning her daughter's comment that he had "immersed [him]self in [Ehrlich's] personage far beyond what one would expect from a great artist's portrayal."[7] Admitting that her husband, who dictated most of his correspondence, had written very few letters, she also enclosed a handwritten missive that Ehrlich had sent to her after speaking at a medical conference.

Having collaborated successfully on *The Roaring 20s*, Bogart, Mark Hellinger, Raoul Walsh, Jerry Wald and Richard Macauley went to work on *They Drive by Night* (1940), based on an I. A. Bezzerides novel, *Long Haul*, filmed in England two years earlier. Hellinger quickly cranked out a story treatment, and Wald and Macauley (after their disastrous work on *Torrid Zone*) fashioned another brisk, exciting screenplay, this time about the uncertain, dangerous trucking profession, that again teamed Bogart with George Raft.

Bogart is billed fourth (below Raft, Ann Sheridan and Ida Lupino), a notch lower than in his previous Warners A film, but is actually above the title in *They Drive by Night*. He appears, unshaven and asleep, in the opening scene, as Paul Fabrini shares yet another grueling wildcat trucking run with his more ambitious brother, Joe (Raft). The first half of the film is an excellent exposé of the relentless challenges, problems and dangerous situations faced by Depression-era drivers, especially those who attempted to remain independent rather than accept a salary from a trucking company.

Attempting to make enough extra dough to pay off the overdue loan on their rig, the Fabrinis are forced off the road by some careless joy riders. At Barney's roadside diner, Joe phones Mike Williams (Charles C. Wilson), boss of the San Francisco outfit to whom they are contracted, to collect the $300 owed them. Williams, refusing to help them replace a cracked wheel on the truck, and angered over their inability to deliver the load, tips off Farnsworth (Jack Mower), a weasel-like, little loan shark who wants his $300, "plus interest."

"I'd like to kick that chiseler's teeth out," growls Paul.

They Drive by Night (1940): Joe Fabrini (George Raft) restrains his hot-headed brother, Paul (Bogart), from "wrap[ping] a crank around [the] neck" of their chiseler boss, Mike Williams (Charles C. Wilson) in Raoul Walsh's film about the dangers faced by Depression-era truck drivers (original lobby card).

While waiting for the new wheel, they meet Cassie Hartley (Ann Sheridan), a knockout, red-headed waitress, whom all the truckers (as well as Barney, the owner of the joint) are hitting on. But Cassie, as smart as she is sultry, will have none of it. When Joe mentions that he prefers working for himself, she counters, "You're working for the finance company." Macauley and Wald's script (the sexiest ever written for a classic Production Code-era Warners film) is rife with double entendres. After Joe refers to Cassie's "classy chassis," another driver offers to "finance it."

"You couldn't even afford the headlights," she fires back. Seated at the lunch counter, Bogart and Raft do a perfectly timed, mutual double take as they check out her exquisite derriere.

Farnsworth slithers into the diner, intent on repossessing their rig, but their fellow drivers, in a display of solidarity, tell lies about the truck, then throw him through the swinging doors into the parking lot. Williams has hired another driver to pick up their load, so the Fabrinis hop into the repaired rig to pay him a visit. "We ought to wrap a crank around your neck!" Paul threatens as they try to grab some dough. Tired of getting the brush-off, Joe knocks the asinine boss to the floor.

Back on the road, they spot the lone figure of a woman, standing on the shoulder in the pouring rain. Cassie climbs up into the rig, admitting that she quit her job: "Barney had twelve hands, and I didn't like any of them." Later, she adds, "He was always trying to tie my apron strings."

"There's nothing wrong with that," Joe remarks.

"There is if you're not wearing an apron," she points out.

The clever sexual references (veiled just enough to sail over the heads of PCA censors) continue with Paul's frequent references to returning home to spend "just one hour" with his wife, Pearl (Gale Page), after being away for two weeks. They first attempt to help two other truckers who fall asleep, crash and burn, before Paul is dropped off and Joe helps Cassie get a room in Los Angeles. "I've always liked redheads," he tells her.

"You shouldn't," she warns him. "Red means 'stop.'"

"I like everything about you," he admits. "I like the way you fill out your clothes." Exhausted, he falls asleep on the bed. Forced to curl up in a chair, Cassie first covers him with a quilt. This scene, beautifully played by Raft and Sheridan, innocently shows how two strangers can immediately build a genuine rapport. In the morning, when Cassie kisses Joe goodbye, he suggests, "Don't practice that on anyone else. Save it for me."

The fatal accident on the road has affected Paul drastically. Unable to sleep, he tells his wife, "Every time I closed my eyes, I could see those two guys, burning." To make matters worse, Farnsworth and a police officer arrive to repossess the truck, then stand watch outside. "If you get thirsty," Paul offers, "come on in and I'll give you a mickey." Meanwhile, Joe meets with Ed Carlsen (Alan Hale), an old pal who owns a trucking company, and his wandering wife, Lana (Ida Lupino), who has unsuccessfully tried to work her wiles on Joe.

Without consulting his brother, Joe, eliminating the middle man, drops their dough on a large load of lemons, prompting Paul to ask angrily, "What am I, a stooge?" They haggle with George Rondolos (George Tobias) for a $500 profit (standing behind Tobias, Bogie unleashes some nonverbal shtick), then pay off Farnsworth. Now, Joe pushes even harder; and, when Paul asks to pull over to get some sleep, he refuses. Passed out at the wheel, Paul loses control on a dangerous curve, Joe tumbles out into a ditch, and the truck crashes through a guardrail, then over a cliff.

Seriously injured, Paul loses his right arm, a tragedy Pearl, who wished her husband at home to start a family, views as a potential blessing. Carlsen then hires Joe as his traffic manager; but Paul, unable to drive, sits around the house, complaining bitterly about his bad luck.

Up to this point, *They Drive by Night* is a powerful, straightforward Warners look at labor issues; but, rather than further exploring Paul's problems and possible recovery, the remainder of the narrative shifts to Lana Carlsen's relentless adulterous pursuits, which culminate in the carbon-monoxide murder of her inebriated husband, and subsequent framing of Joe after he rejects her continued advances. Ida Lupino furiously chews the scenery as Lana lapses into total psychosis, going insane on the witness stand during Joe's trial. This over-the-top material effectively eliminates Paul's plight—and Bogart's presence—from the picture.

As Lana's business partner, Joe is able to give his brother a job as dispatcher; and, appearing on screen for a few seconds, Bogie makes it look as if everything is now hunky-dory for Paul. Following Lana's paranoiac confession that she deliberately left Ed in the garage with the car's engine running—"The doors made me do it! The doors made me do it!"—Joe tries to turn over his half-interest in the company to the workers, but they will have none of it.

Raft and Bogart are a terrific team in *They Drive by Night*, but both could have benefited from a script that left the story in their hands. In a tough, non-criminal role, Bogie briefly was able to explore his ever-developing, angst-ridden persona; while Raft, shorn of the ex-con trappings of Cliff Taylor in *Invisible Stripes*, created a truly decent character: hard-working, tolerant, alcohol-free, calm in every crisis (only throwing a punch as a last resort), treating his girl with respect and sensitivity, and staying on the same level with his associates. Ann Sheridan, blending her usual self-assuredness with a genuine sweetness, makes Cassie Hartley one of her most appealing Warners characters. Raoul Walsh's direction is top-drawer in the rugged action scenes and during the verbal duels between the amorous males and Cassie; and, though the film's second half is a disappointment, the Lupino "insanity scenes" anticipate the psychotic meltdown of Cody Jarrett in his future masterpiece, *White Heat*.

To promote *They Drive by Night*, publicity director S. Charles Einfeld, with the support of a half million Teamsters, sent a 15-ton truck cross-country, for eventual presentation to Ann Sheridan. Between Chicago and Los Angeles, the trailer was painted with the signatures of drivers, mayors and fan-club members, and anyone who glimpsed "the Sheridan truck" became a prospective patron of the film.

Cagney's politics were called into question during the summer of 1940, when Los Angeles Grand Jury D.A. Burton Fitts included his name on a list of people who had "shown interest in Communist Activity." Congressman Martin Dies was holding a hearing in San Francisco, thus launching the first such public attack on the U. S. Constitution that would be magnified by the House Committee on Un-American Activities (HUAC) seven years later. Knowing that his charitable contributions to liberal causes had landed him on the list, Cagney held a press conference in San Francisco, where he admitted to being a Democrat intending to campaign for FDR, but that he couldn't possibly be a "Communist" and be so supportive of democracy. His effort was successful, but he was infuriated that he had been forced to bow to something so truly un-American.

More pleasant was Jim and Willie's adoption of two children, a boy they named James, Jr., and a girl, Casey. Oddly, the couple had a separate house built on their property for the children to live in, so as not to interrupt their father while he was studying one of his film roles.

Cagney was far more pleased at the prospect of starring in a screen adaptation of Aben Kandel's 1936 best-selling New York novel *City for Conquest*, which he appreciated for its inclusion of subplots set during the years 1907–1927 in his birthplace (the Lower East Side) and boyhood home (Yorkville), as well as one involving boxing. He also was thrilled by the filmmakers assigned to the project: his brother William as producer, Raoul Walsh as director, and John Wexley as screenwriter.

Then the bottom began to fall out. The superlative, no-nonsense Walsh was dumped in favor of "prestige" director Anatole Litvak, who worked slowly and was fond of endless retakes. Then Wexley's script was read by both Jim and Bill Cagney, who concurred that the playwright new little about the period and even less about boxing. Robert Rossen was then brought in to rewrite it.

Cagney trained for the boxing sequences with Harvey Perry, ate a healthy diet, rose at 5:30 each morning to run 10 miles, wrestled, shadow boxed, and slept 10 hours each night— rigid discipline that melted off 10 pounds and left him feeling fantastic at 41. The regimen not only inspired a powerhouse character, but also helped Jim endure the pomposity of Litvak, whom he considered a "squirrelly son of a bitch" and "natural-born asshole."[8] In return, the director—who blamed the conflict on his star's inability to play the part—later said, "Only once in my life did I ever have any difficulty and this was with Jimmy Cagney."[9]

Cagney's disdain for Litvak's "European" directing style, involving lengthy tracking and panning shots that created endless blocking problems for the actors, was observed by the supporting actor who played Googi, the mobster pal of Jim's Danny Kenny: future master stage and screen director Elia Kazan. Nearly 50 years later, Kazan wrote about Litvak's condescending, commanding "Germanic" attitude, and Cagney's straightforward, energetic approach to acting — one that had nothing in common with his own Group Theatre "Method" training. Nonetheless, Kazan considered Cagney a "complete actor," noting that some of his own colleagues in the Group practiced "artistic snobbery."[10]

Cagney's greatest disappointment with *City for Conquest* came when the film was butchered in the cutting room. The complex multiple-plot structure could not be accommodated by a standard two-hour running time, and several sequences involving various aspects of Danny Kenny's life were dumped. "What remained was a trite melodrama," lamented Cagney. "When I realized what they had done, I said to hell with it, and that cured me of seeing my pictures thenceforth. I even wrote a letter of apology to the author."[11]

Litvak opens *City for Conquest* with a majestic montage of New York infrastructure. Again, Ward Bond (as an Irish cop) welcomes viewers into a Warner Bros. world, listening to the philosophizing of an "Old Timer" (Frank Craven), a bewhiskered bum who introduces a scene involving Danny and Eddie Kenny, Peggy Nash and Googi Zucco as children in an East Side slum. Though constructed differently (incorporating more camera setups and editing, supporting Cagney's claim that Litvak shot a lot of coverage), the scene recalls the opening of *Angels with Dirty Faces*, even down to the organ grinder cranking out "East Side, West Side."

The next scene fades in on a close-up of a punching bag, the camera pulling back to reveal the adult Danny Kenny working out at a gym, as his pal, "Mutt" (Frank McHugh), looks on. As bystanders listen to the Primo Carnera-Max Baer championship bout (which occurred on June 14, 1934) on the radio, Danny hits the street with Peggy (Ann Sheridan), "his girl" since childhood. At an apartment house, they sit down to chat at the top of the stairs, and are immediately bawled out by Mrs. Nash (Blanche Yurka). In the flat Danny shares with his brother, Eddie Kenny (Arthur Kennedy) is giving piano lessons to a musically challenged boy. Impressed by Eddie's talents and artistic aspirations, Danny encourages him to keep writing his "New York Symphony."

Intent on raising enough dough to support his brother, Danny agrees to fight "Kid" Callahan (Bob Steele), an arrogant boxer who had tangled with him at the gym. Throwing only *two* punches (off camera), Danny knocks him cold, a stunning feat that impresses promoter Scotty MacPherson (Donald Crisp). During their locker-room discussion about future fights, Danny informs him, "I think I need a good reason to sock a guy." (In a San Francisco bout on August 25, 1930, Max Baer delivered two powerhouse punches to the head of opponent Frankie Campbell, actually knocking his brain loose. After lying unconscious for an hour, Campbell finally was taken to a hospital, where he died from massive cerebral hemorrhages. Charged with manslaughter, Baer was acquitted, but the incident haunted him for the rest of his life. After defeating Carnera for the heavyweight title in 1934, Baer lost it to James J. "Cinderella Man" Corbett the following year.)

At a posh nightclub, Danny becomes jealous when Peggy trips the light fantastic with egotistical dancer Murray Burns (Anthony Quinn). (Following their vigorous terpsichore, Sheridan's tradition of going bra-less is openly apparent.) When Burns and a waiter make obnoxious cracks about Peggy, Danny decks them both.

Sitting in their truck at a construction site, Danny tells Mutt, "You'll take it and like it," just before they are visited by their childhood chum, Googi Zucco (Elia Kazan). (Here, Cagney delivers a line associated with Bogart.) In the evening, as Danny and Peggy observe the city skyline, she speaks of their long-term relationship, emphasizing her need to escape the stifling

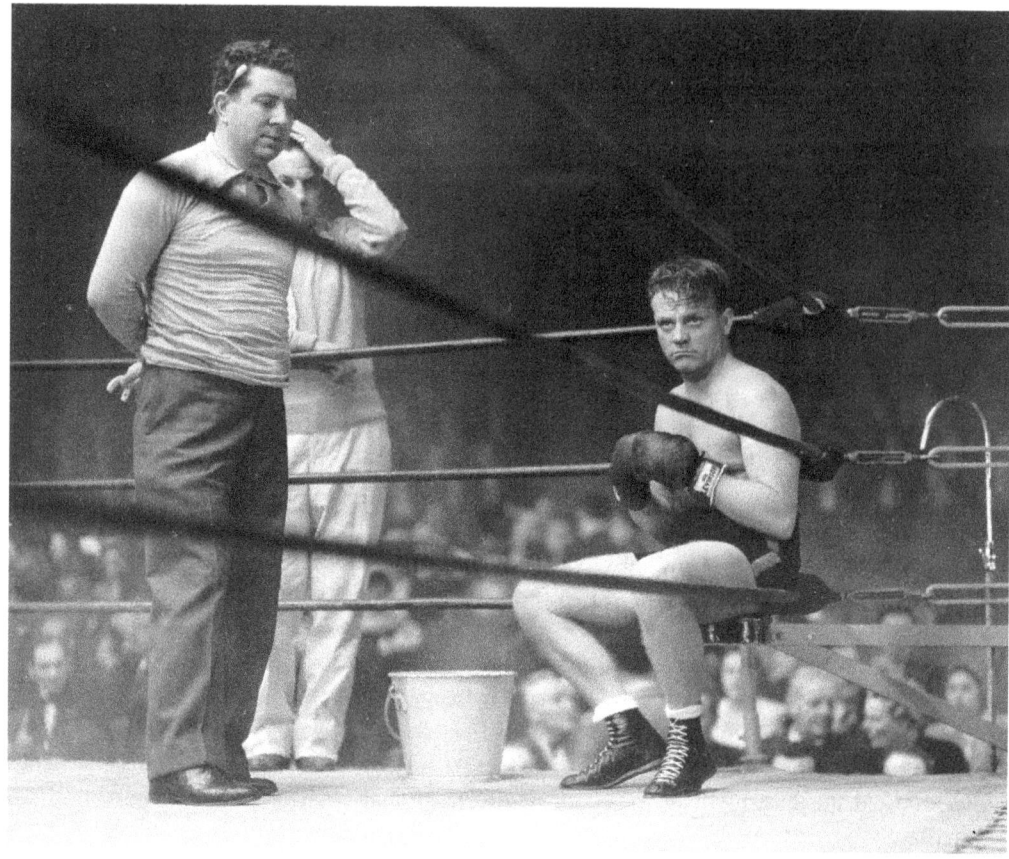

City for Conquest (1940): In this realistic ringside shot, "Mutt" (Frank McHugh) is concerned about boxer Danny Kenny (Cagney), who has been blinded by rosin dust smeared on the gloves of his opponent.

environment of their origin. "You've got to have ambition," she insists, reflecting her decision to sign on as the female sidekick in the "Burns and Company" dance "team," a move that further feeds Danny's jealousy.

Peggy tours with Burns, who manhandles her in their dressing room; while Danny, as "Young Samson," knocks out every opponent in the ring. Paying her a visit, he accidentally injures her shoulder when trying to punch out Burns. Badly shaken by the incident, she continues with the abusive hoofer, now accepting a professional name change to "Maurice and Margolo."

Briefly reunited, Danny and Peggy judge a dance contest, where they are asked to take to the floor. "You know, I don't know anything about dancin'," Danny claims. (This line is the first of two Cagney in-jokes spoken by the actor.) They now plan to marry; but, after Peggy is enticed with the news that Maurice and Margolo have been asked to appear in a big-time show, she sends a crushing letter to Danny.

In Chicago, Young Samson is scheduled to fight "Cannonball" Wales (Joe Gray) for the welterweight championship. Aware of Wales' impending defeat, a trainer smears rosin dust on the thumbs of his gloves; and Danny, struggling to see through badly swollen eyes, staggers into the 15th round before finally hitting the canvas. Having trained heavily, Cagney connects with several real punches, then convincingly portrays oncoming blindness. This degree of authenticity, combined with Litvak's fondness for lengthy montages, adds up to a dynamic cinematic bout. Reduced to a "human punching bag, beaten to a pulp," Danny is taken to his dressing room.

The doctor reports finding a gritty substance in Danny's eyes, and MacPherson fumes, "The dirty, low-down rats!" (making *City for Conquest* the fifth Cagney film in which a version of the phrase "dirty rat" is spoken). Meting out a little Mob justice for Dutch (Jerome Cowan), Wales' promoter—who asks, "What have you been sniffin' lately?"—Googi whacks him, dumping the body in the river. Sacrificing his own life to help his old pal, Googi is gunned down by Cobb (Ben Welden), Wales' manager.

"As blind as a bat," Danny admits when he learns that his eyes cannot be surgically treated for at least a year. Peggy attempts to visit him, but MacPherson angrily sends her away. Back at their flat, Danny listens to an off-key canary rehearsing with Eddie for a new show. He pretends to like the mediocre songs, but continues to push his brother to become a serious composer. "I don't know anything about music," he insists. (The second Cagney in-joke, this comment, like the earlier dancing reference, gives Danny a quality opposite to that of the actor, who not only studied the guitar, but also wrote songs and composed tunes.) As Eddie presumably finishes his "New York Symphony," Danny, desperate for "something to do," meets with Scotty to set up a newsstand.

A newspaper instantly hits the streets, advertising Edward Kenny conducting "The Magic Isle Symphony" at Carnegie Hall. Some of the footage cut from the longer version of the film obviously was included prior to this scene, which awkwardly and unconvincingly tries to tie up all the loose ends. After conducting the concert, attended by Peggy and Scotty, but caught on the radio by Danny, Eddie sermonizes about the significance of the symphony, for which his brother is given credit. There is no narrative build-up to the Carnegie Hall performance (one minute, Eddie can't get anyone to listen to him; the next, he's conducting at the most prestigious venue in the land); and the completely lackluster musical performance, intercut with close-ups of Scotty and, especially, Peggy, being moved to tears, comes off as phony and nearly as contrived as Danny beginning to regain his sight moments later. "You're always my girl," Danny tells Peggy after she arrives at the newsstand.

A final scene of "The Old Timer" clumsily concludes *City for Conquest*, a film with much unrealized potential. Cagney, who gives a solid, thoroughly believable performance, was justified in his contempt. Despite the gaping holes in the plot, Ann Sheridan provides many emotional high points; and Elia Kazan, lending Googi a Method persona far ahead of its time, is magnificent. (This was the first of two major supporting roles Kazan would play on screen, the other coming the following year in Warners' *Blues in the Night*. His influence on Marlon Brando is apparent in every nuance and gesture, and he is the very blueprint for Robert De Niro.)

Based on a story by Valentine Williams and Wolfgang Wilhelm, Milton Krims' screenplay for *A Dispatch from Reuters* (1940) is remarkably faithful to the life of Paul Julius Reuter. Born Israel Beer Josaphat in Kassel, Germany, on July 21, 1816, Reuter, the son of a rabbi, abandoned the Jewish faith in 1845, when he was baptized under the name that would be attached to his famous financial news agency. In Gottingen, Reuter met Carl Friedrich Gauss, who had, with Wilhelm Weber, established the first electromagnetic telegraph in 1833.

In 1848, Reuter left Germany for Paris, where he worked in the news agency later known as the Agence France Presse. To compensate for a break in telegraph service between Paris and Berlin, Reuter opened an institute in Aachen that used carrier pigeons to connect this German location to Brussels, Belgium. Until a telegraph link was built in 1851, he successfully provided Paris Stock Exchange information to prominent financiers. That year, he made a permanent move to London, where he founded the Reuters news agency. In 1857, he became a naturalized British subject.

To link Britain with mainland Europe, Reuter built a telegraph line through the English channel; then, in 1863, extended it to the west coast of Ireland. Off the coast of Cork, London-bound ships from the United States would dump buoys containing copies of news reports into the sea, where they were picked up by Reuters associates, who then telegraphed the information to the English before the ships arrived. In 1871, the "media mogul" was declared Paul Julius Baron von Reuter by the Duke of Saxe-Coburg-Gotha. He died a wealthy and famous noble in Nice, France, in 1899.

A Dispatch from Reuters avoids any references to religion (though Reuter became the second Jewish character Robinson played in a Warners biopic), and avoids historical details that would have made the complicated (and somewhat rushed) narrative easier to understand. However, the film accurately hits Reuter's significant career high points, as well as some salient personal ones, including his marriage to Ida Maria Elizabeth Clementine Magnus (Edna Best), daughter of Dr. Magnus (Otto Kruger), a physician in Aachen who, in one scene, benefits from the carrier-pigeon service when news arrives about a poisoned medicine he is about to administer to children.

As written by Krims, Robinson plays Reuter as a determined entrepreneur who will only provide information that is "accurate and impartial." Refusing to provide exclusive access to anyone, he seeks to benefit all of mankind with his service. In reality, Paul Julius Reuter, to beat the competition, was a sort of "news bootlegger" who heisted reports from ships as they passed his outpost in Ireland. This aspect is depicted in the film, but any references to wealth and nobility (character traits that didn't fit the Warner Bros. mold) are excluded. Ironically, though never revealed in the film, Robinson again was playing a man who made his fortune by less than legal or ethical means.

The film opens in 1833 Gottingen, where Professor Gauss (Paul Weigel) is sending signals over wires, and the youthful Reuter (Dickie Moore) begins his belief that "News is the most important thing in the world." In 1899, referred to as "The Pigeon Fool," he and his remarkably lazy assistant, Max Wagner (Eddie Albert), use the birds successfully to convince bankers, including the pompous Otto Bauer (Gene Lockhart), to subscribe to the service. When Bauer offers Reuter a partnership for the exclusive rights, he responds that he intends to "build a future for myself based on service to the community."

Robinson's Reuter is determined yet kindly, and his relationships with his wife, Wagner, and fellow experimenter Franz Geller (Albert Bassermann) show him as sensitive and considerate, even when facing deadlines and crises. His most trying potential calamity occurs during the American Civil War, when his British backer, Sir Randolph Persham (Nigel Bruce), who has invested heavily in the Confederacy, faces financial ruin; and in the aftermath, when Abraham Lincoln is assassinated on April 14, 1865. Reuter, the first newsman to publish a report of the murder, is accused of fabricating the story to smash the stock market, but a special session of Parliament establishes the truth. Closing the film, the media mogul corrects those who have been mispronouncing his name as 'Rooter' by quietly saying, "And, gentleman, the name is pronounced '*Roy*-ter.'"

Reuniting director William Dieterle and cinematographer James Wong Howe, *A Dispatch from Reuters* doesn't measure up to *Dr. Ehrlich's Magic Bullet*, but the impressive production benefits from uniformly first-rate performances. Albert Bassermann is pure charm as Reuter's beloved collaborator and friend; Otto Kruger is great support in a reprise of his *Dr. Ehrlich* relationship with Eddie; Gene Lockhart is typically exasperating as the banker; Nigel Bruce,

A Dispatch from Reuters (1940): In his second Warners biopic, Robinson plays communications pioneer Paul Julius Reuter, supported by Eddie Albert as his slacker assistant, Max Wagner (original lobby card).

as always, is entertaining as himself; and Edna Best (a British stage actress who appeared in a few films, including Hitchcock's *The Man Who Knew Too Much* [1934]), is intelligent and selfless as Reuter's supportive wife.

Whereas *Dr. Ehrlich* features a concluding speech that indirectly addresses European fascism, Reuters sneaks in some brief, more subtle commentary at the midpoint of *Dispatch*. After Lenchen, Reuter's prize pigeon, is killed by a newly built telegraph line, the saddened newsman (he is shown kissing the bird in several scenes) views it as a metaphor for the inevitable growth of technology. Having used the pigeon for his marriage proposal, he has the beloved bird stuffed. "She built our future for us," he tells his wife, noting that Lenchen's epitaph should be "A Victim of Progress." He admits, "I believe in progress, just as I believe in a smaller world where men may come closer to each other and get to know each other. That's the ultimate objective of all progress— knowledge — and through knowledge, the truth."

When *A Dispatch from Reuters* was released in December 1940, the public, now disinterested in biopics, stayed away. The following summer, studio suits, concerned that Robinson was getting too old to attract audiences, had discussed canceling his contract with Jack Warner. The mogul, however, knew that a lawsuit from Eddie would cost him much more; plus, he was planning to produce an adaptation of Jack London's novel *The Sea Wolf*, which the actor already had approved.

While filming during the autumn of 1940, Robinson enjoyed working with fellow New York Jewish actor John Garfield (born Julius Garfinkel), who shared his liberal political concerns. In fact, Eddie saw the role of Wolf Larsen as an opportunity to portray a fascist "superman," and the atmosphere of the ship as reflecting the social order of Nazism. He later said that Garfield "was one of the best young actors I ever encountered, but his passions about the world were so intense that I feared any day he would have a heart attack. It was not long before he did."[12]

10

Perilous Pard and That Bastard Bogart

The box-office success of *They Drive by Night* put Raoul Walsh firmly in the director's chair for *High Sierra*, also starring Ida Lupino and — moving into the male starring role — Bogart, as a gangster tailored for him by John Huston. Huston adapted the screenplay from the recently published novel by W. R. Burnett, who served as his assistant under the supervision of Mark Hellinger, who, in turn, endured the "management" of Hal Wallis. After Huston finished his work, he wrote to Wallis, "It would be very easy for this to be made into the conventional gangster picture, which is exactly what it should not be. With the exception of *Little Caesar*, all of Burnett has suffered sadly in screen translation."[1]

Bogie had read the story in *Redbook* prior to its publication in book form; but when he sent a note to Wallis, requesting the role of Roy "Mad Dog" Earldon, he was completely ignored. The role (with the gangster's surname shortened to "Earle") was offered to *the* Warners heavy hitter — Paul Muni — who accepted but then failed to respond to any of the screenplay drafts sent for his perusal. Truth to tell, Muni didn't want to die in another film.

Huston didn't give a damn about Muni. The director was still incensed over the self-absorbed actor's rewrites of his script work on *Juarez*; not to mention that the over-the-top, fire-and-greasepaint actor — the stylistic opposite of the economical, naturalistic Bogart — was completely wrong for the role. While both actors began their careers on the stage, Bogart effortlessly transformed his style for the camera, while Muni usually continued to play for the back row of the theater even while in a tight cinematic close-up.

When Jack Warner ordered Hellinger to pressure the two writers, Huston responded with characteristic profanity. Finally, seven days after the screenplay was completed on July 10, 1940, the ever-egotistical Muni, angered at Warner's scuttling of a Beethoven biopic promised to him (not Robinson), furiously tore up his $5,000-per-week contract and left the studio.

Then, as usual, the role was offered to George Raft. But, this time, it was Bogart himself who talked Raft out of a primo role. Knowing that the "tough guy" was thoroughly sick of playing heavies and thugs, Bogie described the role as more of the same, prompting Raft personally to report his refusal to Jack Warner. Bogart now was in, and began makeup tests on July 23, while Raft was sent to New York to promote *They Drive by Night*. Huston was deliriously happy. He disliked Raft, whom he considered a clueless, buffoonish Mafia type.

S. Charles Einfeld began a national publicity campaign to distribute news articles and artwork building up Bogie's reputation as a formidable gangster character. To capture Burnett's description of the gangster as having "coarse dark hair [with] silvery streaks" and "dark eyes [that] were weary and sad," Bogart had his head shaved on the sides to provide a gray-white contrast to his black hair on top. Thoroughly dedicated to the role, he also took part in the auditions for the handicapped farm girl who is aided by Earle in the film. Born Joan Brodel, lovely Joan Leslie was only 15 when she was signed by Warner Bros., though she had been acting on stage and in films from the age of three.

Having briefly worked with Bogie in *They Drive by Night*, Ida Lupino was cast as Marie Garson, the misguided waif who falls in love with Earle. She had been very nervous during the shooting of the earlier film, her first at Warners, but now looked forward to such an important project with Bogart.

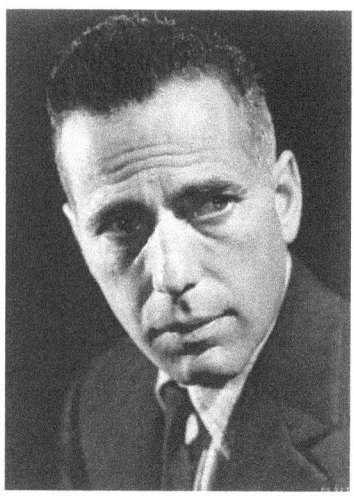

High Sierra (1941): Bogart pleased Raoul Walsh by capturing W.R. Burnett's physical description of Roy "Mad Dog" Earle, including having his head shaved on the sides.

Walsh began shooting *High Sierra* on August 5, 1940. Armed with a 44-day schedule, he benefited from a budget allowing him to film at several locations, including a fishing camp, the Arrowhead Springs Resort, and Mount Whitney in the Sierra Nevadas. (Burnett had hit upon the idea of using such a location while trout fishing at June Lake, near Yosemite.) To create a powerful, gritty realism, the thrilling car chase involving Earle and the authorities was filmed entirely on location near Lone Pine, and no studio back-screen shots were used. For Earle's fatal fall down the mountainside, Bogart was doubled by Buster Wiles, who plunged 89 feet through brush and around boulders, bouncing five times before he came to a stop. Incredibly, the fearless stunt man asked to do it again, but Walsh was satisfied with the take.

Huston visited the set several times, observing Bogie imbibing his "three-cocktail" lunches. Lupino became quite enamored with her costar, enjoying their time off-camera and posing for a humorous, "suggestive" photo beside their hotel swimming pool. Dialogue coach Irving Rapper claimed that she was in love with Bogie, but her husband, actor Louis Hayward, was often on the set, as was Mayo, to incite the usual quota of arguments and brawls.

Bogart had played bad-asses who end up on the wrong end of a gun several times at Warner Bros., but *High Sierra* was the first film to hint at the Bogie persona that would dominate the studio's style throughout the 1940s. This was also the first A film to promise him top billing, an achievement that was undermined, when, on September 18, 1940, Wallis asked Jack Warner if Lupino, who'd been so important to the success of *They Drive by Night*, deserved the number-one spot. When the new billing was issued the next day, Lupino, who had broken out with a rash, didn't report for work at Lone Pine. She called in sick again the following morning, but did appear a day later, acting with Bogie as if nothing had happened.

When the film was released in early 1941, reviewers heaped praise on Walsh, Huston, Burnett—and Bogart, who did not immediately benefit, however. True to form, the studio expected him to accept further supporting roles, or leads in lesser projects.

While shooting *High Sierra*, Bogart was called before the Red-baiting Dies Committee. John L. Leech, a Communist Party snitch, referred to as a "pathological liar" in official FBI records, mentioned Bogie's name to Burton Fitts, who also had pegged Cagney as a pinko. Like his fellow Wiseguy, Bogie also had donated money to San Joaquin Valley workers, during a lettuce harvesters strike in 1936.

On Friday, August 16, 1940—the day the hotel holdup was scheduled to be filmed—production was stalled while Bogie appeared before Dies, who used several different strategies in an attempt to get him to admit that he, or fellow Hollywood actors, were either Communists or had contributed cash to the Party. Cool and calm, Bogart answered, "No" to all questions, then (accurately) denied knowing Leech, and concluded by clearly admitting the resentment he felt over having his Constitutional rights trampled under foot. Returning to the set, he gave "Mad Dog" Earle a little extra fire as the mobster and his gang hit the Tropico Springs Hotel. Back at Jack Warner's office, *perhaps* the whole Commie affair had played a part in the mogul's decision to give Lupino top billing.

Bogart carried his liberal leanings over into presidential politics, joining Robinson, John Garfield, Melvyn Douglas and Claude Rains in the Hollywood for Roosevelt campaign. During a *Salute to Roosevelt* radio show, broadcast on NBC and CBS, he performed with Garfield, Henry Fonda, Walter Huston, Groucho Marx and Lucille Ball. A week prior to the 1940 contest between FDR and Republican Wendell Wilkie, the Tinsel Town group placed a full-page ad, headlined "Why We of Hollywood Will Vote for Roosevelt" and listing 200 names, including Bogie's.

High Sierra opens with Roy Earle, granted a pardon by the Governor of Indiana, being released from Mossmoor Prison. First showing him in close-up from the waist down, the camera tilts up to show the back of the ex-con's head as he exits the prison gate, then turns around to reveal the pale visage he has developed during years in stir. He pauses to watch some children playing in a park, then seeks out "Big Mac" to receive "orders" for his next job, but instead finds an unpleasant underling, Jack Kranmer (Barton MacLane), a retired cop, who tells him about the scheduled heist at the Tropico Springs Hotel in California.

On his way west, Earle stops at his old homestead in Illinois, where a weary old timer (reflecting the reality of Depression foreclosures) asks, "You from the bank?" Recognized by the frightened man (Erville Alderson), he continues on his journey. On a lonely highway in the Southwest, he barely avoids a collision with another car after a jackrabbit runs out into the road (Walsh's own visual reference to the 1924 accident that cost him his left eye). At a gas station, Mount Whitney looms in the background as he introduces himself as "Mr. Collins" to "Pa" Goodhue (Henry Travers), his daughter, Mabel Baughman (Minna Gombell), and granddaughter, Velma Baughman (Joan Leslie), members of an Ohio family whose farm was repossessed.

At Shaw's Camp, Earle joins his "gang," "Red" Hattery (Arthur Kennedy) and "Babe" Kozak (Alan Curtis), two greenhorns who constantly fight over Marie Garson. In a reprise of Bogart's introduction, Walsh first shows Ida Lupino, seated on the cabin step, looking down, before she raises her head to check out the new arrival. Earle also meets Algernon (Willie Best), a camp attendant who teams him up with a friendly mutt called "Pard" (Bogart's own dog, "Zero"), described by the gangster as "a born panhandler." Both dog and master were based on Burnett's actual experiences at June Lake.

Willie Best, sometimes known as "Sleep 'n' Eat," was one level up from Stepin Fetchit on the stereotypical Black servant scale, but this busy African American performer was a talented comic actor who appeared in many top A films during the Golden Age. His Algernon might be on the lazy side, but the film, for which Hal Wallis was ultimately responsible, depicts him as quite resourceful, particularly in his invention of a fishing rod that automatically catches a fish while he enjoys a siesta. A typical comic element of its era, there is no equivalent in the screenplays or direction of John Huston.

Following a meeting with Louis Mendoza (Cornel Wilde), their "inside man," Earle cases the hotel. While driving through Tropico Springs, he is held up by an accident in the street. Recognizing Pa and Velma, he stops to help.

"Oh, a wiseguy is in on this!" grumbles the other driver, but Earle, learning that Pa has 13 cents in his pocket and $5 in his shoe, squeezes $50 from the accusatory motorist. As Velma climbs out of the driver's seat, Earle realizes that she is a "cripple" with a clubfoot. That evening, while stargazing with the girl, he tells her he learned about astronomy in a place "where we didn't have much else to do."

"Times have sure changed," declares "Big Mac" (Donald MacBride, in one of his best Warners performances), who pulled the strings for Earle's pardon. Not long for this world, Mac, confined to his bed, attempts to sneak booze against the orders of "Doc" Banton (Henry Hull). "All the A-1 guys are gone," he tells Earle, "dead, or in Alcatraz." He discusses the hotel heist, then hands Earle an envelope containing instructions to be followed after his death. "I'm going to die," he admits. "So are you. So are we all."

Convinced by Banton that a specialist could correct Velma's handicap, Earle and "Doc" pay her a visit. Pa asks Roy if he plans to marry the girl, then explains that she has a fellow back in Ohio. As they drive away, Banton tells Earle that he's like "'Johnny' Dillinger ... just rushin' toward death."

Back at the camp, Earle discovers that Red and Babe have come to blows over Marie. Even before the heist begins, the inexperienced gang is divided by their drunken attempts to bump off each other. Roy hands Marie his .45, telling her to lash out at Babe; but when she refuses, he pistol-whips the mug in the jaw.

Later that night, Earle wrestles through a dream as Marie watches. In the morning, she pleads with him to let her stay. Roy tells her that his plans don't include her, that she "could never mean anything" to him.

"Is she pretty?" she asks about Velma.

"Yeah," he replies, "and *decent*." Here, Walsh incorporates a reaction shot, allowing Lupino to register Marie's anguish with a subtle facial expression.

Earle pays for the operation, then drops by to check on Velma. He mentions a "big business deal" and his intention to travel around the world. "I'd sure like to marry you," he admits. "I ain't too old, and I'm going to have a lot of dough some day." Rejected, he nonetheless promises to "come back and see Velma walk."

In preparation for the big heist, Earle orders Algernon to lock up Pard, but the dog escapes through a window and chases them down the road. "What I ought to do is put a bullet through his head," Roy threatens. "Of all the fourteen-carat saps—starting out on a caper with a woman and a dog."

"One move out of you, son, and I'll fill your pants full of lead," Earle snarls to a bellboy (Richard Clayton) as the gang enters the hotel. Hinting at Bogart's addiction to tobacco, Roy then smashes a display case to steal a pack of cigarettes. As Red and Babe hammer away at the jewel safe, a hotel watchman (William Gould) walks in, pulls his piece, and is gunned down by Earle.

Roy and Marie make their getaway in his car, as the others, including the cringing Mendoza, follow, only to careen off the road and explode into a fireball. "Small timers for small jobs," Earle alleges. "They lost their heads. This one was just too big." Later, they learn that Mendoza has survived.

Earle displays his decent side when he suggests that Marie will constantly "be in trouble" if she stays with him. Dropping in on Big Mac to deliver the jewels, he finds the boss dead in bed, and Kranmer, "suggesting" that they divide the dough. "Listen, chiseler," Earle defiantly fumes. Kranmer tries to grab the box, but Roy resists, then is nicked by a bullet before hitting the floor and gunning him down.

Banton treats Earle's wound before he returns to see Velma walk. While Marie waits outside in the car, he becomes irritated by the completely recuperated girl's ungrateful attitude and the behavior of her beau, Lon Preiser (John Eldredge), who failed to visit or help his "fiancée" until she was able to dance. "Take your hands off me," Earle orders him. "I don't like you, and I don't like your friends." Sending Pard in ahead of her, Marie crashes the party.

Earle delivers the jewels to the fence mentioned in Big Mac's note. With the big boss gone, the mob is now being run by "Larry" (a most *un*-Mob-like moniker) in Kansas City. But Roy holds out a diamond ring for Marie. Displaying his naïveté in romantic matters, he places it on the pinkie finger of her left hand. While discussing Pard's possible connection to the botched heist, he asks, "How could a poor little dog be the cause of it all? That's just plain dumb!"

High Sierra (1941): Knowing the end is near, Roy Earle (Bogart) sends Marie Garson (Ida Lupino) to safety before speeding into the Sierras with the cops in hot pursuit.

The recovered Mendoza has turned stool pigeon, and front-page headlines declare "Mad Dog" Earle "Public Enemy Number One." Aggravated by the unwarranted nickname and title, Earle is recognized by a man whom he pistol-whips and locks in a motel closet. With Marie and Pard put safely on a bus to Las Vegas, he knocks over a general store for some dough, whips another "Mad Dog" spotter, then speeds off with the coppers in hot pursuit.

"I've done all the time I'm ever gonna do," he had told Marie, who replied, "You're all I've got in the world." With these remarks in mind, Earle frantically attempts to outrun the patrol cars by heading into the Sierras, but eventually runs out of road.

As law enforcement officers and newspaper and radio reporters gather below Mount Whitney, Huston and Burnett's script takes a swipe (the second in the film) at the sensationalism and bloodthirstiness of the American media (going strong, even in 1941). Warners regular Jerome Cowan appears as Healy, a journalist for *The Chronicle*, and Sam Hayes plays a radio announcer giving a play-by-play of Mad Dog's last stand, noting that "morbidly curious bystanders" are nearby.

Prodded by the police, Marie can't force herself to ask Earle to surrender; and a sharpshooter is sent to find a position above him on the rocks. Pard runs off to find his master, and Earle, using a bullet (a nice gangster touch), writes a note informing the cops that Marie remained innocent during the whole caper. Hit by a single rifle shot, he tumbles down the mountainside. As the dog licks his hand, Healy crassly asks Marie, "He's not much now, is he?"

"Mister, what does it mean when a man crashes out?" she inquires, realizing that Roy has now found the "freedom" he was seeking. During her brief time with him, she, too, had discovered a way out of her own trap. The film ends with a close-up of Lupino's tear-streaked face as the camera pulls up to focus on the peak of the mountain.

Bogart gives a flawless, fully realized, moving performance as Roy Earle, his first criminal whom the audience wished wouldn't come to a bad end in the final reel. Avoiding the histrionics of her *They Drive by Night* characterization, Lupino is a thoroughly believable, capable female companion for him. The supporting cast — particularly Zero — is excellent across the board. Bogie, who considered Jack Warner a cheapskate, not only wore his own clothes, but also supplied his own dog, whose dedication to Earle is a truly touching and ultimately tragic component of the film.

Raoul Walsh's consistently realistic, gritty approach to the material, particularly his insistence that the chase scene be shot entirely on location, provided the perfect environment for Bogart's breakout role. *High Sierra* proved an important effort for both director and star.

Walsh's next Warners project was a period piece, *The Strawberry Blonde* (1941), his first collaboration with Cagney. The plot of the film already was a bit hoary, but Jim enjoyed working with his two stunning female costars, Olivia de Havilland and Rita Hayworth, so much that he and his brother, again on board as associate producer, invited his mother to the set to watch the shooting of the beer garden scene. Carrie Cagney advised Walsh on the authenticity of the 1890s set; but, claiming that she was overweight, turned down the director's request that she appear in the scene.

Based on the play *One Sunday Afternoon* by James Hagan, this romantic comedy benefits from the sharp dialogue of Julius and Philip Epstein. Cagney and de Havilland are billed above the title, and Hayworth has the top "with" spot. An instrumental version of "Bill Bailey, Won't You Please Come Home" introduces dentist T. L. "Biff" Grimes (Cagney) and his best friend, Greek barber Nicholas "Nick" Pappalas (George Tobias) as they play a friendly game of horseshoes. In the neighboring yard, separated by a stone wall, a group of pretentious college students lend their voices to "Bill Bailey," deliberately irritating Biff.

Pestered by his wife, Amy (de Havilland), to go out for a walk — a respectable activity requiring a bath — Biff complains to Nick about having only two patients in the past eight months. He wonders if people in the neighborhood know he's "a jailbird," but his buddy suggests they merely "have good teeth."

A group of street musicians strikes up "And the Band Played On," prompting a discussion about the "Strawberry Blonde," Virginia Brush, and the dreaded Hugo F. Barnstead. "You knock him down," Nick suggests. "I kick him."

Regretful for revisiting painful memories, Biff speaks his mantra, "I take nothing from nobody." The phone rings, and he responds, "I don't pull teeth on Sunday, unless it's a child." The caller insists that he treat "Alderman Barnstead," and a taste for vengeance brews in his mind. "It's more than a coincidence," he tells Nick. "It's poetic justice."

A tuba floating in mid-air, accompanied by "And the Band Played On," initiates a flashback, set 10 years in the past, that comprises the majority of the narrative. Biff's unemployed father, William "Old Man" Grimes (Alan Hale) attempts to put the moves on Mrs. Mulcahy (Una O'Connor) before ducking into the neighborhood tavern. "The ladies all prefer me bark to their husband's bite," he tells the old broad. Outraged that his son might be working as a bartender, Old Man Grimes is informed by Biff that he is the new bouncer, a job necessary to pay for his correspondence course in dentistry.

Ordered to eject the moocher, Biff counters, "There are a lot of other bums in here. Let me throw one of them out." Staging a brawl, Biff tells him, "You're my Old Man. I brought you up," before tossing him into a lamp post. (The stunt man in the shot looks nothing like

Alan Hale.) Biff then dukes it out with the boss, "Big Joe" (Edward McNamara), coming away with a black eye.

At Nick's barber shop, Biff can't keep his story straight while describing being hit by a "spittoon," a "beer bottle" or a "broom handle."

"Hey, fellas, here comes the Strawberry Blonde," announces one of the boys, as Virginia Brush (Rita Hayworth) saunters down the sidewalk. After persuading Biff to help him sell tickets for a boat ride, blustery Hugo F. Barnstead (Jack Carson) pitches one to Virginia, picking her up in the process.

Old Man Grimes constantly blames his lazy, inebriated lifestyle on pain from his teeth. Intending to pull one, Biff gives him a major dose of nitrous oxide, creating a severe laugh attack. "I'm gettin' sillier by the minute," he declares before chasing Biff around the room. Barnstead arrives, calling up to the window that two girls are waiting for them in the park. The Old Man wants to go, but Biff gasses him again, yanks the tooth with a pliers, and runs out.

The celebrated Raoul Walsh, whose eyepatch was a necessity. John Ford wore one to emulate his hero, but resisted admitting it.

Virginia Brush is joined by Amy Lind, a "modern" woman who agitates for female suffrage and wears her nurse's uniform while out on dates. Virginia speaks of behaving in a manner that will discourage male trifling, and Amy responds, "Why, goodness. Why did we come here, if not to be trifled with?" The two suitors arrive, and Hugo easily gets fresh with Virginia, but Biff is frightened off by Amy's "unwomanly" attitudes.

The men switch partners on the second date, during the "boat ride." Just as Biff and Virginia are about to board the vessel, the gangway is pulled up. Only 750 passengers are allowed, but they had peddled 3,000 tickets—the first indication that Barnstead is less than honest in his business dealings. Following an evening at the local beer garden—during which Cagney and Hayworth briefly dance together—Biff walks Virginia home, where she gives him a kiss. As he leaves, he repeats the romantic move on a horse.

Three weeks later, Biff waits in the park, anxious for their reunion. Amy meets him instead, then Nick arrives with news that Virginia and Hugo were married that afternoon. To save face, Biff tells him that he was waiting for Amy. She drops her suffragette pose, and Biff (inspired by Cagney's own aversion to tobacco) says, "Never smoked a cigarette ... I never inhale myself." The sequence concludes with a proposal; and just as quickly, the next scene, set 18 months later, depicts the married couple at home, where Biff is continuing his dental studies.

At dinner with the Barnsteads, Biff is offered an executive vice-president position at Hugo's contracting firm. Following the addition of a foreman job for his Old Man, he is given a nice office but nothing to do. On a regular basis, he signs documents he doesn't bother to

The Strawberry Blonde (1941): Temporary bouncer T. L. "Biff" Grimes (Cagney) must eject his "Old Man," William (Alan Hale), from the premises in Raoul Walsh's delightful period comedy (original lobby card).

read. While at a construction site, William is killed when a brick wall collapses, a tragedy multiplied by a graft charge leveled at Biff by two policemen friends, Charlie Brown (Max Hoffman, Jr.) and Mat Hughes (Pat Flaherty).

Biff is convicted and sentenced to five to seven years in the Big House, enduring hard labor but also continuing his studies, eventually allowed to practice prison dentistry. Unfortunately, he drills through a bridge while working on the Warden (Wade Boteler), who sends him to solitary. By the time he is released, he has earned his dental diploma. Though casting him in a sympathetic role, Warners couldn't resist making Jim a jailbird (albeit an innocent one). Walsh's fast-paced prison montage provides a brief, less torturous version of events depicted in *Each Dawn I Die*.

The film's most effective scene, beautifully played by Cagney and de Havilland, reunites Biff and Amy in the park where they first met. De Havilland, a very subtle actress, usually spoke very quietly, and is matched by Cagney, who, throughout the film, delivers his lines at a slower tempo than usual, an approach that sets Grimes apart from his fast-talking, electric wiseguy characters.

The floating tuba returns to end the flashback, and Virginia rudely escorts Hugo into Biff's office for a tooth extraction. Yanking the molar without using anesthetic, Biff sends his old nemesis howling from the room. Satisfied with a "little revenge," he tells Nick, "I'm the dope. He's the wiseguy," then admits his pleasure over *not* marrying Virginia. "I'm happy. He's not."

Biff provokes a rousing fight with all the next-door collegians, then prepares for a walk with Amy, to the tune of "And the Band Played On." Her whisper into his ear suggests a pregnancy, and the couple strolls happily into the final fadeout.

Biff Grimes is a calmer Cagney, but the actor still manages to work in some trademark fisticuffs, dance moves, and even some never-before-seen gymnastics. The supporting cast, especially Rita Hayworth, is compelling, with only Alan Hale briefly going over the top during the laughing-gas scene. A lighthearted, charming period piece with occasional serious overtones, *The Strawberry Blonde* (particularly on the heels of *High Sierra*— was a departure for the action-oriented Walsh, though his usual quota of machismo manages to creep in.

Power-mad ship's captain "Wolf" Larsen in *The Sea Wolf* (1941) was another role turned down by George Raft, who eventually became the worst judge of good parts in Hollywood history. But this time it wasn't Bogart, but Robinson, who benefited, creating one of his most memorable and complex screen characters.

Robert Rossen's final draft of the screenplay pleased Robinson, who had admired the novel since childhood. Though he doesn't physically resemble Jack London's description of the tall, blonde Scandinavian Wolf Larsen, Eddie's interpretation is the most psychologically developed character of his Warners career. Along with *Angels with Dirty Faces, The Adventures of Robin Hood* and *The Sea Hawk* (1940), *The Sea Wolf* is one of Michael Curtiz's finest pre-*Casablanca* masterpieces, and one of the most complex films in his entire catalog.

Robinson, Ida Lupino and John Garfield (appearing in his 12th Warners film) all are billed above the title, while the studio made sure to emphasize the film's fidelity to the novel by listing London's name twice in the opening credits, even though the script greatly deviates from the author's original as the narrative progresses. The maritime atmosphere is established instantly, heavily enhanced by the evocative musical score by Erich Wolfgang Korngold. Curtiz had worked with him many times, and the Austrian composer's contribution to the Errol Flynn pirate epics *Captain Blood* (1935) and *The Sea Hawk* became synonymous with the cinematic sea. *The Sea Wolf* was the first and last Warner Bros. Wiseguys film to feature one of his complete original scores. (His work on *A Midsummer Night's Dream* consisted mainly of arranging the famous Mendelssohn score, as well as writing "additional music.")

The "pre-noir," expressionistic style that Curtiz brought to his Warners horror films of the 1930s, particularly *The Walking Dead*, permeates *The Sea Wolf*, not only visually, but dramatically and thematically. The depiction of a group of dark, desperate and doomed characters predated John Huston's "inauguration" of film noir in *The Maltese Falcon* by six months. In a way, *The Sea Wolf*, set in 1900, is a combination of the Warners gangster and Flynn adventure genres wrapped up stunningly by Curtiz.

As sailor George Leach, John Garfield opens the film in his trademark, down on his luck mode, sweating profusely in a San Francisco saloon as he hides out from the police. After Johnson (Stanley Ridges) refuses an "offer" to sail aboard *The Ghost*, and is followed out of the dive by a press gang, the ship's agent (Ralf Harolde) tries to slip Leach a mickey. Needing no such "inducement," the fugitive knocks him to the barroom floor, claiming, "I'll ship on the first and quickest one out of here."

While rowing out to *The Ghost*, Cooky (Barry Fitzgerald), bottle firmly in hand, laughingly warns Leach about the "foulest ship in creation" and "the cold, merciless heart of Wolf Larsen." Steaming behind them, the passenger boat *Martinez* carries escaped convict Ruth Webster (Ida Lupino), who is attempting to elude two cops by hooking up with Humphrey Van Weyden (Alexander Knox), a soft-spoken stranger who admits he can do nothing to help her. Ruth fights them off and jumps overboard, just before a freighter rams the boat. The scene, juxtaposing miniatures with studio tank shots of travelers tossed about by the collision, is brief but convincing.

The *Martinez* sinks, and Van Weyden, having survived, pulls the unconscious Ruth onto some wreckage as a mysterious schooner sails toward them out of the fog. As Curtiz cuts, then tracks in, closer, the name "Ghost" is visible on her starboard bow. Literally creeping into the film like a specter, the ship immediately is established as a character with its own personality. Van Weyden walks onto the deck, pushing open some small doors to reveal a figure pacing in the background as the crew works between them. The camera cuts closer, and Robinson strides toward it, giving the viewer a good close-up gaze at the captain's grimy, slightly scowling face.

Van Weyden, observing the first mate lying supine on the wet deck, remarks that "no one seems to care," then gets no response from Larsen after thanking him for the rescue. Another sailor announces, "He's dead, sir," and Larsen matter-of-factly repeats the words, calls the corpse a "dirty drunken sot," then asks the crew, "Any of you fellas got a Bible or a prayerbook?" He receives nothing but quiet laughter in return.

Larsen tells Van Weyden he has the look of "a preacher," eliciting more laughter.

"I'm a writer," Van Weyden replies.

"What do you write about?" asks the captain.

"Whatever I see," he says.

"Is this the first time you ever saw a man die?"

"It's the first time I've ever seen such indifference to death."

"Well, you haven't seen enough to be a good writer," Larsen accuses. "This voyage ought to do you a lot of good."

Van Weyden asks if he will be put ashore, and is informed that he will replace the dead mate, even if proving useless in the position. "You're soft, like a woman," Larsen adds, explaining that *The Ghost* touches no ports nor the usual shipping lanes, and that he obeys only "The Law of the Sea." Demoted to cabin boy, Van Weyden instead replaces Leach, who refers to his "promotion" to boat puller as a "dirty, filthy, heartbreaking job." Called "a filthy scum" by the captain, he protests, "He isn't talking to a dog. He's talking to a man," and gets beaten to the deck for his trouble.

While toiling in the galley, Van Weyden is taunted by the sadistic Cooky, who is reading aloud the writer's notes about the captain and crew, "a gallery of rogues ... a brutal, callous and inhuman lot." Promising to show the scribblings to the captain, Cooky, gleefully chuckling, pulls a knife, informing him that, aboard the ship, stabbing is "not a criminal offense."

Pursued by his "brother's ship," Larsen expects the crew to "fight or drown," but lies to them that they "are hunting seals." While dining with his "officers," he suffers one of his recurrent, debilitating headaches, then asks the drunken Dr. Louis (Gene Lockhart) about the condition of Ruth, a friend of the "literary cabin boy." "Louis has a perfect record aboard this ship," he informs them. "He hasn't cured a patient yet."

In the captain's cabin, Van Weyden peruses the many books on the shelves, spying the monumental works of Herbert Spencer, Charles Darwin, Friederich Nietsche, Edgar Allan Poe and Thomas DeQuincey, before picking up a volume of John Milton. Larsen enters, asking him to read some of the "great poem," then recites the infamous line, "Better to reign in Hell than serve in Heaven," adding, "Milton really understood it all.... Maybe it would be better if I never opened a book."

Larsen grabs the notes given to him by Cooky. "You write very well," he compliments his cabin boy, then reads the frank, unflattering description of the crew and their master.

The Sea Wolf (1941): Robinson, in a brilliant performance as the megalomaniacal "fascist superman" Captain Wolf Larsen, is well-supported by (standing, left to right) Howard da Silva, John Garfield and Stanley Ridges in Michael Curtiz's noir, maritime masterpiece (original lobby card).

Van Weyden disagrees that the voyage will change him, receiving a punch in the gut for addressing the skipper as "Larsen."

"You'll say *Captain* Larsen, or *Sir*. Remember, there's a difference in our social standing on board this vessel." But Larsen enjoys having the scribe around, revealing his life story so they can write a book together.

Leach barges in, announcing that "the woman … I think she's dying." Typically, Doc Louis, passed out on the job, is slapped awake by Larsen. Babbling deliriously about her imprisonment, Ruth inspires the cruel Cooky to allege, "She's not a lady. She's one of us!" To save her life, Leach, his arm slashed during a fight with the crazed cook, submits to a blood transfusion.

Ruth asks Larsen to "give her a break," but he orders Louis to "take her below," prompting the boat puller to throw a marlin spike at him. "Leach, according to the laws of the sea, I could hang you for this, but I won't," the captain snarls. "You're going to save me that trouble. Before this voyage is over, you'll hang yourself." Beaten again, Leach is ordered taken below.

"You should have let me die!" Ruth tells Louis.

Back in Larsen's cabin, Van Weyden recites his description, which "isn't on paper yet," of the captain:

> A brute, completely without feeling or thought. A cruel, merciless creature who kills for the sake of killing, who tortures for hearing the anguished cries of his victims. But, as this first impression wears

off, one realizes that this is a highly complex individual, a mass of contradictions, a man who is tortured by a brain he should never have been given. But, with that brain, he is able to think, to see clearly that all these things he denies in other men — the need for respect, for dignity — exist in himself.... Since he has found it so difficult in the outside world to maintain that dignity, he creates a world for himself, a ship on which he alone can be master, on which he alone can rule. The next step is a simple one. An ego such as this must constantly be fed, must constantly be assured of its supremacy, so it feeds itself upon the degradation of people who've never known anything but degradation. It is cruel to people who have never known anything but cruelty. But to dare to expose that ego, in a world where it would meet its equal ...

"It's a lie!" Larsen rages. "It's a lie!"

Louis knocks at the door, requesting, "I want you to forbid the men to laugh at me." Now sober, he wants to be treated with the respect he formerly enjoyed, as "Dr. Lou*is* J. Prescott."

Larsen calls all hands on deck, announces Louis' wishes, then kicks "the doctor" down the stairs from the bridge. The crew laughs and tears into him, so he crawls up the ratlines; and, as the captain tries to talk him down, he states, "I fear no man, no man!" then jumps to his death.

"It was an accident," Larsen asserts. "He slipped."

A classic Curtiz romantic scene follows, with Ruth visiting the bruised and bloodied Leach down in the hold. The director tracks into a profile two-shot, cuts closer to each character, then moves in to a tight close-up of Lupino's face, as Korngold's love theme, led by accordion and violin, subtly accompanies them. Unlike his scores for the Flynn epics, the music for this film never drives the scenes, instead remaining a moody complement, providing a sonic equivalent of Curtiz's noir style.

Under cover of darkness, the crew, organized by Leach, mutinies, tossing Larsen over the side. Back on board, the captain locks all but Cooky below, then asks to see Van Weyden in his cabin. Wracked by another headache, he loses his sight. Alternating between (apparently) sincere sympathy and (definitely) insidious evil, he manages to pressure the writer into staying with him. On deck, he hides his increasing blindness, promises liquor to the crew, and reveals that Cooky provided a list of all the men involved in the mutiny. For turning informer, the stool pigeon is keel hauled and bitten by a shark.

Van Weyden tells Leach and Johnson that Larsen is blind. While the captain attempts to pilot the ship, the three men prepare to escape in a lifeboat. In true Warners tough-guy mode, Leach is forced to punch out Ruth when she refuses to go with them. At sea, they discover a note from the captain and their water barrels filled with vinegar.

Approached by another ship in the fog, Larsen panics, revealing his blindness to the crew. Floating up to the now-derelict *Ghost* (a la "The Flying Dutchman") in their lifeboat, the four deserters board her, and Leach is locked in the cabin as she begins to sink. "He's not only blind, he's mad," Leach warns the others.

Larsen can now make out only shadows as he holds a gun on Van Weyden, who offers to take him to a doctor. "In the best literary tradition of the sea," the captain states, "I, Wolf Larsen, sink with my own ship, in sight of land," a small island two miles away, where he was headed when "his brother caught up" with him. Looking a bit like "Little Caesar" while holding his rod on Van Weyden, he finally guns down the writer after warning him not to recite any more of his biographical book. Now completely blind, he assumes he missed after hearing the scribe's voice. Van Weyden talks Larsen into giving Ruth the key to free Leach, then falls dead in the water and the captain goes down with *The Ghost*. A traditional Hollywood close-up of the couple and a long shot of the lifeboat sailing off toward the horizon end the film.

The Sea Wolf is one of the finest examples of how Robinson, eminently versatile and vastly underrated (and never nominated for an Academy Award), became one of the first film actors to play a gallery of different, well-developed characters, rather than consistently relying on a singular personality (like nearly all the male actors associated with MGM or Paramount). Cagney and Bogart, too, soon would have further opportunities to deviate from their established archetypes, but both of them had to work harder at it. After making cinematic statements against the Third Reich by playing "the good guys" in *Confessions of a Nazi Spy* and *Dr. Ehrlich's Magic Bullet*, Eddie saw a prime opportunity to play the other side of the coin, a would-be fascist superman, one with a psychological complexity that eventually degenerates into megalomania, paranoia and insanity, physically manifested in the loss of his sight, an affliction that directly ends his power over the world of *The Ghost*.

The supporting cast complements him admirably, with Garfield giving his usual strong, measured performance, and Lupino getting suitably intense at the right moments. A classic maritime film may have been inadequate without the scene-stealing, near-lunatic Barry Fitzgerald, whose similar credits of the era include *The Ebb Tide* (1937), based on a *very* dark Robert Louis Stevenson novel, and John Ford's expressionistic saga *The Long Voyage Home* (1940). Gene Lockhart, who often played annoying scoundrels (as in *A Dispatch from Reuters*), could also be subtle and likeable, and his disgraced doctor lends some tragic heart to this mostly cold-blooded film.

The studio occasionally tackled a complicated novel like *The Sea Wolf*, but Jack Warner and Hal Wallis couldn't help recycling the same old tired tales, shoving Bogie into a remake of *Kid Galahad*, made less than four years earlier, after — who else? — George Raft turned down the part. Originally titled "Carnival," *The Wagons Roll at Night* (1941) cast him as bush-league circus manager Nick Coster, under the direction of Warners journeyman Ray Enright. Using the original Francis Wallace story on which Seton I. Miller had based *Kid Galahad*, Fred Niblo, Jr., and Barry Trivers retained entire scenes and dialogue from the earlier screenplay, merely transferring them to a circus setting. Angry that he'd been relegated to a recycled programmer after completing *High Sierra*, Bogart, during the shoot, taunted a lion with his cane, only to have the gigantic cat urinate on his prized LaSalle car, ruining the bright yellow paint job.

Warners considered *The Wagons Roll at Night* so unimportant that no one is billed above the title, though Bogart has the top spot, above Sylvia Sidney, on the after-title "starring" panel. On the road with Nick Coster's Original Coney Island Carnival, Flo Lorraine (Sidney) impersonates a gypsy fortune teller, while "the boss" is busy throwing a dissatisfied customer out of his wagon. She accuses Coster of "always flying off the handle," then offers a business suggestion: "What this turkey needs is a shot in the arm."

"Hoffman the Great" (Sig Ruman), the carnival lion tamer, is wallowing in his perpetual state of inebriation. Reminding him that he was fired by the Ringling Bros. Circus, Coster commands "a gallon of coffee" and a shower via "the fire hose."

"A real man can drink and still do his work," Hoffman mumbles while staggering toward the performance cage. As the lions stalk through the wooden entrance chute, he jabs one with his walking stick, causing it to break free. In town, the cat prowls into a grocery store and leaps onto the counter. The proprietor, Matt Varney (Eddie Albert), calmly places a baby into an apple barrel, then holds the lion at bay with a pitchfork until Coster and his cohorts arrive.

Coster realizes that the "shot in the arm" they need is Varney, the local hero, who signs on for a week as Hoffman's assistant. "Doc" (Cliff Clark), the carnival barker, promotes him as "The Grocery Boy Lion Tamer," and he is billed above Hoffman on the banner that spans the entrance. His "training" consists of sweeping up after the lions, but he is sent into the performance cage with only a whip as Hoffman does his act. "I guess I've dreamed all my life of something like this," he admits.

Coster reveals his plan to groom Matt as the new lion tamer "Varney the Great." Discovering Hoffman in a near-comatose state, he persuades Matt to go solo, then can't force himself to watch the neophyte coax five lions through a ring of fire. "I shouldn't have sent him in there," he tells his assistants standing outside the tent.

"He was better than you ever were," Coster tells Hoffman after giving him the boot. At Bert's Bar, Varney tries to explain the situation, but Hoffman responds by accusing him of being involved with Flo. Matt hits him hard and is thrown into the street. While Coster is away, Hoffman returns to the carnival and attacks Varney. During the scuffle, the old man is mauled by one of the lions through the bars of a cage. A "village yokel" from the bar claims that Matt tried to murder him, then runs off to inform the cops.

Flo makes the difficult decision to hide Varney at "Nick's farm," where his sister, Mary (Joan Leslie), lives with Mr. and Mrs. Harry Williams (Aldrich Bowker and Clara Bandick). Coster has repeatedly forbade the carnival folk to have any contact with Mary, whom he sent to a convent to keep "clean." Always criticizing their way of life—and indirectly offending Flo—he growls, "We're a lot of mugs and grifters and riff-raff.... It's a sleazy game we're in."

At the farm, Matt sleeps in Nick's room, and receives breakfast in bed from Mary. Soon they are pitching the woo by a pond, where Matt tells her she's "a lot prettier" than Nick. The usually straightforward Ray Enright gets a little ambitious in this scene, tilting the camera down to focus on their reflection in the water as they kiss.

Flo reluctantly tells Nick where Matt is hiding out. Predictably, he fumes about "road show vermin crawlin' all over the house," then drives off to bring him back. By grooming Matt as the "star" lion tamer, Coster tries to control his sister's would-be suitor. Regardless of Varney's innate decency, Nick believes he can transform the naïve young man into the kind of person he despises—a man like himself. This element of self-loathing fits the then-emerging Bogart persona, and adds depth to a two-dimensional character in a cookie-cutter production. Without his occasional sympathetic moments, Nick Coster, who refers to the carnival as "a racket," could have become a watered-down, non-criminal version of Bogie's stock supporting gangster.

Doc, noticing that Matt isn't paying attention to his dangerous work, tells Flo that the lad must be in love with her. Paraphrasing one of Harry Carey's lines in *Kid Galahad*, he says, "I've known you for a long time, Flo. You can't beat aces." Flo's momentary joy is shattered when Matt reveals he's in love with Mary, then takes a bus back to the farm.

Angered over the insubordination of his performers, Coster is pawed by "Caesar" as he passes the lion's cage, but heads to the farm to confront Varney. Mary explains that she is truly in love with Matt, but Nick slaps her. Knocked down by a right from Varney, he retreats back to the carnival, where Flo admits that she, too, is in love with the lad. Of course, he won't listen to the truth, proclaiming Matt a "two-timer."

Caesar goes berserk and kills Bundy (Jack Mower), one of the trainers. Persuading the authorities not to destroy the lion, Nick pretends to make up with Matt, then (in a classic Bogart close-up) subtly registers pure evil in his eyes when Caesar rolls by in a cage. "That cat's a celebrity now. He killed a guy," he says. Describing Varney of the Lions' "big break ... in the big town," he plans a "sensational" act with "just one cat" for the spectators in Chicago.

Flo rushes to the farm to tell Mary of Nick's machinations, and Doc warns Matt about Caesar. Coster assures Varney that his gun filled with blanks will scare off the lion, then

The Wagons Roll at Night (1941): In this remake of *Kid Galahad*, circus manager Nick Coster (Bogart) attempts to stop lion tamer Matt Varney (Eddie Albert) from putting the moves on his young sister, Mary (Joan Leslie) (original lobby card).

removes the cartridges right before the event. Flo and Mary frantically speed to the circus, then plead with Nick backstage as Caesar overtakes Matt in the cage. Nick runs in and blasts away, but is severely mauled before Matt can drag him out, pick up the piece and finish off the lion.

"I was wrong about the kid.... He's a swell guy," Nick tells his sister. Turning to Flo, he apologizes, then asks her to "see that these kids get married and get started right." Laughing for the first time in the film, he says, "I wonder if they can use a smart promoter where I'm goin'" before he dies.

Again, a Warners rehash is made competent by a fast pace and good performances. Bogart may have justifiably hated the role, but gave more than was required, and Sylvia Sidney is suitably sympathetic in the part originally played by Bette Davis in *Kid Galahad*. A vast improvement on the wooden Wayne Morris in the earlier film, Eddie Albert, at times working his way through dreadful "hick" dialogue, is more appealing than in his previous Warner Bros. Wiseguys effort, *A Dispatch from Reuters*. Perhaps the most pleasant aspect of *The Wagons Roll at Night* is the still 16-year-old Joan Leslie, this time playing Bogie's sister, rather than the girl who breaks his heart.

On November 23, 1940, the day after Bogart finished shooting *The Wagons Roll at Night*, his 72-year-old mother, Maud, passed away from cancer. He had brought her from New York to Hollywood, where Mayo had faithfully cared for her. When asked about her, Bogie complimented her toughness, then alluded to the fact that no one had ever been able to get close to her.

While in New York, Gladys Robinson had seen Laura and S. J. Perelman's play *The Night Before Christmas* and convinced Eddie that it would make a good Warners film. After talking Hal Wallis into shelling out $30,000 for the screen rights, Robinson then had second thoughts, irking the producer and Jack Warner, who again considered giving him the axe. In the meantime, he again fled to MGM, where Mervyn Leroy was directing *Unholy Partners* (1941), in which he was cast as yet another crusading newspaper editor, eventually giving his life to defeat racketeering.

When Bogart discovered that Jack Warner had bought the rights to Irwin Shaw's Broadway stage success *The Gentle People*, he began lobbying to star in the prestige film version, again with Ida Lupino, who had been cast as the female lead. He went so far as to send a telegram to producer Henry Blanke, claiming that he'd heard he was to play Geoff, a waterfront racketeer who shakes down local fishermen.

Blanke neglected to reply to Bogie. As always — Mad Dog Earle notwithstanding — he wasn't the studio's first choice. Cagney and Raft, whose films made more money, still topped the A list. Never mind that neither actor was interested in *The Gentle People*.

Stubborn to the last, Bogart went above Wallis' head, directly to Jack Warner. After reading his telegram, stating that he was "the most logical person" for the part, the boss gave in, but then — according to available accounts — ended up casting Lupino's pal John Garfield in the film, released as *Out of the Fog* (1941), at her request. The fact that Lupino was paid $40,000 for her work on this film, as opposed to the $16,500 that would have been earned by Bogie, provides a sufficient explanation.

Moviegoers' enthusiastic responses to Cagney's comic turn in *The Strawberry Blonde* inspired another romantic comedy, *The Bride Came C.O.D.* (1941), also scripted by the brothers Epstein, but this time reuniting Jim with Bette Davis. Unfortunately, the results were less than expected, resulting in one of the worst films featuring either actor.

Occasionally a lot of talent does little to compensate for a bad idea. With William Cagney as associate producer (under Hal Wallis), William Keighley as director, and the Epsteins as dialogue masters, there can be no other good reason for the inferiority of *The Bride Came C.O.D.* A shoddy attempt at a Frank Capra-like screwball comedy, it is neither funny nor inventive, instead relying (at three different points) on Bette Davis landing bum-first onto a cactus. This low-rent slapstick isn't humorous on any of the occasions it happens to her, and is even more obnoxious when it befalls Cagney. The Epsteins must have *really* hated the film's premise to have contributed such an atypical, atrocious script.

Following a four-day "whirlwind" courtship, "Texas Oil Heiress" Joan Winfield (Davis) accepts a marriage proposal from popular radio crooner and bandleader Allen Brice (Jack Carson), a scoop broadcast nationwide by "Tattletale" Tommy Keenan (Stuart Erwin). Appalled, Joan's father, Lucius K. Winfield (Eugene Pallette), hires Steve Collins (Cagney), an independent pilot whose plane is about to be repossessed, to "kidnap" his daughter and land her safely in Amarillo. The fee? $10 per pound, times 110 pounds, equals $1,100. (Did buxom Bette weigh only 110 pounds in 1941?)

Joan, with a parachute draped on backwards, tries to bail out. Steve crashes, and they share a cold night in the desert (Cagney "imitates" a coyote at one point), then discover a ghost town called "Bonanza." The sole resident, "Pop" Tolliver (Harry Davenport), a raven-toting old geezer who stayed on after the mine closed in 1914, fries greasy breakfasts, locks Steve in the rattle-trap hoosegow for "kidnapping," then helps the down-on-his-luck flyer prevent Joan from marrying Brice. Following a series of predictable and dimwitted mishaps—except for a hilarious accident sequence during which Pop and Joan try to escape through the desert in an ancient auto that backfires, then blows up, on aviation fuel—Steve gets his dough and the dame.

The are a few Epstein dialogue diamonds in the rough. Sheriff McGee (William Frawley), having flown in from Los Angeles, can't believe Tolliver has been isolated in Bonanza for 30 years. "Never seen a movie?" the lawman asks.

"Not a real one," the old timer replies.

"Sounds Un-American to me," he responds.

Injecting some subtle, Stan Laurel-like shtick into the generally non-comical proceedings, Cagney is *very* funny during a scene set in the abandoned mine. Steve has found an exit, but decides not to tell Joan, allowing her father time to arrive and stop the marriage to Brice. As she sleeps beside him, he attempts to eat a smuggled-in sandwich, but begins to choke when she unexpectedly stirs. Displaying the impeccable Cagney comic timing, Steve explains that he was dreaming of "eating a big steak dinner" and "started chewing too fast." Joan kisses him, tastes mustard, and the jig is up.

In the most unbelievable fight scene of Cagney's career, Steve is beaten in the street by Brice, whom he has accused of singing off-key. During an earlier, truly awful, sequence of bad vocalizing, Cagney and Davis actually *sing* their lines to each other through a closed door.

Jim managed to enjoy making the film, mostly resisting over-the-top antics to deliver a thoroughly professional performance, but Bette must have been seething as she played perhaps the most stupid character in her classic Hollywood career. During the closing scene, Cagney gets the last "howl," when Steve, during their wedding night at Tolliver's ramshackle Palace Hotel, again does his coyote "impression" while waiting in bed for Joan (now weighing in at 118 pounds).

Dumped from *Out of the Fog*, Bogart was offered a consolation film, *Manpower*, another Raoul Walsh effort to team him with George Raft. As soon as Raft learned that Bogie was aboard, however, he began campaigning around the studio to get his former costar booted from the project. Raft's claim was that Bogart simply was miscast as his buddy, while others knew the truth of the matter: George couldn't stand the competition.

Bogart finally was dropped from the project after he began arguing with Raft's double, Mack Gray, during a wardrobe test; but imagine Raft's dismay when his replacement—heavy hitter Eddie G.—was brought aboard. Rather than the tuna fisherman of *Tiger Shark*, Robinson became a power lineman in *Manpower*, battling his coworker Raft for the fair hand of Marlene Dietrich. The shoot was not a happy one for Walsh, who constantly had to direct in the midst of two feuds: a producers' power struggle between Mark Hellinger and Hal Wallis; and another, more volatile, actors' scrap between Robinson and Raft on Stage 11 of the Burbank studio. Displeased with having to compete with Eddie (in particular) and with the downward spiral of his career (in general; and of his own making), Raft was difficult from the outset, becoming ferociously jealous over Robinson's attention to Dietrich. Eventually the production ran a week over schedule, with the budget escalating to $920,000.

Those working on the film may have let its title go to their heads. Fed up with Wallis' interference (which had begun during *High Sierra*), Hellinger asked Jack Warner to let him out of his contract in February 1941. He planned to stay for the *Manpower* shoot, but quit two weeks before Walsh fired up the cameras in late March. Wald was then promoted, with a salary increase, from writer to associate producer.

Raft, not wanting the audience to perceive him as weak, objected to a scripted scene that depicted Johnny Marshall, in the pouring rain, losing his grip on Hank McHenry (Robinson), who then falls to his death. Raft refused to shoot the scene, insisting that a faulty rope be responsible for Hank's plummet.

The tension finally peaked on April 26, 1941, during the shooting of a fight scene featuring Robinson and Ward Bond. Robinson's volatility can be witnessed when he punches out the imposing Bond, his sledgehammer right striking so realistically that it can almost be felt off-screen. Robinson, Raft and Cagney — all diminutive men — were as formidable as John Wayne when it came to packing a powerful punch.

Portraying Johnny stopping Hank from carrying on the brawl, Raft roughed up Robinson a little too much, then swore at him when the latter objected. Raft then punched Robinson in the side, prompting Bond and Alan Hale to separate them. With Robinson's permission, Hal Wallis filed Screen Actors Guild charges against Raft; but when the film became a box-office hit in July, recouping more than its overrun budget, Wallis and Robinson dropped the charges.

Robinson, Dietrich and Raft all are billed above the title, each on a separate panel, in the same size type (actually steel rivets, emphasizing the film's macho moniker). Lightning strikes during a raging thunderstorm, indicating the volatile nature of the entire enterprise. (Rain saturates a major portion of the 103-minute running time.) Power lines go down, surgeons can't see their patients in the operating room, and a late-night lover (shown 1941 Production Code-style, alone in a medium close-up) asks, "Hey, honey, what's the address here?"

Off work for the past hour, Hank attempts to cut a rug with a hesitant dame at a smoky nightclub, while his much slicker pal, Johnny, puts his confident, calm moves on a more receptive chick. Ordered back to work, Hank tries to follow Johnny's lead, but is helped on his way by an insistent bouncer. Indicating the advanced level of their male bonding, Johnny admits, "Every time I've seen you up at bat, you strike out. Even if dames don't love you, *I* do."

At the job site, rain pours down as "Omaha" (Frank McHugh) and Eddie Adams (Ward Bond) aid Hank and Johnny in emergency repairs. Johnny is hit by a falling cross arm, and Hank, trying to help, is electrocuted when he steps on a sparking transformer. Both injured men are taken down to a panel truck, where Eddie performs CPR on the unconscious Hank. Johnny recovers and, immediately concerned about his friend, who has been in a state of arrest for 30 minutes, takes over the resuscitation duties. "Ah, it's no good, Johnny," Eddie sighs. "You can't bring him back."

Johnny refuses to stop, however. "How do you feel, mug?" he asks as Hank regains consciousness. Incredibly, old Hank is just fine — suggesting that he also was suffering from hypothermia brought on by the torrential, chilling rain; under normal circumstances, seven minutes of arrest is enough to cause irreversible brain damage.

Engaging in their usual sophomoric shenanigans, Hank's cohorts visit him at the hospital, where Omaha steals flowers from an adjacent room and "Jumbo" Wells (Alan Hale) harasses Hank's roommate, Sidney Whipple (Walter Catlett, who spends the entire film in traction), and every nurse he sees. "For this room, we always draw lots, and I lost," one of the young women claims.

A slight variation on his *They Drive by Night* character, Raft's Johnny is an outwardly concerned, decent man who uses frank, borderline-insulting remarks to protect those he cares about. He again prefers to stay calm, and borders on teetotalism, but doesn't hesitate to let his fists fly if pushed in that direction. After leaving the hospital, he accompanies Antoine "Pop" Duval (Egon Brecher) to prison to pick up his "innocent" daughter, Fay

(Dietrich), who has done a year-long stretch for "pinching a guy's wallet" in a San Francisco gin joint.

Walsh consistently emphasizes the tough-as-nails, blue-collar atmosphere by combining the workers' easy-going attitudes with a visual emphasis on steel: high-voltage towers, large tools, and even a spinning hubcap to symbolize the car ride back from the Big House. The constant camaraderie between the men carries over from the workplace to the home front, as all the men bunk together at a local boarding house, where the poker playing never ends and even the aging, bulky Jumbo slides down the banister rear-first.

When Hank, now promoted to foreman, returns from the hospital, Adams' comments naturally gravitate toward dames. "You've been turned down so many times," he tells Hank, "you're beginning to look like a bedspread." For the first time in the film, Robinson, a head shorter than Ward Bond, knocks the more imposing man to the floor.

During a dangerous job involving heavily iced power lines, Pop Duval dies instantly when hit by a falling wire. (Considering the earlier resuscitation miracle, someone should have been able to save him in such a hypothermia-friendly environment.) The cynical Johnny isn't impressed by Fay's attitude, but the sympathetic Hank, visiting her at the Midnight Club, a clip joint run by "Smiley" Quinn (Barton MacLane), offers her $150 from Pop's "insurance policy," though she only accepts $50 (75 percent of which is skimmed by Smiley).

A classic Raoul Walsh scene—in which Hank, Johnny and Jumbo go shopping for women's nightgowns—is followed by the smitten suitor's delivery of the "birthday present" to Fay's apartment, where she is being propositioned by Al Hurst (Ben Welden), an unwanted lothario, whom he nearly beats to death. This violent attack is the preview for his marriage proposal; and, though she admits, "I'm wrong for you ... I'm not in love with you," he doesn't view these statements as inimical to a successful marriage. (Since both films were released nearly a decade earlier, Robinson enduring a retread of *Two Seconds* and *Tiger Shark* didn't seem to matter to Jerry Wald and Richard Macauley, again indulging their prodigious recycling tendencies.)

The wedding reception is an undisguised remake of the same event in *Tiger Shark*, with Eddie doing another of his convincing inebriation scenes as Hank is carted away by his bride and best buddy. Continuing their hijinks, McHugh and Hale do a little table-top choreography as Omaha and Jumbo drunkenly smash the wedding cake.

The remainder of the film focuses on Hank's naïve inability to recognize his wife's unhappiness. She actually attempts to be a "good wife" during the honeymoon, but eventually declares her love for Johnny—all of this done most *un*convincingly by Marlene Dietrich, who is as icy as the power lines that kill her on-screen father. One of Golden Age Hollywood's most distantly glacial actresses, she often was little more than a fascinatingly sculpted face, a Teutonic accent, and a shapely pair of legs. The two actresses who play her fellow clip-joint coworkers (Eve Arden and Joyce Compton) both exude more warm attraction in their brief scenes, making the depiction of two tough guys falling in love with an iceberg of such Titanic proportions even more unbelievable. Her synthetic blonde wig adds a visual stiffness to the overall dramatic inflexibility.

The volatility of the actors is well represented in two fight scenes, one set at the Midnight Club, where Johnny decks Smiley, beats two other men with a chair, then polishes off two more mugs with one of the wooden legs as he goes out the door. The other incident involves Hank's second pummeling of Eddie Adams, prompted by the larger man's insensitive remark about Fay. Hank calls him a "wiseguy" after smashing him (with a real punch) to the locker-room floor. This is the film's most tense moment, which is defused when the

Manpower (1941): Johnny Marshall (George Raft) helps break up a fight between Hank McHenry (Robinson) and Eddie Adams (Ward Bond). In reality, Bond and Alan Hale had to separate Robinson and Raft, who scuffled after shooting this scene, directed by Raoul Walsh (original lobby card).

two men shake hands. One can only speculate if Robinson's general anger on the set was increased by his distaste for Ward Bond's ultra-conservative politics, which became more blatant during and after World War II.

Johnny is nearly killed when a plane crashes into a power line, knocking him to the ground. (All of the emergency calls are carried out in darkness, rain and icy conditions.) At the hospital, Dietrich makes her most erotic gesture by taking a cigarette from Raft's mouth and smoking it herself, though she also performs this gesture with a total lack of emotion. Of course, Hank, still without a clue, invites Johnny to recuperate at their home. "Hi-ya, family," he says to them as he returns from work. While on the job, Johnny has been enjoying al fresco dining with Fay and friendly baseball games with the neighborhood boys. "Beat It! I'll take the rap," he says in Raft-fashion after smashing a window.

During a 10-day road assignment (Walsh rehashes his own material from *They Drive by Night*) also written by Wald and Macauley (featuring female and slot-machine harassment at a diner), Hank wires Fay to join them; but she packs and, accompanied by her two friends, drops in at the Midnight Club to ask Smiley for a job reference. Her timing is perfectly atrocious, and she is pinched in a police raid. While Hank is out at the site, Johnny answers a phone call from the slammer and agrees to bail her out. In a display of his steely eyed, tough-guy brutality, he slaps Fay hard, twice, knocking her down the steps in front of the police station. "Don't turn on the waterworks for me," he tells her. "It don't register." Raft shows how effective an actor, if cast properly, can be with an essentially one-note, understated performance; while Dietrich is merely tedious.

During a savage rainstorm, Adams quits, prompting Johnny to tender his resignation, though he agrees to do "one more" job for Hank. But when Fay admits to Hank that she is in love with Johnny, he *finally* realizes the truth and immediately flies into a jealous, murderous rage. Climbing up a tower, he takes after Johnny with a huge wrench, but fatally falls after his friend valiantly attempts to hold onto a strap that slips out of his hand. This event, a reverse of Robinson's accidental high-rise killing of Preston Foster in *Two Seconds*, provides *Manpower* with a dynamic remedy to the 20 minutes of feeble "love triangle" that precedes it, and also looks ahead to the apocalyptic refinery demise of Cagney in Walsh's *White Heat*. One of Warners' best directors of montage sequences, he builds the sequence dramatically by having his actors ascend geographically. (As he had used a mountain in *High Sierra*, he incorporates a tower here, then would provide his most unforgettable example in *White Heat*).

"Every time I get tangled with a dame," Hank says before he expires, "I do the wrong thing ... take care of her, Johnny." Walsh offers a last-minute twist when Fay walks to a rural bus stop. Johnny follows, but both of them are hidden from view when the bus arrives. The vehicle driving off while the couple walks back down the road is hardly the usual Hollywood closing clasp, but it still falls within classic generic conventions.

Dropped from *Manpower*, the insensed Bogart became even more outraged when his material slid back to the *Return of Dr. X./Virginia City* level. Now a studio messenger appeared, handing him the script for *Bad Men of Missouri*, to be directed by his *Wagons Roll* chum Ray Enright. Bogart's role? Western outlaw Cole Younger!

Ordered to meet with Enright, Bogie scrawled a message to Steve Trilling: "Are you kidding? ... This is certainly rubbing it in — since Lupino and Raft are casting pictures, maybe I can."[2] He had left the city and was relaxing aboard his boat at Balboa, where he couldn't be reached.

Jack Warner sent a legal notice to Bogart via registered mail — which went unanswered — then suspended him, and *Bad Men of Missouri* (1941) was filmed with Dennis Morgan in the Younger role. For months, Bogie remained defiantly estranged from Warners, until gossip monger Louella Parsons — who knew that suspended players were "off limits" — contacted the studio publicity department, demanding that he be able to appear on her radio show, *Hollywood Hotel*. Warner capitulated, having no idea what magnificence lie in store for "that bastard Bogart" just around the corner.

11

The Black Bird

John Huston renegotiated his Warner Bros. contract in 1941, grabbing a pay raise and the right to direct one film in return for his services as screenwriter. He chose to fill both production roles on a new adaptation of Dashiell Hammett's *The Maltese Falcon*, which he felt had been given short shrift by Warners, who had purchased the film rights for $8,500 in 1930. The studio's semi-serious version released the following year was followed by a screwball comedy attempt in 1936. "They were such wretched screenplays," he said, "no understanding, just assholes, idiots of what Dashiell Hammett had done."[1] The erudite Huston had the *radical* idea that a film could actually be faithful to its literary material. He later said:

> I wanted to be a director, and I think that Warner Bros. would have preferred for me to remain as a writer, rather than gamble on my talents as a director. They had no idea whether I'd be any good or not. It was in the way of an indulgence on their part, a very sporting one.[2]

Dashiell Hammett, born in St. Mary's County, Maryland, in 1894, worked for the Pinkerton detective agency in Baltimore, Spokane and San Francisco from 1915–21. Using his firsthand experiences with deception, corruption and violence, he sought to create a private investigator who differed from the accepted Sherlock Holmes deductive reasoner. His first two novels, *Red Harvest* and *The Dain Curse* (both 1929) were originally published in *The Black Mask*, the magazine that inaugurated the "hard-boiled detective," and followed the violent cases of a character called "The Continental Op."

The Maltese Falcon, published in 1930, was the first and only Hammett work to feature Sam Spade, for whom there was "no original." In 1934, Hammett revealed, "He is a dream man in the sense that he is what most of the private detectives I worked with would liked to have been and quite a few of them in their cockier moments thought they approached."[3] His other novels, *The Glass Key* (1931) and *The Thin Man* (1934) also were adapted into popular films.

On May 22, 1941, Huston met with Henry Blanke and studio manager Tenny Wright to discuss the new film, which would begin shooting on June 10, 1941, with a slim B-film budget of $381,000. The Warners suits "acted out of friendship toward me, out of good will," said Huston. "They agreed to give me a shot at it, and if it didn't come off all that well, they wouldn't be too disappointed as it was to be a very small picture."[4]

In the days that followed, Blanke cast three supporting actors, Mary Astor (four weeks at $2,500 per), who had just signed a two-picture contract; freelance character star Peter Lorre (five weeks at $2,000); and cinematic neophyte Sydney Greenstreet (four weeks at $2,500), whom Huston had seen on stage in *There Shall Be No Light* at Los Angeles' Biltmore Theatre. By June 5, the crew assignments had been made, but the lead role of Sam Spade had yet to be cast.

Bogart had participated in wardrobe tests with Astor the previous day, but the part was promised to — naturally — George Raft, whose contract didn't grant story approval but did rule out B-film assignments. Huston argued with Blanke and casting director Steve Trilling, but they insisted the role had to be offered to bad boy George. The studio, wanting to borrow Henry Fonda from 20th Century–Fox for the upcoming film *The Male Animal*, also told Raft that he could decline the Spade part if he wished to be loaned to Darryl F. Zanuck's outfit. Considering *Falcon* another unimportant picture—and not wanting to work with a first-time director—he turned it down.

Jack Warner had confoundedly tolerated Raft's antics—including his dishonest financial dealings with the studio, violent behavior and constant use of goons who accompanied him to film sets—for far too long. On June 10, Bogart was taken off suspension and happily reported to the studio to begin acting for Huston, a collaboration that would create some of the best Hollywood films over the next decade. The supporting roles were filled out with Jerome Cowan as Spade's ill-fated partner, Miles Archer; the great Gladys George (who had played Panama in *The Roaring Twenties*) as Iva, Archer's widow and Spade's mistress; Elisha Cook, Jr., as the weasel-like gunsel, Wilmer Cook; Barton MacLane as Lieutenant Dundy; and Ward Bond as Spade's pal, Detective Tom Polhaus.

Huston had the advantage of assembling the ideal cast, avoiding the problems Roy Del Ruth encountered for the 1931 programmer, which is populated with actors who merely play stock Warners characters of the era: especially Dudley Digges as a decidedly *non*-obese, over-the-top "Fat Man," and the usually interesting Dwight Frye, who has *nothing* to do as Wilmer Cook.

Even Walter Huston briefly appears as the ill-fated Captain Jacobi, an unbilled cameo he did to wish his son good luck. In return, John—who could be brutal to fellow filmmakers—made his father do numerous takes, after which the elder Huston went home rather bruised and very irritated. The following day, Mary Astor, impersonating John's secretary, called Walter, claiming, "Mr. Huston is sorry, but something happened to the film in the lab and we'll have to retake your sequence this afternoon. Could you be ready to shoot at one o'clock?"

Walter replied, "You tell my son to get another actor or go to hell!"[5]

Huston laboriously sketched rough storyboards of each shot, then held rehearsals, but these efforts ultimately saved time during the actual shooting. Inspired by his mentor, William Wyler, with whom he had worked on *Jezebel* (1938), he filmed many scenes in long takes, and wasted little stock on re-takes. Impressed by Hammett's unique prose style, he attempted to create a visual counterpart through a combination of lighting, angles and camera movement. Nearly every chapter and section is faithfully scripted, and nearly all the dialogue is represented verbatim or in carefully edited passages. Often, an excellent novel proves a huge hindrance to screenwriters (as *The Maltese Falcon* did for Maude Fulton and Brown Holmes, who jettisoned Hammett's complexities to create a simple, seriocomic skeleton for their 1931 attempt), but such was not the case with Huston, who became one of the first filmmakers at a major Hollywood studio to fill the duties of both sole screenwriter and director on the same feature film.

To wring realistic performances from his cast, Huston also took the unorthodox route of shooting the film in sequence, rather than choosing to structure it later in the cutting room. This caused some concern among the studio suits, but the director stood his ground and delivered the goods. Mary Astor said, "He'd had the wit to keep Hammett's book intact. His shooting script was a precise map of what went on. Every shot, camera move, entrance, exit was down on paper, leaving nothing to chance, inspiration or invention."[6]

Huston said:

The Maltese Falcon (1941): Sam Spade (Bogart) is visited by his mistress, Iva (Gladys George), wife of his late partner, Miles Archer, in John Huston's seminal film noir masterpiece (original lobby card).

> The story was a dramatization of myself, of how I felt about things. Hammett's mentality and philosophy were quite congenial to me … I attempted to transpose his highly individual style into camera terms with sharp photography, geographically exact camera movements, and striking but not shocking setups.[7]

Hammett's sensibilities indeed were agreeable to Huston, as the writer often became involved in left-wing political causes; like the famous "Hollywood Ten," he spent some time in the slammer because of his convictions.

Due to the Production Code, the only passages Huston had to alter were those of a sexual nature, including one involving Brigid sleeping over with Spade (which he diluted), and a later incident in which Spade, searching for a $1000 bill, insists that she "take her clothes off" in his bathroom (which he replaced with Spade simply trusting her on this count). The 1931 version includes the original material, including a gratuitous nude scene of Bebe Daniels in the bathtub, while eliminating important plot structure and character development that would have dramatically improved the film. After all, it was these pre-Production Code scenes that led to the outcry for censorship, which ultimately forced filmmakers to be much more creative when slipping in sexy material.

Other overt Hammett references that posed a problem for Huston were those involving profanity (seven different swear words) and the gay characters. In the novel, a desk clerk at the St. Mark's Hotel is a "red-haired dandy," and Effie Perine calls Joel Cairo "queer," while Spade once uses the term "fairy"; but more innocuous dialogue, such as the private eye's references to Lieutenant Dundy as Tom Polhaus' "boyfriend" sailed right through the PCA screening.

After viewing the dailies of the early scenes, Hal Wallis became worried over Bogart's leisurely approach to Spade, thinking the actor had abandoned his familiar, fast-paced delivery. Ordered to re-shoot, Huston managed to crank Bogie back up to his famous staccato style. The rehearsals paid off during the many long takes, with the camera moving from one character to the next, often for minutes at a time. Huston created a style based on "real-time" movement for a concrete reason. He wanted the audience to be privy only to events actually experienced by the detective. "The book was told entirely from the standpoint of Sam Spade, so also was the picture,"[8] he explained.

By the third week of the shoot, Huston was two days ahead of schedule. Even the arrival of Greenstreet, whose inexperience required extra rehearsal, didn't slow him down. The climactic scene, set in Spade's apartment and played in real time (comprising 20 percent of the film), could have posed an intimidating challenge for the most seasoned veterans; but Huston carefully choreographed and rehearsed the interactions of Bogart, Astor, Lorre, Greenstreet and Cook, inaugurating in fine fashion "the Huston style" while creating one of the most powerful, unforgettable scenes in motion picture history. Bogart's performance alone is "the stuff dreams are made of."

Having created a masterpiece sequence, Huston ends it (and the film) with a monosyllabic line from Ward Bond, who gets the last word — and the last laugh. Described by Hammett as having "thick" facial features, Tom Polhaus, played substantially as written, proved perfect casting for Bond. Following Spade's explanation that the "dingus" is "the stuff dreams are made of" (Bogart wrote the line), Polhaus responds, "Huh?" and the characters walk into the fade-out.

The screenplay had included the actual concluding scene from the novel (in which Iva Archer reunites with Spade in his office), but it was eliminated at the last minute, allowing the production to wrap at $327,182, a full $54,000 under budget, an economic fact that endeared Huston to Jack Warner and Hal Wallis. Though Warner originally had planned to give Astor top billing above the title, with Bogart below (in type 75 percent of the title's size), he reconsidered, declaring *The Maltese Falcon* the first "Bogart film," with the actor's name *above* the title and in the same size type.

Astor remarked that, rather than an actor becoming absorbed into his character, the reverse occurred with Sam Spade, a literary creation that benefited by becoming Bogart. During the shoot, Bogie followed Cagney's acting "method" of *listening* to the other performers, looking right at them, and telling them the truth. Astor's comment is only half true, however, because Samuel Spade and Humphrey Bogart, equally strong, charismatic entities (one literary and one literal) form the ideal *union* on screen.

Hammett's physical description of Spade in the novel more closely resembles Boris Karloff's "Hjalmar Poelzig" in Universal's horror classic *The Black Cat* (1934) than any character ever played by Bogart. From the very first paragraph, Hammett vividly visualizes his hard-boiled hero, then instantly establishes his attitude:

> Samuel Spade's jaw was long and bony, his chin a jutting v under the more flexible v of his mouth. His nostrils curved back to make another, smaller v. His yellow-gray eyes were horizontal. The v motif was picked up again by thickish brows rising outward from twin creases above a hooked nose, and his pale brown hair grew down — from high flat temples — in a point on his forehead. He looked rather pleasantly like a blond satan.
> He said to Effie Perine: "Yes, sweetheart?"

From the outset, Huston was handed the perfect role for Bogart, one that already existed on the page before he even set out to *adapt* anything for his screenplay. Hammett's dialogue became music in Bogie's mouth, and drove the actor's performance, which — thanks to the director's unorthodox shooting schedule — he was able to build dynamically from the first scene to the last. Moreover, dialogue phrases like "Yes, sweetheart," "And when you're slapped you'll take it and like it" and "I won't play the sap for you" became indelibly tied to the actor. His milestone interpretation of Sam Spade determined the development of the Bogart persona for the rest of his career.

Bogie's approach created one of the most dynamic performances ever filmed, proving how an actor with an already strong persona could reinvent himself in a particular role, one that becomes even more powerful when viewed against the smug, patronizing, one-dimensional version of the character played by Ricardo Cortez in the 1931 film. In chapter three, Hammett describes one of Spade's unique facial mannerisms — "He drew his lips back over his teeth in an impatient grimace" — a tick that Bogie had already used in some previous films, but here ineradicably adds to his style. Spade *carefully* rolls his own cigarettes throughout the novel (one of Hammett's descriptions comprises an entire paragraph), giving Bogart a truly legitimate cinematic excuse to indulge his tobacco addiction. Like so many other elements superbly rendered by Huston in this film, the smokes also establish an essential atmospheric element of film noir.

Bogie enjoyed himself during production, especially during his martini lunches with Huston and fellow actors at the Lakeside Country Club. Huston's scheduling and approach to shooting *Falcon* had allowed the entire troupe to develop close friendships, also allowing Bogie to break free from Mayo's grasp for a time. In fact, Huston absolutely hated Mayo, and could not fathom why the actor wanted anything to do with her.

The Maltese Falcon not only netted Huston a new pal, but a new career of legendary proportions, one the director began with supreme narrative economy, a written prologue establishing pertinent details about the Black Bird that Hammett saved for chapter 13, more than halfway into the complicated novel:

> In 1539, the Knight Templars of Malta, paid tribute to Charles V of Spain, by sending him a Golden Falcon encrusted from beak to claw with rarest jewels — but pirates seized the galley carrying this priceless token and the fate of the Maltese Falcon remains a mystery to this day ...

Though the Black Bird is not revealed until the final scene, the statuette is shown behind this prologue and the atmospheric titles, the most stunning to grace a Golden Age Warners film.

Huston and Arthur Edeson's compositions, many involving complicated camera movements, are as consistently perfect as the writing and casting, some of them giving a widescreen impression though shot in the standard 1.33 to 1 ratio. In the initial scene, showing the two detectives seated at their desks (Archer at left, Spade at right, with their names looming above them on the office window), Jerome Cowan and Bogart are literally brushing against the edges of the frame with their backs, an image that not only impresses visually but also shows the personal gulf between them.

Aside from a major condensation involving Spade's search of Brigid O'Shaughnessy's room and the arrival and burning of the ship *La Paloma*, and a few brief passages not essential to the plot, the film closely follows the novel. Brigid, using the name "Miss Wonderly," hires Spade and Archer to shadow Floyd Thursby, a violent man who has followed her "sister" to San Francisco. When Archer is murdered, Spade meets Sergeant Tom Polhaus at the scene, then is questioned at his apartment by the cop and his lieutenant, Dundy, about this murder and the subsequent killing of Thursby.

In his office the next day, Spade is visited by Iva Archer, widow of the deceased — and

The Maltese Falcon (1941): A cast that dreams are made of: Lieutenant Dundy (Barton MacLane), after cuffing Sam Spade (Bogart) on the chin, stands by as Sergeant Tom Polhaus (Ward Bond) tells the detective to "stop it ... take it easy." The entire incident was sparked by Brigid O'Shaughnessy (Mary Astor), who pistol-whipped little Joel Cairo (Peter Lorre), seeker of "The Black Bird" (original lobby card).

his girlfriend. Retained by Brigid—from whom he is able to extract *some* accurate information about Thursby—the detective then is visited by the mysterious, effeminate Joel Cairo, who offers him $5,000 to find "the Black Bird," holds him at gunpoint, is temporarily knocked unconscious, then sticks him up again! Shadowed conspicuously by Wilmer Cook, who keeps a vigil outside his apartment, Spade meets that evening with Brigid and Cairo, who yells for help while the detective is trying to ditch Dundy and Polhaus at the door. Spade convinces the cops that Brigid's pistol-whipping of the little man was actually a way to "test" them, Cairo leaves, and she stays late, still half-lying about the true history of the Black Bird.

At the Hotel Belvedere the following morning, Spade confronts Cook in the lobby—"People lose teeth talking like that"—then later meets Casper Gutman, the "Fat Man," in his room. When Sydney Greenstreet makes his screen debut, his obesity is shocking, although his elegant dress and carriage present a somewhat more attractive figure than Hammett's original:

> The fat man was flabbily fat with bulbous pink cheeks and lips and chins and neck, with a great soft egg of a belly that was all his torso, and pendant cones for arms and legs. As he advanced to meet Spade all his bulbs rose and shook and fell separately with each step, in the manner of clustered soap-bubbles not yet released through the pipe through which they had been blown.

Huston compensates for Greenstreet's less grotesque appearance by using low angle shots basically placing the camera in the actor's crotch.

Feigning anger over Gutman's unwillingness to reveal the secrets of the Black Bird, Spade storms out, then drops in on District Attorney Bryan (John Hamilton), whom he frustrates with his own concealment of the facts. Delivering razor-sharp dialogue in his rapid-fire style, Bogart is exhilarating as Spade asks the stenographer, "Getting this all right, son? Or am I going too fast for you?" Returning to the Fat Man's lair, he masterfully disarms Cook of two .45 pistols, then insists, "Let's talk about the Black Bird."

Providing the intrigue of a sweeping adventure in the middle of the film, Gutman finally tells the tale, then slips Spade a mickey. As in the novel, the detective attempts to leave, but is tripped and kicked in the head by the psychotic "boy." Regaining consciousness, he then searches Brigid's room and witnesses the burning *La Paloma*. Back at the office, the mortally wounded Captain Jacobi stumbles in and drops a large, newspaper-wrapped package to the floor, babbling, "You know—the Falcon," before he expires.

"We've got it, Angel! We've got it!" rejoices Spade, instructing Effie to report the death of Jacobi but not mention "the bundle." He then leaves to check the Black Bird at the Union Bus Terminal before investigating a hysterical phone call supposedly made by Brigid (which turns out to be a ploy to lure him away from the office). "You're a good man, Sister," he tells Effie on his way out.

The remaining 27 minutes of the film involve the brilliant final confrontation between Spade and all the principal Falcon seekers at his apartment, including the detective's insistence that Cook serve as the "fall guy" for the murders, haggling over his fee, Effie's delivery of the statuette, his revelation that Brigid bumped off Archer, and the arrival of Dundy and Polhaus. Bogart crescendos like a brilliant musician, unleashing mesmerizing though supremely controlled pyrotechnics as Spade tells her, "Maybe you love me and maybe I love you ... I'll have some rotten nights after I've sent you over, but maybe that will pass." The overlapping dialogue in this breathtaking scene (something the film shares with *Citizen Kane*, along with Huston and Edeson's photographing of actual ceilings in the sets), combined with the real-time performances of Bogart and Astor, helps make the film timeless.

Though Bogart is the peak of the performance pyramid, the entire cast is the exemplary, essential foundation. In his film debut, Greenstreet is dazzling, with Lorre providing the ideal physical counterpoint, as well as a hysterical, whimpering foil to the Fat Man's monumentally calm, yet sometimes slightly giddy, demeanor. Lorre's outburst when Cairo realizes the Falcon is a fake—"You imbecile! You bloated idiot" (taken verbatim from the novel)—is alternately wicked and hilarious. (Cairo is arguably the Hungarian actor's finest English-language performance, perhaps rivaled only by his tour de force characterization in Robert Florey's heartbreaking *The Face Behind the Mask* [Columbia, 1940].) Though not referred to by any homosexual term in the film, Cairo's curly "hairdo" (which is "smooth" in the novel) and carrying of a phallic cane/umbrella, which he holds close to his face during his initial discussion with Spade (matched by Elisha Cook's neurotic behavior when emasculated from his .45s on two occasions), was Huston's way of suggesting Hammett's original "queer" depiction. The director's uncanny eye for casting is also supported by Hammett's line, in chapter seven, that Cairo's "eyes, though the throttling pressure on his throat made them bulge, were cold and menacing."

Huston, in casting Dundy, gave the usually unlikeable Barton MacLane a chance to play a somewhat more ambiguous character (as in the novel), nearly matching Ward Bond (in his best performance in a film not directed by John Ford) as Polhaus. Hammett's colorful and tough dames are also well-represented: Astor as the conniving, self-interested Brigid; Gladys George as the troubled Iva; and, especially, the superb Lee Patrick as the ineffable Effie Perine. Only one female in the novel (Gutman's daughter, Rhea) is not included.

Huston's attention to detail, apparent from his faithful adaptation, is also represented by what *isn't* in Hammett's original. In the novel, when Spade tells Brigid she's being sent up, he mentions, "Well, if you get a good break you'll be out of San Quentin in twenty years and you can come back to me then." In 1930 this was an accurate statement; but, after California opened the Tahachapi women's penitentiary in 1933, female prisoners were no longer sent to San Quentin — hence Spade's mention of "Tahachapi" in the 1941 script.

The film, which cost a mere $381,000, did moderate business at the box office, but was a critical favorite, garnering praise for Huston and Bogart, and Academy Award nominations for Best Picture, Best Screenplay, and Best Supporting Actress for Astor. Jack Warner was pleased with the positive press, and agreed with Hal Wallis that the somewhat disappointing financial returns were the result of insufficient publicity. Though they had ended up with something light years ahead of a B film, *The Maltese Falcon* unfortunately had been marketed that way.

The following spring, *Falcon* was topped for Best Picture by the John Ford masterpiece *How Green Was My Valley* (1941), joining *Citizen Kane* in the losers' circle. Astor won, and Huston (for his screenplay) and Greenstreet were nominated, but — in one of scores of instances of inexplicable Academy behavior (though this time a travesty) — Bogart was ignored. The *style* of the picture certainly was noticed. Arguably, the entire film noir cycle — perhaps the only truly American "art film" genre — rarely produced other films to rival this initial effort.

> **Bart Aikens**
> Film Noir Aficionado and "Garage Cinema" Pioneer, Hollywood
> on
> ***The Maltese Falcon***
>
> The only man I think Sam Spade likes and respects is Tom Polhaus — Ward Bond — a fair-minded detective who halts Brigid O'Shaughnessy's assault on Joel Cairo by pushing her into a chair and scolding, "That's no way to act!"
>
> Two of Spade's most amusing moments for me are when he describes Lieutenant Dundy as Polhaus' "boyfriend" and "playmate."

12

Whacking the Axis

Cagney's next Warner Bros. picture, *Captains of the Clouds* (1942), filmed during the summer of 1941, reflected the growing pro-war climate in the United States. Norman Reilly Raine resurrected the insubordinate Cagney of his *Fighting 69th* script, and, teaming with Arthur T. Horman and Richard Macauley, created the character of Brian MacLean, a Canadian bush pilot who volunteers to train flyers under the British Commonwealth Air Training Plan.

Cagney enjoyed shooting on location in North Bay, Ontario, where Michael Curtiz and cinematographers Sol Polito and Wilfred M. Cline — augmented by the aerial camera work of Elmer Dyer, Charles Marshall and Winton C. Hoch — captured the stunning beauty of Canadian forests and lakes in Technicolor. Curtiz also allowed Cagney to improvise much of his own dialogue in scenes with old pals Alan Hale and George Tobias (in another of his endless "ethnic" roles), and young Warners heartthrob Dennis Morgan. Some of the action proved grueling, particularly a sequence involving Cagney, Hale and Morgan landing a plane and jumping out of the cockpit before sprinting out of camera range. Due to logistics and blocking problems, Curtiz called for several takes. "We wore out three sets of cadets," recalled Cagney.[1]

Captains of the Clouds was Jim's second Warners aviation picture in a row (and his fourth overall), but his very first to feature material connected to World War II. This preparedness extravaganza also introduced his red hair to the cinema, an element that adds to his ever-cocky, Irish-Canadian, aerial daredevil. Curtiz carefully introduces each of the four main bush pilots: "Blimp" Lebec (Tobias), a light-hearted French-Canadian; Francis Patrick "Tiny" Murphy (Hale) and Johnny Dutton (Morgan), two cooperative carriers; and MacLean, who uses every dirty trick in the book to steal others' business. A fifth pilot, "Scrounger" Harris (Reginald Gardiner), an Englishman displaced by the Blitz, also flies along their routes.

Captains is a clumsy attempt to remake two earlier Cagney films and string them together. The first half, focusing on MacLean's arrogant attitude in the sky (his unnecessarily dangerous routines) and on the ground (his pursuit of Dutton's girl, Emily Foster [Brenda Marshall]), is based on *Devil Dogs of the Air*; while the second, featuring MacLean's reckless, fatal disregard for military orders, is a World War II color update of *The Fighting 69th*.

None of the other bush pilots can tolerate MacLean, but after he receives a skull fracture from his plane's propeller, Dutton flies through fog to Churchtown, where he picks up Dr. Neville (J. Farrell MacDonald). During MacLean's recuperation from surgery, while Dutton and Murphy are off taking over his accounts, Emily works her wiles on Brian, who vows to show her all the major cities, where he will be waiting for other men, "with a baseball bat, beating them off." But after Murphy tells MacLean the truth about Dutton's role in saving his life, he leaves Emily to return to work. Flashing a classic Cagney "broad-bashing" scowl, he effortlessly picks her up and sets her on a table.

Captains of the Clouds (1942): In his first Technicolor film, Cagney is joined by Dennis Morgan in Warners' propaganda tribute to the Royal Canadian Air Force, directed by Michael Curtiz (original lobby card).

MacLean warns Dutton, "You marry Emily, and you'll have no more airline than a jackrabbit," then resorts to violence to teach his new partner some sense.

"That sure was a businesslike shellackin'," Murphy compliments, "but that won't stop him from marrying her."

Determined to end the affair, MacLean flies back to the camp, flashes $4,000 in Emily's face, and they elope. Dutton follows them, starts another fight in their hotel room, then enlists in the Royal Canadian Air Force, an impulsive act that, coupled with MacLean's abandonment of Emily (and the four grand) after the wedding night, awkwardly closes the film's first half and abruptly opens the second.

At Willie's Chinese Restaurant, their favorite hangout, MacLean, Murphy, Lebec and Harris listen to Winston Churchill deliver a speech over the radio. Instantly, they unanimously decide to join the RCAF and outlandishly land their planes on a runway at the Air Force base. Ordered to leave and enlist in the proper manner, they do so, only to discover they are too old to fight and, regardless of their flight experiences, have to start over "at the beginning"—to train, not to be fly boys, but instructors.

The film's second hour is an endless parade of training exercises, shifting the narrative from mediocre, but visually stunning (thanks to Ontario *and* Brenda Marshall) adventure to staid, preachy propaganda. The many plot contrivances are large enough to fly an RCAF plane through, especially the constant presence of Dutton as MacLean's trainer (a rehash of the O'Brien-Cagney relationship in *Devil Dogs*). At one point during a training flight, MacLean, as he ignores orders and spins recklessly, inexplicably (in a Cagney improvisation) speaks Yiddish to Dutton.

"All he wants to do is get across and fight," Dutton informs their commander.

Delivering a line essential to all military preparedness films, a cadet adds, "Don't we all?" Max Steiner's jaunty musical score constantly accompanies the happiness these men express at the very notion of bombing "Herr Shicklgruber." (The name "Hitler" is never mentioned.)

Court-martialed for seriously injuring a cadet while ignoring flight regulations, MacLean joins the washed-out Murphy, singing and *dancing* together in a bar. Cagney made a personal musical contribution, writing new verses for the Canadian war song, "Bless 'Em All," which he and Hale sing during the scene. Picking up a newspaper, MacLean rattles off statistics about Air Marshall William A. "Billy" Bishop. Again, their patriotic zeal immediately moves them to action.

The actual Billy Bishop appears in the next scene, taking part in an RCAF wings awarding ceremony, during which the two sky devils dive at the cadets' formation. Murphy hot dogs a bit too much, passes out, crashes and is burned to an unrecognizable crisp. The diving incident is even more ludicrous than the bush pilots' earlier base landing, but Cagney recalled it as one of his favorite moments, one credited with inspiring several young American men to enlist in the RCAF.

Emily makes her contrived reappearance during the second half, running into Dutton at a club and telling the truth about her "marriage." "Don't you see, Johnny? You owe Brian a lot." Yes, he does, if only to bring Cagney back into the film, which becomes even more deadly dull after MacLean disappears.

Also stripped of his civilian pilot's license, MacLean returns to re-enlist, using the identity of "Francis Patrick Murphy." Two transports of pilots and instructors have crashed, and the RAF is desperate for more Canadian flyers. MacLean tells Dutton, "There's only one thing that's important—that I can fly that bomber!" Soon, the reunited pair are joined in the air by fellow fly boys Lebec and Harris.

In sight of England, a lone Messerschmidt dives its deadly swastika at the gallant Canadians. Lebec and Harris are both killed by machine-gun fire, but MacLean, against orders (of course), breaks formation and plummets toward the "Heinie," going kamikaze to blast both of them into the sea. As Dutton and company fly toward Old Blighty, Churchill's voice accompanies Warners' credit to all the military personnel depicted in the film.

By the time *Captains of the Clouds* was released on February 12, 1942, the student pilots on screen already were involved in combat with Germany. Saddled with such straightforward propaganda, Michael Curtiz was stylistically hamstrung; but his next two Warners projects, produced back-to-back, and also reflecting the realities of World War II, are saturated with his cinematic prowess. Released during the second half of 1942, both *Yankee Doodle Dandy* and *Casablanca* are not only two of the greatest Warner Bros. Wiseguys titles, but also two of the best motion pictures ever produced in the United States.

On the very talons of the *Maltese Falcon*, Bogart was rushed into *All Through the Night* during the autumn of 1941, playing big-time Brooklyn gambler Alfred "Gloves" Donahue, in a script by Leonard Spigelglass and Edwin Gilbert — with additions by the Epstein Brothers — blending gangster overtones with levity and a mob of Nazi fifth columnists. Incredibly, this brew was based on fact. Producer Jerry Wald had heard a story from his brother, Malvin — who worked for the Brooklyn *World*—that Jewish gangsters often tipped off the paper's editor regarding the activities of Nazis holding meetings in Yorkville. At times, the Hebrew wiseguys even wreaked a little physical havoc on Adolf's boys in the borough.

The exemplary cast, which includes Frank McHugh, Barton MacLane, William Demarest and a young Jackie Gleason, is also loaded with refugees from Hitler's Reich: Peter Lorre, back for his second of several films with Bogart; Conrad Veidt, in a warm-up for *Casablanca*; and Kaaren Verne, Lorre's ex-wife. The film, completed in mid-October 1941 (seven weeks before the Japanese attack on Pearl Harbor), was released on January 10, 1942 (one month after the United States entered the war), and was an early entry in the official wartime "all Hollywood films should fight the Axis" campaign waged by the Office of War Information.

Bogart's move at Warners from second-rate (late 1930s series) to top gangster (*High Sierra*), to cool-headed noir hero in *The Maltese Falcon* just prefaced the government "takeover" of the film industry. As the studios geared up to "help win the war" by including Axis-oriented material in the majority of their prestige and popular genre films, Bogie became Warners' top anti-Nazi star until the end of the conflict.

As Bogie, Conrad Veidt and Kaaren Verne are billed above the title in the opening credits, the melody of "Deutschland Uber Alles" invades Adolph Deutsch's score. The pals of Gloves Donahue use toy soldiers to plan an English counter-attack against the Krauts, while the "boss" himself enters the eating establishment, demanding his daily fix of Miller's Bakery cheesecake. Served National cheesecake as a close "substitute," he is infuriated. "You tell Charlie to take his cheesecake from Miller's, or else," he threatens as he leaves the joint.

This culinary outrage leads Gloves into a night-long odyssey of discovering the body of Papa Miller (Ludwig Stossel) stashed in his bakery basement; "Miss Hamilton" (Verne), a sultry Teutonic songbird coerced into supporting the Reich to save her father; a "goggle-eyed little rat named Pepi" (Lorre); Hal Ebbing (Veidt), a top Nazi operative masquerading as an antiques auctioneer who always carries a dachshund; and an attempt to blow up "the newest American battleship." During his anti-terrorist endeavors, Gloves also struggles to evade the local coppers, who have accused him of murdering Joe Denning (Edward Brophy), the partner of Duchess Club owner Marty Callahan (Barton MacLane). Murdered by the Nazi goons, Joe is discovered with "a glove found near the body ... identified as the property of Gloves Donahue, man about town and a well-known figure in the sporting world."

Some typical period "racial humor" invades the film when Deacon, a.k.a. "Saratoga," Donahue's African American valet (Sam McDaniel, brother of the immortal Hattie), is shining his shoes. "Excuse me, boss," Saratoga apologizes.

"Hey, Saratoga?" Gloves asks.

"Yassir?" he replies.

"Isn't that my tie you got on?" Gloves observes.

"Yassir."

"And my shirt?"

"Yassir."

"What are you doing with my belt?"

"You don't want your pants to fall down, do you, boss?" concludes Saratoga.

Barney (Frank McHugh), Gloves' chauffeur, enters to announce his marriage, and Annabelle (Jean Ames), his new bride, is disgusted when he runs out with the rest of the gang. Stomping her foot, she complains, "Married twenty minutes, and already I'm a widow!"

"Don't worry, Miss," counsels Saratoga. "Things ain't always as black as dey looks."

This inclusion of an Uncle Tom character in an anti-fascist film is a cinematic reflection of the segregated reality of the United States in early 1942 and the rampant discrimination that would be experienced by African American servicemen drafted into fighting against the racist Axis powers over the next three years. (The military would finally be desegregated by Execu-

All Through the Night (1942): Professional gambler Alfred "Gloves" Donahue (Bogart) and his sidekick, "Sunshine" (William Demarest), are guarded by Pepi (Peter Lorre), a little "goggle-eyed" Nazi saboteur, in Warners' fact-inspired wartime wiseguy film (original lobby card).

tive Order 9981, issued by President Harry S. Truman on July 26, 1948.) Interestingly, Warner Bros., the New Deal studio, would also create a positive, somewhat progressive, depiction of a Black character, another Bogart sidekick, later that same year, in a little film called *Casablanca*.

Aided by Gloves, Miss Hamilton — actually Uda Hammel, born in Nurnberg in 1917 — accidentally discovers that her father, Ludwig, recently died of "natural causes" at the Dachau concentration camp. During his efforts to rouse his fellow tough guys into action, Gloves tells Callahan:

> Trackin' down this Hamilton doll, I uncovered a nest of fifth columnists, fivers, *spies* to you. Pepi was one of them. That's what Joe found out, and that's why Pepi knocked him off.... Listen, Marty, I know you're no mental giant, but try to juggle this, all of you. I got a first-hand report tonight on what it's like on the other side, from that Hamilton babe — and, brother, I'm telling you, we gotta watch our steps. Those babies are strictly no good from way down deep. They're no bunch of petty racketeers tryin' to muscle in on some small territory. They wanna move in wholesale, take over the whole country.... Now listen, Big Shot, they'll tell you what time you get up in the morning and what time you go to bed at night. They'll tell you what you eat, what kind of clothes you can wear, what you drink. They'll even tell you the morning paper you can read.

Donahue's speech has the desired effect. "I'll help you track down them coyotes, Partner," vows one of Barney's "cowboy" pals.

Another "wrangler" admits, "I tackled 'em in 1918, and I ain't afraid to tackle 'em now!"

Even Saratoga is allowed in on the game at this point. "Me, too," he chimes in. "They're gonna make a warmonger out of me yet."

The most entertaining scene involves Gloves and "Sunshine" (William Demarest) impersonating "two munitions experts from Detriot" who have traveled to New York to set the charge to blow up the battleship. After punching out the real saboteurs, they attend a 3 a.m. meeting, where they unleash an onslaught of rapid Germanic gibberish that even party organizer Steindorff (Martin Kosleck) can't understand. After Gloves' boys, supported by Callahan's mob, crash the party, Donahue confronts Ebbing on the docks, where a speed boat has been loaded with explosives. Forced to drive the boat, Gloves takes it to the limit, turns a quick left, dives into the water, and sends Ebbing and the threat to national security exploding into an unmanned lumber barge!

Declared "National Hero Number One" for defeating the Nazi fifth column in a single night, Gloves remains modest. When Miss Hamilton declares, "It's about time someone knocked the Axis back on its heels," he counters, "It's about time someone knocked those heels on their Axis."

Bogart improvises throughout the film, including the use of his trademark terms "kid" (for Verne) and "sweetheart" (for cop James Burke). Edging more toward ambivalently heroic characters, he vowed to foil the enemy, not only on screen, but also in real life. Too old to be drafted, he took the skipper's exam and joined the United States Coast Guard Auxiliary of Southern California, using his 38-foot boat *Sluggy* to patrol the coast on weekends.

Robinson returned to Warner Bros. in the late autumn of 1941, still slated to star in *The Night Before Christmas*, now titled *Larceny, Inc.* (1942), about a criminal and his dimwitted sidekicks who buy a luggage store so they can tunnel into the bank vault next door. Rather than accept his usual fee, Robinson, knowing that the U.S. soon would be involved in the war, had Warners donate the $100,000 to the U.S.O. It was further evidence that he was focusing more on social issues, particularly anti-Semitism and the aggression of the Third Reich, and less on vehicles like *Larceny, Inc.* When he and Gladys sponsored a December 3 Shrine Auditorium concert to promote the Russian Benefit Committee, the FBI logged another leftist strike against him, although he merely was doing all he could to support those already fighting Hitler.

World War II isn't directly mentioned in *Larceny, Inc.*, but there are references to the "defense tax" and how "defense priority" affects city construction projects. J. Chalmers "Pressure" Maxwell (Robinson) first appears as a catcher in a baseball game held in the yard at Sing Sing, where he and his pal, Jug Martin (Broderick Crawford), are waiting to be released. In the prison office, Pressure meets with the Warden (Joseph Crehan), who feels enough sympathy to let the ex-con leave wearing his own pinstriped suit!

Back on the street, Pressure is reunited with Denny (Jane Wyman), daughter of late Mob boss Dutch Costello, who "met an untimely demise in a phone booth." Promising to go "legitimate," he fails to secure a $25,000 bank loan to finance a dog track, then decides to "borrow the dough *our* way." With his "partner," "Weepy" Davis (Edward Brophy), posing as a "man from the gas company," Pressure explores the basement of the luggage store next to the bank, then agrees to buy it from Homer Bigelow (Harry Davenport) for $1,000.

Pressure orders Jug to walk in front of a car, then demands money from the bewildered driver. Bigelow is paid off, Weepy steals a pick axe, and Jug begins to dig through the basement floor to tunnel toward the bank vault. The screenplay, adapted by Everett Freeman and Edwin Gilbert from a play by Laura and S. J. Perelman, relies on comedy much broader than that featured in Robinson's earlier crime spoofs. After a neighboring merchant, Mademoiselle Gloria (Barbara Jo Allen), pays a visit, she tells Pressure, "I wish you'd drop over sometime and look over my lingerie."

"Why don't you drop in sometime," he replies, "and look over my trunks."

Weepy intends to speed up the excavation operation by stealing a pneumatic drill from the WPA. Noticing an attractive woman in a barber shop, he tells Pressure she looks "love starved."

"Get back into that alley and make love to that drill," he replies. Soon, Weepy returns, with the power tool hidden in a Christmas tree.

Concerned about other merchants who might catch on to their plan, Pressure organizes them and meets with contractor J. J. McCarthy (William B. Davidson), pretending to be concerned about the completion of their torn-up street. Construction soon resumes, and Pressure is caught off guard: "How did I know that McCarthy was going to take me seriously?"

Denny discovers the drilling and takes steps to make sure the store is busy "every minute." Still digging, they are interrupted by Mr. Aspinwall (Grant Mitchell), an officer from the bank, who, intending to expand his building, offers Pressure $12,000 for the store. Busier than ever, Pressure is visited by the grateful merchants, then receives another offer from the bank, this time for $15,000. Enjoying the recent surge, he decides to keep the store open until the amount is increased to $20,000. "Goodbye, all you filthy capitalists!" says Denny as she leaves.

The arrival of Leo Dexter (Anthony Quinn), an escaped con seeking a piece of the action, pushes Pressure to ask Aspinwall for the 15 grand, a sum the bank won't have until the following week. When Bigelow wanders back in, Pressure agrees to sell the joint back to the old man for three grand. Dressed as Santa Claus, Jug stands watch while Leo drills away downstairs. Bigelow brings the three G's, but Dexter's stooge, Smitty (Joe Downing), pistol-whips him. The old man crawls to set off the burglar alarm, Smitty repeats his knock-out number on Pressure, and Dexter dynamites the basement wall, but the police arrive to arrest the gang. As the store burns, Pressure struggles to drag Bigelow out to safety, then hands the $3,000 to Denny.

Armed with a drawing for his new Maxwell Luggage store, Pressure tells Jug and Weepy he'll need 50 G's to build it. Both of them refuse to be hit by a car, and the boss insists, "We go our separate ways." His way takes him directly in front of a police sedan, but he staggers to his feet and all three run down the street (Three Stooges style) into the final fadeout. Directed by Lloyd Bacon, *Larceny, Inc.*, though an entertaining, consistently funny, well-acted film, fared poorly at the box office, and its frustrations soon would end Robinson's relationship with Warner Bros. (Nearly six decades later, Woody Allen would borrow the film's premise for his *Small Time Crooks* [2000].)

Philip and Julius Epstein were back for the final film of Cagney's Warner Bros. contract, *Yankee Doodle Dandy* (1942), joining screenwriters Robert Buckner and Edmund Joseph to create a cinematic portrait of multitalented theatrical legend George M. Cohan. Jim could not have asked for a better swansong, or a more appropriate patriotic shot in the arm for filmgoers thrust into a wartime environment. Bill Cagney had been wanting to find a vehicle that would powerfully wipe out any public suspicion about his brother's leftist, "un-American" attitudes; and the story of Cohan, who was seriously ill at the time, seemed tailor-made for him. Cohan wanted Fred Astaire to play him on the screen, but the elegant dancer, knowing he was completely wrong for the part, turned it down. Cagney revealed:

> Psychologically, I needed no preparation for *Yankee Doodle Dandy*. I didn't have to pretend to be a song-and-dance man. I was one.... [O]nce a song-and-dance man, always a song-and-dance man. In that brief statement, you have my life story; those few words tell as much about me professionally as there is to tell.[2]

Cohan spent several weeks working on the screenplay with Buckner, recalling the details

Larceny, Inc. (1942): As con man J. Chalmers "Pressure" Maxwell, Robinson, supported by Broderick Crawford and Jane Wyman, plays the final role under his Warner Bros. contract (original lobby card).

of his life, all of which were connected to the theater. He refused to allow any "romantic" scenes referring to his two marriages, so the fictional character of Mary (Joan Leslie) was invented to embody the positive qualities of both Cohan wives. When the draft of the script was sent to Cagney, he was astounded at its dead seriousness, with absolutely no inkling that Cohan was the creator of 42 Broadway comedies. Jim suggested that the Epsteins (who received no screen credit) rework the script before he started shooting the film with Michael Curtiz.

Screen tests began October 31, 1941, on Warners' Stage 3. Cagney was thrilled when his sister, Jeanne, was cast as Josie Cohan, George's sole sibling. The casting decision was not his, but made by Curtiz, who personally asked her to audition. The actors chosen for Cohan's parents also pleased him: the peerless Walter Huston (who had worked with Cohan on the stage) as Jerry and able Rosemary De Camp (who was 11 years *younger* than Cagney) as Nellie. Huston initially turned down the role, but Cagney exercised quick damage control, ordering the screenwriters to add a death scene for Jerry, an opportunity the shrewd actor couldn't resist.

Joan Leslie, who already had appeared with Bogart in *High Sierra* and *The Wagons Roll at Night*, was still only 17 years old. Always respectful of fellow actors, Cagney invited Joan to join him in his morning improvisational "rewriting" sessions, during which Curtiz allowed him to devise more appropriate dialogue.

Principal photography began on December 3, five days before FDR declared war on Japan. Shooting his first scene on December 12, Cagney, energized by the patriotic atmosphere, gave the part all he had — as an actor, singer and dancer — and continued to add his own unique contributions to the script, none of which were interfered with by Curtiz or the Warners executives.

Cagney played a variation on his own personality in the dialogue scenes, but expertly recreated Cohan's stage technique, particularly his choreography (again enhanced by Johnny Boyle), which combined stiff-legged strutting with a cocked-head, corner-of-the-eye glance at the audience. Cohan loved Jim's performance, but withheld his approval until his wife saw the film. After watching *Cagney*, Mrs. Cohan turned to her husband and said, "*You* were wonderful."

The only *Doodle* actor Jim disliked was contract player S. Z. "Cuddles" Sakall, a Hungarian who purposely spoke heavily accented, broken English—an affectation (like that of Margaret Lindsay) that drove him up the wall. In their one scene together, Sakall kept improvising bits of comic mumbling that overlapped Cagney's own dialogue. Angered, Jim took Curtiz aside, asking him to curtail Cuddles' shtick. The director refused to insult his fellow countryman, so Cagney took care of the problem himself, but Sakall still managed to slip in a mumbler that remains in the final cut.

Curtiz and William Cagney were very concerned about finding the right actor to portray one of the film's most important characters: President Franklin D. Roosevelt. After testing dozens of performers, they chose Captain Jack Young, an imitator who eventually played FDR in four feature films from 1942–44. Though Young appears on screen, his voice ultimately was overdubbed by Art Gilmore, another Roosevelt impressionist.

The Warners front office, very concerned with the vocal aspects of the soundtrack, even insisted that Cagney make a test recording before he was allowed to sing in his musical scenes. Jim loved to sing, but knew the limitations of his baritone voice. In the first place, Cohan's tenor had been just as unsure—a reality that led the composer to write his songs with simple melodies in major keys—so Cagney felt comfortable combining actual singing with talking some of the lyrics. Though Joan Leslie was an accomplished singer, the studio insisted that her songs be overdubbed by vocalist Sally Sweetland.

The film opens in 1942, as Cohan makes a long-awaited comeback, starring as FDR in the Rodgers and Hart Broadway show *I'd Rather Be Right*. (A singing and dancing Roosevelt is quite a fantastical characterization.) Following a rousing performance, he receives a letter from the President, requesting his presence at the White House, where an African American butler (Clinton Rosemond) leads Cohan up a flight of stairs to FDR's study. (This set is the film's recreation of Roosevelt's actual study, which he set up in the upstairs Yellow Oval Room, where he conducted most of his official business. The more familiar Oval Office, redesigned in 1933 by FDR and architect Eric Gugler, is on the *first* floor, in the West Wing of the White House, and includes no second storey.)

During his meeting with FDR, Cohan recalls his life story. Prior to the flashback, which comprises most of the 125-minute film, FDR mentions a newspaper review of *I'd Rather Be Right* that champions Cohan as a "better president" than the real Commander in Chief. Reminding Roosevelt that the comment was published in a *Republican* paper, Cohan begins his reminiscence "about 60 years ago," when Mr. and Mrs. Jerry Cohan were billed on vaudeville marquees. Jerry, dressed in a "stage Irish" costume, does a solo routine, then rushes home for Nellie's delivery of their son, George. It's the Fourth of July (Cohan actually was born on July 3, 1878), and a small U.S. flag is placed into the newborn's tiny hand.

Thrust onto the stage at an early age, George is teamed with a donkey. "I was a good Democrat, even in those days," Cohan (in a voice-over) informs FDR. At age 13, he plays the lead in *Peck's Bad Boy* and, developing an insufferably cocky attitude, declares himself a "star."

Yankee Doodle Dandy (1942): The Four Cohans: Nellie (Rosemary De Camp), Jerry (Walter Huston), Josie (Jeanne Cagney) and George (James Cagney). Jim won his Best Actor Academy Award in this Michael Curtiz wartime flagwaver (original lobby card).

In Philadelphia on the Fourth of July, prominent producer Edward Albee tries to hire "The Four Cohans," but George's arrogance nixes the offer, a selfish move that earns the boy a sound spanking from Jerry. Curtiz's casting couldn't have been more perfect: Douglas Croft, who plays the young George, proved equally as unruly to the director on the set.

A few years later, George, made up with white hair and long beard, is playing "his mother's father." After the performance, he is visited backstage by an aspiring young hoofer named Mary (Joan Leslie), who mistakes him for a wise old man. Hired to perform a specific song in the vaudeville show, Mary is urged by George to sing one of his original compositions. When the outraged manager drops the curtain, ending Mary's effort, George kicks him in the bum and is promptly fired.

Seeking a solo career as a composer of musical comedies, George, accompanied by Mary, auditions at the office of prominent Broadway producers Dietz (George Tobias) and Goff (Chester Clute). They perform "Harrigan" while pitching George's new show, referred to as "trash" by Dietz. Dissatisfied with the scripted version, Cagney reworked the entire number to feature his voice more extensively.

At Madame Bartholdi's Boarding House, where the Cohans — theatrical people — are forced to lodge, George informs his parents that he sold the show. Teaming up with Samuel H. Harris (Richard Whorf), he continues to lie by telling Schwab (S. Z. Sakall) that they have sold a major musical play to Dietz and Goff.

Little Johnny Jones features Cagney singing and dancing his way through two Cohan classics, "Yankee Doodle Boy" and "Give My Regards to Broadway." Following this enormous box-office smash, George re-forms "The Four Cohans" during a montage showing the happy family entertaining endless appreciative audiences.

Cohan writes the love song "Mary" for his wife, but faces a dilemma when stage star Fay Templeton (Irene Manning) wants to sing it in *Forty-five Minutes from Broadway*. He intends to break the news gently, arriving home with an enormous bouquet of flowers and a box of candy, but sweetheart Mary already knows all about the switch. The staging of the show *George Washington, Jr.* features another Cagney terpsichorean tour de force, during "You're a Grand Old Flag," which briefly features Wallace Clark as Theodore Roosevelt.

In 1912 the elder Cohans retire to their farm, while Josie leaves to get married. Focusing on playwriting, George pens the serious effort *Popularity*, which belies its title by bombing at the box office. Three years later, the *Lusitania* is sunk by the Germans; and, when the United States enters World War I in 1917, he writes his "biggest hit," "Over There," which warns the enemy to "beware" the arrival of American troops. As Cagney sits alone at a piano on a darkened stage, Curtiz and cinematographer James Wong Howe begin the scene in long shot, then gradually track in as Cohan plunks out the familiar melody.

A subsequent sequence showing him accompanying Nora Bayes (Frances Langford) as she belts out the song for a gathering of soldiers is followed by a unique scene that marks the passing of time, consisting primarily of a single long take, with the camera constantly moving through a miniature cityscape, pausing to show billboards and neon signs advertising a series of Cohan productions. This stunning sequence was designed by Don Siegel, who was responsible for all the remarkable montage scenes.

Prior to Cohan being called to his father's deathbed, the film depicts Nellie and Josie as already having died. (Josie Cohan died in 1916, a year prior to her father, but Nellie survived her husband by more than a decade, passing away in 1928.) The finest dramatic moment of the film is Cagney's brilliant playing of the son's final words to the father, who has lapsed into senility. Asked if he made a curtain-call speech, George repeats his famous stage expression, "My mother thanks you. My father thanks you. My sister thanks you — and *I* thank you," then weeps on his dead father's chest. After he finished the scene, Jim turned toward Curtiz, who, fighting back a flood of tears, said, "Jesus Christ, Jimmy. Beautiful, beautiful." Cagney later admitted, "That may have been the ultimate compliment."[3]

Cohan retires, leaving Sam Harris to produce shows on his own. Years later, Harris, now flat broke, persuades his former partner to return to the theater in *I'd Rather Be Right*, during which Cohan's FDR sings about the Axis and Hitler, threatening that the United States will "put ants in his Japants." The Rodgers and Hart musical starring Cohan actually was staged in 1937; but, for the film, the lyrics were updated to reflect the current wartime situation.

The flashback ends, and Roosevelt presents the Congressional Medal of Honor to Cohan, "the first person in his profession" to receive it. This scene was based on an actual event on June 29, 1936, when FDR awarded Cohan a Congressional Gold Medal for his role in building World War I morale with "You're a Grand Old Flag" and "Over There." The film errors in calling it the Medal of Honor, which is awarded only to combat veterans.

The film's degree of accurate detail can be seen on the clock sitting on the President's desk. When Cohan begins the flashback, the clock indicates 9 p.m. Now it has advanced exactly 115 minutes, to 10:55 p.m.

"I'm just a song and dance man," Cohan tells FDR. "Everybody knows that." Bidding farewell to the President, he repeats his stage expression of family gratitude, then does a seemingly effortless dance down the staircase. This famous, Bill "Bojangles" Robinson-style choreography apparently was improvised on the spot by Cagney. In the street, troops are marching to the tune of "Over There." Cohan joins the march, and is asked by a sergeant (Frank Faylen), "What's the matter, old timer? Don't you remember this song?"

Robert Buckner devised the framing story featuring Roosevelt, but using the President as an actual character was a culmination of Jack Warner's support for FDR, hints of which began to appear in the studio's films at the time of the 1932 election. Cagney was a longtime Democrat, and enjoyed the inclusion of the FDR material.

The shoot was a taxing one, but Jim loved every minute; and his total immersion in the role, mentally and physically, is obvious in every aspect of his tremendous performance, which earned him the New York Film Critic's Best Actor Award, as well as the Oscar. His teaming with brother Bill and sister Jeanne, cowriting of several scenes with Curtiz, on-camera improvisations, hiring of the Epstein brothers, and extensive work with Johnny Boyle added up to the most personal project he ever made at Warner Bros.

During the New York premiere on May 29, 1942, a war-bond rally raised $4,750,000 for the U.S. Treasury Department. The subsequent universally positive critical response and eight Academy Award nominations were overwhelming — a reality that induced the brothers Cagney to announce to the brothers Warner that they had formed Cagney Productions, to make films to be released through United Artists. The public, too, were wild about Jim as George, and now realized that he was much more than just a "gangster" or "wiseguy actor."

The United States was now fully involved in World War II, and Jim alternated starring in his own films — which included *Johnny Come Lately* (1943) and *Blood on the Sun* (1945) — with stumping for the war effort (as a member of the Hollywood Victory Committee, set up by SAG, of which he now was President) and appearing in propaganda shorts like MGM's "You, John Jones" (1943), directed by his nemesis Mervyn LeRoy and featuring Ann Sothern and Margaret O'Brien.

On December 8, 1941, five days after Curtiz began shooting *Yankee Doodle Dandy* — and the day of FDR's war declaration — a studio analyst at Warner Bros. received a copy of an unproduced play by Murray Burnett and Joan Alison called "Everybody Comes to Rick's." Following the President's announcement, Jack Warner enthusiastically turned up the anti-Nazi heat, eliminating plans for prestige productions in favor of war-related pictures. A wartime economy meant increased employment for workers who would fill theaters showing, not glitzy epics, but films relevant to the moment.

Hal Wallis was keen to find a major vehicle for Bogart. On December 11, when FDR declared war on Nazi Germany, Wallis was given a 12-page report recommending "Everybody Comes to Rick's" as a colorful, suspenseful and timely potential box-office winner, perhaps to star Bogart, Cagney or Raft. For the meantime, however, Jack Warner, wanting a sequel to *The Maltese Falcon*, inquired if Dashiell Hammett would be interested in writing a continuation of his novel, including all the major characters except Mary Astor's, who had gone to the Big House, possibly to death row. Although ill, Hammett considered the proposal, but declined when Warner offered an insufficient advance.

Warner then decided to cast Bogart, Astor and Greenstreet in *Across the Pacific* (1942), with John Huston again at the helm. And, while "Everybody Comes to Rick's" was in preproduction, why not star Bogie in yet another picture turned down by Raft, *The Big Shot* (1942)? After crawling out of the gangster quagmire of the 1930s, Bogart now shuffled back into a wiseguy vehicle. Mary Astor refused to play the female lead, then Vincent Sherman bowed out, leaving producer Walter MacEwen to hire Lewis Seiler as director.

The Big Shot opens with Joseph "Duke" Berne dying in the hospital ward of the Big House, appropriately signifying the final time Bogart would play a gangster in a Warner Bros. film. "It's just a matter of hours," a doctor announces, "maybe moments."

Cagney at the end of his contract with Warner Bros. in 1942 (courtesy James Cagney).

"I was a wiseguy," Berne recalls. "I had all the angles figured. A wiseguy — big shot." He asks for a cigarette, blows some smoke that triggers a flashback, and begins a film noir narration that, for the first time, allows the viewer inside the mind of a Bogart criminal. His first Warners Wiseguy, in *The Petrified Forest*, is called Duke, and so is his last, a fact that Bogie solidifies by playing Berne as a variation on Mantee, complete with five o'clock shadow and menacing monotone, but balancing the portrayal with the intelligence of his subsequent criminal characters.

A three-time loser, Berne, paroled after serving all but six months of a five-year sentence, will be sent up for life if arrested again. Unable "safely" to return to his criminal ways, nor find "honest" employment, he asks himself, "Why feed a dead man, even if he is walking around?" Reflecting Bogart's recent characters who possess positive qualities, Berne engages audience sympathy from the outset.

At Sardo's restaurant, Berne is accosted by two of his old Mob associates, Sandor (Howard Da Silva) and Frenchy (perennial hood Joe Downing, who is particularly malicious this time around). Duke wants nothing to do with another heist, so Frenchy honors his cowardice by ordering a glass of milk. Mercilessly taunting the former "big shot," he says, "Maybe you want it in a bottle with a nipple on it," then slaps him repeatedly. Berne controls his temper, then smashes the glass of milk after they leave the café.

Informed that his former cohort in crime, Attorney Martin T. Fleming (Stanley Ridges), has cooked up an armored car caper, Berne visits the law office, where his old flame, Lorna (Irene Manning), now Fleming's wife, is killing time. Duke agrees to mastermind the hit, then returns to Sardo's and knocks Frenchy to the floor, soaking him with milk after the goon drops a cigarette into the glass.

Later that night, Lorna drops in at Berne's room to plead with him to go straight, but they are interrupted by a knock from Frenchy, who spies her coat draped over a chair. Lorna pulls a rod on Duke, and he agrees to ditch the armored car job, leaving the others to continue without him. Following a furious gun battle with the cops, Sandor is burned to death in the getaway car, but Frenchy escapes after shielding himself with an innocent female bystander who is pressured by the police into identifying Berne as the assailant.

At Fleming's apartment, Duke, claiming he "was out, walking alone," needs a more convincing alibi. The shyster refuses to help, but Berne threatens "to put the finger" on him if he doesn't cooperate. George Anderson (Richard Travis), a struggling car salesman, agrees to testify that he was demonstrating a new model to Duke at the time of the robbery. Berne casually saunters into the police station, but is double-crossed at the trial after Frenchy squeals to Fleming about Lorna's late-night visit. The prosecution calls Anderson's girl, Ruth Carter (Susan Peters), who reveals that they were together at 9 p.m. on the Friday evening in question, and Berne's phony alibi is exposed.

The Big Shot (1942): "I was a wiseguy," admits Joseph "Duke" Berne, Bogart's last Warner Bros. gangster, here held at gunpoint by former flame Lorna Fleming (Irene Manning) (original lobby card).

In the Big House together, Anderson is serving a year for perjury, while Berne, sent up for life, warns him, "Stay away from guys like me." Duke falls in with Frank "Dancer" Smith (Chick Chandler), agreeing to operate a spotlight in an upcoming show for the inmates. Lorna, on the outside, leaves Fleming to help devise an escape plan, including smuggling in a rod and rope aboard the warden's car.

During Dancer's (blackface) performance of "Sweet Georgia Brown," Berne knocks out the electricity and they make a break for it. Dancer is shot down by a guard, but Duke climbs over the wall to Lorna, waiting in her car. Anderson, for his effort to stop the escape, is indicted for murder after a wounded guard dies.

Holding Quinto (Murray Alper), a recently paroled mug, at gunpoint, Fleming learns that Lorna has taken Berne to a cabin at Bald Ridge. For a few hours, Duke enjoys a tranquil domestic existence (another first for a Bogart wiseguy), mixing batter for buckwheat cakes while sitting in a rocking chair, and fondly recalling memories of his "Old Lady" trying to pay their mortgage. He pretends to complain about the fresh winter air, claiming he needs "four-parts cigarette smoke and one-part air. Then maybe a guy can breathe."

His brief respite ends when a radio announcer reports on the Anderson case. "He don't mean anything to me," he tells Lorna. "I ain't stickin' my neck out!" (A few months later, Bogie would deliver a paraphrase of this line and insure his screen immortality.) Just as a police car and two motorcycles arrive, Duke and Lorna speed off through the snow. "I've got to get to the warden before they get to me," Duke vows. During the chase, Lorna is shot to death.

At Fleming's apartment, Berne phones Warden Booth (Minor Watson) to confess to the murder he is about to commit, but the shyster pulls a rod and fires. Duke guns him down, but is seriously wounded in return. Cigarette smoke ends the flashback as he takes his final drag. "It's dark in here," he remarks. "What kind of cheap dump is this, tryin' to save on electricity?" Drawing the cigarette away from his face, he utters his last words — "big shot" — and it falls to the floor as his hand goes limp.

The film's frequent emphasis on cigarettes, particularly the dialogue referring to Duke's need for smoke and the final image of a burning butt after he dies, is an eerie, prophetic element when viewed in retrospect. The mood of *The Big Shot* is consistently downbeat, its noir aspects looking ahead to the future of the genre, while its content reaches back into the Warners history of Bogart bad-asses and the Depression theme of a down-on-his-luck, innocent man being framed by an unscrupulous attorney.

An underrated film, *The Big Shot* deserves to be considered something more than the last gangster project Bogie made before *Casablanca*. Duke Berne is a fusion of several of his previous characters; but, in his decision to put himself in harm's way — sticking out his neck — to save a truly decent man, Bogie already was paving the way for the immortal Richard "Rick" Blaine.

Bogart again is surrounded by sterling support. Stanley Ridges gives another of his quietly loathsome performances, and the stunning Irene Manning (fresh from her brief role in *Yankee Doodle Dandy*) provides an early example of the many dangerously irresistible noir gun molls and femmes fatale who followed in her wake during the 1940s.

Across the Pacific went into production before *The Big Shot*, but was released nearly three months afterward. John Huston enjoyed the opportunity for a second collaboration with his three *Falcon* alumni, and asked a fourth veteran to play an elaborate joke on the set. Managing to keep his plan a secret, Huston smuggled in Peter Lorre for a walk-on as a ship's waiter. With his back to the camera, Lorre brushes past Greenstreet and Astor as he carries a tray. During the shoot, Lorre managed to plant a kiss on Astor's neck, and they broke into laughter when the prank was discovered.

Huston couldn't help surprising his stars with unexpected cameos. In between making *The Maltese Falcon* and *Across the Pacific*, he directed *In This Our Life* (1942) with Bette Davis, catching her off guard by having his father appear as a disgusted bartender, as well as using Bogart to cast his shadow on an office door.

Midway through production on *Pacific*, Bogart, after visiting the Finlandia Baths on Sunset Boulevard one evening, arrived home to find a soused Mayo waiting for him in the living room. Lunging at him with a butcher knife, she stabbed him in the back. He was seriously wounded, but refused to call the police, instead paying a doctor $500 to bandage him up and keep quiet. When he reported late to the set, Huston found him in his dressing room, attempting to get his clothes over the bandages. Bogie didn't miss a day of work.

Before shooting began, Huston had received a commission in the U.S. Army Signal Corps, but obtained a 60-day deferment. With nine days left in the shooting schedule, he was ordered to report for duty, so Vincent Sherman came in to film the final scene, in which Bogie's Rick Leland singlehandedly fights off a Japanese attack. Because of FDR's controversial Executive Order 9102, signed on March 18, 1942, which "relocated" 110,000 West Coasters of Japanese ethnicity (62 percent of whom were American citizens) into internment camps, Warners had to cast Chinese actors as the enemy.

Across the Pacific can be considered the first true A-film Bogart starring vehicle, and he receives his own credit panel before the title. The narrative opens on November 17, 1941, with

Across the Pacific (1942): John Huston's wartime "follow up" to *The Maltese Falcon* stars Bogart as espionage agent Richard Leland, who jokes that he's "J. Edgar Hoover," supported by Keye Luke and Mary Astor (original lobby card).

the U.S. Army court-martial of Captain Richard Lomas Leland at Governor's Island, New York. Having "disgraced his uniform," he exchanges it for a trench coat and fedora, the trademark attire Bogart repeatedly would wear for the rest of his career.

In Halifax, Leland tries to enlist in the Royal Canadian Army artillery, but is rejected by a major (Lester Matthews) aware of his "dishonorable" status. "Maybe Chiang Kai-shek won't be so particular," Leland says, then buys passage on the Japanese freighter *Genoa Maru*, scheduled to sail down the East Coast, through the Panama Canal, and across the Pacific. In the steamship office, he observes Alberta Marlow (Mary Astor) conferring with the clerk (Keye Luke).

On board, Leland meets the corpulent Dr. Lorenz (Sydney Greenstreet), Chair of Sociology at a university in the Philippines, and his "man," T. Oki (Kam Tong). The following morning (after enjoying a smoke in bed), Leland walks on deck, with his trench coat caped over his robe. Checking out the scantily clad Miss Marlow, he asks, "Are your legs always blue? If you catch pneumonia, what will become of our romance?" She replies that the Philippines will provide the proper climate for dressing in shorts, and he adds, "There's a Canadian for you. Let them take their clothes off and they're happy."

Richard Macauley's screenplay, based on the story "Aloha Means Good-bye" by Robert Garson, and undoubtedly augmented by Huston, is loaded with choice dialogue, developing further the Bogart and Astor chemistry established in *The Maltese Falcon*. Following a dinner topped off by bread pudding, Leland and Miss Marlow share a kiss on deck. "Are you getting sick?" he asks.

"I don't know," she replies. "How do girls usually react when you kiss them?"

Plied with whiskey by Lorenz, Leland reveals his military disgrace: "I'll hire out to whoever will pay for my services— Chiang Kai-shek, Hirohito," then becomes ill himself. When the boat drops anchor at New York, he leaves Miss Marlow at the dock while going off to "borrow money from a friend." He is followed by an unidentified man (Paul Stanton) whom he ditches; and — 32 minutes into the film — Leland's true modus operandi is revealed. Here, the audience is treated to the first real Bogart "hero," not a gambler who happens upon enemies of the United States, but an Army Intelligence agent assigned to foil a Japanese plot (the details of which are saved for the final reel).

Warned about a "Japanese gunsel" boarding the *Genoa Maru*, Leland spots him trying to assassinate Lorenz. Pushing Marlow to the deck, he draws his .45 and shoots the gun from the would-be killer's hand. Hastily the offender is walked down the gangplank, into a storage building, and shot. Leland, comparing his rod to the one Lorenz carries in his suit jacket, remarks, "Mine's bigger than yours."

Marlow, asking Leland if he's a "G-Man," is informed, "If it'll make you happy, I'm J. Edgar Hoover."

The memorable Bogart-Astor exchanges continue after Marlow is badly sunburned on deck. "You certainly are a girl of many colors," Leland says in her cabin, as she covers her breasts with an unfastened shirt. "First, your legs get blue, then your face turns green, now you're red all over."

"Seeing me in pain *does* give you pleasure," she replies.

Denied passage through the Panama Canal, the *Genoa Maru* drops the passengers at Cristobal, where Leland arranges for rooms at the Pan American hotel, managed by his old "friend," Sam Wing On (Lee Tung Foo). Having earned Lorenz's trust by telling a tale about "trouble with a dame" and the subsequent theft of regimental funds, Leland agrees to sell him the current flight plan of the Canal Patrol.

On December 6, 1941, Leland, pretending to open a bank account, reports to A. V. Smith (Charles Halton), who agrees to provide the patrol schedule. Back at the hotel, Lorenz refuses to pay for the information, and his cohort, Joe Totsuiko (Victor Sen Yung), administers a karate knockout to Leland, who then is beaten with a cane. Regaining consciousness, he is aided by Sam, who provides him with a gun and the information necessary to track down the enemy.

At a movie theater, Leland confers with a cohort, who is assassinated, then blasts his way out. He follows the Japanese hit man to a base in the jungle, is captured and taken to Lorenz. "Looks like you boys are planning to knock over the Canal," he declares.

Miss Marlow, knowing nothing about the plot, was coerced into the voyage to help her father, whose real identity is Dan Morton (Monte Blue), a disgraced drunkard who "absconded with the company funds," then assumed a new identity on the Bountiful Plantation in Panama, where Lorenz and his Japanese pals have stashed their aircraft and torpedo parts. Totsuiko boasts of the Japanese appetite for war, inspiring Leland to threaten, "You may start it, but we'll finish it."

Totsuiko murders the incoherent Morton, but Leland grabs the killer's gun and runs into the jungle, pistol-whips a machine gunner, shoots down the plane as it takes off, and single-handedly wipes out every Japanese saboteur. Lorenz is too cowardly to commit hari kiri, and Leland tells him, "You've got a date with Army Intelligence." As the Canal Patrol roars overhead, he adds, "Right on time, eh, Doc? If any of your friends in Tokyo have trouble committing hari kiri, those boys will be glad to help them out." Having completed his mission, the rugged hero walks into the fadeout with Marlow.

Rushed into production, both to capitalize on *The Maltese Falcon* and to support the war effort, *Across the Pacific* (the boat never reaches that ocean) features an outlandish premise buoyed by sharp dialogue and solid performances. Having played Leland, a true American hero, and "Duke" Berne, a reversion to gangster type, simultaneously, Bogie again may have been wondering about which direction his Warners career was going, but his next role would forever settle all doubts. Never again would Jack Warner, threatening suspension, force him to play a gangster. But Bogie's ambiguous "heroes" still would possess the dark qualities demonstrated through his wiseguy persona, giving the cinema, whether in a witty wartime drama or a moody film noir, its most powerful icon.

Hal Wallis moved from being a production executive to a hands-on producer responsible for a quartet of films every year, each billed as "A Hal B. Wallis Production," with a raise in salary and a percentage of the profits. Now that he was no longer production chief, opportunities arose for other artists, including Mark Hellinger, who returned for duties to include writing, producing and directing, and Howard Hawks, who would be a supervisor and director also having control over writing and editing, with his name above the title of each "Howard Hawks Production." He was to make five films, one per year, receiving $100,000 for each, while working exclusively for Jack Warner.

Legend suggests that Jerry Wald and Robert Buckner's original plan for the film adaptation of "Everybody Comes to Rick's," titled *Casablanca*, was to cast Ronald Reagan as Rick Blaine and Ann Sheridan as his love interest; but after Hal Wallis saw *Across the Pacific*, it was Bogart all the way. However, a more likely explantion is that Reagan, whose draft deferments had expired, was being promoted in studio publicity to keep his name familiar to the filmgoing public. (Arthur Kennedy, Dennis Morgan and George Brent also were mentioned for the Rick part.) Wallis eliminated any thoughts of Sheridan and Mary Astor as prospects, instead opting for a European actress, eventually working a trade: Warners darling Olivia De Havilland for David O. Selznick's Ingrid Bergman. Wallis had attempted, unsuccessfully, to grab Bergman for *All Through the Night*.

In January 1942 Wallis assigned the screenplay to Aeneas Mackenzie and Wally Kline, who were ordered to expand the play's love story, while eliminating any material that might offend the PCA, especially the character of Lois, who had broken up Rick's marriage before becoming Victor Laszlo's (Paul Henreid) mistress (not his wife). Their work didn't satisfy Wallis, who then gave the love-story subplot to Casey Robinson, who had scripted several popular Bette Davis vehicles, and now crafted the character of Ilsa Lund (Bergman), the loyal Mrs. Laszlo whose family were victims of the Nazis. The official rewrite then went to the Epstein brothers, who retooled the dialogue, giving choice lines to police prefect Louis Renault (Claude Rains), whose complex relationship with Rick is a crucial element. At one point, the Epsteins were required to travel to Washington, D.C., to work on Frank Capra's *Why We Fight* series, but eventually returned to the *Casablanca* project.

On April 2, 1942, Jack Warner sent an unexpected memo to Wallis, recommending *George Raft* for the Rick part. Wallis refused, explaining that the role was being tailored specifically for Bogart, who had signed a seven-year contract, at $2,750 per week, on January 1. On April 6, Wallis assigned yet another writer, Howard Koch, to the project, ordering him to flesh out Blaine's political views and how he is ultimately moved by the Nazi occupation and French resistance. Koch later said, "It was a picture the audiences needed. The American ... the world audience. What it said was that there were values that were worth making sacrifices for, and it said it in a very entertaining way."[4]

Bogie's stock got a shot in the arm on May 21, when Jack Warner, having attended the

Washington, D.C., premiere of *Across the Pacific*, sent a telegram to the studio, referring to him as a big star and their equivalent of Clark Gable. Two weeks later, Warner and his wife, Ann, dined at the White House with FDR, who asked the mogul to make an adaptation of *Mission to Moscow*, the memoirs of Joseph E. Davies, former U.S. Ambassador to the Soviet Union. Of course, Warner accepted, honored to release a major film to support an American ally.

Warner spent several weeks casting the role of Sam, Rick's piano-playing pal. The role required an African American actor, and Wallis at first wasn't concerned about the gender. Singers Lena Horne, Ella Fitzgerald and Hazel Scott (who married Adam Clayton Powell, Jr., in 1945 and was blacklisted five years later) were considered, but the studio, for obvious reasons, began insisting on a male performer. Understandably, Wallis wanted to cast Clarence Muse, a fine actor, singer and songwriter, but he was *always* working.

Next, Wallis tested Arthur "Dooley" Wilson, a drummer who had played the part of Little Joe opposite the great Ethel Waters in the 1940 Broadway version of *Cabin in the Sky* and had recently moved to Hollywood. (He had earned his nickname after appearing, in whiteface, as "Irish" characters on the Chicago stage.) Though he wasn't enthusiastic about Wilson, Wallis signed him, commenting that he *might* be able to play the role. The actual keyboard work was done off-camera by studio pianist Elliot Carpenter. Perhaps the least convincing aspect of the film is Wilson's nonexistent keyboard "technique," but his enthusiastic, superb performance distracts attention away from his hands.

Michael Curtiz began shooting *Casablanca* on May 25, but Koch remained on the set to collaborate with the director and Bogart on extensive rewrites. Some location shots were filmed at Van Nuys Airport, but most of the production was confined to the studio soundstages. At this point, the project still seemed rather ludicrous. Just days before, Bogie and Bergman, while having lunch together, had discussed strategies of getting released. Bergman, however, had screened *The Maltese Falcon* several times, attempting to develop an approach to acting with him. In fact, she was taller than Bogie, who had to attach three-inch wooden blocks to his shoes and sit on pillows for certain scenes. Eventually, as expected, Mayo began phoning the studio, paranoically thinking her husband was "involved" with Bergman.

The first scene filmed by Curtiz was the flashback of Rick and Ilsa at the Café La Belle Aurore in Paris, with Sam (and Carpenter off camera) playing Herman Hupfeld's "As Time Goes By." Casey Robinson had written the scene and given it to Wallis just four days earlier, when it was almost completely rewritten by the Epstein brothers. While composing his score after the film was edited, Max Steiner wanted to jettison "As Time Goes By" in favor of an original song, but it was too late to re-shoot the scenes: Bergman already had cut her hair short to appear in Samuel Goldwyn's *For Whom the Bell Tolls* (1943).

The now-famous "La Marseillaise" scene, one of the most powerful moments in world cinema, flawlessly presented through images and music — the only dialogue being Victor Laszlo's command to the orchestra, "Play 'La Marseillaise.' Play it!"— was as moving on the set as it is on-screen. Many of the actors were European refugees, some Jews who had left behind relatives who suffered fates far more horrible than anything suggested in *Casablanca*.

The film still had no ending, much less the powerful, unforgettable conclusion that would become an American cultural treasure. Several versions were filmed, and the uncertainty about whom Ilsa would end up with added extra realism to Ingrid Bergman's performance, which is an integral element of the complex web of relationships that is resolved when Major Strasser (Conrad Veidt) is shot, Ilsa flies off with Victor, and Rick walks off into the fog with Renault. Howard Koch later said, "If *Casablanca* had ended ... with Bogart going off with

Bergman, the romantic ending ... there wouldn't be any legend today."⁵ More than that, Bergman ending up with Paul Henreid, who delivers a one-note, stiff, humorless performance, rather than Bogie, the film's true hero, is a testament to Ilsa's devotion to her freedom-fighter husband.

Bogart's monologue in the scene was four pages long. After being rewritten for the third time, it was given to him the night before Curtiz expected to shoot. During lunch the next day, Bogart and Curtiz loudly argued over how he was to deliver the lines. The disagreement continued for two hours, until Wallis arrived to mediate. Following another hour of wrangling, Bogie finally agreed to do the scene. Whatever actor and director had shouted about was academic, because Bogie delivered one of the most powerful concluding monologues ever filmed, an effort that rivals his magnetic performance at the conclusion of *The Maltese Falcon*.

Curtiz and Wallis wrapped the production, 11 days late and $75,000 over budget, in early August. After the film was shown to a preview audience, some viewers wondered aloud what became of Rick and Louis after they strolled down the runway, so Wallis suggested shooting an epilogue depicting the two, now in uniform, aboard a freighter on their way to battle the Nazis! However, the Allies serendipitously landed in North Africa—at Casablanca, to be exact—and Jack Warner wanted to waste no time taking advantage of the resulting public-relations bonanza.

Fortunately, for *Casablanca*—and for film history—Wallis substituted a single line for the proposed epilogue. As the two walk into the fog, Bogart recites the immortal line, "Louis, this could be the beginning of a beautiful friendship."

Steiner's dynamic "Arabic" music (reminiscent of his earlier score for John Ford's *The Lost Patrol* [RKO, 1934]) opens the film, blending in French ("La Marseillaise") and German ("Deutschland Uber Alles") melodies. Following a brief narration about the treacherous route taken by European refugees, many of whom "wait in Casablanca," the film's tension is established instantly when the murder of two German couriers carrying Letters of Transit is announced, and a "suspicious character" carrying Free French literature is gunned down beneath a poster of the Nazi-collaborator, Vichy Marshal Phillipe Petain. This image quickly cuts to the famous slogan of the French Revolution, "Liberte, Egalite, Fraternite," sculpted above the Palace of Justice.

As a plane flies over Rick's Café Americain, Major Strasser is met at the airport by Renault, who claims, "Unoccupied France welcomes you to Casablanca," then explains that his men "are rounding up twice the usual number of suspects." The actual murderer, however, will be at the club that night: "He'll be at Rick's. Everybody comes to Rick's."

Curtiz gives Bogart a fine introduction after Sam sings "It Had to Be You" and "Shine." Following various patrons' comments about Rick, his right hand is shown in close-up, signing a marker advancing a customer 1000 francs, before he picks up a cigarette as the camera pans to his face. When Ugarte (Peter Lorre), the real suspect, arrives, the repartee between the two actors (and good friends) is extraordinary, their dialogue perfectly timed but naturally delivered, like master musicians interweaving counter-melodies. "You despise me, don't you?" asks Ugarte.

"Well, if I gave it any thought, I probably would," replies Rick.

Because of Rick's attitude, Ugarte entrusts the Letters of Transit to him, for "an hour, perhaps longer." Sam strikes up "Knock on Wood," and Rick slips the letters into his piano. When Renault informs Rick of Ugarte's impending arrest, Bogart utters the legendary line, "I stick my neck out for nobody." The Captain then mentions the arrival of resistance fighter and concentration camp escapee Victor Laszlo, who "will offer a fortune to anyone who'll furnish him with an exit visa." Later, when Ugarte hysterically pleads for his life (as only Peter Lorre could), Rick repeats, "I stick my neck out for nobody."

Rick may not go out of his way for any individual, but he does treat everyone with comparable consideration. When Signor Ferrari (Sydney Greenstreet) futilely asks to purchase the café, then the services of Sam, Rick replies, "I don't buy or sell human beings," telling him to ask the piano player directly. Sam, who is Rick's one true friend, wouldn't work for anyone else, claiming he already makes more money than he has time to spend.

Renault has done his research, and knows that Rick tends to side with lost causes, having run guns to Ethiopia and fought with the Loyalists in Spain, both resistance efforts against fascism. Rick informs the Captain that he settled in Casablanca for "my health. I came ... for the waters," adding that "I was misinformed" (a line paraphrased from an earlier Curtiz film, *The Adventures of Robin Hood*, in which Claude Rains plays Prince John). Known for playing suave characters, Rains is at his most complex as Renault, at one point telling Ilsa that, if he'd been born a woman, he'd be in love with Rick.

Ingrid Bergman, too, is at her best, merging quiet sensuality with an appealing, bashful innocence, and her glances at Sam when she first arrives at Rick's are priceless. Dooley Wilson's subtle nonverbal acting is a perfect complement, and he effortlessly indicates that Sam and Ilsa share an understanding about *something* involving Rick. "Some of the old songs, Sam" she requests; and, after he tries to meander through "Avalon," she appeals, "Play it once, Sam — for old time's sake. Play it, Sam. Play 'As Time Goes By.'"

During the song, Rick storms in, snarling, "I thought I told you never to play ..." Again, the actors' eyes powerfully convey a past association the characters might wish to forget. Breaking a precedent, he agrees to have a drink with Ilsa, Laszlo and Renault, who claims, "She was asking about you earlier, Rick, in a way that made me extremely jealous." The Captain then affectionately calls him "Ricky." Reinforcing her affection for the piano player, Ilsa asks Rick, "Say goodbye to Sam for me. There's still nobody in the world who can play 'As Time Goes By' like Sam."

"He hasn't played it in a long time," Rick admits. At closing time, as a searchlight strafes the outside of the café, Rick sits in the dark with a glass and a whiskey bottle (one of the truly iconic Bogart images, stunningly lit by Arthur Edeson). Sam wants him to go to bed, but realizes that his preoccupation won't make for peaceful sleep. "Let's get out of here," Sam proposes, "We'll take the car and drive all night. We'll get drunk. We'll go fishing and stay away until she's gone." Rick tells him to go home, but Sam defiantly insists, "No, sir. I'm staying *right here.*"

Revealing that "it's December 1941 in Casablanca," Rick pounds his fist onto the table: "Of all the gin joints in all the towns in all the world, she walks into mine." He then orders Sam, "You played it for her. You can play it for me. If she can stand it, I can. Play it!" Yet another performance of "As Time Goes Boy" leads to a romantic flashback of happier times in Paris before the Nazis rolled in, a sunny drive along the Champs Elysees, a boat ride on the Seine, the champagne toast of "Here's looking at you, Kid," dancing the night away, and Ilsa's shyness when Rick speaks of marriage. She admits there was another man in her life, adding, "He's dead."

The Germans strike, leading to the scene at the La Belle Aurore and another "Here's looking at you, Kid." Bogart reportedly devised the line himself, after demonstrating some poker techniques for Bergman.

"Kiss me, kiss me, as if it were the last time," Ilsa pleads as German guns fire in the dis-

Casablanca (1942): Bogart and Ingrid Bergman as Rick Blaine and Ilsa Lund, the Hollywood cinema's most beloved romantic couple, in Michael Curtiz's surprise wartime masterpiece that has become a national treasure.

tance; then Rick, in a puff of smoke and pouring rain at the train station, reads a note explaining, "I cannot go with you or ever see you again" as Sam comforts his "boss." The flashback concludes, and Rick, feeling his bourbon, knocks over his glass as Ilsa returns to the club, frustrating him further.

Bogart perhaps knew as well as any actor how to play a drunk scene with believable subtlety. As Rick waxes cynical while slurring only slightly, Ilsa explains Laszlo's influence on her. Then the booze makes Rick reveal his own pain by becoming truly hurtful: "Tell me. Who was it you left me for? Was it Laszlo, or were there others in between, or aren't you the kind that tells?" Not surprisingly, Ilsa, a tear in her eye, retreats, while Rick drops his head onto the table.

Strasser offers to give Laszlo an exit visa in exchange for "information," but the anti-fascist reminds him that even a concentration camp couldn't "persuade" such behavior from him. Laszlo's next attempt takes him to the Blue Parrot Café, owned by Signor Ferrari, who acts as the local black market broker. Outside the restaurant, Ilsa is finally able to tell Rick that she was married to the freedom fighter, "even when I knew you in Paris."

The "fat hypocrite" tells Laszlo that he may be able to get only one visa, for Ilsa. "It would take a miracle to get you out of Casablanca," Ferrari informs him, "and the Germans have outlawed miracles." Rick may be their only hope for two, he adds.

Later, when a German and a Frenchman fight over Yvonne (Madeleine LeBeau), a beautiful broad at the Café Americain bar, Rick breaks it up, maintaining that he doesn't allow "politics" in the joint. One nod to the Soviet allies comes when Sasha (Leonid Kinskey), the bartender, approving of Rick's "sentimental" move allowing a Bulgarian (Helmut Dantine) to win at roulette, kisses him on both cheeks. "Well, you crazy Russian," exclaims Rick, slapping him on the back.

The film's most compelling moment arrives when Rick, again disallowing politics, refuses to help Laszlo, then breaks another precedent. A group of Nazis give voice to "Watch on the Rhine," Lazslo demands that the band play "La Marseillaise," and Rick nods his approval, a political act of defiance that incites Renault to express "shock" over discovering gambling in the house, which is then closed down. With exquisite comic timing, an employee enters the frame to hand the Captain some cash. "Your winnings, Sir," he exclaims.

"In the meantime, everybody stays on salary," Rick generously announces in the wee hours; but when Isla appeals for the Letters of Transit, he replies, "*I'm* the only cause I'm interested in."

"If you don't help us," she pleads, "Victor Laszlo will die in Casablanca."

"What of it?" he asks. "I'm going to die in Casablanca. It's a good spot for it."

Ilsa pulls a gun. "Go ahead and shoot," Rick responds. "You'll be doing me a favor."

Disarmed, she admits she still loves him, explaining that she believed Laszlo had been killed trying to escape from the concentration camp; then, just before they were to leave Paris together, she learned of her husband's survival. "I ran away from you once. I can't do it again," she reveals, asking Rick to "think … for all of us."

"All right, I will," he replies. "Here's looking at you, Kid."

Laszlo unselfishly asks Rick to use the letters to take Ilsa out of the country. After the Vichy police break in to arrest the concerned husband, Rick visits Renault, claiming he and Ilsa will be using the Letters of Transit and that a ruse will be staged to allow them to "chuck [Laszlo] into a concentration camp for years." (An additional scene, in which Rick visits Laszlo in jail to tell him about the Letters of Transit, was shot but not included in the final film.) At the Blue Parrot, Rick tells Ferrari that Sam gets "twenty-five percent of the profits," but the big man replies, "I happen to know that he gets ten percent, but he's worth twenty-five."

Renault attempts to arrest Laszlo, but Rick pulls a rod. Pretending to phone the airport, the Captain calls Strasser instead. On the runway, Rick defies his own cynical attitude by convincing Ilsa to get on the Lisbon plane with her husband, who will need support in the dangerous days ahead. The combination of camera movement, compositions and editing in the scene is flawless, and a testament to the prodigious talent of Michael Curtiz.

"If that plane leaves the ground, and you're not with him, you'll regret it," Rick assures Ilsa, "maybe not today, maybe not tomorrow, but soon, and for the rest of your life."

"But what about us?" she asks.

"We'll always have Paris," he replies. "We didn't have. We'd lost it, until you came to Casablanca. We got it back last night." Claiming, "I've a job to do, too," and that she can't follow him, he explains, "Ilsa, I'm no good at being noble, but it doesn't take much to see that the problems of three little people don't amount to a hill of beans in this crazy world. Someday, you'll understand that." As she tears up, he lets her have it one more time: "Here's looking at you, Kid."

Rick tells Laszlo that Isla, *pretending* that she still loved him, visited him only to get the Letters of Transit. "Welcome back to the fight," Laszlo replies. "This time I know our side will win."

The propeller fires up, and a series of rapid, tight, stunning close-ups prefaces the Laszlos' walk to the plane. Strasser arrives and tries to phone the radio tower, but Rick guns him down in self defense. "Major Strasser has been shot," Renault announces to some underlings. "Round up the usual suspects." He opens a bottle of Vichy Water, tosses it into a waste can, then offers to arrange passage for both of them to a Free French garrison as they stroll off into the fog of legend.

Casablanca (1942): Bogie's grace, subtlety and intensity in the role of Rick Blaine helped make him the greatest movie star of all time. The film didn't hurt Ingrid Bergman's career, either (original half-sheet poster).

The final cut premiered at Thanksgiving 1942 and went into general release in January 1943, when the Allies began a summit at Casablanca and created additional weeks of publicity for Warner Bros. The film was a box-office smash, won Oscars for Best Picture, Best Director and Best Screenplay, and landed a Best Actor nomination for Bogart, who soon would shed his expatriate club-owner's skin for that of war hero.

Playing Rick Blaine with grace, subtlety and intensity, carefully yet dynamically transitioning from callous self-interest to moral ambiguity, to selfless heroism against the ultimate evil, insured Bogart of immortality. It is one of the screen's genius characterizations, and the favorite of millions of viewers nearly seven decades later. "*Casablanca*, for my father, was the most important movie that he made," said Bogart's son, Stephen. "*Casablanca* is just one of those timeless beauties that lasts forever."[6]

Bogart, Bergman and Henreid all reprised their roles for a *Screen Guild* Players radio broadcast on April 26, 1943.

Rudy Pearson
Professor, College of the Pacific, Sacramento, California
on
Casablanca

Casablanca is a great example of how many people in the United States would like reality to be. Add in an unusual historical era with a dash of Warners cultural bad-boy image, and you have an excellent foundation for the all-American story.

Pushing forward an American ideal can be seen in the relationship between Rick and Sam, an unusual pairing for the 1940s. However, if one remembers the WWII effort to compare American democracy to fascism and totalitarianism, there was a historical connection. There are two historical trends that clearly show the effort to build and promote this unusual racial relationship.

First, the Roosevelt Administration had been developing a rapport with the African American community for some time. The Black Cabinet, Mary McLeod Bethune and Eleanor Roosevelt are well-known figures in this relationship. FDR himself hailed the significance of Jesse Owens and Joe Louis in upholding the superiority of the United States. All of these "promotions" were pioneering moments for race relations, and pulled many African Americans into the Democratic Party.

Secondly, the Office of War Information was following this earlier idea when it made some effort to encourage better roles for African Americans in the movies than in real life. Movie military personnel were integrated, while the official U.S. military remained segregated during WWII.

This, of course, represented an American who claimed the higher ground of democracy and fairness. And, promoting this ideal would help the OWI recruit African Americans into the service and into war industry jobs. Manpower was needed and previous barriers of race and gender had to change.

Therefore, the movie relationship of Rick and Sam fits into something larger than movie roles. Despite Rick's cynicism and individualism, there is a reliance on his best friend, Sam. This underlines a U.S. moral conviction of an ideal, of a nation that was caring and sharing, and a black-and-white relationship that helped challenge a contemporary stereotype that could be seen on any street during the 1940s.

Having been fully involved supporting the war effort, including a European trip to entertain the troops, Robinson briefly returned to Warner Bros. in late 1942, but there were no real opportunities. At 20th Century–Fox, he joined the all-star cast of *Tales of Manhattan*. The following year, he starred in *Destroyer* at Columbia and the omnibus film *Flesh and Fantasy* at Universal. The roles offered by Warners — in the horror film *A Beast with Five Fingers* (eventually filmed as *The Beast* ... in 1946) and the newspaper yarn *The Good Die Poor* — didn't interest him. And a supporting role as a cantankerous old geezer in *The Treasure of the Sierra Madre* (for which Walter Huston was also being considered) was just that — a *supporting* role — so he turned it down.

His continuing war-effort activities involved him with the U.S.O., but also with the Committee for the Protection of the Foreign Born, ostensibly created to aid refugees, and the National Council for American-Soviet Friendship — associations that would add to the FBI's growing file of his "subversive" dealings, irregardless of his true intentions. Compounding the problems beginning to brew from his political affiliations, his personal life, too, was becoming increasingly complicated. His wife, who suffered from bipolar disorder, repeatedly threatened to file for divorce.

Robinson's relationship with Warners continued to worsen. J. L. had become fed up with his rejection of every potential film. Eddie responded with a long letter to the mogul, explaining his dissatisfaction with the scripts offered him, including *Larceny, Inc.*, which he admitted pitching to the studio, as a vehicle for *another* actor.

Warner finally had enough of Robinson's displeasure. And combined with the fact that he was the oldest star on the lot, not to mention a high-salaried one, Eddie was given his walking papers on August 6, 1943, after 13 years as a Warners contract actor. He was paid $50,000 each for the two films he still owed the studio.

Another kind of war raged between Hal Wallis and Jack Warner, who was becoming increasingly jealous of the producer's successes. The situation had reached a breaking point at the 1943 Oscars, where Wallis had a heyday, including being presented with the Irving G. Thalberg award. When *Casablanca* was announced as Best Picture, Warner raced up the aisle ahead of Wallis and grabbed the statuette, which he took back to the studio and kept out of his "rival's" mitts. Thereafter, Warner refused to allow his top cast and crew to work for Wallis, who was let out of his contract in April 1944. After much legal wrangling, they ended their battle that December with a payoff and a promise of profit shares on the films Wallis had produced.

Mark Hellinger also hit the road again. Following a difficult war assignment for William Randolph Hearst, he returned stateside to an equally thorny Warner, who received his resignation shortly thereafter. J. L., who now was the sole executive producer, was perfectly happy to assign the top productions to Henry Blanke and Jerry Wald, who knew how to massage the mogul's enormous ego.

Outspoken leftist John Howard Lawson (who later was blacklisted as one of the Hollywood Ten) wrote the screenplay for *Action in the North Atlantic* (1943), a tale of the Merchant Marine who deliver war materiel to Murmansk and the Red Army. In a scene set in Manhattan's seamen's hall, the National Maritime Union (a Communist-supported organization) is shown uniting against fascism. Appropriately, Lawson suggested that Lloyd Bacon base his visual and editing style on Soviet montage (particularly Sergei Eisenstein's legendary *Battleship Potemkin* [1925]). Bogart, too, attempted to add his own liberal content, particularly the presence of an African American captain, but his suggestion was cut from the script.

Bogie, always comfortable as a sailor, shared Cagney's appreciation of Bacon, and enjoyed working with the director, even though the film ultimately disappointed him. He was required to exert himself in some action scenes, but the script didn't present any new acting challenges. He was disgruntled with much of the dialogue, and also had difficulty learning his lines, due to continued domestic turmoil, thus having to memorize them on the set each morning. None of the actors ever had to set foot on a real ship, with huge sets being constructed in the studio and the camera set on a crane that swung it from side to side.

At one point, contract player Bernie Zanville, making his film debut, became fed up and yelled at Bogie. But the fact that a "nobody" was chewing out the star made him laugh, and this incident began a friendship between the two actors. When the studio insisted that Zanville be given an Anglo screen name, Bogart suggested "Dane Clark," and the neophyte actor accepted it.

The film begins with a written prologue quoting FDR about "delivering the goods ... damn the torpedoes, full speed ahead!" First Mate Joe Rossi (Bogart) narrates the opening as he stands aboard the deck of the *Northern Star* with Captain Steve Jarvis (Raymond Massey), who speaks of his chief officer being "in trouble in every deep-water port in the world." Below deck is a poker-playing crew including Alfred "Boats" O'Hara (Alan Hale), Johnny Pulaski (Dane Clark), "Chips" Abrams (Sam Levene), "Caviar" Jinks (J. M. Kerrigan) and "Tex" Mathews (Western character actor Glenn Strange, one year before he played Universal's Frankenstein Monster in the first of three films).

A German U-boat hits the vessel with two torpedoes, causing them to abandon ship. Though shot in the studio, relying on miniatures and rear-projection, this blazing scene is exciting, with the added realism of the Nazis actually speaking German. Tex, who attempts to swim through burning oil, is the only sailor who doesn't make it to the lifeboat, which is rammed and shattered by the submarine, forcing the others to grab onto a raft. "We'll hunt you down and slice you like a piece of cheese!" Jarvis shouts to the Nazi Captain (William von Brincken).

"They can't hear you," Rossi tells him.

"But God can!" Jarvis replies. After 11 days afloat, the survivors are rescued, and Rossi immediately speaks of getting another ship, which he calls "home," while Jarvis returns to his wife (Ruth Gordon). Back on land, Rossi sports the familiar Bogart fedora.

At the Casino Club, Rossi eyes Pearl (Julie Bishop), who sings Cole Porter's "Night and Day," then he slugs a loudmouth whose "loose lips might sink ships." She complains about his uncouth violence, but Rossi replies, "He should have had his teeth kicked in."

At the Maritime Union, Pulaski incurs the wrath of his fellow sailors when he argues about leaving the sea to be with his wife and coming child. "So you want a safe job, huh?" one of them asks. "Go ask the Czechs and the Poles and the Greeks. They were figuring on safe jobs. They're lined up in front of guns, digging each other's graves. The trouble with you, Pulaski, is you think America is just a place to eat and sleep. You don't know what side your future is buttered on." Stopping the speech, O'Hara tears the union badge from Pulaski's jacket, causing him to rejoin the crew.

Jarvis drops by to pick up Rossi, who "got spliced" with Pearl the previous day, and asks her to call his wife while they are at sea aboard the newly commissioned S.S. *Seawitch*. Cadet Robert Parker (Dick Hogan), having sailed on the Northern Star and fresh from the Merchant Marine Academy, arrives on board. Some footage is dedicated to training exercises, with Dane Clark continuing to inherit the wiseacre mantle of Cagney. During a convoy conference, merchant seamen from the Allied countries (including the U.S.S.R.) enthusiastically hail each other, and the *Seawitch* is ordered to Murmansk.

The convoy, attacked by a wolf pack of U-boats, is forced to disperse, a prolonged section that comprises one-third of the film. Isolated from the other ships, the *Seawitch* is tailed by a lone sub carefully remaining just out of range. Ordering a complete blackout and silence aboard the ship, Jarvis plans to elude the Nazi surveillance while drifting until dawn. Meanwhile, the U-boat captain orders dawn patrol bombers to determine the ship's position. Two planes attack, causing moderate casualties. One is shot down, but the other clips the Captain before crashing into the ship's bow, killing Parker. Demonstrating another of his abilities, Rossi operates to remove a bullet from Jarvis' leg. "You're the skipper from now on," the injured C.O. tells him.

But the waters still aren't safe, as the U-boat blasts them broadside. Rossi orders gasoline spread over the ship and set ablaze to create the impression of their immobilization. The submarine surfaces, and the *Seawitch* rams away, truly "slicing it like a piece of cheese." Soviet planes fly overhead as they sail into Murmansk. One of the sailors shouts, "Comrade! Comrade!" to some Russian women, while O'Hara comments to Pulaski, "It's the first time I've ever wanted to kiss a longshoreman."

This somewhat overlong film is capped off by the actual voice of Roosevelt:

> From the freedom-loving peoples of the United Nations to our merchant seamen on all the oceans goes our everlasting gratitude. With their aid, we shall build a bridge of ships to our allies, over which we will roll the implements of war. We will see to it that men and materials will be delivered, where they're needed and when they're needed. Nothing on land, in the air, on the sea, or under the sea, shall prevent our complete and final victory.

Jack Warner certainly did his part for FDR and the OWI with this picture, and Lloyd Bacon (who had directed Cagney in *Here Comes the Navy*) loved making another rousing maritime project. *Action in the North Atlantic* marked the seventh time Bogart worked with the director.

For the first time, though his character is briefly described as a hell-raiser, Bogart plays an obviously heroic character from the very outset of a narrative; and, even if he felt no new acting challenges, his performance as Rossi, a tough guy with a sensitive side, is as plausibly

Action in the North Atlantic (1943): Bogart's first full-blown war film, directed by Lloyd Bacon. As Joe Rossi, a first mate in the Merchant Marine, Bogie saves the life of his Captain, Steve Jarvis (Raymond Massey), as Alfred "Boats" O'Hara (Alan Hale) looks on (original lobby card).

"modern" as those of many later actors who claimed him as an influence. He is particularly good while reading from the Bible, then delivering Rossi's own sermon over eight flag-draped dead before their burial at sea. Raymond Massey, often known for his stage histrionics, also creates one of his most restrained, believable characterizations.

While performing as a tank commander in Columbia's excellent North Africa combat film *Sahara* (1943), Bogart filmed a cameo for Warners' *Thank Your Lucky Stars* (1943), an all-star "showcase" featuring Bette Davis, Olivia de Havilland, Errol Flynn, John Garfield and Ann Sheridan. Mark Hellinger produced, while musical specialist David Butler directed. Originally scheduled to *sing and dance* with de Havilland and Ida Lupino as a jive trio called the Rhythmaniacs, he was prevented by Columbia's tight shooting schedule. As a replacement, Bogie, coincidentally receiving top billing (the credits are alphabetical), is relegated to being "intimidated" by the ever-irritating "Cuddles" Sakall.

The film opens at KFWB Radio, Hollywood, with Dinah Shore singing "Thank Your Lucky Stars" on the *Eddie Cantor Show*. Shore calls Garfield a sweet and gentle boy, as he roughs up Cantor in the wings, then takes center stage to mangle "Blues in the Night." Hellinger and Butler appear on the street, where Cantor also plays Joe, a bus driver who pilots a route around the stars' homes. Back in the studio, Cuddles immediately chews the scenery, working in plenty of the babbling gibberish that so exasperated Cagney in *Yankee Doodle Dandy*. Cantor nearly matches Cuddles' serving of thickly sliced ham, then is followed by the absurd overkill of Spike Jones and his band.

Most of the performers appear as themselves, but Dennis Morgan and Joan Leslie play "Tommy Randolph," a singer, and "Pat Dixon," a songwriter. Dixon sits on a swing that Randolph describes as having been used by Bogart for "making love" to Lupino, whom Leslie impersonates. *The Roaring Twenties* is mentioned, and she does an extended Cagney impression, including some shtick from *Yankee Doodle Dandy* (in which she plays his wife).

The war is first mentioned indirectly when Cuddles and Edward Everett Horton mention the Allied Charities' "Cavalcade of Stars" to Cantor by his swimming pool. Incredibly, Mike Mazurki is Cantor's piano player during an outdated, Al Jolson-style number (sans blackface). Cantor spends the rest of the film describing every detail of his career over the phone to Horton.

Jack Carson and Alan Hale do a straw-hat-and-cane song and dance together, and two mock-Native Americans speak of making "Edward G. Robinson ... an honorary chief." Ann Sheridan sings "Love Isn't Born, It's Made"; then, halfway through the film, Bogart, complete with Duke Mantee stubble, calling Cuddles "Fatso," "Blubber" and "Jughead," inquires about Cantor's whereabouts. Cuddles pulls his tie and yells in his face, ordering him out of the theater. "Gee, I hope none of my movie fans hear about this," he says as he shuffles down the stairs. After *Casablanca*, this appearance, an unfunny parody of his old stereotypical gangster, was the most ridiculous imaginable.

Shore's velvet tones, on "The Dreamer," again briefly provide a pleasant diversion; then a reappearance of the "American Indians" (plus Canter dressed as a chief) includes Horton's reference to General Custer as "a very nice fella." (Warners' whitewashing of Custer had been featured in Raoul Walsh's *They Died With Their Boots On*, starring Errol Flynn, the previous year.) Stereotypes are even more rampant in the "Ice Cold Katie" number, as Willie Best appears as "Private Jones" and Hattie McDaniel sings! Interestingly, at a time when the U.S. military was still segregated, the only soldier appearing in the film is an African American.

The Cavalcade of Stars finally arrives, with Shore performing another elaborate number, and none other than Errol Flynn singing and dancing the Cockney song "That's What You Jolly Well Get" in a London pub set—the most charming and entertaining scene in the film. Bette Davis also *attempts* to sing, entering a lavish cocktail party to warble "They're Either Too Young or Too Old," a commentary on the only men left behind by the draft. At least as awful as Garfield, George Tobias even tries to flex his vocal cords, during "I'm a Dreamer," before Alexis Smith lays on some very capable terpsichore, and Sheridan, Flynn, Davis, McDaniel, Morgan, Leslie and *multiple* Cantors close the show.

Overlong and overblown at 127 minutes, the film seems twice as lengthy (particularly whenever the annoying Cantor or Cuddles are on screen), and modern viewers may thank their lucky stars when it finally drags to a halt. Though Robinson and Cagney were no longer under contract, the film has the distinction of being the sole Warners production to mention all three Wiseguys.

Following four months of shooting *Sahara*, during which his fights with Mayo reached an alarming state, Bogart prepared again to work for Michael Curtiz, joining his *Casablanca* cohorts Claude Rains, Sydney Greenstreet, Peter Lorre and Helmet Dantine for *Passage to Marseille* in May 1943. Bogie liked Casey Robinson and Jack Moffitt's script, which dealt with French fascism, but soon was disappointed by Warners' shift to an entirely different film, tentatively titled "The Pentacle," casting him as a wife murderer. He refused the new project, and Jack Warner complained that he wasn't honoring his contract. In return, Bogie agreed to play the killer only if the script was rewritten.

"The Pentacle" then was scheduled for May, and *Passage to Marseille* was slated for the following month. Five days before Curtis Bernhardt was to begin shooting the former, the script, now titled *Conflict*, was delivered to Bogart, who, after reading some of the dialogue, again refused to do it. Jack Warner threatened to replace him with Jean Gabin in *Marseille*, and actually phoned personally on May 6, arguing for 30 minutes with Bogie, who asked to be suspended. Warner was really irked at this point, and told Hal Wallis to go ahead with Gabin in *Marseille*, but the French actor wasn't interested. Then Sydney Greenstreet, scheduled to appear in both films, threatened to back out.

Finally, on June 3, Bogart learned of the death of his hero, Leslie Howard, whose plane from Lisbon had been shot down by German fighters. Saddened by this tragedy, he phoned Steve Trilling and agreed to do whatever films the studio had planned.

The Warners suits had been concerned that depicting the French penal colony of Cayenne, located on the Caribbean coast of South America, would draw protests from France. In 1938 the Boris Karloff vehicle *Devil's Island* had proved so controversial that its release was held up for two years. Incredibly, *Marseille*— including a sequence in which Jean Matrac (Bogart) guns down a German crew attempting to flee a shot-down plane — drew protests from American church groups who objected to the killing of "helpless men." (Yet, the same folks who objected to this cinematic slaughter of the Axis enemy said nothing about Hitler's treatment of the Jews.)

The Office of War Information cut the scene from export prints, but Warners kept it in the domestic release, which also included a subsequent sequence during which Captain Malo (Victor Francen), a French officer, reprimands Matrac, who replies, "Look about you ... and tell *me* who are the assassins."

Bogart again argued on the set with Michael Curtiz, and his usual punctuality was being seriously affected by an increase in his late-night drinking habits, made worse by the continuing battles with his wife. During the shoot, Bogie also was busy preparing to go on tour as a member of the Hollywood Victory Committee, which provided major acting talent to the U.S.O. Photos were taken of him receiving his inoculations, and a loyalty check was made by the War Department, just in case he had any "Communist connections." The report concluded that he was "clean on all counts," his only flaws being a violent temper which led to frequent arguments with his wife.

Passage to Marseille, featuring flashbacks within flashbacks, is the most convoluted and confusing of all the Warners Wiseguy films. The first *Casablanca* connection in the picture is Max Steiner's music, featuring a melody from "La Marseillaise" accompanying a written prologue:

> This is the story of a Free French Air Squadron. It is also the story of France. For a nation exists, not alone in terms of maps and boundaries, but in the hearts of men. To millions of Frenchmen, France has never surrendered.
> And today, she lives, immortal and defiant, in the spirit of the Free French Air Force, as it carries her to the skies over the Rhineland.

The action opens "Somewhere in Germany," with Free French planes (actually U.S. "Flying Fortresses") bombing Nazi installations. Bogart is introduced immediately, as Matrac mans a machine gun. The Germans speak their native language, but the French speak English. (Wisely, the American and British actors didn't attempt phony accents.) The unbelievable nature of the narrative is established instantly, as Matrac drops a note from the plane to his wife, Paula (Michelle Morgan), waiting in a field below!

The squadron's base is hidden in barns and haystacks "Somewhere in England," where Captain Freycinet (Claude Rains, sporting an eye patch) is the commanding officer. A very staid Matrac is wished well by the Captain before the planes take off for a "special occasion," the bombing of Berlin. British war correspondent Manning (John Loder) says of Matrac, "I can't get him out of my mind. I feel I've seen him somewhere before.... I've never seen a stronger face, or a stranger one. Not a fellow to take liberties with, I should say."

Freycinet initiates the first flashback, a story to be kept "off the record ... later, I think it might be told," beginning off New Caledonia aboard the *Ville de Nancy*, a Marseilles-bound tramp freighter skippered by Captain Malo. Aside from the crew of "hard-bitten old salts" are three cabin passengers, one of whom is the "ample" Major Duval (Sydney Greenstreet), "a dominating, narrow-minded martinet" who'd been a World War I hero. "Time always proves I'm right," boasts Duval as he argues about the "invincibility" of the Maginot Line.

"Two days out of Colon," the *Nancy* sails through an area rife with German torpedo activity, where they rescue a group of emaciated men, including Matrac, Marius (Peter Lorre), Renault (Philip Dorn), Garou (Helmut Dantine) and Petit (George Tobias) aboard a drifting lifeboat. Duval deduces that they are Devil's Island fugitives, while Malo mentions that their location, currently 1,500 miles from Cayenne, makes such an assertion highly unlikely. Though the exhausted men have been "without food for 20 days, without water for five," both Bogie and Lorre are constantly puffing away on their killer cigarettes.

Grilled by Duval, Renault claims that they have sailed from Venezuela, and Matrac insists, "We have no leader. We're all equal. We're a group of free men." Marius declares they were heading to France out of patriotism, carrying an iron box of gold dust, also containing their passports, which fell overboard during an enormous swell on the Orinoco River.

"All convicts are liars," spouts the reactionary Duval, who wants to "turn them over to the police," but Malo refuses to lock them in the brig. Freycinet meets with the men, and agrees that they should be allowed to fight for France. Here, Renault begins the flashback within the flashback set in the equatorial jungle, where "men die, or else go insane." The "patriots" all gather together in a swamp to discuss the splendors of France (Lorre rolls smokes) and devise a way to serve their country: enlist Matrac, who fought against the Nazis as early as 1938.

The section featuring Matrac working as an anti-"dirty fascist flunky" journalist during the Munich Crisis is a *flashback within a flashback within a flashback*! He married Paula, but was framed for murder by the Nazis after defending the destruction of his printing press, receiving a 50-year sentence at the penal colony. Because of his "intense and fiery nature," he lands in solitary confinement. Not only was the "cage" set recycled from *Devil's Island*, but Harry Cording (who menaced Boris Karloff in the earlier film) arrives to beat Bogie senseless with a club. This portion of the film concludes with the escape of the patriotic group in the "canoe" of Grand-pere (Vladimir Sokoloff), who, "too old to fight," remains behind.

Malo announces to the men that, on June 23, France, under Marshal Petain, signed an armistice with Germany, the establishment of the Vichy government, "the blackest day in the history of our motherland." Shades of Rick Blaine enter Bogart's character at this point, as Matrac asks Freycinet if he can abandon ship off Marseilles during the night. "I don't care about my country," he alleges. "The France you and I loved is dead, Captain. She's been dying for a long time. I saw her die in the Rhineland and in Munich. Now that her death is complete, I can stop lying and tell the truth. I'm trying to get back to a woman. I never intended to fight."

"If you won't fight, why should we help you escape?" asks Freycinet.

"I'll leave that to your conscience," Matrac replies.

"Your wife is waiting for the man who went away," the Captain points out. "A man who

Passage to Marseille (1944): Devil's Island escapees Jean Matrac (Bogart) and Marius (Peter Lorre, supine on deck) aboard the *Nancy*, which sails through a series of convoluted flashbacks into combat with the Germans (original lobby card).

loved his country. The patriot. Would you betray such a woman? I leave that to *your* conscience." In a role reversal from his Vichy-leaning Renault in *Casablanca*, here Rains' character wholeheartedly supports the Free French.

Unwilling to change course for England, Duval wrests control of the boat, announcing his embrace of "the new order." The men revolt (the debonair Rains punching out Hans Conreid is a treat), Matrac and Marius grab machine guns, and Malo regains control. The men get their chance to fight sooner than expected when a German plane dive bombs the vessel. Marius is shot down, but Matrac furiously machine guns the plane into the sea, then kills the survivors when they climb onto the floating wing.

The narrative returns to "the present," with Freycinet revealing that he promoted the story of the convicts actually being victims of a torpedoed ship. Malo commands a minesweeper, Garou is "the greatest mechanic in England," and Petit works on the ground crew. As for Renault, he pilots the plane on which Matrac serves as gunner. Shot up during the raid, they miss dropping a note to Paula, but manage to land at the base.

Matrac, hit by fire from a Messerschmidt, is dead — bringing Bogie to the peak of his screen heroism by making him a martyr (he really looks like a corpse in his final close-up). The film ends at the military funeral of Matrac, with a reading of the note he wrote for the fifth birthday of his son (whom he never saw). The maudlin nature of the words, backed by an "angelic" choir, are made palatable by Rains' fine reading:

You are the heir of what your father and your friends won for you with their blood. From their hands, you have received the flag of happiness and freedom. My son, be the standard bearer of the great age they have made possible. It will be too tragic if the men of goodwill should ever be lax, or fail again to build a world where youth may love without fear, and where parents may grow old with their children, and where men will be worthy of each other's faith. Take care of your mother, Jean. I hold you in my arms. I kiss you both. May God keep you and love you as I do. Good night and au revoir, till our work is finished. And, until I see you, remember this: France lives. Vive la France.

Rains, Lorre and Dorn, as well as Bogart in an underplayed performance, lend the bewildering *Devil's Island* meets *Casablanca* propaganda film a veneer of credibility (though none of them seem remotely "French"). Curtiz, again working with his *Sea Wolf* collaborator, cinematographer James Wong Howe, created his usual quota of visual interest.

During the filming of *Conflict* that summer, Mayo paid several visits to the set, and the couple actually celebrated their fifth anniversary with the cast and crew on August 20. When his warring wife wasn't present, between takes, Bogie played chess on a hand-carved board she had given him. Halfway through production, he suggested adding a scene that reflected his attitude at the time: After bumping off his wife, Richard Manson (Bogie) tells a bartender about his wish that women were just a few inches high, small enough to carry around, then make life-size only when needed, and shrink down again when they become difficult. Not surprisingly, Steve Trilling and producer William Jacobs shot down this chauvinistic idea.

In November 1943 Bogie and Mayo left for a 10-week tour of West and North Africa and Italy. Having nothing planned, he improvised gangster-style shtick based on his Warner Bros. characters, while she sang show tunes and blues songs. During the 35,000-mile trip, they made a memorable appearance in Casablanca. In Caserta, Italy, they met up with Captain John Huston, who was working for the Army Signal Corps, shooting footage for his documentary *The Battle of San Pietro* (1945). Huston recalled them being drunk, raising some serious hell, finally resulting in their return to the States after Bogie insulted a general who had objected to his carousing in a Naples hotel.

Back in the States, Bogart, rather than returning to Los Angeles, chose to stay in New York. Jack Warner refused to tolerate this latest flexing of his star's ego, and contacted the U.S.O., informing them that, should Bogie continue to be uncooperative, he would be hesitant to send any more of his actors abroad. Likewise, Army and Pentagon brass weren't pleased with Bogie's behavior, and orders were issued for his return. Due to wartime transportation delays, Warner had a hell of a time booking the Twentieth Century Limited, then told Mort Blumenstock, the studio's New York publicity director, to get Bogart on the train.

Blumenstock located Bogie's room at the Gotham Hotel, but again he refused to leave. On the day he was supposed to board the train, he disappeared, but the U.S.O. was on his trail. Shortly before departure time, Bogart called Blumenstock, who told him that his entire career would be in jeopardy if he and Mayo didn't arrive at Grand Central Station to collect the tickets. Four days later, the Bogarts were reluctantly answering questions for reporters at L.A.'s Union Station. However, they did lend their services to "Report from the Front," a three-minute film about the trip produced to raise money for the American Red Cross, narrated by Bogie.

13

Bogie and Baby

The moody, chiaroscuro black-and-white style established in *The Maltese Falcon* and *Casablanca* continued into Warners' film noir cycle, including two major projects teaming Bogart with Howard Hawks—and young Betty Joan Perske, better known as Lauren Bacall.

Betty's mother, Natalie Weinstein-Bacal, a Jewish Rumanian immigrant, had married New Yorker William Perske, but divorced him when the child was five. After the split, Natalie reclaimed the Bacal portion of her maiden name, then changed her daughter's moniker to Betty Bacal. While in high school, aspiring actress Betty and a friend wangled their way into a meeting with Bette Davis at the Gotham Hotel.

During the fall of 1940, the ambitious 16-year-old enrolled at the prestigious American Academy of Dramatic Arts, next to Carnegie Hall. Less than a year later, she was modeling professionally on Seventh Avenue, pursuing stage roles, and marveling at real actors—including Vincent Price in *Angel Street* and Boris Karloff in *Arsenic and Old Lace*—on Broadway.

In 1942 Betty, accompanied by her mother and Aunt Rosalie, saw *Casablanca* at the Capitol Theatre. Bacall later recalled that Rosalie "was mad" about Bogart, thinking he was "sexy." Then an admirer of Bogie's costar in *The Petrified Forest*, she admitted, "I thought he was good in it, but mad about him? ... I couldn't understand Rosalie's thinking at all. Bogart didn't vaguely resemble Leslie Howard. Not in any way."[1]

In 1943 Howard Hawks formed his own company, H-F Productions, with Charles K. Feldman. Two of the properties owned by H-F—Ernest Hemingway's *To Have and Have Not* and Raymond Chandler's *The Big Sleep*—were planned as Bogart vehicles, to be produced by Hawks with no interference from Jack Warner. Before production began on the first property, Hawks sold Warner the rights to the Hemingway novel for $108,500, plus 20 percent of the gross up to $3 million.

Hawks later said:

> I was trying to get Hemingway to write for pictures, and he said, "Howard, I don't want to. I don't know enough about writing for pictures. I'm good at what I'm doing, but I don't want to go to Hollywood." And I said, "You don't have to go to Hollywood. I'll come and meet you, and we'll fish and hunt, and we'll work on a story." I said, "Ernest, I could make a picture out of your worst book."
>
> "What's my worst book?" he said, and I said, "*To Have and Have Not* is a bunch of junk."
>
> He said, "You can't make a picture out of that," and I said, "Yes, we can."[2]

David O. Selznick and Howard Hughes had made initial inquiries, but Bacall accepted an offer from Hawks in May 1943 to shoot a screen test in Hollywood. Then 18, she signed a contract for a mere $100 per week, having a little stage experience but no knowledge of film. Her photo on the cover of *Harper's Bazaar* was all it took. Hawks now set out to be Svengali to Bacall's Trilby, molding a new female star from the ground up, including driving her to secluded spots and ordering her to read aloud in a *low* voice. The director also jettisoned the name Betty in favor of Lauren, inventing a publicity story that it had been her great-grandmother's handle. She later said:

> This was my first ... role in a movie, from nowhere—from Howard Hawks. He said, "I want to put you in a picture, with either Cary Grant or Humphrey Bogart. And I thought, "Cary Grant! Oh, boy!" I thought that would be fabulous. Bogart? I thought, "Oh, I don't know." Little did I know...[3]

Hawks assigned the screenplay for *To Have and Have Not* to Jules Furthman, whose work Jack Warner found too ponderous. The mogul wanted better love scenes and more action, elements eventually supplied by three additional writers, including William Faulkner, whose dissipated lifestyle had led him to Hollywood. By the time all the ink dried, next to none of Hemingway's original story remained (current foreign-policy concerns of the Roosevelt Administration shifted the setting from Cuba to French Martinique); but Warner was pleased with the many similarities to *Casablanca*: the foreign locale, the saloon, the cynical, macho man who becomes a freedom fighter against the Nazis, the romance with a beautiful young woman who invades his domain, even the piano-playing sidekick (Hoagy Carmichael).

The material was perfect for Hawks, who specialized in stories heavy on male bonding, with an interloping, tough female who manages to get under the top man's skin; and his emphasis on the complex Bogart-Bacall relationship helped set the film apart from *Casablanca*. Jack Warner, who preferred Dolores Moran, fought against using an unknown teenager in such an important role, but Hawks wouldn't back down, an insistence that proved good for everyone—including Bogart, who was introduced to Bacall at the director's studio bungalow in the days before shooting began on February 29, 1944. "We'll have a lot of fun together," Bogie told her.[4]

When Hawks first called, "Action!" and cinematographer Sid Hickox rolled the camera, only 36 pages of the script had been completed. The nervous Bacall, writing her own dialogue during rehearsal, was shaking visibly, and Bogart was cracking wise to calm her down. To stem the trembling, she tilted her head and cast her eyes up at Bogie—a practical move that resulted in what came to be known as "The Look." She gradually overcame her trepidation, but was continually ribbed by everyone on the set, including Bogie, who had a blast loosening her up. Eventually he visited her dressing room and, while joking around, kissed her, then handed her a matchbook, on which she wrote her phone number. It was the first time in his career he had made a pass at a leading lady, and this one was young enough to be his daughter. Soon, his recent drink-sodden, irascible attitude disappeared. Bacall remembered, "Bogie ... was a very funny guy. A very witty man, which I never expected. And I, in turn, gave as good as I got."[5]

Bacall greatly admired Hawks, but her growing involvement with Bogart began to threaten their professional relationship. One evening in April, the director ordered her to appear at his home for a conference. He ran a tight ship, on the set and in private, and, though apparently happily married, simply became jealous when his discovery began to gravitate toward his male star. He told Bacall that she was jeopardizing her career and, if she continued, he would be tempted to send her to Poverty Row. The next day, Bogie assured her that this threat was nonsense, then proceeded angrily to confront Hawks and risk scuttling the production.

To Have and Have Not already was two weeks behind schedule, and Warner could not tolerate a major row between director and star. But, rather than trying to pressure Bogie, as he had done in the past, the mogul made a much simpler move. He offered more money. Bogie took the bait, and Hawks regained control of his set.

"Bogie was one of the best actors I've ever worked with," praised Hawks, who also admitted, "I had trouble the first day with Bogart. I think I grabbed him by the lapels and pushed his head up against the wall.... He had a couple drinks at lunch, and that's what caused it. Stopped that."[6]

Hawks recalled, "When two people are falling in love with each other, they're not tough to get along with."[7] Following the shoot, Bacall had to keep practicing for months to maintain her sultry, low voice, a process supported by Hawks' wife, Nancy, a.k.a. "Slim." Hawks said, "Now it's perfectly natural. And the funny thing is that Bogie fell in love with the character she played, so she had to keep playing it the rest of her life."[8]

During the shoot, Bacall had the rare experience of hanging out with two of the Warners Wiseguys when Bogie introduced her to Cagney, who typically informed her, "If you can survive even seven years at Warners, then you can conquer the world." She revealed, "[A]t this point, I still trusted Jack Warner; it didn't make sense to me that he would want to put me into anything but the best. And, in any case, I had Howard to protect me."[9]

Hawks wrapped the film on May 10, then invited Bacall to dine at his home, while her new love interest returned to the realm of "The Battling Bogarts." Bogie's domestic conditions were even worse than they had been before the shoot, but the studio's publicity department continued to circulate stories of the couple's marital bliss. Mayo, during a drunken binge on the *Sluggy*, had broken her foot; and, while she was laid up, Bogie enjoyed the opportunity to meet Bacall in secret. She admitted:

> I'd never known anyone remotely like Bogie. As he revealed more of his life to me, I realized that it had been complicated and rough.... He was a gentle man — diametrically opposed to the kind of parts he played.... He had never had a secret relationship such as we were having.... I wanted to give Bogie so much that he hadn't had.[10]

Later, Bacall added:

> I remember having to tell Bogie I was Jewish. I didn't know what his response would be. He always would say, "I'm a High Episcopalean." Well, of course, he never set foot inside a church.... He could care less. He had not a stroke of prejudice in him, in any area.[11]

One week after the wrap, Bogie wrote her a letter, romantically revealing, "[N]ow I know what was meant by 'To say goodbye is to die a little'— because when I walked away from you that last time and saw you standing there so darling I did die a little in my heart. Steve."[12]

Bogart's name superimposed over the Caribbean opens the film, then the title is followed by "A Howard Hawks Production." The major supporting actors' credits read:

> With
> Walter Brennan
> Lauren Bacall
> Dolores Moran
> Hoagy Carmichael

As in *Casablanca* and *Passage to Marseille*, Bogie will become involved with the Free French: "Martinique, in the summer of 1940, shortly after the fall of France." His seafaring character, Captain Harry Morgan, appears immediately, copping a sarcastic attitude while telling the port authority that he will be taking a client to the waters off Key West. His mate, Eddie (Hawks favorite Walter Brennan), is passed out on the dock, but a cold bucket of salt water wakes him enough to grab another bottle of beer aboard the boat. In the Hemingway environment of deep-sea fishing, Eddie pounds down brew while Horatio the Dog (Sir Lancelot) baits the hooks. The client, Mr. Johnson (Walter Sande), is as asinine as he is inept, complaining about the crew and losing fish, as well as an expensive rod and reel. He claims he doesn't have $825, then promises to pay up after visiting the bank at 10 a.m. the next day.

While entering his hotel room, Morgan hears, "Anybody got a match?" from behind him. He turns around, then tosses a matchbox to a young woman, Marie Browning (Bacall). She lights her cigarette, says, "Thanks" and walks away. She next is seen drinking with Johnson as Cricket (Hoagy Carmichael), the piano player, and his band swing "Am I Blue?" She joins in, then walks back upstairs.

"Let's have it ... Johnson's wallet," Morgan demands, taking Marie into his room, where he calls her "Slim" and she calls him "Steve." Morgan opens the wallet, finding plenty of traveler's checks and a 6:30 a.m. plane ticket inside. The Free French boys arrive, but he refuses to become involved. "You better count those traveler's checks," Morgan orders, asking Johnson to sign a denomination of $825, just as a small war breaks out in the street. Johnson is gunned down, so Morgan pockets the wallet and $60 in cash just as the Vichy Captain Renard (Dan Seymour) and Lieutenant Coyo (Sheldon Leonard) arrive. They confiscate the money and Morgan's passport, so Slim picks another pocket on the dance floor.

She buys a bottle and delivers it to "Steve's" room, then refuses to answer his questions and leaves, slamming the door, but he tails her across the hall. He exits her room, but she soon follows him back across, calls him a "stinker" and kisses him. "What did you do that for?" he calmly asks.

"Been wondering whether I'd like it," she replies.

"What's the decision?"

"I don't know yet," she claims, giving him an even better smack—the kind not usually seen on U.S. screens during the Production Code years. "It's even better when you help," she adds. "You know you don't have to act with me, Steve," she advises him as she leaves. "You don't have to say anything and you don't have to do anything. Not a thing." As she grabs the doorknob, she seductively turns her head back toward him, suggesting, "Oh, maybe just *whistle*." She opens the door, begins to walk through it, turns back again, and says, "You know how to whistle, don't you, Steve? You just put your lips together and — blow."

The scene cuts to a medium shot of Morgan. After the closing door is heard, he thinks, looks back at the doorway, grins, begins the "look at the beautiful dame" whistle, emphasizing the second, lower note by gesturing with his cigarette, then smiling wide and turning as the scene fades. Hawks claimed that he actually wrote this scene:

> It had no relation to the story, and it made such a good scene that Jack Warner ... said, "Howard, where does that come in the picture?" I said, "It isn't in there," and he said, "It better be in when you make it." So, we had a hell of a time adapting that to the picture, and finally it worked in and became the best line in the whole thing.[13]

Morgan meets with the Free French to offer transportation, alleging that a need for money is the only reason. Back at the café, Cricket sings his new number for Slim. "Steve" walks in, asks her to leave, and hands her a plane ticket for 4 p.m. that day.

Eddie arrives at the dock, but Morgan refuses to take him along, resorting to slapping him before handing him money. "I don't want you," he insists, but the rummy stows away.

"Could I have just one?" Eddie asks. "I don't want to get the shakes." (Hawks would use variations on this character in several of his later films, including his Western masterpiece *Rio Bravo* [1959], in which the tables are turned: Walter Brennan plays the unwitting nursemaid to Dean Martin's drunk.)

At his destination, Morgan collects his Free French passengers—a married couple, Paul and Helene de Brusac (Walter Molnar and Dolores Moran)—and heads back toward Martinique, but the boat is fired upon. Paul is wounded, but they are delivered successfully before Morgan and Eddie return to the café to find Slim still there, singing with Cricket. At this point in the film, Bogart appears cheerfully relaxed while projecting Morgan's calm, cool demeanor (including his trademark "rubbing the chin" gesture, one of several techniques deliberately appropriated by Frank Sinatra).

In the cellar, Morgan operates on the injured Paul after Helene objects to his non-physician status. "He probably has as good a chance with me as anybody," he says. As he begins, Helene faints dead away. Following the removal of the bullet, he tries to loosen her clothes, but Slim coolly objects to such behavior.

Back in Morgan's room, Slim offers to perform a domestic duty for him. "You've wanted to do something for me, haven't you?" he asks.

"Mmm hmm," she purrs.

"Mmm hmm," he quietly echoes, then stands up and walks toward her. "Walk around me."

She registers a slightly puzzled look.

"Go ahead. Walk around me. Clear around," he clarifies.

She circles him once, gives a charming little, breathy laugh, then shows him those big cat's eyes.

"You find anything?" he asks.

"No. No, Steve," she discloses. "There are no strings tied to you. *Not yet.*"

He manhandles her over to the door, then turns her toward him in a medium close-up, laying on another great kiss. She responds with a genuine look of satisfaction, then smiles with her *eyes* before hugging him. "Oh, I like that," she whispers, then gently hesitates, "'cept, 'cept for the beard. Why don't you shave and we'll"— she gently slaps his cheek —"we'll try it again?"

A knock from Frenchy (Marcel Dalio), interrupts them, and Steve gives her a look of desire never before seen on Bogart's cinematic face.

Eddie is being questioned by Captain Renard in the café. "Good thing you didn't get me in that tub," Steve says, gently poking her in the belly as he rushes out.

"Look out for those strings, Steve," she warns. "You're liable to trip and break your neck."

The true playfulness that exists between people who have just fallen in love is tangible in this scene, and Bogart's genuine happiness can be seen in every frame. None of his usual darkness is there. He seems as young and innocent as Bacall herself. No moment in their three subsequent films together matches this quality, because the conditions would never again be the same. Although the "whistle scene" is the most famous, this sequence may be the highlight of *To Have and Have Not*. It also is arguably as sexy as the cinema ever *needed* to get, and a towering example of how good taste and playful innuendo ("to have not") can be far superior to the actual depiction of sex that has compromised the integrity of films made decades later ("to have").

Downstairs, the repulsive Renard inquires about their last trip out to sea, accusing them of shooting at a patrol boat. Morgan claims they were attacked by a German submarine, then asks if he can have his passport, cash, the $825 owed him, plus Renard's offer of $500 in exchange for information about the "two passengers" he picked up. The ploy works, and the Vichy goons leave.

Cricket sings "Hong Kong Blues" to a packed house before Slim — a long, cool woman in a black dress, if ever there was one — enters to "go to work." "You won't have to sing much in that outfit," Morgan remarks, then reveals that he is being followed and Eddie is missing.

The Free French plan to rescue a patriot from Devil's Island (a direct "borrowing" from *Passage to Marseille*), but Morgan pretends to maintain his Rick Blaine-like neutrality, then informs Slim that she will be joining Eddie and him on a permanent trip to "Port au Prince, maybe." Bacall's stare into Bogie's eyes is another magnificent moment.

To Have and Have Not (1944): The first of the Bogart and Bacall films, *loosely* adapted from Ernest Hemingway's novel and directed by Howard Hawks, stars Bogie as skipper-cum-Free French fighter Harry Morgan, a.k.a. "Steve," and Baby as Marie Browning, a.k.a. "Slim," ably backed up by Walter Brennan as the memorable "rummy" Eddie (original lobby card).

Bacall is vocally unsure with her big number as Slim sings "How Little We Know," but the brief performance is thoroughly enjoyed by Morgan. Helene hands over her jewelry to him, asking that he keep it until she and her husband can reach safety, but Renard arrives to report that Eddie has been taken into custody.

Requesting cigarettes from a desk drawer, which Slim opens to reveal a gun, Morgan walks around to get a match, grabs the piece and shoots Renard's mute bodyguard (Aldo Nadi) *through* the desk (an inventive action device). Holding the gun on Renard and Coyo, he pretends to be stressed to the breaking point (as Sam Spade does with the Fat Man in *The Maltese Falcon*): "You've been pushing me around long enough. So, you were going to drive Eddie nuts. Picking on a poor old rummy that never … slappin' girls around. That's right, go for it! That boy needs company."

Frenchy disarms and handcuffs them, and Morgan commands them to sit on the couch. "You're both going to take a beating until one of you uses that phone. That means one of you is going to take a beating for nothing. I don't care which one it is. Let's start with you," he tells Renard, then pistol-whips him. In this scene, Bogart actually saves the day with *cigarettes*, then revives his old gangster shtick for a good cause.

Renard orders Eddie's release and signs harbor passes, prompting the Frenchman to embrace Morgan, who counters, "No kissin', Frenchy."

Eddie arrives, and Slim repeats his favorite question to him, "Was you ever bit by a dead bee?"

"Was *you*?" he parries.

"Yeah," she claims. "You know, you gotta be careful of dead bees. They can sting you just as bad as live ones, especially if they was kind of mad when they got killed."

"I feel like I was talkin' to myself," Eddie says.

"I bet I've been bit a hundred times that way," she admits.

"Why don't you bite 'em back?" he asks.

"I would," she tells him, "only I haven't got a *stinger*." Bogart glances at Bacall, looks at Brennan, and registers another of those rare, gleaming smiles.

Slim bids farewell to Cricket, who kicks his band into a sprightly Caribbean number. Giving Bogart those cat's eyes one more time, Bacall takes him out of the joint with wiggling hips and a sunny, love-soaked smile. Brennan follows behind them, carrying their suitcases. Carmichael lays down the final chord.

To Have and Have Not is a loosely plotted film, but an excellent character piece and a particular pleasure to watch any time Bogart and Bacall are together. A chance to see two *real* people actually falling in love on screen is a delight, especially a couple this believable and just this *good*. By this time, Bogart was a consummate professional; but Bacall, in her very first screen performance, looks like one. Her performance is a remarkable screen debut, and the coaching combination of Bogart and Hawks certainly was partially responsible. Beyond the individual performances, there simply is no other couple's chemistry in the classic Hollywood cinema that compares to that of Bogie and Baby, the nickname he gave to her. In 1944 their combination of artistry and reality had never been seen on the screen; and, more than six decades later, makes the film seem as fresh as the day it was released.

Walter Brennan supplies another of his memorable afflicted characters to a Hawks film. Hoagy Carmichael, who cut his teeth hanging out with Louis Armstrong in Chicago joints during the 1920s, is a treat, one of the great American songwriters and a *real* pianist, for a change. This film, released on October 11, 1944, brought some momentary joy to home-front audiences during some dreadfully dark days.

Bacall, who first saw herself on the screen at the sneak preview in Beverly Hills, recalled:

> I, of course, had no idea what it was going to be like.... And all of these cards came in, and they were thrilled with it, and I was just kind of *stunned* by it. You know, you don't realize what you've done. I never knew what was going to happen, but *they* knew: Warners knew, and Howard knew.... You cannot imagine that about *yourself*.... When I came to New York for the first time, after *To Have and Have Not* had been released ... and made a big hit, and I made a big hit in it. Then, we went by train ... I arrived at Grand Central Station, and there were *thousands* of people there, waiting to see me. [The film] was really fairy-tale time ... it worked, and I can see why it worked. All I could think of was where the romance was at the time of the scene![14]

Expecting a holiday, Bogart immediately received another script, *God Is My Co-Pilot*, which cast him as a flyer who is also a religious fanatic. The newly amiable Bogie quickly retreated, and the bristling ego returned. After giving his star more money, Jack Warner wrote to Steve Trilling that he was "sick and tired" of such "ungrateful[ness],"[15] and Bogart, on the heels of a major picture, was barred from working at Warners or any other Hollywood studio.

Jack Warner had Bogart pegged; but, when it came to Bacall, he had never been more wrong about an actor. After he saw *To Have and Have Not*, he bought her contract from Hawks before production began on *The Big Sleep*. Warner also purchased the rights to the 1939 Chandler novel (the author's first) for $20,000 in October 1944, while William Faulkner and Leigh Brackett (who had written the crime novel *No Good from a Corpse*) worked on the screenplay. Hawks later revealed that he hired Brackett, thinking she was a man, but then was even more impressed that she *wrote* like a man.

During the summer, Bogart and Bacall had cooled their trysts following an unexpected visit to the *Sluggy* by Mayo. Some of Bogie's pals intercepted the limping Mrs. Bogart and whisked her off the boat, while Bacall hid in the head until the coast was clear. Prior to beginning *The Big Sleep* shoot on October 10, Bogie limited his contact to sending flowers on her 20th birthday. Mayo, sensing what was in the wind, told her husband she'd "reform" if he'd give her a chance. He agreed but, one week into production on the new film, he moved out, finally fed up with the hollow promises of a violent alcoholic.

While working on *The Big Sleep*, Bogart and Bacall enjoyed the rave reviews they received for their chemistry in *To Have and Have Not*; but, only two weeks after leaving Mayo, Bogie returned home to give it one more try. Bacall reported to the studio with swollen and bloodshot eyes, applying ice packs before appearing on the set. Now Bogie arrived late, his heavy drinking again affecting his work.

In late October, Bogart took some time to campaign for FDR's fourth bid for the Presidency, and joined over 30 other Hollywood stars for a 60-minute broadcast sponsored by the Democratic National Committee on November 6. Approved by Jack Warner, he hosted the spectacular, which included pitches and performances by John Garfield, Judy Garland, Rita Hayworth, Gene Kelly and Lana Turner. Clarence Muse, representing FDR's African American supporters, also took part, singing "Free and Equal Blues" with songwriter Earl Robinson. Cagney also was there, forming a barbershop quartet with Danny Kaye, Keenan Wynn and Groucho Marx to take a direct shot at the right wing with a parody of "The Old Grey Mare":

> The old Red Scare
>   It ain't what it used to be
>   Ain't what it used to be
>   Ain't what it used to be ...

Illness plagued *The Big Sleep* set, causing a delay in production as Hawks recovered from the flu and Bogie suffered from laryngitis, made worse by the return of the constant inebriation that had accompanied his "reconciliation" with Mayo. He drank for a solid three weeks, until a point of crisis occurred after the cast and crew were dismissed for the Yuletide holiday. Now staying in a hotel, he celebrated his 45th birthday on Christmas Day by giving a gold watch to Bacall, then proceeded to get dangerously drunk. That night, he appeared back on his own doorstep, stewed out of his mind. After threatening Mayo, he passed out. Examined by a doctor, he was ordered to see a psychiatrist before returning to work.

Jack Warner, understandably, was not amused. Hawks tried to "shoot around Bogie" on December 26 and, by the following day, closed down production until the star could return. *The Big Sleep* was shaping up to be one of the most confusing films ever made, due in part to the fact that Faulkner and Brackett worked separately, never seeing each other's work, but simply turning in their pages to Hawks independently over a span of only eight days. At the last minute, Jules Furthman was brought in to help create a less-bewildering ending. Hawks, in an attempt to speed up production, then made the screenplay even more baffling by cutting 13 pages, a total of *11 scenes*. Following a two-day rest, Bogart appeared back at the studio on December 28. Now at least temporarily sober, he gave one of the best performances of his career.

At one point, Bogie, as confounded as anyone about the film's plot, asked Hawks, "Who pushed Taylor off the pier?" No one knew who had whacked the "mystery chauffeur" whose disappearance necessitates the hiring of Philip Marlowe. Hawks didn't know the answer, nor did — of all people — Raymond Chandler. The director later explained:

I found out for the first time that you don't have to be too logical. You should just make good scenes. Faulkner and Leigh Brackett ... They said the stuff was so good, there's no sense in making it logical. So we didn't. Because, once during the picture, Bogart said, "Who killed this fellow?" And I said ..."I don't know." So we sent a wire to the author ... and asked him, and he told us the name of the fellow, and I wired him back and I said, "He was down at the beach when that happened. It couldn't have been done that way." So, nobody knew who killed that person. It didn't hurt the picture.[16]

Hawks wrapped *The Big Sleep* on January 12, 1945, but its release would be delayed until August 23, 1946. The film didn't play well for a preview audience in March 1945, so Jack Warner decided to allow Hawks additional time to rework the film while another Bacall vehicle, an inferior muddle called *Confidential Agent*, was released. Charles Feldman reported to Warner that additional scenes with Bacall displaying the insolence she had pioneered in *To Have and Have Not* should be filmed. Also, the studio decided to complete and release its features connected to World War II, which finally was drawing to a close in Europe, and save *The Big Sleep* for after the armistice. Back on the home front later that month, Mayo finally had agreed to give Bogie a divorce, which was finalized on May 10, after which he had no further contact with her.

Bogart had begun working on *The Two Mrs. Carrolls*, directed by Peter Godfrey and produced by Mark Hellinger, who gave him time off to tie the knot with Bacall on May 21, just 11 days after his divorce, at Malabar Farm near Lucas, Ohio. She later wrote, "I couldn't have wished for a man as incredibly good as this man was. And even so I didn't realize every quality of Bogie's on that day. He was to surprise and delight me continually in the ensuing years."[17]

Back in Hollywood on June 15, 1945, *Conflict* finally was released. In the midst of all his cynically heroic World War II characters, Bogie's delusional, cold-blooded wife murderer seemed an aberration to audiences, but the presence of Sydney Greenstreet playing psychologist Mark Hamilton, a complex foil to his frequent costar, adds to the interesting, low-budget noir atmosphere conjured by director Curtis Bernhardt. No longer enjoying sole billing above the title, Bogart shares it with Alexis Smith and Greenstreet, whose hands open the film as they write a fifth-anniversary invitation to Richard Mason (Bogie) and his wife, Kathryn (Rose Hobart).

Hardly the happy couple, they bicker from the outset, with Kathy accusing Dick of being in love with her sister, Evelyn Turner (Smith), who arrives to accompany them to Hamilton's home for dinner and a "psychological" debate about love with the doctor and Professor Norman Holdsworth (Charles Drake). Evelyn is young and beautiful, while Kathy's "Bride of Frankenstein"-streaked hair reflects her contempt for Dick. During the drive home, Dick stares at Evelyn in the rear view mirror and slams the car into a tree, breaking his leg. He recovers with only a pronounced limp, but feigns paralysis, remaining in a wheelchair.

"It's funny how virtuous a man can be when he's helpless," Kathy replies when Dick fakes an apology for their argument about Evelyn. Pretending he must meet with a business associate, he tells Kathy to leave for their Mountain Springs vacation, then wait for him to arrive. While driving along a treacherous road in the fog, she is halted by a parked car, then hailed by Dick (Bogie wearing his usual trench coat and fedora), who, using a cane, walks to her from the roadside. Her meek, unconvincing "No, no, Richard, don't" dissolves to his plummeting the car off a cliff, where it is buried by a falling pile of freshly cut logs that form a pentacle.

Back at home, Hamilton calls, vowing to "look after" him during Kathy's absence. Dick phones the police to "report a missing woman" while staring at an engineering drawing of a

Conflict (1945): Bogart, Alexis Smith and Sydney Greenstreet share above-the-title billing in this noir programmer that casts Bogie as a callous wife killer (original title lobby card).

pentacle pattern. Lieutenant Workman (James Flavin) arrives, having no evidence of her whereabouts, and Dick enjoys attention from Evelyn. He mentions that Kathy had been acting strangely, adding, "She'd imagined that I had fallen in love with you."

During a visit from Hamilton, the police report finding Kathy's ring in the possession of a hobo (John Harmon) who claims he filched it from a "lady's pocket book" on a downtown street. Hamilton invites Dick to ease his stress at Rainbow Lake, and Evelyn agrees to join them. At home, Dick consults Phillips (Edwin Stanley), his butler, about the aroma of Mrs. Mason's perfume in the room, then discovers some of her personal items he had discarded with the body and car.

At the fishing lodge, Hamilton mentions the impending arrival of Holdsworth, which worries Dick as he spies a pentacle of small logs over a fire pit, then receives a phone call presumably from "Mrs. Mason." Evelyn and Holdsworth enjoy the night air, and Hamilton describes his theory that all those who commit premeditated murder are egomaniacs who believe in the "perfect crime."

Evelyn reveals that she failed to reply to Holdsworth's marriage proposal, and Dick assumes, "You feel about me just as I feel about you." In his room, he admits that he loves her and that "Kathryn was right." Shifting into his rapid-fire dialogue mode, Bogart effectively conveys Mason's obsession as Evelyn rebuffs Dick's claims.

At his engineering office, Dick opens an envelope addressed in Kathy's hand and containing a claim ticket. At a pawnshop, he is handed a locket, engraved "From Richard to

Kathryn" and containing their photos, but cannot buy it until a 90-day waiting period has passed. Neglecting to pay for a taxi, Dick is called "sweetheart" by the cabbie. He returns to the shop with Workman, finding a different pawnbroker and no locket. Wild-eyed, Dick grabs the man but is escorted out by the detective.

Dick and Hamilton take the envelope to a handwriting analyst, who declares it genuine but perhaps written by a close blood relative. He then is tipped off by Phillips about Evelyn taking Kathy's stationery and wearing the same brand of perfume. At Rainbow Lake, he insists on driving Evelyn home, but is interrupted by a call from Hamilton, who reports that, due to the authenticity of the handwriting, "I think it means that Kathryn is still alive." Dick then shows his decent side by telling Holdsworth to try again with Evelyn, and that he's "a nice fellow."

The next day, Dick believes that he sees Kathy walking along a downtown street, then psychotically accuses a landlady of harboring "his wife ... a person who's been murdered." At Hamilton's office, he reports his experience, denying the supernatural and insisting that the woman "couldn't have been" Kathy. The doctor says he needs Dick's confidence to be able to help, and the "mental case" speeds back to the scene of the crime, where Hamilton and the police are waiting for him. Having given Kathy a rose pin just before she left for the mountains, the doctor knew that Dick could only have seen it at the time of her death; after Dick mentioned it during the police interview, he began baiting his elaborate snare.

Contrived, loaded with B-film trappings, and cursed with a nondescript title, *Conflict* nonetheless is a quickly paced, entertaining little film featuring an atypical Bogart characterization. In fact, the production seems less a Warners and more like a Columbia programmer that would have been a good fit for Boris Karloff or Basil Rathbone.

On August 15, 1945, production halted on Bacall's *Confidential Agent* to celebrate the end of World War II. Jack Warner sent telegrams to several political heavyweights, including President Harry Truman, Prime Minister Winston Churchill, Eleanor Roosevelt and Ambassador to the U.S.S.R. Joseph E. Davies, author of *Mission to Moscow* and the force behind the studio's 1943 (soon to be controversial) film version.

Though most film artists, like the public at large, expected a lessening of home-front turmoil now that the war had ended, the knee-jerk start of the Cold War led to an undemocratic atmosphere bearing similarities to that which the Allies had just successfully fought against. Even Jack Warner began to "make a list," including the names of the left-wing writers who had crafted anti-fascist screenplays for Errol Flynn, John Garfield and Bogart. Then the mogul's liberal politics really began to drift to the right on Friday, October 5, when hundreds of striking film technicians—members of the Conference of Studio Unions (an alternative to IATSE)—formed picket lines outside Warner Bros. and were fended off by blasts from fire hoses. However, the strikers remained until the following Monday, when a gang of goons poured from the gates to beat them with clubs. As more strike busters arrived, cars were overturned and the violence escalated. The Screen Actors Guild maintained neutrality during the strike, but many performers sent telegrams of protest, and names such as "Bloody Monday" and "The Battle of Burbank" were coined.

Later that month, the National Labor Relations Board ruled that the technicians had the right to choose their own representation. The studio bosses backed down, but IATSE, the Motion Picture Alliance for the Preservation of American Ideals (MPA), and California's Committee on Un-American Activities all alleged that the strike had been a Communist conspiracy. Lists of sympathizers—fuel for future blacklisting—were compiled, and Jack Warner continued his migration to the right. Hollywood liberals now lost their only ally with power in the industry, a reality that affected all the Warner Bros. Wiseguys, particularly Robinson and Bogart.

The MPA, founded by ultra-conservative director Sam Wood (president) and the anti-labor Walt Disney (vice-president), were at the forefront of the witch-hunters, providing endless lists of "Commie" names to the House Committee on Un-American Activities (HUAC) and other major blacklisters. Top actors who joined included Pat O'Brien (whose participation must have annoyed Cagney), Gary Cooper, Donald Crisp, Irene Dunne, Clark Gable, Adolphe Menjou, Ginger Rogers, Barbara Stanwyck and Robert Taylor. John Wayne eventually served as president, supported by his best buddy Ward Bond, undeniably the biggest reactionary windbag in the history of the blacklist. John Ford, whose politics never agreed with those of the MPA, also joined up with the two premiere members of his "stock company." (The director never could stand his "discoveries" to take a leadership role without his personal involvement.)

When *The Big Sleep* was finally released, with several original (fully scored) scenes cut and replaced by 15 minutes of new footage (shot an entire year after the original wrapped), it was no less confusing than before, but the Bogart-Bacall chemistry won over critics and filmgoers. Following John Huston's innovative lead in *The Maltese Falcon*, Hawks chose to include Philip Marlowe in nearly every scene, allowing the audience to examine the developing case through the detective's experiences. One of the physical gestures Bogie used to set Marlowe apart from Sam Spade was a frequent pulling of his ear, which he and Hawks developed to demonstrate the detective's own bewilderment over the case.

In this final release version, in most of the scenes featuring Bogart and Bacall (shot in late 1944 and early 1945), the couple were still frustrated lovers; while, in several others (filmed in January 1946), they were now a married couple. The opening credits, providing a prime example of film noir imagery, feature a silhouette of a man and woman (*not* Bogart and Bacall) lighting cigarettes as the couple shares above-the-title billing (only Bogie is pre-title on *To Have and Have Not*, and Bacall is billed third). As usual, "A Howard Hawks Production" appears after the title. Just before the supporting players' names appear, the camera moves into a close-up of an ashtray eventually housing two smoldering smokes.

The door nameplate, "Sternwood," framed in close-up, immediately establishes the location from which Philip Marlowe's adventures will emanate. The shadow of a fedora creeps across half of it before the camera moves down to the detective's right hand pressing the bell button. A dissolve leads inside to Norris (Charles D. Brown), the butler, answering the door. Here, Hawks gives Bogart a unique introduction, first using audio only—"My name's Marlowe. General Sternwood wanted to see me"—then having him walk in and politely remove his hat. While Sam Spade begins a new case by having clients come to his office, Marlowe makes a [green]house call, to an invalid who requires the heat of his home botanical center to survive.

An absolutely breathtaking female (Martha Vickers) descends the stairs. Wearing a pair of shorts, she appears to have gams all the way up to her neck, a feature Marlowe instantly notices before he looks up to her face to say, "Morning."

She checks out *his* legs. "You're not very tall, are you?" passes her lips.

"Oh, I try to be," Marlowe replies. "Riley, Doghouse Riley" is the name he offers. "Shamus," the occupation.

She gives him a couple glances, then falls backward into his arms. "You're cute," she sighs as he barely laughs and Norris returns to announce, "The General will see you now, Sir." She slowly crawls out of his grasp and slinks toward the background. Marlowe turns

The Big Sleep (1946): Perhaps the most convoluted linear narrative ever filmed, Howard Hawks' film noir classic features plenty of smoldering scenes with Bogie and Baby (original title lobby card).

around, briefly walking *backwards*, watching her, while moving toward his client's sanctuary. "Who's that?" he asks the butler.

"Miss Carmen Sternwood, Sir," Norris reveals.

"You ought to wean her," suggests Marlowe. "She's old enough."

"How do you like your brandy, Sir?" the General (Charles Waldron) inquires.

"In a glass," replies Marlowe.

Sternwood speaks of his poor health, brought on by extravagance, and his current vicarious need to enjoy others' vices. Asked to describe himself, Marlowe offers, "I'm 38, I went to college. I can still speak English when my business demands it. Used to work for the District Attorney's office.... I was fired for insubordination. I seem to rate pretty high on that."

The father of two live-in daughters, "both pretty — and *pretty wild*," one single (Carmen) and the other divorced (Mrs. Vivian Rutledge), Sternwood is "being blackmailed again." A year earlier, he had "paid a man named Joe Brody $5,000" to leave Carmen alone. At the time, a detective, Sean Regan, had handled the affair. No longer employed by the General, Regan, a former IRA captain who also "traded shots" with Marlowe, has not communicated for about a month.

In an envelope, Marlowe finds the business card of rare book dealer Arthur Gwynn Geiger, which includes a handwritten note referring to several enclosed promissory notes for gambling debts signed by Carmen. Sternwood says he didn't ask about Geiger, because, "if I did, she'd just suck her thumb and look coy."

"Yeah, I met her in the hall, and she did that to me," replies Marlowe, "then she tried to sit on my lap when I was standing up." Bogart delivers the line with classic noir sarcasm, while Waldron registers an almost imperceptible scoff. "If I seem a bit sinister as a parent, Mr. Marlowe," Sternwood explains, it's because my hold on life is too slight to include any Victorian hypocrisy. I need hardly add that any man who has lived as I have, and who indulges for the first time in parenthood at my age, deserves all he gets."

"Pay him," Marlowe commands, pointing out that the notes are signed. Advised to "get rid of" Geiger, he insures the General that word will be delivered. Soaked with sweat, he is asked to visit Mrs. Rutledge. The camera pans with Marlowe until Vivian is revealed, in profile, pouring a drink. Turning to face him, she gives her disparaging opinion of private detectives. In Bogie and Bacall's first scene together, the rhythm established with the rapid fire, sometimes overlapping dialogue, is razor sharp. Vivian is as ruthless as Carmen is shameless. "I don't like your manners," she tells Marlowe.

"I'm not crazy about yours," he fires back. "I didn't ask to see you. I don't mind if you don't like my manners. I don't like them myself. They're pretty bad. I grieve over them long winter evenings, and I don't mind you ritzing me or drinking your lunch out of a bottle, but don't waste your time trying to cross-examine me."

Slamming down her glass on the window sill, she exclaims, "People don't talk to me that way!" She slowly saunters toward him, asking, "Do you always think you can handle people like, uh, trained seals?"

"Uh, huh," he responds. "I usually get away with it, too."

She speculates that her father isn't really concerned with finding Sean Regan, who "just drove off one afternoon without saying a word. They found his car parked in some private garage."

At the Hollywood Public Library, Marlowe bones up on rare first edition books before dropping in at A. J. Geiger's shop. Unsatisfied with the way Bogart initially played this scene, Hawks told him to make it more interesting, so he improvised some business with Marlowe assuming the personality of an eccentric bibliophile. Turning up the brim of his fedora, donning dark shades, and pressing his fingers together in a prayer-like position, Marlowe enters, prissily asking Agnes (Sonia Darrin), the clerk, for first editions that never existed. "You do sell books, hmm?" he inquires, pushing down his glasses and peering over the rim. "Maybe I better see Mr. Geiger."

"He's not in just now," she replies. An old gent enters, and she buzzes him into a back room.

As soon as Marlowe exits the store, the brim goes down, the shades come off, and the cool but determined, manly persona returns. Thunder rolls overhead as he heads across the street to the Acme Book Shop, where he grills the owner (Dorothy Malone) for a description of Geiger. He discusses the same "first editions" with her, revealing, "I'm a private dick on a case." Her knowledge is such that she'd "make a good cop." Determined to wait an hour for Geiger to leave at closing time, and wanting to stay out of the rain, he tells her, "You know, it just happens, I've got a bottle of pretty good rye in my pocket. I'd a lot rather get wet in here."

She locks up the joint and pulls down the shade, closing for the afternoon. Over drinks, her glasses come off and hair comes down, revealing a knockout brunette. "*Hello*," Marlowe drawls enthusiastically. When a car driven by "Geiger's shadow, Carol Lundgren (Tom Rafferty)," pulls up, he pats her on the shoulder, says, "So long, pal," and hits the street.

In the pouring rain, Marlowe trails Geiger's car to a house on Laverne Terrace. Soon, a

Packard pulls up, and a woman runs into the house. Marlowe examines the registration, made out to Carmen Sternwood, then relaxes in his car, smoking cigarettes. Glancing at the front of the house, he sees a bright flash in the window, then hears a woman scream. Three shots blast inside as he runs to the front door. A man runs out the back, drives off in the Packard, and is followed by a man in another car. Marlowe crawls in through the window, discovers the body of Geiger (Theodore Von Eltz), the inebriated Carmen, and an empty camera hidden inside a piece of ceramic sculpture. "You're higher than a kite," he tells Carmen, helping her to the sofa. As the scene dissolves, Marlowe rummages through a strong box, in which he — while tugging at his right ear — discovers the murdered man's secret code book. [The original 1945 version shows Marlowe discovering Geiger, Carmen, and the camera; then making a thorough search of the house before finding the box.]

Marlowe stuffs the book into his pants, closes the window, and escorts Carmen toward the door. Another dissolve leads to inside the Sternwood home, where Norris welcomes him. Vivian joins them, helping Marlowe carry Carmen into her bedroom. "Did you do this?" she asks.

Marlowe cracks wise, advising her to forget about the entire affair, but another mention of Sean Regan creates a tense moment. He then gives Norris the same advice before walking through the rain back to Geiger's house, where the body has disappeared. [In the 1945 version, after Marlowe drags Carmen from the murder scene, he is seen driving her home, then talking to Norris outside in the rain.]

Police Inspector Bernie Ohls (Regis Toomey) arrives at Marlowe's apartment to report the discovery of a Packard belonging to the Sternwoods, "washing around in the surf off Lido Pier. And I almost forgot, there's a guy in it." Marlowe accompanies him to the scene, where the dead man is identified as Owen Taylor, the Sternwood chauffeur. (This content of this scene is reminiscent of *The Maltese Falcon*.)

Vivian is waiting at Marlowe's office the next morning. She apologizes for her previous rudeness, then hands him an envelope containing a photograph of Carmen. In exchange for the negative, the owner wants $5,000. Marlowe inquires why she didn't call the police, so she dials the phone. Some shenanigans with a cop follow, then she asks Marlowe why he nixed the call.

"Because I'm working for your father," he replies, "or because I think I'm beginning to like another of the Sternwoods."

"I prefer the second reason," she says, then suggests that five grand can be borrowed from the gambler, Eddie Mars.

Back at Geiger's book shop, Marlowe, pulling his ear, spies Lundgren and an associate packing crates in the back room. He grabs a taxi, banters with the female cabbie (Joy Barlowe), and tails a station wagon to the Randall Arms apartments, where he sees the name "Joe Brody" on the resident listing. Back at the murder scene, he finds Carmen, who claims that Brody committed the crime. A stranger—with "two boys outside"—enters, asking about Geiger. Marlowe identifies him as Eddie Mars (John Ridgely).

At his office, Marlowe is phoned by Vivian, who claims she hasn't seen Carmen. Waiting outside the Randall Arms, he sees her walk in, then muscles his way into Brody's apartment. Brody (Jean Heydt) pulls a gat, and Marlowe asks the two hiding women — Agnes and Vivian — to come out. He advises Vivian not to pay off Brody, whom he accuses of being Geiger's murderer and the owner of the photograph. Carmen arrives, packing heat and demanding the picture. Brody hands Marlowe the negative, and Vivian takes her sister home.

Brody's explanation is that he'd been watching Geiger's house, where Owen Taylor (Dan

Wallace), "sweet on Carmen," broke in, whacked Geiger, and stole the film. Brody followed the Packard until it skidded off the road; then, playing "copper," he took the film from Taylor and left. Marlowe, of course, believes that Brody engineered the affair of the Packard in the ocean and the hiding of Geiger's body, but says, "All I want to do is find out what Geiger had on the Sternwoods."

Brody walks over to answer the door. Two gunshots blast through the opening, Brody crumples against the wall, and Marlowe pursues the killer, Lundgren, down the stairs and into the street, where he ducks a shot. Tracking him down, Marlowe, gat drawn, forces Lundgren to drive to Geiger's house. Lundgren tries to get tough, but Marlowe knocks him out, discovers the body in the bedroom, and calls Bernie Ohls: "Did you boys find a gun on Owen Taylor when you fished him out of the drink last night ... if they did, it had three empty shells in it. You come up to 7244 Laverne Terrace, off Laurel Canyon Road, and I'll show you where the slugs went." Ohls then grills Lundgren about hiding Geiger's body and shooting Brody.

[Two 1945 scenes occurring at this point were cut in their entirety: The first, set at the office of the D.A. (Thomas Jackson), features Marlowe with Ohls and Captain Cronjager (perennial cop James Flavin) recapping the case. The second shows Vivian waiting at Marlowe's office, wearing a veil that partially obscures her face. In fact, her entire head appears caged, not only inside the wire-like veil, but also encased by an absolutely hideous hat resembling an ancient leather football helmet. No wonder Charles Feldman had written to Jack Warner about replacing the scene with a new, sexier one. The mogul took the advice, then characteristically claimed it was his own idea.]

The 1946 replacement scene features the same dialogue, but is set in a bar, where Vivian is stunningly dressed, sans veil and hat. She reports that her father is pleased with the results of the previous evening, and Marlowe replies, "Yes, I managed to keep the Sternwoods out of it." The General is ready to pay him off, case closed, but Marlowe counters that only the Geiger incident has been finalized. Vivian, insisting that Geiger was their only concern, hands him a $500 check. "Tell me, what do you usually do when you're not working?" she asks.

"Oh, play the horses, fool around," he answers.

"No women?" she quietly inquires.

"I'm generally working on something most of the time," he admits.

"Could that be stretched to include me?" she asks.

"I like you. I told you that before," he reminds her.

"I liked hearing you say it," she reveals, "but you didn't do much about it."

"Well, neither did you," he points out.

"Well, speaking of horses," she says, "I like to play them myself, but I like to see them work out a little first—to see if they're front runners, or come from behind. Find out what their whole cart is—what makes them run."

"Find out mine?" he asks.

"I think so," she replies, playing with a cigarette.

"Go ahead," he encourages.

"I'd say you don't like to be rated," she begins. "You like to get out in front, open up a lead, take a little breather in the back stretch, and then come home free."

Marlowe lights her smoke. "You don't like to be rated yourself."

"I haven't met anyone yet that could do it," she gently boasts. "Any suggestions?"

"I can't tell, until I've seen you over a distance of ground," he explains. "You've got a touch of class, but I don't know how far you can go."

13—Bogie and Baby

"A lot depends on who's in the saddle," she informs him. "Go ahead, Marlowe. I like the way you work. In case you don't know it, you're doing all right."

He sits back in his chair. "There's one thing I can't figure out."

"What makes me run?" she interjects.

"Uh huh," Marlowe murmurs.

"I'll give you a little hint," she offers. "Sugar won't work. It's been tried."

"What'd you try it on me for?" he asks. "Who told you to sugar me off this case? Was it Eddie Mars?"

Cat's-eyes indignation plays on Vivian's face as she plops down her whiskey glass.

"All right," Marlowe says, holding up his right hand. "Don't answer me, but somebody put you up to it, and it wasn't your father. He didn't tell you to pay me off, did he?"

"No," she admits, "he's not well. I used my own judgment."

"Are you sure?" he asks.

This scene is *exactly* what Charles Feldman had ordered: all the insolence and innuendo of the *To Have and Have Not* teaming, plus the added conflict of Bacall's character not being truthful with Bogie's. Here, again, is cinematic sensuality as good as it could get in the 1940s under the Production Code, but Marlowe and Vivian — and their problematic relationship — are more complex than Steve and Slim in the previous film.

Marlowe asks Vivian about her gambler pal, disclosing, "Did you know it was Eddie Mars' blonde wife Sean Regan was supposed to have run off with?"

She registers a slight look of surprise, but says, "Who doesn't?"

"Did you know he owned the house Geiger operated in — that he was mixed up in that racket, too?" he asks.

"No," she denies, "I don't believe it," puffing on her cigarette.

Marlowe pushes a bit. "Then why does it bother you so much?" She smashes out the smoke as he opens up. "What's Eddie Mars got on you?" He studies her continued mangling of the cigarette. "Oh, come now, Angel, stop shaking. I don't want to hurt you. I'm trying to help you." He stands up. "Well, you better run along. You made a deal, and you're going to stick to it, right or wrong. We'll take up the question of you and I when the race is over."

She stands up. He continues, "The only trouble is, we could have ..." Someone bumps into her and Marlowe grabs her. "Pardon me," says the stranger.

"Yes," she agrees. "The only trouble is, we could have had a lot of fun if you weren't a detective."

"We still can," he counters.

"So long, Marlowe." She walks out.

Marlowe calls Mars, then drives to his gambling lodge. The singer at the center of the room is none other than Vivian, who smiles and waves at Marlowe. Bacall's vocals are a slight improvement on her *To Have and Have Not* effort.

Marlowe asks Mars about Sean Regan, but the gambler replies that the murders of Geiger and Brody have closed the blackmail case. Asked about his two-timing wife and Regan, Mars says it's private business. Bogart does a subtle double take as Marlowe asks, "Oh, Eddie, you don't have anybody watching me, do you? Tailing me in a gray Plymouth coupe, maybe?"

Marlowe believes none of it. On his way out, he visits Vivian at the roulette table, where Mars raises her marker. She wins and leaves to meet Marlowe outside.

Marlowe grabs a .38 from a secret compartment in his car, then waits for one of Mars' goons to stick her up. "Somebody's always giving me guns," he tells the stooge, then punches him out. [A version of this scene was originally filmed for the 1945 version, then re-shot for the 1946 release.]

While driving her home, Marlowe stops on the side of the road. He again asks her about Mars, reaffirming his affection for her father and "another one of the Sternwoods."

"I wish you'd show it," Vivian tells him. Marlowe kisses her. "I like that," she admits. "I'd like more." Another kiss. "That's even better." Seventy-six minutes into the film, Bogie and Bacall finally connect.

Vivian realizes that Marlowe *is* trying to use sugar to get what he wants. "So that's the way it is?"

"Kissing is all right," he says. "It's nice. I'd like to do more of it. But, first, I'd like to know what Eddie Mars has on you." He knows that she, Mars and the goon staged the scene at the gambling joint. When she refuses to reveal the contents of her bag, he tells her his efforts to "carry" her are over.

Carmen is waiting in Marlowe's apartment. When he tries to give her the bum's rush, she bites him. He throws her out, goes to bed, then is awakened at 2 *p.m.* by a phone call from Bernie Ohls. The D.A.—at Vivian's request—has ordered him to drop the Sternwood case, so he explains the Mars-Regan connection.

At a diner, Marlowe calls Norris, but is informed by Vivian that they have located Regan in Mexico. On his way out, he is dragged into an alley and beaten by two thugs. Harry Jones (Elisha Cook, Jr.), a former bootlegger hired by the late Brody to tail him, escorts him to his office. Agnes has found Mrs. Mars, and Jones wants $200 for the exchange. Marlowe arrives at their appointed meeting, but the little man is being grilled at gunpoint by another Mars stooge, Canino (B-Western actor Bob Steele), who forces him to drink poison. Alone with the body, Marlowe answers a call from Agnes, who meets with him to sell the information.

At the designated location, an auto garage, Marlowe fakes a blowout, then finds Canino and Art Huck (Trevor Bardette) inside, but the two thugs aren't dumb enough to believe his story. Huck grabs his overcoat from behind (the same maneuver Bogie uses on Elisha Cook in *The Maltese Falcon*) and Canino knocks him out.

Marlowe, tied up on the floor of the house behind the garage, regains consciousness, recognizes Mona Mars (Peggy Knudsen), then welcomes Vivian into the room. "The boys don't take any chances, do they?" he observes. "Where are they? Out digging a grave?"

"Why did you have to go on?" Vivian asks.

"Too many people told me to stop," he replies. "Light me a cigarette, would you, Angel?"

Mona swears she and Regan "were just good friends." She had to hide out to allay police suspicions that Mars had killed him.

"Eddie Mars never kills anybody. He just hires it done," he informs her. She tosses a drink in his face and storms out. "She's all right. I like her," he tells Vivian. [A version of this scene, using a different actress, Pat Clark, in the Mona role, was shot for the 1945 version. It was re-shot in 1946 because Clark gave an embarrassingly wooden performance.]

"You like too many people," she replies, *still* asking him to drop the case. The detail in Bogart's portrayal of Marlowe is impressive: "Don't cut toward your hand," he says as Vivian saws through the rope. Wearing handcuffs, Marlowe tells her to "count to twenty slowly, then scream your head off" before hiding out on the porch.

Canino and Huck rush in to investigate the scream, Marlowe grabs the .38 from his car, and waits. Huck reappears outside, slowly surveys the yard, then runs like hell when Marlowe fires a warning shot. Canino fires two shots from a window, then emerges, using Vivian as a shield. Marlowe hunkers down behind the driver's side fender. "There!" she yells and points. "There, behind the wheel!"

Canino blasts away four more times, emptying his gun. He isn't so bright, after all. His demise is a classic Howard Hawks moment: Marlowe stands up, enlightens him — "Over here, Canino"— then gives him three shots to the belly. The goon stoops, stumbles backward against a huge tree, and slowly slumps over, the car blocking his fall to the ground. Hawks then cuts to a two-shot of Marlowe grabbing the handcuff key from his pocket.

This scene is immediately followed by another graced by dialogue characteristic of Hawks. In Canino's car, Marlowe and Vivian speed into town. "I didn't have a chance to thank you for what you did back there," he says. "You looked good, awful good. I didn't know they made 'em like that anymore." The director's films often feature characters and situations in which one wonders if another "is good enough." Often, the characters are male; sometimes, they are atypical, resourceful women — like Bacall — or Joanne Dru's "Tess Millay" in his landmark Western *Red River* [1948], in which the wounded woman stands up to a psychotic John Wayne).

"I guess I'm in love with you," Vivian tells Marlowe, matter-of-factly, then threatens to confess to killing Regan if he takes her to the police.

"I'm not going to," he replies. Whereas Sam Spade in *The Maltese Falcon* is a "take it and like it" hard-boiled detective, Philip Marlowe has a more sensitive nature and doesn't enjoy violence for the sake of it. "Look, Angel, I'm tired," he admits. "I killed a man back there, and I had to stand by while a harmless little guy was killed. You think I could tell them all that happened because Geiger tried to throw a loop over Carmen?"

Marlowe refuses to ask anything further about her involvement in the Regan-Mars affair. Unlike Sam Spade's romantic entanglement with Brigid O'Shaughnessy, which is always a direct part of the case (as is everything else the detective does in *The Maltese Falcon*), Marlowe's involvement with Vivian often has nothing to do with his professional investigations. Spade sends Brigid up the river, perhaps to the chair, but Marlowe never considers doing any such thing to Vivian. After all, at this point, it's Bogie and his wife!

"I guess I'm in love with you," Marlowe echoes as they head for one last visit to the Geiger house. He phones Mars, reporting the news about the gambler's "best boy," Canino, and lying that he is still at the auto garage. They agree to meet at Geiger's in 10 minutes, so Vivian closes up the house while he hides the car. Two Mars stooges, Pete (Ben Welden) and Sidney (Tom Fadden), prowl the grounds as Mars enters the house with a key. Mars attempts to cut the telephone cord, but Marlowe pulls his gat and frisks him. "It was *Carmen*, wasn't it, Eddie?" he asks, referring to the murder of Regan, who made advances to her when she was high.

Marlowe knows that Mars entered without a gun to strike a bogus deal. As Sid Hickox tracks the camera into a medium close-up of Bogart, Marlowe explains, "When I went out that door, things were going to be different. That's what those boys are doing out there. But everything's changed now, Eddie, because I got here first. All right, Angel, get down on the floor."

Now Bogart launches into his stressed-out, trigger-happy act. Mars tries to talk tough, but Marlowe blasts the ceramic sculpture. "What do you want me to do?" he asks. "Count three, like they do in the movies? That's what Canino said to little Jonesy." He fires one shot, creasing Mars' left arm. He fires a second shot, sending the coward fleeing out the door. "Don't shoot! It's Mars!" can be heard outside as the door closes, machine gun fire splintering it from right to left. The door slowly reopens and Mars' body falls in on its face. (This sequence combines Cagney's end in *The Public Enemy* with that of Paul Muni in Hawks' own *Scarface*.)

Marlowe calls Ohls, reports the incident, claiming that Mars killed Regan. How can this conclusion possibly satisfy the Production Code? "Let me do the talking, Angel," he says. "I don't know yet what I'm going to tell them, but it'll be pretty close to the truth. You'll have to send Carmen away, from a lot of things. They have places for that. Maybe they can cure her. It's been done before. We'll have to tell your father about Regan. I think he can take it."

"You've forgotten one thing," Vivian mentions. "Me."

"What's wrong with you?" inquires Marlowe.

"Nothing you can't fix," she replies, giving him "The Look" as a police siren sounds in the distance.

This concluding material was very daring for a 1946 film. While drugs are never mentioned (a provision of the Production Code), Marlowe continually refers to Carmen as being "high." Perhaps the only drug is booze, enough to have loosened her up for a pornographic photo; but, at one point, he smells her glass and registers a perplexed expression. Some congenital mental illness may also be plaguing the troubled young woman. If she did kill Regan, a murderer is going free (a direct violation of the Code), albeit due to extenuating circumstances. Marlowe's mentioning of "places for that" indicates, in 1940s parlance, a "sanitarium."

Rather than becoming less confusing with each repeated viewing, *The Big Sleep* can remain a confounding experience. But Howard Hawks was right: "good scenes" make an entertaining and interesting film, regardless of plot incoherence. In the case of *The Big Sleep*, narrative clarity is not important at all — not when Bogart and Bacall are the main attraction. Their characters do not ignite each other in the same way as do Steve and Slim in *To Have and Have Not*, not only because they were married while *The Big Sleep* was still being tweaked, but due to the substantially different literary personalities they were interpreting for Hawks. Surrounded by a Warners gallery of fine players, they — partially due to re-shooting — gave another pair of unforgettable performances.

During the summer of 1946, Warner Bros. loaned Bogart to Columbia, where he costarred with Lizabeth Scott in *Dead Reckoning* (1947), directed by John Cromwell. On October 14, 1946, he was back with Bacall (each earning $10,000) for a *Lux Radio Theatre* broadcast of *To Have and Have Not*, hosted by William Keighley. However, shrewd Jack Warner withheld his consent until they both agreed to film a cameo for *Two Guys from Milwaukee* (1946), starring Dennis Morgan and Jack Carson.

Warner was so pleased with the new version of *The Big Sleep* that he tore up Bogart's seven-year contract, offering him a 15-year deal at $200,000 per picture, plus story, screenplay and director approval. In return, Bogie gave immediate, blanket director approval to Hawks, John Huston, Michael Curtiz, John Cromwell and Delmer Daves.

Bogart's first two hand-picked projects were wildly different: *Dark Passage*, a noir thriller pairing him with Bacall and told with subjective camera from his character's perspective; and *The Treasure of the Sierra Madre*, rivalling *The Maltese Falcon* as John Huston's ultimate masterpiece, featuring Bogie as a likeable, down-and-out fellow who becomes a psychotic maniac after discovering gold in the mountains of Mexico.

Bacall met Huston when Bogart took her to a party at Ira Gershwin's home. She later wrote:

> Huston was ... another original. Aside from his extraordinary talent, he's always been a personal mesmerizer.... He adored Bogie and vice versa — he was very funny but devilish and socially unde-

pendable.... I was accepted immediately by him because I loved his friend. He didn't like women much on their own.[18]

On the home front, Bogart was happier than he'd been in years, finally content in a married relationship. He substantially cut back on his drinking, and when he did become overly sarcastic with a friend or visitor, Bacall quickly cut him down to size. Held up by the wedding and the retooling of *The Big Sleep*, Warners' *The Two Mrs. Carrolls*, which had been in the can since June 1945, finally was released on March 4, 1947. As in *Conflict*, Bogie plays a wife murderer, but this time Geoffrey Carroll, an American artist leading a double life in England. Produced *before* his new contract was signed, this Warners film, based on a play by Martin Vale and directed by Peter Godfrey, was the first since *Virginia City* to miscast him.

Bogie is billed above the title with Barbara Stanwyck and Alexis Smith, while English character actor Nigel Bruce is in the top supporting spot. When the film opens, Geoffrey and his girlfriend, Sally (Stanwyck), have only just met. He is sitting by a pleasant Scottish stream, sketching her, as MacGregor (Colin Campbell), calls out, "You've caught a fish!" Carroll orders him to throw it back, not wanting the animal to be "unhappy."

That afternoon, the couple will celebrate their anniversary of "knowing each other for two weeks." As Carroll admits, "Two weeks is the only real happiness I've ever known. I love you, Sally. I love you," Bogie gives perhaps the most wooden performance of his Warner Bros. career. Appearing in his first film since completing *To Have and Have Not*, he had to be uncomfortable working with Stanwyck. His stilted love scenes with her are the complete antithesis of his smoldering passion with "Baby." Or perhaps Bogie knew that Barbara was a witch-hunting member of the Motion Picture Alliance.

Rain pours down, and they seek shelter in a cave. While Carroll runs to collect the fishing gear, Sally shakes out his coat, discovering an unmailed letter containing his plea for a divorce from his invalid wife. She runs off, and he holds his hand to his head, overcome by pain, as Franz Waxman's melodramatic music surges on the soundtrack.

In London, Carroll visits Blagdon (Barry Bernard), a chemist, then returns to his wife and daughter, Beatrice (Ann Carter), who admires his in-progress painting, "The Angel of Death." As he takes a glass of "milk" into his wife's bedroom, he informs Bea that she will be enrolled in a private school. The next scene moves to "the cathedral town of Ashton," where Geoffrey has been living for 18 months with the new Mrs. Carroll, Bea, and the finished "Angel of Death" hanging over the fireplace.

Sally's ex-fiancé, Charles Pennington (Patrick O'Moore), arrives for a visit, announcing that two more guests, Cecily Latham (Alexis Smith) and her mother (the ever-pompous Isobel Elsom), will be joining him. Upstairs in his studio, Geoffrey fumes over his inability to produce a decent painting. Sally passes on the news about "Penny," and Carroll threatens to "break his neck."

"Oh, don't be silly," she naively replies. "You're not jealous of Penny."

"You've got some wrong information," he insists. "I'm jealous of anything or anybody that takes your mind off me for a single second."

Sally grabs his wrists. "I like that."

Carroll refuses to go downstairs. As to Penny, he declares (in an obvious Bogart improvisation), "You know, I have the strangest feeling that this is the beginning of a beautiful hatred."

Cecily, having attended a recent exhibition of Carroll's work, asks him to paint her portrait. "I always paint what I see," he tells her. "Some people find that embarrassing." He also says exactly what he thinks, refusing to take her commission "right now."

The Two Mrs. Carrolls (1947): Warners miscast Bogart one last time, as another wife murderer, in this stilted thriller also starring Barbara Stanwyck, Alexis Smith and Nigel Bruce (original title lobby card).

"Don't I suggest an idea to you?" Cecily asks.

"Yes," he replies, "but nothing I'd care to paint." Carroll's disinterest in the guests (and Bogart's in the role) is so apparent that he spends most of the scene staring at and smoking his cigarette.

Carroll shows Cecily some of his work, but she is more interested in flirting with him. He describes "The Angel of Death," revealing that the model was his first wife, just before her demise.

At the Drury Park horse races with Sally and the Lathams, Carroll, who needs money to pay Blagdon, speaks of painting the portrait of Cecily, whose hand he holds under the bleacher seat. Soon, Sally is visited by Dr. Tuttle (Nigel Bruce, again doing his Dr. Watson shtick), who diagnoses "nothing very serious ... a case of nerves." Troubled by Bea's comment about Van Gogh—"such a brilliant man to have gone insane"—Carroll is attacked by another headache.

Cecily arrives, and Geoffrey kisses her passionately, just before she says she's leaving England for Rio de Janiero. "You're not going any place without me, ever," he commands. She replies that he can join her, *if* he accomplishes his plans in 48 hours. In how many Warners films could Bogie possibly bump off his wife in favor of Alexis Smith, then be spurned by her?

Carroll tells Bea that he is traveling to London to enroll her in Weatherly School, "one of the best in England." Sally (Stanwyck, in full makeup, looks not the least bit ill), walks down from her bedroom, asks to see his new painting, and admits that she knows of Cecily's love for him. He deflects her comments, then leaves on his trip.

During Carroll's absence, Bea describes his behavior, her mother's death and the meetings with Blagdon. In London, the chemist advises him not to move out of the country, and is beaten to death in return. Carroll then steals the evidence of their transactions from the safe. At this point in the film, Bogart dons the fedora and trench coat (a tendency that often aggravated Jack Warner).

Bea and Sally, wanting to see the new painting, unlock the studio and find the canvas: the second Mrs. Carroll as "The Angel of Death" (shot in close-up, in the shadow of pouring rain, accompanied by a thunderous Waxman chord). Tuttle (constantly requesting booze) and the Lathams arrive, followed by Carroll. After they leave, Sally asks him about his first wife, and he brings her some "milk," which she pours out the window. Before walking up to bed, she grabs a gun (badly shot in close-up, the actual location is impossible to discern). Carroll discovers milk on the window sill and outside on the ground (an improbability, considering the ferocity of the thunderstorm).

Conveniently, the Yorkshire Strangler is on the loose (a newspaper headline suggests that he and the London burglar/killer may be one and the same), so Carroll decides to garrote the poor girl. He walks out into the rain, breaks a window, climbs in, and ascends the staircase. Sally phones Penny, but Carroll rips the cable from the wall. Another over-the-top hysterical Stanwyck scene, made worse by bad editing, culminates with Carroll, somehow climbing the side of the house, smashing through the window, and entering, Dracula-style (after all, Bogie *had* played a vampire). Totally insane, he yanks down the bell rope, and she pulls the gun. Bogart makes some great crazed-killer faces as Geoffrey strangles her, but she's not *quite* dead. The Inspector (Leland Hodgson) arrives, offering to "talk it over" with Carroll.

At the bottom of the stairs, Carroll asks the police, "Just a moment, before we go. Would you gentleman like a drink? A glass of milk, perhaps?" They shake their heads, he raises his right hand to his, then makes a "who cares?" gesture as a *really* obnoxious Waxman chord assaults the viewer's ears.

The Two Mrs. Carrolls, based on an English penny-dreadful play, features another Bogart role better suited to Boris Karloff. The acting ranges from occasionally catatonic (Bogart) to histrionic (Stanwyck), and Waxman's insufferably bombastic music only accentuates the film's inadequacies. The presence of Nigel Bruce and a poison-in-the-milk husband obviously suggests Alfred Hitchcock's superior, Academy Award–winning *Suspicion* (1941), costarring Cary Grant and Joan Fontaine. Tedious, contrived, and dated in its time, *The Two Mrs. Carrolls* is arguably the worst Warners film Bogie made during the 1940s. How could he possibly take it seriously? How many killers are stupid enough to create sensational painted evidence of their victims? Chalk it up to Geoffrey Carroll's monumental egomania (just as described by Dr. Hamilton [Sydney Greenstreet] in *Conflict*).

Bogart had read the galley proofs of David Goodis' novel *The Dark Road* several years earlier, then passed them on to Jerry Wald, thinking the bleak story would make a unique thriller. Together, they convinced Jack Warner to purchase the film rights, and hired Goodis to adapt the screenplay concerning Vincent Parry, an innocent man who escapes from prison to find his wife's killer. After Goodis submitted an unsatisfactory draft, Delmer Daves was brought in to direct and rework the script, now titled *Dark Passage*.

The unrelenting darkness and cynicism of the story reflects the Cold War, anti-Communist paranoia of the time. Bogart liked the premise, and enjoyed traveling to San Francisco with Bacall, whose inclusion in the film was a major selling point for Warner, who at first balked at the expense of a location shoot. (Wald and Daves had considered other actresses, including Viveca Lindfors, for the Irene Jansen role.) Warner also had objected to cinematog-

Dark Passage (1947): Bogart and Bacall portray a serious relationship influenced by their real-life marriage in Delmer Daves' atmospheric film noir experiment.

rapher Sid Hickox using a subjective style framed from Parry's perspective, which keeps Bogart's face off-screen for much of the film. With a new, handheld camera, Hickox was able to create a more fluid, convincing first-person technique than that achieved by Paul C. Vogel for Robert Montgomery's *Lady of the Lake* (shot entirely in the first-person), released by MGM while Warners was producing *Dark Passage*.

The San Francisco shoot during the winter of 1946–47 was exciting. Reporters constantly arrived at the Mark Hopkins Hotel, fans tramped around in the rain with their autograph albums, hoping to meet Hollywood's two hottest stars, and 1,500 people arrived at the Golden Gate Bridge, necessitating the intervention of the Highway Patrol. Bacall remembered:

> That movie ... was fun, because of where we were, and it was romantic, because it was San Francisco. Delmer Daves, who directed it, was a lovely, lovely man, and very emotional. I had a scene in *Dark Passage*, I had to get very teary, and Del Daves was sitting right in front of the camera, just crying away, just sobbing, right along with me.[19]

Daves receives sole credit for the screenplay, "From the Novel by David Goodis," in the opening credits. Parry escapes from San Quentin aboard a truck, causing the trash barrel in which he is hiding to crash off and roll down a hill. His point of view is first seen spinning around inside the metal can. Bogart's noir narration is quiet and subdued, instantly creating a somewhat depressive tone, as he is picked up by Sam (Tom D'Andrea), who identifies his passenger after hearing a radio report of the escape. Parry (and, through the use of subjective camera, the audience) punches him out, drags him into some bushes, and exchanges their clothes. While Parry is tying his shoes, a car stops, and a young woman (Bacall), who calls him "Vincent," tells him to climb in for a ride to San Francisco. He hides under a tarp in the backseat, along with her painting materials, to get through a police check point.

At her apartment, she reveals herself as Irene Jansen by way of a newspaper editorial she had written on Parry's behalf. She takes his measurements, then goes out to buy him a new suit of clothes while he showers, shaves, and listens to swing records. Madge Rapf (Agnes Moorehead), a woman Parry recognizes, knocks, but he orders her to leave without answering the door. As Johnny Mercer's "Too Marvelous for Words" plays on the record player, Irene returns with the clothes, then speaks of the imprisonment and death of her father, Calvin Jansen, an innocent man convicted of murdering his wife.

That evening, while Irene is out, Parry takes a taxi driven by a garrulous cabbie (Pat McVey) who identifies him, then recommends a plastic surgeon. Bogart's face is kept in shadow as the silhouette of Parry's head is shown for the first time. The cabbie promises to make a 3:00 a.m. appointment with "the doc," then drops Parry at his destination. Inside, his friend, trumpeter George Fellsinger (Rory Mallinson), is asleep on the bed, holding a newspaper featuring the headline "Escaped Killer in S.F." and a photograph of Parry (the only method the film uses to show the pre-surgery version) on the front page. He tells George about Irene, recalling that "she came to my trial every day."

"*Madge* framed you," Fellsinger insists. "Madge wanted to hook you, and when she found out she couldn't have you, she framed you. Sent you up for life. We both know that."

Parry meets the cabbie at the office of "Walter Coley, Specialist" (Houseley Stevenson), who requires only 90 minutes and $200 to complete the operation. The anesthetic is administered, and a brief montage sequence combines events from the past day with surreal images of the slightly sinister doctor. After Parry regains consciousness, Bogart's head is now seen in the light, partially mummified in bandages.

Thirty-seven minutes into the film, the subjective camera is abandoned. Coley tells Parry to consume only liquids and not speak, forcing Bogart to mime his performance while his face is wrapped.

Back at Fellsinger's room, Parry discovers him beaten to death with his trumpet, then returns to stay with Irene. Exhausted while walking to her apartment, he stumbles upon the car driven by the man he beat and abandoned down the road from San Quentin the previous day. He passes out, then awakens to see Irene's face looking down at him. Parry, with his head bandaged, can only consume liquids, but Bogie makes sure to work in a cigarette. "Parry Friend Found Murdered" announces the headline in the day's *Extra*, the article stating that his fingerprints were found on the trumpet.

Madge returns, hysterical over the newspaper story, pleading to stay in the apartment to avoid the murderous Parry. Her ex-husband, Bob Rapf (Bruce Bennett), arrives, and the two argue about Parry, including accusations of an affair. Irene admits she had been entertaining a man the previous day, sarcastically adding that Vincent Parry had dropped by to murder her. "If you tell the truth, nobody believes you," she tells Parry. "They didn't."

Parry begins to speak just before Irene removes the bandages. Bogart was careful to grow a sufficient amount of beard to suggest the passage of time. George and Ira Gershwin's "Someone to Watch Over Me" is playing as he, clean shaven, walks down the stairs. Taking a long look, Irene declares, "I think I even like you better."

Parry smiles slightly. "Well, don't let it give you any ideas."

"What kind?" she asks.

"Don't change *yours*," he replies. "I like it just as it is."

Irene keeps staring at him, with the same approving grin, as he turns over the record to repeat "Too Marvelous for Words." Daves doesn't rush his storytelling, and takes time to use certain uncomplicated images to emphasize the characters' often subtle emotions, occasionally incorporating on-screen jazz standards (rather than a score) to reinforce those feelings. For 14 seconds, Vincent and Irene say nothing, but just *look* at each other. (Bogart and Bacall both admired Daves' sensitivity and intelligence, considering him one of the nicest, most decent guys in Hollywood.)

Vincent wants to clear himself by seeking out the real killer. Daves cuts to a close-up of Irene as her eyes begin to glisten. "I thought I had a good life here," she says, "but your going away doesn't make it seem good any more. "I've sort of joined your team, and I don't look forward to being without you."

"When I leave here, you're off my team, and lucky to be," he points out. "No, I've got the Indian sign on me. It seems I can't win. I've got to start out and prove who killed them."

"But won't you be leaving your fingerprints wherever you go?" she asks. "The doctor didn't change them. Don't even try, Vincent."

"Yeah, I see what you mean," he sighs. "Well, I guess the only thing for me to do is get the first bus out of town, fast." She wants to know his destination, but he claims he hasn't decided, then insists, "You'd be insane to follow me." She calls a taxi while he packs his bag.

Franz Waxman, providing the antithesis of his overbearing score for *The Two Mrs. Carrolls*, wrote a moody, quiet oboe piece to accentuate the scene of Vincent and Irene's parting. The cabbie rings the bell repeatedly. "Funny how quickly they come, when you don't want them to come at all," she observes.

Parry realizes he needs a new name, finally settling on "Alan Linnell."

"Goodbye, Alan," she says as the bell rings twice more. Daves cuts to a stunning close-up of Bacall as a tear drops from Irene's right eye. "You'd better go."

"There isn't any possible way to say ... Goodbye, Irene," he manages as she opens the door. Vincent walks down the corridor, from foreground to background, getting farther away from Irene, before he sets down his bag and looks back at her. As opposed to the earlier use of subjective camera from Vincent's perspective, here the film shifts to Irene's point of view.

A medium shot of Irene shows her watery eyes providing an emotional counterpoint to her delicate smile (Daves' ability to tell his story with purely visual means is at its height here). The elevator reaches their level, Vincent disappears into it, and the director cuts to a close-up of Irene's melancholy face. Unlike the playful, suggestive Bogart-Bacall love scenes created by Howard Hawks, Daves offers intimate, serious romantic scenes for the married version of the couple, playing characters involved in a more dire situation.

The taxi driver scrutinizes Parry's face, then complains, "I nearly pushed my thumb through that buzzer."

Parry gets out at Harry's lunch wagon, orders ham and eggs, then pretends to be interested in horse-racing results. Unfortunately, the racing season ended the previous month, and an inquisitive man (Douglas Kennedy) at the back of the wagon walks over to grill him about why he has no raincoat (just where is that Bogie trench coat?), why he isn't asleep, what he does for a living. "Linnell" tells the detective he's hiding out "from his wife in Portland," but is forced to go back to a "hotel" to produce his identification. As they are walking down the sidewalk, Parry sees a car approaching (on the "wrong" side of the street) and dashes out in front of it. The detective follows suit and is hit. As Parry runs off, the motorist becomes hys-

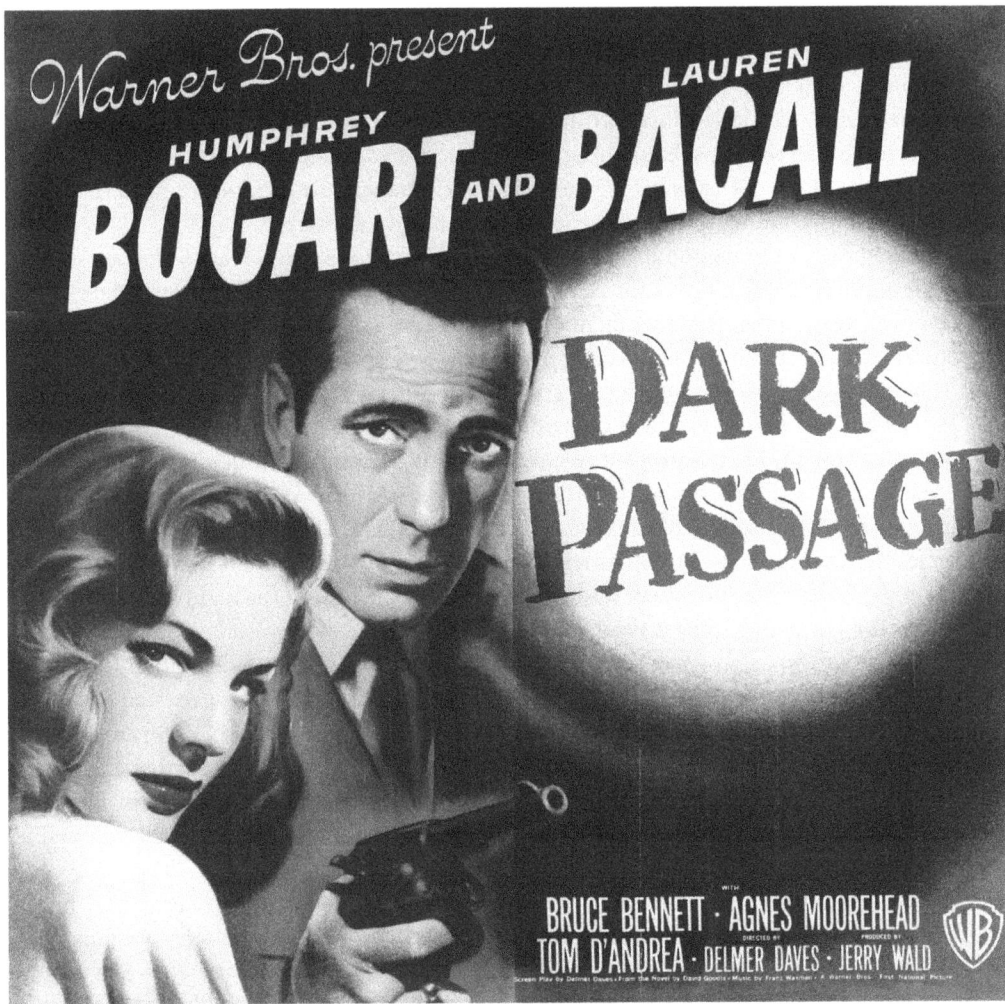

Dark Passage (1947): Bogie and Baby, represented by striking noir graphics (original six-sheet poster).

terical, shouting the film's most bizarre line of dialogue: "My heart feels like a baseball bat is in my chest!"

The cop phones his sergeant with a description, while "Linnell" books a room. The next morning, he glances out the window. A knock at the door startles him, unexpectedly producing Sam, the motorist he beat and abandoned. This "annoying, small-time crook" could collect the $5,000 reward, but demands $60,000 from "the dame" in exchange for not calling the cops. Held at gunpoint, Parry is forced to drive to Irene's apartment as Sam absentmindedly prattles on about Mexico and obtaining phony papers in Arizona. Parry takes a back road, stops, grabs the gun, then forces Sam out beneath the Golden Gate Bridge. "Did you kill Fellsinger?" he asks. Here, Bogie finally gets to turn on his tough guy routine.

Sam denies involvement but admits that he saw another car following the taxi on the night of the murder—"a convertible coupe ... a canvas top ... a bright color ... orange." They grapple over the gun, which gets thrown into the drink before Sam goes toppling down the cliff. "Thanks, my good friend," says Parry, looking down at the body. "Now I know who killed my wife, and George."

Parry goes to Madge's apartment, pretending that Bob recommended her as a date, plies her with candy and compliments, then reveals his true identity. "I know you did it," he admits, threatening to turn over the facts to the police and describing both murders she committed. George, he insists, was killed just to frame him a second time. Madge admits her guilt but refuses to confess to the cops. Launching into a vicious tirade, she screams her twisted views as she attempts to open a drawer in a dressing table. She tries to run, but crashes through a plate glass window, falling multiple stories to her death in the street.

Utilizing the San Francisco location, Daves has Parry take a streetcar to the bus station, where he inquires about a ticket for Benton, Arizona. While waiting for enough fares to be sold, he overhears strangers—a woman with two children, and a man—discussing the current social climate, in which "nobody seems to ever give a hang about the other fellow."

"There was a time when folks used to give each other a helping hand," the man continues. Parry plugs the jukebox, which coincidentally plays "Too Marvelous for Words," as the man tells the woman, "You know, we've got something in common—being alone."

"Alan" calls Irene, describing the fatal meeting with Madge. He asks her to get a map of South America, then locate a little coastal town called Pieta, where he will be waiting in "a little café, right on the bay." A cop enters the station, but Parry gets on the bus. A dissolve miraculously spans time and space, leading to the little café, where the band kicks into "Too Marvelous for Words" as Irene arrives to dance with Vincent.

The story of *Dark Passage* is contrived and improbable, the ending is outlandish (especially for a noir narrative), and Daves' pacing is slow and deliberate, but his visual emphasis, highlighted by sparse dialogue and unusual characters, creates a unique, entertaining 106-minute film. Each supporting actor is cast perfectly in a colorful role, particularly Agnes Moorehead and Tom D'Andrea, who are practically psychotic in their selfishness, Houseley Stevenson as Dr. Coley, and Pat McVey as the cabbie. As Irene, Bacall shows a vulnerable, caring side this time around.

Bogie, beginning as an unseen voice, then shown wrapped in bandages, and finally appearing in his customary visage, is allowed dynamically to build the intensity of his characterization from start to finish. First quietly narrating his travails, he switches to a strange style of mime, shows sensitivity in the love scenes and fear when pursued by cops and chiselers, then emerges as the Bogart tough guy to save himself and confront the real killer before concluding in high romantic style. An interesting experiment that differs completely from the first two Bogart-Bacall films, *Dark Passage* fared poorly at the box office.

14

Protecting the Goods

Producer Henry Blanke persuaded Jack Warner to let John Huston shoot *The Treasure of the Sierra Madre* on location in Mexico, which raised the film's budget from $1,879,000 to over $2.5 million. Repeating the magic he worked on Hammett's *Maltese Falcon*, Huston adapted the screenplay from the mysterious B. Traven's complex novel.

Robinson, having turned down Walter Huston's role in *Sierra Madre*, was no longer on the studio payroll. He had been accepting parts primarily for money, in films such as 20th Century-Fox's *Tampico* (1944), Columbia's ludicrous *Mr. Winkle Goes to War* (1944), and a pair of ultra-depressing Fritz Lang noir tragedies, *The Woman in the Window* (1944) and *Scarlet Street* (1945). Two projects of which Eddie thought highly were Billy Wilder's unforgettable noir *Double Indemnity* (1944), with Fred MacMurray and Barbara Stanwyck, and Orson Welles' *The Stranger* (1946), in which he was thrilled to play an intrepid hunter of Nazi war criminals. In 1944 he had traveled to London, becoming the first performer to entertain the Allied troops after the D-Day invasion.

One of Eddie's most beautifully acted roles came in MGM's *Our Vines Have Tender Grapes* (1945), in which he plays a Norwegian-American farmer in Wisconsin who has a remarkable relationship with his young daughter (Margaret O'Brien, in a stunning performance). The screenplay for *Grapes* was penned by Dalton Trumbo, who eventually was blacklisted as one of the Hollywood Ten.

Robinson's ability to land good film roles was affected adversely by rumors of his being a Communist, helped along by major Red baiters like Martin Dies, who had attempted to smear Cagney, and members of the Motion Picture Alliance, which continued to boast such reactionary luminaries as founder Sam Wood (an anti-FDR conservative who believed Hollywood literally was crawling with Reds), Gary Cooper, Robert Taylor, John Wayne, Ward Bond and Adolphe Menjou (whose paranoid beliefs bordered on fascism).

One happy event marked a reunion of sorts between Robinson and Jack Warner, who attended Manny's bar mitzvah at Beverly Hills' Temple Emanu-El in March 1946. As the younger Robinson's godparents, Warner and his wife were very impressed with the service. In fact, Warner told Robinson that he planned to produce a "brotherhood film" depicting three different faiths: Catholic, Protestant and Jewish (a sequence that would feature the bar mitzvah). Although Manny recreated the event on camera, Robinson was not impressed, thinking his son quite an exploited ham. Combined with his wife's continued mental problems, it was too much for him to take, and he asked Warner, who had invested $10,000 in the project, to withhold general distribution. The completed film eventually was sent only to religious groups.

To the suits at Warner Bros., *The Treasure of the Sierra Madre* promised to be a thoroughly depressing project. In the first place, Huston's Mexico, rather than being the usual "exotic" fantasy locale created in and around Hollywood, would be as realistic as possible.

Likewise, this was an all-male film totally devoid of romance, with its star becoming a greed-crazed, murderous psychopath.

Secondly, Huston's source was uncompromisingly pessimistic. The mysterious novelist B. Traven, who claimed to be an American, reportedly was a reclusive German expatriate who fled to England, then Mexico, after escaping a firing squad during the unsuccessful 1918 Communist revolution in Bavaria. *The Treasure of the Sierra Madre*, first published in Berlin, was based on a 19th-century German ballad about three Americans who strike it rich abroad. One leaves to celebrate, then returns with wine; and the other two, each wanting half the treasure instead of one third, stab him to death. As he lies dying, he reveals that he poisoned the wine. This bleak premise appealed to the cynical, dour Traven, who created the damned trio of Dobbs, Curtin and Howard.

As top support for Bogart — who cherished the acting possibilities offered by his unusual role as Fred C. Dobbs — Huston brilliantly cast his father, Walter, as Howard, the crusty old prospector; B-Western favorite Tim Holt (son of 1930s star Jack Holt, who also has a small role) as Curtain, Dobbs' young companion whom he eventually attempts to murder; Bruce Bennett as the interloper Cody; and — at the request of B. Traven — himself as "White Suit," the man whom Dobbs repeatedly panhandles. Traven was excited about seeing Bogie in the lead, but initially considered Walter Huston, at 63, too young to play the old geezer, who he insisted be over 70. One of the finest actors ever to grace the stage and screen, Walter simply removed his false teeth, allaying all of the author's concerns. Bacall wrote, "Walter Huston [was] a devastatingly attractive and witty man and beautiful actor."[1]

John Huston began shooting *Sierra Madre* on the Warners lot on March 17, 1947. Following three weeks of studio and back-lot work, he then moved his cast and crew to the village of Jungapeo, near San Jose de Purura, 140 miles from Mexico City. For the next two months, the company planned to use the ritzy Hotel Reforma as its home base, a comfortable respite from the hot and dusty exterior locations. When Bruce Bennett arrived on the set, he was particularly impressed by the rapport between Huston and Bogart, whom he considered a peerless actor. While on location, the Hustons tried smoking marijuana together, but John became sick, vowing never to touch reefer again. For his part, Bogie stuck with Dos Equis beer.

Many Mexican actors, stunt performers, and local villagers were employed in bit parts and as extras, giving the film the authenticity John Huston desired. In the role of Gold Hat, the bandido who kills Dobbs, he made the inspired decision of casting Alfonso Bedoya. As his technical advisors, he hired Ernesto A. Romero and Antonio Arriaga. Huston loved the country, and had spent two years riding with the Mexican cavalry as a young adult. When the *Sierra Madre* shoot concluded, he actually brought a local orphan boy back to Los Angeles as his adopted son. During the last years of his life, he lived near Puerto Vallarta.

As the location work reached the eight-week point, Huston had fallen behind schedule, and Bogie became irritated. The director had assured him that he'd be able to compete in the Honolulu Classic yacht race from California to Hawaii, an event that, due to the attack on Pearl Harbor, had been postponed since 1942. Bogie had spent $15,000 to prepare, including hiring a seven-man crew, and constantly ranted about it in Huston's presence. One night, he got in his friend's face during dinner, claiming they were being overtaxed to make "a fucking masterpiece" and loudly shouting until Huston actually made the tough guy cry by viciously twisting his nose. Ultimately, Bacall asked the director to ease up on her husband and, on May 30, the company left for Mexico City. With the Mexican location work completed, they still had nearly six weeks of shooting back in California, where Jack Warner was *not* pleased with the rushes he had seen, particularly the filthy, unshaven appearance of Bogart.

Following more toiling in the mining country of California, and on the Warners back lot and sound stages, Bogart reached his final sequence. He already had acted for 100 days on the film, and was nearly worn out while performing the most difficult scene in the script, when Dobbs goes insane after discovering that Curtain, whom he thought dead, is missing. Huston dismissed him on July 22, 18 days after his dream of racing to Honolulu had been dashed.

On August 1, Jack Warner watched the film and, to everyone's relief, called it the best film the studio had produced. However, B. Traven, who had arrived at Warners using the name "Hal Croves," expecting the $500 per week promised by Huston for his work as "adviser," angrily walked out after two days on the set (behavior quite peculiar for an author espousing radical socialist views). Production head Tenny Wright had offered Croves only $100, and the author blamed the director, who thereafter would be denied the rights to any of his novels. That was B. Traven's loss. As far as Bogart was concerned, it was time to return to the sea as captain of the *Santana*.

To John Huston, Traven's literary property is the real star of his film. Max Steiner's first dramatic chord sounds over the Warner Bros. logo, the credits begin with "The Treasure of the Sierra Madre," then a *second* panel reads, "Starring Humphrey Bogart." But Huston considers *all* his supporting actors to be stars, following Bogart's billing with "AND" Walter Huston, Tim Holt, Bruce Bennett, Barton MacLane and Alfonso Bedoya.

A close-up of a poster publishing the results of the February 14, 1925, National Lottery widens as the camera pulls back to reveal a man's hands tearing up his ticket. A second close-up shows the disappointed face of Fred C. Dobbs, framed beneath a tattered fedora. This initial image of Bogart (especially with his fashion trademark in such a sorry state) immediately announces the down-and-out status of this character. Heading across the Tampico street and down the sidewalk, he panhandles fellow gringos for change. Obviously ashamed of the shape he's in, he asks a tall man dressed in white (John Huston), "Hey, Mister? Can you stake a fellow American to a meal?" Huston cuts to a low-angle shot, behind Bogart, making his own character seem to tower over the poor Dobbs as he hands over a peso. This opening scene is a masterful montage, created by Huston from actual location shots, filmed *behind* Bogart's double, Joseph Smith, and back-lot and studio shots of Bogie.

Dobbs enjoys his food, but is annoyed by a boy (Robert Blake) at his left shoulder who tries to sell him another lottery ticket. "If you don't get away from me, I'm going to throw this water right in your face," he threatens. The boy steps back, then walks behind him to emerge at his right shoulder. Dobbs is a man of his word: the kid gets soaked. But the boy's persistence touches a tinge of guilt in the ragged, unshaven drifter. He buys 1/20 of a ticket, a "sure winner," "so's I don't have to look at your ugly face." Looking at the number, Dobbs says, "Thirteen," and chuckles.

In a local park, Dobbs shares his cigarettes with another down-and-outer (Tim Holt, who won the role over Ronald Reagan, who obviously would have been disastrous, and John Garfield, who was unavailable). Noticing a man, clad in white and reading a newspaper while having his shoes shined, Dobbs goes back into his panhandling act: "Hey, uh, can you stake a fellow American to a meal?" Without looking up at the beggar, the man digs a peso from his pocket, places it in Dobbs' hand, and returns to his paper. Huston cuts to a medium close-up of himself as the man in white, smoking a good cigar, lowering the paper long enough to glare at the bum, then raising it back up again.

The Treasure of the Sierra Madre (1948): Fred C. Dobbs (Bogart) and his "partner," Bob Curtin (Tim Holt), before setting out on their ill-fated gold-mining expedition, in John Huston's masterful adaptation of the famous novel by the mysterious B. Traven (original lobby card).

This time, Dobbs uses the dough to get a shave and haircut. Back on the sidewalk, he notices his dirty fedora is now too big, then briefly follows a prostitute after she saunters past. (One of the few females in the film, this cameo character is *always* reported as being played by Ann Sheridan. Though there is a still photograph showing the "Oomph Girl" in costume with the other actors, the actress in the actual scene resembles Sheridan *not one iota*, instead an authentic knockout Latina. If it is Ann, the makeup is incomprehensibly think. Decide for yourself.) For the third time, Dobbs hits up the gringo in white: "Hey, Mister? Will you stake a fellow American to a meal?"

"Such impudence never came my way," White Suit whines. "Early this afternoon, I gave you money. While I was having my shoes polished, I gave you more money." Huston cuts to a close-up of a baffled Dobbs. "Now, you put the bite on me again. Do me a favor, will ya? Go occasionally to somebody else. This is beginning to get tiresome."

"Excuse me, Mister," Dobbs replies. "I never knowed it was you. I never looked at your face. I just looked at your hands and the money you gave me. Beg pardon, Mister, I promise I'll never put the bite on you again."

Cutting to a close-up of himself with the cigar from over Bogart's right shoulder, Huston shows White Suit saying, "This is the very last you get from me. Just to make sure you don't forget your promise, here's another peso."

"Thanks, Mister, thanks," says Dobbs, looking at his benefactor this time.

"But, from now on," White Suit commands, "you have to make your way through life

14—Protecting the Goods

without my assistance," then strides off. Later, in a cantina, one man in silhouette waits while another, also hidden in shadows, walks in. "Hey, buddy," inquires Fred C. Dobbs. "Can you stake a fellow American to a meal?"

"I won't give you a *red cent*," growls Pat McCormick (Barton MacLane), "but, if you want to make some money, I'll give you a job." Dobbs wants to know the catch, and is informed he can earn $8.00-per-day working on an oil rig. While waiting for the ferry, he recognizes Curtin, his companion from the park. Huston's directorial pacing, combined with the narrative economy of his screenplay, has accomplished all the establishing action in a mere *seven* minutes.

Working "sixteen, eighteen hours a day," Dobbs and Curtain have yet to see a cent of pay. "You'll be paid as we step off the ferry," McCormick claims. Back in Tampico, the "agent" with the dough is nowhere to be seen, so Pat hands Dobbs a bill, telling him to be "at the Cantina Madrid ... no later than three o'clock." At 7:02 p.m., McCormick hasn't arrived, so Dobbs and Curtin get a room at the local flop house, where Howard (Walter Huston), a grizzled old geezer, is discussing gold prospecting with another vagabond (Jack Holt). During his brief, rapid-fire dissertation on the dangers of the precious metal, the old man foreshadows every situation that will follow.

A few days later, Dobbs and Curtain are again sitting idle. "Do you believe what that old man who was doin' all the talkin' at the Oso Negro said the other night?" asks Dobbs, "about gold changin' a man's soul so's he ain't the same kind of a guy as he was before finding it?"

"Guess that all depends on the man," replies Curtin.

"That's exactly what I say," agrees Dobbs. "Gold don't carry any curse with it. It all depends on whether or not the guy who finds it is the right guy. The way I see it, gold can be as much of a blessing as a curse."

Curtain spots Pat McCormick emerging from the Hotel Bristol. The boss is squiring "Senorita Lopez" (Jacqueline Dalya), whom he sends back to the hotel, before dragging Dobbs and Curtin into a cantina, where he explains that *he* has yet to be paid. (Some past commentators on *Sierra Madre* have incorrectly noted the "Ann Sheridan" prostitute as being the "only" woman in the film.) Curtain insists on getting "what's coming to us," then threatens McCormick, who breaks a bottle in his face and punches Dobbs. The two beat McCormick senseless (the obvious doubles in the long shots are one of the film's few flaws), then grab only what he owes them from his wallet.

At the fountain in Tampico, the two scrappers bathe their wounds as Dobbs speaks of their stupidity in waiting around for another job. They discuss the prospects of digging for gold, then seek out the old man, who agrees to join them if they can raise $600. Lamenting not having "a red cent," Dobbs is startled by the lottery boy, who runs in to announce his winning of 200 pesos.

Bandits, led by Gold Hat (Alfonso Bedoya), attack the train heading out of Tampico, and the three would-be prospectors blast away, helping to scare them off. Outfitted with mules and provisions, they begin their ride into the mountains toward a desolate area where few have ever attempted to go. Taking a break, Dobbs and Curtin are excited over gold streaks in some rocks, but Howard, ahead of them on the trail, comes back down to identify it as "pyrite—Fool's Gold." Later, the old man stays up, eating and playing the harmonica, while the two younger men lie in an exhausted sleep.

After climbing through a jungle and up the mountainside, the two greenhorns are ready to give up. Howard taunts them, but when Dobbs threatens to hit him with a rock, Curtin intervenes. "Ah, leave him alone. Can't you see the old man's nuts?"

"Ha!" Howard grumbles. "Nuts! Nuts, am I? Ha! Let me tell you something, my two fine bedfellows. You're so dumb, there's nothing to compare you with. You're dumber than the dumbest jackass. Look at each other, will ya? Did you ever see anything like yourself for bein' dumb specimens?" Laughing gleefully, he launches into a merry dance (a jig Walter Huston had learned in his early vaudeville days). "You're so dumb, you don't even see the riches you're treading on with your own feet!" The elder Huston had played some memorable roles in films, including *The Criminal Code* (Columbia, 1930), *The Devil and Daniel Webster* (MGM, 1932), *Dodsworth* (Goldwyn, 1936) and, of course, *Yankee Doodle Dandy*, but never had he created such a matchless *character* as this, complete with slobber flying from his mouth as he continues to dance, advising his companions, "Yeah, don't expect to find nuggets of molten gold. It's rich, but not that rich. And here ain't the place to dig. It comes from some place further up. Up there." Pointing up the mountain, he continues, "Up there is where we've got to go. Up there!"

Howard possesses so much detailed knowledge about every aspect of gold mining that Walter Huston's effortless performance suggests he actually was a prospector or engineer rather than one of the world's great actors. As soon as the old man begins weighing the sand-like ore they have panned, Dobbs, lying on his back in the tent, smoking a cigarette, asks, "When are we going to start dividing it up?" Making a disgusted face, Howard nonetheless replies, "Any time you say," while the level-headed Curtain objects, "What's the use of dividing it at all? I don't see any point. We're all going back together when the time comes. Why don't we wait until we get paid for the stuff, and then just divide up the money?"

"Either way suits me," adds Howard. "You fellas decide."

"Oh, I'm for dividing it up as we go along," Dobbs emphasizes. "Make each guy responsible for his own goods."

"I reckon I'd just as soon have it that way," Howard agrees. "I don't happen to like the responsibility of guarding your treasure any too well."

"Well, who asked you to?" Dobbs says, raising a nervous laugh from Howard, who adds, "Only I thought I was the most trustworthy of the three." Challenged again by Dobbs, the old man explains the difference between being trustworthy and being honest, then describes a possible outcome to their little adventure (which later proves quite prophetic).

The mine caves in on Dobbs the next day, and Curtain pulls him to safety. "I owe my life to you, partner," says Dobbs.

During a campfire discussion about what each man will do with his goods, Dobbs and Curtain, with gleams in their eyes, eventually become silent as Huston cuts to close-ups of their slightly smiling faces. Registering another of his disapproving expressions as his eyes move from one man to the other, Howard warns, "If I were you boys, I wouldn't talk or even think about women. It ain't good for your health."

Howard wants to set a ceiling at $25,000 each, while Dobbs, his greed continually growing, wants "fifty thousand, anyway—seventy-five would be more like it." Satisfied with $25,000, the old man doesn't want to remain on the mountain for a year to mine more than that. When Curtain mentions the word "hog," Dobbs takes it personally.

During the night, Dobbs gets up to check his goods, which he has hidden under a rock. He returns to the tent, discovers Curtain gone, and becomes suspicious. The following morning, he begins to babble to himself about not going to sleep, getting even with anyone who'll disturb his goods, and having to travel to the village for provisions—venting every paranoid thought about the gold to his burro. When Howard questions him, he accuses the old man of trying to get rid of him.

14—Protecting the Goods

A gila monster crawls under a rock, but when Curtin tries to kill it, Dobbs thinks he is digging for the goods hidden under it. Curtin taunts him about being too yellow to put his hand into the hole, and Dobbs blows up, threatening to kill his partner. While Dobbs cools off, Curtin leaves for the village, where he meets Cody (Bruce Bennett), an inquisitive Texan, who asks to join him. Back at camp, as they discuss how to deal with an interloper, Cody walks in. "No vacancies, you understand?" Dobbs tells him. All three try to deny that gold has been found at the site, then band together to make sure the intruder doesn't "murder us all in our sleep."

In the morning, Dobbs accuses Cody of stealing their water. Called uncivilized, Dobbs knocks him down. Howard advises him to leave, but he refuses, challenging them to make a choice — kill him, run him off, or take him in as a partner — then describing the cons associated with each alternative. "Do the mug in, I say," Dobbs recommends as they discuss the situation. "Let majority decide," says Howard. The verdict: "All three of us haul out our cannons and let him have it.... Let's make it short and sweet for him."

The "firing squad" approaches Cody, but a bandit gang can be seen moving up the mountainside. Gold Hat and his hombres arrive, claiming they are Federales. Dobbs asks about their badges, and the leader defiantly replies, "We ain't got no badges. We don't need no badges. I don't have to show you any *stinking badges!*" Dobbs threatens him. "Give us your gun, and we'll leave you in peace," he replies. Dobbs blasts a chunk out of his sombrero, prompting an offer to trade a gold watch, which Howard shoots with his pistol.

During the ensuing gunfight, Cody is killed, preventing them from having to commit cold-blooded murder. "One less gun," Dobbs now says. Looking down the mountain, they hear the bandits regrouping, then Gold Hat commanding them to ride off. "This may be just a trick to lure us out," warns Curtin.

"I don't think so," says Howard, "They ain't good enough actors for this kind of a trick." (Walter Huston was in a position to know; besides, his son wrote the line.)

"Federales—look at 'em. I could kiss every one of 'em," admits Dobbs as they watch the bandits being driven off.

"Name's James Cody, Dallas, Texas" Howard says while searching the dead man's wallet. "Reckon she's his girl," he adds, handing a photo to Dobbs.

"Hmm, not bad," replies Dobbs, as Howard attempts to read a letter. While Dobbs rolls a cigarette, the more literate Curtin takes over, reading the words of Cody's wife, revealing that he was a poor farmer trying to strike gold to support his family. "Well, I guess we better dig a hole for him," is Dobbs' sensitive assessment.

Each man now has about $35,000, and the lode is thinning out. Dobbs is satisfied —"I don't want to keep that dame waitin', whoever she is"— but Howard announces that the mountain must be "put back in shape.... We've wounded this mountain. It's our duty to close her wounds. It's the least we can do to show our gratitude for all the wealth she's given us."

"You talk about that mountain like it was a real woman," says Curtain.

"She's been a lot better to me than any woman I ever knew," Dobbs divulges.

"Goodbye, mountain, thanks," Howard says as they lead their mules away from the site. At their camp that night, Curtin offers to give "a fourth" of his money to Cody's widow. Howard concurs, but Dobbs responds, "You two guys must have been born at a revival meeting." Suddenly, as Howard is playing his harmonica, with all three men in the frame, a hand, holding a scythe, enters at left. (John Huston offers no warning, and the audience and Howard see the knife simultaneously.) "We got company," the old man announces.

The scene cuts to a close-up of a dour Mestizo face, then back to the shot of all three men, with the stranger silhouetted in the left foreground. Dobbs reaches for his pistol, but Howard advises, "Steady, boys." The Mestizo and a companion behind him both remove their hats. "Buenos noches," says the one with the knife. Two more "Indians" join them. Howard responds agreeably in Spanish, addressing them as amigos.

"Gracias, senors," the man replies, and all four (Manuel Donde, Ildefonso Vega, Francisco Islas, Alberto Valdespino) sit down by the fire. Curtin offers coffee, while Dobbs tosses them some tobacco. Their guests hand over native tobacco in return. A little boy has fallen into water and lies unconscious, the leader tells Howard, who agrees to go with them. Planning to return in the morning, he tells Dobbs and Curtin, "Look after my goods while I'm gone, will ya?"

An entire community watches Howard while he works on the boy, who slowly awakens, spitting up some water. The natives cross themselves and remove their hats as he leaves the village, then return the next day as the three are back on the trail, insisting that Howard be repaid as their guest. Dobbs and Curtin offer to guard his goods and meet him in Durango.

Resting on the trail, Dobbs complains to Curtin about having to transport the old man's burro, wishing it would plummet down "two-thousand feet of gorge," then insists they camp for the night. "We take all his goods and go straight up north, leave the old jackass flat," he tells Curtin.

"You aren't serious, are you?" Curtin asks. "You don't really *mean* what you're saying."

"Fred C. Dobbs don't say nothin' he don't mean," he replies.

"As long as I'm here and can do anything about it," vows Curtin, "you won't touch a single grain of the old man's goods."

"I know exactly what you mean," says Dobbs. "You want to take it all for yourself and cut me out."

"No, Dobbs," he swears. "I'm on the level with the old man, just as I'd be on the level with you, if you weren't here."

"Get off your soapbox, will ya?" Dobbs orders. "You only sound foolish out here in this wilderness. I know you for what you are. For a long time, I've had my suspicions about you. Now I know I've been right." Dobbs' delusions have reached a dangerous stage. He has begun to project his own paranoid insecurities onto his partner, claiming that Curtin plans to "bump me off … and bury me out here in the bush, like a dog." Dobbs pulls his pistol, but Curtin knocks him down, removes the bullets and hands over the weapon. "I'll bet you $105,000 you go to sleep before I do," Dobbs challenges, then laughs to himself.

The next morning, Curtin is exhausted on the trail, and Dobbs waits for him to nod off. That night by the fire, when he finally crashes, the gold-crazed maniac marches him to his "funeral," then shoots him twice (off screen, behind a tree). But Curtin is still alive, and plays dead when Dobbs returns to the scene a while later, then crawls to another camp, where some Indians find him. Now Dobbs constantly talks to himself, offering self-advice and laughing madly after discovering that Curtin is gone. Bogart brilliantly, believably, creates a one-man tour de force in his remaining scenes.

Howard is living like a king among the peasants, lounging in a hammock, offered limes and tobacco by an attractive young woman, and drinking tequila. Curtin arrives, and the old man patches him up. "I'll pull out of this, if only to get that guy," he threatens.

"Well, I reckon we can't blame him too much," Howard counters. "He's not a real killer, as killers go. I think he's as honest as the next fella, or almost. The big mistake was leaving you two fellas out there in the depths of the wilderness with more than a hundred thousand between you. Mighty big temptation, partner, believe me."

A burro dies as Dobbs struggles along the trail, choked with thirst and caked with dirt. He finds a muddy hole, lays down beside a drinking mule, and shoves his head into the water. The reflection of a sombrero-clad hombre appears beside him as he drinks. It is Gold Hat, who requests tobacco, then questions his claim that two friends are "following on horseback." The bandit wants the hides tied to the burros. Dobbs draws his gun and pulls the trigger, but the chambers are empty. Gold Hat knocks him down, then chops him twice with a machete (off camera, behind a burro). The bandits tear off the hides, dumping all the gold dust onto the ground. Having abandoned all the real wealth, they then attempt to sell the burros in Durango.

Federales arrive and seize the thieves, who are forced to dig their own graves before they are summarily executed by a firing squad. Howard and Curtin ride in, learn that Dobbs is dead, and pick up their "goods" at the village office. A young boy informs them that the bandits believed the bags were filled with sand used to make the hides heavier. Riding hell-bent for the ruins outside of town, they are swept by a ferocious "sand" storm. Nothing remains but torn, empty bags.

Howard laughs uncontrollably. "Ah, laugh, Curtin, old boy! It's a great joke played on us by the Lord, or fate, or nature, or whatever you prefer, but whoever or whatever played it certainly had a sense of humor! The gold has gone back to where we found it!" Howard continues to laugh, the villagers laugh — and Curtin laughs. "It's worth ten months of suffering and labor, this joke is," Howard adds. If ever a film offered a clear-cut moral, here it is.

Howard is all set up as a medicine man: "I'll be worshipped and fed and treated like a high priest for telling people things they want to hear. Good medicine men are born, not made."

Curtin has no idea about his own fate. "You know, the worst ain't so bad when it finally happens — not half as bad as you figure it'll be before it's happened. I'm no worse off than when I was in Tampico. All I'm out is a couple hundred bucks, when you come right down to it — not very much compared to what Dobbsy lost." Howard offers to give Curtin his share of the provisions and hides, if he'll buy a ticket to Dallas to visit Cody's widow. The two survivors ride their separate ways, the camera tracking in to a close-up of an empty bag caught on the needles of a tiny cactus.

The final scene is pure John Huston, an original the director added to Traven's material to temper the author's relentless futility. As with *The Maltese Falcon*, Huston personally adapted a popular novel, then directed it in a superbly paced, unadorned yet visually stunning manner, creating a film with a dynamic, fully developed central character surrounded by a gallery of equally interesting individuals, each portrayed by an actor ideal for the role. Like his earlier dual effort, he created a motion picture for the ages.

Bogart's arc in *Sierra Madre* is one of the most vivid disintegrations of character ever filmed. Considered by many to be his greatest performance, Fred C. Dobbs is the most unique and unexpected in his entire cinematic catalog. As he morally sinks lower into the depravity and violence begot by greed, his physical appearance follows suit. Jack Warner was right about Bogart's looks. As his hair becomes more unkempt and curly, his beard thickens, and the grime continues to build, he degenerates into a near-simian state. Bogie had played a gangster with a vicious streak in previous films, but none of them became as completely inhuman as Dobbs before getting whacked in the final reel. His death is actually the only cold-blooded murder in the film, unless the executions are counted. Just before the film's release, Bogart told New York *Post* critic Archer Winsten, "I play the worst shit you ever saw."[2] In 1948, Bogart fans who admired his brilliant interpretations of Sam Spade, Rick Blaine and Philip Mar-

The Treasure of the Sierra Madre (1948): Bogart, giving what many consider his finest cinematic performance, is consistently upstaged by the charismatic Walter Huston, who won a Best Supporting Actor Oscar for his role as Howard, the crusty old prospector (original half-sheet poster).

lowe had a difficult time accepting their hero as this psychotic reprobate — proof that he was not only a major Hollywood star, but a truly great actor.

Tom A. Pennock
Film Buff and Collector, Battle Creek, Michigan
on
The Treasure of the Sierra Madre

The film depicts how money changes people. It's really the love of money, rather than the pursuit of it. It turns out to be more work than it's worth.

Bogart as Fred C. Dobbs epitomizes human greed and selfishness in his superb, paranoiac performance. This self-centered, bitter man no longer trusts anyone, including his friend, Bob Curtin. Looney and delusional, Dobbs is eventually undone by his own conscience — especially when he tries to kill Curtin, and then wondering if he is really dead.

In the end, Dobbs loses, and Curtin and Howard share the last laugh. Realizing they have lost their fortunes to the wind, they leave the disappointment behind and go on with their lives.

President Harry Truman had been getting tough on Communism, and his "Truman Doctrine" mandated active intervention, economic and otherwise, in the affairs of countries under growing Red influence and control. This Cold War mentality affected the home front as well, with the federal government requiring loyalty oaths from its employees. Representatives of HUAC, including chairman J. Parnell Thomas, had visited Hollywood; and, in September 1947, began issuing subpoenas to those they wished to question at hearings the following month.

In response, John Huston teamed with director William Wyler, writer Philip Dunne and actor Alexander Knox to form the Committee for the First Amendment, to protest HUAC's attack on the basic freedoms guaranteed to every American. Bogart and Bacall—along with Henry Fonda, Ava Gardner, Paulette Goddard, Benny Goodman, Myrna Loy, Gregory Peck and Billy Wilder—were among the first of 140 members to sign up. Devoted to fighting the truly un-American activities of HUAC, they planned to have representation in Washington, D.C., on a daily basis, declaring themselves anti-Communist, and being extra careful not to welcome members who had ever been actual members of the Party.

On October 20, 1947, HUAC officially began its hearings, questioning "friendly witnesses" Louis B. Mayer and Jack Warner, who admitted that he had fired 11 "Communist" writers, including Dalton Trumbo. On the second day, the rabidly right-wing Adolphe Menjou happily testified, praising the Motion Picture Alliance and paranoically claiming there were actors who *act* like Communists, individuals who could easily work "subversive" actions into their performances, though no names were actually mentioned.

However, Menjou then moved on to describe a September 1946 Screen Actors Guild strike mediation meeting, crediting SAG acting president Ronald Reagan for being on the "right" side, while others had been on the "wrong" side that would have allowed Communist "domination" of the labor unions. Menjou named four actors on that "wrong side," supporters of the Conference of Studio Unions (CSU): Hume Cronyn, Paul Henreid, Alexander Knox and Edward G. Robinson.

The day after Menjou created this additional suspicion of Robinson (in fact, Adolphe wanted to "hang" Eddie!), Howard Rushmore, former film critic for *The Daily Worker*, tried to save his own one-time Commie bum by naming names, including Robinson, whom he painted as a joiner of "Communist fronts." On October 23, Gary Cooper, Robert Montgomery (a close friend of Cagney's), George Murphy and director Ray McCarey were friendly witnesses, with Ronald Reagan pledging to aid HUAC in any way possible.

The next day, the Committee for the First Amendment ran full-page ads in the Los Angeles papers, including Article I of the Bill of Rights and 100 signatures, including those of Bogart, Bacall, Huston and Gladys Robinson. (Eddie was shooting *All My Sons* at Universal.) On October 25, a group of CFA performers—including Bogie and Bacall, Huston, Lucille Ball, Gene Kelly, Myrna Loy and Fredric March—recorded material for *Hollywood Fights Back*, a radio program that aired nationally the following day.

That same Sunday, the CFA sent representatives, including Huston, Bogart and Bacall, to Washington to protest formally at the HUAC hearings; but, following efforts in D.C. and during a five-city tour, they returned to Hollywood, having accomplished little. On November 2, *Hollywood Fights Back* aired again, with Bogie representing the CFA:

> We saw American citizens denied the right to speak by elected representatives of the people. We saw police take citizens from the stand like criminals, after they'd been refused the right to defend themselves. We saw the gavel of the committee chairman cutting off the words of free Americans. The sound of that gavel, Mr. Thomas, rings across America! Because every time your gavel struck, it hit the First Amendment to the Constitution of the United States.

On November 24, a group of film-industry financiers and producers, including Jack Warner, met at the Waldorf-Astoria in New York, issuing a statement that they wouldn't hire any of the Hollywood Ten artists until they had publicly cleared themselves, including admissions that they were not members of the Communist Party. The group also made declarations that basically outlawed *anyone* who was suspected of "subversive" beliefs or actions, thereby giving the green light to blacklisting in Hollywood.

That same day, during a session at the House of Representatives, Helen Gahagan Douglas, wife of Melvyn Douglas and a Member of Congress from California, asked for a list of "subversive" films. John Rankin, an anti-Semitic Mississippi Democrat, responded by rattling off the actual names of actors who had signed an anti-HUAC petition; among them were her own husband, "Melvyn Hesselberg," "Daniel Kaminsky" (Danny Kaye) and "Emmanuel Goldenberg."

Bacall wrote, "[S]ome of the most talented and creative writers, directors, and a few actors were deprived of the right to work, though they were guilty of nothing.... It suddenly became risky, even dangerous, to be a Democrat."[3] Huston concluded, "Communism was as nothing compared to the evil done by the witch-hunters. They were the real enemies of this country."[4]

The Treasure of the Sierra Madre raked in $3.5 million at the box-office, won the Golden Globe as best picture, and made a haul at the Academy Awards, winning Best Supporting Actor for Walter Huston and *two* Oscars (Best Director and Best Screenplay) for his son. The film didn't win Best Picture, but this oversight doesn't seem as wrongheaded as the fact that Bogart wasn't even nominated for Best Actor. As good as Bogie is in an unforgettable performance, the truth is that Walter Huston, who invented or adapted many of Howard's mannerisms from previous roles, steals every scene that he's in. In fact, at one point during production, Bogart grumbled, "One Huston is bad enough, but two are murder."[5]

Jack Warner was ultimately dissatisfied with the film's performance, as cost overruns negated any profits, and thereafter curtailed expensive prestige productions, especially those requiring location shooting. One film that was hit hard by this edict was the next Huston-Bogart epic, *Key Largo*, an adaptation of the 1939 Maxwell Anderson play originally slated to be filmed in the Florida Keys. Instead, the entire production, with the exception of some establishing shots, was shot in the studio at Burbank.

Bacall again was paired with Bogart, who once more portrayed a cynical man who is forced into heroic acts by dangerous circumstances. But this time, he would be victorious over his old nemesis from a decade earlier: Robinson, as notorious, sadistic gangster Johnny Rocco. Curiously, Huston originally wanted Charles Boyer for the role. Years later, Eddie provided a first-hand recollection of the Bogie-Bacall relationship:

> She was all hardness and rough on the outside, but she was mush in her heart. She was even—and she'd kill me for saying this—dear and warm and utterly devoted to her husband, her family, and her nation. But, brother, she shellacked and varnished herself so that no one would know it. I still know it, and the risk of embarrassing her with a word she'd hate, I think she is lovable.[6]

Jerry Wald produced *Key Largo*, with Huston and Richard Brooks writing the screenplay. Prevented from shooting on location, Huston and Brooks were allowed to *write* in southern Florida, where they bathed in the humid atmosphere while completing the majority of the script. When Huston first read the play, he was furious that the entire thing was written in blank verse. On Broadway, the play, which starred Paul Muni as a Spanish American War deserter who fights off a bandit gang, ran for only 125 performances.

Shooting was scheduled to begin on December 15, 1947, but first the screenplay had to be approved by the PCA's Joseph Breen, who objected to Johnny Rocco's similarity to Charles "Lucky" Luciano, who recently had been deported to Cuba. After this element was toned down, the script was given the green light.

Robinson was guaranteed 10 weeks' work (at $12,500 per), while Wald also scored Claire Trevor for six weeks and Lionel Barrymore for 10 (both at $5,000). Though Warner had eliminated expenses by confining the production to the studio, costs still ran high, due to the num-

Key Largo (1948): While directing the film that re-teamed Bogart and Robinson, who created the most evil gangster of his career, John Huston confers with Eddie during the famous bathroom scene.

ber of top stars in the cast, plus Huston's independent working methods that elbowed out Wald and gave the director almost complete control over the shooting and editing.

Huston chose the legendary Karl Freund as cinematographer, and the two rehearsed tirelessly with the cast for three weeks, especially to create Robinson's powerful introduction, originally scripted as a simple walk down the stairs, but changed to an unforgettable image of Rocco in the bathtub, smoking a cigar. Eddie's only Warners "nude scene" was inspired by Huston's walking in on Richard Brooks bathing with a fan blowing near the tub. Later, Huston said that his star looked like "a crustacean with its shell off."[7]

Robinson contributed some lighthearted comments to Warners publicity, claiming that he preferred to rest up before whacking someone on camera, a process that allowed "make-believe evils" to be "committed with an unfettered mind, free from complications.... I always nap before murder, It's a habit with me. That's why I like a cozy cat-nap before I kill."[8] The publicity department also claimed that Eddie and Bogie met with Arthur Grube, a retired U.S. Secret Service agent, who served as technical adviser on counterfeiting.

The bathtub scene and a subsequent sequence involving Rocco's henchmen led off production (an atypical move for Huston, who usually preferred to shoot in continuity). By January 2, 1948, only two weeks into the 48-day schedule, Huston was already four days behind, so Wald replaced the meticulous Freund with Sid Hickox, who ultimately made no difference, as Huston continued demanding unorthodox camera angles that slowed progress.

Key Largo was the first film in which Bacall's long hair was swept back from her temples and clamped with a barrette. Warners publicity claimed that the bizarre Freund, after closely scrutinizing her appearance, proclaimed that "the Look also has ear appeal": "Indeed, the lady has shapely ears. They cling closely to her head and they have nicely rounded lobes—not too prominent. Neat, I guess, is the word for those cute little ears."[9]

By February 14, Huston was three *weeks* behind schedule, but the Bogart-Bacall chemistry was so powerful that Wald and Warner began to accept the fact that the director was creating another very special motion picture. But, while the romance angle in the earlier Bogart-Bacall films is the most powerful element, here it eventually is overwhelmed by the crescendo created by Huston's near-horror-like juxtaposition of the hurricane outside the house with the psychotic tornado called Johnny Rocco *inside*.

Bogart was now the studio's biggest star, yet he never acted like it, knocking on Robinson's dressing room door to call him to the set each morning. Bogie also wanted Eddie's name to be listed above his in the credits and on the posters; though, with his name to the left, he technically still had top billing. Robinson enjoyed the company of Bogart, Bacall and Huston, all fellow liberals and members of the CFA. But, by the time the shoot ended in March 1948, the CFA had disbanded, and the heavily pressured Bogart had publicly admitted in a *Photoplay* article that he was "no Communist" and that the trip to Washington had been a mistake.

Huston indirectly addresses HUAC in the *Key Largo* script, when Frank McCloud responds to Johnny Rocco's "Why'd you stick your neck out?" by quoting from FDR's January 1942 Declaration of War speech. Angered over the unconstitutional hearings, the director used the gangsters as a metaphor for the witch-hunters who had compromised his friend. He and Richard Brooks also worked in material referring to Bogart's love of the sea. The boat on which McCloud fights it out with Rocco at the film's end was named *Santana* after the actor's own yawl that he loved so much.

Bacall remembered the shoot as "one of my happiest movie experiences." The multitalented Barrymore—who presented each of his costars with a signed original etching—had loved the daily serving of tea and cookies in her dressing room, as did Eddie, "a marvelous actor and a lovely, funny man" who "did 'Molly Malone' with a Yiddish accent which was wildly funny."[10]

A Key West-bound bus is pulled over by a patrol car. As Sheriff Ben Wade (Monte Blue) walks over to question the driver (Joe P. Smith), Huston cuts inside the bus, cleverly introducing Bogart (as Frank McCloud) with two views: the camera, placed behind his right shoulder, shows his profile (screen left) and a reflection of his face in the side mirror (screen center). McCloud then turns to survey the passengers behind him, giving the audience a close-up of his face. The authorities are "looking for a couple Indians, broke out of jail, young bucks in fancy shirts."

McCloud is dropped at the Largo Hotel, where some tough guys tell him the joint is closed. While drinking a beer at the bar, he sits down beside Gaye Dawn (Claire Trevor), a drunken, loud-mouthed broad listening to horse races on the radio. A buzzer sounds, and one of the mugs, Toots Bass (Harry Lewis), takes a drink upstairs. Returning, Bass tells Gaye, "He wants you," and she excuses herself as "I've Got a Right to Sing the Blues" plays over the airwaves.

On the dock behind the hotel, McCloud meets James Temple (Lionel Barrymore), the wheelchair-bound owner, and his daughter-in-law, Nora (Bacall), just before the Sheriff and his deputy, Clyde Sawyer (John Rodney), arrive to inquire about "the Osceola brothers." Temple sends them on their way, then tells McCloud, "Those two brothers and my boy,

George, grew up together. There's no harm in 'em. They just went to Palm Grove and got a little snootful and started to take Florida back for the Indians. Came mighty near succeeding, too, and I sent word for them to come in and give themselves up. Not that I'm supposed to know where they are, you understand." Inside the bar, the old man informs Bass that McCloud was his son's commanding officer, "in the Italian campaign together, from Salerno to Cassino. And my boy, George, was killed in Cassino."

A scream is heard emanating from upstairs, just before the scene cuts to Curley Hoff (Thomas Gomez) strong-arming Gaye into a room. Temple yells up at Hoff, demanding that they behave or leave. Nora shows McCloud to his room, revealing that the five lodgers, including a "Mr. Brown," have rented the entire hotel, then asks about George's death. When Nora steps out, Hoff enters, claiming that they have traveled to Key Largo from Milwaukee "for the deep sea fishing." The phone rings, and Nora receives news of an impending hurricane.

During a scene in which McCloud discusses George's "heroism" with Temple and Nora, Huston works in an indirect reference to his famous World War II documentary, *The Battle for San Pietro*:

> Once, outside San Pietro, George and a couple of others established a forward observation post. They got a direct hit, and the others were killed. That left it up to George. For three days and three nights, he stayed awake, directing our fire. Most of that time, I was on the other end of the line. To keep himself awake, he talked into the phone — talked and talked. Most of his talk was about you two. You'd be surprised how much I know about you both.

Outside, McCloud and Nora run into Hoff, who introduces him to Ralph Feeney (William Haade). Bogart briefly demonstrates his nautical knowledge as McCloud helps secure a boat against the coming foul weather. "Where did you learn about boats?" Nora asks.

"My first sweetheart was a boat," he admits. Observing the lodgers' yacht, he advises Hoff to move it away from the reef. Here, Huston takes the time realistically to show Bogie and Bacall working together to double up the bow lines. Three small boats of Seminoles arrive, and McCloud meets Mama Choby (Felipa Gomez), a 112-year-old woman, and the Osceolas, Tom (Roderic Redwing) and John (Jay Silverheels), who tells Nora, in pidgin English, "We here give ourselves up to police. What Mr. Temple say, we do. Him good friend to Indian."

Thunder rolls and rain pours down. Hoff answers the phone, claims that Temple and Nora aren't in, then pulls a .38 on McCloud. Upstairs, behind a blowing fan, a cigar-smoking man (Robinson) reads a newspaper and enjoys a drink while soaking in a bathtub. Hoff times his actions perfectly, arriving to help "Mr. Brown" on with a robe just as he is toweling off. Across the hall, Brown looks down at a wounded man, Deputy Sawyer, whom he slaps three times.

"Brown? Hey you, Brown!" Temple shouts from another room. Chomping on his cigar, Brown walks in to find everyone congregated together. Temple asks if they are thieves, and Bass replies, "That's right, Pop, we're going to steal all your towels."

"We'll be out of here in a couple of hours," Brown says. "Try to put up with us that long, eh?"

Sawyer regains consciousness. "You won't get away with it, Rocco," he says as he staggers in. Bass trips him to the floor.

"Johnny Rocco, *of course*," says McCloud in a tight close-up. Walking over, the mobster acknowledges his identity. "The one and only Rocco," McCloud explains to the old man, who recalls, "But they threw you out of the country."

"Yeah. Yeah, that's right," Rocco admits. "After living in the U.S.A. for more than thirty years, they called me an undesirable alien. Me, Johnny Rocco, like I was a *dirty Red* or somethin'."

"You're right, you shouldn't have been deported," Temple agrees. "You should have been *exterminated*."

McCloud apologizes for the old man's harsh comments, then describes Rocco's legendary criminal activities. Tapping into the gangster's gargantuan ego, he adds, "Welcome back, Rocco. It was all a mistake. America is *sorry* for what it did to you."

"I'll be back up there one of these days," vows Rocco, "and then you're going to *really* see something." As Temple continues to berate him, he asks McCloud, "Okay, you know all about me. Now, what's with you, *Wiseguy*?"

Questioned about his war service, McCloud answers, "I believed some *words*.... They went like this." Here is Huston's excerpt from FDR's Declaration of War: "We are not making all this sacrifice of human effort and human lives to return to the kind of a world we had after the last World War. We're fighting to cleanse the world of ancient evils, ancient ills." Even though Jack Warner now had sided with the right, the director managed to work in material that may have reminded the mogul of his lengthy pro-Roosevelt stance.

"What's that all about?" puzzles Rocco, gesturing with his cigar.

"We rid ourselves of your kind once and for all," interjects the old man. "You ain't comin' back!" Taunted as a cripple, Temple fights to rise from his wheelchair (an extraordinary, painful effort for the arthritic Barrymore) and challenge the laughing mobster. He takes a swing and falls to the floor. McCloud helps him up, while Nora begins to beat Rocco's chest with her fists and scratch his face.

Rocco responds by planting a kiss on her. "You're a wildcat," he says. "You smell blood, huh? Got your appetite up, huh?" Interrupted by a call from Miami, he lets her go. The skipper (Alberto Morin) arrives to warn Rocco about the coral reef, but the tyrant grabs him by the collar, shoves a .45 in his face, and threatens, "You move that boat, and I'll blow your brains out."

Back upstairs, Angel (Dan Seymour) shaves Rocco, who complains about being double-crossed by the politicians he'd put in office. Turning his attention back to the "wildcat," he compares her to the young Maggie Mooney, a.k.a. Gaye Dawn, then slowly walks over to her.

Huston cuts to a tight facial close-up of Bacall as Rocco whispers something into Nora's ear. Nothing the director could have written could rival what is possible in the viewer's imagination. First, Nora walks away from the degenerate gangster, then turns to strike him again, but he grabs her wrists. She hesitates for two seconds, then spits directly in his face. In close-up, he glares at her in utter surprise and indignation. As she turns her face away from his gaze, McCloud intervenes.

"Look at him, the great Johnny Rocco," says Temple, "with Nora's spittle hanging from his face."

Robinson has been carefully building the intensity of his performance throughout the scene. Now Rocco explodes, "Shut up, old man!"

"Come over here," Temple continues. "I'd like to spit on ya."

Rocco frantically grabs a .38 from Hoff, threatening, "You're not going to stop me from wiping you all out." McCloud points out that he'd have to kill everyone, even his own goons, to avoid leaving witnesses, and Rocco again replies, "Wiseguy." The tension finally is broken by Gaye, demanding to be let out of her room to reload her tank.

Rocco changes into his clothes, then asks about the weather, but McCloud has no satisfactory reply. "I thought you knew all the answers," he jeers. "I thought you was a *wiseguy* from way back." Bass laughs idiotically, and Rocco calls him a "dumbbell," then asks, "What's worse, Curley—a dumbbell or a *wiseguy*?"

"A wiseguy, I guess," Curley replies.

McCloud and Temple get Rocco to admit that he'll never have enough. "You," he says, pointing at McCloud, "do you know what you want?"

"Yes," he admits, "and I had hopes once, but I gave them up."

"Hopes for *what*?" asks Rocco.

McCloud, showing no sign of fear, replies, "A world in which there's no place for Johnny Rocco."

The mobster tosses him a .45, then grabs Hoff's .38, challenging him to pull the trigger. "One Rocco, more or less, isn't worth dying for," announces McCloud, tossing the rod aside. Sawyer picks it up and slowly inches toward the door. Rocco shoots him in the chest, but when the deputy tries to fire back, the .45 is empty. Another blast from the gangster sends him over the railing into the bar below.

Temple believes that McCloud is fearless, sending Bogie into his Rick Blaine mode: "What do I care about Johnny Rocco, whether he lives or dies? I only care about *me*—me and *mine*. If Rocco wants to come back to America, let him. Let him be President. I fight nobody's battles but my own.... Me, die to rid the world of a Johnny Rocco? No thanks."

Nora, surprised by his selfish comments, accuses McCloud of cowardice. Bacall's intensity inspires some fine, subtle nonverbal expressions of guilt from Bogart.

Huston's pacing is razor-sharp, as the hurricane begins to churn at the film's exact midpoint (50 minutes), when Hoff and Angel row out in a gale to send Sawyer's body down to Davy Jones' Locker. On the phone with Ziggy in Miami, Rocco is cut off when the storm knocks out the power. Gaye tries to sneak some bourbon, but the mobster disgustedly announces, "One thing I can't stand is a dame that's drunk," recounting her alcoholic background for the entire group. "You know, I gave her her first chance," he adds, "took her out of the chorus, made her a singer. Mention that while you're at it. Why ain't you a singin' star instead of a lush?" Rocco makes her the proposition of a drink for a song.

"Without any accompaniment?" she asks.

"Now, look, do you want a drink, or don't ya?" he replies.

Gaye begins by describing her "gorgeous ... low-cut" gowns and the lone "baby spot" used to illuminate her in the darkness of the club. Rocco and his boys applaud facetiously. "Well, go ahead, sing," he orders.

Huston insisted that Trevor perform "Moanin' Low" a cappella and off-key, allowing a piano off-camera only to give her an idea of the proper melody. Most of the performance is delivered in a single medium shot, with reaction shots of Rocco, McCloud and Nora, and Temple being cut in at various points. Huston cuts to a two-shot showing Gaye, leaning against the wall in the left foreground, and Hoff, listening in the background at right. A close-up of Hoff, chewing gum and shaking his head, is followed by a tight close-up of Rocco delivering an even more dismayed expression. The performance disintegrates, Gaye grabs for the bar, and asks, "Can I have that drink now, Johnny?"

"No," he replies in disgust. She pathetically pleads for it, but he tells her, "You were rotten." McCloud gets up, pours a drink, and hands it to her. She two-fistedly takes it like medicine, saying, "Thanks, fella," before Rocco slaps McCloud three times. Robinson really connects with Bogart, causing his head to recoil noticeably. Huston cuts in a close-up reaction shot of Nora, then a tight close-up of McCloud. "You're welcome," he replies.

Warners publicity emphasized, "Miss Claire Trevor made her motion picture song debut under handicaps that would have discouraged a less courageous actress."[11] Indeed, her performance in the scene is brilliant, her naturalistic nonverbal expressions during the pauses between lines are heartbreaking. Gaye Dawn necessarily becomes a bit raucous when hitting the hooch, but Trevor was one of the most subtle, quiet actresses of the Golden Age, often at her best playing a hooker with a heart of gold, notably in William Wyler's *Dead End*, with Bogart, and John Ford's *Stagecoach* (United Artists, 1939), with John Wayne. Just as *Key Largo* brought Robinson back to create a latter-day degeneration of his most familiar role, Trevor, too, returned to offer a look at the inevitable collapse experienced by her archetypal character.

Slowly walking back to his seat after being slapped by Rocco, McCloud casts his shadow across Temple and Nora, who registers a delicate look of approval for his defiance of the gangster. "I'm sorry about the things I said upstairs," she whispers to him. "I know they aren't true. Will you forgive me?"

"Of course," he replies, as she speaks of his bravery. "Maybe it is a rotten world," she acknowledges, "but a cause isn't lost as long as someone is willing to go on fighting." She also reveals that George told her the truth about San Pietro: "He had it the other way. You were the one on the hill." After sharing suggestive romantic scenes in the midst of serious conflicts in three films, Bogie and Bacall — directed together for the first (and only) time by the socially conscious Huston — now play characters quietly debating serious philosophical values during a turbulent situation.

As Temple graphically describes a past hurricane, pure fear begins to play across the Mob boss' face. "You don't like it, Rocco, do you? The storm," observes McCloud. "Show it your gun, why don't you? If it doesn't stop, shoot it."

Temple prays to God to send the storm "crashing down," caring not if all are sacrificed to "destroy" the criminal plague. Rocco draws his rod to shoot the old man, then shoves it in McCloud's belly and pulls the trigger twice. The gun is empty.

After the hurricane rages, McCloud gently caresses the sleeping Nora's hair. She awakens, asking, "Will we ever see you again, Frank? Will we?"

"I hope so," he answers.

Temple wants him to stay on at Key Largo. While the old man presents his case, Huston cuts to a beautiful chiaroscuro close-up of Nora as she lovingly looks up at McCloud. Compared to the sensual gazes that Bacall levels at Bogart in their earlier pairings, here she projects an innocent longing that is just as powerful. McCloud admits that he has no "folks," and Temple responds, "I'd be proud to have you regard us as your family."

Bass reports that the boat is gone, throwing Rocco and the boys into a panic. Gaye enjoys a good laugh, while the mobster hatches an alternative plan to have McCloud take them to Cuba aboard the craft that still remains moored to the pier. The Osceola brothers arrive to berate Temple for not giving them shelter, and the old man realizes that Rocco had left them outside to die.

The mobster quietly threatens McCloud with torture if he doesn't cooperate. Sheriff Wade, searching for Sawyer, questions them, then discovers the deputy's body, washed up by the hurricane. Rocco claims the "Indians" committed the crime. Apprehended on the pier, the Osceola brothers try to run, but Wade guns them down. Accused of being an accessory to the murder, Temple, learning of his friends' deaths, is distraught, while McCloud's eyes seethe with anger.

The boys from Miami finally arrive. Ziggy (Marc Lawrence) is "a sight for sore eyes," laughs it up at Gaye's expense, then inspects the counterfeit dough that Hoff has been carrying around in a black case. Conferring in the dark, McCloud, Nora and Gaye discuss his chances of making a break when they leave to board the boat. "You were right," he tells Nora. "When your head says one thing, and your whole life says another, your head always loses." Temple agrees that he has to "make a fight of it."

Rocco pays the old man, then asks Nora, "Want to come along, sister?" and whispers in her ear one more time. Gaye, feigning hysteria at the prospect of being left behind, pleads with him, grabs his .45 and hands it to McCloud just before they head out the door. Aboard the *Santana*, Rocco and Angel lounge in the cabin, while Feeney stays on deck with the seasick Bass. Hoff is concerned that the abandoned Gaye will "squeal" on Ziggy. "Well—" replies Rocco, raising a laugh from both men.

Key Largo (1948): John Huston assembled a cast as powerful as the film's hurricane: Bogart, Robinson, Bacall, Lionel Barrymore and Claire Trevor (original press book publicity).

Turning hard to port, McCloud sends Feeney over the stern, then shoots Bass, who clips him before crumpling to the deck, and Hoff, who emerges through the cabin door. Climbing onto the canopy above the bridge, he opens a hatch to watch for the others. Realizing that Gaye took his piece, Rocco pries the .38 from Hoff's dead hand, then orders Angel on deck. The underling hesitates, and the now paranoid Rocco whacks him, then offers "Soldier" a partnership and half the loot. "It's all yours, Soldier," he says from the cabin, tossing his money bag on deck, "and plenty more after we get to Cuba."

When dough doesn't faze McCloud, Rocco reverts to the "other" Mob alternative: threats and intimidation. "Soldier! You're not big enough to do this to Rocco. I'll kill you! You'll never bring me in! Never!" In desperation, he finally pretends to give up his gun, picking up the pistol dropped by the dead Angel and tossing it on deck.

Rocco slowly creeps out of the cabin, .38 in hand. McCloud fires one slug, and the gangster goes down, but twice pulls himself up to a kneeling stance to receive more doses of lead. McCloud ties off the wheel, observes the annihilated gang lying at his feet, and, "about twelve miles off Boot Key Harbor," radios the U.S. Coast Guard, who put him through to the Largo Hotel, where Wade is apologizing for killing the Osceola brothers.

"I'm the one to blame," says Temple. "If they hadn't trusted me, they wouldn't have turned up here, and they'd still be alive. It seems we can't do anything but harm to those people even when we go to help 'em."

"No, Mr. Temple," Gaye disagrees, "it wasn't you, and it wasn't the law or anybody. It was only *Johnny Rocco*. Nobody in the whole world is safe as long as he's alive." She then leaves with the Sheriff.

Nora answers the phone. "He's alright, Dad. He's coming back to us," she reports, then opens the storm shutters to let the sunlight filter in. The final image shows the smiling McCloud at the helm of the *Santana*, heading for Key Largo.

In its publicity campaign, Warners distributed five phonograph records, each containing a five-minute "interview" with one of the stars: "On the air for you! Put 'em on your favorite radio station five different days!"[12] The five-day hallyhoo plan also included separate teaser ads for Bogart, Robinson, Bacall, Barrymore and Trevor, intended to peak potential audience interest before the film's release. Three national sponsors ran full-page ads with a *Key Largo* tie-in: Mayer Gloves, using Bacall as a model in *Mademoiselle* and *Seventeen* magazines; Eversharp Pen, with Bogie displaying the goods, in *Life*; and Deltah Pearls, featuring a gorgeous portrait of Bacall, in *Movie Show Magazine*.

Huston ran significantly over schedule, but the budget increase wasn't as hefty as on *Sierra Madre*. *Key Largo* grossed $3.5 million, placing within the top 20 box-office hits of 1948. Nonetheless, the film was the last to star Bogart and Bacall, as well as being Huston's Warner Bros. swansong. He was fed up with J. L. and — due to the HUAC blacklisting — the country at large, which induced him to form his own company, Horizon, and live and work outside the United States whenever possible.

Robinson really hadn't played another *serious* gangster part at Warners since *Little Caesar* 17 years earlier. While the original film chronicles the rise and fall of a Mob boss based on Al Capone, *Key Largo* uses "Lucky" Luciano as the inspiration for a gang leader already on his way out, an obsolete figure in the postwar world — a reality that accounts for the bitterness and frustration that inspire him to commit acts of cruelty. This gangster is not only a self-serving criminal, he's an evil fascist who leaves the Seminoles out in the hurricane to die, a scourge who, in the opinion of Temple, must be "exterminated." Enrico Bandello was allowed an appeal to "Mother of Mercy," but there is no such potential redemption for Johnny Rocco.

Frank McCloud heroically eliminates this societal blight; and, in the process, Bogart was able to exact his cinematic revenge for the blastings he received from Robinson a decade earlier. Unfortunately, he didn't get a chance to do the same with Cagney!

Bogie's calm underplaying provides the perfect complement to Eddie's brazen, though completely believable, performance. Ten years after being eliminated as so many gangsters, he was able to vanquish Public Enemy Number One and add a "gang terminator" to his gallery of complex Warners heroes.

Thomas Gomez is excellent in one of his best roles, and is well supported by all the wiseguy actors. Marc Lawrence, though his appearance as Ziggy is brief, is always a gangland treat. Not surprisingly, Claire Trevor earned the official top acting honors, including the Academy Award for Best Supporting Actress.

15

Cagney Apocalypse

Robinson had returned to Warner Bros. for *Key Largo*. Now, Cagney was persuaded to revert to psychotic gangster form to beef up *White Heat*, which had been planned as a low-budget crime thriller. Incredibly, Warners had spent only $2,000 on the rights to Virginia Kellogg's original story.

In need of financing, the brothers Cagney accepted a new contract requiring that Jim star in only one studio film per year. Better still, they could produce their own films for Cagney Productions on the Warners lot; and now that Jim had Bill to deal with Jack Warner, he knew he could avoid direct conflicts with The Shvontz. After he signed on May 6, 1949, the *White Heat* budget was increased and Raoul Walsh came on board to direct the screenplay by Ivan Goff and Ben Roberts, which was rewritten five times (with help from Cagney and Walsh) before it was approved. Most of Cagney's suggestions were honored, except his request that pal Frank McHugh play a supporting role.

The script, which originally championed the literarily stiff, procedural "T-Men," evolved into a focus on the volatile, exciting Arthur "Cody" Jarrett, a role tailored specifically for Cagney and his on-screen *mother*. In this film, the gangster would be fighting against forces from *both* sides. Flying in the face of the PCA, the gangster would defy official governmental forces (the Treasury Department) *and* the insubordinate mugs in his own gang. Dishing out *white heat*, Cody Jarrett is *only* an individualist, a straight shooter against the hypocrisy of modern capitalist society.

Armed with a 42-day schedule and a $1-million budget, Walsh rolled the cameras in mid–May. Trumpeting the return of their star, the Warners publicity machine issued a four-page press release claiming that Cagney had been looking for a good gangster part. To set the facts straight, Jim wrote his own four-page release, explaining how he'd invested his earlier gangsters with redeeming elements of humor, and that his interest in *White Heat* stemmed from its depiction of modern detective methods and the essential stupidity of the criminal.

Like Robinson in *Key Largo*, Cagney helped resurrect, in intense, psychotic fashion, an obsolete genre characterization, here taken to absolute extremes made possible by his unique, powerful persona, and culminating in a terrifying apocalypse resembling an atomic blast. Goff and Roberts had written a superb script, but Cagney transformed Cody Jarrett into a seminal screen character. In all of the films in which he plays a heavy—but in *White Heat* in particular—Cagney stunningly imbues his character with complexities far beyond the written page. No other actor could have starred in this tailor-made film and made it work.

Ma Jarrett (Margaret Wycherly)—a character nearly as savage and unsympathetic as her son—was based on Kate "Ma" Barker, an Ash Grove, Missouri, woman who dutifully cared for all four of her boys, members of the notorious Barker-Karpis gang that carried out a series of bank robberies and kidnappings during the early 1930s. The popular image of Barker as an actual criminal mastermind is a myth, reportedly encouraged by none other than J. Edgar Hoover, who had to justify the BOI's gunning down of the old lady in January 1935.

As visual reinforcement for Cody Jarrett's mother complex, Cagney asked Walsh if the headache-wracked gangster could sit in Ma's lap after one of his debilitating attacks. More than anything else, Jim wanted to see if he and the director could get away with it. "We did it, and it worked," Cagney later admitted.[1] Of course, he'd already sat in Lucille Laverne's lap in his very first film, *Sinner's Holiday*, nearly 20 years earlier.

Walsh assembled an incomparable supporting cast, including Virginia Mayo as Cody's trashy wife, Verna, Edmond O'Brien as T-Man Hank Fallon, and Steve Cochran as "Big Ed" Somers, Verna's man on the side. Virginia Mayo recalled:

> I had some great roles with Raoul Walsh, and *White Heat* was wonderful, just fabulous. Jimmy was so strong. Then you had to react to him. That's how powerful he was. In the garage, I'm trying to get away, because I know he's going to come after me. He really scared me. I could hardly speak, and he choked it out of me.
>
> He enjoyed working with me, I found out. He said, "I want you to be in my next picture, which is a musical, *The West Point Story*."[2]

The credits sequence opens with a locomotive steaming through a tunnel as Cagney and Mayo are billed in large type before the title, which fills the screen with an enormous "WHITE HEAT," presented in wavy, white letters. On the California state line in the High Sierras, a train is shadowed by a sedan speeding along a parallel road. Inside are Cody Jarrett and several gang members, who block the tracks with the car, while two more goons aboard the train knock out the conductor. Cody climbs onto the bridge above the tunnel, draws his rod, and waits for the train to be stopped. As it slows down, he jumps onto a car and orders the engineer to pull the brake. When a couple of the boys fire into a U.S. Mail car, another mug says, "Sounds bad, Cody."

"Why don't you give 'em my address, too?" he replies.

The boys dynamite the car, and the engineer warns, "You won't get away with it, Cody."

"Cody, huh?" Jarrett asks. "You've got a good memory for names—*too* good." He fires two slugs into the engineer's belly, then repeats the treatment for an assistant. Walsh gives the audience a literal taste of *white heat* when the second man falls against a lever releasing excess steam from the engine, cooking Zookie Hommell (Ford Rainey), one of the gang.

"It ain't safe with a crackpot givin' orders," says "Big Ed" Somers, as he and a fellow goon enter the gang's hideout, a remote Lake Tahoe cabin 300 miles from the crime scene.

"Smells good, Ma," Cody, leaning over a hotplate, tells his mother before kicking open the bedroom door. Snoring loudly, Verna is sound asleep (what an entrance for Virginia Mayo), but her husband insists she help with the groceries. "He's getting worse. He needs a doc," Giovanni "Cotton" Valetti (Wally Cassell) tells Cody, pointing to the scalded Zookie, his face and hands bandaged, mummy-style, as he lies on a sofa.

"When the time comes," replies Cody, with a slight hint that he *might* give a damn. After taunting Big Ed, he sits down to check his rod, but is overcome by an incapacitating headache, falls to the floor, and involuntarily fires a shot. Ma rushes him into a bedroom, where he lies facedown on the bed as she massages the back of his neck. "It's like having a red-hot buzz saw inside my head," he tells her.

"Don't let them see you like that," Ma advises. "Might give some of them ideas."

Walsh cuts to a close-up two-shot as Cody sits on Ma's lap and hugs her. "Always thinking about your Cody, aren't ya?" he asks.

"That's right," she replies, patting his chest. He struggles to stand up, then sits on the bed, giving Ma an affirmative nod.

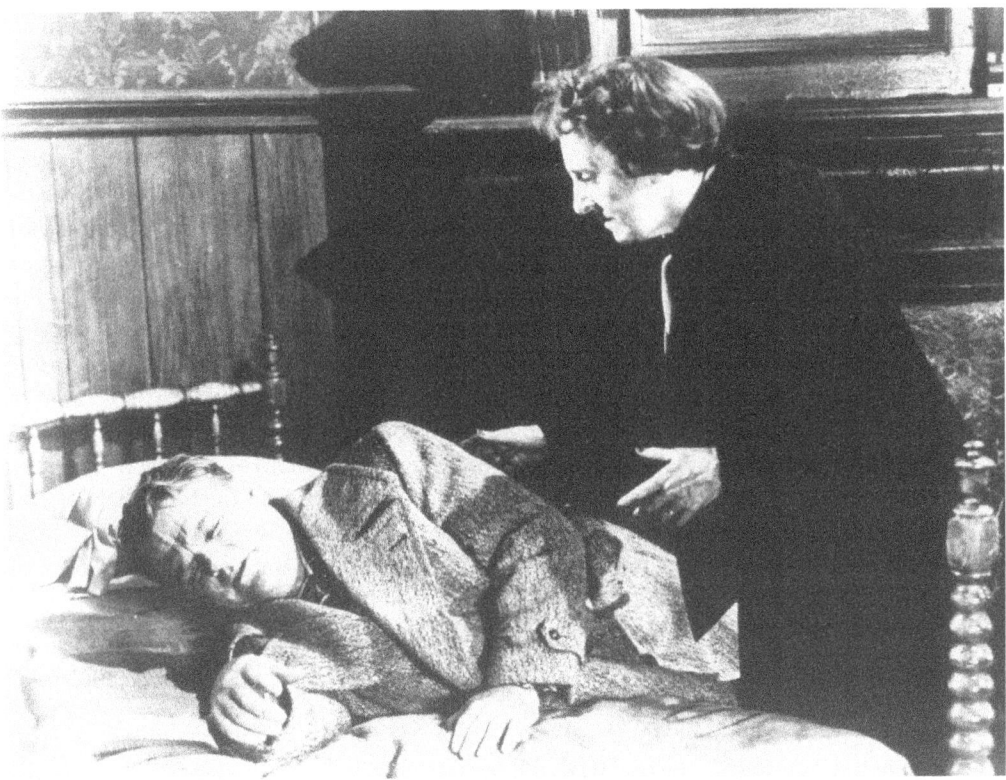

White Heat (1949): Psychotic Arthur "Cody" Jarrett (Cagney), racked by a debilitating headache, is comforted by his Ma (Margaret Wycherly) in Raoul Walsh's apocalyptic postwar gangster opus.

She pours him a shot of whiskey and hands him the glass, toasting, "Top of the world, son."

"I don't know what I'd so without you, Ma," he admits before downing the booze.

"Now go on out. Show 'em you're all right," she says. Cody Jarrett may be a monster, but even the worst monster has a mother.

Cody decides to blow the joint under cover of an impending storm. In the bedroom, he packs the stolen dough in a suitcase, then enjoys a private moment with Verna. "You're cute," he tells her. "Come 'ere."

Hugging him, she mentions spending a little of the loot. "I'd look good in a mink coat, Honey."

"You'd look good in a shower curtain," he points out.

Zookie asks if he did well on his first job, but Cody can't risk taking him along. "We'll send a doc back right away," he claims. Outside, Ma worries about the injured man informing the cops, so Cody commands Cotton to be a "specialist." Handing the reluctant executioner a rod, he says, "Go back and make it easy for him." As they head for the cars, Cody explains to Ma that the cops will find "a corpse without a record — nothing to tie him to the tunnel job or us." A shot is heard, then Walsh cuts inside the cabin to show Cotton blasting two more slugs into the ceiling before handing Zookie a pack of smokes. Cody may be a psycho-sadistic killer without a conscience, but some of his associates aren't wiseguys at all, just working-stiff criminals, actually decent guys at the core.

At the Tahoe County Morgue, U.S. Treasury Agent Philip Evans (John Archer) is called in by police who have a frozen body discovered by hunters. Dust deposits on the dead man's clothes and Cotton's fingerprints on the cigarette pack give him solid evidence against the Jarrett gang.

Cody, Ma and Verna are holed up at a Milbanke Motel in Los Angeles. Verna stands on a chair, modeling a mink coat, while her husband relays the news about Zookie. Ma has gone out to buy strawberries. "She just *had* to get some for her boy," Verna snarls. Cody kicks the chair, knocking her, rear-first, onto a sofa. The mink falls off, exposing her slip and nylon stockings underneath. Cagney improvised this move, putting quite a scare into Virginia Mayo.

A T-Man, spotting Ma at the market, marks her car bumper. But Ma is no fool, doing her best to ditch the cops. Only Evans reaches the motel, where he confronts Cody as they are preparing to lam out of the joint. Grabbing a rod from his coupe, Cody shoots him in the shoulder before they speed off. These location scenes, shot on the streets of Los Angeles, lend the film a gritty, urban atmosphere that would be echoed by countless subsequent noir and crime films. Chased by the cops, Cody escapes by pulling into a drive-in theater (a specific incident borrowed by Peter Bogdanovich for a major portion of his directorial debut, *Targets* [1968], Boris Karloff's last great film). He switches to a plan "cooked up" before the "tunnel job," telling Ma and Verna that he'll confess to an Illinois state crime that occurred simultaneously. "Couldn't be in both places at once, could I?"

"You're the smartest there is, Cody," praises Ma, who sits *between* her son and his wife.

"Sure, it's smart, but what about me?" asks the mink-clad Verna. "What do I do for the next two years?"

"Same as you did before he married you," replies Ma.

"You better not, Baby," warns Cody. "I'll be back."

The broads put on an act for the T-Men, so Evans calls in undercover man Hank Fallon, an educated specialist who spends most of his time in the Big House. Aware that "Scratch" Morton pulled the Springfield job, then "went underground," Fallon concludes, "A hoodlum turns himself in on a phony rap and beats the gas chamber. Jarrett outsmarted you."

"That's just what we wanted him to think," Evans reveals. "We're working *with* the Springfield police. We *arranged* for the confession to check. So, what happens? Jarrett does a stretch in the penitentiary. In case he gets lonely and wants to talk to someone, we're going to let one of our own boys do a stretch, right in the same cell." Fallon's objective: "Stick with him until you find out where he unloaded $300,000 in federal currency without a single bill showing up. Also, try to learn the identity of the very special fence that engineered this deal."

Fallon scrutinizes records and photographs of the Illinois Pen inmates, weeding out mugs he busted so they may be transferred elsewhere. One wiseguy who draws his attention is Bo Creel (Ian MacDonald), a thief who could identify him "in the dark," but scheduled for release before Fallon's "sentence."

Evans prepares him for the unusual nature of the assignment: "You see, there's insanity in the Jarretts. Some of it rubbed off on Cody. His father died in an institution. When he was a kid, he used to fake headaches in order to get his mother's attention away from the rest of the family. It worked. As he grew up, the fancied headaches became real, until, now, they tear him to pieces. Any minute, he's apt to crack open at the seams. There goes our case. So you'll be working against time."

Cody's madness is never totally explained, but the screenplay offers several angles. Rather than arguing definitely for congenital insanity, Evans cites environmental and psychosomatic reasons. His father was insane, but Cody's motivation was his mother, drawn inexorably to "her boy" by his attention-seeking behavior.

But Evans doesn't rule out a hereditary component. He continues, "The only person he's ever cared about or trusted is his mother. No one else has ever made a dent, not even his wife. His mother's been the prop that's held him up. He's got a fierce, psychopathic devotion for her. All his life, whenever he got in a spot, he just put out his hand, and there was Ma Jarrett. Without her, maybe Cody—just like his old man."

"You mean, I'm supposed to take Mama's place?" assumes Fallon. "I'll practice up on my lullabies."

Using the alias "Victor Pardo," Fallon enters the Big House. While waiting in the immunization line, he notices Bo Creel, who has been laid up with pneumonia, working as a medic. To avoid exposure, he starts a brawl and is dragged off to solitary confinement. Back in the cell block, he listens to his mates discussing the continued operations of the Jarrett gang, led by Ma during Cody's absence. Unknown to "her boy," the old broad has her hands full, observing the carrying-on of Verna and Big Ed, who plans to have Cody whacked in the Joint.

In the prison shop, Roy Parker (Paul Guilfoyle), a fellow inmate, attempts to drop a large motor on Cody as he dumps buckets of metal filings. "Pardo" dives and knocks him out of the way, saving his life. "Why should you care if a guy named Cody Jarrett gets his, if you don't want somethin'?" he asks.

Cody is visited by Ma, who informs him about Verna and Big Ed. "What's mine is mine, but I ain't goin' to let it make me sick," he says. "I'll take care of them when I get out."

"That's what I told myself," replies Ma, wild-eyed (and sporting a toothy grin reminiscent of Lon Chaney's vampire in *London After Midnight* [1927]). "And I'll help ya, Cody, like always. You'll be out soon—back on top of the world."

"With you around, Ma, nothing can stop me," he assures her.

Ma asks him about the "accident" in the shop, then vows, "*I'll* take care of Big Ed."

"No, no, Ma," Cody disagrees, "you won't have a chance."

"Any time I can't handle his kind, I'll know I'm gettin' old," she explains. "No one does what he's done to you, son, and gets away with it." Despite Cody's protests, she stands up, vowing, "I'm going after him, Cody, to keep him from having you knocked off in here."

"Ma! Ma! Ma!" Cody shouts, grabbing onto the wire mesh. Back in the shop, his mood is somber, then incensed as he threatens to "take care of" Parker. The noise of the machines, combined with Ma's voice in his head, triggers one of his savage migraines, and he crawls along the floor to Pardo, who drops some tools to provide cover, then massages the back of his head while offering positive reinforcement. Cody stands up, gradually recovers, looks at Pardo, then grasps both of his hands and pats him on the cheek. In shot-reverse-shot close-ups, Cagney's subtle nonverbal acting is brilliant, injecting a brief look at whatever tenderness still exists in Jarrett's twisted psyche.

That night, in the darkness of their cell, Cody and Pardo quietly discuss the headache, Ma, and the "petty-ante stretch" set up to "take the heat off ... for another job." Cody calls him "Kid," a term indicating the establishment of trust between them. Pardo, claiming he can rig the prison electrical system, agrees to "crash out" with him, but only if they do it alone. "All right, Kid," Cody agrees. "It's a deal. And, if it works, I'll pay ya back."

Pardo meets with his "wife" to pass on news of the prison break. The T-Men then plan their surveillance, including the use of a tracking device that will be attached to the getaway car. However, before the escape can be carried out, Cody, while eating in the mess hall, receives word, through a string of inmates, that his mother is dead. Trying to eat, Cody first is incredulous, then agonized. Rising up in anguish, he goes completely ballistic. Unleashing a painful wail, he slams down his tin cup, crawls onto the table, rolls over other inmates, the table-top and down onto the floor, then punches out four guards before being subdued. As he is carried out, his plea, "I've got to get out of here! I've got to get out of here! I've got to get out!" is barely decipherable beneath the flood of sorrowful shrieks pouring out of him. Walsh covers all the action in long shot, lending a consistent, documentary-like tone, refusing to cut in a typical "star" close-up.

To successfully pull off this startling scene of mess-hall madness, Cagney drew upon youthful memories of hearing painful wails while visiting a mental hospital on Ward's Island. Many of his fellow actors and the 300 extras were not told what to expect, their resulting looks of shock and fear being absolutely genuine. This scene contains the most powerful acting Cagney ever committed to celluloid, and its undiminished ability to distress an audience is perhaps equaled only by the film's apocalyptic ending.

Tommy Ryley (Robert Osterloh) brings soup to the strait-jacketed Cody, who, pretending he's Pardo, calls him "Vic." When the guard isn't looking through the barred window in the door, Cody offers to take Ryley along on the escape in exchange for the gat he has stashed. The prison doctor declares Jarrett "violent and homicidal" while awaiting the arrival of psychiatrists who will "commit him to the institution." The warden phones Evans, informing him of Cody's impending release to the asylum. "Tomorrow they'll be a pardon coming through for one of your inmates, Vic Pardo," Evans replies. "Rush it through, will you?" Now that Jarrett is a raving maniac, the Treasury plan is canceled.

Cody, released from the strait-jacket and armed with Ryley's .38, takes the doctors and Roy Parker hostage. Using "The Reader" (G. Pat Collins), the prison's lip-reading informant, as a decoy, Cody orders him dressed in the strait-jacket. On their way out to the car, Parker pleads, "You wouldn't kill me in cold blood, would ya?"

"No," Cody replies, "I'll let you warm up a little."

Evans intends to pick up Fallon, but receives word about the breakout. "He'll stay with Jarrett until he gets what he's after," the T-Man informs his associates.

At a temporary hideout, Cody ties up the two psychiatrists, grabs a chicken leg, then walks outside to the trunk of the penitentiary sedan, in which the little prison hit-man has been confined. "How you doin', Parker?" Cody inquires.

"It's stuffy in here," he replies. "I need some air."

"Oh, stuffy, huh? I'll give it a little air," Cody announces before blasting four slugs into the car, then enjoying the rest of the chicken.

Abandoned by the rest of the gang, Verna and Big Ed are more than a bit anxious. "Stay here and shoot it out," she tells him. "Me, I'm goin'. I want to live."

"Cody might have some ideas about that," warns Big Ed.

"I'll go someplace he'll never find me," she vows.

"The world ain't big enough, Sugar," he tells her. "Not when he finds out what you did to his Ma."

Verna hesitates. "You'd tell him?"

"*If* you run out on me," he replies.

"But I only did it for you, Ed," she explains. "She had you covered."

"Cody still ain't gonna like to hear that she got it in the back," he reminds her. "Feel more like stayin' now?"

After darkness falls, Verna lies awake, frightened by every sound. She gets up, dresses, and climbs out a window, but Cody is waiting for her in the garage. He grabs her around the neck, causing her to plead and lie in equal measure. "You let Ma die," he accuses, "didn't even raise a finger to help her. You just stood there and watched Big Ed kill her. Maybe you thought it was funny, an old woman takin' on a guy like that, huh?" Mayo recalled being frightened of Cagney while shooting this scene, and her naturalistic performance is superb.

"He got her in the back," she admits, then offers to help him get into the booby-trapped house. Inside, Cody rings the bell attached to the front door, then cases the downstairs, rod drawn, while Verna walks upstairs, where Ed is waiting. She claims she tried to leave, but couldn't. As Ed embraces her, the door opens slightly, and Cody's left eye can be seen peering in. She occupies Ed with a drink, and Cody quietly sneaks in behind him. The cornered rat tosses down his glass and runs out of the room, but Cody blasts two bullets through the door (a classic Cagney device). Verna follows Cody to the top of the stairs, where the contented killer glances at his wife, briefly points at the body lying below, then offers his arm to her. Executing the subtlest of double-takes, then gently directing Mayo's attention with one of those legendary hands, Cagney, using no dialogue, accomplishes an acting feat just as effective as, but 180 degrees away from, Cody's ranting lunatic display in the mess hall. Pardo, Ryley and the Reader walk in. Cody announces, "Catch!" and kicks Big Ed's body to the bottom of the staircase.

Cody and the boys meet with some of Big Ed's former associates to plan the robbery of a $426,000 payroll from a chemical plant. They've invested 12 grand in a gas truck to use as a Trojan horse, and expect to fence the traceable bills through Cody's "manager," known as "The Trader" (Fred Clark), who arrives in the guise of a fisherman. Pardo gains extra points with Cody by tripping up the visitor with angling questions, then pulling his rod on the "phony." Cody laughs, then introduces him to Trader, whom he tells, "Vic's my partner, fifty-fifty."

"Cody Jarrett going fifty-fifty?" questions Trader.

"I split even with Ma, didn't I?" Cody replies.

That night, Pardo sneaks out, tangles with one of Cody's gorillas, then claims he was heading to L.A. to visit his wife. Cody admits that he, too, is lonely. Pardo asks about Verna, but he shakes his head, explaining, "All I ever had was Ma, and now — Your mother alive?"

"No, no," Pardo replies, "she died before I even knew her."

"I was walkin' around out there, talkin' to mine," Cody reveals. "That sound funny to you? Well, some might think so. My old lady never had anything, always on the run, always on the move. Some life. First there was my old man, died kickin' and screamin' in a nuthouse, then my brother. And after that, was takin' care of me, always tryin' to put me on top. 'Top of the world,' she used to say.… That was a good feelin' out there, talkin' to her, just me and Ma. Good feelin'. Liked it." Looking at Pardo, he adds, "Maybe I am nuts."

Following a few drinks, Cody takes Verna off to bed, while Pardo stays up to "repair" her radio. Cagney, at age 49, demonstrates his physical prowess by giving the much taller Mayo a piggyback ride, walking up the stairs, without using his hands, relying on her arms and legs wrapped around him.

The next morning, Pardo attaches his makeshift signaling device to the chassis of the truck. While stopping at a gas station, he uses soap to write a message to the police on the restroom mirror, then alerts the attendant to the "dirty" facility. At a rendezvous with Trader, they pick up their driver — Bo Creel, who has been working at the chemical plant. Meanwhile, Evans receives the message and dispatches radio cars to track the signal.

Creel drives the Trojan truck into the plant, then uses his identification card to enter the accounting office, where he pistol-whips the guard. While the gang uses a cutting torch on the safe, Creel recognizes Pardo. "Hey, Cody, that guy's a copper," he discloses. "He's a T-Man. I know him. His name is Fallon."

White Heat (1949): Cody Jarrett (Cagney) disapproves of the slatternly lifestyle of his unfaithful wife, Verna (Virginia Mayo), the kind of trashy broad Raoul Walsh loved to depict in his films (original lobby card).

Fallon grabs a sawed-off shotgun. "A copper. A copper," Cody announces. "How do you like that, boys? A copper — and his name is Fallon." With tears beginning to well in his eyes, he laughs. "And we went for it. *I* went for it. Treated him like a kid brother. And I was going to split fifty-fifty with a copper." He laughs again, nearly crying this time. Indicating the betrayal Cody is feeling from his surrogate mother, Cagney dazzlingly displays two strong emotions simultaneously.

Fallon orders the gang to raise their hands, but Zookie sneaks up and pistol-whips him from behind. Creel wants him whacked, but Cody plans to use him as a hostage to get past the army of cops surrounding the joint. In custody, Verna offers to talk Cody out in exchange for a deal. "Lock her up," orders Evans.

Cody starts talking to Ma, using the shotgun to blast away at the cops. Blinded by tear gas, he accidentally shoots Zookie in the back. Fallon escapes, making his way out to inform Evans about the whereabouts of Daniel Winston, "The Trader." The cops pick off members of the gang as they attempt to make their way through the maze of the refinery, but Cody and Ryley get as far as the huge chemical tanks on the outer perimeter of the plant. "Don't fire unless you've got a perfect target," commands Evans, who adds a colossal understatement, "That place is a stack of dynamite."

The chuckling Cody is completely insane at this point, his delusions of grandeur increasing by the moment. "They think they've got Cody Jarrett," he tells Ryley. "They haven't got

Cody Jarrett. You hear, they haven't got him. And I wanna show ya, they haven't got him." He *runs* up the steps to the top of a tank, and, when Ryley tries to surrender, fires two shots into his back. "Come and get me!" he shouts to Evans.

Fallon, using a high-powered rifle with a scope, hits Cody three times, but he refuses to die. Dragging himself back to his feet, he fires his .38 *into* the tank twice, raising large bursts of flame. The cops run like hell. Looking skyward, Cody, smiling maniacally, proudly announces, "Made it Ma! Top of the world!" The tank explodes into a gigantic fireball, its near-atomic, mushroom-like image of flame and smoke being followed by three more erupting tanks. Cagney's startling acting and Walsh's potent imagery combine to create one of the most chilling images in the history of the cinema, its goosebump-raising potential never lessened by repeated viewings. (The refinery setting is another major *White Heat* element appropriated by Peter Bogdanovich for *Targets*.)

After this holocaust, a sober summation by the T-Men is superfluous and anticlimactic, to say the least. "Cody Jarrett," declares Evans. "Finally got to the top of the world," adds Fallon, "and it blew right up in his face." Firefighters uselessly pour water into the blaze, one more tank explodes, and "The End" sails into the image, backed by a screen-filling wall of fire.

White Heat was Raoul Walsh's best film since *High Sierra*, another powerful thriller set in the same vicinity. But this time he directed a different Warners Wiseguy, his first work with Cagney since *The Strawberry Blonde* in 1941. (Of course, he directed both Cagney and Bogart in *The Roaring Twenties*.) *White Heat*, combining the classic Warners gangster and prison genres with the crime-procedural brand of film noir, is arguably the finest work of Walsh's impressive career, and the director always gave Cagney credit for adding the fascinating layers of depth to Cody Jarrett, particularly the decision to make the mobster unique by playing him as a mental case. Perhaps the richest performance of his career, it—like Rocky Sullivan in *Angels with Dirty Faces*—should have brought Jim an Oscar; but, as in 1938, the Academy still didn't give Best Actor awards for gangster portrayals. Cagney's Academy Award for *Yankee Doodle Dandy* was won as much by the patriotic character and subject matter as by the actual performance (but Jim preferred it that way).

No stranger to noir, the classically trained Edmond O'Brien was one of the finest actors of the Golden Age, equally comfortable in colorful period parts or naturalistic streetwise roles. *White Heat* gave him the opportunity to play a dual role, a savvy cop and his polar opposite, a tough-talkin' inmate.

White Heat was the sixth Warners film to depict a relationship between a Cagney character and his mother. Interestingly, it was the first to *bump off* his Ma, a character who would never again appear in a Cagney film released by Warners. Margaret Wycherly, an accomplished stage actress, is magnificent as Ma Jarrett, psychologically the polar opposite, the absolute moral inversion, of her loving Christian mother to the future World War I hero, Alvin C. York (Gary Cooper), in Warners' *Sergeant York* (1941), directed by Howard Hawks.

As Verna, Virginia Mayo expertly plays the kind of trashy broad that Walsh loved to depict in his films, belting back booze, wearing gaudy jewelry and furs, and being "polite" enough to spit out her chewing gum before kissing Cody. Steve Cochran is perfectly cast as Big Ed, the self-seeking wiseguy who'll do anything to double-cross the boss, including helping bump off his mother.

16

Three Wiseguys Who Knew Jack

Humphrey Bogart

On February 18, 1950, *Chain Lightning*, starring Bogart as test pilot Matthew Brennan, was released. Directed by Stuart Heisler, it would prove to be Bogie's final film actually made at Warner Bros.

While testing a new jet built by Leland Willis (Raymond Massey) for the U.S. Air Force, Brennan disobeys orders, remaining in the air to carry out further trials of his own design. Massey begins a voice-over, initiating a flashback that comprises most of the 94-minute running time.

In 1943 Lt. Colonel Brennan, piloting a B-17 over Hitler's Europe, has flown a record 24 missions. During a meeting with Carl Troxell (Richard Whorf), he lodges several complaints about the flaws of the "Flying Fortress." Ordered Stateside after a tough mission, he attempts to obtain permission to marry his sweetheart, Red Cross nurse Joan Holloway (Eleanor Parker), but his commanding officer is busy with "the Prime Minister."

Back in the States, Brennan is introduced to Willis at a cocktail party, where he runs into "Jo," who has arrived with Troxell, now the developer of a new jet. In a scene unique to his career, Bogie plays the chords in a two-man piano arrangement, while singing a World War II ditty. Bitter over Brennan's failure to write to her in England, Jo tries to ignore him, but he insists on taking her home, then leaves frustrated.

Troxell asks Willis to hire Brennan as Chief Test Pilot. Jo, working as Willis' secretary, is ordered to get him on board. In the air, he is truly happy, performing every conceivable trial on the JA3 experimental jet, while Jo, who "didn't want him here," is "scared—scared stiff."

Troxell demonstrates a model of his new ejection pod to Brennan, but the pilot is not supportive, considering the invention a "keg of dynamite." After Willis is injured in a plane crash, Brennan proposes a headline-grabbing JA3 flight from Nome, Alaska, over the North Pole, to Washington, D.C. Though the maximum range of the jet is 4,000 miles, Willis plans to implement Brennan's own idea: seal the wings, making the entire ship a gigantic fuel tank, then fly at a higher altitude, to reach a distance of 5,300. His payoff *if* he reaches the destination: $30,000.

Angered over Brennan's "grandstanding," Troxell vows to demonstrate a new jet, the JA4, complete with ejection pod, before the JA3 reaches Washington's National Airport. Over the North Pole, the cabin air pressure drops, causing Brennan to pass out briefly, but he regains control as it levels off. Out of fuel and menaced by a lightning storm, he still executes a triumphant landing. Collecting his check, he vows to give up flying to marry Jo, who, at the very moment of his proposal, receives a phone call with news of Troxell's death while testing the pod.

Ed Bostwick (Morris Ankrum) approaches Brennan, asking him to demonstrate a dupli-

Chain Lightning (1949): Bogart's final film actually made at Warner Bros., this disappointing aviation soap opera paired him with the stunning Eleanor Parker, who signed this title lobby card (original lobby card).

cate JA4 to redeem Troxell. In an attempt to arouse Brennan's sense of guilt, Bostwick plays back the flight recording of Troxell's death. Brennan throws him out, refusing to commit suicide, then informs Jo that, after one last flight aboard the JA3, he'll be "through with the whole weeping, wailing bunch of you."

The flashback ends with a needless *repeat* of the opening scene. Jo arrives, informing Willis and the Air Force personnel that Brennan is testing, not the JA3, but the *JA4*. As he receives approbation from the ground, he ejects the pod. The jet crashes and burns, the pod lands, and Jo rushes out to greet the triumphant pilot. Driving a jeep down the runway, General Hewitt (Roy Roberts) declares, "Now you're in aviation, Willis. Now you see how a deathtrap can be turned into a life raft."

"Why did you take a chance, Matt? Why did you do it?" asks Jo.

"Well, there I was, up 60,000 feet," Brennan replies. "It was the quickest way to get down to *you*."

An endless exercise in tedious aviation testing and development procedures, *Chain Lightning* offers ample evidence why Bogart finally became fed up with Warner Bros. While not as bad as *The Two Mrs. Carrolls*, this production proved a thankless vehicle for the powerful star of *The Treasure of the Sierra Madre* and *Key Largo*, the two Bogart films immediately preceding it. Bogie gives his standard reluctant hero performance (finally showing some intensity near the conclusion), but is surrounded by supporting actors playing cardboard characters in a contrived screenplay. In particular, Raymond Massey, whose restrained performance helps anchor *Action in the North Atlantic*, is thoroughly wasted as a one-dimensional, constantly cranky, conservative industrialist.

Walter Huston passed away suddenly on April 7, 1950, one day after his 64th birthday. Lauren Bacall remembered:

> We were ... on the boat when [the] news came ... Walter had been staying at the Beverly Hills Hotel — we'd all been together just a few nights before. It was all ... very sad. I was more than ever aware of John's very real love for his father. John Huston's life had not been based on attachments. He felt things, of course, but I don't believe that a life blow had ever been dealt him until Walter died. There was a small service ... It was beautiful and moving. There was a moment about halfway through when a deep, half muffled sob emanated from John. A chilling sound. I looked at him and thought of him differently from then on.[1]

After walking through *Chain Lightning*, Bogart starred in one of his finest non-Warners films, *In a Lonely Place*, playing the complex, moody and violent writer Dixon Steele for director Nicholas Ray. This Columbia noir classic was followed by *The Enforcer* (1951), a "Murder Inc." thriller slated to be directed independently by Bretaigne Windust for United States Pictures, then released by Warner Bros. Windust, a Broadway director whose greatest triumph was *Arsenic and Old Lace* (1941–44) with Boris Karloff, occasionally dabbled in the cinema, but his contribution to *The Enforcer* proved negligible. He began shooting the film, then fell seriously ill, so Bogie saved the day by bringing in none other than Raoul Walsh, who directed during Windust's lengthy hospitalization but refused to take on-screen credit.

As Assistant D.A. Martin Ferguson, set to convict Mob boss Albert Mendoza (based on Louis "Lepke" Buchalter), Bogart is *really* on the side of law and order this time. Screenwriter Martin Rackin patterned Ferguson on Brooklyn A.D.A. Burton B. Turkus, who convinced wiseguy Abe Reles to turn informer, spilling the beans about the entire Murder Inc. organization.

The film opens with the cops transporting Joseph Rico (Ted de Corsia), the State's nervous witness, to the D.A.'s office in an armored car. Captain Ted Nelson (Roy Roberts) opens the door, and Bogart is — smoking a cigarette. "If you won't talk, I'll send you to the chair," Ferguson threatens Rico, then shows him that Mendoza is locked safely in the slammer. Moments later, a Mob marksman unsuccessfully tries to whack the terrified informant. While in a washroom, Rico crawls out the window onto a ledge, and when Ferguson attempts to help him back in, he falls to his death, just seven hours before the beginning of Mendoza's trial.

Forced to review all the arrest reports, Ferguson initiates a flashback recounting Murder Inc.'s ordering of James "Duke" Malloy (Michael Tolan) to kill "his girl," Nina Lombardo. Soon, Malloy is found hanging in his jail cell, so Ferguson and Captain Nelson investigate "Philadelphia," "Big Babe" and "Smiley," three names mentioned by the dead man. "Philadelphia" Tom Zaca (Jack Lambert) is apparently insane, "Smiley" Schultz is smoldering in a furnace, and "Big Babe" Lazich (Zero Mostel) is afraid to talk. In this scene, the cops first hear the Mafia terms "contract" and "hit."

Ferguson threatens to lock up Babe's wife (Greta Granstedt) and institutionalize his son (Louis Lettieri), so the big man, launching a series of multiple flashbacks, describes the organization and operations of "The Troupe." Joe Rico, depicted as a reluctant, cringing squealer in the opening scene, is a true tough guy here.

Babe identifies Nina Lombardo's body in a dredged-up station wagon belonging to Thomas O'Hara (Don Beddoe), who, found bleeding on a sidewalk, recalls the hit for Fer-

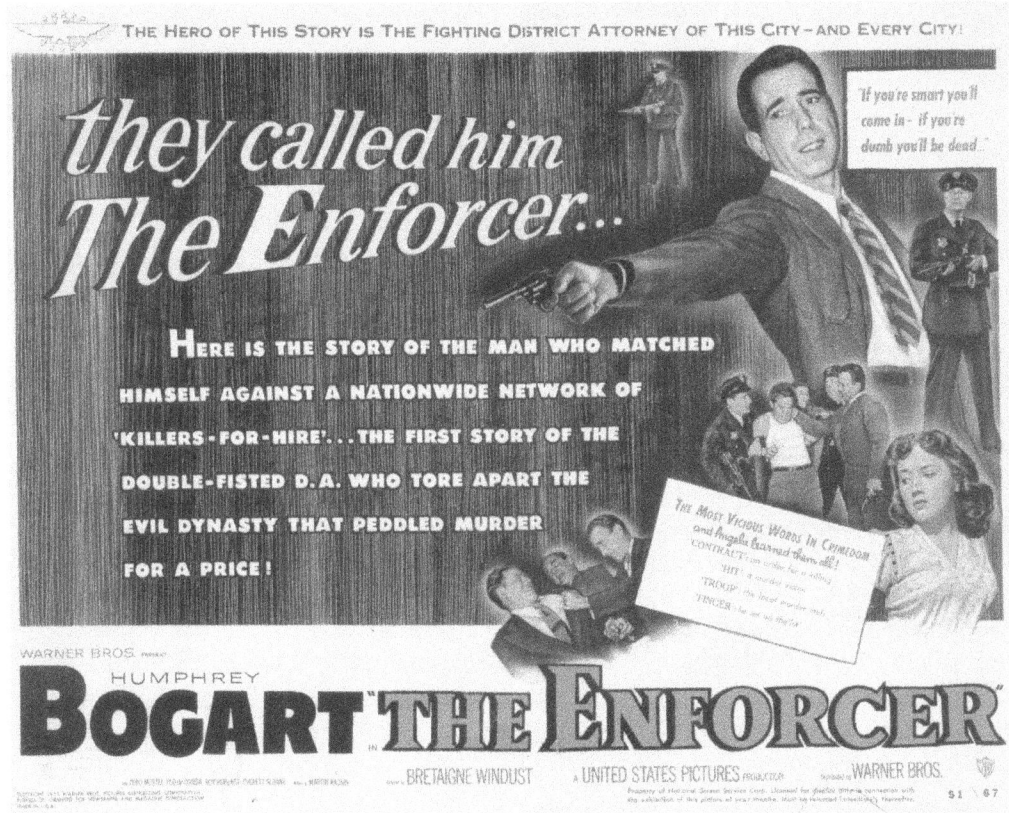

The Enforcer (1951): Released by Warner Bros., this independently produced exposé of Murder Inc. borrows from *The Big Sleep* and stars Bogart as Assistant District Attorney Martin Ferguson, a character based on Mob-busting Brooklyn Assistant D.A. Burton B. Turkus (original title lobby card).

guson. Teresa Davis (Patricia Joiner), the murdered girl's roommate, provides further information, including Nina's original name of "Angela Vetto," daughter of a murder witness. Ferguson then leans on the now-lucid Philadelphia, who recollects delivering bodies to a 12th Street undertaker. More bodies in car coffins are then dredged out of the marsh.

Following a visit from murderous hit man Herman (Bob Steele), Rico meets with Ferguson to cut a deal regarding Mendoza (Everett Sloane) and the formation of the organization — the final flashback before the narrative returns to the D.A. and Nelson lamenting the sorry state of their evidence. In a last-ditch effort, Ferguson visits Mendoza in his cell, where he confronts the killer with photographs of his victims. Scrutinizing Nina's photo, Mendoza asks the guard for a call to his "lawyer," who then phones Herman to order a "rush job."

In the courthouse record room, Nelson is listening to Rico's taped interviews. Ferguson enters and paces the room, as the statement, "And the girl, staring at him with the big, blue eyes" emerges from the recorder. Playing it back twice more, he then examines the coroner's report on Nina Lombardo, who is listed as having *brown* eyes. "The finger man pointed out the wrong girl, and Duke killed the wrong girl," he tells Nelson. "The one they wanted was her roommate — the one we talked to. I knew she was lying about something. She's Angela Vetto." Calling for a four-hour delay, Ferguson claims he has "an eyewitness who can put Mendoza in the chair."

Tailed down the main drag by Herman and a fellow stooge, Teresa/Angela is saved in the nick of time by Ferguson, who attracts her attention by using a loudspeaker. Just as Herman pulls his heater to whack the girl, the D.A. guns him down. Here, Bogart, shooting Bob Steele in a tense moment, reprises Marlowe's blasting of Canino in *The Big Sleep*, which "inspired" several elements in this film. "I want to see that smile fade on Mendoza's face when he looks into those big, blue eyes again," he tells Angela.

Louis "Lepke" Buchalter, in addition to ordering countless Murder Inc. hits (including that of the infamous Dutch Schultz), was said to have whacked at least 100 victims personally. Sentenced to walk the last mile to the Sing Sing electric chair on March 4, 1944, he is the only Mob boss ever executed by state or federal authorities. The fictionalized exploits of *The Enforcer* add up to little more than standard B noir, but Raoul Walsh's no-nonsense, hard-hitting direction, combined with the presence of Bogart and Steele, creates an entertaining variation on the classic Warner Bros. style.

Set in 1925 Damascus, Columbia's *Sirocco* (1951), an undisguised takeoff on *Casablanca* featuring Bogie as a gun-runner, was followed by his most memorable non–Warners performance. Having lost out on his one Academy Award nomination for a Warners film (*Casablanca*), he took home Oscar gold for *The African Queen* (1951), directed and produced independently by John Huston for a United Artists release. Bacall revealed, "The idea of awards was diametrically opposed to Bogie's concept of non-competitive acting ... such things for actors are meaningless unless they all play the same part."[2]

While on location in Africa, Bogie and Bacall both became fast friends with his electric costar Katharine Hepburn, who invited them for dinner after their return to California. One particular evening, they joined Kate, Spencer Tracy (one of Bogie's favorite actors and a great pal) and — James Cagney. Bacall remembered:

> The three actors were contemporaries—each had left his individual mark—and they liked and admired each other. As they exchanged stories and reminisced, Katie and I sat spellbound.... Bogie always said that if he were asked to choose the best actor in movies, Spence would win hands down— and without doubt the greatest movie personality ever seen was Cagney. It has passed through my mind that, in a way, he too thought it was pretty terrific to be with Spence and Jimmy that night.[3]

The Eisenhower-Nixon ticket triumphed in the 1952 election, and Jack Warner sent a sarcastic telegram to Bogie and Bacall: "Thanks for helping elect Eisenhower. Without love. Jack Warner."[4] With Truman — who had waged his own "anti-Red" campaign — gone from the White House, conservative forces strengthened the McCarthyites even further. The blacklist continued, and the Motion Picture Alliance for the Preservation of American Ideals continued to "name names" and otherwise impinge upon the civil rights of fellow actors.

During the autumn of 1952, Warners began developing a screenplay titled "Rock of Gibraltar," assigned to Nicholas Ray, but Bogart, continuing to accept lucrative offers from other studios, kept turning down the scripts sent by the studio. He had signed his last contract with the company in 1946, appearing in only four films. On September 22, 1952, his turbulent 15-year association with Jack Warner came to an end. Two years later, while appearing on the television show *Person to Person*, he told Edward R. Murrow, "I miss my battles with Jack. No one ever gave me such good insults as he did.... I had some wonderful years at Warners studio ... and I realize they were largely responsible for what was to follow in my career."

Deadline U.S.A. (1952), a 20th Century–Fox newspaper versus the Mob expose, was followed by MGM's *Battle Circus* (1953), a Korean War medical drama. Next, Bogie was persuaded by John Huston to fly to Italy to shoot *Beat the Devil* (1953), costarring Peter Lorre, Jennifer Jones, Gina Lollobrigida and Robert Morley as an eccentric group of fortune hunters interested in an African uranium deposit. Released by United Artists, this confounding "mess" (as Bogie called it) bombed at the box office. In 1954, he bounced back with two of his finest late-career performances, in Columbia's *The Caine Mutiny*, directed by Hollywood Ten veteran Edward Dmytryk, and Paramount's *Sabrina*, directed by Billy Wilder and costarring Audrey Hepburn and his old nemesis William Holden (as his younger brother). Later that year, he also costarred with Ava Gardner and Edmond O'Brien in *The Barefoot Contessa*, a Hollywood exposé written and directed by Joseph L. Mankiewicz and released by United Artists.

On May 30, 1955, two decades after the landmark Warners film version of *The Petrified Forest*, Bogart reprised his Duke Mantee characterization for the television program *Producer's Showcase*, a stilted live production also featuring Bacall as Gabby and Henry Fonda as Alan Squire. Three feature films followed during the second half of the year: Paramount's *We're No Angels*, a comedy about escaped Devil's Island convicts costarring Aldo Ray, Peter Ustinov and Basil Rathbone, marked the final time Bogie was directed by Michael Curtiz; 20th Century–Fox's *The Left Hand of God*, in which he plays an American pilot masquerading as a *priest* in post–World War II China, reunited him with Edward Dmytryk; and Paramount's *The Desperate Hours*, tautly directed by William Wyler, cast him as a gangster one last time. Thirteen years after playing his final Warners Wiseguy, he was able to add a real wrinkle to his classic thug, as an escaped lifer who terrorizes a conservative suburban family (headed by Fredric March) while awaiting delivery of some dough.

In January 1956 Bogart was to return to Warners to costar with Bacall in "Melville Goodwin, U.S.A." Wardrobe tests were filmed, but Bogie had fallen ill, troubled by a persistent cough. Dr. Maynard Brandsma, a lung-and-throat specialist who treated many Hollywood heavyweights, diagnosed cancer of the esophagus. Immediate surgery was required, but he wanted to appear in the Warners film first. Brandsma told him to forget it, that he might be dead before the shoot ended. On February 29, he underwent a nine and one-half hour operation at Good Samaritan Hospital to remove his esophagus and re-attach the stomach. An enormous incision had been made from his shoulder to his hip. (Brandsma later would discover John Ford's stomach cancer.) Warners went ahead with "Melville Goodwin, U.S.A." (released as *Top Secret Affair* [1957]), with Kirk Douglas in the lead and Susan Hayward replacing Bacall. Released on May 9, 1956, Columbia's boxing drama *The Harder They Fall* proved to be Bogie's last picture. "We didn't work together again, unhappily," said Bacall, "because we worked very well together."[5]

John Huston wanted to see his friend. Bacall was more than game, helping him to play a practical joke on her husband at the hospital. She asked Bogie's nurse to keep him in the bathroom, then brought in Huston, who crawled under the covers into his bed. She revealed:

> It was funny—John's machine-gun laugh. Bogie's understated one. Two really good old friends so glad to see one another. Later I walked John to the elevator and told him as much as I knew. He was in America for only a few days. "Bogie's going to be all right, honey—he'll be fine...."[6]

During a later visit to their Holmby Hills home, Huston was shocked to see Bogie shrunk to about 90 pounds, being lowered downstairs in the dumbwaiter. "We all knew he wasn't going to live," he said, "but he was still having those goddamn treatments ... Betty didn't want him to read in the paper that he was going to die, so everyone who knew him put the best face on they could."[7]

Frank Sinatra, Bogie's cohort in the original incarnation of "The Rat Pack" (a term coined by Bacall while observing them in a dissipated state in Las Vegas), paid many visits to his friend and inspiration. One day, the dreaded Jack Warner called, *asking* if he could visit Bogie. He spent 15 minutes in the bedroom, nervous though actually finding humor in his former contract player's admission that he'd be going to work at Columbia as soon as he "was well." That quarter-hour may have been one of the most uncomfortable of the mogul's professional life.

After suffering terribly, Bogart mercifully passed away during the early morning of January 14, 1957. Having experienced a horrific nocturnal experience, Bacall later asked, "Why did Bogie have to go through a night like that one?"[8]

Huston penned Bogart's eulogy, and Warner Bros. scheduled a moment of silence observed during the funeral. Bacall sent a copy to Jack Warner, and the mogul responded with a warm note acknowledging Bogie's major contribution to the studio.

In part, Huston said:

> Humphrey Bogart died early Monday morning…. At no time during the months of illness did he believe he was going to die…. He loved life…. Bogie was lucky at love and he was lucky at dice. To begin with he was endowed with the greatest gift a man can have: talent. The whole world came to recognize it…. We have no reason to feel sorry for him—only for ourselves for having lost him. He is quite irreplaceable. There will never be another like him.[9]

Edward G. Robinson

Following *Key Largo*, Robinson starred in *The Night Has a Thousand Eyes* (1948) at Paramount and *House of Strangers* (1949) at 20th Century-Fox; but, in March 1949, he, along with Paul Muni, John Garfield, Melvyn Douglas and others, was named as a "Red" during trials in Washington. Because of his "guilt by association" with liberal causes, he was unable to find any film work, aside from a cameo in Warners' lighthearted musical comedy *It's a Great Feeling* (1949), the first time he appeared on screen in color.

Doris Day had signed her first Hollywood contract, with Warners, in 1948, undergoing a true trial by fire while acting for Michael Curtiz in two films, *Romance on the High Seas* and *My Dream Is Yours*. *It's a Great Feeling*, a nearly plotless Warners tribute to itself directed by David Butler, was only her third assignment, but she already was using her deft combination of flawless singing, naturalistic acting and effortless physical comedy to steal the show. As aspiring actress Judy Adams from Gurkees Corners, Wisconsin, she works as a waitress in the studio commissary while awaiting her first big break, which arrives as *Mademoiselle Fifi*, to be directed by Jack Carson.

Carson — who plays "himself"— is so loathed by all the Warners directors (Raoul Walsh, Michael Curtiz, King Vidor and David Butler all appear briefly) that he is *forced* to direct his own project, in which he will costar with Dennis Morgan and the new female lead. Morgan's early 1930s-style crooning is hopelessly old-fashioned alongside the dynamic, nuanced Day sound of 1949. While he was rooted in Rudy Vallee, she could swing with Sinatra.

Day, combined with a constant parade of star cameos, makes the film worth watching. Gary Cooper sips a malt; Ronald Reagan gets a haircut; Jane Wyman — Mrs. Reagan — appears with their young daughter, Maureen; Sydney Greenstreet unleashes his trademark laugh; Danny Kaye impersonates a train; Joan Crawford goes into her man-killer act; Eleanor Parker and Patricia Neal attempt to give Judy advice; and musical director Ray Heindorf gives in to Judy's shameless flattery. Robinson's cameo is the best of them all, as he arrives on the lot just as Charlie (Pat Flaherty), the studio gate guard, refuses to admit Carson and Judy, who plans to shoot a screen test. The charm of this appearance is created by an alternation between his indelible screen image and his own gentle personality.

"Never mind, I'll take over," Robinson, adopting his mobster persona, tells Carson as he approaches the copper. "Now, listen, flatfoot. You heard my pal. He wants to give the kid a break. Now, knock off and let him in. C'mon, now. Scram. Out of the way." Charlie refuses to overlook studio security, so Robinson must take him aside. "Come here, Wiseguy," he commands.

"Now, look, Charlie," he says, dropping the pretense, "I've got a reputation for being tough. Now, you got to do what I say, otherwise people will start talking. They'll stop going to see my pictures. The studio will lose money. They'll close up shop — shut down. *You'll* be out of a job."

The parody of "Little Caesar" resumes as he pushes Charlie back toward the car and grabs him by the lapels. "Now, look here. You're not going to open that big, fat trap anymore, are ya?"

"No, Mr. Robinson," the guard replies.

"And my friends can go through, can they?" he continues.

"Yes, Mr. Robinson," Charlie agrees.

"Then smile!" he orders.

"Thanks, Eddie," Carson chimes in.

Robinson responds, "Ain't nothin'."

As Carson drives onto the lot, Charlie tells Eddie, "What I won't do to keep my job."

Robinson removes the cigar from his mouth, thumbs himself in the chest, looks straight into the camera, and admits, "Me, too."

Another unforgettable cameo is provided by Errol Flynn, who appears in the final scene as Judy's fiancé, Jeffrey Bushdinkle, at their Wisconsin wedding. In fact, Errol's allure is so strong that she abandons any thoughts of a Hollywood career in favor of marrying him.

Thinking his brief role in *It's a Great Feeling* would lead to more work at the studio, Robinson met with Jack Warner, who ranted about Communism and how Hollywood's Jewish artists should completely distance themselves from any leftist affiliations. Warner offered him no work but said he would try to pull strings at the FBI. Finally, he told Robinson to warm up to SAG president Ronald Reagan. Eddie was advised to "come clean" publicly, but he refused to "back down" as Bogie finally had. Reagan, who secretly served as an FBI informant on Hollywood "Commies," refused to help in any way, instead concentrating on lending SAG support to right-wing causes such as the Crusade for Freedom, an anti-Communist movement.

In 1950 Robinson left the U.S. to work with director Gregory Ratoff, who cast him in London Films' *Operation X* (released as *My Daughter Joy* by Columbia in the U.S.), an outlandish, bizarre film about a megalomaniacal businessman who tries to marry off his daughter to a sultan in exchange for a secret ingredient that will allow him to rule the world. Nearly two years passed before he landed another film role, as a genius actor in one segment of the United Artists anthology film *Actors and Sin* (1950), written, produced and directed by his liberal friend Ben Hecht.

Robinson continued to have political problems as long as HUAC existed, testifying twice and attempting to alter his public persona by starring in the road company of the anti-Communist play *Darkness at Noon* during the autumn of 1953. He eventually became a working character actor again, including roles in three films released in 1953: *Vice Squad* (United Artists), a low-budget cop drama costarring Paulette Goddard; *Big Leaguer* (MGM), a baseball picture shot at the New York Giants Florida training camp by director Robert Aldrich; and *The Glass Web* (Universal), a Jack Arnold 3-D crime melodrama.

During 1954 he worked in only one feature, *Black Tuesday* (United Artists), again resurrecting his ruthless gangster shtick for a disappointing production. The following year proved more fiscally sound, with two films for Columbia — *The Violent Men*, a Western costarring Barbara Stanwyck and Glenn Ford, and *Tight Spot*, a Ginger Rogers vehicle in which he was cast as a U.S. attorney — as well as another United Artists crime thriller, *A Bullet for Joey*, an interesting Cold War police procedural teaming him with his old nemesis, George Raft, for the first time in 14 years. His next two projects, *Illegal* (1955) and *Hell on Frisco Bay* (1956), were both released by Warner Bros.

Illegal, directed by Lewis Allen and based on the play *The Mouthpiece* by W. R. Burnett and Frank J. Collins, features Robinson as Victor Scott, a determined D.A. with gubernatorial aspirations, who sends Edward Clary (DeForest Kelley) to the chair for first-degree murder. While Clary is walking the last mile, Scott receives new evidence proving his innocence. Unable to stop the execution, Scott, racked with guilt, resigns from office and briefly takes to the bottle, landing in the slammer himself. He defends a fellow jailbird and becomes a first-rate defense attorney, but soon falls under the thumb of mobster Frank Garland (Albert Dekker), having successfully defended one of his goons on a murder charge. During his extravagant defense, he ridiculously drinks a evidentiary bottle of poison, then barely lives long enough to have his stomach pumped. When Ellen Borden (Nina Foch), a former colleague in the D.A.'s office (a married woman whom he secretly loves), is charged with a murder that implicates her as a Mob informant, Scott risks his life to defend her.

One of the highpoints of the trial is the testimony of Garland's mistress, Angel O'Hara (Jayne Mansfield, in her third screen appearance), a classic noir dumb blonde dressed in black. Burnett and Collins' play had been adapted by Warners twice previously, as *The Mouthpiece* (1932), starring Warren William, and *The Man Who Talked Too Much* (1940), starring George Brent, but Robinson's bravura performance lends *Illegal* its own unique appeal. Just before signing with Warners for *Illegal*, Lewis Allen directed two independent crime thrillers released by United Artists, *Suddenly* (1954), starring Frank Sinatra as a psychotic would-be Presidential assassin, and the aforementioned *A Bullet for Joey*, in which Eddie plays a Canadian cop who goes after Raft's mobster.

Robinson was offered second billing, behind Alan Ladd (who also produced), for *Hell on Frisco Bay*, directed by Frank Tuttle. Both stars reverted to the typecasting of their early years for the film, with Ladd playing Steve Rollins, a former cop fresh from San Quentin, bent on avenging himself on Robinson's Victor Amato, boss of the San Francisco waterfront mob who framed him for manslaughter.

Shot in color and Cinemascope (a common choice for filmmakers during the first years of its use), *Hell on Frisco Bay* was robbed of the noir atmosphere it needed. Robinson, again required to give nothing more than his Mob-boss best, is ably supported by Paul Stewart as Joe Lye, his right-hand man, but Ladd, often a tedious actor, is solidly wooden throughout. The female contingent provides interesting contrasts: Joanne Dru as Rollins' estranged wife, Fay Wray as a washed-up movie star now involved with Lye, Jayne Mansfield in a tiny part as a blonde bimbo who dances with Victor's brother, Mario (Perry Lopez), and D. W. Griffith and John Ford favorite Mae Marsh as Rollins' landlady.

Robinson received top billing in the disastrous *Nightmare* (1956) for United Artists, then costarred unforgettably as Dathan, creator of the Golden Calf, in Cecil B. DeMille's stolid Paramount Biblical epic, *The Ten Commandments* (1956), and as Frank Sinatra's cantankerous, *conservative* older brother in Frank Capra's hilarious Columbia comedy, *A Hole in the*

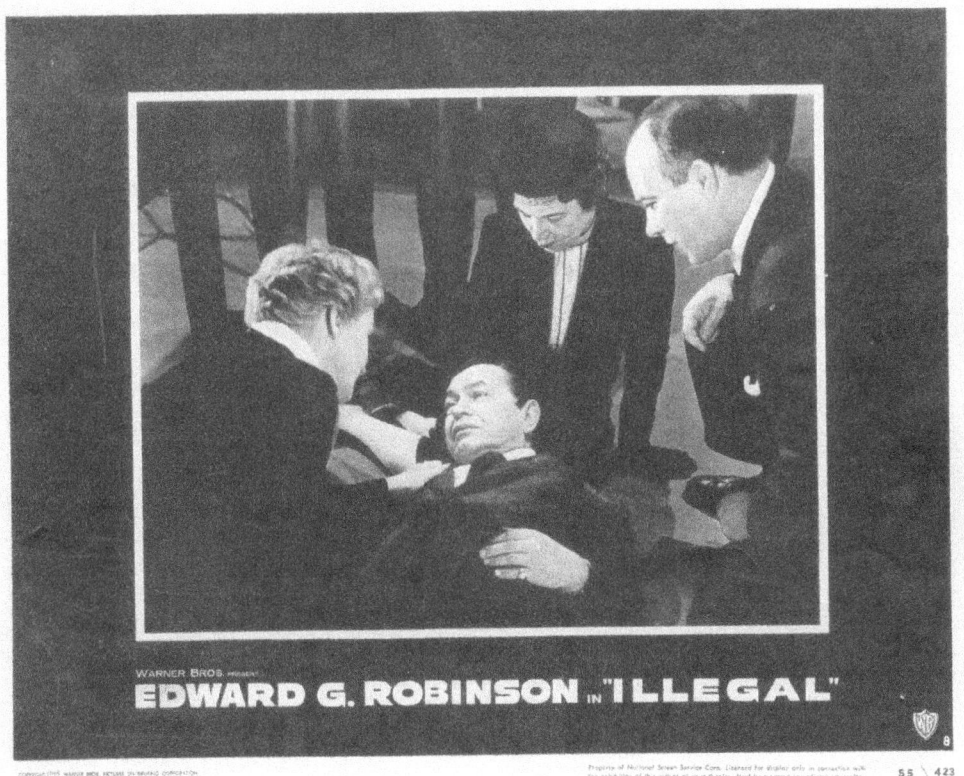

Illegal (1955): Victor Scott (Robinson), nearly committing suicide to prove a point in the courtroom, is attended by Ellen Borden (Nina Foch), left, an unidentified woman, and Ralph Ford (Edward Platt) in Warners' third adaptation of the W.R. Burnett–Frank J. Collins play *The Mouthpiece* (original lobby card).

Head (1959). A lifelong admirer of Eddie G., Sinatra (who first saw *Little Caesar* at age 15) loved working with him.

Feature roles were few and far between over the next five years, with major studio offers coming from 20th Century-Fox (*Seven Thieves* [1960]), Columbia (*Pepe* [1960], a cameo role, and *Good Neighbor Sam* [1964]), Paramount (*My Geisha* [1962]) and MGM (*Two Weeks in Another Town* [1962], *The Prize* [1963] and *The Outrage* [1964]). He disliked *Two Weeks*, but was pleased to be reunited with his old Warners costar, Claire Trevor, who played his wife, rather than a moll, this time.

Sinatra chose to pay a colorful tribute to his wiseguy inspiration in a Warners film (Eddie's final as a gangster) in 1964. In 1935 Cagney had been considered for the role of Robin Hood. Three decades later, Frank gave Eddie a brief brush with the English legend in *Robin and the 7 Hoods*, a Sinatra-produced Prohibition-era spoof combining elements of three classic Warners genres: the gangster film, the epic adventure and the musical. Sinatra stars as "Robbo," with able support from Dean Martin (as Little John), Sammy Davis, Jr. (as Will Scarlet) and Bing Crosby (as Allen A. Dale). The film, also featuring Allen Jenkins (in a supporting role) as well as Robinson (in a one-scene cameo), is a 1960s widescreen, "Rat Pack" descendant of Eddie G.'s Mob spoofs *The Little Giant*, *A Slight Case of Murder* and *Larceny, Inc.*

Jack Warner ordered an old-fashioned musical with an original score, to be directed by

Hell on Frisco Bay (1956): Robinson plays his first Cinemascope Mob boss, Victor Amato, here pointing his piece at Joanne Dru (original lobby card).

Gene Kelly, who was ready to begin rehearsals in Hollywood, when Sinatra, busy with other commitments, stalled the project. Eventually, the versatile Gordon Douglas replaced Kelly, and shooting began on October 31, 1963. Set during a time when government at the local level was corrupt and the federal government seemed uninterested in the average Joe, the film offers an updated rendering of the classic Robin Hood Norman-versus-Saxon motif. While the gang-influenced Sheriff of Chicago is the 1920s parallel of the 1100s Sheriff of Nottingham, the (unmentioned) President Herbert Hoover, whom Depression victims came to view as an absentee leader, could be the counterpart of King Richard the Lionheart.

Like Eddie G.'s Golden-Age gangster parodies, in which he subtly displays an ineptly self-reliant quality, *Robin and the 7 Hoods* offers Sinatra in a satire eschewing buffoonery, slapstick and sight gags for a sophisticated style in which the comedy arises naturally from the absurd counterculture of gangsterism. The nature of the competing operations of Robbo and Guy Gisbourne (Peter Falk), not to mention the Chicago police, provides the springboard for hilarious situations grounded in a historical setting — a period during which Robinson and Cagney benefited as the archetypal cinematic gangsters.

Violence, other than that committed against inanimate objects, is downplayed in *Robin and the 7 Hoods*. The only on-screen murder is that of Eddie's "Big Jim," who is gunned down by *singing* mugs at his birthday party! The scene opens with a close-up (courtesy of William Daniels' stunning Cinemascope work) that tracks out to a long shot of a banquet reminiscent of *Little Caesar*. After a cut to Big Jim blowing out *all* the numerous candles, he announces, "I ain't gonna make no speech. I just want to thank all you bums for this wonderful birthday party. You know, one thing I learned when I first started out. A man what ain't got friends is poor, and he's gonna stay poor until he goes out and buys some good ones. *Me*? I got the best!"

The Mob boss then introduces the corrupt cops surrounding him as "friends who would go out and cut a right arm off for me. All I've got to tell them is whose. You know, the reason I got such loyal friends is because I'm thoughtful. All the time I'm boss in Chicago, I never asked *nobody* to work on a holiday ... only one time, I asked — one St. Valentine's Day. A little clean-up job."

The scene cuts to a close-up as Jim concludes, "I just want to thank all you mugs again. The only thing I'm sorry, is that my good pal Robbo ain't here from New Orleans, where he's takin' in the races. Well, that's all I gotta say for now. Now, everybody get drunk!"

The entire roomful of tuxedoed goons, proposing a birthday toast, draw their heaters and whack the boss. A lap dissolve segues from the shocked don to a crepe-draped oil painting of his image, accompanied by the commentary of Guy Gisborne: "Big Jim was a *shmendrick*. He was a no-good leader. The man was tight. He don't part with a dime. And, besides, he was a slob. And, on top of everything else, he wasn't even an American citizen. Well, things are going to be different from here on in Chicago." Indeed they will be, as Robbo and his gang bust into the board room to begin the big change.

Though he isn't listed in the on-screen credits, Robinson is plugged and pictured (with burning cigar) in the official Warner Bros. pressbook, noting his "return to the ... lot for the first time in nine years."[10] Recalling the film, Frank Sinatra, Jr., said simply, "Edward G. Robinson was one of the great actors that the Twentieth Century produced."[11]

Robinson's final Warners film, John Ford's *Cheyenne Autumn*, also was released in 1964. Spencer Tracy originally was cast as "Great White Father" Carl Schurz, Secretary of the Interior, but was unable to travel to the location. Ford replaced Tracy with Robinson, but then shot Eddie's scenes in the studio. To complete the climactic scene of Schurz cordially meeting with the Cheyenne, back-screen projection of washed out images of the actual location was used behind Eddie and the other actors.

Ford, who was called "Natani Nez" (tall leader) by the Navahos, wanted to cast several native actors in lead Cheyenne roles, but even the filmmaker considered America's greatest couldn't override Jack Warner when it came to casting a picture. Since he held the purse strings, Warner had final say on pre- (cast) and post-production (editing). The mogul was not going to risk a multi-million-dollar budget on unknown Native American performers in significant parts. The same reasoning that led him to cast Bogart as a Mexican now resulted in Mexican actors (Ricardo Montalban, Gilbert Roland and Dolores del Rio) being cast as Cheyenne characters. Though most of the "Indian" parts would have been played by Navahos, the role of "Little Wolf," if Ford had his way, would have gone to his close friend, the formidable, part-Cheyenne Woody Strode, who had given excellent performances in two of the director's masterpieces, *Sergeant Rutledge* (Warner Bros., 1960) and *The Man Who Shot Liberty Valance* (Paramount, 1962). Since Strode was also African American, Jack Warner gave the part to Montalban; and he, like the other Latino and Anglo actors who played Cheyenne roles, speaks English throughout most of the film. The bit and extra roles, however, are played by the Monument Valley Navahos.

The film opens on the Cheyenne Reservation in the Southwest "Indian Territory" on September 7, 1878. More than a year has passed since the White Man forcibly relocated the tribe here from its "green and fertile country, 1,500 miles to the north." Captain Thomas Archer

(Richard Widmark) is not pleased with the U.S. Congressional Committee, "the gentlemen from the East" who don't care that "the Cheyenne have been forgotten ... to most people ... a footnote in history." Promised medicine and food, they have received nothing. Of the 1,000 men, women and children marched to the parched desert location, only 286 remain alive. The Quaker schoolteacher Deborah Wright (Carroll Baker) naïvely believes the abandoned tribe will still attend her class, but the soldier explains the difference between the "pitiful reservation Indians" and the innate warrior nature of the true Cheyenne, whom he respects. Fed up with empty promises, the survivors begin to march back to "Yellowstone country."

After crossing the river that marks the north border of the reservation, the warriors lie in wait for the cavalry. Red Shirt (Sal Mineo) fires the first shot, sparking retaliatory cannon fire from the Army. "Even a dog may go where he likes," says Dull Knife (Gilbert Roland), "but not a Cheyenne." Newspapers print propaganda with inflated casualty reports, and concerned businessmen form a group to visit Secretary of the Interior Schurz, who had attempted to eliminate corruption in the Indian Bureau by infusing Quakers into the equation. Cigar in hand, Robinson gives a fine performance as the embattled Schurz, perhaps the only Washington bureaucrat who considers the Cheyenne to be human beings. In a brief scene, the Secretary recalls to Senator Henry (Denver Pyle) their noble fight at Gettysburg, even though they "had never seen a Negro slave." Spencer Tracy had been first choice, but the role seems tailor-made for Eddie.

Several members of Ford's "stock company," including Harry "Dobe" Carey, Jr., Ben Johnson, George O'Brien and Patrick Wayne, appear in supporting cavalry roles. Ford's son-in-law, Ken Curtis, doing a slight variation on his Festus Haggin character in the *Gunsmoke* television series, plays Joe, a racist saddle tramp, who shoots a Cheyenne he meets in the desert, begging for food. "I always wanted to kill me an Injun," he says repeatedly. Ford deals with racism in earlier films, most notably in *The Searchers* (1956) and *Sergeant Rutledge*, but *Cheyenne Autumn* is his official "apology" to a people he had depicted as one-dimensional villains in earlier Westerns such as *Stagecoach* (1939) and *Rio Grande* (1950).

As an Irish-American at the turn of the 20th Century, Ford considered himself a minority, therefore often depicting the downtrodden underdog in his films; though his concession to a major studio—depicting a specific, sensitive historical subject within the conventions of "epic" cinema—brought down heaps of negative criticism from "liberal" journalists. Truth to tell, U.S. film critics in 1964 still considered the Western an "inferior, juvenile" genre, and *Cheyenne Autumn* only received sensible reviews in Europe, where Ford was considered a major artist.

Ford follows a tragic scene of White buffalo slaughter with a comic-relief sequence set in Dodge City involving Wyatt Earp (James Stewart), Doc Holliday (Arthur Kennedy) and Jeff Blair (John Carradine). Joe and his three cronies enter the saloon, spouting an exaggerated story about "Indian fighting," but Earp ignores the paranoia in favor of his poker game. When the phony cowpokes confront the Marshal, he shoots Joe in the foot, then cuts out the bullet. The "Fordian" shtick goes on far too long during the ludicrous "Battle of Dodge City," during which Earp and Holliday accompany a mob onto the prairie to fight the oncoming hordes (only a lone "Indian" is seen). Ford would have been better served by eliminating this superfluous sequence from his serious, though ponderous, attempt to depict the plight of the Cheyenne. (For years, it was cut from release prints, but later included in a restored, full-length version.)

In the snows of northern Nebraska, the Cheyenne nation splits, half moving on, the others seeking the protection of Fort Robinson, where the Quaker hopes to save the children.

Archer arrives to find that those who have surrendered have been ordered to march back to the reservation through the freezing winter. Captain Wessels (Karl Malden), the by-the-book Prussian commander, insists on obeying the order, but Dull Knife and "Spanish Woman" (Dolores del Rio) vow to die where they stand.

Incensed, Archer takes two weeks' leave to visit Washington, where Schurz asks to see him. Archer tells the Secretary the truth about conditions at the fort, referring to the imprisonment of the Cheyenne in a freezing warehouse as "murder." After he leaves to return to Nebraska, Schurz walks toward some portraits hanging on his office wall. Ford cuts to a stunning shot showing Robinson's reflection in a framed daguerreotype of Abraham Lincoln, as Schurz asks, "Old friend, what would *you* do?"

Ford held a lifelong devotion to the Great Emancipator. His brother, Francis, had effectively portrayed Lincoln in a series of silent films, and John had featured the 16th President in his own *The Iron Horse* (1924), *The Prisoner of Shark Island* (1937), which focuses on the assassination, and *Young Mr. Lincoln* (1939), starring Henry Fonda as the pre-presidential, Illinois "jack-leg lawyer."

Robin and the 7 Hoods (1964): Eddie G. as Mob boss "Big Jim" Stevens, who gets whacked by his crew in the opening scene of this Warners "Rat Pack" musical spectacular (original press book publicity).

At Fort Robinson, Ford depicts the drunken Wessels being relieved of duty, just before the Cheyenne break out of their warehouse jail. Unarmed women are shot down, and babies fall, crying in the snow. The scene ends with the authoritarian Wessels, utterly shocked, staggering through the aftermath of the massacre. The survivors march farther north, where they meet up with those who had moved on, in the hills of Dakota, 1,200 miles from the reservation. The cavalry lines up for an assault, but is interrupted by Archer, who has brought Schurz with him. The Secretary informs the commander that the land they stand on is Department of the Interior property, and that he will "parlay with the Indians."

"You've made one of the most heroic marches in history," Schurz tells Little Wolf (Ricardo Montalban) and Dull Knife. "You deserve to go back to your homeland and stay there in peace." Having no tobacco for their peace pipe, they accept cigars from the Secretary. (A more perfect way for Robinson to end his Warners career cannot be imagined. Ford also was a big fan of cigars; and, like Eddie G., also died of cancer.) To insure the peace, Dull Knife shoots down the war-crazed Red Shirt, and Archer and Deborah are reunited.

The release of Paramount's *A Boy Ten Feet Tall* (1965), shot on location in Kenya three years earlier (when Robinson suffered a serious heart attack), was followed by his last great role, professional gambler Lancey Howard (a character he considered close to his own personality), in MGM's *The Cincinnati Kid* (1965), costarring Steve McQueen and his Golden Age Warners cohort Joan Blondell. 1966 promised several key roles, including Dr. Zaius in *Planet of the Apes*, an impoverished Jewish immigrant in *The Angel Levine*, and a Turkish warlord in *Cervantes*, but a grim auto accident nearly proved fatal, landing him in intensive care and then home for a lengthy convalescence, during which Frank Sinatra was often at his side. He finally went back to work two years later, in six films, including *The Biggest Bundle of Them*

All for MGM and *Never a Dull Moment* for Walt Disney. On April 24, 1968, he made his first public political appearance in two decades, supporting the Martin Luther King Friendship Rally at the Hollywood Bowl.

The Columbia Western *MacKenna's Gold* (1969), featuring Eddie as a blind gold prospector alongside Gregory Peck, Omar Sharif and Raymond Massey, was followed by a small role in the Cinerama extravaganza *Song of Norway* (1970). His last screen role, for MGM, was completed as he was struggling with throat cancer, in a poignant death scene in the unsettling science-fiction thriller *Soylent Green* (1973), which reteamed him with his *Ten Commandments* costar, Charlton Heston. At that time he also was dictating his autobiography, *All My Yesterdays*, to writer Leonard Spigelglass.

Unfortunately, Robinson's home life was bitterly disappointing. Finally divorcing his mentally ill wife in 1957, he was forced to sell his beloved art collection, which long had attracted prominent visitors to his home. His son, Manny, who briefly tried his hand at acting, also suffered from serious attitude and alcohol problems.

Among Robinson's honorary pallbearers on January 28, 1973, were Warners heavyweights Mervyn LeRoy, Hal Wallis and, incredibly, Jack Warner. A little more than a year later, on February 26, 1974, his namesake, Edward G. Robinson, Jr., died a burned out wreck at age 40. Regardless of Eddie's personal feel-

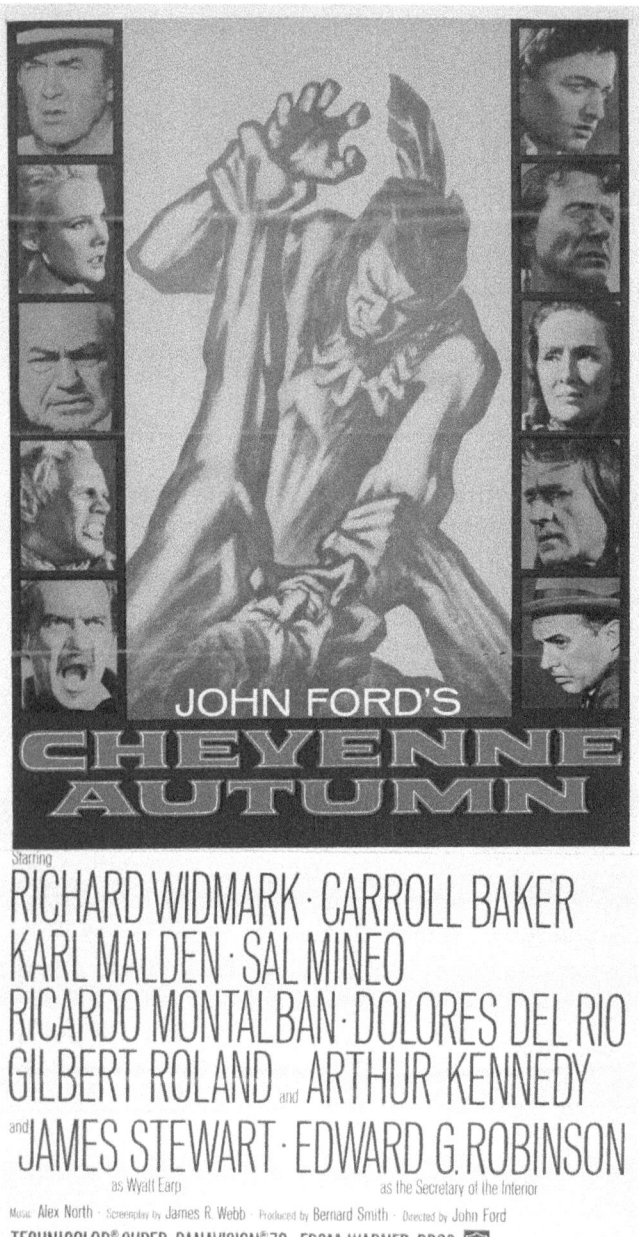

Cheyenne Autumn (1964): In John Ford's epic tribute to the Native American tribe, Robinson is superb as "Great White Father" Carl Schurz, United States Secretary of the Interior, perhaps the only Washington bureaucrat in the film who considers the Cheyenne to be human beings. Eddie couldn't have asked for a better way to end his association with Warner Bros. (original three-sheet poster).

ings and battles with the studio's chief, his unique, versatile performances at Warner Bros., which made him a major star, have insured him of cinematic immortality.

James Cagney

Cagney had blasted his way through *White Heat*. Still smoldering from that intense experience, he planned a new Warners musical, *The West Point Story* (1950), based on an incident in which George M. Cohan had persuaded the superintendent to let him live at the academy for a week while writing a scene for a new show. During pre-production, which included his personal approval of the screenplay, director and cast, Jim began another William Cagney Production, to be released by Warners, *Kiss Tomorrow Goodbye* (1950), which would feature his final gangster characterization for the studio.

Robinson signed this personal publicity portrait for Oklahoma representative (and avid autograph collector) Ewing C. Sadler during the late 1930s. Sadler later served as assistant attorney general of Oklahoma.

Cagney didn't want to do *Kiss*, but appreciated that it was based on a novel by Horace McCoy (whose hard-boiled, Depression-era works include *They Shoot Horses, Don't They?*), would be produced by brother Bill, and costar the Yiddish actor Luther Adler, a major force in the Group Theatre. They also cut a deal whereby Warners would pay the first $500,000 in receipts to the banks that had financed the Cagneys' poorly received *The Time of Your Life* (United Artists, 1948). Also appearing in *Kiss Tomorrow Goodbye* are old Warners stalwarts Ward Bond and Barton MacLane as corrupt cops on the take. Regardless of Bond's notorious reputation for Red-baiting, the Cagneys admired him as an actor, having also featured him in *The Time of Your Life*.

Jim had become an independent producer to make films providing an antidote to the wiseguy persona he had been expected to maintain at Warner Bros. After losing money on his own gentler, contemplative works, he again played a vicious gangster to raise some much-needed dough. Though the plot bears similarities to *White Heat*, particularly a jail break and a planned major heist, the presentation of the mad criminal differs considerably from the previous film. No matter how sadistic Cody Jarrett's behavior may be, the viewer still likes him, because of the way Cagney deliberately played him. Rather than repeat a similar characterization for *Kiss Tomorrow Goodbye*, Jim chose to play the killer as totally *un*likable. And, while Cody is a fully realized character with psychological depth whose tendencies have resulted from hereditary insanity and a bad environment, Ralph Cotter is merely a self-interested, cold-blooded killer whose behavior is not presented as the result of nature and/or nurture. The screenplay provides no details.

Cagney had attempted to break from his violent criminal image by playing placid philo-

Kiss Tomorrow Goodbye (1950): Accepting the role because he needed the dough, Cagney played his final gangster as a vicious bastard with no redeeming features, costarring with Barbara Payton, Ward Bond, Luther Adler and Barton MacLane (original title lobby card).

sophical types, but here he vividly proves his dislike for the wiseguy image — a clever way to portray the character in his final Warners gangster picture. Interestingly, in the small role of Cotter's brother, his polar opposite —"one of the few honest men left in the world"— is William Cagney.

Directed by Gordon Douglas, *Kiss Tomorrow Goodbye* opens at the murder trial of seven "evil" defendants: Holiday Carleton (Barbara Payton), Cotter's former girlfriend; Charles Weber (Ward Bond) and John Reese (Barton MacLane), former police officers; Keith Mandon (Luther Adler), former attorney; Peter Cobbett (John Halloran), former guard at the State Penal Farm; Victor Mason (Rhys Williams), former front for mobsters; and Joseph "Jinx" Rainer (Steve Brodie), Cotter's former right-hand man. "There should be eight," but Cotter is already dead.

Cobbett is the first to take the stand, initiating a flashback to the prison farm, four months earlier. While working in a field, Cotter fakes a fever to get "a drink of water," then retrieves two pistols hidden in a tire inner-tube stashed in the creek. Signaled by their getaway car, Cotter and Carleton (Neville Brand) make a break, but the young man is clipped by a guard. Cotter, not wanting to be slowed down, registers a malicious expression as he shoots the wounded man in the head. In the nearby bushes, a *female* associate guns down one of the mounted guards and guides Cotter to the car, driven by Jinx Rainer. Sitting in the backseat, the young woman, Holiday Carleton, laments the death of her brother. At a parking garage, Cotter meets Vic Mason, who expects to be paid $1,000 for his services, including information about Holiday.

At her apartment, Cotter gets comfortable; but, when he makes disparaging remarks about her dead brother, she throws a knife at him, cutting his neck behind the left ear. He looks at her silently, calmly walks into the bathroom, wets a towel to soothe the wound, then suddenly, brutally whips her across the face, giving her three more hard swats before she grabs him and apologizes. She reveals her feelings of loneliness, and Cotter kisses her. For his mobster swansong, Cagney returns to his broad-bashing of old, turning up the intensity, then immediately countering it with a sexual component.

In broad daylight, Cotter and Jinx heist Hartford's supermarket. The owner protests, so Cotter pistol-whips him in the face with a .45. At Mason's garage, he divides the dough, offering the mechanic one-quarter, plus the grand for the escape expenses. Mason, objecting to the hit on a neighborhood store, calls Cotter "stark, staring nuts." Replying with an evil, teeth-gritting grimace, Cotter kicks him hard, ordering, "*Never* say that again."

Cotter enjoys a cup of coffee with Holiday as a knock is heard at the apartment door. A voice in the hall claims, "It's Vic Mason, Ralph," then Inspector Weber and John Reese burst in to shake him down for his cut from the market heist. Both of them are ordered to leave town, "on separate buses." Now completely broke, Cotter asks for the return of his .45 automatic, which Reese unloads, then tosses onto a chair. "An automatic is the only thing," Cotter tells Holiday, who is told to dispose of the revolver he used during the prison break.

Cotter and Jinx, who still has his two-grand cut, plan to record the coppers during a subsequent shakedown. At Mason's garage, Cotter inquires about a car, but the mechanic replies, "I wouldn't cut you down if you were hangin'," then squeals to Weber. Sneaking back in, Cotter viciously pistol-whips and kicks him. Weber and Reese return to the apartment, where Jinx operates the recording equipment in the bedroom closet. Cotter mentions a payroll job, and Weber takes the bait.

Cotter—using the alias "Paul Murphy"—and Jinx visit "Doc" Greene (Frank Reicher), a quack philosopher who preaches metaphysical mumbo jumbo to local yokels. Following his lecture, the charlatan is introduced to them by Margaret Dobson (Helena Carter, who appropriates phony, pretentious diction, a la Margaret Lindsay, that must have driven Cagney to distraction). Forced to employ mild duress, Cotter is referred to Keith "Cherokee" Mandon, a lawyer known for his association with the Mob. Margaret gives them a ride to a drug store, during which she explains Greene's philosophical theory of the "mathematical conception of the fourth dimension."

The cinematic version of Ralph Cotter is not the obvious scholar of Horace McCoy's novel, but Cagney's intelligent interpretation sets the character apart from his earlier gangsters. Cotter may be a cold, ruthless criminal, but he is also an erudite one. Responding to Margaret's elucidation, he counters, "I don't hold with the theory that the fourth dimension is either philosophical or mathematical. I think it's purely intuitional. I don't mean to start an argument, or sound pretentious, but that's the way I feel about it." Later, Cotter tells a police officer that he is "a kind of 20th-century Fagin."

The narrative returns to the trial, as Mandon, being questioned by the prosecutor, claims he was coerced into aiding the fugitives. In flashback, Mandon initially refuses to advise Cotter, who pulls his .45, then takes the lawyer to the apartment to hear the incriminating recording. Weber and Reese arrive to discuss the payroll job, Mandon emerges from the bedroom, and Jinx plays the record. Gordon Douglas tracks into a tight, chiaroscuro close-up of Ward Bond's face as Weber listens incredulously, then the image focuses on Cagney and Adler in the background as the Inspector turns to face his enemies. Weber swats the tone arm from the record, slashing his hand on the needle, then threatens to whack the lot of them. "Pulling that trigger, Charlie, will be just like putting a bullet through your own head," Mandon informs him. "Now, you ought to know that there's more than a single copy of that record.... Those records are gonna be played for the mayor, Charlie, for the District Attorney, and, of course, for the Chief of Police."

Behind Holiday's back, Cotter picks up Margaret for a drive into the country. On a winding highway, she drives 100 mph; then Cotter, striking an insane expression, presses down on her foot, increasing the speed to 120. She stops to light a smoke, but Cotter tosses the cigarette away, planting a kiss just as two motorcycle cops pull over. "We don't want Ezra Dobson's daughter killed on our beat," one of them declares. As they drive off, Cotter briefly asks about her father, then returns to necking.

The next morning, Holiday tosses a coffee pot, cup, cream pitcher and sugar bowl past the laughing Cotter, smashing them against the living room wall, before sitting on his lap and starting a make-out session of her own. Mandon then accompanies him to City Hall, where he burns his prison record and obtains a gun permit from Weber, even though the Inspector has been given 48 hours "to get him, dead or alive."

Against Mandon's advice, Cotter continues to squire Margaret, then incurs the mighty wrath of her $30-million father after they elope across the state line. Dobson (Herbert Heyes) storms directly into their bedroom (of course, they are sleeping in Production Code-approved twin beds), wakes them, and launches into a tirade. Cotter listens quietly, keeping silent until the old man leaves, then calmly discusses the situation with Margaret before going back to sleep with the .45 under his pillow. In the morning, he signs an annulment renouncing all claims, refuses a $25,000 payoff check, and apologizes to Dobson.

Cotter plans to whack three collectors employed by Rohmer, a local bookie. Dressed in a cop's uniform, he approaches them about a "parking ticket," then forces them to drive "way out in the country." One of the mugs shouts, "It's a heist!" and is gut shot in return. Rohmer calls Weber, ordering him to find the three missing men, but Cotter arrives with his third of the cut: 17 grand. "I will take care of Rohmer," the mobster promises. Meanwhile, the police question the injured Mason, who identifies Cotter and directs them to Holiday's apartment.

As the trial continues, Jinx is on the stand, admitting his trepidation at working with the unstable Cotter. "Do you know how it feels to be scared?" he asks the prosecutor, as the flashback returns. Jinx divides the bookie's dough, then announces his "retirement," but Cotter threatens to add his partner to the "three dead men in the quarry." Mandon knocks, then takes Cotter outside to discuss his "marriage." Holiday eavesdrops though an open window as the lawyer relays a message from Ezra Dobson, who is demanding "Murphy's" presence.

Dobson is pleased to see "Paul," praising his "complete disregard for money" and apparent high regard for Margaret. "But you don't know anything about me," he replies. "I'm a total stranger to you. I might be a thief. I might be a convict. I might even be a murderer."

"The man who accepts Margaret," Dobson continues, "will also have to accept the management of her estate ... [a] fortune ... greater than mine." He then pulls the annulment petition from his jacket. "You're still married, you see," he discloses. "Think it over, and let me know tomorrow."

On his way out, Cotter embraces Margaret, who, discovering his .45, sinks it in the patio fountain. Ever confident in his own twisted abilities, he tells her he'll return in an hour. Back at the apartment, he demands his money, but Holiday tosses onto the table a spent bullet, the one he had used to kill her brother, retrieved by Cobbett. Drawing the very gun that fired the fatal shot, Holiday threatens Cotter, who offers to leave her all the dough, then mentions the copy of the record he sent to his own brother, who will testify against her and the rest of the gang.

"You changed me. You made me just the same as you are," she claims. "And you've got nobody to blame but yourself."

He tries to convince her that he's fleecing Margaret's millions for their own use. "Tomorrow, everything will be different. We'll be rich," he tells her. "All I've got to do is tell Dobson, 'Yes' tomorrow."

"You can *kiss tomorrow goodbye*," she replies. "You shouldn't have killed my brother."

Unarmed, Cotter tosses his fedora at her face, but she shoots him in the belly, knocking him to the floor. He grabs the neck of a broken champagne bottle and staggers to his feet. She pulls the trigger again, but the gun doesn't fire. "I told you not to trust a revolver," he grimaces. She squeezes again, blasting a second shot into his chest. Teetering, he gazes painfully at her, falls on his back, lifts his head to look at her one last time, then slowly rolls his head to stare directly at the ceiling as he dies.

Concluding the trial, the prosecutor plays the record for the jury. The last voice heard on the platter is that of the dead Cotter, as it eerily skips, "I'll remember. I'll remember. I'll remember." On the stand, Cotter's brother (William Cagney, with his hair dyed black) confirms the identity of the voice.

Released in the immediate wake of the superlative *White Heat*, *Kiss Tomorrow Goodbye* fared poorly at the box office and quickly disappeared. One of Cagney's most seldom-seen films, it is also one of the most underrated. The title is appropriate in more ways than one, with Cagney playing more kissing scenes (with two different women) than in any other film he made at Warners— an interesting element, since he claimed being uncomfortable with screen romance. Truly appropriate for his final Warners gangster role is Cotter's murder at the hands of a woman — cinematic justice for playing so many broad-bashing mugs at the studio over the years.

While shooting *Kiss*, Jim also rehearsed the dance numbers for *The West Point Story*, playing Elwin Bixby, a fading Broadway director who reluctantly signs on to helm the academy's annual student musical after an attempted con by theatrical producer Harry Eberhardt (Roland Winters). Roy Del Ruth was back in his Warner Bros. director's chair, working with Cagney for the first time in 17 years. Also in the cast are Jim's *White Heat* partner Virginia Mayo (again playing his "love interest") and the inimitable Doris Day. Mayo recalled that Cagney "sent me to his dancing teacher. He said, 'I want you to learn this routine, because we have to do it in the picture.' It was easy, you know, because I could do *that*. Easy, standing on my head."[12]

Cagney characteristically took the dancing seriously, again hiring Johnny Boyle as choreographer, but his cartoon-like performance throughout the film — perhaps the worst in his entire Warners career — suggests that he thought the rest of the material unworthy of earnest consideration. His introduction in the opening scene is one of the most over-the-top in Hollywood history. As Bixby watches a rehearsal for a forthcoming show, he literally goes apoplectic, yelling at the top of his lungs as he absurdly jumps, flails, stomps and trips his way onto the dance floor, where he demonstrates the proper terpsichore. After this tirade, Cagney, his voice hoarse, is obviously winded.

Whenever "Bix" encounters a situation or remark he dislikes, Cagney mugs away, combining hammy facial expressions with an annoying exaggeration of a famous grunt he uses to much better effect in some of his earlier Warners films. At times, he even resorts to screwing up his face while making noises like a clucking chicken!

"Bix" immediately receives a sound bawling out from Eve Dillon (Mayo), who nags him throughout the film, throwing up her arms in frustration and slapping his hands away when he mentions marriage. (Mayo, who had slimmed down since *White Heat*, repeatedly shows off her gams to good effect.) Eberhardt, accusing Bix of formerly stealing away singer-dancer Jan Wilson (Doris Day), now wants his own nephew, Tom Fletcher (Gene Nelson), filched from West Point. While walking in front of obvious studio back-screen projection of the military academy, Eve expresses a patriotic admiration countered by Bix's affirmative remarks about Benedict Arnold.

The old-fashioned musical numbers—particularly the rehearsal of "The Kissing Rock," featuring cadets dancing with *each other* (the "women" wear signs around their necks)—are redeemed by Cagney's sporadic deference, but he doesn't completely refrain from screaming and stomping like a madman. "Is he always this violent?" an officer asks Eve. He punches out a cadet, "Bully Boy" Gilbert (Alan Hale, Jr.), while demonstrating a dance, and is barred from the post; but Eve, behind his back, agrees to his "becoming a cadet." (Cagney was 50 when the film was made.) Bix's behavior is Cagney's overblown "homage" to material in *Footlight Parade*. Then, after he accepts cadet status, it's *The Fighting 69th* (and the other Cagney-O'Brien service pictures) all over again.

Bix hatches a plan to dump Gilbert and trick Jan Wilson away from Hollywood to play "The Princess." (Later, Alan Hale, Jr., returning for a musical number, effortlessly lifts Cagney onto the stage like a sack of flour.) Cagney's acting is far more subtle in his scenes with the perpetually naturalistic Doris Day (whose singing and facial expressions show the influence of her only potential musical equal, the great Patty Andrews). After making this film (and *Love Me or Leave Me* for MGM five years later), Cagney called Day one of the finest actresses with whom he ever worked. She almost single-handedly rescues *The West Point Story* from Del Ruth's heavy-handedness.

Jan falls in love with Fletcher, who had told Bix he'd never leave the Point for any reason, including a singing career or marriage. Bix does his best to ship Jan back to Tinsel Town, but Fletcher goes AWOL and is arrested. The Commandant cancels the show, but Eve discovers that a visiting head of state could secure amnesty for the offenders. During a weekend leave, Bix takes a group of cadets to Washington, D.C., and New York, where they hunt down the French Premier. Cagney speaks French in the scene: "I picked it up from a chick at the Folies Bergere," Bix claims.

A parade is given in honor of the Premier, the show goes on (with Bix substituting for a cadet he accidentally punches out), and the military presents him with the show to produce on Broadway, leaving the chiseling Eberhardt out in the cold. Cagney executes some fine solo choreography, and his final dance number with Mayo is a true highlight.

Warners next cast Cagney as Lew Marsh, an alcoholic newspaper editor, in *Come Fill the Cup* (1951), a film that brought back stark memories of watching his father descend into a booze oblivion. Fired from his position at the *Sun-Herald*, Marsh achieves sobriety with the aid of Charley Dolan (James Gleason), then is encouraged by publisher John Ives (Raymond Massey), whose nephew, Boyd Copeland (Gig Young), needs help with his own addiction. Matters are complicated further by Copeland's marriage to Marsh's former girlfriend, Paula Arnold.

Novelist Harlan Ware based Marsh on Jim Richardson, City Editor of the *Los Angeles Examiner*, whom Cagney consulted to develop some behavioral traits common to alcoholics. However, his portrayal again was compromised by meddling from Jack Warner, who insisted that a gangster subplot be added to the material gleaned from Ware's novel. In his continu-

Come Fill the Cup (1950): Cagney, though a non-Method actor, drew on painful childhood memories to interpret the character of Lew Marsh, a recovering alcoholic, in this promising film that was compromised by Jack Warner's decision to add a gangster subplot (original lobby card).

ous stupor, Copeland has become involved with wiseguy Lennie Garr (Sheldon Leonard), who, at one point, holds him and Marsh at gunpoint, giving them the awful choice of either taking a shot or *being* shot. When Dolan dies in a car accident, Marsh suspects that Copeland is responsible, but another reporter discovers that a brake hose had been punctured by mechanic Kip Zunches (King Donovan), a Garr goon.

Copeland is frightened into sobriety, but attempts suicide during a painful withdrawal. Marsh checks him into a hospital, promising to help upon his release, then enlists the mayor and local law enforcement in an effort to bring down Garr's mob. By the film's end, Garr is killed during a struggle with Marsh and Copeland, who is reunited with Paula.

Another disappointing change from Ware's novel was dropping a strong African American character—who helps Marsh get sober—for a more standard Irish-American reformed drunk (though James Gleason gives his usual fine performance). Cagney was not pleased, thinking another potentially great film was ruined. The stock newspaper man versus the Mob material is forced and heavy-handed, but the scenes involving recovery are realistic and well-played by Cagney, Gleason and Young (a real-life alcoholic who, at age 65 in 1978, murdered Kim Schmidt, his 31-year-old bride of three weeks, then turned the gun on himself).

While shooting *Come Fill the Cup*, Cagney also contributed a cameo to Warners' *Starlift* (1951), an all-star, musical "variety show" in which familiar faces briefly appear to cheer up soldiers in need of a morale boost. Roy Del Ruth's main challenge was working multiple

A Lion Is in the Streets (1953): Cagney plays Hank Martin, a Louisiana peddler-cum-gubernatorial candidate, in Raoul Walsh's uneven political drama (original press book publicity).

performers into the 103-minute running time. Gary Cooper, Gordon MacRae, Virginia Mayo, Randolph Scott and Jane Wyman all wander in at various points, but the film's true saving grace is Doris Day, in her second of three screen appearances with Jim.

Cagney agreed to play Captain Flagg (alongside Dan Dailey's Sergeant Quirt) in 20th Century–Fox's remake of *What Price Glory?* (1952) because it was a musical, a fact that angered director John Ford, who dumped all the songs. In another "William Cagney Production" released by Warner Bros., *A Lion Is in the Streets* (1953), Jim plays Hank Martin, a Louisiana gubernatorial candidate patterned on Huey P. Long. Luther Davis based his screenplay on Adria Locke Langley's novel, the rights to which Cagney had purchased in 1947. "Every player runs across a character in a book or play, or in life that he feels he understands fundamentally," Jim explained. "That's the way I reacted to Hank Martin."[13]

The Cagney boys made the film a true family affair, casting sister Jeanne as the woman who shoots Martin, and hiring brother Edward as story editor. Director Raoul Walsh and old buddy Frank McHugh (cast in a rare "heavy" role) happily re-teamed with Jim, who also cast a very young Anne Francis (as his girlfriend on the side!) and Lon Chaney, Jr., in supporting roles. Before shooting began, Cagney toned up for a solid week by working with a hand plow on his Northridge, California, farm.

In vivid Technicolor, an orange Warner Bros. logo introduces Cagney's name before the title, superimposed over the statue of "Honest Abe" at the Lincoln Memorial in Washington, D.C. As a growling lion paws at the base of the statue, Raoul Walsh's credit appears. In pouring rain, Verity Wade (Barbara Hale) and two children struggle down a muddy road toward a schoolhouse. More children scamper through the muck, and when a tiny girl falls into a rut, she is helped out by a friendly peddler, Hank Martin. He introduces himself to Verity, then dances back into the rain and down the road, singing, "I've met the girl I'm going to marry."

Hank is next seen driving his own truck loaded with all manner of wares—and indeed has his wife, now Verity Martin. Having lived in the vehicle, he now settles into a ramshackle house—on their wedding day. During an evening celebration with local sharecroppers, they are interrupted by cotton baron Robert L. Castleberry IV (Larry Keating), who "has this whole county in his thievin' pocket." At the home of attorney Jules Bolduc (Warner Anderson), the Martins meet Castleberry, whom Hank calls "a bloodsuckin' thief."

"If you ever make such statements again to a living soul, I will swear out a warrant for your arrest, on a charge of criminal libel," Castleberry threatens. "Criminal libel, Sir, can get you *five years* on the chain gang."

"I've been readin' up a lot about criminal libel, in Jules' law books," Martin reveals, "and five years is right, all right—less'n if it happens to be true, which it is."

"I have warned you," he replies, as the African American butler, Moses (Sam McDaniel, Bogie's valet, Saratoga, in *All Through the Night*), enters with a tray of drinks.

"Castleberry?" Martin asks, grasping the butler's arm. "I suppose Moses, here, counts as a living soul, don't he?"

Castleberry is stone silent.

"Moses," Martin continues, pointing to his adversary, "Robert L. Castleberry is a *thief*—and the weights he uses in his cotton gins weigh *short*."

While making deliveries with Verity, Hank meets his old friends, Spurge McManamee (Lon Chaney, Jr.), and his daughter, "Flamingo" (Anne Francis), who flies into a rage when she realizes they are married. Spurge and Flamingo, in separate boats, row them through the swamp to "the settlement," where Hank intends to peddle his wares. Flamingo takes a detour into a slough, directly toward an enormous alligator. Verity tries to fight it off as Spurge fires his rifle. To dissuade fatherly violence toward Flamingo, Verity claims that the deviation was her idea. That night, Flamingo visits Hank, promising to wait for him, "like a mule in a barn," and he cannot resist her charms.

Martin plans to fight Castleberry's criminal libel suit by using approved cotton gin weights. Just in case, he has rounded up 50 men to provide protection against the 20 deputies hired by the "thief." Concerned about his intentions, his wife remarks, "Hank, you're not a—a *gangster*. There's one charge against you now."

Jeb Brown (John McIntire), offered payment for a load of cotton by Frank Rector (Frank McHugh) at the Castleberry warehouse, asks to try his own weights. Martin is handed an arrest warrant issued in another county, so he calls in his forces, then proves the company has been using false weights in their payouts. A deputy tries to shoot Smith (Burt Mustin), and Brown retaliates, landing in jail for murder. At Castleberry's office, Martin meets Guy Polli (Onslow Stevens), who offers to influence the trial process in return for a political "thank you." Before due process can begin, Brown is gunned down in his cell by a Castleberry goon. Critically wounded, he is determined to proceed with the trial, with his wife, Jennie (Jeanne Cagney), at his side. As he dies, Martin proves his innocence and whips the crowd into a fervor.

Polli buys Castleberry and Company, and Martin runs to unseat Governor Charles Snowden (Fay Roope). A rainstorm hits on election day, keeping rural voters at home, so Martin pays a visit to Polli's domain, where Flamingo is waiting. Polli claims that Samuel T. Beach (James Millican) and Rector, not Castleberry himself, were responsible for the swindle, then offers to deliver "city votes" in exchange for a list of demands. On his way home, Martin's car becomes stuck in the road, so he tramps through the mud to find a new baby daughter and the election in a dead heat. He addresses the "folkses" over the radio, mentioning the lack of roads in rural areas, education and his intention not to concede. He concludes by calling his supporters to arms. "I'd follow him to Kingdom Come," proclaims Spurge.

Verity attempts to see Bolduc, who has been summoned by the Sheriff. "Ma'am, what is it?" asks Moses. "A lynchin'?"

"No, Moses," she replies, "certainly not that kind. This is a lynching of a whole state, a whole sovereign state. This is a lynching led *by my husband*."

Martin, leading the mob, is headed off by Bolduc, who informs Jennie that Samuel T. Beach shot her husband, then produces a written statement signed by a man who "swore he was with ... Beach at the time the murder took place. This crooked statement was signed and sworn to by — Hank Martin!"

Jennie grabs Smith's rifle and orders Bolduc to "cease his lyin'," but Verity impulsively confesses, "The affidavit is false," proving that her husband used the Castleberry affair to advance his own political ends. Martin pleads with the crowd, but Jennie shoots him down. He struggles to his feet, claims, "I told you I would lead you to Glory," then falls back to the ground, where he dies.

Cagney, who uses a subtle "Southern" accent in the film, was right about Hank Martin. In a true Cagney Production, he is thoroughly believable as a unique, powerful character, rather than playing yet another criminal or showman for Warners. Unfortunately, the film, bold in its depiction of political corruption (and the two brief scenes hinting at the treatment of Blacks in the South), is a rather disjointed affair, primarily due to editing ordered by attorneys for the Huey P. Long Estate. The truly ironic component of *A Lion is in the Streets* is that, in his final above-the-title role in a Warner Bros. release, Cagney is killed by his own sister!

For Paramount and director Nicholas Ray, Jim made his first Western in 16 years, *Run for Cover* (1955), then went to MGM for the outstanding Cinemascope musical *Love Me or Leave Me* (1955), based on the true story of 1920s pop-jazz singer Ruth Etting (Doris Day) and her manager-husband-manipulator, minor Chicago mobster Martin ("The Gimp") Snyder (a complex characterization for which Jim received a Best Actor Oscar nomination). Day (who *should* have won an Oscar for her sublime, moving performance — while supremely singing *great* songs), said of Cagney, "He's the most professional actor I've ever known. He was always 'real.'"[14] Interestingly, Cagney, the dancer and lover of musicals, had to limp throughout the film.

Made by Orange Productions for a Warner Bros. release, the film version of the Thomas Heggen-Joshua Logan Broadway hit *Mister Roberts* (1955), offered Cagney another prestige role, that of the hated Captain of the U.S.S. *Reluctant*. Due to the depiction of the Captain as a nasty, over-the-top tyrant, the U.S. Navy initially resisted approving the script; so John Ford, who had served with great distinction during World War II, being wounded while filming the Battle of Midway and directing the Field Photo Unit during the D-Day Invasion, was brought in to smooth the waters. Jim was particularly impressed when Ford called personally to offer him the role, his first in a widescreen Warnercolor film.

Star Henry Fonda, who had played Roberts in the stage version more than 1,000 times, was offended by Ford and screenwriter Frank Nugent's addition of "unnecessary" humor (particularly the over-the-top depiction of the Captain) into what was a superb script. Fonda really had little to complain about, considering that Jack Warner and producer Leyland Hayward, who both thought him too old and too long absent from Hollywood, didn't want him in the film. Josh Logan, who directed the stage version, actually cast Marlon Brando in January 1954; but Ford, when consulted, replied, "Bullshit! That's Fonda's part."[15]

To make matters worse, the alcoholic Ford was pounding down beer like there was no tomorrow, constantly keeping a case by his director's chair. At one point during location shooting in Hawaii, while lodging at the Niamalu Hotel at Waikiki Beach, the director, inebriated and wrapped in a large towel, appeared poolside. Climbing up the ladder to the high diving board, in front of several cast members, he dropped the towel and jumped off, stark naked, into the water.

Continuing to consume alarming quantities, Ford ruptured his gallbladder and was sent to the hospital. Leland Hayward recalled, "Ford was pissed all day. Ward Bond, for Christ's sake, was directing the picture. At least he kept the cameras turning when Ford came to and until he passed out again."[16] Eventually, Ford was replaced by Cagney's old Warners nemesis Mervyn LeRoy (who later claimed he was responsible for 90 percent of the completed film). However, Jack Lemmon, who plays Ensign Pulver, said that "Pappy" had completed half the picture, adding, "I think [LeRoy] did a superb job directing the scenes the way he thought that John Ford would shoot them."[17]

At one point, Josh Logan also was brought in to polish certain scenes, including the moving, climactic sequence during which Pulver reads a letter from Mister Roberts. Lemmon and the rest of the cast agreed that the scene needed to be re-shot, but when the young actor visited the recuperating Ford, he lied to the formidable director about his opinion of the original take.

The tension on the set in Hawaii occasionally was alleviated, however, when Cagney would break out his guitar. Critics have faulted him for hamming it to the hilt as Captain Morton, but he was directed to play the character that way, and Warners was delighted with his performance. Studio publicity lauded him for playing "the tyrannical skipper with more than the usual amount of gusto," noting that "preview audiences attest Cagney, the comedian, tops anything he's ever done before."[18]

While on location, Jim, out of necessity, became involved in the off-camera shenanigans. Lemmon recalled:

> One night, we were all invited to one of the junior [Naval] officer's houses ... for meatballs and spaghetti. So we all went, and Cagney commandeered a jeep, and he was driving. There were two or three of us in the jeep, and he drove us over to the house. We were all there, and the party's going on, and everybody's drinking and having a good time.
> Someone made me ... play the piano, which I do at times. Some lady sat down beside me — an attractive young lady was sitting beside me. And that's all. She was just sitting there. Now, in this sort of living room, there was an opening in the wall, like a counter, and there was open space into the kitchen. And suddenly, I hear a commotion in the kitchen, and screaming. I look in, and there's a

guy in there with a butcher knife in his hand, and his arms up in the air. About three other guys have got ahold of his arm, and are trying to wrestle him down, and everything.

He's hollering ..."I'll kill the son of a bitch!" Apparently, it was a junior officer ... It was his wife who sat on the bench, and he just assumed something, I guess, that I was making a pass at his wife, which was totally untrue. I hadn't even talked to her. She was talking to me about songs, and trying to pick them out on the piano, and I was trying to put chords to it.

Anyway, the next thing I know, I feel two hands on my collar, from behind. And I'm lifted straight up into the air, and pulled away from the piano, and pushed towards the door. It was Cagney. He had me, and he got me, and he said, "Just keep goin'!" He got me outside, down the steps, and he said, "Get in that jeep!"

And I said, "Yes, sir." I jumped into the jeep, and Cagney jumped in, drove me back to the bachelor officer's quarters. We were all right, but he saved my neck. This guy really was ready to go with that knife.[19]

Mister Roberts opens with a long shot of U.S. Naval vessels at sea, then cuts to a close-up of Henry Fonda standing on the bridge, peering through binoculars. As he drops the lenses from his eyes, "Mister Roberts" fills the bottom half of the screen, below his chin. Several stunning images of ships in the setting sun, and a silhouette of Roberts against the sea are followed by Fonda and Cagney's shared top billing. Though three directors (four, if Ward Bond is included) worked on the film, John Ford's distinctive contributions are easy to spot. And even when he wasn't actually directing, his longtime collaborator, cinematographer Winton C. Hoch, who won an Oscar for his Technicolor work on *The Quiet Man* (1951), was behind the camera.

The *Reluctant*, or "The Bucket," as known to her men, is a Navy cargo ship operating in the back areas of the Pacific during the waning days of World War II. As Chief Petty Officer Dowdy (Ward Bond) announces reveille, one of the sailors snarls, "Okay, Chief. You done your duty. Now get your big, fat can outta here!" Here, Ford's imprint is established instantly. The director often referred to Ward Bond as a "horse's ass," not only because of the actor's arrogant personality, but also due to the size and equine-like contour of his rear end. By 1955 Bond had known Ford for 27 years, alternately acting as his best friend and whipping boy, and he appeared in more of the director's films than any other actor. Fond of making asinine jokes about Bond's bum in public, Ford also frequently featured it in his films, both verbally (by adding dialogue to the script) and visually (designing actual compositions using it as a focal point). The fact that the director often considered Hollywood's greatest based elements of his cinematic sensibility around an actor's ass is astonishing; but, then, John Ford was in no way a conventional filmmaker or human being.

With the first Bond bum reference out of the way, a symbol more central to the plot is shown: the Captain's beloved palm tree, awarded by Admiral Finchley, potted in a small bucket marked, "Keep Away!" Mr. Roberts lopes along the deck, gazing out to sea, before sitting down to jaw with "Doc" (William Powell) about Ensign Frank Pulver (Jack Lemmon), the palm tree, and the unfulfilling tedium of their cargo duty. Roberts constantly requests to be transferred, "preferably to a destroyer," but the Captain "screams like a stuck pig" every time.

As Doc leaves, Roberts stands up, once again to gaze out over the water. The scene cuts to a medium-long shot as C.P.O. Dowdy enters, screen right: Ford has Ward Bond keep his back to the camera — bum prominent, framing it by placing his hands on his hips — until cutting to a medium two-shot of Fonda and Bond, who then turns to face the camera before sitting down. This image is the second nod to Bond's bum during the initial 10 minutes. Roberts and Dowdy walk out of the frame, and the scene cuts to Captain Morton, in pajamas, robe and Naval cap, emerging from his cabin to water the palm tree. In his final film released by Warner Bros., Cagney had to play second fiddle to a character actor's posterior.

There are obvious phallic images, as well. When a group of liberty-starved sailors (including Ford perennial Harry "Dobe" Carey, Jr.) observe and pant over nurses showering on a nearby island, Swede drops a fully extended spyglass to his crotch, holding it like an erection as he complains, "How do you use this thing?"

Cagney finally speaks, as the Captain observes the ensuing brawl. "Hold it, right there, Mista!" he shouts. "What's that man doing on deck without a shirt?" He then orders Roberts to put the offender on report. Later, when a sailor passes out from the heat, Roberts allows the men to abandon their shirts, causing Morton to go ballistic.

On the island, Pulver meets the bevy of nurses while requisitioning aspirin. Thinking he has made a date with the head nurse, he invites her to visit the ship that afternoon, when six actually arrive. Here, Ford includes a simultaneously judicious and gratuitous use of the widescreen image: the nurses, backs to the camera, line up at screen left, as Ward Bond enters, screen right, his rear end wiggling its way from foreground to background as he unleashes his familiar "horse whinny" (horse's-ass shtick he originally unleashed on screen in Ford's *My Darling Clementine* [20th Century-Fox, 1946]). A subsequent shot, moments later, again features the bums of Bond and the nurses. Discovering the sailor's view of the shower, the nurses leave the ship.

Thanks to Roberts' gift of a bottle of Scotch to a port director, the sailors are given liberty at Elysium, the "Polynesian Paradise." When natives row out to greet them, Morton orders, "Get them cannibals off this vessel! Get them off!" then cancels the liberty. Roberts protests, then agrees to be blackmailed, buying the crew a break with a promise of future obedience to the Captain's whims.

Following a stage-like structure, the film does not show the actual liberty, just the appalling aftermath (though one can imagine the sort of comic drunken brawling Ford would have favored). "Can they walk?" Dowdy asks when the Shore Patrol arrives with two truckloads of inebriated sailors.

"Walk?" the S.P. replies. "Some of them can't even crawl."

Two more trucks pull up. An Army M.P. (James Flavin) has singled out a handful of men, wearing leis and sporting parasols, who crashed Colonel Middleton's testimonial dinner dance, initiating a brawl that sent 38 soldiers to the hospital. (This typical "Fordian" shtick is repeated, ad nauseam, in *The Wings of Eagles* [1957], the director's tribute to Frank "Spig" Wead, in which Ward Bond plays "John Dodge," an amusing spin on Ford himself.) In addition, two young women "were somewhat mauled," while six others, their clothes torn from them, "ran screaming into the night." Dolan (Ken Curtis) stumbles aboard with a nanny goat stolen from Rear Admiral Whitworth, intent on turning the Captain's palm tree into "chow."

The *Reluctant* is kicked out of port, causing the Captain to issue outrageous orders, followed by, "*Right*, Mr. Roberts?" A man of his word, Roberts has no choice but to obey, causing confusion among the crew, who assume he is bucking for a promotion. Roberts asks Doc to transfer him to a shore hospital, where he can "lie around" until the ship sails, then is briefly cheered up by Pulver's intention to create a super firecracker to toss under Morton's bunk. While in his laundry "laboratory," Pulver inadvertently blows up his entire stash, filling the hold with soap suds.

Inspired by radio reports of V-E Day, Roberts, to the strains of John Philip Sousa, marches up to the bridge, rips the palm tree from its bucket, and tosses it into the ship's wake. Of course, the Captain emerges with his watering can, goes nuts, then issues a general alarm, calling all hands to battle stations. "*Who* did it?" he ominously asks over the intercom. "*Who*

Mister Roberts (1955): Captain Morton (Cagney) holds Lieutenant (j.g.) Douglas Roberts (Henry Fonda) to their Faustian bargain in the John Ford–Mervyn LeRoy adaptation of the smash Thomas Heggen-Joshua Logan Broadplay play (original lobby card).

did it?" While the microphone is still on, he rants furiously to Roberts about not honoring their agreement, spluttering and choking himself sick.

The crew regain their respect for Roberts, forge a letter, and finally land him a transfer off the *Reluctant*. When he admits to Doc, "I love those guys. I think they're the greatest guys on this Earth," Roberts could be John Ford himself, speaking about his beloved U.S. Navy. A social ritual scene typical of Ford, during which the crew present their hero with a brass "palm tree" medal and bid him farewell, also gives the audience its final glimpse of the very grateful and humble Lieutenant (j.g.) Douglas Roberts. The closing scene features Pulver reading a letter (including Fonda-specific references to Omaha and Iowa City) to the crew from "Doug," who made it into actual combat. Referring to his "preposterous hunk of brass," Roberts admits, "I'd rather have it than the Congressional Medal of Honor."

Pulver anxiously opens a second envelope and immediately crumples the letter inside.

"What's the matter, Frank?" asks Doc.

The subtle agony on Jack Lemmon's face is the highlight of his entire performance. The camera slowly tracks into a close-up as he continues to stare at the letter with an empty look in his eyes.

"Frank, what is it?" Doc demands. There is no editing: the camera remains on Pulver.

"Mr. Roberts is dead," he finally reveals, killed by a kamikaze pilot while drinking coffee in his cabin. Storming up to the bridge, Pulver grabs the palm tree and bucket, tosses them overboard, and announces his action to the Captain. The film ends with Cagney, placing one of those expressive hands to his head.

Within the context of his character, Cagney gives a fine performance. Captain Morton is a boisterous, two-dimensional tyrant, but Jim's acting is not as inappropriately over-the-top as his extreme, lighting-fast emotional shifts in *The West Point Story*. Despite Fonda's objections to the screenplay, he is superb in the film, one of the most entertaining and moving Hollywood productions of the 1950s.

The film had a built-in audience. The play, in New York and on the road, ran for six years to record audiences and grosses. The book, by Thomas Heggen, had gone into 20 printings, selling more than 2 million copies, by the time the film was completed. Ed Sullivan, a big fan of the play, devoted his entire June 19, 1955, *Toast of the Town* program to promote the film, drawing over 50 million viewers to their television sets.

Mister Roberts (1955): A cast featuring Henry Fonda, James Cagney, William Powell, Jack Lemmon and Ward Bond simply couldn't miss, especially when teamed with a sensational Broadway play and the direction of John Ford and Mervyn LeRoy, two heavyweight directors with solid connections to the Warner Bros. Wiseguys (original press book publicity).

Fonda, Cagney and Lemmon, accompanied by the ubiquitous palm tree, reenacted a live version of the scene in which the confused Captain meets Pulver for the first time, giving the audience a rare opportunity to see Jim on stage, without benefit of re-takes. Leland Hayward also appeared; and, when Sullivan asked about the necessity of using two directors, he offered a carefully prepared, sanitized explanation:

> Well, we didn't really want to, Ed. Jack Ford got terribly ill in the middle of the picture, and was rushed off to the hospital, late Sunday night for an operation. Mervyn stepped in and started directing the next morning, at nine o'clock. And I think the two of them together made a great team. Next to Jack Ford and Mervyn LeRoy, the best team I know is Josh Logan and Tom Heggen.

Cagney and Fonda also recreated the scene of Roberts' Faustian deal with the Captain to give the sailors liberty. Jim's 25-year absence from the stage was apparent, as he briefly hesitated several times, getting through by improvising his lines, while Hank's emotional intensity in a part he'd played for six years never faltered. Near the end of the scene, the tension built, until sparks really flew between these two peerless performers.

The Warners publicity blitz included full-page ads in a dozen national magazines, including *Life*, *Look*, *Photoplay* and *Modern Screen*. One particular newspaper ad must have exasperated Fonda: "Mister Godfrey (Arthur) says *Mister Roberts* is 'A terrific picture, infinitely better than the play!'" Many years later, Hank's daughter, Jane Fonda, summed it up when she said, "My father never thought the movie was as good as the play, but it was, and still is, an audience favorite."[20]

This last Warners effort by Cagney was followed by the musical *The Seven Little Foys* (1955), in which Jim (who played George M. Cohan for free) dances with Bob Hope, and *Short Cut to Hell* (1957), which he directed, unsuccessfully, for Paramount; *Tribute to a Bad Man* (1956), directed by Robert Wise, and *These Wilder Years* (1956) for MGM; *Man of a Thousand Faces* (1957), with Cagney excellent as Lon Chaney, and *Never Steal Anything Small* (1959) for Universal; and *Shake Hands with the Devil* (1959), filmed in Ireland, *The Gallant Hours* (1960), with Cagney as Admiral "Bull" Halsey directed by Robert Montgomery, and *One, Two, Three* (1961) for United Artists. The last film, directed by Billy Wilder, who insisted that Cagney overact outrageously throughout, induced Jim to retire — a period of cinematic dormancy he maintained until being persuaded by Milos Forman to play the police commissioner in *Ragtime* (1981) alongside his beloved friend Pat O'Brien. The fact is that he had become much more interested in raising prize cattle and promoting soil conservation. "Acting is not the beginning and end of everything," he said.[21]

By the time Cagney played an Irish revolutionary in *Shake Hands with the Devil*, his association with cinematic violence was really beginning to bother him. In the early Warner Bros. films, little on-screen explanation was offered for his characters' abusive behavior toward women. "The writers ... have written it into the scripts and the directors have followed it up by directing it into the pictures," he said.[22] But after his Warners "comeback" in *White Heat*, his criminal characters began to be depicted as either wracked with mental problems or full-blown insanity. As part of the publicity campaign for *Shake Hands*, he wrote an article in which he attempted to explain why he again was playing an aggressive character:

> Twenty-five years ago I was a hoofer. Somebody stuck a gun in my hands and I've been living cinematically by the gun ever since. Some people think I was born with a gun in my hand.
> The truth is, I hate violence.... This time I'm not playing a gunman. I'm a revolutionary ... and the gun is part of my professional equipment, as much a part of it as the stethoscope I carry as a doctor, which is the revolutionary's daytime profession ...
> During my career, thousands of words have been written about me. Most of them dwelt on the fact that I am, by vocation, a farmer; that off screen I lead a quiet life and don't get into trouble.
> But none of these stories has anywhere near the impact of one of my pictures. People get an impression of me from the screen that sticks much more thoroughly than anything they read.[23]

In 1973 Cagney gladly narrated the prelude to a special Edward G. Robinson tribute presented during the Academy Awards ceremony. The following year, he received an honor when the American Film Institute presented him with its Life Achievement Award. Held on March 13, the banquet included a song by emcee Frank Sinatra, and testimonials by former costars Mae Clarke, Doris Day and Jack Lemmon. Also praising Jim were John Wayne and Ronald Reagan (who now liked Cagney because his politics had turned increasingly conservative in wealthy old age), and Bob Hope, Charlton Heston, George Stevens, Cicely Tyson, George C. Scott and Shirley MacLaine.

In 1976, Cagney admitted:

> Not long ago I drove down Ventura Boulevard past Warner Bros. where I made over forty of my sixty-two movies, and I didn't turn a hair. It didn't interest me one damn. In thinking about all my reasons for quitting, I can boil them down to one: when I stopped caring, I stopped acting.[24]

Now quite ill after several minor strokes, Cagney made one more screen appearance, in the television movie *Terrible Joe Moran* (1984), which unfortunately was ruined by director Joseph Sargent's use of a Cagney impersonator to overdub all his dialogue. On Easter Sunday, March 30, 1986, Jim passed away, of cardiac arrest, at his Verney Farm. Having been very generous to his two adopted children, he left everything to Willie, who lived another eight years, passing away at age 95 on October 10, 1994.

Summing up his career, Cagney revealed:

[M]y aim was never stardom. I never gave it a thought in my early years, and after I was given the designation, I didn't think about it then. With me, a career was a simple matter of putting groceries on the table. I've never thought of myself as anything but a journeyman actor, going where the job happened to be, doing the job, and making my way back home.[25]

Cagney was a top-billed star during his entire 12-year career as a Warner Bros. contract actor, and only left the studio when *he* made the decision. Perhaps the ultimate compliment ever written about him came from British film scholar Patrick McGilligan:

[H]e presented a type that can best be summed up as the "anti-hero." Cagney was really the first. Gable, the smiling chiseller; Bogart, the charismatic loner; Brando, the brooding misfit; and James Dean, the rebel—all owe a hefty measure of their tradition to Cagney.... Almost every American male performer since Cagney's heyday can trace the lineage of his style to the actor's influence.[26]

"You walk in, plant yourself, look the other fella in the eye, and tell the truth."[27]

—James Cagney

Appendix

The Warner Bros. Wiseguys Films

Sinners' Holiday (October 11, 1930) **James Cagney**; Joan Blondell, Lucille Laverne; directed by John G. Adolphi; 55 minutes

The Doorway to Hell (October 18, 1930) **James Cagney**; Lew Ayres, Dwight Frye; directed by Archie Mayo; 78 minutes

The Widow from Chicago (November 23, 1930) **Edward G. Robinson**; Alice White, Neil Hamilton; directed by Edward Cline; 64 minutes

Little Caesar (January 9, 1931) **Edward G. Robinson**; Douglas Fairbanks Jr., Glenda Farrell; directed by Mervyn LeRoy; 80 minutes

Other Men's Women (January 17, 1931) **James Cagney**; Grant Withers, Joan Blondell, Mary Astor; directed by William Wellman; 70 minutes

The Public Enemy (April 23, 1931) **James Cagney**; Joan Blondell, Mae Clarke, Jean Harlow; directed by William Wellman; 84 minutes

The Millionaire (May 1, 1931) **James Cagney**; George Arliss, David Manners, Florence Arliss; directed by John G. Adolphi; 82 minutes

Smart Money (July 11, 1931) **Edward G. Robinson, James Cagney**; Evalyn Knapp, Boris Karloff; directed by Alfred E. Green; 90 minutes

Blonde Crazy (November 14, 1931) **James Cagney**; Joan Blondell, Louis Calhern; directed by Roy Del Ruth; 73 minutes

Five Star Final (September 26, 1931) **Edward G. Robinson**; Boris Karloff, George E. Stone; directed by Mervyn LeRoy; 89 minutes

Taxi! (January 23, 1932) **James Cagney**; Loretta Young, George E. Stone; directed by Roy Del Ruth; 70 minutes

The Hatchet Man (February 4, 1932) **Edward G. Robinson**; Loretta Young, Leslie Fenton; directed by William A. Wellman; 74 minutes

The Crowd Roars (April 16, 1932) **James Cagney**; Joan Blondell, Ann Dvorak, Frank McHugh; directed by Howard Hawks; 85 minutes

Two Seconds (May 18, 1932) **Edward G. Robinson**; Preston Foster, J. Carroll Naish; directed by Mervyn LeRoy; 68 minutes

Winner Take All (July 16, 1932) **James Cagney**; Marian Nixon, Virginia Bruce, Clarence Muse; directed by Roy Del Ruth; 68 minutes

Tiger Shark (September 22, 1932) **Edward G. Robinson**; Zita Johann, Richard Arlen; directed by Howard Hawks; 80 minutes

Big City Blues (1932) **Humphrey Bogart**; Joan Blondell, Eric Linden; directed by Mervyn LeRoy; 65 minutes

Three on a Match (October 28, 1932) **Humphrey Bogart**; Joan Blondell, Ann Dvorak, Bette Davis; directed by Mervyn LeRoy; 64 minutes

Silver Dollar (December 22, 1932) **Edward G. Robinson**; Bebe Daniels, Aline MacMahon; directed by Alfred E. Green; 84 minutes

Hard to Handle (January 28, 1933) **James Cagney**; Mary Brian, Ruth Donnelly, Allen Jenkins; directed by Mervyn LeRoy; 81 minutes

The Little Giant (April 14, 1933) **Edward G. Robinson**; Helen Vinson, Mary Astor; directed by Roy Del Ruth; 74 minutes

Picture Snatcher (May 6, 1933) **James Cagney**; Ralph Bellamy, Patricia Ellis, Alice White; directed by Lloyd Bacon; 77 minutes

The Mayor of Hell (June 23, 1933) **James Cagney**; Madge Evans, Allen Jenkins, Frankie Darro; directed by Archie Mayo; 90 minutes

I Loved a Woman (September 22, 1933) **Edward G. Robinson**; Kay Francis, Genevieve Tobin; directed by Alfred E. Green; 90 minutes

Footlight Parade (September 30, 1933) **James Cagney**; Joan Blondell, Ruby Keeler, Dick Powell; directed by Lloyd Bacon, Busby Berkeley; 104 minutes

Lady Killer (December 28, 1933) **James Cagney**; Mae Clarke, Margaret Lindsay; directed by Roy Del Ruth; 76 minutes

Dark Hazard (February 3, 1934) **Edward G. Robinson**; Genevieve Tobin, Glenda Farrell; directed by Alfred E. Green; 72 minutes

Jimmy the Gent (March 17, 1934) **James Cagney**; Bette Davis, Alice White, Allen Jenkins; directed by Michael Curtiz; 67 minutes

He was Her Man (May 18, 1934) **James Cagney**; Joan Blondell, Victor Jory; directed by Lloyd Bacon; 70 minutes

Here Comes the Navy (June 28, 1934) **James Cagney**; Pat O'Brien, Gloria Stuart, Frank McHugh; directed by Lloyd Bacon; 86 minutes

The Man with Two Faces (August 4, 1934) **Edward G. Robinson**; Mary Astor, Mae Clarke; directed by Archie Mayo; 72 minutes

The St. Louis Kid (November 1, 1934) **James Cagney**; Patricia Ellis, Allen Jenkins; directed by Ray Enright; 67 minutes

Devil Dogs of the Air (February 7, 1935) **James Cagney**; Pat O'Brien, Margaret Lindsay; directed by Lloyd Bacon; 86 minutes

G-Men (April 18, 1935) **James Cagney**; Ann Dvorak, Margaret Lindsay, Robert Armstrong; directed by William Keighley; 86 minutes

The Irish in US (August 1, 1935) **James Cagney**; Pat O'Brien, Olivia de Havilland, Frank McHugh; directed by Lloyd Bacon; 84 minutes

A Midsummer Night's Dream (October 9, 1935) **James Cagney**; Dick Powell, Joe E. Brown; directed by Max Reinhardt, William Dieterle; 132 minutes

The Frisco Kid (November 30, 1935) **James Cagney**; Margaret Lindsay, Ricardo Cortez, George E. Stone; directed by Lloyd Bacon; 77 minutes

Ceiling Zero (January 16, 1936) **James Cagney**; Pat O'Brien, June Travis; directed by Howard Hawks; 95 minutes

The Petrified Forest (February 6, 1936) **Humphrey Bogart**; Bette Davis, Leslie Howard; directed by Archie Mayo; 83 minutes

Bullets or Ballots (June 6, 1936) **Edward G. Robinson, Humphrey Bogart**; Joan Blondell; directed by William Keighley; 81 minutes

Two Against the World (July 11, 1936) **Humphrey Bogart**; Beverly Roberts, Henry O'Neill; directed by William McGann; 64 minutes

China Clipper (August 22, 1936) **Humphrey Bogart**; Pat O'Brien, Beverly Roberts; directed by Ray Enright; 85 minutes

Isle of Fury (October 10, 1936) **Humphrey Bogart**; Margaret Lindsay, Donald Woods; directed by Frank McDonald; 60 minutes

Black Legion (January 30, 1937) **Humphrey Bogart**; Dick Foran, Erin O'Brien-Moore; directed by Archie Mayo; 83 minutes

The Great O'Malley (February 13, 1937) **Humphrey Bogart**; Pat O'Brien, Ann Sheridan; directed by William Dieterle; 71 minutes

Marked Woman (April 10, 1937) **Humphrey Bogart**; Bette Davis, Lola Lane, Jane Bryan; directed by Lloyd Bacon; 96 minutes

Kid Galahad (May 26, 1937) **Edward G. Robinson, Humphrey Bogart**; Bette Davis, Wayne Morris; directed by Michael Curtiz; 101 minutes

San Quentin (August 7, 1937) **Humphrey Bogart**; Pat O'Brien, Ann Sheridan, Barton MacLane; directed by Lloyd Bacon; 70 minutes

Swing Your Lady (January 8, 1938) **Humphrey Bogart**; Frank McHugh, Louise Fazenda, Allen Jenkins; directed by Ray Enright; 72 minutes

A Slight Case of Murder (February 26, 1938) **Edward G. Robinson**; Jane Bryan, Ruth Donnelly; directed by Lloyd Bacon; 85 minutes

Crime School (May 28, 1938) **Humphrey Bogart**; Gale Page, Billy Halop, Huntz Hall, Leo Gorcey; directed by Lewis Seiler; 86 minutes

Racket Busters (July 16, 1938) **Humphrey Bogart**; George Brent, Gloria Dickson, Allen Jenkins; directed by Lloyd Bacon; 71 minutes

Men Are Such Fools (July 16, 1938) **Humphrey Bogart**; Priscilla Lane, Wayne Morris; directed by Busby Berkeley; 70minutes

The Amazing Dr. Clitterhouse (July 20, 1938) **Edward G. Robinson, Humphrey Bogart**; directed by Anatole Litvak; 87 minutes

Boy Meets Girl (August 27, 1938) **James Cagney**; Pat O'Brien, Marie Wilson, Ralph Bellamy; directed by Lloyd Bacon; 80 minutes

Angels with Dirty Faces (November 24, 1938) **James Cagney, Humphrey Bogart**; Pat O'Brien; directed by Michael Curtiz; 97 minutes

King of the Underworld (January 7, 1939) **Humphrey Bogart**; Kay Francis, James Stephenson; directed by Lewis Seiler; 69 minutes

The Oklahoma Kid (March 3, 1939) **James Cagney, Humphrey Bogart**; Rosemary Lane, Donald Crisp; directed by Lloyd Bacon; 85 minutes

Dark Victory (April 20, 1939) **Humphrey Bogart**; Bette Davis, George Brent, Ronald Reagan; directed by Edmund Goulding; 105 minutes

Confessions of a Nazi Spy (April 27, 1939) **Edward G. Robinson**; Francis Lederer, George Sanders; directed by Anatole Litvak; 102 minutes

You Can't Get Away with Murder (May 20, 1939) **Humphrey Bogart**; Billy Halop, Gale Page; directed by Lewis Seiler; 69 minutes

Each Dawn I Die (July 22, 1939) **James Cagney**; George Raft, Jane Bryan, George Bancroft; directed by William Keighley; 92 minutes

The Roaring Twenties (October 23, 1939) **James Cagney, Humphrey Bogart**; Rosemary Lane; directed by Raoul Walsh; 104 minutes

The Return of Doctor X (November 23, 1939) **Humphrey Bogart**, Wayne Morris, Rosemary Lane; directed by Vincent Sherman; 60 minutes

Invisible Stripes (December 30, 1939) **Humphrey Bogart**; George Raft, William Holden; directed by Lloyd Bacon; 81 minutes

The Fighting 69th (January 26, 1940) **James Cagney**; Pat O'Brien, George Brent, Alan Hale; directed by William Keighley; 90 minutes

Dr. Ehrlich's Magic Bullet (February 23, 1940) **Edward G. Robinson**; Ruth Gordon, Otto Kruger; directed by William Dieterle; 103 minutes

Virginia City (March 16, 1940) **Humphrey Bogart**; Errol Flynn, Miriam Hopkins, Randolph Scott; directed by Michael Curtiz; 121 minutes

It All Came True (April 6, 1940) **Humphrey Bogart**; Ann Sheridan, Jeffrey Lynn; directed by Lewis Seiler; 97 minutes

Torrid Zone (May 18, 1940) **James Cagney**; Pat O'Brien, Ann Sheridan, Andy Devine; directed by William Keighley; 88 minutes

Brother Orchid (June 7, 1940) **Edward G. Robinson, Humphrey Bogart**; Ann Sothern; directed by Lloyd Bacon; 91 minutes

They Drive by Night (July 27, 1940) **Humphrey Bogart**; George Raft, Ida Lupino; directed by Raoul Walsh; 93 minutes

City for Conquest (September 21, 1940) **James Cagney**; Ann Sheridan, Donald Crisp; directed by Anatole Litvak; 104 minutes

A Dispatch from Reuters (October 19, 1940) **Edward G. Robinson**; Eddie Albert, Nigel Bruce; directed by William Dieterle; 89 minutes

High Sierra (January 21, 1941) **Humphrey Bogart**; Ida Lupino, Alan Curtis, Arthur Kennedy; directed by Raoul Walsh; 100 minutes

The Strawberry Blonde (February 22, 1941) **James**

Cagney; Olivia De Havilland, Rita Hayworth; directed by Raoul Walsh; 97 minutes

The Sea Wolf (March 21, 1941) **Edward G. Robinson**; John Garfield, Ida Lupino, Alexander Knox; directed by Michael Curtiz; 100 minutes

The Wagons Roll at Night (April 25, 1941) **Humphrey Bogart**; Sylvia Sidney; Eddie Albert; directed by Ray Enright; 84 minutes

Manpower (August 9, 1941) **Edward G. Robinson**; George Raft, Marlene Dietrich, Alan Hale; directed by Raoul Walsh; 105 minutes

The Bride Came C.O.D. (July 12, 1941) **James Cagney**; Bette Davis, Stuart Erwin, Jack Carson; directed by William Keighley; 92 minutes

The Maltese Falcon (October 3, 1941) **Humphrey Bogart**; Mary Astor, Peter Lorre, Gladys George; directed by John Huston; 100 minutes

All Through the Night (January 10, 1942) **Humphrey Bogart**; Kaaren Verne, Peter Lorre; directed by Vincent Sherman; 107 minutes

Captains of the Clouds (February 12, 1942) **James Cagney**; Dennis Morgan, Brenda Marshall; directed by Michael Curtiz; 113 minutes

Larceny Inc. (April 24, 1942) **Edward G. Robinson**; Jane Wyman, Broderick Crawford; directed by Lloyd Bacon; 95 minutes

Yankee Doodle Dandy (June 6, 1942) **James Cagney**; Joan Leslie, Walter Huston, Jeanne Cagney; directed by Michael Curtiz; 113 minutes

The Big Shot (June 13, 1942) **Humphrey Bogart**; Irene Manning, Richard Travis, Stanley Travis; directed by Lewis Seiler; 82 minutes

Across the Pacific (September 4, 1942) **Humphrey Bogart**; Mary Astor, Sydney Greenstreet; directed by John Huston; 97 minutes

Casablanca (November 26, 1942) **Humphrey Bogart**; Ingrid Bergman, Sydney Greenstreet; directed by Michael Curtiz; 102 minutes

Action in the North Atlantic (June 12, 1943) **Humphrey Bogart**; Raymond Massey, Julie Bishop; directed by Lloyd Bacon; 126 minutes

Thank Your Lucky Stars (1943) **Humphrey Bogart**; Errol Flynn, Bette Davis, John Garfield; directed by David Butler; 127 minutes

Passage to Marseille (February 17, 1944) **Humphrey Bogart**; Claude Rains, Peter Lorre; directed by Michael Curtiz; 110 minutes

To Have and Have Not (October 11, 1944) **Humphrey Bogart**; Lauren Bacall, Walter Brennan; directed by Howard Hawks; 100 minutes

Conflict (June 15, 1945) **Humphrey Bogart**; Alexis Smith, Sydney Greenstreet, Rose Hobart; directed by Curtis Bernhardt; 86 minutes

Two Guys from Milwaukee (July 26, 1946) **Humphrey Bogart**; Lauren Bacall, Dennis Morgan; directed by David Butler; 90 minutes

The Big Sleep (August 23, 1946) **Humphrey Bogart**; Lauren Bacall, John Ridgely, Martha Vickers; directed by Howard Hawks; 114 minutes

The Two Mrs. Carrolls (March 4, 1947) **Humphrey Bogart**; Barbara Stanwyck, Alexis Smith; directed by Peter Godfrey; 99 minutes

Dark Passage (September 5, 1947) **Humphrey Bogart**; Lauren Bacall, Bruce Bennett, Agnes Moorehead; directed by Delmer Daves; 106 minutes

Treasure of the Sierra Madre (January 6, 1948) **Humphrey Bogart**; Walter Huston, Tim Holt; directed by John Huston; 126 minutes

Key Largo (July 16, 1948) **Humphrey Bogart, Edward G. Robinson**; Lauren Bacall, Lionel Barrymore; directed by John Huston; 101 minutes

It's a Great Feeling (August 1, 1949) **Edward G. Robinson**; Doris Day, Jack Carson, Errol Flynn; directed by David Butler; 84 minutes

White Heat (September 2, 1949) **James Cagney**; Virginia Mayo, Edmond O'Brien, Margaret Wycherly; directed by Raoul Walsh; 114 minutes

Chain Lightning (February 18, 1950) **Humphrey Bogart**; Eleanor Parker, Raymond Massey; directed by Stuart Heisler; 94 minutes

Kiss Tomorrow Goodbye (August 4, 1950) **James Cagney**; Barbara Payton, Ward Bond, Luther Adler; directed by Gordon Douglas; 102 minutes

The West Point Story (December 22, 1950) **James Cagney**; Virginia Mayo, Doris Day, Gordon MacRae; directed by Roy Del Ruth; 107 minutes

The Enforcer (February 24, 1951) **Humphrey Bogart**; Zero Mostel, Ted de Corsia, Everett Sloane; directed by Raoul Walsh (credited to Bretaigne Windust); 87 minutes

Come Fill the Cup (October 24, 1951) **James Cagney**; Phyllis Thaxter, James Gleason, Gig Young; directed by Gordon Douglas; 113 minutes

Starlift (December 14, 1951) **James Cagney**; Doris Day, Gordon MacRae, Virginia Mayo; directed by Roy Del Ruth; 103 minutes

A Lion is in the Streets (September 23, 1953) **James Cagney**; Barbara Hale, Anne Francis; directed by Raoul Walsh; 88 minutes

Mister Roberts (July 30, 1955) **James Cagney**; Henry Fonda, William Powell, Jack Lemmon; directed by John Ford, Mervyn LeRoy; 123 minutes

Illegal (October 28, 1955) **Edward G. Robinson**; Nina Foch, DeForrest Kelley, Jayne Mansfield; directed by Lewis Allen; 88 minutes

Hell on Frisco Bay (July 1956) **Edward G. Robinson**; Alan Ladd, Joanne Dru, William Demarest; directed by Lewis Allen; 98 minutes

Robin & the 7 Hoods (June 24, 1964) **Edward G. Robinson**; Frank Sinatra, Dean Martin, Sammy Davis, Jr.; directed by Gordon Douglas; 123 minutes

Cheyenne Autumn (October 3, 1964) **Edward G. Robinson**; Richard Widmark, Karl Malden, Carroll Baker; directed by John Ford; 156 minutes

Chapter Notes

Preface

1. John Huston, letter to Scott Allen Nollen, 15 February 1982.
2. Henry Brandon, conversation with Scott Allen Nollen, St. Paul, Minnesota, July 1988.

Introduction

1. Paul Buhle and Dave Wagner, *Radical Hollywood: The Untold Story Behind America's Favorite Movies* (New York: The New Press, 2002), p. 164.
2. Midge Farrell, conversation with Scott Allen Nollen, Los Angeles, November 1996.

Chapter 1

1. Edward G. Robinson, with Leonard Spigelglass, *All My Yesterdays: An Autobiography* (New York: Hawthorn Books, Inc., 1973), p. 54.
2. James Cagney, *Cagney by Cagney* (New York: Doubleday and Company, Inc., 1976), p. 11.
3. Cagney, *Cagney by Cagney*, p. 14.
4. A. M. Sperber and Eric Lax, *Bogart* (New York: William Morrow and Company, Inc., 1997), p. 24.

Chapter 2

1. "Al Jolson in *The Singing Fool*, "A Warner Bros. Vitaphone Picture" souvenir book (Warner Bros. Pictures, 1928), p. 8.
2. Cagney, *Cagney by Cagney*, p. 35.
3. Cagney, *Cagney by Cagney*, p. 39.
4. Cagney, *Cagney by Cagney*, p. 39.
5. Robinson, *All My Yesterdays*, pp. 113–144.
6. Robinson, *All My Yesterdays*, p. 117.
7. Cagney, *Cagney by Cagney*, p. 43.
8. Darryl F. Zanuck, in Patrick McGilligan, *Cagney: The Actor as Auteur* (New York: A. S. Barnes and Company, 1975), p. 168.
9. Cagney, *Cagney by Cagney*, p. 45.

Chapter 3

1. Cagney, *Cagney by Cagney*, p. 46.
2. Robinson, *All My Yesterdays*, pp. 3–4.
3. Robinson, *All My Yesterdays*, p. 126.
4. Robinson, *All My Yesterdays*, p.117.
5. Cagney, *Cagney by Cagney*, p. 48.
6. James Cagney, in McGilligan, *Cagney: The Actor as Auteur*, p. 211.
7. Patrick McGilligan and Paul Buhle, *Tender Comrades: A Backstory of the Hollywood Blacklist* (New York: St. Martin's Press, 1997), p. 140.
8. Howard Hawks, in Joseph McBride, *Hawks on Hawks* (Berkeley: University of California Press, 1982), p. 54.
9. Cagney, *Cagney by Cagney*, p. 49.
10. Hawks, in McBride, p. 54.
11. Cagney, *Cagney by Cagney*, p. 52.
12. Cagney, *Cagney by Cagney*, p. 53.
13. Hawks, in McBride, p. 34.
14. Hawks, in McBride, p. 35.
15. *The Man with Two Faces* pressbook (Warner Bros.-First National Pictures, 1934), p. 6.

Chapter 4

1. Robinson, *All My Yesterdays*, p. 130.
2. Robinson, *All My Yesterdays*, p. 135.
3. Cagney, *Cagney by Cagney*, p. 54.
4. Cagney, *Cagney by Cagney*, pp. 64–65.
5. Midge Farrell conversation.
6. Robinson, *All My Yesterdays*, p. 142.
7. Cagney, *Cagney by Cagney*, p. 57.
8. Mae Clarke, letter to Scott Allen Nollen, 1983.
9. Robinson, *All My Yesterdays*, p. 150.
10. Cagney, *Cagney by Cagney*, p. 60.
11. Cagney, *Cagney by Cagney*, p. 62.
12. *The Man with Two Faces* pressbook, p. 6.
13. *The Man with Two Faces* pressbook, p. 4.
14. *The Man with Two Faces* pressbook, p. 14
15. *The Man with Two Faces* pressbook, p. 5.

Chapter 5

1. Cagney, *Cagney by Cagney*, p. 63.
2. Robinson, *All My Yesterdays*, p. 156.
3. Cagney, *Cagney by Cagney*, p. 65.
4. Cagney, *Cagney by Cagney*, p. 67.
5. John Dover Wilson, ed., *The Complete Works of William Shakespeare* (London: Octopus Books Limited, 1981), p. 194.
6. Hawks, in McBride, p. 56.

Chapter 6

1. Robinson, *All My Yesterdays*, p. 165.
2. *Bullets or Ballots* pressbook (Warner Bros.-First National Pictures, 1936), p. 2.
3. *Bullets or Ballots* pressbook, p. 7.
4. *Bullets or Ballots* pressbook, p. 21.
5. *Bullets or Ballots* pressbook, p. 24.
6. *Bullets or Ballots* pressbook, p. 26.
7. *Bullets or Ballots* pressbook, p. 27.
8. Robinson, *All My Yesterdays*, p. 178.
9. Henry Brandon, discussion with Scott Allen Nollen, 30 December 1988.
10. Henry Brandon discussion.
11. Scott Allen Nollen, *Boris Karloff: A Gentleman's Life* (Baltimore: Midnight Marquee Press, 1999), p. 110.
12. Robinson, *All My Yesterdays*, p. 182.
13. Robinson, *All My Yesterdays*, p. 181.
14. Robinson, *All My Yesterdays*, p. 193.
15. Robinson, *All My Yesterdays*, p. 89.
16. Ronald Reagan, conversation with Scott Allen Nollen, West Branch, Iowa, August 1992.

Chapter 7

1. Cagney, *Cagney by Cagney*, p. 72.
2. Cagney, *Cagney by Cagney*, p. 76.

Chapter 8

1. Cagney, *Cagney by Cagney*, pp. 84–85.
2. Cagney, *Cagney by Cagney*, p. 86.
3. Cagney, *Cagney by Cagney*, p. 93.

Chapter 9

1. John Huston, in Lawrence Grobel, *The Hustons* (New York: Charles Scribner's Sons, 1989), p. 211.
2. Robinson, *All My Yesterdays*, p. 211.
3. Huston, in Grobel, p. 216.
4. Pat O'Brien, in McGilligan, *Cagney: The Actor as Auteur*, pp. 176–177.
5. Robinson, *All My Yesterdays*, p. 217.
6. Robinson, *All My Yesterdays*, p. 76.
7. Robinson, *All My Yesterdays*, p. 213.
8. James Cagney, in John McCabe, *Cagney* (New York: Carroll and Graf Publishers, Inc., 1997), p.194.
9. Anatole Litvak, in McGilligan, *Cagney: The Actor as Auteur*, p. 81.
10. Elia Kazan, in McCabe, p. 193.
11. Cagney, *Cagney by Cagney*, p. 96.
12. Robinson, *All My Yesterdays*, p. 218.

Chapter 10

1. Huston, in Grobel, pp. 209–210.
2. Sperber and Lax, p. 145.

Chapter 11

1. Huston, in Grobel, p. 212.
2. John Huston, in *John Huston: The Man, the Movies, the Maverick* (Point Blank documentary film, 1988).
3. Dashiell Hammett, *The Maltese Falcon* (Franklin Center, Pennsylvania: The Franklin Library, 1987), editor's note.
4. John Huston, in Grobel, p. 213.
5. Walter Huston, in Grobel, p. 221.
6. Mary Astor, in Grobel, p. 221.
7. John Huston, in Grobel, p. 219.
8. John Huston, in Grobel, p. 219.

Chapter 12

1. Cagney, *Cagney by Cagney*, p. 102.
2. Cagney, *Cagney by Cagney*, p. 104.
3. Cagney, *Cagney by Cagney*, p. 106.
4. Howard Koch, in *You Must Remember This: A Tribute to Casablanca*. *Casablanca* DVD (Turner Entertainment, 2002).
5. Koch, in *Casablanca* DVD. .
6. Stephen Bogart, in *Casablanca* DVD.

Chapter 13

1. Lauren Bacall, *By Myself* (New York: Alfred A. Knoft, 1978), p. 69.
2. Howard Hawks, in *The Men Who Made the Movies: Howard Hawks* (Turner Classic Movies, 2002).
3. Lauren Bacall, in *Private Screenings: Lauren Bacall* (Turner Classic Movies, 2005).
4. Bacall, *By Myself*, p.101.
5. Bacall, in *Private Screenings*.
6. Hawks, in McBride, p.102.
7. Hawks, in McBride, p. 101.
8. Hawks, in McBride, p.102.
9. Bacall, *By Myself*, p. 132.
10. Bacall, *By Myself*, pp. 109–110.
11. Bacall, in *Private Screenings*.
12. Bacall, *By Myself*, p. 114.
13. Hawks, in *The Men Who Made the Movies*.
14. Bacall, in *Private Screenings*.
15. Sperber and Lax, p. 269.
16. Hawks, in *The Men Who Made the Movies*.
17. Bacall, *By Myself*, p. 155.
18. Bacall, *By Myself*, p. 166.
19. Bacall, in *Private Screenings*.

Chapter 14

1. Bacall, *By Myself*, p. 171.
2. Humphrey Bogart, in Sperber and Lax, p. 335.
3. Bacall, *By Myself*, p. 173.
4. John Huston, in Grobel, p.300.
5. Humphrey Bogart, in Grobel, p. 292.
6. Robinson, *All My Yesterdays*, p. 181.

7. John Huston, in Grobel, p. 306.
8. Edward G. Robinson, in *Key Largo* pressbook (Warner Bros. Pictures, 1948), p. 10.
9. Karl Freund, in *Key Largo* pressbook, p. 9.
10. Bacall, *By Myself*, p. 182.
11. *Key Largo* pressbook, p.10.
12. *Key Largo* pressbook, p. 2.

Chapter 15

1. Cagney, *Cagney by Cagney*, p. 126.
2. Virginia Mayo, in *White Heat: Top of the World*. *White Heat* DVD (Turner Entertainment, 2005).

Chapter 16

1. Bacall, *By Myself*, p. 194.
2. Bacall, *By Myself*, pp. 215–216.
3. Bacall, *By Myself*, p. 212.
4. Jack Warner, in Sperber and Lax, p. 469.
5. Bacall, in *Private Screenings*.
6. Bacall, *By Myself*, p. 259.
7. John Huston, in Grobel, p. 444.
8. Bacall, *By Myself*, p. 281.
9. John Huston, in Bacall, *By Myself*, p. 295.
10. *Robin and the 7 Hoods* pressbook (Warner Bros. Pictures, 1964), p. 16.
11. Frank Sinatra, Jr., in *Robin and the 7 Hoods* DVD (Warner Home Video, 2001).
12. Virginia Mayo, in *White Heat: Top of the World*.
13. James Cagney, in *A Lion is in the Streets* pressbook (Warner Bros. Pictures, 1953), p. 7.
14. Doris Day, in McGilligan, *Cagney: The Actor as Auteur*, p. 135.
15. John Ford, in Joseph McBride, *Searching for John Ford* (New York: St. Martin's Press, 2001), p. 545.
16. Leland Hayward, in McBride, *Searching for John Ford*, p. 550.
17. Jack Lemmon, in *Mister Roberts* DVD (Warner Home Video, 1998).
18. *Mister Roberts* pressbook (Warner Bros. Pictures, 1955), p. 27.
19. Lemmon, in *Mister Roberts* DVD.
20. Jane Fonda, in *Mister Roberts* DVD.
21. Cagney, in McGilligan, *Cagney: The Actor as Auteur*, p. 154.
22. Cagney, in McGilligan, *Cagney: The Actor as Auteur*, p. 159.
23. James Cagney, in *Shake Hands with the Devil* pressbook (United Artists Pictures, 1959).
24. Cagney, *Cagney by Cagney*, p. 156.
25. Cagney, *Cagney by Cagney*, p. 160.
26. McGilligan, *Cagney: The Actor as Auteur*, p. 207.
27. Cagney, *Cagney by Cagney*, p. 158.

Bibliography

Primary Sources

Interviews

Brandon, Henry. Conversation with author. St. Paul, Minnesota, July 1988.
Brandon, Henry. Telephone Interview by author, 4 March 1989.
Farrell, Midge. Conversation with author, Los Angeles, November 1996.
Lee, Anna. Telephone Interview by author, 12 August 1989.
Reagan, Ronald. Conversation with author, West Branch, Iowa, August 1992.

Interview Footage in Documentary Films

Bacall, Lauren. *Private Screenings: Lauren Bacall.* Turner Entertainment, 2005.
Hawks, Howard. *The Men Who Made the Movies: Howard Hawks.* Turner Entertainment, 2002.
Huston, John. *John Huston: The Man, the Movies, the Maverick.* Point Blank, 1988.
Koch, Howard. *You Must Remember This: A Tribute to Casablanca.* Turner Entertainment, 2002.
Lemmon, Jack. *Mister Roberts.* Warner Home Video, 1998.
Mayo, Virginia. *White Heat: Top of the World.* Turner Entertainment, 2005.
Sinatra, Frank Jr. *Robin and the 7 Hoods.* Warner Home Video, 2001.

Correspondence

Brandon, Henry. Letter to author, April 1989.
Clarke, Mae. Letter to author, 1983.
Huston, John. Letter to author, 15 February 1982.
Johann, Zita. Letter to author, 11 January 1985.

Archives

University of Southern California, Los Angeles. The Papers of Edward G. Robinson.
University of Wisconsin, Madison. Wisconsin Center for Film and Theatre Research. Warner Bros. Files.

Memoirs

Arliss, George. *My Ten Years in the Studios.* Boston: Little, Brown and Company, 1940.
Bacall, Lauren. *By Myself.* New York: Alfred A. Knopf, 1978.
Bogart, Stephen. *Bogart: In Search of My Father.* New York: E. P. Dutton, 1995.
Cagney, James. *Cagney by Cagney.* New York: Doubleday and Company, Inc., 1976.
Robinson, Edward G., with Leonard Spigelglass. *All My Yesterdays: An Autobiography.* New York: Hawthorn Books, Inc., 1973.
Warner, Jack. *My First Hundred Years in Hollywood.* New York: Random House, 1964.

Warner Bros. Studio Publicity Materials

"Al Jolson in *The Singing Fool*: A Warner Bros. Vitaphone Picture" souvenir book. Warner Bros. Pictures, 1928.
Bullets or Ballots press book. Warner Bros.-First National Pictures, 1936.
Key Largo pressbook. Warner Bros. Pictures, 1948.
A Lion is in the Streets pressbook. Warner Bros. Pictures, 1953.
The Man with Two Faces pressbook. Warner Bros.-First National Pictures, 1934.
Mister Roberts pressbook. Warner Bros. Pictures, 1955.
Robin and the 7 Hoods pressbook. Warner Bros. Pictures, 1964.

Secondary Sources

Books on James Cagney, Edward G. Robinson and Humphrey Bogart

Gansberg, Alan L. *Little Caesar: A Biography of Edward G. Robinson.* Lanham, Maryland: The Scarecrow Press, Inc., 2004.
Hirsch, Foster. *Edward G. Robinson.* New York: Pyramid, 1976.
McCabe, John. *Cagney.* New York: Carroll and Graf Publishers, Inc., 1997.
McGilligan, Patrick. *Cagney: The Actor as Auteur.* New York: A. S. Barnes and Company, 1975.
Parish, James Robert, and Alvin H. Marill. *The Cinema of Edward G. Robinson.* New York: A.S. Barnes, 1972.
Sperber, A. M., and Eric Lax. *Bogart.* New York: William Morrow and Company, Inc., 1997.

Books on the History of the Cinema

Balio, Tino, ed. *The American Film Industry*. Rev. ed. Madison: University of Wisconsin Press, 1985.

Buhle, Paul, and Dave Wagner. *Radical Hollywood: The Untold Story Behind America's Favorite Movies*. New York: The New Press, 2002.

Everson, William K. *Classics of the Horror Film*. Secaucus, N.J.: Citadel Press, 1974.

Grobel, Lawrence. *The Hustons*. New York: Charles Scribner's Sons, 1989.

Hirshhorn, Clive. *The Warner Bros. Story*. New York: Crown, 1979.

McBride, Joseph. *Hawks on Hawks*. Berkeley: University of California Press, 1982.

McBride, Joseph. *Searching for John Ford*. New York: St. Martin's Press, 2001.

McGilligan, Patrick, and Paul Buhle. *Tender Comrades: A Backstory of the Hollywood Blacklist*. New York: St. Martin's Press, 1997.

Nollen, Scott Allen. *Boris Karloff: A Gentleman's Life*. Baltimore: Midnight Marquee Press, 1999.

Parish, James Robert. *The Tough Guys*. Carlstadt, N.J.: Rainbow Books, 1976.

Schatz, Thomas. *The Genius of the System: Hollywood Filmmaking in the Studio Era*. New York: Pantheon Books, 1988.

Sennett, Ted. *Warner Brothers Presents*. New Rochelle, N.Y.: Arlington House, 1971.

Literature

Hammett, Dashiell. *The Maltese Falcon*. Franklin Center, Pennsylvania: The Franklin Library, 1987.

Wilson, John Dover, ed. *The Complete Works of William Shakespeare*. London: Octopus Books Limited, 1981.

Index

Numbers in ***bold italics*** indicate pages with photographs.

Abel, Walter 130
Academy of Motion Picture Arts and Sciences (AMPAS) 50
Across the Pacific (1942 film) 1, 233, 236–239, ***237***, 240, 347
Action in the North Atlantic (1943 film) 247–***249***, 314, 347
Actors and Sin (1950 film) 319
Acuff, Eddie 100, 111
Adler, Luther 327–328
Adolphi, John G. 18–19
The Adventures of Robin Hood (1938 film) 94, 139, 201, 242
The African Queen (1951 film) 316
After All (play) 41
Albee, Edward 231
Albert, Eddie 2, 51–52, 190–***191***, 205, ***207***
Alderson, Erville 195
Aldrich, Robert 319
Alexander, John 100, 102
Alexander, Ross 94, 108
Alison, Joan 233
All My Sons (1949 film) 293
All Quiet on the Western Front (1930 film) 21
All Through the Night (1942 film) 2, 224–227, ***226***, 239, 335, 347
Allen, Barbara Jo 227
Allen, Lewis 320
Allen, Woody 228
Alper, Murray 235
Alperson, Edward L. 98, 137
The Amazing Dr. Clitterhouse (1938 film) 1, 131–134, ***132***, 139, 181, 346
American Film Institute (AFI) 5–6
American League for Peace and Democracy 106
American Legion 106
Ames, Jean 225
Amy, George 77
"And the Band Played On" (song) 198, 201
Anderson, Eddie ("Rochester") 156
Anderson, Maxwell 12, 14, 294
Andrews, Patty 332
Andrews, Robert Hardy 109
Angel Street (play) 255
Angels with Dirty Faces (1938 film) 113, 137–145, ***138***, ***142***, 147, 155, 158–159, 169, 187, 201, 311, 346
"Angels with Dirty Faces" (1939 radio show) 142
Ankrum, Morris 312

Anti-Nazi League 106, 152
Apfel, Oscar 38
Arbuckle, Roscoe ("Fatty") 10, 14
Archer, John 305
Arden, Eve 211
Argus, Edwin 22
Arlen, Richard 51, 53
Arliss, Florence 29
Arliss, George 28–29, ***29***
Armstrong, Robert 88
Arnold, Edward 54
Arnold, Jack 319
Arnow, Max 120
Arriaga, Antonio 284
Arsenic and Old Lace (play) 126, 255, 314
Arthur, Chester A. 56
Arthur, Jean 85
"As Time Goes By" (song) 240, 242
Astaire, Fred 228
Astor, Mary 6, 28, 59, 61, ***80***–81, 106, 214–215, 217, ***219***–221, 233, 236–238, ***237***, 239
"Avalon" (song) 242
Aylesworth, Arthur 83
Ayres, Lew 2, 20–22, ***21***

Baby Mine (play) 14
Bacall, Lauren (wife of HB) v, 255–263, ***260***, 265–275, ***267***, 277–282, ***278***–279, ***281***, 284, 293–296, 298, 300–302, ***301***, 314, 316–317; on *Dark Passage* 278; on Humphrey Bogart 256–257, 263, 317–318; on *To Have and Have Not* 261
Bacon, Lloyd 61–62, 66, 76–77, 85, 90, 92, 94, 114–115, 118, 124, 130, 134, 147, 150, 165–168, 180–181, 228, 247–248
Bad Men of Missouri (1941 film) 213
Bad Sister (1931 film) 41
Baer, Max 187
Baker, Carroll 324
Baker, Tommy 182
Baldwin, Earl 85, 91, 123, 126
Baldwin, Faith 129
Ball, Lucille 195, 293
Bancroft, George 138–139, 157
Bandick, Clara 206
Barbary Coast (1935 film) 85, 94, 97
Bardette, Trevor 150, 272
The Barefoot Contessa (1954 film) 317
Barker, Kate ("Ma") 86, 303

Barlowe, Joy 269
Barrat, Robert 62, 66, 73, 83–84, 111
Barrow, Clyde 86
Barrymore, John 15, 43, 63
Barrymore, Lionel 294, 296, 298, ***301***–302
Barty, Billy 94
Basserman, Albert 172, 190
Battle Circus (1953 film) 316
"The Battle Cry of Freedom" (song) 175
The Battle of San Pietro (1945 film) 254, 297
Battleship Potemkin (1925 film) 247
Baum, W. Carter 90
Baxter, Alan 157
The Beast with Five Fingers (1946 film) 246
Beat the Devil (1953 film) 316
The Beautiful and the Damned (1924 film) 15
Beavers, Louis 104
Beddoe, Don 314
Bedoya, Alfonso 284–285, 287
Beery, Noah, Sr. 29
Beethoven, Ludwig van 110, 193
Beiderbecke, Bix 142
Belasco, David 17
Bellamy, Ralph 1, 61–62, 134–136, 181
The Bells (play) 9
The Bells of Conscience (EGR play) 9
Bennett, Bruce 279, 284–285, 289
Bennett, Joan 103
Bercovicci, Leonardo 130
Bergman, Ingrid 239–***245***, ***243***
Berkeley, Busby 66–69, 128–129
Bernard, Barry 275
Bernhardt, Curtis 251
Best, Edna 190
Best, Willie ("Sleep 'n' Eat") 195, 250
Bethune, Mary McLeod 246
Bezzerides, I.A. 183
Biberman, Abner 158, 162
Bickford, Charles 12
Big City Blues (1932 film) 41, ***52***, 345
Big Leaguer (1953 film) 319
The Big Shot (1942 film) 233–236, ***235***, 347
The Big Sleep (1946 film) 1, 255, 261–263, 266–275, ***267***, 315–316, 347

353

Big Town (radio show) 120
The Big Trail (1930 film) 159
Biggers, Earl Derr 28
The Biggest Bundle of Them All (1968 film) 325–326
"Bill Bailey, Won't You Please Come Home?" (song) 198
Bioff, Willie 156
Birth of a Nation (1915 film) 159
Bishop, William A. ("Billy") 224, 247
Black, Maurice 25
The Black Cat (1934 film) 217
Black Legion (1937 film) 2, 110–113, *111*, 346
The Black Mask (magazine) 214
Black Tuesday (1954 film) 320
Blackmail (1939 film) 171
Blackmer, Sidney 25
Blake, Robert 285
Blanke, Henry 93, 132, 214, 247, 283
"Bless 'Em All" (song) 224
Blessed Event (1933 film) 50
Block, Ralph 73
Blonde Crazy (1931 film) 39–41, *39*, 42, 345
Blondell, Joan 17–19, 27–28, *39*, 44, 46, *52*, 53, 59, 66–*69*, 75–*78*, 103–104, 106, *107*, 120, 325
Blood on the Sun (1945 film) 233
Blue, Monte 238, 296
Blues in the Night (1941 film) 189
"Blues in the Night" (song) 249
Blumenstock, Mort 254
Body and Soul (1931 film) 41
Bogart, Dr. Belmont (father of HB) 12–13, 84
Bogart, Humphrey v, *52*, *54*, *101*, *105*, *107*, *108*, *111*, *115*, *117*, *119*, *123*, *126*, *128*, *131*, *132*, *143*, *148*, *155*, *166*, *176*, *181*, *184*, *194*, *197*, *207*, *216*, *219*, *226*, *235*, *243*, *245*, *249*, *253*, *260*, *264*, *267*, *276*, *278*, *281*, *286*, *292*, *301*, *313*, *315*; Academy Award 316; on acting 316; alcohol abuse 14, 84, 251, 262, 284; birth 12; childhood 12; death 318; early films 17; education 12–13; on Jack Warner 316; marriages 14, 17, 110, 116, 155, 257, 263; military service 13; political beliefs and activities 71, 194–195, 266, 275, 277, 293; as sailor 13, 227, 284–285; stage performances 13–14, 84, 99–100; on *The Treasure of the Sierra Madre* 291, 294; on Warner Bros. 316; World War II tour 254
Bogart, Maude Humphrey (mother of HB) 12–13, 207–208
Bogdanovich, Peter 306, 311
Boland, Mary 13, 17
Bonaparte, Napoleon 110, 118
Bond, Ward 2, 86, 100, 133, *148*, 153, 175, 187, 210–*212*, 215, 217, *219*, 221, 266, 283, 327–328, 337–339, 341

Booth, John Wilkes 159
Booth, Shirley 14
Borg, Veda Ann 119
Borzage, Raymond 64
Boteler, Wade 200
Bowker, Aldrich 206
Boy Meets Girl (1938 film) 1, 134–136, *135*, 141, 346
A Boy Ten Feet Tall (1965 film) 325
Boyer, Charles 294
Boylan, Malcolm Stuart 85
Boyle, Johnny 98, 230, 233, 331
Boys Town (1938 film) 141
Brackett, Leigh 261–263
Bradley, Harry C. 69
Brady, Alice 13, 17
Brady, William, Jr. 13–14, 84
Brady, William, Sr. 13–14
Brand, Neville 328
Brando, Marlon 189, 337
Brandon, Henry 2–3, 110–113
Brecher, Egon 111, 210
Breen, Joseph 83, 119, 294
Brennan, Walter 257–258, *260*–261
Brent, George 130–*131*, 150–151, 154, 168–*169*, 239
Brian, Mary 57–59, *58*
The Bride Came C.O.D. (1941 film) 208–209, 347
Bright, John 30–31, 34, 39, 44, 53–54, 71, 118
The Bright Shawl (1922 film) 10, 16
Brincken, William von 247
Broadway's Like That (1930 film) 17
Broderick, Johnny 103
Brodie, Steve 328
Bromfield, Louis 177
Brooks, Richard 294–295
Brophy, Edward 123, 225, 227
Brother Orchid (1940 film) 1, 152, 180–183, *181*, 346
Brown, Charles D. 182, 266
Brown, Joe E. 90, 93–94
Brown, Rowland 137
Browning, Tod 17
Bruce, Nigel 190–191, 276–277
Bruce, Virginia 48–49
Bryan, Jane 115, 117, 124–*125*, 157, 165–*166*
Bryan, William Jennings 56
Buchalter, Louis ("Lepke") 314, 316
Buckner, Robert 150, 155, 228–229, 233, 239
A Bullet for Joey (1954 film) 320
Bullets or Ballots (1936 film) 103–*107*, *105*, 117, 120, 346
"Bullets or Ballots" (1939 radio show) 106
Burgess, Dorothy 44
Burke, Frankie 138
Burke, James 227
Burnett, Murray 233
Burnett, W.R. 23, 25–26, 73, 193–194, 320
Burnside, Norman 134, 171

Busch, Niven 44, 81
Busley, Jessie 177
Butler, David 249, 318
"By a Waterfall" (song) 68
Byron, Arthur 65, *80*

Cabin in the Sky (stage show) 240
Cagney, Carolyn Nelson ("Carrie") (mother of JC) 10–11, 198
Cagney, Casey (adopted daughter of JC) 186
Cagney, Edward (brother of JC) 10
Cagney, Frances Willard Vernon ("Willie") (wife of JC) 11, 42, 97, 186
Cagney, Harry (brother of JC) 10
Cagney, James 3, *21*, *27*, *30*, *32*, *35*, *39*, *43*, *45*, *47*, *58*, *63*, *64*, *72*, *76*, *78*, *79*, *84*, *86*, *87*, *89*, *92*, *97*, *135*, *138*, *142*, *143*, *148*, *156*, *157*, *161*, *179*, *200*, *223*, *231*, *234*, *305*, *310*, *328*, *333*, *340*, *341*; Academy Award 233, 311; on acting 342–343; on Anatole Litvak 186; on *Angels with Dirty Faces* 137–138; birth 10; as boxer 11, *47*–49, 186–189, *188*; on *Captains of the Clouds* 222; childhood 10–11; children of 186; on *City for Conquest* 186; dance school of 12, 17; as dancer 11, 12, 17, 68–*69*; death 7, 343; education 11; on Edward G. Robinson 34; as farmer 342; on *The Fighting 69th* 168; on *G-Men* 86; on George Arliss 28; on George Raft 156; as guitarist *150*, 337; on Hollywood 342–343; marriage 11; on *The Oklahoma Kid* 148; on *Picture Snatcher* 62; political beliefs and activities 71–72; Screen Actors Guild (SAG) activism 65, 76, 86, 90, 116; on screen fights 18, 62, 84; on screen violence 342; on *Sinner's Holiday* 18; on *Smart Money* 34; stage performances 11–12; on *Taxi!* 48; on *Yankee Doodle Dandy* 228
Cagney, James (adopted son of JC) 186
Cagney, James, Sr. (father of JC) 10–11, 332
Cagney, Jeanne (sister of JC) 11, 229, *231*, 233, 336
Cagney, William ("Bill") (brother of JC) 10, 49–50, 134, 168, 186, 228, 233, 303, 327, 331, 334
Cagney Productions 233, 303, 327
Caine, Georgia 132
The Caine Mutiny (1954 film) 317
Caites, Joe 124
Calhern, Louis 40, 81, 173
California Christian Church Council 106
Campbell, Colin 275
Campbell, Frankie 187
Cane, Charles 64
Cannery and Agricultural Workers Industrial Union (CAWIU) 72

Cantor, Eddie 249–250
Capone, Al 16, 23–24, 31, 41, 156, 302
Capra, Frank 50, 152, 208, 239, 320
Captain Blood (1935 film) 94, 201
Captains of the Clouds (1942 film) 222–224, **223**, 347
Carey, Harry 118, 206
Carey, Harry, Jr. ("Dobe") 324, 339
Carmichael, Hoagy 43, 142, 256, 258, 261
Carnera, Primo 187
Carpenter, Elliott 240
Carradine, John 324
Carse, Betty 53
Carson, Jack 199, 208, 250, 274, 318
Carson, Kit 147
Carter, Ann 275
Caruso, David 7
Casablanca (1942 film) 6, 141, 177, 201, 224–226, 236, 239–246, **243**, **245**, 250–251, 253–257, 316, 347
Cassavetes, John 6
Cassell, Wally 304
Catlett, Walter 53, 210
Cavanaugh, Hobart 73, 113
Ceiling Zero (1936 film) 96–97, 346
Ceiling Zero (play) 96
Chain Lightning (1949 film) 312–314, **313**, 347
Chalked Out (play) 155
Chandler, Chick 235
Chandler, Raymond 255, 261–263
Chaney, Lon, Jr. 335
Chaney, Lon, Sr. 17, 307, 342
Chang, Anna 42
Chaplin, Charles 10, 92
Charters, Spencer 127
Cheyenne Autumn (1964 film) 323–**326**, 347
"Chicago" (song) 60
China Clipper (1936 film) 108–109, 346
Chodorov, Edward 64
Churchill, Berton 60
Churchill, Marguerite 100
Churchill, Winston 223–224, 265
Cianelli, Eduardo 114
The Cincinnati Kid (1965 film) 325
Citizen Kane (1941 film) 5–6, 220–221
City for Conquest (1940 film) 186–**189**, 188, 346
Clark, Cliff 205
Clark, Dane 247
Clark, Fred 309
Clark, Pat 272
Clark, Wallace 232
Clarke, Mae v, 1–3, 31–32, **32**, 59, 68–**72**, **80**–82, 98, 342
Clayton, Richard 196
Clement, Clay 158
Cleveland, Grover 56, 148
Cline, Eddie 23

Cline, Wilfred M. 222
Clive, E.E. 109–110
Clute, Chester 231
Cochran, Steve 304, 311
The Cocoanuts (1929 film) 66
Cohan, George M. 10, 12, 228–233, 327, 342
Cohan, Jerry 229–230
Cohan, Josie 229, 232
Cohan, Nellie 229–230
Cohen, Sammy 168
Cohn, Harry 85
Colbert, Claudette 16
Collier, William, Jr. 25
Collins, Frank J. 320
Collins, G. Pat 165, 308
Columbia Pictures 41, 85, 99, 220, 246, 248–249, 274, 283, 314, 316–318, 320–321, 326
Come Fill the Cup (1951 film) 332–**333**, 347
Committee for the First Amendment (CFA) v, 293, 296
Committee for the Protection of the Foreign Born 246
Compton, Joyce 211
Conan Doyle, Sir Arthur 146
Conference of Studio Unions 265, 293
Confessions of a Nazi Spy (1939 film) 2, 152–154, **153**, 171, 205, 346
Confidential Agent (1945 film) 263, 265
Conflict (1945 film) 250–251, 254, 263–265, **264**, 275, 347
Cook, Donald 31
Cook, Elisha, Jr. 215, 217, 220, 262
Cooke, Ray 44
Coolidge, Calvin 159
Cooper, Gary 266, 283, 293, 311, 318, 334
Coppola, Francis Ford 6, 25
Corbett, James J. ("Cinderella Man") 187
Cording, Harry 252
Cormack, Bart 16
Corrigan, Emmett 56
Cortez, Ricardo 80–82, 94, 100, 218
Cosmopolitan Productions 96
Cowan, Jerome 178, 189, 197, 215, 218
Cradle Snatchers (play) 14
Cramer, Richard 40
Craven, Frank 77, 187
Crawford, Broderick 227, **229**
Crawford, Joan 152, 318
Crehan, Joseph 155, 163, 227
Crime School (1938 film) **126**–128, 141, 155, 346
The Criminal Code (1930 film) 288
Crisp, Donald 132, 149, 173, 182, 266
Croft, Douglas 231
Cromwell, John 274
Cronyn, Hume 293
Crosby, Bing 78–79, 142, 321
Crouse, Russel 126

The Crowd Roars (1932 film) 44–46, **45**, 162, 345
Crusade for Freedom 319
Curtis, Alan 195
Curtis, Ken 324, 339
Curtiz, Michael 6, 18, 74, 76, 94, 99, 116, 137–**144**, 155, 163, 174, 176–177, 201–204, 222–224, 229–233, 240–245, 250–251, 254, 274, 317–318
Custer, General George 250

Dailey, Dan 334
The Daily Worker (newspaper) 130–131, 293
The Dain Curse (novel) 214
Dalio, Marcel 259
Daly, George 24
Dalya, Jacqueline 287
Damita, Lili 95
The Dancing Town (1927 film) 14
D'Andrea, Tom 278
Daniels, Bebe 56
Daniels, William 322
"Danny Boy" (song)
Dantine, Helmut 243, 250, 252
Dark Hazard (1934 film) 68, 73–**74**, 345
Dark Passage (1947 film) 274, 277–282, **278**, **281**, 347
The Dark Road (novel) 277
Dark Victory (1939 film) 150–151, 154, 346
"Darktown Strutter's Ball" (song) 42
Darrin, Sonia 268
Darkness at Noon (play) 319
Darro, Frankie 63–**64**
Darwin, Charles 202
Da Silva, Howard **203**, 234
Davenport, Harry 208, 227
Daves, Delmer 274, 277–278, 280
Davidson, William B. 228
Davies, Joseph B. 240, 265
Davies, Marian 96, 134
Davis, Bette 2, 3, 41, 53, 74–75, 90, 99–103, **101**, 110, 114–118, **115**, **117**, 150–151, 154, 207–209, 236, 239, 249–250, 255
Davis, Luther 334
Davis, Sammy, Jr. 321
Davis, Virginia 53
Day, Doris 142, 318, 331–332, 336, 342
Day, Shirley 47
Dead End (1937 film) 120, 133
"Dead End" Kids 20, 64, 120, 124, **126**–127, 138–141, 155, 164, 167
Dead Reckoning (1946 film) 274
Deadline U.S.A. (1952 film) 316
De Camp, Rosemary 229, **231**
de Corsia, Ted 314
Deering, John 152, 160
de Havilland, Olivia 90–93, 198, 200, 239, 249
Dekker, Albert 320
Dell, Gabriel 126, 139
del Rio, Dolores 323, 325

Del Ruth, Roy 39, 42, 47–49, 59–61, 68, 215, 331, 333–334
Demarest, William 225–*226*
DeMille, Cecil B. 142, 320
DeNiro, Robert 189
DeQuincey, Thomas 202
The Desperate Hours (1955 film) 317
Destroyer (1943 film) 246
Deutsch, Adolph 121, 225
"Deutschland Uber Alles" (song) 153, 225, 241
The Devil and Daniel Webster (1932 film) 288
Devil Dogs of the Air (1935 film) 81, 85–*87*, 113, 222–223, 345
The Devil with Women (1930 film) 17
Devil's Island (1940 film) 120, 251–252, 254
Devine, Andy 178–*179*
Dewey, Thomas E. 114–115
Diaz, Porfirio 10
Dickson, Gloria 130, 142
Dies, Martin 152, 186, 194–195, 283
Dieterle, William 93, 113, 171, 173–174
Dietrich, Marlene 209–213
Digges, Dudley 64, 215
Dillinger, John 86, 90, 196
"Dinah" (song) 43
Dinehart, Alan 75
Disney, Walt 266, 326
A Dispatch from Reuters (1940 film) 2, 171, 180, 189–*191*, 205, 207, 346
Dmytryk, Edward 317
Dr. Ehrlich's Magic Bullet (1938 film) 1, 113, 134, 151–152, 171–*174*, 172, 183, 190, 205, 346
Dr. Socrates (1935 film) 85, 145
Doctor X (1932 film) 163
Dodd, Claire 58, 66–67, *69*
Dodge City (1939 film) 155, 174, 176
Dodsworth (1936 film) 288
Don Juan (1926 film) 15
Donde, Manuel 290
Donnelly, Ruth 57–59, *58*, 123, *125*
Donovan, King 333
Donovan, William ("Wild Bill") 168
Doorway to Hell (1930 film) 2, 5, 20–23, *21*, 30, 86, 345
Dorn, Philip 252, 254
Double Indemnity (1944 film) 283
Douglas, Gordon 322
Douglas, Helen Gahagan 294
Douglas, Kirk 142, 317
Douglas, Melvyn 152, 195, 294
Downing, Joe 124, 155–156, 228, 234
Dracula (1931 film) 21, 29
Drake, Charles 263
"The Dreamer" (song) 250
Drifting (play) 13–14
Dru, Joanne 273, 320, *322*
Duff, Warren 137, 150, 158, 167

Duffy, Rev. Francis 168, 170
Dumbrille, Douglas 58, 69, 175
Dunn, Emma 73, 157
Dunne, Irene 266, 293
Dvorak, Ann 45–46, *45*, 53–55, *54*, 86, 88, 90
Dyer, Elmer 222

Each Dawn I Die (1939 film) 113, 156–158, *157*, 166, 200, 346
"Each Dawn I Die" (1943 radio show) 158
East Is West (1930 film) 17
"East Side, West Side" (song) 138, 187
The Ebb Tide (1937 film) 205
The Ebb Tide (novel) 205
Eburne, Maude 40, 80
Edeson, Arthur 156, 218, 220, 242
The Edgar Bergen and Charlie McCarthy Show (radio show) 178
Ehrlich, Hedwig 183
Ehrlich, Dr. Paul 134, 171, 174, 183
Einfeld, S. Charles 186, 193
Eisenhower, Dwight D. 316
Eisenstein, Sergei 247
Eldredge, John *80*, 145, 197
Elliott, Robert 21, 38
Ellis, Patricia 62, 83–*84*
Elsom, Elizabeth 275
Eltz, Theodore von 269
End of Poverty in California (EPIC) 72
The Enforcer (1951 film) 314–316, *315*, 347
Enright, Ray 83, 109, 205–206, 213
Epstein, Julius 198, 208, 224, 228–229, 233, 239–240
Epstein, Philip 198, 208, 224, 228–229, 233, 239–240
Erickson, Carl 55
Erwin, Stuart 96, 208
Esway, Alexander 110
Etting, Ruth 336
Evans, Madge 63–*64*
Every Sailor (stage show) 11

The Face Behind the Mask (1940 film) 220
Fadden, Tom 273
Fairbanks, Douglas, Jr. 25, *26*, 36, 109
Fairbanks, Douglas, Sr. 159
Falk, Peter 322
Farrell, Charles 17, 41
Farrell, Glenda v, 25–*26*, 53, 73–*74*
Farrell, Midge 3, 6–7, 65
Faulkner, William 256, 261–263
Faylen, Frank 233
Fazenda, Louise 121
Federal Bureau of Investigation (FBI) 86–90, 152, 246, 304, 319
Federal Communications Commission (FCC) 108
Feldman, Charles 263, 270–271
Fenton, Leslie 32, 41, 69
Fessier, Michael 177

Fetchit, Stepin 79
Fields, Lew 11–12
Fields, Stanley 26
Fields of Glory (1920 film) 10
The Fighting 69th (1940 film) 113, 168–170, *169*, 222, 332, 346
"The Final Problem" (short story) 146
Finkel, Abem 110, 114
Finn, Jonathan 155
Fisher, Fred 60
Fitts, Burton 186, 194
Fitzgerald, Barry 201, 205
Fitzgerald, Ella 240
Fitzgerald, F. Scott 15
Fitzgerald, Geraldine 151
Fitzroy, Emily *80*
Five Star Final (1931 film) 37–39, 63, 106–108, 345
Flaherty, Pat 200, 318
Flavin, James 264, 270, 339
Flesh and Fantasy (1943 film) 246
Flint, Helen 112
Florey, Robert 220
Floyd, Charles ("Pretty Boy") 86–87
Flynn, Errol 94–95, 136, 151, 155, 174–177, *176*, 201, 249–250, 265, 319
Flynn, Rita 32
Foch, Nina 320–*321*
Fonda, Henry v, 51, 152, 195, 215, 293, 317, 337–342, *340*, *341*
Fonda, Jane 342
Fontaine, Joan 277
Foo, Lee Tung 238
Footlight Parade (1933 film) 66–*69*, 332, 345
For Whom the Bell Tolls (1943 film) 240
Foran, Dick 100–*101*, 110, 134, 168
Forbstein, Leo F. 103
Ford, Glenn 320
Ford, Francis 325
Ford, John 2, 17, 85, 152, 175, 181, 205, 220–221, 266, 300, 320, 323–326, 334, 337–342
Forman, Milos 342
Forty-five Minutes from Broadway (stage show) 232
42nd Street (1933 film) 66
Foster, Preston 47, 213
Fox Film Corporation 41, 159
Foy, Brian 106–108, 120
Francen, Victor 251
Francis, Anne 2, *334*–335
Francis, Kay 66–*67*, 145–*147*
Francis, Noel 34
Frankenstein (1931 film) 19, 21, 34, 71
Franklin, Dean 168
Franklin, Dwight 94
Franz, Dennis 7
Frawley, William 209
"Free and Equal Blues" 262
Freeman, Everett 227
Freund, Karl 295–296
Friderici, Blanche 41

The Frisco Kid (1935 film) 94–**97**, 346
Frye, Dwight 21, 215
Fulton, Maude 215
Fung, Willie 42
Furthman, Jules 256

G-Men (1935 film) 86–90, **89**, 345–346
Gabin, Jean 251
Gable, Clark 23, 240, 266
The Gallant Hours (1960 film) 342
Gardiner, Reginald 222
Gardner, Ava 293, 317
Garfield, John 14, 134, 156, 171, 191–192, 195, 201, **203**, 205, 208, 249–250, 262, 265, 285
Gargan, Edward 127
Garland, Judy 262
Garson, Robert 237
Gateson, Marjorie 69
Gaudio, Antonio ("Tony") 51, 116
Gauss, Carl Friederich 189
The Gentle People (play) 208
George, Gladys 160–**161**, 215–**216**, 220
George, Grace 13
George Washington, Jr. (stage show) 232
"Georgia on My Mind" (song) 43
German-American Bund 106, 151–154
Gershwin, Ira v, 274
"Get Happy" (song) 23
Gibson, Wynne 12
Gilbert, Edwin 224
Gilbert, John 66, 227
Gilmore, Art 230
Gish, Dorothy 10
"Give My Regards to Broadway" (song) 232
Glasmon, Kubec 30–31, 34, 39, 53–54
The Glass Key (novel) 214
The Glass Web (1953 film) 319
Gleason, Jackie 225
Gleason, James 98, 332–333
Gleason, Lucile 98
God Is My Co-Pilot (1945 film) 261
Goddard, Paulette 293, 319
The Godfather (1972 film) 7, 25, 32–33
Godfrey, Arthur 342
Godfrey, Peter 263, 275
Goebbels, Dr. Joseph 2, 153
Goff, Ivan 303
Gold Diggers of 1933 (1933 film) 66
Goldenberg, Morris (father of EGR) 9
Goldwyn, Samuel 10, 85, 94, 97, 120, 133, 240
Gombell, Minna 195
Gomez, Felipa 297
Gomez, Thomas 297, 302
Gone with the Wind (1939 film) 151
Good Neighbor Sam (1964 film) 321
Goodis, David 277–278

Goodman, Benny v, 293
Goodwin, Harold 23
Gorcey, Leo 126, 138–139, 167
Gordon, Gavin 58
Gordon, Mary 90–**92**, 113
Gordon, Ruth 171–**172**, 248
Gould, William 196
Goulding, Edmund 150, 154
Graetz, Paul 109
Grand National Pictures 98, 116, 137
Grand Street Follies of 1928 (stage show) 17
Granstedt, Greta 314
Grant, Cary 256, 277
Grant, Ulysses S. 56
Grapewin, Charlie 100
Gray, Joe 188
Gray, Mack 209
Great Guy (1936 film) 98
The Great O'Malley (1937 film) 110, 346
The Great Train Robbery (1903 film) 15
Green, Alfred E. 34, 55, 65
Greenstreet, Sydney 214, 217, 219–221, 236–237, 242, 250–252, 263–**264**, 277, 318
Gribbon, Harry 12
Griffith, D.W. 159, 320
Grube, Arthur 295
Gugler, Eric 230
Guilfolye, Paul 307

Haade, William 117, 297
Hagan, James 198
Haines, William Wister 110
Hale, Alan 168–**169**, 175–**176**, 185, 198–**200**, 210, 222, 224, 247, **249**–250
Hale, Alan, Jr. 332
Hale, Barbara 335
Hall, Huntz 126, 139, 164
Hall, Porter 100
Hall, Thurston 133, 156
Haller, Ernest 163
Halloran, John 328
Halop, Billy 126, 139, 155
Halton, Charles 172, 238
Hamilton, John 220
Hamilton, Margaret 124
Hamilton, Neil 13, **22**, 23
Hammett, Dashiell 6, 214–221, 233, 283
Hanlon, Bert 125
Hansen, Chuck 86
Hard to Handle (1933 film) 57–59, **58**, 345
The Harder They Fall (1956 film) 317
Harding, Warren G. 138
Hardwicke, Cedric 131
Hardy, Oliver 2
Hari, Wilfred 173
Harlow, Jean **30**, 32–33, 72
Harmon, John 124, 264
Harolde, Ralf 34, 49, 62, 201
Harper's Bazaar (magazine) 255
Harrigan, William 88

Harris, Jed 12
Harris, Sybil 127
Harrison, Benjamin 148–149
Hart, Gordon 110
Hart, Lorenz 230, 232
Hartley, Esdras 118
Harvey, Lew 150
Harvey, Paul 100, 124
The Hatchet Man (1932 film) 41–**42**, 81, 178, 345
Hatton, Raymond 69
Hawks, Howard 42, 44–46, 50–52, 85, 96–97, 156, 239, 255–258, 260–263, 265–275, 280, 311; on *The Big Sleep* 262–263; on Humphrey Bogart 45, 256–257; on James Cagney 45; on *To Have and Have Not* 255
Hawks, Nancy ("Slim") 257
Hayden, Harry 107
Hayes, Helen 14
Hayes, Sam 197
Hayle, Grace 68
Hayward, Leland 337
Hayward, Louis 194
Hayward, Susan 317
Hayworth, Rita 198–199, 201, 262
He Was Her Man (1934 film) 76–**78**, 345
Hearst, William Randolph 6, 9, 72, 96, 247
Hecht, Ben 62–63, 134, 319
Heggen, Thomas 336, 340–341
Heggie, O.P. 84
Heindorf, Ray 318
Heisler, Stuart 312
Hell on Frisco Bay (1955 film) 320, **322**, 347
Hellinger, Mark 159, 163, 183, 193, 209, 239, 247
Hell's Bells (play) 14
Hemingway, Ernest 255
Henreid, Paul v, 239–240, 245, 293
Hepburn, Audrey 317
Hepburn, Katharine 316
Herald, Heinz 171
Herbert, Hugh 93–94, 129
Here Comes the Navy (1934 film) 77–81, **79**, 85, 113, 248, 345
Hernandez, Juano 142
Heston, Charlton 326, 342
Heyburn, Weldon 127
Heydt, Jean 269
Heydt, Louis Jean 158
Heyes, Herbert 330
Hickman, Howard C. 108
Hickox, Sid 107, 118, 256, 277–278, 295
High Sierra (1941 film) 1, 168, 193–198, **194**, **197**, 201, 205, 213, 226, 229, 311, 346
Hinds, Samuel S. 112
Hirohito 238
Hitchcock, Alfred 191, 277
Hitler, Adolf 106, 152, 154, 159, 171, 224, 227, 232, 251
Hobart, Rose 263
Hoch, Winton C. 222, 338

Hodgson, Leland 277
Hoffman, Max, Jr. 200
Hogan, Dick 248
Hohl, Arthur 75–**76**
Holden, William 165–168, **166**, 317
A Hole in the Head (1959 film) 320–321
The Hole in the Wall (1928 film) 16
Holiday Inn (1941 film) 79
Hollywood Fights Back (radio show) 293
Hollywood Hotel (radio show) 106
Hollywood Victory Committee 233, 251
Holmes, Brown 73, 215
Holmes, Stuart 148
Holt, Jack 284, 287
Holt, Tim 284–**286**, 292
Holy Terror (1931 film) 41
"Home on the Range" (song) 66
"Honeymoon Hotel" (song) 68
"Hong Kong Blues" (song) 259
Hoover, Herbert 56, 60, 106, 159, 322
Hoover, J. Edgar 86–87, 89–90, 237–238, 304
Hope, Bob 342
Hopkins, Arthur 84
Hopkins, Miriam 85, 175–176
Hopton, Russell 60, 69, 77, **89**
Horman, Arthur T. 222
Horne, Lena 240
Hoskins, Allen ("Farina") 64
House Committee on Un-American Activities (HUAC) 5, 68, 86, 186, 266, 292–293, 296, 302, 319
House of Strangers (1949 film) 318
How Green Was My Valley (1941 film) 221
Howard, Leslie 99–103, **101**, 120, 251, 255
Howe, James Wong 150, 171, 173, 178, 232, 254
Huber, Harold 65, 77, 124, 155
Hughes, Howard 255
Hughes, John 97
Hull, Henry 196
Hull, Warren 100
Hunter, Ian 93
Hupfeld, Herman 240
Huston, John v, **1**, 3, 6, 131–132, 134, 137, 171, 174, 193–195, 201, 214–221, 233, 236–237, 254, 266, 274–275, 283–302, **293**, 314, 316–318; on *The Maltese Falcon* 214–216
Huston, Walter 195, 215, 229, **231**, 246, 284, 287–288, **292**, 294, 314
Hymer, Warren 19

I Am a Fugitive from a Chain Gang (1932 film) 26, 112, 160, 171
I Am the Law (1938 film) 134
"I Don't Want to Play in Your Yard" (song) 148
I Loved a Woman (1934 film) 65–**67**, 345
Ibsen, Henrik 9

"Ice Cold Katie" (song) 250
I'd Rather Be Right (stage show) 230, 232
Illegal (1955 film) 320–**321**, 347
"I'm Forever Blowing Bubbles" (song) 33, 63, 160, 178
Impatient Maiden (1932 film) 71
In a Lonely Place (1950 film) 314
In Old Arizona (1929 film) 159
In This Our Life (1942 film) 236
Ince, Ralph 41
Inescourt, Frieda 113
International Alliance of Theatrical Stage Employees (IATSE) 156, 265
International Labor Defense (ILD) 71
Invisible Stripes (1940 film) 165–168, **166**, 185, 346
Invitation to Murder (play) 84
The Irish in Us (1935 film) 90–93, **92**, 346
The Iron Horse (1924 film) 325
Islas, Francisco 290
Isle of Fury (1936 film) 108–110, 346
It All Came True (1940 film) 177, 346
"It Had to Be You" (song) 124, 241
It's a Great Feeling (1949 film) 318–319, 347
It's a Wise Child (play) 17

Jackson, Horace 129
Jackson, Selmer 48
Jackson, Thomas 25, 270
Jacobs, William 109
Jacquet, Frank 127
James, Henry 9
Janney, Leon 20
Janney, William 47
Jason, Sybil 113
Jaws (1975 film) 50
The Jazz Singer (1927 film) 15–16
Jenkins, Allen 11, **54**–55, 57, 63–65, 75, 83, 91–92, 94, 114, 121, **123**–124, 131–**132**, 181, 321
Jewell, Isabell 97, 114
Jezebel (1938 film) 151, 215
Jimenez, Soledad 118
Jimmy the Gent (1934 film) 74–**76**, 345
Johann, Zita 2, **50**–51
Johnny Come Lately (1943 film) 233
Johnson, Ben 324
Joiner, Patricia 315
Jolson, Al 16, 17, 66, 250
Jones, Dickie 112
Jones, Jennifer 316
Jones, John Paul 168
Jones, Spike 121
Jordan, Bobby 124, 126, 139
Jory, Victor 77, 94, 156
Joseph, Edmund 228
Juarez (1939 film) 134
Juarez, Benito 134
Juarez and Maximilian (play) 10, 133

Kai-shek, Chiang 238
Karloff, Boris 19, 34–39, **35**, **37**, 51, 65, 76, 90, 98–100, 108, 113, 116, 120, 126, 141, 163, 165, 217, 251–252, 255, 265, 277, 306, 314
Karloff, Dorothy Stine 98
Karsner, David 55
Katz, Lee 163
Kaufman, George S. 80–81
Kaye, Danny v, 262, 294, 318
Kazan, Elia 187, 189
Keane, Edward 161
Keating, Larry 335
Keaton, Buster 10
Keeler, Ruby 66, 68
Keighley, William 17, 86, 94, 103, 105, 107, 139, 156, 168–169, 177, 179, 208, 274
Kelley, DeForest 320
Kellogg, Virginia 303
Kelly, Gene v, 262, 293, 322
Kelly, George ("Machine Gun") 87
Kelly, John 21
Kelly, Paul 161, 167
Kendall, Cy 127
Kennedy, Arthur 187, 195, 239, 324
Kennedy, Douglas 280
Kenyon, Charles 65
Kerr, Don Thaddeus 162
Kerrigan, J.M. 247
Key Largo (1948 film) 1, 294–303, **295**, **301**, 313, 318, 347
Kibbee, Guy 40, 43, 45, 48, 53, 93–94
The Kibitzer (play) 16
Kid Galahad (1937 film) 116–118, **117**, 122, 129, 205–207, 346
Kilian, Victor 12, 175, 178
Kilmer, Joyce 168
Kimble, Lawrence 177
King, Joseph 94, 104
King, Martin Luther 326
King of the Underworld (1939 film) 145–**147**, 177, 346
Kingsley, Sidney 120
Kinnell, Murray 31
Kinskey, Leonid 243
Kiss Tomorrow Goodbye (1950 film) 327–331, **328**, 347
Kline, Wally 239
Knapp, Evelyn 19, **29**, 30, 36
Knowlden, Marilyn 138
Knox, Alexander 201, 293
Knudsen, Peggy 262
Knute Rockne, All American (1940 film) 168
Koch, Howard 239–240
Kohler, Fred 94
Korngold, Erich Wolfgang 93, 201, 204
Kosleck, Martin 2, 153, 227
Kreuger, Ivan 53
Krims, Milton 152, 189–190
Kruger, Otto 172, 190
Ku Klux Klan (KKK) 110–112, 142, 152
Kubrick, Stanley 6
Kuhn, Fritz 154

Lackteen, Frank 173
The Lady from Shanghai (1949 film) 6
Lady Killer (1933 film) 2, 68–*72*, 345
A Lady to Love (1930 film) 16–17
Laemmle, Carl, Sr. 17
Lambert, Jack 314
Lancelot, Sir 257
Landau, David 44
Landon, Alf 106
Lane, Lola 114
Lane, Nora 75
Lane, Priscilla *128*–129, *159*–160
Lane, Richard 181
Lane, Rosemary 150, 163–165, *164*
Lang, Fritz 283
Langford, Frances 232
Langley, Adria Locke 334
Larceny, Inc. (1942 film) 227–*229*, 246, 321, 347
Larkin, John 36
Lasky, Jesse 13
The Last Gangster (1937 film) 118
The Last Mile (1932 film) 137
The Last Mile (play) 137
Late Night Final (play) 37
Laurel, Stan 2, 92, 209
Laverne, Lucille 17, 25, 304
Lawes, Lewis E. 155
Lawrence, Marc 167, 300, 302
Lawson, John Howard 247
LeBeau, Madeleine 243
Leech, John L. 194
The Left Hand of God (1955 film) 317
Leigh, Rowland 94
Leigh, Vivian 151
Lemmon, Jack 337–338, 340–342
Leonard, Sheldon 258, 333
Leong, James B. 42
LeRoy, Mervyn 23–25, 37, 44, 47, 53–54, 57, 107, 208, 233, 326, 337, 340
Leslie, Joan 194–195, 206–*207*, 229–231, 250
Lester, Bruce 134
Lettieri, Louis 314
Levene, Sam 247
Lewis, Harry 296
Lewis, Vera 160
Life (magazine) 302
The Life of General Villa (1914 film) 159
The Lights of New York (1928 film) 16
Lincoln, Abraham 175–176, 325
Lindbergh, Charles 108
Linden, Eric 45, *52*, 53
Lindfors, Viveca 277
Lindsay, Howard 122, 125–126
Lindsay, Margaret 70, 85, 88, 91, 94–*97*, 109–110, 230
A Lion Is in the Streets (1953 film) 2, *334*–336, 347
Lissauer, Herman 94
Litel, John 96, 115, 124, 155, 163
Little Caesar (1931 film) 7, 23–27, 24, *26*, 30–31, 34, 36, 53, 73, 105, 122, 193, 302, 321–322, 345
The Little Giant (1933 film) 59–*61*, 180, 321, 345
Little Johnny Jones (stage show) 231–232
Litvak, Anatole 152, 186–189
Livingston, Margaret 35
Lloyd, George 124
Lloyd, Roy 12
Lockhart, Gene 98, 190, 202, 205
Loder, John 252
Logan, Joshua 336–337, 340
Lollobrigida, Gina 316
London, Jack 9, 191
London After Midnight (1927 film) 307
London Films 99, 319
Lonesome Manor (stage show) 12
Long, Huey P. 334, 336
Long Haul (novel) 183
The Long Voyage Home (1940 film) 205
Lopez, Perry 324
Lord, Robert 37, 57, 59–60, 110
Lorre, Peter 214, 217, *219*–220, 225–*226*, 236, 241, 250, 252–254, *253*, 316
Louise, Anita 93–94
Love, Montagu 172
Love Affair (1931 film) 41
"Love Isn't Born, It's Made" (song) 250
Love Me or Leave Me (1955 film) 332, 336
Lovelace, Richard 41
Loy, Myrna v, 41, 152, 293
Luciano, Charles ("Lucky") 114, 294, 302
Lugosi, Bela 165
Lukas, Paul 152
Luke, Keye *237*
"Lullaby of Broadway" (song) 93
Lundigan, William 168
Lupino, Ida 183–186, 193–198, *197*, 201, 205, 208, 249–250
Lux Radio Theater (radio series) 103, 106, 142, 158, 274
Lyndon, Barre 131
Lynn, Jeffrey 160 168–*169*, 177

MacArthur, Charles 134
Macauley, Richard 160, 163, 177–179, 183–184, 211–212, 222, 237
MacBride, Donald 196
MacDonald, Ian 306
MacDonald, J. Farrell 91, 222
MacEwan, Walter 233
MacGowan, Kenneth 12
MacKellar, Helen 107
MacKenna, Kenneth 14
MacKenna's Gold (1969 film) 326
Mackenzie, Aeneas 239
Mackintosh, Louise 58
MacLaine, Shirley 342
MacLane, Barton 88–*89*, 95–96, 103–*105*, *107*, 118, 156, 195, 211, 215, *219*–220, 225, 285, 287, 327–328
MacMurray, Fred 283
The Mad Genius (1931 film) 43, 63
Mademoiselle (magazine) 302
Madison, Noel 25, 65, 88, 90
Magee, Frank 107
Maggie the Magnificent (play) 17
Magnus, Maria Elizabeth Clementine 190
Mahin, John Lee 50
Malden, Karl 325
The Male Animal (1942 film) 215
Mallican, James 336
Mallinson, Rory 279
Malone, Dorothy 268
The Maltese Falcon (1931 film) 214–215, 218
The Maltese Falcon (1941 film) 6, 177, 201, 214–221, *216*, *219*, 224, 226, 233, 236–237, 239–241, 255, 260, 266, 269, 272–274, 283, 291, 347
The Maltese Falcon (novel) 6, 214–221
Malyon, Eily 152
Man of a Thousand Faces (1957 film) 342
The Man Who Came Back (1930 film) 17
The Man Who Changed His Mind (1936 film) 98
The Man Who Could Work Miracles (1937 film) 99
The Man Who Knew Too Much (1934 film) 191
The Man Who Shot Liberty Valance (1962 film) 323
The Man Who Talked Too Much (1940 film) 320
The Man with Two Faces (1934 film) 2, *80*–82, 345
Mankiewicz, Franz 11
Mankiewicz, Herman J. 11
Mankiewicz. Joseph L. 11, 317
Manners, David 2, *29*
Manning, Irene 232, 234–*235*
Manpower (1941 film) 52, 209–213, *212*, 347
Mansfield, Jayne 320
March, Fredric v, 293, 317
Marked Woman (1937 film) 110, 114–116, *115*, 118, 128, 346
Marquis, Rosalind 114
"La Marseillaise" (song) 240–241, 244, 251
Marsh, Mae 320
Marsh, Marian 38, 107
Marshall, Brenda 222–223
Marshall, Charles 222
Marshall, Tully 165
Martin, Dean 258, 321
Marx, Groucho 152, 195, 262
The Marx Brothers 66
Massey, Raymond 247, *249*, 312–314, 326
Mathews, Dorothy 20
Matthews, Lester 237
Maxwell, Edwin 69
Mayer, Louis B. 72, 106, 118, 293

Mayo, Archie 18, 64, 80–81, 99–103, 110
Mayo, Virginia 304, 306, 309–311, **310**, 331–332, 334
The Mayor of Hell (1933 film) 63–65, **64**, 126, 128, 345
Mazurki, Mike 250
McAllister, Neil
McCarey, Ray 293
McCarthy, Joseph 68, 316
McCollum, Barry 12
McCoy, Horace 327
McDaniel, Hattie 225, 250
McDaniel, Sam 225, 335
McDonald, Frank 109–110
McGann, William 107, 110
McGill, Barney 27
McHugh, Frank 23, 43–46, 67, 77–79, 85–86, 90–94, 98, 104, 121, 134, 160–163, **161**, 168–169, 187–**188**, 210, **212**, 225, 303, 335
McIntire, John 335
McLaglen, Victor 17, 41
McMahon, Aline 38, **55**–56
McNamara, Edward 199
McQueen, Steve 325
McRae, Gordon 334
McVey, Pat 279
McWade, Robert 58, 95
Meeker, George 73
Meet the Wife (play) 13–14
"Melancholy Baby" (song)
"Melville Goodwin, U.S.A." (proposed film) see *Top Secret Affair*
Men Are Such Fools (1938 film) **128**–131, 346
Mencken, Helen (wife of HB) 14
Mendelssohn, Felix 93–94
Menjou, Adolphe 266, 283, 293
Mercer, Beryl 31, 33
Mercer, Johnny 279
Merriam, Frank E. 72
"Merrily We Roll Along" (song) 86
Methot, Mayo (wife of HB) 75, 110, 114–116, 134, 155, 207, 218, 240, 250, 254, 257, 262–263
Metro-Goldwyn-Mayer Pictures (MGM) 5, 16–17, 18, 55, 96, 118, 134, 151, 208, 233, 278, 316, 319, 321, 326, 332, 336, 342
Middleton, Charles 175
Midnight (1934 film) 84
A Midsummer Night's Dream (1935 film) 93–94, 96, **135**, 201, 346
A Midsummer Night's Dream (Shakespeare play) 93–94
Milland, Ray 40
Miller, Seton I. 44, 90, 104, 116, 205
Miller, Sidney 64
Miller, Vernon C. 86–87
Millhauser, Bertram 75
The Millionaire (1931 film) 2, 28–30, **29**, 345
Mineo, Sal 324
"The Minstrel Boy" (song) 91
Mission to Moscow (1943 film) 240, 265

Mister Roberts (1955 film) 336–342, **340**, **341**, 347
Mister Roberts (play) 336
Mr. Samuel (play) 17
Mr. Winkle Goes to War (1944 film) 283
Mitchell, Grant 228
Mizner, Wilson 48–49, 57, 59–60
Moffitt, Jack 250
Molnar, Walter 258
Monogram Pictures 121, 165
Montalban, Ricardo 323, 325
Montgomery, Robert 278, 293, 342
Moore, Dickie 48, 190
Moorehead, Agnes 279
Moran, "Bugs" 32
Moran, Doris 256, 258
Morgan, Byron 37
Morgan, Dennis 163, 168–**169**, 213, 222–**223**, 239, 250, 274, 318
Morgan, Michelle 251
Mori, Toshia 42
Morin, Alberto 298
Morley, Robert 316
Morris, Adrian 101
Morris, Wayne 116–**117**, 128–129, 163–**164**
Morton, Samuel ("Nails") 32
A Most Immoral Lady (play) 17
Mostel, Zero 314
Motion Picture Alliance for the Preservation of American Ideals (MPA) 265–266, 275, 283, 293, 316
The Mouthpiece (1932 film) 320
Movie Show Magazine 302
Mowbray, Alan 49
Mower, Jack 183, 206
The Mummy (1932 film) 51
Muni, Paul 10, 26, 46, 85, 96, 110, 131, 134, 145, 152, 171, 174, 193, 274, 294
Munson, Ona 38
Murphy, George 293
Murrow, Edward R. 316
Muse, Clarence 47, 48, 240, 262
Mussolini, Benito 159
Mustin, Burt 335
My Darling Clementine (1946 film) 339
My Daughter Joy (1950 film) 319
My Dream Is Yours (1949 film) 318
My Geisha (1962 film) 321

Nadi, Aldo 260
Naish, J. Carroll 41, **50**
The Narrow Corner (1933 film) 109
Nash, Frank 86
National Committee for American-Soviet Friendship 246
National Labor Relations Board 265
National Maritime Union 247
National Recovery Act (NRA) 68, 75
The Nazi Spy Conspiracy in America (book) 151
Neal, Patricia 318

Nelson, Gene 332
Nelson, George ("Baby Face") 90
Never a Dull Moment (1968 film) 326
Never Steal Anything Small (1959 film) 342
Niblo, Fred, Jr. 168, 205
Nietsche, Friederich 202
The Night Before Christmas (play) 208, 227
The Night Has a Thousand Eyes (1948 film) 318
The Night Ride (1930 film)
Nightmare (1956) 320
Nixon, Marian 48
Nixon, Richard 316
No Good from a Corpse (novel) 261
Noble, Ray 93
Nolan, Lloyd 88
Nugent, Frank 337
Number 37 (play)
NYPD Blue (TV show) 7

O'Brien, Edmond 304, 311, 317
O'Brien, George 41, 324
O'Brien, Margaret 233, 283
O'Brien, Pat 17, 51, 77–**79**, 81, 85, **87**, 88, 90–91, 96–98, 108–110, 113–**114**, 118–**119**, 134–136, **135**, 137–**143**, **138**, **142**, 168–170, **169**, 178–180, **179**, 223, 266, 332, 342
O'Brien-Moore, Erin 111
O'Connor, Robert Emmett 31, 42, 62
O'Connor, Una 177, 198
Office of War Information (OFI) 246, 248, 251
O'Flynn, Damian 115
The Oklahoma Kid (1939 film) 147–**150**, **148**, 163, 179, 346
The Old Maid (1939 film)
Oliver, Edna Mae 14
Olson, Moroni 165, 175
O'Moore, Patrick 275
One Sunday Afternoon (play) 198
One, Two, Three (1961 film) 342
O'Neill, Henry 100, 104, 107, 130, 154, 167
Only Angels Have Wings (1939 film) 97
Operation X (1950 film) see *My Daughter Joy*
Ornitz, Samuel 71
O'Shea, Oscar 130
Osterloh, Robert 308
Other Men's Women (1931 film) 27–28, **27**, 345
Our Vines Have Tender Grapes (1945 film) 6, 283
Ouspenskaya, Maria 173
Out of the Fog (1941 film) 208
The Outrage (1964 film) 321
Outside, Looking In (play) 12
Outside the Law (1930 film) 17
"Over There" (song) 232–233

Padden, Sarah 77
Page, Bradley 76
Page, Gale **126**–127, 132, 155, 185

Pallette, Eugene 208
Paramore, Edward, Jr. 147
Paramount Pictures 5, 14, 18, 79, 317–318, 320, 325, 342
Parker, Bonnie 86
Parker, Eleanor 312–*313*, 318
Parker, Willard 124
Parsons, Louella 213
Passage to Marseilles (1944 film) 250–254, ***253***, 257, 259, 347
Patrick, Lee 167, 220
Pawley, Edward 88–***89***, 150
Payton, Barbara 328
Peck, Gregory v, 293, 326
Peck's Bad Boy (play) 230
Pendleton, Nat 43, 121
Penny Arcade (play) 17
Pepe (1960 film) 321
Perelman, Laura 208, 227
Perelman, S.J. 208, 227
Perkins, Osgood 96
Perry, Harvey 91, 186
Perry, Linda 107
Perske, William 255
Person to Person (TV show) 316
Petain, Phillipe 241
Peters, Susan 234
The Petrified Forest (1936 film) 7, 99–104, ***101***, 106–107, 110, 112, 116, 146, 165, 234, 255, 317, 346
"The Petrified Forest" (1940 radio show) 103
"The Petrified Forest" (1955 TV show) 317
The Petrified Forest (play) 84, 99, 102
Phelps, Buster ***54***
Phillips, Mary (wife of HB) 14, 17
Picture Snatcher (1933 film) 1, 61–***63***, 345
The Pillars of Society (play) 9
Pitter Patter (stage show) 11
Pitts, Zasu 177
Planet of the Apes (1968 film) 325
Platt, Edward ***321***
Poe, Edgar Allan 202
Polito, Sol 103, 139, 222
Porter, Cole 248
Porter, Edwin S. 15
Popularity (play) 232
Powell, Adam Clayton, Jr. 240
Powell, Dick 49, 66–68, 93
Powell, William 338
Power, Tyrone 103
Pratt, Purnell 19, 38
Price, Vincent 255
The Prisoner of Shark Island (1937 film) 325
The Prize (1963 film) 321
Producer's Showcase (TV series) 317
Production Code of 1934 31, 33, 36, 38, 43, 47, 49, 57, 60, 62, 68, 70, 73, 81, 83–84, 88, 90, 107, 126, 140, 155, 158, 183–185, 210, 216, 271, 274, 294
The Public Enemy (1931 film) 2, 7, 30–33, ***30***, ***31***, 34, 36, 42, 53, 55, 59, 63, 70, 77, 116, 157, 274, 345

Punsley, Bernard 126, 139
Purvis, Melvin 86
Pyle, Denver 324

Qualen, John 77
The Quiet Man (1952 film) 338
Quinn, Anthony 187, 228

The Racket (play) 16, 23
Racket Busters (1938 film) 130–***131***, 346
Rackin, Martin 314
Rafferty, Tom 268
Raft, George 42, 52, 156–158, ***157***, 165–168, ***166***, 171, 177, 193, 201, 205, 209–210, ***212***, 214–215, 233, 239, 320
Ragtime (1981 film) 342
Raine, Norman Reilly 129, 158, 168, 222
Rainey, Ford 304
Rains, Claude 152, 195, 239, 242, 250–251, 253–254
Ralston, Marcia 129
Rankin, John 294
Rappe, Virginia 14
Rapper, Irving 194
Rathbone, Basil 98, 118, 265, 317
Ratoff, Gregory 319
Rawlinson, Herbert 155
Ray, Aldo 317
Ray, Nicholas 314, 316, 336
Raymond, Gene 14
Reagan, Maureen 318
Reagan, Ronald 2, 3, 121–122, 124, 136, 151, 168, 239, 285, 293, 318–319, 342
Red Harvest (novel) 214
Red River (1948 film) 273
Redwing, Roderic 297
Reed, Philip 75
Reed, Tommy 81
Reeves, George 178
Reicher, Frank 174, 329
Reinhardt, Max 93–94
Reles, Abe 314
The Return of Dr. X (1939 film) 2, 163–165, ***164***, 213, 346
Reunited (stage show) 11
Reuter, Paul Julius 189–191
Reynolds, Craig 97
Ricciardi, William 51
Richards, Addison 83, 97, 108
Richetti, Adam C. 86–87
Ridges, Stanley 157–158, 201, ***203***, 234–235
Ridgley, John 163, 269
Rin Tin Tin 15
Rio Bravo (1959 film) 52, 258
Rio Grande (1950 film) 324
Risdon, Elizabeth 160
Ritz Girls of 19 and 22 (stage show) 11
Rivera, Diego 134
Rivkin, Allen 62
The Roaring Twenties (1939 film) ***159***–163, ***161***, 183, 215, 250, 311, 346
Roberts, Ben 303

Roberts, Roy 313–314
Robertson, John 10, 16
Robertson, Willard 157
Robeson, Paul 102
Robin and the 7 Hoods (1964 film) 321–323, ***325***, 347
Robinson, Bill ("Bojangles") 233
Robinson, Casey 239–240, 250
Robinson, Earl 262
Robinson, Edward G. v, ***22***, ***24***, ***26***, ***35***, ***37***, ***42***, ***50***, ***55***, ***61***, ***74***, ***80***, ***86***, ***105***, ***107***, ***117***, ***125***, ***132***, ***153***, ***172***, ***181***, ***203***, ***212***, ***229***, ***295***, ***301***, ***321***, ***322***, ***325***, ***326***, ***327***; on Bette Davis 116; birth 9; on *Brother Orchid* 180; childhood 9; children 61, 326; death 325–326; early films 10, 16–17; education 9; on Humphrey Bogart 117–118, 180; on Jack Warner 106; on Kay Francis 66; language fluency 9; on Lauren Bacall 294; on *Little Caesar* 23–24; marriage 27, 246, 326; military service ***10***; on Paul Muni 134; plays written by 9; political beliefs and activities 106, 152, 191–192, 212, 227, 266, 283, 293, 318–319; on *A Slight Case of Murder* 126; on *Smart Money* 36; stage name 9; stage performances 9–10, 133; on *The Widow from Chicago* 23; World War II tours 246, 283
Robinson, Edward G., Jr. ("Manny") 61, 82, 283, 326
Robinson, Gladys Lloyd (wife of EGR) v, 27, 34, 36–37, 41–42, 56, 61, 82, 208, 246, 293, 326
Robson, Flora 166
Rockne, Knute 168
Rodgers, Richard 230, 232
Rodgers, Walter 56
Rodney, John 296
Rogers, Ginger 266, 320
Roland, Gilbert 323–324
Romance on the High Seas (1948 film) 318
Romero, Ernesto A. 284
Rooney, Mickey 93
Roope, Fay 336
Roosevelt, Eleanor 246, 265
Roosevelt, Franklin Delano (FDR) 49, 55–56, 60, 68, 75, 106, 152, 159–160, 186, 195, 229–230, 232–233, 236, 240, 246–248, 262, 283, 296, 298
Roosevelt, Theodore 65, 232
Root, Wells 50
Rose, Stuart 17
Rosemond, Clinton 230
Rosenbloom, Maxie ("Slapsie") 133, 157
Rossen, Robert 114, 130, 160, 186, 201
Royal Canadian Air Force (RCAF)
The Ruined Lady (play) 13
Ruman, Sig 154, 172, 205
Run for Cover (1956 film) 336
Runyon, Damon 122, 125

Rushmore, Howard 293
Russian Benefit Committee 227

Sabrina (1954 film) 317
Sahara (1943 film) 249–250
The St. Louis Kid (1934 film) 83–**84**, 345
Sakall, S.Z. ("Cuddles") 230–231, 249–250
Salisbury, Leah 23
San Quentin (1937 film) 113, 118–120, **119**, 127, 158, 346
Sande, Walter 257
Sanders, George 153
Sargent, Joseph 343
Saturday's Children (1939 film) 14
Saturday's Children (play) 14
Savage, Daniel Boone 122–**123**
Sawyer, Joseph 94, 100, 110–111, 118, 153, 155, 160
Scarface (1932 film) 42, 45–46, 90, 156, 274
Scarlet Street (1945 film) 283
Schaefer, Rosalind Keating 68
Schenck,,Joseph 61, 123, 126
Schildkraut, Rudolph 10
Schultz, Dutch 104, 316
Scorsese, Martin 6
Scott, George C. 342
Scott, Hazel 240
Scott, Lizabeth 274
Scott, Randolph 175–176, 334
Scottsboro Boys 71
Screen Actors Guild (SAG) 65, 76, 90, 116, 233, 265, 293, 319
The Sea Hawk (1940 film) 201
The Sea Wolf (1941 film) 9, 191–192, 201–205, **203**, 347
The Sea Wolf (novel) 9, 191–192, 201
The Searchers (1956 film) 324
Seff, Manuel 66–67
Seiler, Lewis 126, 177, 233
Selznick, David O. 255
Sen Yung, Victor 238
Sergeant Rutledge (1960 film) 323–324
Sergeant York (1941 film) 311
The Seven Little Foys (1955 film) 342
Seven Thieves (1960) 321
Seventeen (magazine) 302
Seventh Heaven (play) 14
Seymour, Dan 298
Seymour, Harry 124, 258
Seymour, James 66
Shake Hands with the Devil (1959 film) 342
Shakespeare, William 49, 93
"Shanghai Lil" (song) 66, 68
Sharif, Omar 326
Shaw, Irwin 208
Sheehan, John 57
Sheridan, Ann 111, 113, 118, **138–139**, 141, 177–**179**, 183–**184**, 186, 239, 249–250, 286
Sherman, Vincent 164, 233, 236
Sherwood, Robert 84, 102
"Shine" (song) 241

Shirley, Ann 53
Shore, Dinah 249–250
Short Cut to Hell (1957 film) 342
Show Boat (1936 film) 102
Shumway, Lee 23
Sidney, Sylvia 205, 207
Siegel, Don 6, 232
Silver Dollar (1932 film) 55–56, 345
Silverheels, Jay 297
Sinatra, Frank v, 259, 317–318, 320–323, 342
Sinatra, Frank, Jr. 323
Sinclair, Upton 72
The Singing Fool (1928 film) 16
Singleton, Penny 121
Sinner's Holiday (1930 film) 18–21, 27, 155, 304, 345
Sirocco (1951 film) 316
The Skyrocket (play) 17
A Slight Case of Murder (1938 film) 122–126, **125**, 154, 180, 321, 346
A Slight Case of Murder (play) 122
Slim (1937 film) 51
Sloane, Everett 315
Small Time Crooks (2000 film) 228
Smart Money (1931 film) 34–36, **35**, 55, 345
Smith, Al 142
Smith, Alexis 250, 263–**264**, 275–**276**
Smith, Joe P. 296
Snapshots of 1923 (stage show) 12
Sokoloff, Vladimir 252
Something to Sing About (1937 film) 98, 135
Song of Norway (1970 film) 326
The Sopranos (TV show) 7
Sothern, Ann 180, 233
Soubier, Clifford 111
Sousa, John Philip 339
Southern, Hugh 149
Soylent Green (1973 film) 326
Sparks, Ned **52**
Spencer, Herbert 202
Spewack, Bella 134
Spewack, Sam 134
Spielberg, Steven 6, 50
Spigelglass, Leonard 224, 326
Stagecoach (1939 film) 175, 300, 324
Stand In (1937 film) 120, 135
Stanley, Edwin 264
Stanley, Eric 124, 129
Stanton, Paul 238
Stanwyck, Barbara 266, 275–277, **276**, 283, 320
Starlift (1951 film) 333–334, 347
Starr, Frances 37–38
Steele, Bob 272, 315–316
Steiner, Max 176, 224, 240, 251
Stephens, Harvey 149, 155
Stephenson, James 146
Stevens, George 342
Stevens, Landers 24
Stevens, Onslow 336
Stevenson, Houseley 279
Stevenson, Margot 166
Stevenson, Robert Louis 205

Stewart, James 324
Stone, George E. 25–26, **43**, 44, 94–95, 104, 155
The Story of Louis Pasteur (1936 film) 110, 113
Stossel, Ludwig 225
Strange, Glenn 247
Strange, Robert 155
The Stranger (1946 film) 6, 154, 283
The Strawberry Blonde (1941 film) 198–201, **200**, 208, 311, 346–347
Strode, Woody 323
Stuart, Gloria **79**
Suddenly (1954 film) 320
Sugarman, Abe 112
Sullivan, Ed 341
Sullivan, Elliott 130, 161
Sunkissed (1930 film) see *A Lady to Love*
Suspicion (1941 film) 277
Sutherland, Sidney 65
"Sweet Georgia Brown" (song) 235
Swifty (play) 13
Swing Your Lady (1938 film) 120–**123**, 126, 128–129, 146, 165, 346

Tabor, H.A.W. 55
Talbot, Lyle 53–**54**
Tales of Manhattan (1942 film) 246
Tampico (1944 film) 283
Targets (1968 film) 306, 311
Tasker, Robert 118
Taxi! (1932 film) 2, 42–44, **43**, 130, 345
Taylor, Robert 266, 283
The Ten Commandments (1956) 320
Tenbrook, Harry 124
Terrible Joe Moran (1984 TV movie) 343
Terry, Sheila 65
Thalberg, Irving 16, 246
Thank Your Lucky Stars (1943 film) 249–250, 347
"Thank Your Lucky Stars" (song) 249
"That's What You Jolly Well Get" (song) 250
There Shall Be No Light (play) 214
These Wilder Years (1956 film) 342
Thew, Harvey 55
They Died with Their Boots On (1941 film) 150
They Drive by Night (1940 film) 183–186, **184**, 193–194, 198, 210, 346
They Shoot Horses, Don't They? (novel) 327
"They're Either Too Young or Too Old" (song) 250
The Thief of Baghdad (1924 film) 159
The Thin Man (novel) 214
Things to Come (1936 film) 99
This Man's Town (play) 17
Thomas, J. Parnell 292
Thompson, Slim 101

Three on a Match (1932 film) 41, 53–55, **54**, 90, 99, 345
Thunder in the City (1937 film) 110
Tiger Shark (1932 film) 2, 44, **50–53**, 77, 209, 211, 345
Tight Spot (1954 film) 320
The Time of Your Life (1948 film) 327
To Have and Have Not (1944 film) 255–262, **260**, 263, 266, 271, 274–275, 347
"To Have and Have Not" (1946 radio show) 274
To Have and Have Not (novel) 255
Toast of the Town (TV show) 341
Tobias, George 178, 185, 198, 222, 231, 250, 252
Tobin, Genevieve 65, 73, 100
Tolan, Michael 314
Toler, Sidney 73
Tone, Franchot 158
Tong, Kam 237
"Too Marvelous for Words" (song) 279–280
"Too Ra Loo Ra Loo Ral" (song) 91
Toomey, Regis 28, 88, 269
Toones, Fred ("Snowflake") 65, 79
Top Secret Affair (1957 film) 317
Torrid Zone (1940 film) 177–180, **179**, 183–185, **184**, 346
Touch of Evil (1958 film) 6
Tracy, Lee 50
Tracy, Spencer 50, 141, 152, 316, 323
Tracy, William 138
Traven, B. 283–286
Travers, Henry 155, 195
Travis, June 96
Travis, Richard 234
The Treasure of the Sierra Madre (1948 film) 246, 274, 283–**292**, **286**, 294, 313, 347
The Treasure of the Sierra Madre (novel) 283–284
Tree, Dorothy 78, 154
Trevor, Claire 120, **132**–133, 294, 296, 299–302, **301**, 321
Tribute to a Bad Man (1956 film) 342
Trilling, Steve 213, 251, 261
Trivers, Barry 205
Trotsky, Leon 134
Trowbridge, Charles 127
Truman, Harry S. 226, 265, 292, 316
Trumbo, Dalton 283, 293
Tunney, Gene 49
Turkus, Burton B. 314–315
Turner, Lana 262
Turrou, Leon 151
20th Century-Fox Pictures 215, 246, 283, 316–318, 321, 334, 339
20,000 Years in Sing Sing (1933 film) 50, 141
Two Against the World (1936 film) 106–110, **108**, 346
Two Guys from Milwaukee (1946 film) 274, 347

The Two Mrs. Carrolls (1947 film) 263, 275–277, **276**, 280, 313, 347
Two Seconds (1932 film) 46–47, 211, 213, 345
Two Weeks in Another Town (1962 film) 321
Tyler, Tom 182
Tyson, Cicely 342

Unholy Partners (1941 film) 208
United Artists 61, 233, 316–317, 319–320, 327, 342
Universal Pictures 5, 17, 19, 21, 29, 41, 71, 84, 217, 246–247, 293, 319, 342
Up the Ladder (play) 13
Up the River (1930 film) 17
Ustinov, Peter 317

Valdespino, Alberto 290
Vallee, Rudy 318
Vega, Ildefonso 290
Veidt, Conrad 225, 240
Velez, Lupe
Verne, Kaaren 225
"The Very Thought of You" (song) 92–93
Veterans of Foreign Wars (VFW) 106
Vice Squad (1953 film) 319
Vickers, Martha 266
Vidor, King 318
Vigran, Herbert 177
Villa, Pancho 159
Vinson, Helen 59–**61**, 178–**179**
The Violent Men (1954 film) 320
Virginia City (1940 film) 42, 174–178, **176**, 213, 275, 346
Vitaphone Corporation 15–16, 17
Vogel, Paul C. 278

Wadsworth, Henry 97
The Wagons Roll at Night (1941 film) 2, 52, 205–**207**, 229, 347
Wald, Jerry 160, 163, 177–179, 183–184, 209, 211–212, 224, 239, 247, 277, 294–296
Waldridge, Harold 38, 70
Waldron, Charles 267
The Walking Dead (1936 film) 99–100, 113, 141, 163, 201
Wallace, Dan 269–270
Wallace, Francis 205
Wallace, Morgan 35
Wallis, Hal B. 17, 23–24, 34, 51, 65, 74, 76, 86, 88, 93, 99, 101, 103, 106, 114, 121, 134, 152–154, 168, 179, 193–194, 205, 208–210, 217, 221, 239–240, 246–247, 251, 326
Walsh, Raoul 6, 41, 159–163, 183–184, 186, 193–195, 198–201, **199**, 209, 211–213, 250, 303–305, 308, 310–311, 314, 316, 318, 334–335
Walters, Polly 34
Walthall, Henry B. 108
Wanger, Walter 13, 16, 120
Ware, Harlan 332
Warner, Abe 15–17
Warner, Ann 152

Warner, H.B. 38
Warner, Harry 15–17, 57, 61, 83, 93, 96
Warner, Jack L. 1, 5, 6, 15–17, **18**, 20, 23–24, 44, 49, 57, 59–60, 66, 68, 74, 76, 82, 85, 88, 94, 99, 103, 106, 110, 118, 121, 129, 131, 135, 150–152, 154, 156, 159, 168, 180, 193–195, 198, 205, 208–209, 213, 215, 217, 221, 233, 239–241, 246–248, 251, 254–256, 258, 261–263, 265–266, 270, 274, 277, 283–285, 293–294, 296, 303, 316–319, 321, 323, 326–327, 332–333, 337
Warner, Rose 15
Warner, Sam 15–16
Warren, Harry 93
"Watch on the Rhine" (song) 244
Waterloo Bridge (1931 film) 71
Waters, Ethel 240
Watkin, Pierre 136
Watson, Minor 236
Waxman, Franz 275, 277, 280
Way Down East (play) 23
Wayne, John 28, 159, 266, 273, 283, 300, 342
Wayne, Patrick 324
We Americans (play)
Wead, Frank ("Spig") 96–97, 108–109
Webb, Clifton 13
Weber, Joe 11
Weber, Wilhelm 189
Weigel, Paul 190
Weinstein-Bacal, Natalie 255
Weiss, Hymie 31–32
Weitzenkorn, Louis 37, 106
Welch, Niles 56
Welden, Ben 114, 117, 189, 211, 273
Welles, Orson 6, 154, 283
Wellman, William A. 27, 30–32, 41, 63, 118
Wells, H.G. 99
We're No Angels (1955 film) 317
The West Point Story (1950 film) 327, 331–332, 341, 347
Westmore, Perc 74
Wexley, John 131, 137, 152, 186
Whale, James 19, 71, 102
What Price Glory? (1952 film) 334
What Price Glory? (play) 14
"When Irish Eyes Are Smiling" (song) 91
"When Your Lover Has Gone" (song) 39
White, Alice **22**–23, 62–**63**, 75
White Heat (1949 film) 19, 33, 158, 186, 213, 303–311, **305**, **310**, 327, 331–332, 342, 347
The Whole Town's Talking (1935 film) 85, 181
Whorf, Richard 231, 312
Why We Fight (film series) 239
Widmark, Richard 324
The Widow from Chicago (1930 film) **22**, 23, 345
Wild Boys of the Road (1933 film) 36, 53, 63, 112

Wilde, Cornell 195
Wilder, Billy v, 283, 317, 342
Wiles, Buster 194
Wilhelm, Wolfgang 189
Wilkie, Wendell 195
William, Warren 54, 90
Williams, G. Mennen 71
Williams, Guinn ("Big Boy") *169*, 175–*176*
Williams, Rhys 328
Williams, Valentine 189
Wilson, Arthur ("Dooley") 240, 242
Wilson, Charles C. 183–*184*
Wilson, Marie 134–136, *135*
Windust, Bretaigne 314
The Wings of Eagles (1957 film) 339
Wings of the Navy (1939 film) 157
Winner Take All (1932 film) 47–49, *47*, 345
Winston, Archer 291
Winters, Roland 331
Wise, Robert 342
Withers, Grant 19, 27–28, *27*
Wolfe, Ian 2, 164
Wolfson, P.J. 62
The Woman in the Window (1944 film) 283
Women Go On Forever (play) 17
Women of All Nations (1931 film) 41
Wood, Sam 266, 283
Woods, Donald 94, 109
Woods, Edward *30*
Woods, Harry 83
Woollcott, Alexander 80–81
Wray, Fay 320
Wray, John 156
Wright, Tenny 214, 285
Wycherly, Margaret 303, *305*, 311
Wyler, William v, 120, 215, 293, 300, 317
Wyman, Jane 116, 227, *229*, 318, 334
Wynn, Keenan 262

Yamaoka, Otto 42
"Yankee Doodle Boy" (song) 232
Yankee Doodle Dandy (1942 film) 224, 228–233, *231*, 236, 249–250, 288, 311, 347
You Can't Get Away with Murder (1939 film) *155*, 167, 346
"You, John Jones" (1943 short film) 233
Young, Gig 332–333
Young, Jack 230
Young, Loretta 41–*43*, 75
Young Man with a Horn (1949 film) 142
Young Mr. Lincoln (1939 film) 325
"You're a Grand Old Flag" (song) 232
Yurka, Blanche 187

Zanuck, Darryl F. 5, 16–18, 20–21, 37, 59, 61, 112, 179, 215; on *The Public Enemy* 31; on *Taxi!* 44

www.ingramcontent.com/pod-product-compliance
Ingram Content Group UK Ltd.
Pitfield, Milton Keynes, MK11 3LW, UK
UKHW050544150426
5217IPUK00026B/2064